REFERENCE

DATE DUE

RETURNED AUG 1 8 2002 AUG 1 5 2002	

DEMCO, INC. 38-2931

D1465990

DICTIONARY OF
MICROPROCESSOR SYSTEMS

DICTIONARY OF MICROPROCESSOR SYSTEMS

IN FOUR LANGUAGES   *English*
German
French
Russian

EDITED BY

DIPL.-ING. DIETER MÜLLER

Dresden (German Democratic Republic)

ELSEVIER

Amsterdam — Oxford — New York

1984

AUTHORS:

Dipl.-Ing. Dieter Müller   English and German
Dipl.-Ing. René Schulz   French
Jurij Vladimirovič Chapancev   Russian

EXPERT:

Prof. Dr. sc. techn. Dietrich Eckhardt

Published in coedition with VEB Verlag Technik, Berlin
This book is exclusively distributed in all non-socialist countries with the exception of the Federal Republic of
Germany, West-Berlin, Austria and Switzerland by
Elsevier Science Publishers
Molenwerf 1
P. O. Box 211, 1000 AE Amsterdam, The Netherlands

Distributors for the United States and Canada
Elsevier Science Publishing Company, Inc.
52 Vanderbilt
New York, NY 10017
ISBN 0-444-99645-1

Library of Congress Cataloging in Publication Data

Müller, Dieter, 1935 -
   Dictionary of microprocessor systems.
   Includes index.
   1. Microprocessors — Dictionaries — Polyglot.
2. Dictionaries, Polyglot.   I. Schulz, René.
II. Chapancev, Jurij Vladimirovič.   III. Title.
QA76.5.M773   1983   001.64   83-11720
ISBN 0-444-99645-1 (Elsevier Science Pub. Co.)

COPYRIGHT © 1983 VEB VERLAG TECHNIK, BERLIN

*All rights reserved. No part of this publication may be reproduced, stored in a retrieval system, or transmitted in any form or by
any means: electronic, mechanical, photocopying, recording, or otherwise, without the prior written permission of the publisher.*

Registered trade marks, designs and patents are not explicitly marked in this dictionary.

Printed in the German Democratic Republic by Grafischer Großbetrieb Völkerfreundschaft Dresden

VANDERBILT UNIVERSITY
LIBRARY
NASHVILLE, TENNESSEE

PREFACE

Microprocessor technology is the most universal and, thereby, in an equal measure, also the most important field of application for microelectronics. Due to an exceptionally rapid development rate over a period of just ten years, microprocessor technology has attained a present-day rating of decisive significance for complex and further technological progress in all industrial states. Moreover, microprocessor technology not only offers new solution patterns and more economic possibilities for the automation of information processing and control engineering, but is also the basis for products showing fundamentally new properties, coupled with curtailed requirements for labour and material and a lower energy consumption. This field has, therefore, matured into a key technology, able to assist in solving such basic problems as enhancing productivity, economizing on raw materials, creating efficient environmental protection measures, as well as effectively improving both working and living conditions. Consequently, nowadays hardly a single sector of social production, reproduction or consumption can be conceived that has not been invaded by microprocessor technology. The spectrum extends from EDP technology to office automation, from missile technology to vehicle electronics, from machine tool technology to laboratory automation, from medical technology to the household goods field. As a result, the number of specialists and students interested in extending the field of application of microprocessors has increased apace, thus also increasing the numbers of skilled personnel who are anxious to fully utilize microprocessor technology for solving their working and educational assignments. It has therefore become essential to accurately evaluate the specialist literature in foreign languages as microprocessor technology crosses a great many borders in its applications to production and development techniques, so that a veritable flood of information and documentation in various languages is produced to keep up with the unrelenting, dynamic extension of knowledge in this field. Finally, in the interests of export to international markets it has become absolutely essential to participate in international communication in this specialist field and to provide product information in foreign languages.

This volume is intended to make accessible to a broad range of interested parties the specialist vocabulary of microprocessor technology, computer technology and programming. For greater topicality the terms have been chosen not only from the most renowned specialised works but have also been culled from a multitude of recent specialist periodicals and conference reports. Even so, new developments lead to further new terms so that perfection can only be an ultimate goal. Suggestions for additional terms or for other improvements will be gratefully received by the publishers.

Finally, I should like to express my thanks to all involved in the production of this specialist dictionary. First and foremost, the authors of the French and Russian translations, Mr. Schulz and Mr. Chapancev, as well as the staff of the foreign language department of Verlag Technik whose suggestions markedly influenced the selection of the vocabulary of the present edition. I am equally indebted to my colleagues for their specialist advice and to Prof. Eckhardt, Dr. sc. techn. (Dresden) for his meticulous, expert appraisal of the manuscript. Last, but not least, special thanks are due to my wife both for her helpful support and for her patient understanding during the two-year period of manuscript compilation.

D. Müller

DIRECTIONS FOR USE

1. Examples of alphabetical sequence

delay distortion
delayed feedback
delay element
delay equalizer
delay line

feste Befehlslänge
fester Speicherplatz
fester Zustand
feste Wortlänge
Festformat

bit de mémoire
bit de parité
bits de tête
bits par seconde
bit zéro

адрес команды
адресный тракт
адрес обращения
адресовать
адрес операнда

test equipment
tester
testing terminal
testing time
test instruction

Kontrolleinheit
Kontrolleinrichtung
kontrollieren
kontrollierendes System
Kontrollmeldung

signal électrique
signalement d'erreur
signal externe
signalisation
signal multiple

регистр данных памяти
регистрировать
регистрирующее устройство
регистр кода операции
регистр команд

2. Signs and abbreviations

( ) magnetic-core memory (storage) = magnetic-core memory *or* magnetic-core storage
[ ] data net[work] = data net *or* data network
/ display / to = to display
  schalten / in Kaskade = in Kaskade schalten
  format de poche /en = en format de poche
  импульсным управлением / с = с импульсным управлением
< > these brackets enclose explanations
s. = see
s.a. = see also
<US> = American English

A

A 1	abbreviated addressing	abgekürzte Adressierung f	adressage m abrégé	сокращенная адресация
A 2	abbreviated designation	Kurzbezeichnung f	brève désignation f	сокращенное обозначение
A 3	abort / to	abbrechen <Befehlsausführung, Vorgang>	interrompre	прерывать
A 4	abort	Abbruch m	rupture f	прерывание, преждевременное прекращение
A 5	abrupt change	plötzliche (sprungartige) Änderung f	changement m abrupt, modification f subite	внезапное (скачкообразное) изменение
A 6	abrupt p-n junction	abrupter pn-Übergang m	jonction f p-n abrupte	ступенчатый p-n переход
A 7	absolute address, specific address	absolute (tatsächliche) Adresse f	adresse f absolue	абсолютный (действительный) адрес
A 8	absolute addressing	absolute Adressierung f	adressage m absolu	абсолютная адресация
A 9	absolute assembler	absoluter Assembler m <liefert absolute Speicheradressen>	assembleur m absolu	абсолютный ассемблер, ассемблер, работающий с абсолютными адресами
A 10	absolute code, specific (one-level) code	absoluter Kode m	code m absolu	абсолютный код
A 11	absolute coding, absolute programming	absolute Programmierung f	programmation f absolue	программирование в абсолютных адресах
A 12	absolute error	absoluter Fehler m	erreur f absolue	абсолютная погрешность
A 13	absolute loader	absoluter Lader m, Absolutlader m	chargeur m absolu	абсолютный загрузчик
A 14	absolute loading	absolutes Laden n, Laden mit absoluten Adressen	chargement m absolu	абсолютная загрузка, загрузка с абсолютным адресом
A 15	absolute maximum rating	absolute Grenzdaten pl	limites fpl absolues	предельно допустимые параметры
A 16	absolute program	absolutes (unverschiebliches) Programm n	programme m absolu	программа, написанная в абсолютных адресах
	absolute programming	s. A 11		
A 17	absolute value	Absolutwert m	valeur f absolue	абсолютное значение
A 18	absolute value sign	Absolutwertzeichen n, Betragszeichen n	signe m de valeur absolue	символ абсолютного значения
A 19	absorb power / to	Leistung verbrauchen (aufnehmen)	consommer (absorber) la puissance	поглощать энергию
A 20	abstract	Kurzdarstellung f	abrégé m	реферат, резюме
	abstract code	s. P 678		
	AC	s. A 222		
A 21	accelerated life test	zeitraffende Lebensdauerprüfung f	test m accéléré de longévité	ускоренное испытание на долговечность
A 22	accelerated test technique	beschleunigte Prüftechnik f	technique f de test accéléré	способ ускоренного испытания
A 23	acceleration time	Anlaufzeit f, Beschleunigungszeit f	temps m d'accélération	время разгона [магнитной ленты]
A 24	accelerator	Beschleuniger m <Prozessorzusatzeinrichtung für bestimmte Arithmetikfunktionen>	accélérateur m	ускоритель
A 25	accept / to	annehmen, akzeptieren	accepter	принимать
A 26	acceptance	Annahme f	acceptation f, admission f	принятие
A 27	acceptance test	Abnahmeprüfung f	test m d'acceptation	приемное испытание
A 28	acceptor	Akzeptor m, Elektronenaufnehmer m	accepteur m	акцептор
A 29	acceptor doping	Akzeptordotierung f	dotation f d'accepteur	введение акцепторной ┌примеси
A 30	access / to	zugreifen	accéder	обращаться
A 31	access	Zugriff m	accès m	доступ, обращение
A 32	access address	Zugriffsadresse f	adresse f d'accès	адрес доступа (обращения)
A 33	access control	Zugriffssteuerung f	commande f d'accès	управление обращением (доступом)
A 34	access cycle	Zugriffszyklus m	cycle m d'accès	цикл обращения
A 35	accessibility	Zugangsmöglichkeit f	accessibilité f	доступность
A 36	accessible	zugänglich, erreichbar	accessible	доступный, достижимый
A 37	access mechanism	Zugriffsmechanismus m	mécanisme m d'accès	механизм выборки <ЗУ на магнитном диске>
A 38	access method	Zugriffsmethode f	méthode f d'accès	метод доступа (обращения)
A 39	access mode	Zugriffsart f	mode m d'accès	режим доступа
A 40	accessories	Zubehör n, Zubehörteile npl	accessoires mpl	принадлежности, запасные части
A 41	access request	Zugriffsanforderung f	requête f d'accès	запрос на обращение
A 42	access speed	Zugriffsgeschwindigkeit f	vitesse f d'accès	скорость доступа
A 43	access technique	Zugriffstechnik f	technique f d'accès	способ доступа
A 44	access time	Zugriffszeit f	temps m d'accès	время доступа
A 45	access violation	Zugriffsverletzung f, Zugriffsverbotverletzung f	violation f d'accès	нарушение обращения
	AC characteristics	s. D 593		
	accidental error	s. R 18		
A 46	accordance, concordance, coincidence	Übereinstimmung f	concordance f, coïncidence f	соответствие
A 47	account	Konto n, Faktur f, Rechnung f <Beleg>	compte m, facture f	расчет
A 48	accountancy	Abrechnungswesen n	comptabilité f	делопроизводство
A 49	account card	Kontenkarte f	carte f de compte	учетная карточка
A 50	accounting	Abrechnung f, Buchung f	décompte m	расчет, учет, подведение итога
	accounting computer	s. A 51		
A 51	accounting machine, accounting computer	Abrechnungsautomat m, Buchungsautomat m	machine f comptable, automate m comptable	бухгалтерская машина
A 52	accounting period	Abrechnungszeitraum m	période f comptable	расчетный период
A 53	accounting technique	Abrechnungstechnik f	technique f de comptabilité	метод учета
A 54	AC-coupled	wechselstromgekoppelt	couplé à courant alternatif	связанный по переменному току

A 55	**accumulate / to**	akkumulieren, sammeln, summieren	accumuler	накапливать, суммировать
A 56	**accumulator,** accumulator register	Akkumulator *m*, Akkumulatorregister *n*, Akku *m* <Datensammelregister im Rechenwerk>	accumulateur *m*	аккумулятор, регистр-аккумулятор
A 57	**accumulator adjust instruction**	Akkumulatoreinstellungsbefehl *m*, Akkumulatorkorrekturbefehl *m* <Pseudotetradenkorrektur>	instruction *f* d'ajustement d'accumulateur	инструкция настройки аккумулятора
A 58	**accumulator architecture**	Akkumulatorbasis-Architektur *f* <Struktur mit zentralem Akkumulator>	structure *f* sur base d'accumulateur	структура, главным элементом которой является аккумулятор
A 59	**accumulator operate instruction**	Akkumulatorbefehl *m*	instruction *f* d'accumulateur	команда управления работой аккумулятора
A 60	**accumulator register**	s. A 56		
	accumulator shift	Akkumulator-Stellenverschiebung *f*	décalage *m* d'accumulateur	сдвиг [содержимого] аккумулятора
A 61	**accuracy check**	Genauigkeitsprüfung *f*	vérification *f* de précision	контроль точности
A 62	**accuracy control system**	Genauigkeitsüberwachungssystem *n* <Fehleranzeige- und -korrektursystem>	système *m* de surveillance de précision	система контроля по точности <система коррекции и индикации ошибок>
A 63	**accuracy limit**	Genauigkeitsgrenze *f*, Fehlergrenze *f*	limite *f* de précision	предел точности
A 64	**AC current output power**	Wechselstromleistung *f*	puissance *f* alternative (de courant alternatif)	выходная мощность по переменному току
A 65	**AC/DC,** alternating current/direct current	Wechselstrom/Gleichstrom *m*	c.a./c.c., courant *m* alternatif/courant continu	переменный ток/постоянный ток
A 66	**AC dump**	Wechselspannungsausfall *m*, Ausfall *m* der Wechselspannungsversorgung	défaillance *f* de tension alternative	внезапное отключение напряжения переменного тока
A 67	**AC electroluminescent display**	Wechselstrom-Elektrolumineszenzanzeige *f*	affichage *m* électroluminescent à courant alternatif	электролюминесцентная индикаторная панель переменного тока
A 68	**achievable reliability**	erreichbare Zuverlässigkeit *f*	fiabilité *f* accessible	реальная [действительная] надежность
A 69	**ACIA,** asynchronous communications interface adapter	ACIA-Schaltkreis *m*, Asynchronübertragungs-Schnittstellenanpassungsbaustein *m*	module *m* ACIA, module d'adaptation d'interface à transmission asynchrone	асинхронный адаптер связи
A 70	**acknowledgement**	Empfangsbestätigung *f*, Rückmeldequittung *f*, Anerkennung *f*	reconnaissance *f*, quittance *f*	подтверждение приема, квитирование
	AC-PDP	s. A 71		
A 71	**AC plasma-display panel,** AC-PDP	Wechselstromplasmaanzeige *f*	affichage *m* plasma à courant alternatif	плазменная панель переменного тока
A 72	**AC [power] supply**	Wechselspannungsstromversorgung *f*	alimentation *f* en courant alternatif	источник питания переменного тока
A 73	**action macro**	Arbeitsmakro *n*	macro *m* de travail	макродействие, макроисполнение
A 74	**activate / to**	aktivieren, anregen, in Betrieb setzen	activer, mettre en marche	активировать
A 75	**activate button,** start button	Startknopf *m*	touche *f* (bouton-poussoir *m*) de démarrage (mise en marche)	кнопка пуска
A 76	**activation**	Aktivierung *f*, Anschaltung *f*, Ansteuerung *f*	activation *f*	активизация
A 77	**active area**	wirksame Fläche *f*	surface *f* active	активная область
A 78	**active component**	aktives Bauelement *n*	composant *m* actif	активный компонент
A 79	**active current**	Strom *m* im aktiven Betrieb, Arbeitsstrom *m* <im Gegensatz zu Ruhestrom>	courant *m* de travail	ток нагрузки
A 80	**active element**	aktives Element *n*	élément *m* actif	активный элемент
	active-high signal	s. H 80		
	active-low signal	s. L 290		
	active page	s. C 872		
	active power	s. R 64		
A 81	**active power dissipation**	Arbeitsverlustleistung *f*, Leistungsverbrauch *m* im aktiven Betrieb	puissance *f* de perte de travail	рассеяние потребляемой мощности
A 82	**active region**	aktiver Bereich *m*	domaine *m* actif	активная зона
A 83	**active transducer**	aktiver Wandler *m*	convertisseur *m* actif	активный преобразователь
	actual instruction	s. E 33		
	actual value	s. I 227		
A 84	**actuate / to**	betätigen	actionner	запускать
	AC voltage	s. A 223		
A 85	**adaptability**	Anpassungsfähigkeit *f*	faculté *f* d'adaptation	адаптивность
A 86	**adaptable system**	anpassungsfähiges System *n*	système *m* adaptable	адаптивная система
A 87	**adapter**	Anpassungsbaustein *m*, Zwischenstück *n*, Adapter *m*	adaptateur *m*	адаптер
A 88	**adapter circuit,** matching circuit	Adapterschaltung *f*, Anpassungsschaltung *f*	circuit *m* adapteur, circuit d'adaptation	схема адаптера
A 89	**adapter plug**	Anpaßstecker *m*, Übergangsstecker *m*	fiche *f* adaptative	согласующий разъем, переходный разъем
	adapting	s. A 90		
A 90	**adaption,** adapting, matching	Anpassung *f*	adaptation *f*	адаптация, согласование
A 91	**adaptive architecture**	anpassungsfähige Rechnerstruktur *f*, selbstanpassende Struktur *f*	structure *f* adaptative	адаптивная архитектура

	adaptive control	s. S 137		
A 92	**adaptive system**	adaptives System n, selbstanpassendes System, Anpassungssystem n	système m adaptatif	адаптивная система
	ADC	s. A 263		
	ADC controller	s. A 264		
A 93	**ADCCP, advanced data-communications control procedure**	ADCCP-Protokoll n, modernes Datenübertragungssteuerverfahren n	procédure f moderne de commande de télécommunication	процедура с расширенными возможностями управления передачей данных ‹протокол управления каналом передачи данных›, протокол ADCCP
	A-D converter	s. A 263		
	A-D converter controller	s. A 264		
A 94	**add / to**	addieren	additionner	складывать, суммировать
A 95	**added facility**	Zusatzeinrichtung f, Zusatzausrüstung f, Zusatzmöglichkeit f	dispositif (équipement) m supplémentaire	дополнительное оборудование
A 96	**added instruction kit**	Zusatzbefehlsbausatz m	jeu m d'instructions supplémentaires	дополнительный набор команд
A 97	**adder**	Addierwerk n	addeur m	сумматор
A 98	**add instruction**	Additionsbefehl m	instruction f d'addition	команда сложения
A 99	**addition**	Addition f	addition f	сложение, суммирование
A 100	**additional**	zusätzlich	additionnel	дополнительный
A 101	**additional circuit**	Zusatzschaltung f	circuit m additionnel	дополнительная схема
A 102	**addition time**, add time	Additionszeit f	temps m d'addition	время сложения
A 103	**add-on unit**	Zusatzeinheit f, Anbaueinheit f	unité f supplémentaire	дополнительное (дублирующее) устройство
A 104	**address / to**	adressieren	adresser	адресовать
A 105	**address**	Adresse f	adresse f	адрес
A 106	**addressability**	Adressierbarkeit f	adressabilité f	адресуемость
A 107	**addressable latch**	adressierbarer Zwischenspeicher m, adressierbares Auffangregister n	mémoire f intermédiaire adressable	адресуемый регистр-фиксатор
A 108	**addressable memory**	adressierbarer Speicher m	mémoire f adressable	адресуемая память
A 109	**address arithmetic unit**	Adreßrechenwerk n	unité f arithmétique d'adresses	арифметическое устройство обработки и модификации адресов
A 110	**address array**, address field	Adreßfeld n	champ m d'adresse	поле адреса
A 111	**address buffer**	Adreßpuffer m	tampon m d'adresse[s]	буфер адреса
A 112	**address bus**	Adreßbus m	bus m d'adresse	шина адреса
A 113	**address byte**	Adreßbyte n	octet m d'adresse	адресный байт
A 114	**address calculation**	Adreßrechnung f	calcul m d'adresse	вычисление адреса
A 115	**address capability**	Adressierungsvermögen n	capacité f d'adresses	возможности задания адреса
A 116	**address character**	Adressenzeichen n	caractère m d'adresse	символ адреса
A 117	**address code**	Adreßkode m, Adressenverschlüsselung f	code m d'adresse	код адреса
A 118	**address constant**	Adreßkonstante f	constante f d'adresse	адресная константа
A 119	**address counter**	Adreßzähler m ‹seltenere Bezeichnung für Befehlszähler›	compteur m d'adresse	счетчик адреса
A 120	**address decoder**	Adreßentschlüßler m	décodeur m d'adresse	дешифратор адреса
A 121	**address delay time**	Adreßverzögerungszeit f, Adreßsignalverzögerungszeit f	temps m de retardement d'adresse	время запаздывания [сигналов] адреса, время задержки [сигналов] адреса
	address driver	s. A 139		
A 122	**addressed device**	adressiertes Gerät n	appareil m adressé	адресуемое устройство
A 123	**addressed memory**	adressierter (volladressierter) Speicher m	mémoire f adressée	адресованная память
A 124	**address fetch cycle**	Adreßholezyklus m, Adreßabrufzyklus m	cycle m d'appel d'adresse	цикл выборки адреса
	address field	s. A 110		
A 125	**address format**	Adreßformat n, Adreßfeldstruktur f eines Befehls	format m d'adresse	формат адреса
A 126	**address incrementation**	Adreßerhöhung f	incrémentation f d'adresse	инкрементирование адреса
A 127	**addressing**	Adressierung f	adressage m	адресация
A 128	**addressing capability**	Adressierungsmöglichkeit f	possibilité f d'adressage	возможности адресации
A 129	**addressing capacity**	Adressierungskapazität f, Adressierungsbereich m	capacité f (volume m) d'adressage	диапазон адресации, емкость адресуемой памяти
A 130	**addressing concept**	Adressierungskonzeption f	concept m d'adressage	концепция адресации
A 131	**adressing format**	Adressierformat n	format m d'adressage	формат адресации
A 132	**addressing level**	Adressierungsniveau n	niveau m d'adressage	уровень адресации
A 133	**addressing method**	Adressiermethode f	méthode f d'adressage	метод адресации
A 134	**addressing mode**, address mode	Adressiermodus m, Adressierungsart f, Adreßmodus m	mode m d'adressage	тип (режим) адресации
A 135	**addressing signals**	Adressiersignale npl	signaux mpl d'adressage	адресные сигналы
A 136	**addressing technique**	Adressierungstechnik f	technique f d'adressage	способ адресации
A 137	**address latch**	Adreßhalteregister n	registre m de maintien d'adresse	регистр-фиксатор адреса
A 138	**address line**	Adreßleitung f, Adressierleitung f	ligne f d'adresse, ligne d'adressage	адресная линия
A 139	**address line driver**, address driver	Adreßleitungstreiber m	bascule m de ligne d'adresse	усилитель-формирователь адресных сигналов
A 140	**address mapping**	Adreßzuordnung f, Adreßabbildung f	attribution (représentation) f d'adresse	преобразование логических адресов в абсолютные
	address mode	s. A 134		
A 141	**address mode field**	Adressierungsmodusfeld n eines Befehls	champ m de mode d'adressage d'une instruction	поле [инструкции] для обозначения типа адресации
A 142	**address modification**	Adressenmodifikation f, Adressenänderung f	modification f d'adresse	модификация (изменение) адреса

A 143	address part	Adreßteil m	partie f d'adresse	адресная часть
A 144	address path	Adressenweg m	voie f d'adresse	адресный тракт
A 145	address path width	Adreßwegbreite f, Adreß- busbreite f	largeur f de voie (bus) d'adresse	ширина адресной шины
A 146	address pointer	Adressenzeiger m ‹Adreß- register›	pointeur m d'adresse	указатель адреса
A 147	address range	Adreßbereich m	champ m d'adresse	диапазон адресов
A 148	address register	Adressenregister n	registre m d'adresse	регистр адреса
A 149	address segmentation	Adreßunterteilung f, Adreß- raumgliederung f	découpage m (segmentation f) d'adresse	сегментация адреса
A 150	address selection	Adressenauswahl f, Adressenansteuerung f	sélection f d'adresse	выбор адреса
A 151	address space	Adreßraum m	espace m d'adresse	адресное пространство
A 152	address specification	Adressenangabe f	spécification f d'adresse	спецификация адреса
A 153	address stack	Adressenkellerspeicher m	mémoire-cave f d'adresse	адресный стек
A 154	address strobe	Adreßstrobe m, Adreß- markierimpuls m	impulsion f de marquage d'adresse	строб адреса
A 155	address substitution	Adressensubstitution f	substitution f d'adresse	замена (подстановка) адреса
A 156	address transfer	Adressenübertragung f	transfert m d'adresse	пересылка адреса
A 157	address translation	Adressenübersetzung f, Adreßwandlung f	transposition f d'adresse	трансляция адреса
A 158	address type	Adreßart f ‹z. B. Speicher- adresse, E/A-Adresse›	type m d'adresse	тип адреса
A 159	address value	Adreßwert m	valeur f d'adresse	значение адреса
A 160	address word	Adreßwort n	mot m d'adresse	адресное слово
	add time	s. A 102		
	A-D interface	s. A 265		
A 161	adjacent circuit	benachbarte Schaltung f	circuit m adjacent	соседняя (смежная) схема
A 162	adjacent contacts	benachbarte Kontakte mpl	contacts mpl adjacents	соседние (смежные) кон- такты
A 163	adjacent element	Nachbarelement n	élément m adjacent	соседний (смежный) элемент
A 164	adjacent layer	angrenzende Schicht f	couche f adjacente	соседний (смежный) слой
A 165	adjustable capacitor, trimmer	Trimmer m	trimmer m	подстроечный конденсатор
A 166	adjustable DC potential	regelbare Gleichspannung f	tension f continue réglable	регулируемое напряжение постоянного тока
A 167	adjustable gain	regelbare Verstärkung f	gain m réglable	регулируемый коэффи- циент усиления
A 168	adjustable head	einstellbarer Kopf m	tête f ajustable	перемещаемая головка
A 169	adjustable length	einstellbare Länge f	longueur f ajustable	регулируемая длитель- ность
A 170	adjustable point	einstellbares Komma n	virgule f réglable	регулируемая запятая
A 171	adjustable striking	einstellbarer Anschlag m	butée f réglable	регулируемое усилие
A 172	adjustable threshold	einstellbarer Schwellwert m	valeur f de seuil réglable	регулируемый порог
	adjustable threshold MOS	s. A 361		
A 173	adjusting operation	Einstelloperation f, Justage- operation f	opération f d'ajustement	операция настройки (юстировки)
A 174	adjustment	Justierung f	ajustement m	юстировка
A 175	adjustment instruction	Regulierbefehl m, Einstell- befehl m, Berichtigungs- befehl m	instruction f d'ajustement	команда настройки
A 176	admissible character	zulässiges Zeichen n	caractère m admissible	допустимый символ
A 177	admissible error	zulässiger Fehler m	erreur f admissible	допустимая погрешность
A 178	advance / to	fortschalten, vorrücken	avancer, progresser	продвигать, опережать
A 179	advance control, carriage control	Vorschubsteuerung f	commande f d'avancement	управление подачей
A 180	advanced circuit tech- nique	fortschrittliche (moderne) Schaltkreistechnik f	technique f de circuits avancée	прогрессивная (современ- ная) схемотехника
A 181	advanced concept	fortschrittliche Konzeption f	conception f avancée	прогрессивная (передо- вая) концепция
	advanced data-commu- nications control procedure	s. A 93		
A 182	after point alignment	stellengerechte Anordnung f	disposition f correcte	поразрядная установка
A 183	aging	Alterung f	vieillissement n	старение
A 184	air-conditioned in- stallation	klimatisierte Installation f	installation f à air con- ditionné	установка с кондициони- рованным воздухом
A 185	air conditioning	Klimatisierung f	air m conditionné	кондиционирование воздуха
A 186	air-conditioning requirement	Klimatisierungsanforderung f	exigence f d'air conditionné	требования к климати- ческим условиям
A 187	air-conditioning system	Klimaanlage f	système m à air conditionné	система кондициониро- вания воздуха
A 188	alarm message	Fehlermeldung f, Gefahren- meldung f	message m d'alarme	аварийное сообщение
	AIG	s. A 229		
A 189	algebraic expression	algebraischer Ausdruck m	expression f algébrique	алгебраическое выраже- ние
A 190	algebraic function	algebraische Funktion f	fonction f algébrique	алгебраическая функция
A 191	ALGOL ‹algorithmic language›	ALGOL n ‹algorithmische Programmiersprache›	ALGOL m ‹langage algo- rithmique›	АЛГОЛ ‹алгоритми- ческий язык›
A 192	algorithm	Algorithmus m	algorithme m	алгоритм
A 193	algorithm for pattern recognition	Mustererkennungs- algorithmus m	algorithme m de reconnais- sance de figures	алгоритм распознавания образов
A 194	algorithmic	algorithmisch	algorithmique	алгоритмический
A 195	algorithmic minimizing	algorithmische Minimi- sierung f	minimisation f algorith- mique	минимизация алгоритма
A 196	align / to	ausrichten, abgleichen	aligner, équilibrer	выравнивать, налаживать
A 197	aligner	Justiergerät n	appareil m à ajuster	эталонный прибор; устройство для точной регулировки

A 198	**alignment**	Ausrichtung *f*, Abgleich *m*	alignement *m*, équilibrage *m*	выравнивание, наладка
A 199	**alignment pin**	Paßstift *m*	goupille *f* ajustée	штифт для настройки (синхронизации) компонентов устройства
A 200	**allocate / to,** to assign	zuordnen, zuweisen	attribuer, assigner	распределять, размещать, назначать
A 201	**allocation,** assignment	Zuordnung *f*, Zuweisung *f*	attribution *f*	распределение, размещение, назначение
A 202	**allowed state**	erlaubter Zustand *m*	état *m* permis (autorisé)	разрешенное состояние
A 203	**alloy-diffused**	diffusionslegiert	allié par diffusion	легированный диффузией
A 204	**alloy diffusion technique**	Diffusionslegierungstechnik *f*	technique *f* d'alliage par diffusion	метод диффузионного легирования
A 205	**alloying addition**	Legierungszusatz *m*	supplément *m* d'alliage	легирующая примесь
A 206	**alloying technique**	Legierungstechnik *f*	technique *f* d'alliage	метод легирования
A 207	**alloy junction**	legierter Übergang *m*, Legierungsschicht *f*	jonction *f* alliée	сплавной переход
A 208	**alloy[-type] transistor**	Legierungstransistor *m*	transistor *m* à alliage	сплавной транзистор
	all-purpose computer	*s.* G 40		
A 209	**alphabetic[al]**	alphabetisch ‹buchstabenmäßig›	alphabétique	алфавитный
A 210	**alphabetic character**	Alphabetzeichen *n*, Buchstabe *m*	caractère *m* alphabétique	алфавитный символ
A 211	**alphabetic code**	alphabetischer Kode *m*	code *m* alphabétique	алфавитный код
A 212/3	**alphanumeric**	alphanumerisch ‹Buchstaben und Ziffern enthaltend›	alphanumérique	алфавитно-цифровой
A 214	**alphanumeric code**	alphanumerischer Kode *m*	code *m* alphanumérique	алфавитно-цифровой код
A 215	**alphanumeric display**	alphanumerisches Sichtanzeigegerät *n*	appareil *m* de visualisation alphanumérique	алфавитно-цифровой дисплей
A 216	**alphanumeric keyboard**	alphanumerische Tastatur *f*	clavier *m* alphanumérique	алфавитно-цифровая клавиатура
A 217	**alphanumeric output**	alphanumerische Ausgabe *f*	sortie *f* alphanumérique	алфавитно-цифровой выход
A 218	**alphanumeric representation**	alphanumerische Darstellung *f*	représentation *f* alphanumérique	алфавитно-цифровое представление
A 219	**alteration,** change, modification	Änderung *f*, Modifizierung *f*	altération *f*, modification *f*	изменение, преобразование, модификация
A 220	**alteration program**	Änderungsprogramm *n*	programme *m* de modification	программа корректировки (преобразования)
A 221	**alternate code**	Austauschkode *m*	code *m* interchangeable	код замены, альтернативный код
A 222	**alternating current,** AC	Wechselstrom *m*	courant *m* alternatif	переменный ток
	alternating current / direct current	*s.* A 65		
A 223	**alternating voltage,** AC voltage	Wechselspannung *f*	tension *f* alternative	напряжение переменного тока
A 224	**alternation**	Halbwelle *f*	demi-onde *f*	половина периода
A 225	**alternative**	alternativ, wechselweise	alternatif	альтернативный, избирательный
A 226	**alternative branching**	Alternativverzweigung *f*	branchement *m* alternatif	альтернативное ветвление
A 227	**alternative program**	Zusatzprogramm *n*	programme *m* supplémentaire	дополнительная программа
A 228	**alter switch,** change-over switch	Umschalter *m*	commutateur *m*	переключатель, состояние которого опрашивается программой
	ALU	*s.* A 308		
A 229	**aluminium gate,** AlG	Aluminium-Steuerelektrode *f*, Aluminium-Gate *n*, Al-Gate *n*	gate *m* à l'aluminium	алюминиевый затвор
A 230	**ambient conditions,** environmental conditions	Umgebungsbedingungen *fpl*	conditions *fpl* d'environnement	внешние условия
A 231	**ambient temperature,** environmental temperature	Umgebungstemperatur *f*, Raumtemperatur *f*	température *f* ambiante	температура окружающей среды
A 232	**ambient temperature range**	Umgebungstemperaturbereich *m*	champ *m* de température ambiante	диапазон изменения температуры окружающей среды
	american standard code for information interchange	*s.* A 321		
A 233	**amount**	Betrag *m*, Anzahl *f*	montant *m*, nombre *m*	количество, сумма
A 234	**amplification**	Verstärkung *f*	amplification *f*	усиление
A 235	**amplification factor**	Verstärkungsfaktor *m*	facteur *m* d'amplification	коэффициент усиления
A 236	**amplified signal**	verstärktes Signal *n*	signal *m* amplifié	усиленный сигнал
A 237	**amplifier**	Verstärker *m*	amplificateur *m*	усилитель
A 238	**amplifier circuit**	Verstärkerschaltung *f*	circuit *m* amplificateur	усилительная схема
A 239	**amplifier load**	Verstärkerbelastung *f*	charge *f* d'amplificateur	нагрузка усилителя
A 240	**amplifier response**	Verstärkerfrequenzgang *m*	réponse *f* harmonique d'amplificateur	характеристика усилителя
A 241	**amplifier stage**	Verstärkerstufe *f*	étage *m* d'amplificateur	усилительный каскад
A 242	**amplitude adjustment**	Amplitudeneinstellung *f*	ajustage *m* d'amplitude	регулировка амплитуды
A 243	**amplitude characteristic**	Amplitudenkennlinie *f*	caractéristique *f* d'amplitude	амплитудная характеристика
A 244	**amplitude level**	Amplitudenniveau *n*, Höhenpegel *m*	niveau *m* d'amplitude	амплитудный уровень
A 245	**analog[ue]**	analog	analogique	аналоговый
A 246	**analog amplifier**	Analogverstärker *m*	amplificateur *m* analogique	усилитель аналоговых сигналов
A 247	**analog channel**	Analogkanal *m*	canal *m* analogique	канал [передачи] аналоговых сигналов
A 248	**analog circuit**	Analogschaltkreis *m*	circuit *m* analogique	аналоговая схема
A 249	**analog circuitry**	Analogschaltung *f*	montage *m* analogique	аналоговая схемотехника
A 250	**analog comparator**	Analogkomparator *m*, Analogvergleicher *m*	comparateur *m* analogique	аналоговый компаратор, схема сравнения аналоговых сигналов

A 251	analog computer	Analogrechner m	calculateur m analogique	аналоговая вычислительная машина, АВМ
A 252	analog data	Analogdaten pl	données fpl analogiques	данные, представленные в аналоговой форме
A 253	analog display unit	Analogsichtgerät n	appareil m de visualisation analogique	устройство индикации аналоговых сигналов
A 254	analog input	Analogeingabe f, Analogeingang m	entrée f analogique	ввод аналоговых сигналов, аналоговый вход
A 255	analog input amplifier	Analogeingangsverstärker m	amplificateur m analogique d'entrée	предварительный усилитель аналоговых сигналов
A 256	analog interface	Analogschnittstelle f, Anschlußstelle f für Analogsignale	interface f analogique	аналоговый интерфейс
A 257	analog I/O system	Analog-E/A-System n	système m d'E/A analogique	система ввода-вывода аналоговых сигналов
A 258	analog module	Analogbaustein m ‹mit Analogsignalen arbeitender Baustein›	module m analogique	аналоговый модуль
A 259	analog output	Analogausgabe f, Analogausgang m	sortie f analogique	вывод аналоговых сигналов, аналоговый выход
A 260	analog recording	Analogaufzeichnung f	enregistrement m analogique	запись аналоговых сигналов
A 261	analog representation	analoge Darstellung f	représentation f analogique	аналоговое представление
A 262	analog switch	Analogsignalschalter m	commutateur m analogique	аналоговый переключатель
A 263	analog-[to-]digital converter, A-D converter, ADC	Analog-Digital-Umsetzer m, ADU m	convertisseur m analogique-numérique (A-N)	аналого-цифровой преобразователь, АЦП
A 264	analog-[to-]digital converter controller, A-D converter controller, ADC controller	ADU-Steuereinheit f	unité f de commande de convertisseur A-N	АЦП-контроллер
A 265	analog-[to-]digital interface, A-D interface	Analog-Digital-Schnittstelle f, A-D-Schnittstelle f	interface f analogique-numérique (A-N)	аналого-цифровой интерфейс
A 266	analytic code	analytischer Befehlskode m	code m analytique	аналитический код
A 267	analyzer	Analysator m ‹Prüfgerät›	analyseur m	анализатор
A 268	ancillary	Zusatz m, Zubehörausstattung f	auxiliaires mpl	дополнительное устройство
A 269	AND	UND n ‹logischer Operator ,,Konjunktion"›	ET	И ‹логическая операция «КОНЪЮНКЦИЯ»›
A 270	AND circuit, AND gate	UND-Schaltung f, UND-Gatter n, UND-Glied n	circuit m (porte f) ET	схема И
A 271	AND element	UND-Element n ‹logisches Element›	élément m ET	логический элемент И
	AND gate	s. A 270		
A 272	AND NOT, NAND, EXCEPT	negiertes UND n, UND-NICHT n	ET-NON, NAND	И-НЕ
A 273	AND operation	UND-Operation f ‹Boolesche Operation›	opération f ET	операция И
A 274	anisotropic etching	anisotropes Ätzen n	rongement m anisotrope	анизотропное травление
A 275	anisotropic semiconductor	anisotroper Halbleiter m	semi-conducteur m anisotrope	анизотропный полупроводник
A 276	anticoincidence circuit	Antikoinzidenzschaltung f ‹Exklusiv-ODER-Schaltung›	circuit m d'anticoïncidence	схема несовпадения ‹схема выполнения операции «ИСКЛЮЧАЮЩЕЕ ИЛИ»›
A 277	application, use, employment	Anwendung f, Einsatz m, Verwendung f	application f	применение, использование
A 278	application aids	Anwendungshilfen fpl	aides fpl à l'application	дополнительный (вспомогательный) набор прикладных программ
A 279	application-dependent data segmentation	anwendungsabhängige Datenunterteilung f	segmentation f des données dépendante de l'application	сегментация данных по областям применения
	application field	s. R 27		
A 280	application notes	Anwendungsbeschreibung f	description f d'application	комментарий прикладной программы
A 281	application-oriented	anwendungsorientiert	orienté application	ориентированный на прикладное программирование
A 282	application package	Anwendungspaket n ‹Programmpaket zur universellen Anwendung›	pack m d'application	пакет прикладных программ
A 283	application problem	Anwendungsproblem n, Einsatzproblem n	problème m d'application	прикладная задача
A 284	application program	Anwendungsprogramm n	programme m d'application	прикладная программа, программа пользователя
A 285	application software	Anwendungs-Software f, Anwendungssystemunterlagen fpl	logiciels mpl d'application	прикладное программное обеспечение
A 286	application study	Anwendungsstudie f	étude f d'application	исследование [области] применения
A 287	application support	Anwendungsunterstützung f	assistance f à l'application	служебная программа
A 288	application technique	Anwendungstechnik f	technique f d'application	методы прикладного программирования
A 289	applied circuit synthesis	angewandte Schaltungssynthese f	synthèse f de circuit appliquée	прикладные методы синтеза схем
A 290	applied voltage	angelegte Spannung f	tension f appliquée	приложенное напряжение
A 291	apply / to, to use, to employ	anwenden, verwenden, einsetzen	appliquer, utiliser	применять
A 292	approach	Lösungsweg m, Annäherung f	approximation f	приближение

A 293	approximate design	Näherungsentwurf m	projet m approximatif	приближенный расчет
A 294	approximate solution	Näherungslösung f	solution f approximative	приближенное решение
A 295	approximate value	Näherungswert m	valeur f approximative	приближенное значение
A 296	APT <automatically programmed tools>	APT <Programmiersprache für NC-Anwendungen>	APT <langage pour applications NC>	АРТ <язык программирования для станков с числовым управлением>
A 297	arbiter	Schiedsrichter m, Entscheider m <Zuteilungssystem>	arbitre m	арбитр
A 298	arbitrary parameter	freier Parameter m	paramètre m arbitraire	произвольный (свободный) параметр
A 299	arbitrary placement	willkürliche (freie) Anordnung f	emplacement m arbitraire	произвольное размещение
A 300	arbitrate / to	entscheiden, schiedsrichtern	arbitrer	принимать решение
A 301	arbitration	Schiedsspruch m <Zuweisungsentscheidung>	arbitrage m	арбитраж
A 302	architectural compatibility	strukturelle Kompatibilität (Verträglichkeit) f, Architekturübereinstimmung f	compatibilité f structurelle	архитектурная (структурная) совместимость
A 303	architecture	Architektur f, Aufbau m	architecture f	архитектура
A 304	argument	Argument n	argument m	аргумент
A 305	arithmetic[al]	arithmetisch	arithmétique	арифметический
A 306	arithmetic facilities	Arithmetikmöglichkeiten fpl, Arithmetikeinrichtungen fpl	possibilités fpl arithmétiques	арифметические возможности; арифметические устройства
A 307	arithmetic instruction	Arithmetikbefehl m, Rechenanweisung f	instruction f arithmétique	арифметическая инструкция
A 308	arithmetic-logic unit, ALU	Arithmetik-Logik-Einheit f, Rechenwerk n, ALU f	unité f arithmétique et logique	арифметическо-логическое устройство, АЛУ
A 309	arithmetic notation	arithmetische Schreibweise f	notation f arithmétique	арифметическая запись, арифметическое представление
A 310	arithmetic operation	arithmetische Operation f, Rechenoperation f	opération f arithmétique	арифметическая операция
A 311	arithmetic processor, ARP	Arithmetikprozessor m, Arithmetikzusatzprozessor m, ARP <Multilängen- und Gleitkommaarithmetik>	processeur m arithmétique (supplémentaire), ARP m <longueurs multiples et virgule flottante>	арифметический процессор, [дополнительный] процессор для выполнения арифметических операций
A 312	arithmetic register	Rechenregister n	registre m arithmétique	регистр арифметического устройства
A 313	arithmetic section	s. A 314		
	arithmetic shift	arithmetische Verschiebung f	décalage m arithmétique	арифметический сдвиг
A 314	arithmetic unit, arithmetic section	arithmetische Einheit f, arithmetisches Rechenwerk n, Arithmetikwerk n	unité f arithmétique	арифметическое устройство
	arm	s. B 261		
	ARP	s. A 311		
A 315	array	Feld n, <reguläre> Anordnung f	champ m	массив
A 316	array declaration	Feldvereinbarung f	déclaration f de champ	объявление массива
A 317	array processing	Feldverarbeitung f	traitement m de champ	обработка массива; матричная обработка
A 318	array structure	Feldstruktur f	structure f de champ	структура массива
A 319	artificial intelligence	künstliche Intelligenz f	intelligence f artificielle	искусственный интеллект
	ARU	s. A 366		
A 320	ascending sequence	aufsteigende Reihenfolge f	séquence f ascendante	возрастающая последовательность
A 321	ASCII, american standard code for information interchange	ASCII m, amerikanischer Standardkode m für Informationsaustausch	ASCII m, code m standard américain pour l'échange d'informations	ASCII, американский стандартный код информационного обмена
A 322	ASR, automatic send-receive set	ASR-Einrichtung f, automatische Sende-/Empfangs-Gerätekombination f	émetteur-récepteur m automatique	автоматическое приемо-передающее устройство
A 323	assemble / to	montieren, zusammensetzen, assemblieren	assembler	собирать, компоновать, транслировать
A 324	assembler, assembler program, assembly program, assembly routine	Assembler m, Assemblerprogramm n, Assemblierer m, Kode-Umwandlungsprogramm n, Programmumsetzer m <übersetzt Quellkodeprogramme in Objektkodeprogramme>	assembleur m	ассемблер, программа-ассемблер, компонующая программа
	assembler code	s. A 335		
A 325	assembler development system	Assemblerentwicklungssystem n, Entwicklungssystem n auf Assemblerbasis	système m de développement à assembleur	средства составления и отладки программ языка ассемблера
	assembler directive	s. A 336		
A 326/7	assembler error message	Assemblerfehleranzeige f <Erkennung von Formalfehlern beim Assemblieren>	message m d'erreur d'assembleur	сообщение об ошибках программы ассемблера
	assembler instruction	s. A 336		
	assembler language	s. A 330		
	assembler program	s. A 324		
	assembler run	s. A 337		
A 328	assembly	Zusammenbau m, Montage f	assemblage m	сборка, ассемблирование
A 329	assembly error	Assemblierfehler m	erreur f d'assemblage	ошибка в исходном тексте, обнаруженная программой ассемблера

	English	German	French	Russian
A 330	assembly language, assembler language	Assemblersprache f	langage m d'assembleur	язык ассемблера
A 331	assembly language level	Assemblersprachebene f, Assemblerniveau n	niveau m d'assembleur	уровень языка ассемблера
A 332	assembly language program	Assemblerkodeprogramm n, Programm n in Assemblerkode	programme m en code d'assembleur	программа на языке ассемблера
A 333	assembly language programming	Programmierung f in Assemblersprache (Assemblerkode)	programmation f en langage d'assembleur	программирование на языке ассемблера
A 334	assembly operation assembly program	Montageoperation f s. A 324	opération f d'assemblage	операция сборки (компоновки)
A 335	assembly program code, assembler code	Assemblerkode m	code m d'assembleur	машинный код программы ассемблера
A 336	assembly program instruction, assembler instruction (directive)	Assemblerbefehl m, Assembleranweisung f, Anweisung f an den Assembler	instruction f de programme d'assemblage, instruction-assembleur f	инструкция (команда, директива) ассемблера
A 337	assembly program run, assembler run	Assemblerlauf m	marche f d'assembleur	прогон программы ассемблера
	assembly routine	s. A 324		
A 338	assembly system	Montagesystem n	système m d'assemblage	смонтированная система
	assign / to	s. A 200		
	assignment	s. A 201		
A 339	assignment instruction	Zuordnungsbefehl m	instruction f d'assignation	инструкция присваивания
A 340	assignment statement	Ergibtanweisung f	instruction f de résultat	оператор присвоения
A 341	assignment symbol	Ergibtzeichen n	symbole m de résultat	знак присвоения
A 342	assists	Unterstützungen fpl ‹auf Mikroprogrammebene›	assistances fpl ‹au niveau de microprogramme›	средства поддержки ‹на уровне микропрограмм›
A 343	associated	zugehörig	associé	связанный, объединенный
A 344	associated software	zugehörige Software f (Systemunterlagen fpl)	logiciels mpl associés	сопряженное программное обеспечение
A 345	associative memory	Assoziativspeicher m	mémoire f associative	ассоциативное запоминающее устройство
A 346	astable, unstable, instable	instabil, unbeständig	instable	неустойчивый
A 347	astable circuit	instabile Schaltung f	circuit m instable	схема с неустойчивым состоянием
A 348	asymmetrical pulse train	asymmetrische Impulsfolge f	suite f d'impulsions asymétriques	несимметричная импульсная последовательность
A 349	asynchronous	asynchron, taktunabhängig, nicht synchronisiert	asynchrone	асинхронный
	asynchronous communications interface adapter	s. A 69		
A 350	asynchronous computer	Asynchronrechner m	calculateur m asynchrone	ЭВМ с переменным циклом выполнения операций
A 351	asynchronous data transfer	asynchrone Datenübertragung f	transfert m asynchrone de données	асинхронная передача данных
A 352	asynchronous input	asynchrone Eingabe f	entrée f asynchrone	асинхронный ввод [данных]
A 353	asynchronous logic	asynchrone (ungetaktete) Logikschaltung f	montage m logique asynchrone	асинхронная логическая схема
A 354	asynchronous mode	Asynchronmodus m	mode m asynchrone	асинхронный режим
A 355	asynchronous multiplexer	asynchroner Multiplexer m ‹Schnittstellenmultiplexer für asynchrone Übertragungswege›	multiplexeur m asynchrone	асинхронный мультиплексор
A 356	asynchronous operation	Asynchronoperation f	opération f asynchrone	асинхронная операция
A 357	asynchronous operation	asynchroner Betrieb m	régime m asynchrone	асинхронная работа
A 358	asynchronous output	asynchrone Ausgabe f	sortie f asynchrone	асинхронный вывод [данных]
A 359	asynchronous time-division multiplexing	asynchrones zeitgeteiltes Multiplexen n, asynchrones Zeitmultiplexen n	multiplexage m asynchrone à division de temps	асинхронное временное объединение ‹цифровых сигналов данных›, асинхронное мультиплексирование с временным уплотнением
A 360	asynchronous transmission	asynchrone Übertragung f	transmission f asynchrone	асинхронная передача
	ATE	s. A 405		
A 361	ATMOS, adjustable threshold MOS	ATMOS f, MOS-Technik f mit einstellbarem Transistorschwellwert ‹Isolierschicht-FET für Speicherzelle›	ATMOS f, technique f MOS à valeur de seuil ajustable	МОП-структура с регулируемым порогом
A 362	attach / to	anlagern, anhängen, hinzusetzen	attacher, joindre	присоединять, прикреплять
A 363	attached input-output	angelagerte Eingabe-Ausgabe f, integrierte Eingabe-Ausgabe f ‹E/A-Tore sind Teil von CPU- oder Speicher-SK›	entrée-sortie f intégrée	интегрированный ввод/вывод ‹порты ввода/вывода являются частью центрального процессора или запоминающего устройства›
A 364	attachment	Anbaugerät n, Anschlußgerät n	appareil m adjoint (complémentaire)	дополнительное устройство; присоединение, прикрепление
	attenuation	s. D 11/2		
A 365	audio response	akustische Antwort (Beantwortung) f, Tonfrequenzgang m	réponse f acoustique	речевой вывод
A 366	audio response unit, ARU	Sprachausgabeeinheit f ‹Rechner-Telefon-Anschlußgerät zur Sprachausgabe›	unité f de sortie audio	устройство речевого вывода

A 367	**augend**	Augend *m*, erster Summand *m*	terme *m* d'addition	первое слагаемое
A 368	**augment / to**	vermehren, zunehmen	augmenter	прибавлять, дополнять
A 369	**authorized**	berechtigt, autorisiert	autorisé	санкционированный, авторизованный
A 370	**autocode**	Autokode *m*	autocode *m*	автокод
A 371	**autodecrement**	selbsttätiges Vermindern *n*	autodécrémentation *f*	автоматическое декрементирование
A 372	**autodecrementing addressing mode**	Adressierungsart *f* mit eingeschlossener Verminderung der Adresse	mode *m* d'adressage à auto-décrémentation	автодекрементный способ адресации
A 373	**autoincrement**	selbsttätiges Vergrößern *n*	auto-incrémentation *f*	автоматическое инкрементирование
A 374	**autoincrementing addressing mode**	Adressierungsart *f* mit eingeschlossener Erhöhung der Adresse	mode *m* d'adressage à auto-incrémentation	автоинкрементный способ адресации
A 375	**autoindexing**	Selbstindizierung *f* ‹automatisches Erhöhen oder Vermindern eines Index›	auto-indexage *m*	автоиндексация
	autoloader	s. A 396		
A 376	**automata theory**	Automatentheorie *f*	théorie *f* des automates	теория автоматов
A 377	**automated assembly**	automatisierte Montage *f*	assemblage (montage) *m* automatisé	автоматизированная сборка
A 378	**automated construction**	automatisierte Konstruktion *f*	construction *f* automatisée	автоматизированное конструирование
A 379	**automated logic design**	automatisierter Logikentwurf *m*	projet *m* logique automatisé	автоматизированное логическое проектирование
A 380	**automated speech recognition**	automatisierte Spracherkennung *f*	reconnaissance *f* de la parole automatisée	автоматизированное распознавание речи
A 381	**automatic[al]**	automatisch ‹maschinell›	automatique	автоматический
A 382	**automatic averaging**	automatische Mittelwertbildung *f*	évaluation *f* automatique de moyenne	автоматическое усреднение
A 383	**automatic calling unit**	automatische Anrufeinheit *f*	unité *f* automatique d'appel	устройство автоматического вызова
A 384	**automatic character recognition**	automatische Zeichenerkennung *f*	reconnaissance *f* automatique de caractères	автоматическое распознавание символов
A 385	**automatic checking**	automatisches Testen *n*, automatische Prüfung *f*	test *m* automatique	автоматический контроль
A 386	**automatic circuit exchange**, automatic exchange	automatische Wählvermittlung (Vermittlung) *f*	communication *f* automatique	автоматический обмен
A 387	**automatic control engineering**	Automatisierungstechnik *f*	technique *f* d'automatisation	техника автоматического регулирования и управления
A 388	**automatic controller**	automatisches Steuergerät (Regelgerät) *n*	commande *f* (régulateur *m*) automatique	автоматический контроллер
A 389	**automatic data processing**	automatische Datenverarbeitung *f*	traitement *m* automatique de données	автоматизированная обработка данных
A 390	**automatic data processing machine**	automatische Datenverarbeitungsanlage *f*	installation *f* automatique de traitement de données	автоматизированная система обработки данных
A 391	**automatic design system**	automatisches Entwurfssystem *n*	système *m* de conception automatique	система автоматического проектирования
A 392	**automatic drawing digitizing**	automatische Zeichnungsdigitalisierung *f*	transformation *f* automatique de dessins en numérique	автоматическое преобразование графической информации в цифровую форму
A 393	**automatic error correction**	automatische Fehlerkorrektur *f*	correction *f* automatique d'erreurs	автоматическая коррекция ошибок
	automatic exchange	s. A 386		
A 394	**automatic form feeding**	automatische Formularzuführung *f*, automatischer Formulareinzug *m*	acheminement *m* automatique de formulaires	автоматическая подача бланков
A 395	**automatic gate-placement system**	automatisches Gatteranordnungssystem *n* ‹SK-Topologieentwicklung›	système *m* automatique de placement de gate	система автоматического проектирования топологии [микросхем]
A 396	**automatic loader**, autoloader	automatischer Lader *m*	chargeur *m* automatique	автоматический загрузчик
A 397	**automatic logging**	automatische Meßwerterfassung *f*	enregistrement *m* automatique de mesure	автоматическая регистрация
A 398	**automatic message exchange (switching)**	automatische Nachrichtenvermittlung *f*, Speichervermittlung *f*	communication *f* automatique à mémoire	автоматическая коммутация сообщений
A 399	**automatic programming**	automatische Programmierung *f* ‹Programmwicklung mit Rechnerunterstützung›	programmation *f* automatique	автоматическое программирование
	automatic recovery program	s. R 126		
A 400	**automatic reset**	automatische Nullstellung (Rückstellung) *f*	remise *f* a zéro automatique, RAZ automatique	автоматическая установка в ноль
A 401	**automatic restart**, autorestart	automatischer (selbständiger) Wiederanlauf *m*	redémarrage *m* automatique	автоматический повторный запуск, автоматический рестарт
	automatic send-receive set	s. A 322		
A 402	**automatic speech recognition**	automatische Spracherkennung *f*	reconnaissance *f* automatique de la parole	автоматическое распознавание речи
A 403	**automatic switchover**	automatischer Umschalter *m* ‹zwischen zwei Rechnern›	commutateur *m* automatique	автоматический коммутатор
A 404	**automatic teaching machine**, teaching machine	Lehrautomat *m*	automate *m* enseignant	обучающая машина

A 405	automatic test equipment, ATE	automatische Prüfeinrichtung *f* ‹Prüfautomat›	dispositif *m* automatique de test	автоматическое испытательное оборудование
A 406	automatic tester	Prüfautomat *m*	automate *m* de vérification	устройство автоматического контроля
A 407	automatic text processing	automatische Textverarbeitung *f*	traitement *m* automatique de textes	автоматическая обработка текстов
A 408	automatic translation	automatische Übersetzung *f*	traduction *f* automatique	автоматическая трансляция
A 409	automation	Automation *f*, Automatisierung *f*	automation *f*, automatisation *f*	автоматизация
A 410	automode	automatische Betriebsweise *f*	régime (mode) *m* automatique	автоматический режим
A 411	automotive electronics	Kraftfahrzeugelektronik *f*	électronique *f* d'automobile	электронные схемы управления двигателем автомобиля
A 412	autonomous system autopoll[ing] autorestart	s. S 667 automatische Abfrage *f* s. A 401	interrogation *f* automatique	автоматический опрос
A 413	auxiliary carry	Hilfsübertrag *m* ‹Übertrag aus einer Stellenposition unterhalb der Wortlänge, z. B. Halbbyte-Übertrag›	retenue *f* auxiliaire	дополнительный перенос
A 414	auxiliary device	Hilfsgerät *n* ‚Zusatzgerät *n*	appareil *m* auxiliaire	вспомогательное устройство; дополнительное устройство
A 415	auxiliary equipment and supplies	Zusatzeinrichtungen *fpl* und Zubehör *n*	équipement *m* auxiliaire et accessoires *mpl*	комплект дополнительного оборудования и принадлежностей
A 416	auxiliary function	Hilfsfunktion *f*	fonction *f* auxiliaire	дополнительная функция
A 417	auxiliary processor	Hilfsprozessor *m*, Zusatzprozessor *m* ‹für spezielle Funktionen wie GK-Arithmetik, FFT, E/A-Steuerung usw.›	processeur *m* auxiliaire	вспомогательный [специализированный] процессор
A 418	auxiliary routine	Hilfsprogramm *n*	routine *f* auxiliaire	служебная программа
A 419	auxiliary storage	Hilfsspeicher *m*, Reservespeicher *m*	mémoire *f* auxiliaire	вспомогательная память
A 420	availability	Verfügbarkeit *f*	disponibilité *f*	готовность; коэффициент готовности
A 421	available machine time available power	s. A 422 verfügbare (abgebbare) Leistung *f*	puissance *f* disponible	мощность на согласованной нагрузке
A 422	available time, available machine time	verfügbare Rechnerzeit *f*	temps (temps-machine) *m* disponible	доступное [для работы] машинное время
A 423	avalanche	Lawine *f*, Stoßentladung *f*	avalanche *f*	лавина, лавинный разряд
A 424	avalanche breakdown	Lawinendurchbruch *m* ‹Halbleitertechnik›	décharge *f* d'avalanche	лавинный пробой
A 425	avalanche diode	Avalanche-Diode *f*, Durchbruchdiode *f* ‹Zenerdiode›	diode *f* d'avalanche ‹diode Zener›	лавинопролетный диод
A 426	avalanche injection	Lawineninjektion *f*, Elektroneninjektion *f* ‹über Durchbruch›	injection *f* d'avalanche	лавинная инжекция
A 427	avalanche noise	Lawinenrauschen *n* ‹Halbleitertechnik›	bruit *m* d'avalanche	лавинный шум
A 428	avalanche transistor	Lawinentransistor *m*	transistor *m* à avalanche	лавинный транзистор
A 429	average deviation	mittlere Abweichung *f*	écart *m* moyen, déviation *f* moyenne	среднее отклонение
A 430	average execution time	mittlere Ausführungszeit *f*	temps *m* moyen d'exécution	среднее время выполнения
A 431	average propagation time	mittlere Laufzeit *f*	temps *m* moyen de marche	среднее время распространения
A 432	average supply current	mittlere Stromaufnahme *f*	consommation *f* moyenne de courant	среднее значение потребляемого тока
A 433	average transfer rate	mittlere Übertragungsgeschwindigkeit *f*	vitesse *f* moyenne de transmission	средняя скорость передачи [данных]
A 434	averaging	Mittelwertbildung *f*	prise *f* en moyenne	усреднение

B

B 1	backassembler back bias, reverse bias	s. D 418 Sperrvorspannung *f*	tension *f* de polarisation inverse	обратное смещение
B 2	back-biased	in Sperrichtung vorgespannt	à polarisation inverse	обратно смещенный
B 3	back-coupling effect	Rückkopplungseffekt *m*	effet *m* de réaction	влияние обратной связи
B 4	back current, reverse current back direction	Sperrstrom *m*, Rückstrom *m* s. R 369	courant *m* inverse	обратный ток
B 5	back edge, trailing edge	Rückflanke *f*	flanc *m* arrière	задний фронт
B 6	back-end processor	Nachschaltrechner *m*, nachgeschalteter Prozessor *m*	processeur *m* back-end	
B 7	background	Hintergrund *m*, Untergrund *m*	arrière-plan *m*	фоновая задача, фоновый раздел
B 8	background processing	Hintergrundverarbeitung *f* ‹z. B. zu einem im Vordergrund laufenden Echtzeitprogramm›	traitement *m* en arrière-plan	фоновая обработка
B 9	background program	Hintergrundprogramm *n* ‹bearbeitet Aufgaben geringerer Dringlichkeit›	programme *m* en arrière-plan	фоновая программа
B 10	backing storage backing store, backing storage	s. B 10 Hintergrundspeicher *m*, Reservespeicher *m*	mémoire *f* supplémentaire	дополнительное запоминающее устройство
B 11	backlash	Schlupf *m*, toter Gang *m*	pas *m* mort	мертвый ход

B 12	backlog	Rückstand m, Überhang m, unerledigte Arbeit f	restant m, travail m inachevé	невыполненное задание
B 13	backplane	Rückwandplatine f, Rückverdrahtungsplatte f	dos m, plaque f arrière	задняя панель
B 14	backplane interconnection	Rückverdrahtung f, Rückwandverbindung f	connexions fpl arrière, fond m de panier	монтаж соединений на задней панели
B 15	backspace	Rücksetzen (Rückschalten) n um 1 Stelle <Schreib­maschine>	retour m d'une position <machine à écrire>	обратное перемещение, возврат
B 16	back-to-back connection	Antiparallelschaltung f, gegensinnige Parallelschaltung f	couplage m antiparallèle	встречное соединение
B 17	back-to-back cycles, successive cycles	aufeinanderfolgende Zyklen mpl	cycles mpl successifs	последовательные такты
B 18	backup battery	Sicherungsbatterie f, Hilfsbatterie f <Datenerhalt-Sicherung>	batterie f de secours	резервная (вспомогательная) батарея
B 19	backup device	Reservegerät n	appareil m de secours	резервное устройство
B 20	backup equipment	Hilfsausstattung f, Reserveausstattung f	équipement m de réserve	резервное (дублирующее) оборудование
B 21	backup file	Sicherungsdatei f	fichier m de secours	дублирующий файл
B 22	backup memory	Sicherungsspeicher m	mémoire f de secours	резервная (дублирующая) память
B 23	backup system, standby system	Reservesystem n, Aushilfssystem n, Bereitschaftssystem n	système m de réserve	резервная система
B 24	back voltage, reverse voltage	Sperrspannung f	tension f inverse	обратное напряжение
B 25	backward channel	Rückkanal m	canal m arrière	обратный канал
	backward resistance	s. R 372		
B 26	balanced amplifier	symmetrischer Verstärker m	amplificateur m symétrique	дифференциальный усилитель
B 27	balanced circuit	angepaßte (symmetrische) Schaltung f	circuit m symétrique	дифференциальная схема
B 28	balanced error	symmetrischer Fehler m	erreur f symétrique	сбалансированная ошибка
B 29	balanced input	symmetrischer Eingang m	entrée f symétrique	дифференциальный вход
B 30	balanced line	abgeglichene (symmetrische) Leitung f	ligne f équilibrée (symétrique)	симметричная линия
B 31	balanced output	symmetrischer Ausgang m, symmetrische Ausgangsspannung f	sortie f symétrique, tension f symétrique de sortie	симметричный выход
B 32	balanced pulses	symmetrische Impulse mpl	impulsions fpl symétriques	симметричные импульсы
B 33	balanced push-pull amplifier	symmetrischer Gegentaktverstärker m	amplificateur m symétrique push-pull	симметричный двухтактный усилитель
B 34	balanced signal	symmetrisches Signal n	signal m symétrique	симметричный сигнал
B 35	balanced voltage	erdsymmetrische Spannung f	tension f symétrique [par rapport à la terre]	напряжение, симметричное относительно земли
B 36	balance point	Abgleichpunkt m	point m d'équilibrage	точка согласования
B 37	balancing circuit	Abgleichschaltung f	circuit m d'équilibrage	схема компенсации
B 38	balancing machine	Saldiermaschine f	machine f à solder	суммирующая машина
B 39	balancing resistance	Abgleichwiderstand m	résistance f d'équilibrage	компенсирующее сопротивление
B 40	bandwidth	Bandbreite f	largeur f de bande	ширина полосы [частот]
B 41	bank	Bank f <logische Speicher­einheit>	banque m	банк <логическая органи­зация памяти>
B 42	bank address register	Bankadressenregister n, Speicherblockadreßregister n, Speicherbankzeiger m	registre m d'adresses de banque	регистр адреса блока (банка) памяти
B 43	bank switching	Blockumschaltung f <Speichererweiterungs­technik>	commutation f de bloc	переключение блоков (банков) памяти
B 44	bar code	Strichkode m	code m de barres	штриховой код
B 45	barrel shifter	Multipositionsverschieber m <verschiebt in 1 Schritt um mehrere Binärstellen>	décaleur m multiple	схема сдвига на произвольное число позиций
B 46	barrier capacitance, junction (depletion-layer) capacitance	Sperrschichtkapazität f	capacité f de couche de barrage	барьерная емкость, емкость перехода
B 47	barrier layer, junction, depletion layer	Sperrschicht f	couche f de barrage, jonction f	запирающий слой
B 48	barrier layer rectifier, junction rectifier	Sperrschichtgleichrichter m	redresseur m à couche de barrage	выпрямитель с p-n переходом
B 49	barrier potential	Sperrschichtpotential n	potentiel m de barrage	величина потенциального барьера
B 50	base	Basis f <Zahlensystem, Transistorelektrode>, Grundlage f, Träger m	base f, support m	база <электрод тран­зистора>, основание <системы счисления>; основа
B 51	base address, basic address	Basisadresse f	adresse f de base	базовый адрес
B 52	base board, base plate	Grundplatte f, Grundplatine f	plaque f de base	базовая плата
B 53	base bulk resistance	Basisbahnwiderstand m	résistance f série de base	объемное сопротивление базы
B 54	base cell	Grundzelle f	cellule f de base	базовая ячейка
	base circuit	s. C 367		
B 55	base contact	Basiskontakt m	contact m de base	базовый контакт
B 56	base current	Basisstrom m	courant m de base	базовый ток
B 57	base electrode	Basiselektrode f	électrode f de base	базовый электрод
B 58	base element	Grundelement n	élément m de base	базовый элемент
	base-emitter voltage	s. B 70		
B 59	base frequency	Grundfrequenz f	fréquence f de base	основная частота

B 60	base input circuit	Basiseingangsschaltung f <Emitterschaltung>	montage m à entrée de base	схема со входом по базе
B 61	base input current	Basiseingangsstrom m	courant m d'entrée de base	входной ток базы
B 62	base layer	Basisschicht f	couche f de base	базовый слой
B 63	base material	Grundmaterial n, Trägermaterial n	matériau m de base	исходный материал
B 64	base number	Basiszahl f	nombre m de base	основание <системы счисления>
	base plate	s. B 52		
B 65	base region	Basiszone f <Transistor>	zone f de base	область базы
B 66	base register	Basisregister n, Bezugsregister n	registre m de base	базовый регистр
B 67	base resistance	Basiswiderstand m	résistance f de base	сопротивление базы
B 68	base size	Basisflächengröße f	grandeur f de base	размер базы
B 69	base terminal	Basisanschluß m	connexion f de base	вывод базы
B 70	base-to-emitter voltage, base-emitter voltage	Basis-Emitter-Spannung f	tension f base-émetteur	напряжение эмиттер-база
B 71	base transit time	Basiszonen-Signallaufzeit f	temps m de signal de zone de base	время пролета [носителей] через базу
B 72	base voltage	Basisspannung f <Spannung an der Transistorbasis>	tension f de base	напряжение на базе
B 73	base width	Basiszonendicke f	épaisseur f de la zone de base	ширина базы
B 74	BASIC <beginners all-purpose symbolic instruction code>	BASIC n <einfache universelle symbolische Programmiersprache>	BASIC m <langage universel symbolique de programmation>	БЕЙСИК <алгоритмический язык для научных расчетов>
	basic address	s. B 51		
B 75	basic assembler	Basisassembler m	assembleur m de base	базовый ассемблер
B 76	basic building block, basic element (part, unit)	Grundbaustein m	élément m de base	основной модуль
B 77	basic circuit	Grundschaltung f	circuit m de base	базовая схема
B 78	basic clock pulse frequency	Grundtaktfrequenz f	fréquence f d'impulsions de base	основная последовательность тактовых импульсов
B 79	basic construction	Grundaufbau m	structure f de base	базовая конструкция
	basic cycle	s. B 87		
	basic element	s. B 76		
B 80	basic format	Grundformat n	format m de base	базовый формат
B 81	basic function	Grundfunktion f	fonction f de base	базовая (основная) функция
B 82	basic grid, basic raster	Grundraster n	grille f de base	основная координатная сетка
B 83	basic hardware	Grundausrüstung f	équipement m (matériel m) de base	базовый (минимальный) комплект оборудования
B 84	basic instruction	Grundbefehl m	instruction f de base	базовая инструкция (команда)
B 85	basic instruction set	Basisbefehlssatz m	jeu m d'instructions de base	основной набор команд
B 86	BASIC interpreter	BASIC-Interpreter m, Interpreterprogramm n der Programmiersprache BASIC	interpréteur m [de langage] BASIC	интерпретатор команд языка БЕЙСИК
B 87	basic machine cycle, basic cycle	Grundzyklus m, Grundmaschinenzyklus m	cycle m de base	основной машинный цикл
B 88	basic model	Grundtyp m, Grundmodell n	modèle m de base	базовая модель
B 89	basic operating system	Grundbetriebssystem n, Basisbetriebssystem n	système m opérationnel de base	базовая операционная система
B 90	basic operation	Grundoperation f	opération f de base	базовая операция, операция основного набора команд
	basic part	s. B 76		
	basic raster	s. B 82		
	basic sequential access method	s. B 280		
B 91	basic software library	Basissoftware-Bibliothek f	bibliothèque f de programmes de base	библиотека стандартных программ
B 92	basic speed	Grundgeschwindigkeit f	vitesse f de base	расчетное быстродействие
B 93	basic statement	Grundanweisung f	instruction f fondamentale (de base)	основной оператор
B 94	basic system	Basissystem n <kleinste arbeitsfähige Konfiguration>	système m de base	базовая система <минимальный комплект оборудования, обеспечивающий выполнение программ под управлением операционной системы>
	basic teleprocessing access method	s. B 281		
B 95	basic time	Grundzeit f	temps m de base	основное время
	basic unit	s. B 76		
B 96	batch / to	stapelweise verarbeiten	traiter en piles	обрабатывать в пакетном режиме
B 97	batch	Stapel m, Schub m	pile f	пакет
	batch counter	s. P 426		
B 98	batched job	Stapeljob m	travail m en piles	пакетное (пакетированное) задание
B 99	batch loading	schubweises Laden n	chargement m en piles	пакетная загрузка
B 100	batch mode	Stapelverarbeitungsmodus m	mode m d'empilage	пакетный режим
B 101	batch operation	Stapelbetrieb m, Stapelverarbeitungsbetrieb m	régime m d'empilage	обработка в пакетном режиме
B 102	batch process	Chargenprozeß m	processus m à charges	режим пакетной обработки
B 103	batch processing	Stapelverarbeitung f, schubweise Verarbeitung f	traitement m à empilage	пакетная обработка
	batch production	s. V 67		
B 104	batch program	Stapelprogramm n, Stapelverarbeitungsprogramm n	programme m d'empilage	программа обработки в пакетном режиме
B 105	batch pulse	Vorwahlimpuls m	impulsion f de présélection	импульс предварительной установки

B 106	**batch terminal**	Stapelverarbeitungsend-station f, Terminal n für Stapelverarbeitung	terminal m à empilage	терминал управления пакетной обработкой
B 107	**batch testing**	Reihenprüfung f	test m de série	групповые испытания
B 108	**battery-backed system**	batteriegestütztes System n	système m soutenu par batterie	вспомогательная система батарейного питания
B 109	**battery backup**	Batteriestützung f, Absiche-rung f durch Batterie	soutien m par batterie	резервное батарейное питание
B 110	**battery pack**	Batteriesatz m <Hilfsstrom-quelle für Speicher>	jeu m de batteries	батарейный блок
B 111	**battery-powered device**	batteriebetriebenes Gerät n	appareil m à batterie	устройство с батарейным питанием
B 112	**battery power supply**	Batterie-Stromversorgung f	alimentation f à batterie	батарейный источник питания
B 113	**baud**	Baud n, Bd, B <Einheit der Telegrafiergeschwindig-keit>	baud m	бод
B 114	**Baudot code**	Baudot-Kode m <5-Kanal-Fernschreibkode>	code m de Baudot	код Бодо
B 115	**baud rate**	Baudrate f <Übertragungs-geschwindigkeit>	cote f de bauds	скорость передачи данных
B 116	**bay-mounted**	gestellmontiert	monté en châssis	смонтированный на раме
	BBD	$s.$ B 285		
	BCCD	$s.$ B 307		
B 117	**BCD-digit**, binary-coded decimal digit	BCD-Ziffer f, binär ver-schlüsselte Dezimalziffer f	décimal m codé binaire, D. C. B.	двоично-кодированная десятичная цифра
B 118	**BCD digit string**	BCD-Zeichenkette f, Dezimalzeichenkette f	chaîne f de caractères BCD (DCB)	строка цифр, представлен-ных в двоично-десятич-ном коде
B 119	**BCD representation**	BCD-Darstellung f	représentation f BCD (DCB)	представление десятич-ных чисел в двоичном коде, двоично-кодиро-ванное представление десятичных чисел
B 120	**beam lead technique**	Beam-Lead-Technik f, Goldbalkenverbindungs-technik f <drahtfreie Anschlußtechnik>	technique f beam lead	техника изготовления микросхем с балочными выводами
	beginning address	$s.$ I 139		
B 121	**beginning character**	Startzeichen n	caractère m initial	начальный маркер
B 122	**beginning mark**	Anfangsmarke f	marque f initiale	начальная метка
B 123	**benchmark**	Bewertungspunkt m	point m d'évaluation	точка отсчета
B 124	**benchmark problem**	Bewertungsaufgabe f	problème m d'évaluation	эталонная задача, задача оценки характеристик ЭВМ
B 125	**benchmark program (routine)**	Benchmark-Programm n, Bewertungsprogramm n <Programm zur Ermitt-lung der Leistung eines Rechnersystems>	programme m d'évaluation	программа оценки характеристик ЭВМ
	bias	$s.$ B 128		
B 126	**bias current**	Vorspannungsstrom m	courant m de polarisation	ток смещения
B 127	**biased**	vorgespannt	polarisé	смещенный
B 128	**bias voltage**, bias	Vorspannung f	tension f de polarisation	напряжение смещения
	bi-bus driver	$s.$ B 131		
B 129	**bidirectional**	bidirektional, zweiseitig gerichtet, in zwei Rich-tungen arbeitend	bidirectionnel	двунаправленный
B 130	**bidirectional bus**	bidirektionaler Bus m, Zweirichtungsbus m	bus m bidirectionnel	двунаправленная шина
B 131	**bidirectional bus driver**, bi-bus driver	Zweirichtungsbustreiber m <für Buskopplung>	basculeur m de bus bidirec-tionnel	двунаправленный шин-ный формирователь
	bidirectional counter	$s.$ U 75		
B 132	**bidirectional data transfer**	bidirektionale Datenüber-tragung f, Datenüber-tragung auf Zweirich-tungsverbindung	transfert m de données bidirectionnel	двунаправленная пере-дача данных
B 133	**bidirectional line**	bidirektionale Leitung f, Leitung für Zwei-richtungsverbindung	ligne f bidirectionnelle	двунаправленная линия
B 134	**bifurcated contact**	Gabelkontakt m	contact m à fourche	разветвленный контакт
B 135	**BIGFET**, bipolar insulated gate FET	Bipolar-IGFET m <Kombi-nation MOS-Eingangs-und Bipolar-Ausgangs-transistor>	BIGFET m, transistor m à effet de champ à gate isolé bipolaire	биполярный МОП-тран-зистор с изолирован-ным затвором
B 136	**binaries**	Binärwerte mpl	valeurs fpl binaires	двоичные значения
B 137	**binary**	binär, zweiwertig	binaire, dual	двоичный
B 138	**binary arithmetic**	Binärarithmetik f, Rechnen n mit Binärwerten	arithmétique f binaire	двоичная арифметика
B 139	**binary code**	Binärkode m	code m binaire	двоичный код
B 140	**binary-coded address**	binär kodierte Adresse f	adresse f codée binaire	двоично-кодированный адрес
B 141	**binary-coded character**	binär kodiertes Zeichen n	caractère m codé binaire	двоично-кодированный символ
	binary-coded decimal digit	$s.$ B 117		
	binary-decimal-con-version	$s.$ B 150		
	binary digit	$s.$ B 161		
B 142	**binary function**	zweiwertige Funktion f	fonction f binaire	двоичная функция
B 143	**binary loader**	Binärlader m	chargeur m binaire	двоичный загрузчик
B 144	**binary look-up**	binäres Suchen n	recherche f binaire	двоичный поиск
B 145	**binary number**	Binärzahl f	nombre m binaire	двоичное число
B 146	**binary number system**	Binärzahlensystem n, Dual-zahlensystem n	système m de nombres binaires	двоичная система счи-сления

B 147	**binary operation**	*s.* T 364		
	binary point	Kommastelle *f* einer Binär-zahl, Binärkomma *n*	virgule *f* binaire	точка в двоичном числе
B 148	**binary representation**	Binärdarstellung *f*	représentation *f* binaire	двоичное представление
B 149	**binary system**	Binärsystem *n*	système *m* binaire	двоичная система
B 150	**binary-to-decimal con-version,** binary-decimal conversion	Binär-Dezimal-Umwand-lung *f*	conversion *f* binaire-décimale	двоично-десятичное преобразование
B 151	**bipolar**	bipolar	bipolaire	биполярный
B 152	**bipolar device**	Bipolarbaustein *m*, Bau-element *n* in bipolarer Technik	module *m* bipolaire	биполярное устройство
	bipolar IC	*s.* B 153		
	bipolar insulated gate FET	*s.* B 135		
B 153	**bipolar integrated circuit,** bipolar IC	Bipolarschaltkreis *m*, inte-grierter Schaltkreis *m* in bipolarer Technik	circuit *m* intégré bipolaire, CI *m* bipolaire	биполярная интегральная схема, биполярная ИС
B 154	**bipolar microprocessor**	bipolarer Mikroprozessor *m*, Mikroprozessor in bi-polarer LSI-Technik	microprocesseur *m* bipolaire	микропроцессор, изгото-вленный на основе би-полярной технологии
B 155	**bipolar RAM**	bipolarer RAM *m*, Lese-Schreib-Speicher *m* in bipolarer Halbleitertech-nik	RAM *f* bipolaire	биполярное ОЗУ (запо-минающее устройство с произвольным досту-пом)
B 156	**bipolar slices**	bipolare Scheibenelemente *npl* <eines Mikropro-zessors>	éléments *mpl* à tranches bipolaires	биполярные секции <микропроцессоров>
B 157	**bipolar technique**	Bipolartechnik *f*, bipolare [Halbleiterschaltkreis-] Technik *f* <z. B. TTL-, ECL-, I²L-Technik, im Gegensatz zur unipolaren MOS-Technik>	technique *f* bipolaire	биполярная технология
B 158	**bipolar transistor**	Bipolartransistor *m* <im Gegensatz zum unipolaren MOSFET mit Ladungs-trägern beider Polarität arbeitender Transistor>	transistor *m* bipolaire	биполярный транзистор
B 159	**bistable circuit**	bistabile Schaltung *f*	circuit *m* bistable	схема с двумя устойчи-выми состояниями
	bistable multivibrator	*s.* F 126		
B 160	**bit**	bit <Maßeinheit für Infor-mationsgehalt>	bit *m*	бит
B 161	**bit,** binary digit	Bit *n*, Binärziffer *f*	bit *m*, digit (chiffre) *m* binaire	бит, двоичная цифра, двоичный разряд
B 162	**bit-addressable RAM**	bitadressierbarer RAM *m*	mémoire *f* écriture-lecture adressable bit	запоминающее устройство с побитовой адресацией
B 163	**bit addressing**	Bitadressierung *f*	adressage *m* de bit	побитовая адресация
B 164	**4-bit arithmetic,** four-bit arithmetic	4-Bit-Arithmetik *f*	arithmétique *f* à 4 bits	4-разрядная арифметика
B 165	**8-bit arithmetic,** eight-bit arithmetic	8-Bit-Arithmetik *f*	arithmétique *f* à 8 bits	8-разрядная арифметика
B 166	**16-bit arithmetic,** sixteen-bit arithmetic	16-Bit-Arithmetik *f*	arithmétique *f* à 16 bits	16-разрядная арифметика
B 167	**bit capacity**	Bitkapazität *f*	capacité *f* de bit	емкость [ЗУ] в битах
	bit chain	*s.* B 203		
B 168	**4-bit character,** four-bit character	4-Bit-Zeichen *n*, Zeichen *n* im 4-Bit-Format	caractère *m* à 4 bits	4-разрядный символ, 4-разрядное представле-ние символа
B 169	**6-bit character,** six-bit character	6-Bit-Zeichen *n*, Zeichen *n* im 6-Bit-Format	caractère *m* à 6 bits	6-разрядный символ, 6-разрядное представле-ние символа
B 170	**8-bit character,** eight-bit character	8-Bit-Zeichen *n*, Zeichen *n* im 8-Bit-Format	caractère *m* à 8 bits	8-разрядный символ, 8-разрядное представле-ние символа
B 171	**8-bit code,** eight-bit code	8-Bit-Kode *m*, Achtbitkode *m*	code *m* à 8 bits	8-разрядный код
B 172	**4-bit data,** four-bit data	4-Bit-Daten *pl*, Daten *pl* im 4-Bit-Format	données *fpl* à 4 bits	4-разрядные данные
B 173	**8-bit data,** eight-bit data	8-Bit-Daten *pl*, Daten *pl* im 8-Bit-Format	données *fpl* à 8 bits	8-разрядные данные
B 174	**16-bit data,** sixteen-bit data	16-Bit-Daten *pl*, Daten *pl* mit 16-Bit-Wortlänge	données *fpl* à 16 bits	16-разрядные данные
B 175	**bit density**	Bitdichte *f* <Dichte der Informationselemente>	densité *f* de bits	плотность записи в битах
B 176	**4-bit I/O port,** four-bit I/O port, 4-bit-wide I/O port, four-bit-wide I/O port	4-Bit-E/A-Tor *n*, vier Bit breiter E/A-Anschluß *m*	porte *f* d'E/S à 4 bits	4-разрядный порт ввода-вывода
B 177	**8-bit I/O port,** eight-bit I/O port, 8-bit-wide I/O port, eight-bit-wide I/O port	8-Bit-E/A-Tor *n*, acht Bit breiter E/A-Anschluß *m*	porte *f* d'E/S à 8 bits	8-разрядный порт ввода-вывода
B 178	**bit line**	Bitleitung *f*	ligne *f* de bit	разрядная линия
B 179	**bit-manipulating operation**	Bitmanipulationsoperation *f*, Bitoperation *f*	opération *f* de manipulation de bits	операция поразрядной обработки
B 180	**bit-manipulation instruction**	Bitmanipulationsbefehl *m*, Bitbefehl *m*	instruction *f* de manipulation de bits	инструкция поразрядной обработки
B 181	**4-bit microcomputer,** four-bit microcomputer	4-Bit-Mikrorechner *m*, Mikrorechner *m* mit 4-Bit-Verarbeitungsbreite	microcalculateur *m* à 4 bits	4-разрядная микро-ЭВМ
B 182	**8-bit microcomputer,** eight-bit microcomputer	8-Bit-Mikrorechner *m*, Mikrorechner *m* mit 8-Bit-Verarbeitungsbreite	microcalculateur *m* à 8 bits	8-разрядная микро-ЭВМ

B 183	**16-bit microcomputer,** sixteen-bit microcomputer	16-Bit-Mikrorechner *m,* Mikrorechner *m* mit 16-Bit-Verarbeitungsbreite	microcalculateur *m* à 16 bits	16-разрядная микро-ЭВМ
B 184	**4-bit microprocessor,** four-bit microprocessor	4-Bit-Mikroprozessor *m,* Mikroprozessor *m* mit 4-Bit-Verarbeitungsbreite	microprocesseur *m* à 4 bits	4-разрядный микропроцессор
B 185	**8-bit microprocessor,** eight-bit microprocessor	8-Bit-Mikroprozessor *m,* Mikroprozessor *m* mit 8-Bit-Verarbeitungsbreite	microprocesseur *m* à 8 bits	8-разрядный микропроцессор
B 186	**16-bit microprocessor,** sexteen-bit microprocessor	16-Bit-Mikroprozessor *m,* Mikroprozessor *m* mit 16-Bit-Verarbeitungsbreite	microprocesseur *m* à 16 bits	16-разрядный микропроцессор ⌐сылки]
B 187	**bit mode**	Bitbetrieb *m*	régime *m* de bits	побитовый режим [пере-
B 188	**4-bit operand,** four-bit operand	4-Bit-Operand *m,* Vierbitoperand *m*	opérande *m* à 4 bits	4-разрядный операнд
B 189	**8-bit operand,** eight-bit operand	8-Bit-Operand *m,* Achtbitoperand *m*	opérande *m* à 8 bits	8-разрядный операнд
B 190	**16-bit operand,** sixteen-bit operand	16-Bit-Operand *m*	opérande *m* à 16 bits	16-разрядный операнд
B 191	**bit pattern**	Bitmuster *n,* Bitstruktur *f*	dessin *m* (structure *f*) de bits	комбинация битов
B 192	**bit position**	Bitstelle *f,* Binärposition *f*	position *f* de bit	позиция двоичного разряда
B 193	**bit processing**	Bitverarbeitung *f*	traitement *m* de bits	побитовая обработка
B 194	**bit rate**	Bitgeschwindigkeit *f,* Bitfolgefrequenz *f*	vitesse (séquence) *f* de bits	скорость передачи битов
B 195	**4-bit register,** four-bit register	4-Bit-Register *n,* Vierbitregister *n*	registre *m* à 4 bits	4-разрядный регистр
B 196	**8-bit register,** eight-bit register	8-Bit-Register *n,* Achtbitregister *n*	registre *m* à 8 bits	8-разрядный регистр
B 197	**16-bit register,** sixteen-bit register	16-Bit-Register *n*	registre *m* à 16 bits	16-разрядный регистр
B 198	**bit resolution**	Bitauflösung *f*	résolution *f* de bits	разложение на биты
B 199	**bit-serial processing**	bitserielle Verarbeitung *f*	traitement *m* bit-sériel	последовательная обработка битов
B 200	**4-bit slice circuit**	4-Bit-Scheibenschaltkreis *m* <für Mikroprozessoraufbau>	circuit *m* en tranches à 4 bits	4-разрядная секция [микропроцессора]
B 201	**bit-slice microprocessor**	bitscheibenstrukturierter Mikroprozessor *m*	microprocesseur *m* structuré en tranches de bits	разрядно-наращиваемый микропроцессор, секционно-наращиваемый микропроцессор
B 202	**bits per second**	s. B 258		
	bit stream	Bitstrom *m*	courant *m* de bits	поток битов
B 203	**bit string,** bit chain	Bitkette *f*	chaîne *f* de bits	строка битов, последовательность двоичных разрядов
B 204	**bit string comparison**	Bitkettenvergleich *m*	comparaison *f* de chaînes de bits	сравнение последовательности битов
B 205	**bit string data**	Bitkettendaten *pl*	données *fpl* de chaînes de bits	данные, представленные в виде двоичной последовательности
B 206	**bit string element**	Bitkettenelement *n*	élément *m* de chaînes de bits	элемент двоичной последовательности
B 207	**bit string operator**	Bitkettenoperator *m*	opérateur *m* de chaînes de bits	оператор обработки двоичной последовательности
B 208	**bit test**	Bittest *m*	test *m* de bits	проверка состояния разрядов
	4-bit-wide I/O port	s. B 176		
B 209	**8-bit-wide I/O port**	s. B 177		
	blank / to	dunkeltasten <Anzeigestelle>	éclipser	затемнять
	blank	s. B 209 b		
B 209 a	**blank character**	Leerzeichen *n*	caractère *m* vide	символ пробела
B 209 b	**blank space,** blank	Leerstelle *f*	blanc *m,* vide *m,* caractère *m* à ignorer	пробел
B 210	**block**	Block *m* <Datenblock, Geräteblock>	bloc *m*	блок
B 211	**block address**	Blockadresse *f*	adresse *f* de bloc	адрес блока
B 212	**block check character**	Blockprüfzeichen *n*	caractère *m* de vérification de bloc	контрольный символ блока
B 213	**block diagram,** block scheme	Blockdiagramm *n,* Blockschaltbild *n,* Ablaufdiagramm *n* in Blockstruktur	schéma-bloc *m,* organigramme *m*	структурная схема
B 214	**block end**	Blockende *n*	fin *f* de bloc	конец блока
B 215	**block head**	Blockkopf *m,* Blockvorspann *m*	en-tête *m* de bloc	начало блока, описание блока
B 216	**blocking**	Blockierung *f*	blocage *m*	блокировка
B 217	**blocking oscillator**	Sperrschwinger *m*	oscillateur *m* blocking	блокинг-генератор
B 218	**blocking state**	Sperrzustand *m*	état *m* bloqué	запрещенное состояние
B 219	**block length**	Blocklänge *f*	longueur *f* de bloc	длина блока
B 220	**block move**	Blockumspeicherung *f*	mouvement *m* de bloc	поблочная пересылка
B 221	**block-oriented RAM,** BORAM	blockadressierbarer RAM (Lese-Schreib-Speicher) *m,* BORAM	RAM *f* orientée bloc	запоминающее устройство с блочной адресацией
	block scheme	s. B 213		
B 221 a	**block size**	Blockgröße *f*	taille *f* de bloc	размер блока
B 222	**block-structured language**	blockstrukturierte Programmiersprache *f*	langage *m* de programmation à structure de bloc	блочно-структурированный язык
B 223	**block transfer**	Blockübertragung *f*	transfert *m* (transmission *f*) de bloc	пересылка блока
B 224	**block transfer instruction**	Blockübertragungsbefehl *m*	instruction *f* de transfert de bloc	команда пересылки блока
B 225	**board,** plate	Platine *f,* Platte *f,* Brett *n*	platine *f*	панель, плата

	board connector	s. P 450		
B 226	board-level compatibility	Kompatibilität f auf Steckeinheitenniveau, Verträglichkeit f auf Steckeinheitenmodulebene	compatibilité f au niveau de circuit imprimé	совместимость на уровне плат
B 227	board line	Leiterplattenlinie f, Leiterplatten-Produktlinie f	ligne f de circuit imprimé	проводник на [печатной] плате
B 228	board module	Leiterplattenmodul m, Steckeinheitenmodul m	module m à unité enfichable, module à circuit imprimé	сменный модуль
B 229	board size	Leiterplattengröße f, Steckeinheitengröße f	grandeur f d'unité enfichable, grandeur de circuit imprimé	размер платы
B 230	bond / to	bonden, verbinden durch Mikroschweißen	bondériser	соединять, скреплять
B 231	bonding	Mikrokontaktierung f, Mikroverbindung f	bondérisation f	соединение; микросварка
B 232	bonding pad	Bondinsel f	île f de bondage	контактная площадка
B 233	booking data	Buchungsdaten pl	données fpl de comptabilité	бухгалтерские (учетные) данные
B 234	bookkeeping	Buchhaltung f, Buchführung f	comptabilité f	бухгалтерия, делопроизводство
B 235	Boolean, logic[al]	Boolesch, aussagenlogisch, logisch	booléen, boolien, logique	булев[ый], логический
B 236	Boolean algebra	Boolesche Algebra f, Schaltalgebra f	algèbre f booléenne (boolienne)	булева алгебра
B 237	Boolean bit-handling	Boolesche Bitbehandlung f, Bitverarbeitung f nach Booleschen Regeln	traitement m booléen (boolien) de bits	обработка булевых переменных
B 238	Boolean function	Boolesche Funktion f	fonction f booléenne	булева функция
B 239	Boolean logic	Boolesche Logik f <Schaltungslogik>	logique f booléenne (boolienne)	булева логика
	Boolean operation	s. L 245		
	Boolean operator	s. L 246		
B 240	Boolean processor	Boolescher Prozessor m <Logikprozessor>	processeur m booléen (boolien)	процессор обработки булевых функций, логический процессор
B 241	Boolean representation	Boolesche Darstellung f	représentation f booléenne	описание на языке булевых функций
	Boolean variable	s. L 252		
	boost / to	s. B 243		
B 242	booster	Spannungsverstärker m	amplificateur m de tension	усилитель напряжения
B 243	bootstrap / to, to boost	aufladen, anheben	charger, hausser	загружать[ся] автоматически, самозагружаться
B 244	bootstrap area	Bootstrap-Bereich m, Urladerbereich m <Speicherbereich, der für Urlader reserviert ist>	champ m de chargeur primitif	область памяти, зарезервированная под начальный загрузчик
B 245	bootstrap loader	Urlader m, „mitlaufender" Lader m <aufbauendes Ladeprogramm>	chargeur m original	начальный загрузчик, самозагружаемая программа-загрузчик
B 246	bootstrapping	Ladeprogrammaufbautechnik f <Konsolfunktion>	technique f d'établissement de programme chargeur	автоматическая загрузка [программ]
B 247	bootstrapping circuitry	Aufladeschaltung f	montage m de chargement	средства управления начальной загрузкой
B 248	bootstrap routine	Ladeprogramm-Startroutine f	routine f [de démarrage] de chargeur	программа начальной загрузки
	BORAM	s. B 221		
B 249	borrow	Borger m, Mangel m, Subtraktionsübertrag m	manque m, retenue f de soustraction	заем, отрицательный перенос
B 250	bottleneck	Engpaß m, Flaschenhals m	pertuis m	критический элемент (параметр)
B 251	bottom layer	untere Schicht f	couche f inférieure	нижний слой
B 252	bottom limit	untere Grenze f	limite f inférieure	нижняя граница
B 253	bottom-up design	von Grundelementen ausgehender Entwurf m, Entwurf von unten nach oben <Entwurfsprinzip für Systeme oder Programme>	conception f de bas en haut	проектирование снизувверх
B 254	bottom voltage	untere Spannung f	tension f inférieure	нижний уровень напряжения
	bound	s. R 26		
B 255	boundary, boundary layer	Grenzschicht f <Halbleiter>, Grenzfläche f	couche f limite (mitoyenne)	граничный слой
B 256	boundary condition, limiting condition	Randbedingung f, Grenzbedingung f	condition f limite	граничное (ограничивающее) условие
	boundary layer	s. B 255		
B 257	boundary value problem	Randwertproblem n	problème m aux limites	краевая задача
B 258	bps, bits per second	Bit/s, Bits je Sekunde	bps, bits par seconde	бит в секунду, бит/с
B 259	bracket	Halterung f, Trägerarm m	support m	крепление, зажим, фиксатор
B 260	bracket	Klammer f <Zeichen>	crochet m	скобка <символ>
B 261	branch, arm	Zweig m <im Ablauf>	branche f	ветвление
B 262	branch condition	Verzweigungsbedingung f	condition f de branchement	условие ветвления
B 263	branch control	Verzweigungssteuerung f	commande f de branchement	управление ветвлением
B 264	branch decision	Verzweigungsentscheidung f	décision f de branchement	анализ условия ветвления
B 265	branching	Verzweigen n, Verzweigung f	branchement m, bifurcation f	ветвление
B 266	branch instruction	Verzweigungsbefehl m	instruction f de branchement	команда условного перехода
B 267	branch offset	Verzweigungsdistanz f <Adreßdifferenz>	distance f de branchement	приращение адреса <при ветвлении>
B 268	branchpoint	Verzweigungspunkt m <Programm>	point m de branchement	точка ветвления [программы]

B 269	branch target	Verzweigungsziel n <Adresse>	but m de branchement	адрес (метка) перехода
B 270	breadboard [circuit]	Brettschaltung f, Versuchs- schaltung f	montage m d'essai	макет
B 271	breadboard construction	Brettschaltungsaufbau m, Versuchsschaltungs- aufbau m	construction f d'essai	разработка макета
B 272	breadboard kit	Brettschaltungs-Bausatz m, Bausatz m für Versuchs- aufbau	ensemble m de montage d'essai	набор элементов для макетирования
B 273	break / to	unterbrechen	interrompre	прерывать
B 274	break	Unterbrechung f <all- gemein>	interruption f	прерывание
B 275	breakdown	Zusammenbruch m	décharge f	пробой
B 276	breakdown voltage	Durchbruchspannung f	tension f d'allumage, tension d'amorçage	напряжение пробоя
B 277	breakpoint	Haltepunkt m, Unter- brechungspunkt m, bedingter Programmstopp m	point m d'arrêt [condition- nel]	точка останова [про- граммы]
B 278	breakpoint switch	Zwischenstoppschalter m	commutateur m de point d'arrêt	ключ прерывания
B 279	brightness control	Helligkeitssteuerung f	commande f de luminosité	регулирование яркости
B 280	BSAM, basic sequential access method	BSAM n, Basismethode f für sequentiellen Zugriff	méthode f de base à l'accès séquentiel	базисный последователь- ный метод доступа
B 281	BTAM, basic teleprocess- ing access method	BTAM n, Datenfernver- arbeitungs-Zugriffs- methode f	BTAM, méthode f d'accès de base au traitement à distance	базисный телекоммуни- кационный метод доступа
	bubble	s. M 56		
B 282	bubble chip	Blasenspeicherbaustein m	module m de mémoire à bulles	элемент на магнитных доменах
B 283	bubble memory, magnetic bubble memory	Blasenspeicher m, Magnet- blasenspeicher m	mémoire f à bulles [magnétiques]	запоминающее устройство на магнитных доменах
B 284	bucket	Datensammel-Speicher- bereich m	champ m de collection de données	функционально выделен- ная область памяти
B 285	bucket brigade devices, BBD	Eimerkettenelemente npl, Eimerkettenschaltung f <Ladungstransfertechnik>	éléments mpl de chaîne à godets	приборы с передачей заряда, приборы типа «пожарная цепочка»
B 286	buffer	Puffer m, Pufferschaltung f	tampon m	буфер
	buffer	s. a. B 294		
B 287	buffer address	Pufferadresse f	adresse f de tampon	адрес буфера
B 288	buffer amplifier	Pufferverstärker m, Trenn- verstärker m	amplificateur m de tampon	буферный усилитель
B 289	buffered access	gepufferter Zugriff m	accès m par tampon	буферизованный доступ
B 290	buffered device	gepuffertes Gerät n	appareil m à tampon	буферизованное устройство
B 291	buffered FET logic	gepufferte FET-Logik f, gepufferte Feldeffekt- transistorlogik f <GaAs- Schaltungstechnik>	logique f à transistors à effet de champ tamponée	логические схемы на по- левых транзисторах с буферизованными вхо- дами и выходами
B 292	buffered transfer	gepufferte Übertragung f	transfert m à tampon	передача данных с буферизацией
B 293	buffering	Pufferung f	tamponnage m	буферизация
B 294	buffer memory, buffer	Pufferspeicher m	mémoire f tampon	буферное запоминающее устройство
B 295	buffer register	Pufferregister n	registre m tampon	буферный регистр
B 296	buffer stage	Pufferstufe f	étage m tampon	буферный каскад
B 297	bug	Entwurfsfehler m	défaut m de conception	ошибка при разработке
B 298	building block concept, modular principle	Baukastenkonzeption f, Modularprinzip n	concept m modulaire	блочный принцип по- строения
B 299	building block construction	Baukastenkonstruktion f, modularer Aufbau m	construction f modulaire	блочная конструкция
B 300	building block system	Baukastensystem n, Bau- steinsystem n	système m modulaire	блочная (модульная) система
B 301	build-up / to	aufbauen, sich aufbauen	établir, dresser	наращивать, монтировать
B 302	built-in capacity	eingebautes Leistungsver- mögen n	capacité (performance) f incorporée	внутренняя емкость; вну- тренняя производитель- ность
B 303	built-in check, built-in test	eingebaute Prüfung f, ein- gebauter Test m	vérification f incorporée, test m incorporé	аппаратный (встроенный) контроль
B 304	built-in memory	eingebauter Speicher m	mémoire f incorporée	внутреннее запоминаю- щее устройство
B 305	built-in power fail protection	eingebauter Spannungsaus- fallschutz m	protection f contre manque de tension incorporée	встроенная защита от отказов питания
B 306	built-in protection mechanism	eingebaute Schutzvorrich- tung f	dispositif m de protection incorporé	внутренний механизм защиты
	built-in test	s. B 303		
B 307	bulk charge-coupled devices, BCCD	volumenladungsgekoppelte Elemente npl, Volumen- CCD f <Ladungsver- schiebebeschaltung>	éléments mpl couplés par charge de volume, BCCD	приборы со связью через объемный заряд
B 308	bulk processing	Massenverarbeitung f, Ver- arbeitung f großer Daten- mengen	traitement m de masses	обработка информацион- ных массивов
B 309	bulk resistance	Bahnwiderstand m	résistance f de trajectoire	объемное сопротивление
B 310	bulk-silicon ship	Massivsilizium-Chip n <im Unterschied zum Isolator- substrat-Chip>	puce f massive de silicium	чип, выполненный в монолитном кристалле кремния
B 311	bulk storage, mass storage (memory)	Massenspeicher m	mémoire f de masse	массовое запоминающее устройство
B 312	bump	Chipkontaktierungsfläche f, Chipkontaktflecken m	tache f à contact de puce	контактная поверхность чипа
B 313	buried channel	vergrabener (versenkter) Kanal m	canal m caché	скрытый канал

B 314	buried-channel structure	Struktur f mit vergrabenen Kanälen <Schaltkreis-technik>	structure f à canaux cachés	структура со скрытым каналом
B 315	buried collector	vergrabener Kollektor m <Halbleitertechnik>	collecteur m caché	скрытый коллектор
B 316	buried contact	vergrabener Kontakt m	contact m caché	скрытый контакт
B 317	buried layer	vergrabene Schicht f <Halbleitertechnik>	couche f cachée	скрытый слой
B 318	burst mode	Einpunktbetrieb m, Stoßbetrieb m	régime m à coups	монопольный режим
B 319	bus	Bus m, Sammelschiene f <Übertragungsweg mit mehreren Anschluß-stellen>	bus m	шина
B 320	bus acknowledgement	Busanforderungsbestätigung f	confirmation f de demande de bus	подтверждение запроса [шины]
B 321	bus allocation	Buszuweisung f, Buszu-teilung f <Zuweisung der Busführung an einen Bus-master> ⌐m	attribution f de bus	распределение шины
B 322	bus arbiter	Busanforderungsentscheider	arbitre m de bus	арбитр шины
B 323	bus arbitration	Buszuweisungsentschei-dung f	arbitrage m de bus	арбитраж шин
B 324	bus backplane	Bus-Rückverdrahtungs-ebene f	niveau m de connexions arrière de bus	монтаж линий шины на задней панели
B 325	bus-bar system	Sammelschienensystem n, Busschienensystem n	système m barres de bus	физическая реализация проводников шины
B 326	bus clock	Bustakt m, Bussynchroni-sationstakt m	rythme m de bus	синхронизация шины
B 327	bus connection	Busverbindung f, Bus-anschluß m	connexion f de bus	соединение шин
B 328	bus contention	Buskonflikt m <Situation, in der zwei Buspartner gleichzeitig die Steuerung zu erlangen versuchen>	conflit m de bus	конфликтная ситуация, возникающая при по-пытке двух устройств одновременно получить доступ к шине
B 329	bus control circuit, bus controller	Bussteuerschaltung f, Bus-steuerschaltkreis m	circuit m de commande de bus	контроллер шины
	bus control override	s. B 350	⌐bus	
B 330	bus control signal	Bussteuersignal n	signal m de commande de	сигнал управления шиной
B 331	bus cycle	Buszyklus m, Bustransfer-zyklus m	cycle m de bus	цикл шины
B 332	bus driver	Bustreiber m	basculeur m de bus	шинный формирователь
B 333	bus exchange	Busvermittlung f, Bussteue-rungsaustausch m, Wechsel m der Busfüh-rung <Wechsel des aktuel-len Busmaster>	échange m de bus	коммутация шин
B 334	bus exchange line	Busvermittlungsleitung f, Leitung f für Busvermitt-lungssignal	ligne f d'échange de bus	линия сигнала комму-тации шины
B 335	bus exchange logic	Busvermittlungslogik f, Logik f zum Wechsel der Busführung <bewirkt Zuweisung der Bus-masterfunktion>	logique f d'échange de bus	логика коммутации шины
B 336	bus exchange operation	Busvermittlungsvorgang m, Bussteuerungs-Austausch-operation f	opération f d'échange de bus	операция коммутации шины
B 337	bus exchange priority technique	Prioritätsentscheidungsver-fahren n für Busvermitt-lung, Vorrangtechnik f für Bussteuerungswechsel	procédé m de priorité d'échange de bus	способы приоритетной коммутации шин
B 338	bus exchange sequence	Busvermittlungsfolge f, Bussteuerungsaustausch-folge f, Folge f zum Wechsel der Busführung	séquence f d'échange de bus	последовательность ком-мутации шин
B 339	bus exchange signals	Busvermittlungssignale npl, Signale npl zur Reali-sierung eines Wechsels der Busführung	signaux mpl d'échange de bus	сигналы управления ком-мутацией шин
B 340	bus extender module	Buserweiterungsmodul m	module m d'élargissement de bus	модуль расширения шины
B 341	bus floating	Bus-Floating n, Bus-schwebezustand m <Bus hochohmig potentialfrei geschaltet>	bus m flottant <bus en état de grande résistance>	шина, находящая в состоянии высокого импеданса
B 342	bus grant	Busbewilligung f, Bus-gewährung f	autorisation f de bus	предоставление шины
	business computer	s. C 362		
	business data processing	s. C 363		
B 343	bus interface	Busanschlußbild n, Bus-schnittstelle f	interface f de bus	шинный интерфейс
B 344	bus interfacing	Busschnittstellengestaltung f	structure f d'interface de bus	сопряжение шины
B 345	bus locking	Busverriegelung f	verrouillage m de bus	блокирование шин
B 346	bus master	Busmaster m, busführende Einheit f, Bussteuerung ausübende Einheit <initiiert Busvorgänge>	master m de bus	ведущее устройство
B 347	bus operation	Busoperation f, Busvorgang m	opération f de bus	шинная операция
B 348	bus organization	Busorganisation f, Bus-aufbauprinzip n	organisation f de bus	организация шины
B 349	bus-organized structure	busorganisierte Struktur f	structure f organisée bus	шинная структура

B 350	**bus overriding,** bus control override	Überlaufen *n* der Buszuweisungssteuerung, Busblockierung *f* durch einzelnen Buspartner	dépassement *m* de la commande de bus, blocage *m* de bus	передача управления шиной, блокировка шины
B 351	**bus priority control**	Busprioritätssteuerung *f*, Busvorrangsteuerung *f*	commande *f* de priorité de bus	приоритетное управление шиной
B 352	**bus priority structure**	Prioritätsstruktur *f* des Bus, Busprioritätsstruktur *f*	structure *f* de priorité de bus	приоритетная структура шины
B 353	**bus protocol**	Busprotokoll *n*, Bus-Übertragungsprozedurvorschrift *f*	procès-verbal *m* de bus	шинный протокол, протокол обмена по шине
B 354	**bus receiver**	Busempfänger *m*	récepteur *m* de bus	приемник шины
B 355	**bus request**	Busanforderung *f*, Buszuweisungsanforderung *f*	demande *f* de bus	запрос на доступ к шине
B 356	**bus slave**	Bus-Slave *m*, Busvorgänge ausführende Einheit *f*, busführungsabhängige Einheit *f* ‹arbeitet unter Regie eines Busmasters›	slave *m* de bus	ведомое устройство
B 357	**bus structure**	Busstruktur *f*	structure *f* de bus	структура шины
B 358	**bus-structured system**	busstrukturiertes System *n*	système *m* structuré bus	система с магистральной структурой
B 359	**bus timeout**	erzwungene Buszyklusbeendigung *f* bei Überschreiten einer Zeitgrenze	mise *f* au repos de bus	прерывание цикла обмена шины по истечении заданного времени
B 360	**bus traffic**	Busverkehr *m*	trafic *m* de bus	трафик шины
B 361	**bus transaction**	Busoperationsabwicklung *f*, Busoperationsdurchführung *f*	transaction *f* de bus	осуществление шинных операций
B 362	**bus transceiver**	Bustreiber-Busempfänger-Kombination *f*	récepteur-émetteur *m* de bus	шинный приемо/передатчик
B 363	**bus transmitter**	Bussender *m*	transmetteur *m* de bus	шинный передатчик
B 364	**bus vectored interrupt logic**	Buslogik *f* zur Behandlung vektorisierter Unterbrechungen	logique *f* de bus à vecteur d'interruption	логика обработки векторного прерывания
B 365	**bus width**	Busbreite *f*	largeur *f* de bus	разрядность шины
B 366	**busy**	besetzt, beschäftigt	occupé	занятый
B 367	**busy line**	Besetztsignalleitung *f*	ligne *f* occupée	линия сигнала «занято»
B 368	**bypass / to**	umgehen, übergehen	contourner, dépasser	обходить, шунтировать
B 369	**bypass circuit**	Umgehungsschaltung *f*	circuit *m* de dépassement	шунтирующая схема
B 370	**byte**	Byte *n* ‹Informationseinheit mit 8 Binärstellen›	octet *m* ‹comme unité de mesure o›	байт
B 371	**byte access**	Bytezugriff *m*, byteweiser Zugriff *m*	accès *m* d'octet	побайтовый доступ
B 372	**byte address**	Byteadresse *f*	adresse *f* d'octet	адрес байта
B 373	**byte-addressable memory**	byteadressierbarer Speicher *m*	mémoire *f* adressable octet	запоминающее устройство с байтовой адресацией
	byte computer	s. B 378		
B 374	**byte-control protocol**	byteorientiertes Protokoll *n*, byteorientierte Übertragungsprozedur *f*	procès-verbal *m* orienté octet	протокол [управления] с байтовой ориентацией
B 375	**byte data**	Bytedaten *pl*, Daten *pl* im Byteformat	données *fpl* d'octet[s]	побайтное представление данных
B 376	**byte manipulation**	Bytemanipulation *f*, Bytebearbeitung *f*	manipulation *f* d'octet	байтовая обработка
B 377	**byte mode**	Bytebetrieb *m*, byteweiser Betrieb *m*	régime *m* à octets	побайтовый режим [обмена]
B 378	**byte-oriented computer,** byte computer	byteorientierter Rechner *m*, Byterechner *m*	calculateur *m* orienté octets	ЭВМ с побайтовой обработкой данных
B 379	**byte processing**	Byteverarbeitung *f*	traitement *m* d'octets	побайтовая обработка
B 380	**byte rate**	Bytegeschwindigkeit *f*, Bytefolgefrequenz *f*, Byterate *f*	vitesse (fréquence) *f* d'octets	скорость передачи байтов [данных]
B 381	**byte size**	Bytegröße *f*	grandeur *f* d'octet	длина байта
B 382	**byte-string operation**	Bytekettenoperation *f*	opération *f* de chaîne d'octets	операция обработки последовательности байтов
B 383	**byte-swapping**	Bytevertauschung *f*	échange *m* d'octets	перестановка байтов
B 384	**byte-wide interface**	bytebreites Interface *n*, bytebreite Anschlußstelle (Schnittstelle) *f*	interface *f* à largeur d'octet	интерфейс с побайтным обменом

C

C 1	**cabinet mounted unit**	Schrankeinbaueinheit *f*	unité *f* encastrée	блок, смонтированный в стойке
C 2	**cable connection**	Kabelanschluß *m*, Kabelverbindung *f*	connexion *f* de câble	кабельное соединение
C 3	**cache,** cache memory	Cache *m*, Cachespeicher *m*, „Versteckspeicher" *m*, Pufferspeicher *m* im Prozessor-Speicher-Datenkanal ‹ermöglicht bei geeigneter Organisation und Ladestrategie eine effektive Speicherzugriffszeit nahe der Pufferzugriffszeit›	mémoire *f* cachée, cache *f*	кэш-память, буферное запоминающее устройство для обмена данными между процессором и главной памятью
C 4	**cache control register**	Cachespeicher-Steuerregister *m*	registre *m* de commande de cache	регистр управления кэш-памяти
C 5	**cache data**	Cachespeicherdaten *pl*	données *fpl* de cache	данные, хранящиеся в кэш-памяти

C 6	cache hit register	Cachespeicher-Hitregister n, Register n zur Kennung erfolgreicher Cachezugriffe	registre m hit de cache	регистр совпадения кэш-памяти
	cache memory	s. C 3		
C 7	cache tag	Cacheetikett n, Cachespeicher-Inhaltskennung f	marque f de cache	признак слова, хранящегося в кэш-памяти
C 8	cache validity bit	Cachespeicher-Gültigkeitsbit n	bit m de validité de cache	бит достоверности данных кэш-памяти
C 9	CAD, computer-aided design	CAD n, rechnergestütztes Entwerfen n, rechnergestützter Entwurf m	projet m assisté par calculateur	машинное (автоматизированное) проектирование
C 10	CAD-scaled chip	rechnergestützt skalierter Schaltkreis m <Schaltkreis mit durch rechnergestützter Entwurfsüberarbeitung reduzierter Chipfläche>	puce f à surface réduite par assistance de calculateur	автоматизация проектирования микросхем с уменьшенными размерами чипов
C 11	CAD-scaling process	Prozeß m der Chipgrößenreduzierung mittels rechnergestützten Entwurfs	processus m de réduction de puce par assistance de calculateur	уменьшение размеров чипов с помощью системы автоматизации проектирования
C 12	cages, card chassis (frame)	Steckeinheitenaufnahme f, Kartenchassis n, Leiterplattenaufnahmerahmen m	châssis m à cartes	шасси
	CAI	s. C 497		
	CAL	s. C 490		
C 13	calculate / to, to compute	berechnen, ausrechnen	calculer	вычислять, расчитывать
C 14	calculating, calculation	Berechnung f	calcul m	вычисление
C 15	calculating function	Rechenfunktion f	fonction f de calcul	вычислительная процедура
C 16	calculating machine	Rechenmaschine f für Einfachoperationen	calculateur m simple	счетная машина, вычислительное устройство для выполнения элементарных операций
	calculation	s. C 14		
C 17	calculation method	Berechnungsmethode f	méthode f de calcul	метод вычислений
C 18	calculator	einfacher Rechner m <Taschenrechner>	calculateur m <de poche>	калькулятор
C 19	calculator chip	Taschenrechnerschaltkreis m	circuit m de calculateur	БИС калькулятора
C 20	calibrate / to	eichen	calibrer	калибровать
C 21	calibration	Eichung f	calibrage m	калибровка
C 22	calibration curve	Eichkurve f	courbe f de calibrage	калибровочная кривая
C 23	call / to, to invoke	aufrufen, rufen <Programm, Prozedur>	appeler	вызывать, обращаться
C 24	call	Ruf m, Aufruf m <eines Programms>	appel m	вызов, обращение
	call command	s. C 28		
C 25	called subroutine	aufgerufenes Unterprogramm n	sous-programme m appelé	вызываемая подпрограмма
C 26	calling program	aufrufendes Programm n	programme m d'appel	вызывающая программа
C 27	calling sequence	Aufruffolge f von Unterprogrammen	séquence f d'appel	вызывающая последовательность [команд]
C 28	call instruction, call command	Rufbefehl m <für ein Unterprogramm>	instruction f d'appel	команда вызова
C 29	call-reply system	Ruf-Antwort-System n	système m appel-réponse	система типа запрос-ответ
C 30	call statement	Rufanweisung f	instruction f d'appel	оператор вызова
	CAM	s. 1. C 491; 2. C 661		
C 31	cancel / to	rückgängig (ungültig) machen, stornieren	annuler	отменять
C 32	capability-based addressing	möglichkeitsbezogene Adressierung f <auf Zugriffsrechten abgestützte Adressierung in objektorientierten Systemen>	adressage m relatif aux possibilités	адресация, базирующая на принципе допустимости <базирующая на правах доступа>
C 33	capacitance	Kapazität f <eines Kondensators>	capacité f	емкость
C 34	capacitance load, capacitive load, capacity loading	kapazitive Last (Belastung) f	charge f capacitive	емкостная нагрузка
C 35	capacitive coupling	kapazitive Kopplung f	couplage m capacitif	емкостная связь
	capacitive load	s. C 34		
C 36	capacitive reactance	kapazitiver Blindwiderstand m	réactance f capacitive	емкостное реактивное сопротивление
C 37	capacitor storage	Kondensatorspeicherung f	accumulation f à condensateur	запоминающее устройство на конденсаторах, емкостная память
C 38	capacity	Kapazität f, Leistungsfähigkeit f	capacité f, puissance f	производительность
C 39	capacity expansion	Kapazitätserweiterung f	expansion f de capacité	расширение возможностей
	capacity loading	s. C 34		
C 39 a	card	Karte f <Leiterplatte>	carte f	карта
	card	s. a. P 742		
	card batch	s. C 43		
	card chassis	s. C 12		
C 40	card collating, card matching	Lochkartenmischen n, Kartenmischen n	fusion f de cartes	сортировка (подбор) перфокарт
C 41	card column	Lochkartenspalte f, Kartenspalte f	colonne f de carte	колонка перфокарты
C 42	card cycle	Lochkartengang m, Kartengang m	gaine f à cartes	время считывания перфокарты
C 43	card deck, card batch	Lochkartenstapel m, Kartenstapel m, Kartensatz m	pile f de cartes	колода перфокарт

C 44	card feeding	Lochkartenvorschub *m*, Kartenvorschub *m*, Kartenführung *f*	avancement *m* de cartes	подача перфокарт
C 45	card file	Lochkartendatei *f*, Kartendatei *f*	fichier *m* sur cartes	карточный файл
	card frame	*s.* C 12		
	card matching	*s.* C 40		
	card perforator	*s.* C 46		
C 46	card punch, card perforator	Kartenstanzer *m*, Lochkartenstanzer *m*	perforatrice *f* de cartes	карточный перфоратор
C 47	card reader	Lochkartenleser *m*, Kartenleser *m*	lecteur *m* de cartes	устройство считывания с перфокарт
C 48	card row	Lochkartenzeile *f*, Kartenzeile *f*	ligne *f* de carte	строка перфокарты
C 49	card sensing	Lochkartenabtasten *n*, Kartenabtasten *n*	balayage *m* de cartes	считывание с перфокарт
C 50	card unit	Lochkarteneinheit *f*, Lochkartengerät *n*	unité *f* à cartes	карточный блок
	carriage control	*s.* A 180		
C 51	carriage return	Wagenrücklauf *m*	retour *m* de chariot	возврат каретки
	carrier	*s.* C 151		
	carrier concentration (density)	*s.* C 152		
C 52	carrier depletion, charge-carrier depletion	Ladungsträgerverarmung *f*	appauvrissement *m* de charge	обеднение носителями
C 53	carrier injection, charge-carrier injection	Ladungsträgerinjektion *f*	injection *f* de charge	инжекция носителей
	carrier mobility	*s.* C 153		
C 54	carrier transit time	Ladungsträgerlaufzeit *f*	temps *m* de transfert de charge	время пролета носителей
C 55	carry	Übertrag *m*	report *m*, retenue *f*	перенос
C 56	carry bit	Übertragsbit *n*	bit *m* de report	разряд переноса
C 57	carry condition, C condition	Übertragsbedingung *f*	condition *f* de retenue	условие переноса
C 58	carry flag, C-flag	Übertragskennzeichen *n*	marque *f* de report	флаг переноса
C 59	carry look ahead	Übertragsvorausschau *f*, Übertragsvorausberechnung *f*	prévision *f* de retenue	предварительный анализ распространения переноса
C 60	carry-out	auslaufender Übertrag *m*	retenue *f* déversée	выход [сигнала] переноса
C 61	carry propagation	Übertragsfortpflanzung *f*, Übertragsausbreitung *f*	propagation *f* de retenue	распространение [сигнала] переноса
C 62	cartridge, cassette	Kassette *f*	cassette *f*	кассета
C 63	cartridge disk memory	Kassettenplattenspeicher *m*	mémoire *f* à cassette à disque	кассетное дисковое запоминающее устройство
	cartridge storage	*s.* C 72		
C 64	cascadable	kaskadierbar	cascadable	каскадированный
	cascade circuit	*s.* C 65		
C 65	cascade connection, cascade[d] circuit	Kaskadenschaltung *f*, Kettenschaltung *f*	montage (circuit) *m* en cascade	каскадное соединение, каскадная схема
C 66	cascade control	Kaskadenregelung *f*	commande *f* en cascade	каскадное управление
C 67	cascaded carry	Kaskadenübertrag *m*	report *m* de cascade	групповой перенос
	cascaded circuit	*s.* C 65		
C 68	cascaded (cascading) stages	kaskadenartig geschaltete Stufen *fpl*, hintereinandergeschaltete Stufen	étages *mpl* en cascade	последовательно соединенные каскады
C 69	case study	Fallstudie *f*	étude *f* de cas	исследование конкретных условий [применения]
	cash-point terminal	*s.* C 71		
C 70	cash register	Registrierkasse *f*	caisse *f* enregistreuse	кассовый аппарат
C 71	cash terminal, cash-point terminal, point of sale terminal	Kassenterminal *n*	terminal *m* de caisse	кассовый терминал
	cassette	*s.* C 62		
C 72	cassette storage, cartridge storage	Kassettenspeicher *m*	mémoire *f* à cassette	кассетное запоминающее устройство
C 73	cassette tape	Kassettenband *n*	bande *f* en cassette	кассетная лента
C 74	cathode-ray tube, CRT	Katodenstrahlröhre *f*	tube *m* cathodique (à rayons cathodiques)	электронно-лучевая трубка
	cathode ray tube display	*s.* C 841		
	CCC	*s.* C 91		
C 75	CCD, charge-coupled devices	CCD *f*, ladungsgekoppelte Elemente *npl*	éléments *mpl* couplés par charge	приборы с зарядовой связью, ПЗС
C 76	CCD-RAM, charge-coupled RAM, CC-RAM	CCD-RAM *m*, Lese-Schreib-Speicher *m* auf Basis CCD	RAM *f* couplée par charge	запоминающее устройство на основе ПЗС
	C condition	*s.* C 57		
	CC-RAM	*s.* C 76		
C 77	cell	Zelle *f* <Speicherzelle, Schaltungsgrundbaustein>	cellule *f*	ячейка, элемент
C 78	cell array	Zellenfeld *n*, reguläre Zellenanordnung *f*	champ *m* de cellules	регулярная структура ячеек
C 79	cell construction	Zellenaufbau *m*	structure *f* de cellule	ячеистая структура
C 80	cell contents	Zelleninhalt *m*	contenu *m* de cellule	содержимое ячейки
C 81	cell size	Zellengröße *f*	grandeur *f* de cellule	длина (разрядность) ячейки
C 82	cell topology	Zellentopologie *f*	topologie *f* des cellules	топология элемента (ячейки)
C 83	cellular logic	zellulare Logikstruktur *f*	logique *f* cellulaire	клеточная логика (структура)
C 84	central acquisition	zentrale Datenerfassung *f*	acquisition *f* centrale de données	централизованный сбор данных
C 85	central control	zentrale Steuerung *f*	commande *f* centrale	центральное управление
C 86	centralized processing	zentralisierte Verarbeitung *f*	traitement *m* centralisé	централизованная обработка
C 87	central monitoring	zentrale Überwachung *f*	surveillance *f* centrale	централизованное обслуживание
	central processing element	*s.* C 814		

	central processing unit	s. C 815		
C 88	**central processor**	Zentralprozessor m, Hauptprozessor m	processeur m central	центральный процессор
C 89	**centre point**	Sternpunkt m	point m neutre	нулевая точка, нейтраль
C 90	**centre zero measurement**	Messung f mit Mittennullpunkt	mesure f au point neutre	измерение относительно нуля в центре шкалы
C 91	**ceramic chip carrier, CCC**	Keramik-Chipträger m <Mehrlagen-Keramikgehäuse zur Chipaufnahme>	support m de puce céramique	носитель кристалла с керамической подложкой
C 92	**ceramic package**	Keramikgehäuse n	boîtier m céramique	керамический корпус
	CE signal	s. C 197		
	C-flag	s. C 58		
C 93	**chain,** string	Kette f	chaîne f	цепь, последовательность
C 94	**chained addressing**	gekettete Adressierung f	adressage m en chaîne	последовательная адресация
C 95	**chained command (instruction)**	verketteter Befehl m	instruction f en chaîne	команда, включенная в цепочку
C 96	**chain printer**	Kettendrucker m	imprimante f en chaîne	цепное печатающее устройство
C 97	**chance decision**	Zufallsentscheidung f	décision f aléatoire	вероятностное решение
C 98	**chance event**	zufälliger Vorgang m	événement m aléatoire	случайное событие
	change	s. A 219		
C 99	**change dump**	Änderungsauszug m, Speicherauszug m der geänderten Speicherplatzinhalte	extrait m de modification	выдача изменений <избирательная выдача содержимого тех ячеек памяти, состояние которых изменилось с момента предыдущей выдачи>
C 100	**change in load**	Belastungsschwankung f	fluctuation f de charge	колебание (флуктуация) нагрузки
C 101	**change-over contact**	Umschaltkontakt m	contact m inverseur	переключающий контакт
	change-over switch	s. A 228		
C 102	**change record**	Änderungssatz m	enregistrement m de modification	запись изменений (исправлений)
C 103	**change switching**	Umschaltung f	commutation f	переключение, коммутация
C 104	**change tape**	Änderungsstreifen m, Änderungsband n	bande f des modifications	лента изменений (исправлений)
C 105	**channel**	Kanal m	canal m	канал
C 106	**channel activity**	Kanalaktivität f	activité f de canal	активность канала
C 107	**channel adapter**	Kanaladapter m	adapteur m de canal	адаптер канала
C 108	**channel address**	Kanaladresse f	adresse f de canal	адрес канала
C 109	**channel capacity,** channel transmission capacity	Kanalkapazität f, Kanaltransferkapazität f	capacité f [de transfert] de canal	производительность (быстродействие) канала
C 110	**channel check handler**	Kanalprüfroutine f	routine f de vérification de canal	программа контроля канала
C 111	**5-channel code,** five-channel (five-level, five-track) code	5-Kanal-Kode m, Fünfkanalkode m, Fünfspurkode m	code m à cinq canaux	5-дорожечный код
C 112	**8-channel code,** eight-channel (eight-level, eight-track) code	8-Kanal-Kode m, Achtkanalkode m, Achtspurkode m	code m à huit canaux	8-дорожечный код
C 113	**channel command,** channel instruction	Kanalkommando n, Kanalbefehl m	instruction f de canal	команда канала
C 114	**channel control**	Kanalsteuerung f	commande f de canal	управление каналом
C 115	**channel controller**	Kanalsteuereinheit f	unité f de commande de canal	контроллер канала
	channel instruction	s. C 113		
C 116	**channel interface**	Kanalinterface n, Kanalschnittstelle f	interface f de canal	интерфейс канала
C 117	**channel length**	Kanallänge f	longueur f de canal	длина канала
C 118	**channel loading**	Kanalbelegung f	occupation f de canal	загрузка канала
C 119	**channel scheduling**	Kanalzuordnung f	attribution f de canal	составление расписания канала
C 120	**channel selector**	Kanalwähler m	sélecteur m de canal	селектор канала
C 121	**channel stop**	Kanalstopp m <Halbleitertechnik>	arrêt m de canal	перекрытие канала
C 122	**channel switching**	Kanalumschaltung f	commutation f de canal	коммутация каналов
C 123	**5-channel tape,** five-channel (five-level, five-track) tape	5-Kanal-Lochstreifen m, Fünfkanalstreifen m, Fünfspurstreifen m	bande f perforée à cinq canaux	5-дорожечная лента
C 124	**8-channel tape,** eight-channel (eight-track) tape	8-Kanal-Streifen m, Achtkanalstreifen m, Achtspurstreifen m.	bande f à huit canaux	8-дорожечная лента
	channel transmission capacity	s. C 109		
C 125	**character**	Zeichen n	caractère m	знак, символ
C 126	**character code**	Zeichenkode m	code m de caractères	код знака (символа)
C 127	**character-coded**	zeichenverschlüsselt	codé (codifié) en caractères	посимвольно кодированный
C 128	**character density**	Zeichendichte f	densité f de caractères	плотность знаков
C 129	**character generator**	Zeichengenerator m	générateur m de caractères	знакогенератор
C 130	**character handling**	Zeichenbearbeitung f, Zeichenbehandlung f	traitement m de caractères	обработка символов
C 131	**character input**	Zeicheneingabe f	entrée f de caractères	ввод символов
C 132	**characteristic**	Charakteristik f, Kenngröße f, Kennziffer f	caractéristique f	характеристика
C 133	**characteristic curve**	Kennlinie f	courbe f caractéristique	характеристическая кривая
C 134	**characteristic data,** characteristics	Kenndaten pl, Kennlinien fpl	données fpl caractéristiques	идентификационные данные, характеристики
C 135	**character manipulation**	Zeichenmodifizierung f	modification f de caractère	преобразование символов

C 136	**character mode**	Zeichenverarbeitungs-modus *m*, Zeichenmodus *m*, zeichenweiser Betrieb *m*	mode *m* de caractères	символьный режим, режим обработки символов
C 137	**character printer**	Zeichendrucker *m*	imprimante *f* d€ caractères	знакопечатающее устройство последовательного типа
C 138	**character processing**	Zeichenverarbeitung *f*	traitement *m* de caractères	обработка символов
C 139	**character reader**	Zeichenleser *m*	lecteur *m* de caractères	устройство считывания символов
C 140	**character recognition**	Zeichenerkennung *f*	identification (resonnais-sance) *f* de caractères	распознавание символов
C 141	**character representation**	Zeichendarstellung *f*	représentation *f* de carac-tères	символьное представление
C 142	**character search**	Zeichensuche *f*	recherche *f* de caractères	поиск символов
C 143	**character sensing**	Zeichenabtastung *f*	lecture *f* de caractères	считывание символов
C 144	**character sequence**	Zeichenfolge *f*	séquence *f* de caractères	последовательность символов
C 145	**character set**	Zeichensatz *m*, Zeichen-vorrat *m*	jeu *m* de caractères	набор символов
C 146	**character spacing**	Zeichenabstand *m*	espace *m* de caractères	расположение знаков с интервалами
C 147	**character string**	Zeichenkette *f*	chaine *f* de caractères	строка символов
C 148	**character-string field**	Zeichenkettenfeld *n*	champ *m* à chaine de caractères	поле строки символов
C 149	**character-string operand**	Zeichenkettenoperand *m*	opérande *m* de chaine de caractères	операнд строки символов
C 150	**character translator**	Zeichenübersetzer *m*, Zeichenumsetzer *m*	traducteur *m* de caractères	преобразователь [кода] символов
C 150 a	**charge**	Last *f*, Ladung *f*	charge *f*	заряд
C 151	**charge carrier**, carrier	Ladungsträger *m*	porteur *m* de charge	носитель заряда
	charge-carrier concen-tration	s. C 152		
C 152	**charge-carrier density**, [charge-]carrier con-centration, carrier density	Ladungsträgerdichte *f*, Ladungsträgerkonzen-tration *f*	densité (concentration) *f* des porteurs de charge	плотность (концентрация) носителей
	charge-carrier depletion	s. C 52		
	charge-carrier injection	s. C 53		
C 153	**charge-carrier mobility**, carrier mobility	Ladungsträgerbeweglich-keit *f*	mobilité *f* de charge	подвижность носителей
C 154	**charge condition**	Ladungszustand *m*	état *m* de charge	состояние заряда
C 155	**charge conservation**, charge retention	Ladungserhaltung *f*	conservation *f* de charge	сохранение заряда
	charge-coupled devices	s. C 75		
	charge-coupled RAM	s. C 76		
C 156	**charge-coupled shift register**	ladungsgekoppeltes Schiebe-register *m*, CCD-Schiebe-register *n*	registre *m* à décalages couplé par charge	сдвиговый регистр на основе ПЗС
C 157	**charge density**	Ladungsdichte *f*	densité *f* de charge	плотность зарядов
C 158	**charge distribution**	Ladungsverteilung *f*	distribution *f* de charge	распределение заряда
C 159	**charge exchange**	Ladungsaustausch *m*	échange *m* de charge	перезаряд
C 160	**charge pattern**	Ladungsbild *n*, Ladungs-muster *n*	image *f* de charge	потенциальный рельеф
	charge retention	s. C 155		
C 161	**charge space**	Ladungsraum *m*	espace *m* de charge	пространство зарядов
C 162	**charge storage**	Ladungsspeicherung *f*	accumulation *f* de charge	накопление заряда
C 163	**charge store**	Ladungsspeicher *m*	accumulateur *m* de charge	накопитель заряда
C 164	**charge time**	Ladezeit *f*, Aufladezeit *f*	temps *m* de charge	время заряда
C 165	**charge transfer**	Ladungstransport *m*	transfert *m* de charge	передача заряда
	charge transfer devices	s. C 860		
C 166	**chassis assembly**	Chassis-Bausatz *m*	assemblage *m* de châssis	монтажная стойка
C 167	**chassis mounting**	Chassis-Aufbau *m*	montage *m* en châssis	монтаж на основе шасси
C 168	**check / to**, to verify	prüfen, überprüfen, kon-trollieren	vérifier	проверять, контролиро-вать
C 169	**check**, test	Prüfung *f*, Kontrolle *f*, Test *m*	vérification *f*, test *m*	проверка, контроль
C 170	**check algorithm**, check-ing algorithm	Prüfalgorithmus *m*	algorithme *m* de vérification	алгоритм проверки (контроля)
C 171	**check bit**, test bit	Prüfbit *n*, Kontrollbit *n*, Testbit *n*	bit *m* de test (vérification)	контрольный бит
C 172	**check byte**	Prüfbyte *n*	octet *m* de vérification	контрольный байт
C 173	**check character**	Prüfzeichen *n*	caractère *m* de vérification	контрольный символ
C 174	**check circuit**, test circuit	Prüfschaltung *f*, Test-schaltung *f*	circuit *m* de vérification (test)	схема контроля
C 175	**check code**	Prüfkode *m*	code *m* de vérification	контрольный код
C 176	**check computation**	Kontrollrechnung *f*	calcul *m* de vérification	контрольный просчет
C 177	**check digit**	Prüfziffer *f*	chiffre *m* de vérification	контрольная цифра
C 178	**checked operation**	geprüfte Operation *f*	opération *f* vérifiée	проверяемая операция
C 179	**checked quantity**	geprüfte Größe *f*	grandeur *f* vérifiée	контролируемая величина
	check indicator	s. E 238		
C 180	**check information**	Prüfinformation *f*	information *f* de vérification	контрольная информация
	checking algorithm	s. C 170		
C 181	**checking procedure**, test procedure (method), testing technique	Prüfverfahren *n*, Testver-fahren *n*, Prüfmethode *f*	procédé *m* de vérification (test)	тестовая процедура
	checking routine	s. C 188		
C 182	**checking sequence**, test sequence	Prüffolge *f*	séquence *f* de vérification (test)	контрольная последо-вательность
C 182	**checking system**, test system	Prüfsystem *n*, Testsystem *n*	système *m* de vérification (test)	система контроля
C 184	**checking unit**	Prüfeinheit *f*, Kontroll-einheit *f*	unité *f* de vérification	устройство контроля
C 185	**check message**	Kontrollmeldung *f*	message *m* de vérification	контрольное сообщение

C 186	check out / to checkout of system	austesten <Programme> s. S 979	vérifier, tester, essayer <des programmes>	отлаживать [программу]
C 187	checkpoint, test point	Prüfpunkt m, Testpunkt m, Kontrollpunkt m	point m de vérification (test)	контрольная точка
C 188	check program, checking routine, test program (routine)	Prüfprogramm n, Testprogramm n, Testroutine f	programme m de vérification (test)	программа контроля
C 189	check register check run	Prüfregister n s. T 132	registre m de test	контрольный регистр
C 190	check sum, control total	Kontrollsumme f	somme f de vérification	контрольная сумма
C 191	chip	Chip n, „Scheibchen" n, Halbleiterkristallplättchen n mit Logikschaltung, LSI-Schaltkreis m	puce f, circuit m intégré, CI m	бескорпусный компонент интегральной схемы, полупроводниковый кристалл с размещенной схемой, чип
C 192	chip area	Chipfläche f	surface f de puce	площадь чипа
C 193	chip carrier	Chiprahmen m, Chipträgerrahmen m	cadre m à puces	носитель кристалла, кристаллоноситель
C 194	chip complexity	Chipkomplexität f, Schaltkreiskomplexität f	complexité f de puce	сложность микросхемы (чипа)
C 195	chip density chip design	s. C 219 Chipentwurf m, Schaltkreisentwurf m	maquette f de puce, conception f de puce (CI)	проектирование микросхем
C 196	chip device configuration	Elementarzellenaufbau m eines Schaltkreises	structure f élémentaire de circuit	конфигурация компонентов микросхемы
C 197	chip enable signal, CE signal	Schaltkreisfreigabesignal n, Schaltkreisaktivierungssignal n	signal m de libération de CI, signal d'activation de CI	разрешающий сигнал
C 198	chip form	Chipform f, Chipausführung f, Ausführung f eines Schaltkreises	forme f de puce	форма чипа
C 199	chip level	Schaltkreisniveau n, Schaltkreisentwurfsniveau n	niveau m de circuit	уровень интеграции микросхем
C 200	chip maker, IC maker	Schaltkreishersteller m	fabricant m de circuits	изготовитель микросхем
C 201	chip process techniques	Chipherstellungsverfahren npl, Schaltkreis-Prozeßtechniken f	techniques fpl de processus de circuits	техника изготовления микросхем
C 202	chip select signal, CS signal	Chipauswahlsignal n, Schaltkreisauswahlsignal n	signal m de sélection de CI, signal CS	сигнал выбора микросхемы
C 203	chip select time	Chipauswahlzeit f, Schaltkreisauswahlzeit f	temps m de sélection de CI	время выбора микросхемы
C 204	chip set	LSI-Schaltkreissatz m	jeu m de circuits intégrés	набор микросхем
C 205	chip size	Chipgröße f	grandeur f de puce (CI)	размер микросхемы
C 206	chip size constraints	Chipgrößenbeschränkungen fpl, Grenzbedingungen fpl für die Chipgröße	restrictions fpl de grandeur de puce	ограничения на размер микросхемы
C 207	chip testing	Chipprüfung f	test m de puce (CI)	контроль микросхем
C 208	chip user	Chipanwender m, LSI-Baustein-Anwender m <Anwender einzelner LSI-Schaltkreise mit eigener Komplettierungsentwicklung>	usager m de CI	потребитель микросхем
C 209	circuit, circuitry	Schaltung f, Schaltungskomplex m	circuit m	схема, схемотехника
C 210	circuit analysis	Schaltungsanalyse f	analyse f de circuit	схемный анализ
C 211	circuit analyzer	Schaltungsanalysator m, Schaltkreisanalysator m	analyseur m de circuit	схемный анализатор
C 212	circuit arrangement	Schaltungsanordnung f	aménagement m de circuit	расположение схем
C 213	circuit board (card)	Leiterplatte f, Schaltungsplatine f	plaquette f à circuit imprimé, circuit m imprimé	плата
C 214	circuit characteristic	Schaltungskenngröße f	caractéristique f de circuit	характеристика схемы
C 215	circuit complexity	Schaltungskomplexität f	complexité f de circuit	сложность схемы
C 216	circuit component	Schaltungsbauelement n	composant m de circuit	компонент (элемент) схемы
C 217	circuit construction	Schaltungsaufbau m	structure f de circuit	разработка схемы
C 218	circuit delay	Schaltungsverzögerung f, Schaltkreisverzögerung f	retardement m de circuit	задержка переключения микросхем
C 219	circuit density, chip density	Schaltungsdichte f [eines Schaltkreises]	densité f de circuit	плотность упаковки
C 220	circuit design	Schaltungsentwurf m	conception f de circuit	проектирование схем
C 221	circuit design technique	Schaltungsentwurfstechnik f, Schaltkreisentwurfstechnik f	technique f de conception de circuit	методы проектирования схем
C 222	circuit development	Schaltungsentwicklung f	développement m de circuit	совершенствование характеристик схем
C 223	circuit diagram	Schaltbild n, Schaltplan m, Schaltungsdiagramm n	schéma m de circuit	принципиальная схема
C 224	circuit failure	Schaltungsausfall m	défaillance f de circuit	отказ схемы
C 225	circuit fault	Schaltungsfehler m	défaut m de circuit	сбой схемы
C 226	circuit flexibility	Schaltungsflexibilität f, Schaltungsanpassungsfähigkeit f	flexibilité f de circuit	схемная гибкость, согласуемость на уровне схем
C 227	circuit layout, IC layout	Schaltkreis-Layout n, Schaltkreistopografie f, Schaltkreisbelegungsplan m	layout m de circuit (CI)	размещение элементов
C 228	circuit load	Schaltungsbelastung f	charge f de circuit	нагрузка схемы
C 229	circuit logic	Schaltungslogik f, Schaltkreislogik f	logique f de circuit	схемная логика
C 230	circuit modification	Schaltungsabwandlung f, Schaltungsmodifizierung f	modification f de circuit	схемная модификация
C 231	circuit optimization	Schaltungsoptimierung f	optimisation f de circuit	оптимизация схемы
C 232	circuit parameter	Schaltungsparameter m	paramètre m de circuit	параметр схемы

C 233	circuit requirement	Schaltungsanforderung *f*	exigence *f* au circuit	требования к схеме
	circuitry	s. C 209		
C 234	circuit simplification	Schaltungsvereinfachung *f*	simplification *f* de circuit	упрощение схемы
C 235	circuit simulation	Schaltungssimulation *f*	simulation *f* de circuit	моделирование схемы
C 236	circuit speed	Schaltkreisgeschwindigkeit *f*	vitesse *f* de circuit	быстродействие схемы
C 237	circuit switching, line switching	Leitungsvermittlung *f*, Durchschaltvermittlung *f*	communication *f* de lignes	коммутация линий (каналов, цепей)
C 238	circuit switching system	Leitungsvermittlungssystem *n*	système *m* de communication de lignes	система коммутации каналов
C 239	circuit technique	Schaltkreistechnik *f*, Schaltungstechnik *f*	technique *f* de circuit	схемотехника
C 240	circuit tester, IC tester	Schaltkreistester *m*	examinateur (vérificateur) *m* de circuit	тестер для проверки схем
C 241	circuit testing	Schaltungsprüfung *f*	test *m* de circuit	проверка схем
C 242	circular shift, cyclic shift	zyklische Verschiebung *f*, Umlaufverschiebung *f*	décalage *m* cyclique (circulaire)	циклический сдвиг
	circulate / to	s. R 398		
	circulating	s. R 98		
C 243	circulating register	Umlaufregister *n*	registre *m* cyclique (circulaire)	регистр с циклическим сдвигом, динамический регистр
	circulating storage	s. C 909		
	circulation	s. R 399		
	circulation speed	s. R 401		
	C³L	s. C 442		
C 244	clad	kaschiert	contrecollé, doublé	покрытый
	clamper	s. C 245		
C 245	clamping circuit, clamper	Klemmschaltung *f*, Blockierschaltung *f*	montage *m* de blocage	фиксирующая схема, фиксатор
C 246	clamping diode	Klammerdiode *f*	diode *f* agrafe	ограничивающий диод
C 247	classification	Klassifizierung *f*	classification *f*	классификация
	CLC	s. C 280		
C 248	clear / to	<Eins-Zustand> löschen, nullsetzen	remettre à zéro	очищать, устанавливать в ноль
C 249	clearing, zero reset	Löschung *f* (Rücksetzen *n*) auf Null, Nullsetzen *n*	remise *f* à zéro, RAZ	очистка, установка в ноль
C 250	clear to send	sendebereit	disponible à l'émission	готовый к передаче
C 251	clock	Takt *m*	rythme *m*	такт, тактовый сигнал
	clock-actuated	s. C 253		
C 252	clock capacitance	Taktkapazität *f*, Taktbelastungskapazität *f*	capacité *f* de rythme	длина тактовой последовательности
C 253	clock-controlled, clock-actuated	taktgesteuert	commandé par rythmeur	управляемый тактовыми импульсами
C 254	clock cycle	Taktzyklus *m*	cycle *m* d'horloge	цикл синхронизации
C 255	clock cycle time	Taktzykluszeit *f*	temps *m* de cycle d'horloge	длительность цикла синхронизации
	clock driver	s. C 266		
C 256	clocked signal	getaktetes Signal *n*	signal *m* rythmé	синхронизированный сигнал
C 257	clocked system	getaktetes System *n*	système *m* rythmé	синхронизированная система
C 258	clock fall time	Taktabfallzeit *f*, Abfallzeit *f* des Taktimpulses	temps *m* de chute d'impulsion	длительность заднего фронта тактового сигнала
C 259	clock frequency, clock rate	Taktfrequenz *f*, Taktrate *f*	fréquence *f* de rythme, fréquence d'horloge	тактовая частота
	clock generator	s. C 267		
	clocking error	s. T 216		
C 260	clocking scheme	Taktschema *n*, Taktsystem *n*	schéma (système) *m* de rythme	тактирующая схема
C 261	clock input	Takteingang *m*	entrée *f* de rythme	синхронизирующий вход
C 262	clock input voltage	Takteingangsspannung *f*	tension *f* d'entrée de rythme	напряжение входного тактового сигнала
C 263	clock output	Taktausgang *m*	sortie *f* de rythme	тактовый выход
C 264	clock period	Taktperiode *f*	période *f* d'horloge	период тактовых сигналов
C 265	clock pulse	Taktimpuls *m*	impulsion *f* d'horloge	тактовый импульс
C 266	clock-pulse driver, clock driver	Taktimpulsgeber *m*, Taktgeber *m*	générateur *m* de rythme	формирователь тактовых сигналов
C 267	clock-pulse generator, clock generator	Taktimpulsgenerator *m*, Taktgenerator *m*	générateur *m* d'impulsions de rythme	генератор тактовых импульсов, тактовый генератор
C 268	clock-pulse width	Taktimpulsbreite *f*	largeur *f* d'impulsion de rythme	длительность тактового импульса
	clock rate	s. C 259		
C 269	clock requirements	Taktbedingungen *fpl*, Taktanforderungen *fpl*	conditions *fpl* (demande *f*) de rythme	требования к синхронизации
C 270	clock rise time	Taktanstiegszeit *f*, Anstiegszeit *f* des Taktimpulses	temps *m* de montée d'impulsion de rythme	длительность переднего фронта тактового сигнала
C 271	clock signal	Taktsignal *n*	signal *m* d'horloge	тактовый сигнал
C 272	clock timing	Taktdiagramm *n*, Taktablauf *m*	diagramme *m* de rythme	временная диаграмма
C 273	clock transition	Taktimpulsübergang *m*	transition *f* d'impulsion de rythme	переключение синхронизации
C 274	closed library	abgeschlossene Programmbibliothek *f*	bibliothèque *f* de programmes fermée	замкнутая библиотека программ
C 275	closed loop	geschlossene Schleife *f*, geschlossener Wirkungskreis *m* <Betriebsart>	circuit *m* fermé	замкнутая петля, замкнутый цикл (контур)
C 276	closed-loop circuit	Rückführungsschaltung *f*	circuit *m* de réaction	схема обратной связи, схема с обратной связью
C 277	closed-loop control, feedback control	Rückkopplungsregelung *f*	réglage *m* à réaction	регулирование по замкнутому циклу
C 278	closed-shop [operation]	geschlossener Betrieb *m* <Betriebsart>, abgetrennte Verarbeitung *f*	régime *m* fermé	вычислительный центр без доступа пользователей к ЭВМ, операторный режим [эксплуатации ЭВМ]

C 279	closed subroutine	abgeschlossenes Unterprogramm n	sous-routine f fermée	замкнутая подпрограмма
C 280	cluster controller, CLC	Gruppensteuerung f	commande f de groupe, CLC	групповой контроллер
C 281	CMOS, CMOS technique, complementary MOS technique	CMOS f, CMOS-Technik f, Komplementär-MOS-Technik f	technologie f CMOS, technique f MOS complémentaire	комплементарная МОП-технология, КМОП-технология
	CMOS-on-sapphire technology	s. C 282		
C 282	CMOS-SOS, CMOS-on-sapphire technology	CMOS-SOS f, CMOS-auf-Saphir-Technik f <Technologie zur Realisierung von CMOS-Schaltungen auf Saphirsubstrat>	technologie f CMOS-SOS	комплементарные МОП-схемы на сапфировой подложке, КМОП-КНС
	CMOS technique	s. C 281		
	CNC	s. C 531		
C 283	coating	Beschichtung f, Überzug m	revêtement m	покрытие, наружный слой
C 284	coating thickness	Beschichtungsdicke f	épaisseur f de revêtement	толщина покрытия
C 285	coaxial cable	Koaxialkabel n	câble m coaxial	коаксиальный кабель
C 286	coaxial transmission line	konzentrische Übertragungsleitung f	ligne f de transmission coaxiale	коаксиальная линия связи
C 287	COBOL <common business-oriented language>	COBOL n <kommerziell orientierte höhere Programmiersprache>	COBOL m	КОБОЛ <язык программирования для решения экономических задач>
C 288	code / to, to encode	kodieren, verschlüsseln	coder	кодировать
C 289	code	Kode m, Schlüssel m <Verschlüsselungsvorschrift>	code m	код
C 290	code character	Kodezeichen n	caractère-code m, caractère m de code	кодовый знак
C 291	code chart	Kodeschema n	schéma m de code	кодовая таблица
C 292	code check	Kodeprüfung f, Kodefehlererkennung f	vérification f de code	контроль кода
C 293	code compression	Kodeverdichtung f	compression f de code	сжатие кода
C 294	code conversion, code transformation	Kodewandlung f, Kodekonvertierung f, Kodeübersetzung f	conversion (transformation) f de code	преобразование кода
C 295	code converter	Kodeumsetzer m, Kodewandler m	convertisseur m de code	преобразователь кода
C 296	coded address	kodierte Adresse f	adresse f codée	кодированный адрес
C 297	coded character	kodiertes Zeichen n	caractère m codé	кодированный символ
C 298	coded decimal digit	kodierte Dezimalziffer f	nombre m décimal codé	кодированная десятичная цифра
C 299	code density	Kodedichte f	densité f de code	плотность кода
C 300	code digit	Kodeziffer f	chiffre m de code	кодовая цифра
C 301	coded instruction	kodierter Befehl m	instruction f codée	кодированная инструкция
C 302	coded program	kodiertes Programm n	programme m codé	кодированная программа
C 303	coded signal	kodiertes Signal n	signal m codé	кодированный сигнал
C 304	code element	Kodeelement n	élément m de code	элемент кода
C 305	code field	Kodefeld n	champ m de code	кодовое поле
C 306	code generating (generation)	Kodeerzeugung f	génération f de code	генерирование кода
C 307	code line	Kodezeile f, Programmzeile f	ligne f de code (programme)	кодовая строка, строка программы
C 308	code list	Kodeliste f	liste f de code	кодовая таблица
C 309	code pattern	Kodemuster n	dessin m de code	кодовый образец
C 310	code position	Kodestelle f	position f de code	кодовая позиция
C 311/2	code protection	Kodesicherung f	protection f de code	защита кода
	coder	s. C 324		
C 313	code reading	Kode-Kontrollesen n	lecture f de vérification de code	считывание кода
C 314	code redundancy	Koderedundanz f	redondance f de code	избыточность кода
C 315	code segment	Kodesegment n, Programmsegment n	segment m de code	кодовый сегмент
C 316	code space	Koderaum m, Programmkoderaum m, Programmspeicherraum m	espace m de code	кодовое пространство
C 317	code structure	Kodestruktur f, Kodeaufbau m	structure f de code	структура кода
C 318	code system	Kodesystem n	système m de code	кодовая система
	code transformation	s. C 294		
C 319	code translator	Kodeübersetzer m	traducteur m de code	преобразователь кода
C 320	code word	Kodewort n	mot-code m	кодовое слово
C 321	coding	Kodierung f, Verschlüsselung f, Programmnotierung f in Maschinensprache	codage m	кодирование, программирование на машинном языке
C 322	coding aids	Kodierungshilfen fpl	aides fpl de codage	вспомогательные средства кодирования
C 323	coding circuit	Kodierschaltung f	circuit m de codage	кодирующая схема
C 324	coding device, coder, encoder	Kodierer m, Kodiereinrichtung f, Verschlüßler m	codeur m, dispositif m de codage	кодер, кодирующее устройство
C 325	coding field	Kodierfeld n	champ m de codage	поле кодирования
C 326	coding language	Kodiersprache f	langage m de codage	язык кодирования
C 327	coding possibility	Kodiermöglichkeit f	possibilité f de codage	возможность кодирования
C 328	coding sequence	Kodierungsfolge f	séquence f de codage	кодирующая последовательность
	coincidence	s. A 46		
C 329	coincidence circuit (gate)	Koinzidenzschaltung f, Koinzidenzgatter n <Konjunktionsrealisierung>	circuit m de coïncidence	схема совпадения (выполнения операции конъюнкции)
C 330	collate / to	mischen <ordnen>	fusionner	упорядочивать
C 331	collector	Kollektor m, Kollektorelektrode f	collecteur m	коллектор

C 332	**collector barrier,** collector depletion layer	Kollektorsperrschicht *f*	couche *f* de barrage de collecteur	обедненный слой коллектора
C 333	**collector-base current**	Kollektor-Basis-Strom *m*	courant *m* collecteur-base	ток коллектор-база
C 334	**collector capacitance**	Kollektorkapazität *f*	capacité *f* de collecteur	емкость коллекторного перехода
	collector circuit	*s.* C 370		
C 335	**collector contact**	Kollektoranschluß *m*	contact *m* de collecteur	вывод коллектора
C 336	**collector coupling**	Kollektorkopplung *f*	couplage *m* de collecteur	коллекторная связь
C 337	**collector current**	Kollektorstrom *m*	courant *m* de collecteur	коллекторный ток
	collector depletion layer	*s.* C 332		
C 338	**collector-emitter circuit**	Kollektor-Emitter-Schaltung *f*	montage *m* collecteur-émetteur	цепь коллектор-эмиттер
C 339	**collector-emitter voltage**	Kollektor-Emitter-Spannung *f*	tension *f* collecteur-émetteur	напряжение коллектор-эмиттер
C 340	**collector load**	Kollektor[last]widerstand *m*	charge *f* de collecteur	коллекторная нагрузка
C 341	**collector region**	Kollektorzone *f*	zone *f* de collecteur	область коллектора
C 342	**collector transition region**	Kollektorgrenzschicht *f*	couche *f* limite de collecteur	область коллекторного перехода
C 343	**collector voltage**	Kollektorspannung *f*	tension *f* de collecteur	коллекторное напряжение
C 344	**colour graphics**	Farbgrafik *f*, Farbgrafikgeräte *npl*	graphique *m* en couleurs	цветная графика, цветное графическое устройство отображения
C 345	**column**	Spalte *f*	colonne *f*	колонка, столбец
C 346	**column address bits**	Spaltenadreßbits *npl*	bits *mpl* d'adresse de colonne	биты адреса колонки
C 347	**column binary code**	binärer Spaltenkode *m*	code *m* binaire de colonne	поколонный двоичный код
C 348	**column decoder**	Spaltendekoder *m*, Spaltenentschlüßler *m*	décodeur *m* de colonne	дешифратор кода колонки
C 349	**column spacing**	Spaltenabstand *m*, Schreibstellenabstand *m*	écart *m* de colonne	расстояние между колонками
C 350	**combinational (combinatorial) circuit**	kombinatorische Schaltung *f*, Schaltnetz *n*	circuit *m* combinatoire	комбинационная схема
C 351	**combined data and address bus**	kombinierter Daten-Adreß-Bus *m*, D/A-Bus *m*	bus *m* combiné données-adresses	комбинированная шина адрес-данные
C 352	**combined read-write head**	kombinierter Lese-Schreib-Kopf *m*	tête *f* lecture-écriture combinée	[комбинированная] головка чтения/записи
C 353	**combined test**	kombinierter Test *m*	test *m* combiné	комбинированный тест
	COMC	*s.* C 401		
C 354	**command**	Kommando *n*	commande *f*	команда
	command	*s. a.* I 228		
C 355	**command chaining**	Befehlskettung *f*, Kommandokettung *f*	enchaînement *m* d'instructions	формирование (выполнение) цепочки инструкций
C 356	**command language**	Kommandosprache *f*	langage *m* de commande	язык команд
C 357	**command line**	Kommandoleitung *f* <Bus>	ligne *f* à instructions	командная шина
C 358	**command processor,** instruction processor	Befehlsprozessor *m*	processeur *m* à instructions	процессор для обработки команд
C 359	**comment**	Kommentar *m*, Erläuterung *f*, Bemerkung *f*	commentaire *m*	комментарий
C 360	**comment line**	Kommentarzeile *f*	ligne *f* de commentaires	строка комментария
C 361	**commercial application**	kommerzielle Anwendung *f*	application *f* commerciale	применение в экономике
C 362	**commercial computer,** business computer	kommerzieller Rechner *m*, Rechner für kommerzielle Aufgaben	calculateur *m* commercial	ЭВМ для обработки экономической информации
C 363	**commercial data processing,** business data processing	kommerzielle Datenverarbeitung *f*	informatique *f* commerciale	обработка экономической информации
C 364	**commercial instruction set**	kommerzieller (kommerziell orientierter) Befehlssatz *m* <Orientierung auf Zeichenketten und Dezimalzahlen>	jeu *m* d'instructions commerciales	набор команд, ориентированный на обработку экономической информации
C 365	**common architectural elements**	gemeinsame Architekturelemente (Strukturelemente) *npl*	éléments *mpl* communs de structure	общий элемент архитектуры
C 366	**common area**	gemeinsamer Bereich *m*	champ (domaine) *m* commun	общая область [памяти]
C 367	**common-base circuit,** base circuit	Basisschaltung *f*	circuit *m* de base commune	схема с общей базой
C 368	**common bus**	gemeinsamer Bus *m*	bus *m* commun	общая шина
C 369	**common-bus line**	gemeinsame Busleitung *f*	ligne *f* de bus commun	линия общей шины
C 370	**common-collector circuit,** collector circuit	Kollektorschaltung *f*	circuit *m* de collecteur commun	схема с общим коллектором
C 371	**common communication interface**	gemeinsame Kommunikationsschnittstelle *f*, gemeinsamer Übertragungsanschluß *m* zum Informationsaustausch	interface *f* de communication commune	общий интерфейс связи
C 372	**common-emitter circuit,** emitter circuit	Emitterschaltung *f*	circuit *m* d'émetteur commun	схема с общим эмиттером
C 373	**common hardware**	Kleinteile *npl*, Verschleißersatzteile *npl*	[petites] pièces *fpl* de rechange	мелкие запасные части для ремонта и замены блоков ЭВМ
C 374	**common I/O lines**	gemeinsame E/A-Leitungen *fpl*, gemeinsame Leitungen *fpl* für Ein- und Ausgabe	lignes *fpl* d'E/S communes	общие линии ввода-вывода
C 375	**common line**	gemeinsame Leitung *f*	ligne *f* commune	общая (универсальная) линия
C 376	**common logarithm**	dekadischer Logarithmus *m*	logarithme *m* vulgaire (décimal)	десятичный логарифм
C 377	**common memory,** common store	gemeinsamer Speicher *m* <in Mehrprozessorsystemen>	mémoire *f* commune	общая память

C 378	**common mode,** push-push mode	Gleichtaktbetrieb *m*	régime *m* push-push	синфазный режим
C 379	**common mode rejection**	Gleichtaktunterdrückung *f* <Operationsverstärker>	suppression *f* de synchronisme	подавление синфазного сигнала <операционный усилитель>
C 380	**common mode signal**	Gleichtaktsignal *n*	signal *m* de synchronisme	синфазный сигнал
C 381	**common peripherals**	gemeinsame Peripherie *f*	périphérie *f* commune	общие периферийные устройства
	common programs	s. C 382		
C 382	**common software,** common programs	gemeinsame Programme *npl* <in unterschiedlichen Anwendungen nutzbare Programme>	programmes *mpl* communs	универсальное программное обеспечение
	common store	s. C 377		
C 383	**communicate / to**	übermitteln, mitteilen, verkehren	communiquer	связывать, сообщать, передавать
C 384	**communication**	Kommunikation *f*, Nachrichtenverkehr *m*, Nachrichtenübertragung *f*	communication *f*	связь, сообщение, передача
C 385	**communication application**	Nachrichtenverkehrsanwendung *f*, Übertragungstechnik-Anwendung *f*	application *f* de communication	применение в связи
C 386	**communication control character**	Übertragungssteuerzeichen *n*	caractère *m* de commande de communication	символ управления передачей
C 387	**communication engineering**	Nachrichtentechnik *f*	technique *f* des communications	техника связи
C 388	**communication interface**	Kommunikationsschnittstelle *f*, Anschlußstelle *f* zum Informationsaustausch, Übertragungstechnik-Schnittstelle *f*	interface *f* de communication	связной интерфейс
C 389	**communication interface circuit**	Kommunikationsschnittstellenschaltung *f*, Übertragungsinterfaceschaltkreis *m*	circuit *m* à interface de communication	схема интерфейса связи, БИС интерфейса передачи данных
C 390	**communication line**	Fernmeldeleitung *f*	ligne *f* de communication	линия связи
C 391	**communication link,** communications link	Kommunikationsverbindung *f*, Kommunikationsgeräteanschluß *m*, Nachrichtenverbindung *f*	liaison *f* de communication	канал (технические средства) связи
C 392	**communication medium**	Übertragungsmedium *n*, Nachrichtenmittel *n*	milieu *m* de communication (transmission), moyen *m* de communication	средства связи
C 393	**communication mode**	Kommunikationsmodus *m*, Betriebsart *f* des Informationsaustausches	mode *m* de communication	режим (способ) передачи
C 394	**communication module**	Kommunikationsmodul *m*, Anschlußbaustein *m* für Informationsaustauschgeräte <Fernschreiber, Bildschirmgerät, Modem>	module *m* de communication	набор устройств передачи данных
C 395	**communication network**	Kommunikationsnetz *n*, Übertragungsnetz *n* zum Informationsaustausch, Nachrichtenübertragungsnetz *n* ⌐weg *m*	réseau *m* de communications	сеть связи
C 396	**communication path**	Nachrichtenübertragungs-	voie *f* de communication	тракт передачи данных
	communication port	s. C 404		
C 397	**communication procedure**	Übertragungsprozedur *f*, Übertragungsverfahren *n*	procédé *m* de communication	процедура передачи данных
C 398	**communication protocol**	Übertragungsprotokoll *n*	procès-verbal *m* de communication	связной протокол, протокол передачи данных
C 399	**communications**	Nachrichtenwesen *n*, Fernmeldewesen *n*	télécommunications *fpl*, télématique *f*	[дальняя] связь
C 400	**communications channel**	Nachrichtenkanal *m*	canal *m* de communication	канал связи
C 401	**communications controller,** COMC	Kommunikationssteuereinheit *f*	unité *f* de commande de communication	связной контроллер
C 402	**communication signal**	Nachrichtensignal *n*, Nachrichtenübertragungssignal *n*	signal *m* de communication	сигнал канала связи
	communications link	s. C 391		
C 403	**communications modem controller**	Übertragungsmodem-Steuergerät *n*, Modem-Steuergerät *n*	appareil *m* de commande de modem	устройство управления модема
C 404	**communications port,** communication port	Kommunikationsstelle *f*, Informationsaustauschkanal *m* <logisch>, Nachrichtenübermittlungsstelle *f*	point *m* de communication	канал связи (обмена информацией)
C 405	**communications processing**	Nachrichtenverarbeitung *f*	traitement *m* d'informations, traitement de messages	обработка сообщений
C 406	**communication[s] system**	Nachrichtenübertragungssystem *n*	système *m* de télécommunication	система связи
C 407	**communication terminal**	Datenstation *f* für Kommunikation, Nachrichtenübertragungsendstelle *f*	terminal *m* de communication	связной терминал
C 408	**compact code**	kompakter (dicht gepackter) Kode *m*	code *m* compact	[плотно] упакованный код
C 409	**compact construction**	Kompaktaufbau *m*	construction *f* compacte	компактная конструкция
C 410	**compaction**	Verdichtung *f* <von Daten>	compression *f*	сжатие <данных>
C 411	**compactness**	Kompaktheit *f*	compacité *f*	компактность
C 412	**companion processor,** coprocessor	Begleitprozessor *m*, Zusatzprozessor *m*, dazugehöriger Prozessor *m*	processeur *m* adjoint	вспомогательный (дополнительный) процессор

C 413	comparator	Vergleicher m, Vergleichs-einrichtung f	comparateur m	компаратор
C 414	compare instruction	Vergleichsbefehl m	instruction f de comparaison	команда сравнения
C 415	compare logic	Vergleichslogik f, Vergleicherlogik f	logique f de comparaison	аппаратные средства сравнения
C 416	comparing feature	Vergleichsmerkmal n	caractéristique f de comparaison	признак сравнения
C 417	comparing position	Vergleichsposition f	position f de comparaison	разряд сравнения
C 418	comparison operator	Vergleichsoperator m	opérateur m de comparaison	оператор отношения (сравнения)
C 419	compatibility	Verträglichkeit f, Kompatibilität f	compatibilité f	совместимость
C 420	compatibility mode	Kompatibilitätsmodus m, Kompatibilitätsbetriebsweise f	mode m de compatibilité	режим совместимости
C 421	compatible	verträglich, vereinbar, kompatibel	compatible	совместимый
C 422	compatible at-the-board-level	kompatibel auf Steckeinheitenniveau	compatible au niveau de circuits imprimés	совместимый на уровне плат
C 423	compatible microcomputer models	kompatible Mikrorechnertypen mpl	modèles mpl de micro-calculateurs compatibles	совместимые модели микро-ЭВМ
C 424	compatible system	kompatibles System n	système m compatible	совместимая система
C 425	compensating circuit	Kompensationsschaltung f	circuit m de compensation	компенсирующая схема
C 426	compensating errors	sich kompensierende Fehler mpl	erreurs fpl compensées	компенсирующие ошибки, [само]компенсируемые ошибки
C 427	compensating resistor	Kompensationswiderstand m	résistance f de compensation	компенсирующий резистор
C 428	compensation	Kompensation f, Ausgleich m	compensation f	компенсация
C 429	compensation of distortion, distortion elimination	Verzerrungskompensation f	compensation f de distorsions	компенсация искажения
C 430	compensation signal	Kompensationssignal n	signal m de compensation	компенсирующий сигнал
C 431	compensation voltage	Kompensationsspannung f	tension f de compensation	компенсирующее напряжение
C 432	compensator	Kompensator m	compensateur m	компенсатор
C 433	compilation	Kompilierung f, Programmsprachübersetzung f	compilation f	компиляция, трансляция
	compilation time	s. C 438		
C 434	compile / to	kompilieren, zusammenstellen	compiler	компилировать, транслировать
C 435	compiled program	übersetztes Programm n	programme m traduit	скомпилированная программа
C 436	compiler, compiling program	Kompilierer m, Kompilierungsprogramm n, Programmsprachübersetzer m <übersetzt Programme aus Programmsprachkode in Objektkode>	compilateur m	компилятор, компилирующая программа
C 437	compiler-level language	Kompiliererniveau-Sprache f, Übersetzung erfordernde Programmiersprache f	langage m de niveau de compilateur	уровень входного языка компилятора
C 438	compile time, compilation time	Übersetzungszeit f	temps m de compilation	время компиляции
	compiling program	s. C 436		
C 439	complement	Komplement n, Zahlenkomplement n	complément m	дополнение
	1's complement	s. O 58		
	2's complement	s. T 368/9		
C 440	complementary attachments	Ergänzungsgeräte npl	appareils mpl complémentaires	дополнительное оборудование
C 441	complementary circuit	Ergänzungsschaltung f	circuit m complémentaire	схема на дополняющих структурах
C 442	complementary constant-current logic, C^3L	C^3L f, komplementäre Konstantstromlogik f <Schaltungstechnik>	C^3L f, logique f à courant constant complémentaire	комплементарные логические схемы с постоянной инжекцией тока
	complementary MOS technique	s. C 281		
C 443	complementary product	ergänzendes Produkt (Erzeugnis) n	produit m complémentaire	дополняющие изделия, дополняющая продукция
C 444	complementary transistors	Komplementärtransistoren mpl, sich ergänzende Transistoren mpl	transistors mpl complémentaires	комплементарные транзисторы
C 445	complementation	Komplementbildung f	établissement m de complément	образование дополнения
C 446	complement code	Komplementkode m	code m de complément	дополнительный код
C 447	complementer	Komplementierwerk n	complémenteur m	схема образования дополнения
C 448	complement on B	B-Komplement n, Ergänzung f zu B^N	complément m à B	дополнение до B <B^N>
C 449	complement on B-1	(B-1)-Komplement n, Ergänzung f zu B^N-1	complément m à B-1	дополнение до B-1 <B^N-1>
C 450	complement procedure	Komplementierverfahren n, Verfahren n zur Komplementbildung	procédé m de complément	процедура образования дополнения
C 451	complement representation	Komplementärdarstellung f	représentation f complémentaire	представление в виде дополнения
C 452	complete / to	vervollständigen, vollenden	compléter	завершать, заканчивать
C 453	complete breakdown	Totalausfall m	manque m total	полный отказ
C 454	complete carry	vollständiger Übertrag m	retenue f complète	полный перенос

C 455	complete flag, terminate flag	Beendigungskennzeichen n	signe m de fin, marque f de terminaison	флаг окончания
C 456	completely integrated circuit	vollintegrierte Schaltung f	circuit m complètement intégré	законченная интегральная схема
C 457	completely transistorized	volltransistorisiert	entièrement transistorisé	полностью транзисторный
C 458	complete system	Komplettsystem n	système m complet	законченная система
C 459	completion	Vollendung f, Beendigung f	terminaison f	завершение, окончание
C 460	complex automation	komplexe Automatisierung f	automatisation f complexe	комплексная автоматизация
C 461	complex circuit	komplexer Schaltkreis m	circuit m complexe	сложная схема
C 462	complex quantity	komplexe Größe f	quantité f complexe	комплексная величина
C 463	complex system	komplexes (umfangreiches) System n	système m complexe	сложная система
C 464	compliance, grant	Einwilligung f, Gewährung f	consentement m, approbation f	согласие, разрешение
C 465	compliance level, level of compliance	Gewährungsebene f, Bewilligungsebene f	niveau m de consentement	степень соответствия
C 466	component	Bauelement n, Bestandteil n	composant m	компонент, элемент
C 467	component characteristics	Bauelementekennwerte mpl, Bauelementeeigenschaften fpl	caractéristiques fpl de composants	характеристики элементов
C 468	component density	Bauelementedichte f	densité f de composants	плотность элементов
C 469	component life	Bauelementelebensdauer f	longévité f de composants	долговечность элементов
C 470	component operating hours	Bauelementebetriebsstunden fpl <Lebensdauer>	heures fpl de service de composants	срок службы элементов
C 471	component reliability	Bauelementezuverlässigkeit f	fiabilité f de composants	надежность элементов
C 472	component system	Bauelementesystem n, Bausteinsystem n	système m modulaire (de composants)	система элементов
C 473	component technology	Bauelementetechnologie f	technologie f de composants	технология изготовления элементов
C 474	component tester	Bauelementeprüfeinrichtung f, Bauelementetester m	dispositif m de test de composants	тестер для проверки компонентов
C 475	compose / to	zusammensetzen	composer	составлять
C 476	compose edit processor	Zeilenaufbereitungsprogramm n, Druckzeilen-Aufbereitungsprogramm n	processeur m d'édition	программа редактирования строк выходного текста
C 477	composite cable	Kabel n mit mehreren Leitertypen ⌐ f	câble m composé	комбинированный кабель
C 478	composite function	zusammengesetzte Funktion f	fonction f composée	сложная функция
C 479	composite junction	zusammengesetzter Übergang m	jonction f composée	составной переход
C 480	composite line	Vielfachleitung f	ligne f multiple	комбинированная (резервированная) линия
C 481	composite signal	Signalgemisch n	signal m multiple	комбинированный (сложный) сигнал
C 482	compound condition	Verbundbedingung f, zusammengesetzte Bedingung f, Mehrfachbedingung f	condition f compound	объединенное условие
C 483	compound expression	Verbundausdruck m, zusammengesetzter Ausdruck m	expression f compound	составное выражение
C 484	compound statement	Verbundanweisung f	instruction f compound	составной оператор
C 485	compress / to	verdichten	comprimer	сжимать, уплотнять
C 486	computability	Berechenbarkeit f	calculabilité f	вычислимость
C 487	computation	Rechnen n auf Computern, Berechnung (Datenverarbeitung) f mittels Rechenautomaten	calcul m (traitement m de données) à l'aide de calculateur	вычисление, расчет, счет
	compute / to	s. C 13		
C 488/9	computer	Rechner m, Rechenautomat m, [elektronische] Rechenanlage f	calculateur m	электронная вычислительная машина, ЭВМ
	computer-aided design	s. C 9		
C 490	computer-aided learning, CAL, computer-assisted learning	rechnergestütztes Lernen n, Lernen mit Rechnerhilfe	études fpl assistées par calculateur	машинное обучение
C 491	computer-aided manufacturing, CAM	rechnergestützte Fertigung (Fertigungsvorbereitung) f	fabrication f assistée par calculateur	автоматизированное производство с применением ЭВМ, изготовление с поддержкой ЭВМ
C 492	computer-aided programming, computer-assisted programming	rechnergestützte (maschinelle) Programmierung f	programmation f assistée par calculateur	автоматизированное программирование
C 493	computer-aided text processing	rechnergestützte Textverarbeitung f	traitement m de textes assisté par calculateur	автоматизированная (машинная) обработка текстов
C 494	computer application	Rechneranwendung f	application f de calculateur[s]	применение ЭВМ
C 495	computer architecture	Rechnerarchitektur f, Rechner-Strukturaufbau m	architecture (structure) f de calculateur	архитектура ЭВМ
C 496	computer assembly	Rechnerzusammenbau m	assemblage m de calculateur	сборка ЭВМ, монтаж ЭВМ
C 497	computer-assisted instruction, CAI	rechnergestützte Unterweisung f, rechnergestützter Unterricht m	instruction f assistée par calculateur	программированное обучение с помощью ЭВМ
	computer-assisted learning	s. C 490		
	computer-assisted programming	s. C 492		

C 498	**computer-based education scenario**	Unterrichtsgestaltung *f* auf Rechnerbasis	éducation *f* sur base de calculateur	методика обучения с помощью ЭВМ
C 499	**computer-based message system**	Nachrichtensystem *n* auf Rechnerbasis	système *m* de communication sur base de calculateur	система связи с управлением от ЭВМ
C 500	**computer building block,** computer module	Rechnerbaustein *m*, Rechnermodul *m*	module *m* de calculateur	стандартный блок вычислительной машины
C 501	**computer capacity**	Rechnerkapazität *f*, Rechnerleistungsfähigkeit *f*	capacité *f* de calculateur	производительность ЭВМ
C 502	**computer card**	Rechnerkarte *f*, Rechnerleiterplatte *f* ‹zum Rechner gehörende oder den Rechner enthaltende Leiterplatte›	carte *f* de calculateur	плата ЭВМ
C 503	**computer card user**	Rechnerleiterplattenanwender *m*, Anwender *m* von kompletten Rechner-Steckeinheitenmoduln	usager *m* de cartes de calculateur	разработчик средств вычислительной техники на основе покупных плат
	computer centre	*s.* C 550		
C 504	**computer check**	Rechnertest *m*	test *m* de calculateur	машинный контроль
C 505	**computer circuit**	Rechnerschaltung *f*	circuit *m* de calculateur	схема ЭВМ
C 506	**computer code**	Rechnerkode *m*	code *m* de calculateur	код ЭВМ
C 507	**computer-controlled**	rechnergesteuert	à commande par calculateur	управляемый с помощью ЭВМ
C 508	**computer coupling**	Rechnerkopplung *f*	couplage *m* de calculateurs	межмашинная связь
C 509	**computer cycle**	Rechnerzyklus *m*, Rechnerperiode *f*	cycle *m* de calculateur	машинный цикл
C 510	**computer-dependent**	rechnerabhängig	dépendant de calculateur	зависимый от ЭВМ
C 511	**computer design**	Rechnerentwurf *m*	conception *f* de calculateur	проектирование ЭВМ
C 512	**computer development**	Rechnerentwicklung *f*	développement *m* de calculateur	разработка ЭВМ; модернизация ЭВМ
C 513	**computer display**	Rechnersichtanzeige *f*	dispositif *m* de visualisation de calculateur, affichage *m*	устройство отображения
C 514	**computer down-time**	Rechnerausfallzeit *f*	temps *m* de manque de calculateur	время простоя ЭВМ
C 515	**computer education,** computer training	Rechnerausbildung *f*	enseignement *m* de (sur) calculateurs	обучение с помощью ЭВМ
C 516	**computer engineering**	Rechentechnik *f*	technique *f* de calcul	вычислительная техника
C 517	**computer feature**	Rechnermerkmal *n*, Rechnerspezifik *f*	caractéristique *f* de calculateur	характеристики ЭВМ, отличительная особенность ЭВМ
C 518	**computer game**	Rechnerspiel *n*, Computerspiel *n*	jeu *m* de calculateur	машинные игры
C 519	**computer generation**	Rechnergeneration *f*	génération *f* de calculateurs	поколение ЭВМ
C 520	**computer graphics**	Rechnergrafik *f*, Computergrafik *f*	graphique *m* de calculateur	машинная графика
C 521	**computer-independent**	rechnerunabhängig	indépendant de calculateur	машинно-независимый, независимый от ЭВМ
C 522	**computer-independent language**	rechnerunabhängige (rechnertypunabhängige) Programmiersprache *f*	langage *m* indépendant de calculateur	машинно-независимый язык
C 523	**computer industry**	Rechnerindustrie *f*	industrie *f* des calculateurs	производство ЭВМ
C 524	**computer input-output equipments**	Ein-/Ausgabesystemausstattung *f* eines Rechners	équipement *m* d'entrée/sortie d'un calculateur	устройства ввода/вывода ЭВМ, периферийное оборудование ЭВМ
C 525	**computer installation**	Rechnerinstallation *f*	installation *f* de calculateur	установка ЭВМ, монтаж ЭВМ
C 526	**computer instruction**	Rechnerbefehl *m*	instruction *f* de calculateur	машинная инструкция
C 527	**computer interface**	Rechnerinterface *n*, Rechneranschlußstellengestaltung *f*	interface *f* de calculateur	машинный интерфейс
C 528	**computerized**	rechnerbestückt, rechnergeführt	à calculateur	оборудованный средствами вычислительной техники
C 529	**computerized automatic tester**	rechnerbestückter Prüfautomat *m*	automate *m* de test à calculateur	автоматическое испытательное оборудование, работающее под управлением ЭВМ
C 530	**computerized measuring assembly**	rechnerbestückter Meßplatz *m*	place *f* de mesure à calculateur	измерительная установка, управляемая с помощью ЭВМ
C 531	**computerized numerical control,** CNC	rechnergeführte numerische Steuerung *f*, CNC *f*	commande *f* numérique à calculateur, CNC *f*	цифровое управление ‹станками› с помощью ЭВМ
C 532	**computerized test assembly**	rechnerbestückter Prüfaufbau *m*	installation *f* de test à calculateur	испытательная установка, управляемая ЭВМ
C 533	**computer logic**	Rechnerlogik *f*, Rechnerlogikstruktur *f*	logique *f* de calculateur	машинная логика, логические схемы ЭВМ
	computer module	*s.* C 500		
C 534	**computer network**	Rechnernetz *n*	réseau *m* de calculateurs	вычислительная сеть, сеть ЭВМ
C 535	**computer-operated memory test system**	rechnerbetriebenes Speichertestsystem *n*	système *m* de test de mémoire à calculateur	встроенная система контроля памяти
C 536	**computer operation**	Rechneroperation *f*	opération *f* de calculateur	машинная операция
C 537	**computer-oriented**	rechnerorientiert	orienté calculateur	машинно-ориентированный
C 538	**computer performance,** computer power	Rechnerleistung *f*	performance *f* de calculateur	производительность ЭВМ
C 539	**computer peripherals**	Rechnerperipherie *f*	périphérie *f* de calculateur	периферийное оборудование ЭВМ
	computer power	*s.* C 538		
C 540	**computer program**	Rechnerprogramm *n*	programme *m* de calculateur	машинная программа
C 541	**computer programming**	Programmierung *f* eines Rechners	programmation *f* d'un calculateur	программирование на ЭВМ

C 542	computer property	Rechnereigenschaft f	propriété f de calculateur	особенность ЭВМ
C 543	computer run	Rechnerlauf m	marche f de calculateur	работа вычислительной машины, однократное выполнение программы
C 544	computer series	Rechnerserie f	série f de calculateurs	серия ЭВМ
C 545	computer service	Rechnerbetreuung f, Rechnerservice m	maintenance f (service m) de calculateur	техническое обслуживание ЭВМ
C 546	computer store capacity	Rechner-Speicherkapazität f, Speicherkapazität f eines Rechners	capacité f de mémoire de calculateur	емкость памяти ЭВМ
C 547	computer system	Rechnersystem n	système m de calculateur	система ЭВМ
	computer training	s. C 515		
C 548	computer word	Rechnerwort n	mot m de calculateur	машинное слово
C 549	computing accuracy	Rechengenauigkeit f	précision f de calcul	точность вычислений
C 550	computing centre, processing (computer) centre	Rechenzentrum n	centre m d'informatique	вычислительный центр
C 551	computing cycle	Rechenzyklus m	cycle m de calcul	цикл вычисления
C 552	computing element	Rechenelement n	élément m de calcul	вычислительный элемент
C 553	computing error	Rechenfehler m	erreur f de calcul	погрешность вычислений
C 554	computing office	Rechenbüro n	office m de calcul	машиносчетная станция
C 555	computing operation	Rechenoperation f	opération f de calcul	вычислительная операция
C 556	computing power	Rechenleistung f	performance f de calcul	вычислительная производительность
C 557	computing problem	Rechenaufgabe f, Rechenproblem n	problème m de calcul	вычислительная задача
C 558	computing process	Rechenprozeß m	processus m de calcul	процесс вычислений
C 559	computing result	Rechenergebnis n	résultat m de calcul	результат вычислений
C 560	computing rule	Rechenregel f	règle f de calcul	правило вычислений
C 561	computing speed	Rechengeschwindigkeit f	vitesse f de calcul	скорость вычислений
C 562	computing time	Rechenzeit f	temps m de calcul	время вычислений
C 563	concatenated data	verkettete Daten pl	données fpl en chaine	объединенные (сцепленные) данные
C 564	concatenated file	verkettete Datei f	fichier m en chaine	объединенный (составной) файл
C 565	concatenation	Verkettung f	enchaînement m	соединение, сцепление
C 566	concentration-dependent diffusion	konzentrationsabhängige Diffusion f	diffusion f dépendant de la concentration	диффузия, зависящая от концентрации
C 567	concentration distribution	Konzentrationsverteilung f	distribution f de concentration	распределение концентрации
C 568	concentrator	Konzentrator m	concentrateur m	концентратор
C 569	concept	Konzept n, Entwurfsskizze f	concept m	концепция
	concordance	s. A 46		
C 570	concurrent	gleichzeitig existent, nebenlaufend	concurrent	совмещенный, совпадающий, одновременный
	concurrent execution	s. S 434		
	concurrent input / output (I/O)	s. S 435		
	concurrent mode	s. S 436		
	concurrent operation	s. S 437		
	concurrent processing	s. S 438		
	concurrent-processing system	s. S 439		
C 571	concurrent testing	mitlaufende Testung f, simultan zur Aufgabenbearbeitung durchgeführte Prüfung f	test m concurrent	контроль, выполняемый параллельно вычислениям
C 572	condition	Bedingung f	condition f	условие
C 573	conditional assembly	bedingte Assemblierung (Umwandlung) f ‹Quellprogramm enthält bedingte Anweisungen, Bedingung wird erst zum Assemblierzeitpunkt spezifiziert›	assemblage m conditionnel	условное ассемблирование ‹средства программы ассемблера, позволяющие изменять содержание и последовательность исходного текста с помощью специальных директив›
C 574	conditional branch	bedingte Verzweigung f	branchement m conditionnel	ветвление по условию
C 575	conditional breakpoint	bedingter Unterbrechungspunkt m	point m d'interruption conditionnel	точка останова по условию, условная контрольная точка
C 576	conditional code	bedingter Kode m	code m conditionnel	код условия
C 577	conditional expression	bedingter Ausdruck m	expression f conditionnelle	условное выражение
C 578	conditional instruction	bedingter Befehl m	instruction f conditionnelle	инструкция условного перехода
C 579	conditional jump	bedingter Sprung m	saut m conditionnel	условный переход
C 580	conditional operation	bedingte Operation f	opération f conditionnelle	условная операция
C 581	conditional state	bedingter Zustand m	état m conditionnel	состояние, отвечающее определенному условию
C 582	conditional statement	bedingte Anweisung f	instruction f conditionnelle	условный оператор
C 583	condition code	Bedingungskode m	code m de condition	код признака результата
C 584	condition code operation	Bedingungskodeoperation f, Flagmanipulation f	opération f de code de condition	операция установки (анализа) разрядов флагового регистра
C 585	condition code register	Bedingungskoderegister n, Flagregister n	registre m de code de condition	регистр признака результата, флаговый регистр
C 586	condition code setting	Bedingungskodeeinstellung f	ajustement m de code de condition	установка кода условия
C 587	condition flag	Bedingungskennzeichen n	signe m de condition	флаг условия
C 588	condition handler	Bedingungsbehandler m, Bedingungsverarbeitungsprogramm n	programme m de traitement de condition	программа обработки информации о состоянии ЭВМ
	conducting path	s. C 595		
C 589	conducting state, conductive condition	leitender Zustand m	état m conducteur	проводящее состояние

C 590	**conduction**	Leitung f <elektrisch>	conduction f	проводимость
	conduction pattern	s. C 592		
	conductive condition	s. C 589		
C 591	**conductive material**	leitendes Material n	matériau m conducteur	проводящий материал
C 592	**conductive pattern,** con-duction pattern	Leiterbild n	dessin m de conducteurs	рисунок расположения проводников [печатной платы]
C 593	**conductivity**	Leitfähigkeit f	conductibilité f	удельная проводимость
C 594	**conductor**	Leiter m <elektrisch>	conducteur m	проводник
C 595	**conductor line,** conducting path	Leiterzug m	voie f de conducteur	трасса проводника
C 596	**configurable**	konfigurierbar	configurable	конфигурируемый
C 597	**configuration**	Konfiguration f, System-zusammenstellung f	configuration f	конфигурация
C 598	**configuration space**	Konfigurationsraum m, Konfigurationsfreiheits-raum m	espace m de configuration	пространство конфигура-ций
C 599	**conjunction,** logical product	Konjunktion f, logisches Produkt n	conjonction f, produit m logique	конъюнкция, логическое произведение
C 600	**conjunction operation**	Konjunktionsdurchführung f, UND-Verknüpfung f	opération f de conjonction, liaison f ET	операция конъюнкции
C 601	**conjunctive normal form**	konjunktive Normalform f	forme f normale conjonctive	конъюнктивная нормаль-ная форма
C 602	**connect / to**	verbinden, anschließen	connecter, raccorder	соединять, подключать
C 603	**connected back-to-back**	gegeneinandergeschaltet	monté en opposition	включенный встречно
C 604	**connected group**	zusammenhängende Gruppe f	groupe m connecté	связанная группа
	connecting area	s. C 644		
	connecting box	s. C 613		
	connecting cable	s. C 615		
C 605	**connecting compatibility**	Verbindungsverträglichkeit f, Zusammenschaltver-träglichkeit f	compatibilité f de connexion	совместимость по связям
C 606	**connecting lead**	Verbindungsleitung f	ligne f de connexion	соединяющий провод
C 607	**connecting path,** connector pad	Verbindungsweg m, Leistungszug m <technisch>	voie f de connexion	тракт соединения
C 608	**connecting pin,** connector pin	Verbindungsstift m	fiche f de connexion	соединяющий вывод
C 609	**connecting plug,** con-nector plug	Verbindungsstecker m	broche f de connexion	соединяющий штырь
	connecting terminal	s. C 619		⌐провод
C 610	**connecting wire**	Verbindungsdraht m	fil m de connexion	соединяющая перемычка,
C 611	**connect in tandem / to**	in Kaskade schalten	connecter en cascade	соединять каскадно
C 612	**connection**	Verbindung f, Anschluß m	connexion f, raccordement m	соединение, подключение; стык <передача данных>
C 613	**connection box,** con-necting box	Verbindungsblock m, Anschlußleiste f	boîtier m de connexion	соединительная коробка
C 614	**connection buildup**	Verbindungsaufbau m	établissement m de con-nexion	установление связи (соединения)
C 615	**connection cable,** con-necting cable	Verbindungskabel n	câble m de connexion	соединительный кабель
C 616	**connection diagram**	Verbindungsplan m, Ver-schaltungsplan m	schéma m de connexions	схема соединений
C 617	**connection hole**	Kontaktierungsloch n	trou m de connexion	соединительное отверстие
C 618	**connection point**	Verbindungspunkt m	point m de connexion	точка соединения
C 619	**connection terminal,** connecting terminal	Verbindungsanschluß m, Anschlußklemme f	connexion f terminale	соединительная клемма, соединительная колодка
C 620	**connector**	Verbinder m, Anschluß-punkt m	connecteur m	разъем
C 621	**connector contact**	Steckverbinderkontakt m	contact m de connexion	контакт разъема
	connector pad	s. C 607		
	connector pin	s. C 608		
	connector plug	s. C 609		
C 622	**connector receptacle**	Steckdose f, Steckerbuchse f	prise f de courant	гнездо разъема
C 623	**connector slot**	Steckverbinderaufnahme f	prise f de connecteur	щелевое гнездо разъема
C 624	**connect time**	Verbindungszeit f <in einem Teilnehmersystem>	temps m de liaison <dans un système d'abonnés>	время связи
	connect to earth / to	s. E 2		
C 625	**connect to the mains supply / to**	an das Netz anschließen	brancher au secteur	подключать к сети пита-ния
C 626	**consecutive**	fortlaufend, aufeinander-folgend	consécutif	последовательный, сле-дующий один за другим
C 627	**consecutive access**	Zugriff m zu aufeinander-folgenden Zellen	accès m consécutif	последовательный доступ
C 628	**consecutive area**	Folgebereich m	domaine m consécutif	следующая область
C 629	**consecutive instructions**	aufeinanderfolgende Befehle mpl	instructions fpl consécutives	расположение инструк-ций в естественном порядке
C 630	**consecutive numbering**	fortlaufende Numerierung f	numérotage m consécutif	последовательная нумера-ция
C 631	**consistent performance**	gleichbleibende Leistung f	performance f consistante	стабильная производи-тельность
C 632	**console**	Konsole f	console f	консоль
	console control unit	s. C 727		
C 633	**console keyboard**	Konsoltastatur f	clavier m de console	клавиатура консоли
C 634	**console typewriter**	Konsolschreibmaschine f	machine f à écrire de console	пишущая машинка кон-соли
C 635	**constant**	Konstante f	constante f	константа, постоянная
C 636	**constant-current source,** stable power source	Konstantstromquelle f	source f à intensité constante	источник постоянного (стабилизированного) тока, стабилизатор тока
C 637	**constant memory,** con-stant store	Konstantenspeicher m	mémoire f à constantes	память констант

C 638	**constant power,** continuous duty	Dauerleistung f	puissance f continue	постоянная мощность, мощность при длительной нагрузке
	constant store	s. C 637		
C 639	**constant-voltage source**	Konstantspannungsquelle f	source f à tension constante	источник постоянного (стабилизированного) напряжения, стабилизатор напряжения
C 640	**constraint**	Beschränkung f, Grenzwertbedingung f, Randbedingung f	contrainte f	ограничение
C 641	**consumer products**	Konsumgüter npl	produits mpl de consommation	продукция широкого назначения <для широкого круга потребителей>
C 642	**consumption**	Verbrauch m, Leistungsaufnahme f	consommation f	потребление, расход
C 643	**contact alignment**	Kontaktjustierung f	ajustement m de contact	выравнивание положения контактов <при стыковке разъемов>
C 644	**contact area,** connecting area	Kontaktfläche f, Kontaktierungsfläche f	surface f de contact	контактная поверхность
C 645	**contact chattering**	Kontaktprellen n	rebondissement m de contact	дребезг контактов
C 646	**contact float**	Kontaktspiel n	jeu m de contact	ход контакта
C 647	**contact force**	Kontaktkraft f	force f de contact	контактное усилие
	contact fork	s. C 658		
C 648	**contact gap**	Kontaktabstand m	écart m de contact	зазор между контактами
C 649	**contacting**	Kontaktierung f	formation f des contacts	контактирование
C 650	**contactless**	kontaktlos	sans contacts	бесконтактный
C 651	**contact maker**	Kontaktgeber m	contacteur m	контактный датчик, контактор
C 652	**contact pad**	Kontaktstelle f, Kontaktfleck m	point m de contact	контактная площадка
C 653	**contact pin**	Kontaktstift m	pointe f de contact	контактный штифт
C 654	**contact pressure**	Kontaktdruck m	pression f au contact	контактное давление
	contact resistance	s. C 655		
C 655	**contact resistivity,** contact resistance	Kontaktwiderstand m	résistance f de contact	сопротивление контакта, контактное сопротивление
C 656	**contact sense**	Kontaktabfrage f	interrogation f de contact	считывание [состояния] контактов
C 657	**contact-separating force**	Kontakttrennungskraft f	force f de séparation de contact	усилие размыкания контактов
C 658	**contact spring,** contact fork	Kontaktfeder f	ressort m contacteur, lame f de contact	контактная пружина
C 659	**contact surface**	Kontaktoberfläche f	surface f de contact	контактная поверхность
C 660	**contact tab**	Lötanschluß m	connexion f soudée	контакт [для подпайки]
C 661	**content-addressable memory,** CAM	inhaltsadressierter Speicher m <Assoziativspeicher>	mémoire f adressée d'après le contenu	память с адресацией по содержимому <ассоциативная память>
C 662	**contention**	Konfliktsituation f <möglicher Buszustand bei Mehrstationenübertragung>	situation f de conflit	соревнование, конкуренция <ситуация, возникающая при попытке двух или более устройств одновременно захватить управление шиной>
C 663	**contention mode**	konkurrierender Betrieb m	mode m concurrent	режим конкуренции
C 664	**context**	Kontext m, Zusammenhang m <Umgebung einer Programmaktivität in Form von Registerinhalten und Prozeßbeschreibung>	contexte m	контекст
C 665	**context stacking**	Programmzustandskellerung f, Kontextkellerung f	mise f en cave de contexte	запись в стек информации о состоянии программы
C 666	**context switch[ing]**	Kontextumschaltung f, Programmzustandsumschaltung f, Umladen n der Verarbeitungsprozeß-Bezugsregister <bei Unterbrechung einer Programmaktivität zugunsten einer anderen>	commutation f de contexte	замена информации о состоянии программы
C 667	**context switching instruction**	Kontextumschaltbefehl m, Programmzustandswechselbefehl m, Prozeßbezugsregister-Umladebefehl m	instruction f de commutation de contexte	команда замены информации о состоянии программы
C 668	**contextual**	textabhängig	dépendant de texte	контекстный, определяемый по контексту
C 669	**continuation address**	Fortsetzungsadresse f, Folgeadresse f	adresse f de continuation	адрес продолжения
C 670	**continuation line**	Folgezeile f, Fortsetzungszeile f	ligne f de suite	строка продолжения
C 671	**continuation statement**	Folgeanweisung f	instruction f de continuation	оператор продолжения
C 672	**continuity**	Kontinuität f, Stetigkeit f	continuité f	непрерывность
C 673	**continuous [action] controller**	stetiger Regler m	régulateur m continu	регулятор непрерывного действия
C 674	**continuous display**	kontinuierliche Anzeige f	affichage m continu	дисплей, работающий в непрерывном режиме
C 675	**continuous document feeding**	stetige Belegzuführung f	acheminement m de document continu	непрерывная подача документов
	continuous duty	s. C 638		
C 676	**continuous form**	Endlosformular n	formulaire m continu (sans fin)	рулонная бумага

C 677	continuous function	stetige Funktion f	fonction f continue	непрерывная функция
C 678	continuously operating	kontinuierlich arbeitend	opérant en continu	непрерывно действующий
	continuous mode	s. C 680		
C 679	continuous operation	kontinuierlicher Betrieb m, Dauerbetrieb m	opération f continuelle	непрерывная работа
C 680	continuous operation mode, continuous mode	kontinuierliche Betriebsweise f	mode m continu (de régime continu)	непрерывный режим работы
C 681	continuous signal	Dauersignal n	signal m continu (permanent)	непрерывный сигнал
C 682	continuous tape	Endlosband n	bande f sans fin	бесконечная лента
C 683	continuous variable	stetige Variable f	variable f continue	непрерывная переменная
C 684	control	Steuerung f	commande f	управление
C 685	control accuracy	Regelgenauigkeit f	précision f de réglage	точность регулирования
C 686	control action	Regelvorgang m, Steuervorgang m	action f de réglage (commande)	управляющее воздействие
C 687	control adapter	Steuerungsanpassungsbaustein m	adapteur m de commande	адаптер [схемы] управления
C 688	control algorithm	Steuerungsalgorithmus m	algorithme m de commande	алгоритм управления
C 689	control and regulation	Steuerung f und Regelung f	commande f et réglage m	управление и регулирование
C 690	control bit	Steuerbit n	bit m de commande	управляющий бит
C 691	control bus	Steuerbus m	bus m de commande	шина управления
C 692	control card	Steuerkarte f	carte f de commande	управляющая карта
C 693	control character	Steuerzeichen n	caractère m de commande	управляющий символ
C 694	control characteristics	Regelkennlinie f	caractéristique f de réglage	характеристика регулирования
C 695	control check	Kontrollmessung f	mesure f de contrôle	контрольная проверка
C 696	control circuit (circuitry)	Steuerschaltung f, Steuerschaltkreis m	circuit m de commande	схема управления
C 697	control code	Steuerkode m	code m de commande	управляющий код
C 698	control command, control instruction	Steuerbefehl m	instruction f de commande	управляющая команда
C 699	control computer	Steuerungsrechner m, Steuerrechner m	calculateur m de commande	управляющая ЭВМ
	control console	s. C 727		
C 700	control convention	Steuerungsregel f, Steuerungsvorschrift f	convention f de commande	инструкция по управлению
C 701	control cycle	Regelzyklus m	cycle m de commande	цикл управления (регулирования)
C 702	control data	Steuerdaten pl	données fpl de commande	управляющие данные
C 703	control decentralization	Steuerungsdezentralisierung f	décentralisation f de commande	децентрализация управления
C 704	control deviation	Regelabweichung f	écart m de réglage	рассогласование, отклонение
	control device	s. C 718		
C 705	control effectiveness	Regelgüte f	efficience f de réglage	качество регулирования
C 706	control electronics	Steuerelektronik f	électronique f de commande	электронные устройства управления
C 707	control element	Steuerelement n, Regelglied n	élément m de commande	управляющий элемент
C 708	control engineering, control technique	Steuerungstechnik f; Regelungstechnik f	technique f de la commande; technique f de la régulation	техника автоматического управления; техника регулирования
C 709	control equipment	Steuerungsausrüstung f	équipement m de commande	аппаратура управления
C 710	control field	Steuerungsbereich m, Steuerzone f	champ m de commande	область управления
C 711	control flip-flop	Steuer-Flipflop n	bascule f [électronique] de commande	управляющий триггер
C 712	control function	Steuerfunktion f	fonction f de commande	функция управления
C 713	control hierarchy	Steuerungshierarchie f	hiérarchie f de commande	иерархия управления
	control instruction	s. C 698		
C 714	controlled point	Steuerpunkt m	point m de commande	управляемый объект
C 715	controlled system	gesteuertes System n	système m réglé	управляемая система
C 716	controlled time interval	gesteuertes Zeitintervall n	intervalle m [de temps] commandé	регулируемый временной интервал
C 717	controlled transistor	gesteuerter Transistor m	transistor m réglé	управляемый транзистор
C 718	controller, control device	Steuergerät n, Steuereinrichtung f	appareil m de commande	контроллер, управляющее устройство
C 719	control level	Steuerungsebene f, Steuerungsniveau n	niveau m de commande	уровень управления
C 720	control line	Steuerleitung f	ligne f de commande	управляющая линия
C 721	control loop	Regelkreis m	circuit m de réglage	[замкнутый] контур [системы] управления
C 722	control macro	Steuermakro n	macro m de commande	макрокоманда управления
	control memory	s. C 739		
C 723	control mode	Steuermodus m	mode m de commande	режим управления
C 724	control needs, control requirements	Steuerungserfordernisse npl, Steuerungsanforderungen fpl	exigences fpl de commande	требования к управлению
C 725	control operation	Steueroperation f	opération f de commande	операция управления
C 726	control-oriented instruction set	steuerungsorientierter Befehlssatz m	jeu m d'instructions pour commandes	система команд, ориентированная на решение задач управления
C 727	control panel, control console, console control unit	Steuerpult n, Steuerkonsole f	pupitre m (console f) de commande	панель управления
C 728	control processor	Steuerprozessor m	processeur m de commande	управляющий процессор
	control program	s. C 735		
C 729	control protocol	Steuerprotokoll n, Steuerungsprozedurvorschrift f	procès-verbal m de commande	протокол управления
C 730	control pulse	Steuerimpuls m	impulsion f de commande	управляющий импульс
C 731	control punching	Steuerlochung f	perforation f de commande	управляющая пробивка [перфокарты]
C 732	control range	Regelbereich m	plage f de réglage	диапазон регулирования

C 733	**control read-only memory**, control ROM, CROM	Steuer-Nur-Lese-Speicher m, Steuer-ROM m, CROM m <Steuerwerks-speicher für Mikropro-gramme>	mémoire f de lecture seule de commande, CROM f	управляющее постоянное запоминающее устрой-ство, ПЗУ микропро-грамм
C 734	**control register**	Steuerregister n	registre m de commande	управляющий регистр
	control requirements	s. C 724		
	control ROM	s. C 733		
C 735	**control routine**, control program	Steuerprogramm n	programme m de com-mande	управляющая программа
C 736	**control sequence**	Steuerfolge f	séquence f de commande	управляющая последо-вательность
C 737	**control signal**	Steuersignal n	signal m de commande	сигнал управления
C 738	**control state**	Steuerzustand m	état m de commande	состояние управления
C 739	**control store**, control memory	Steuerspeicher m, Steuer-folgenspeicher m, Steuer-werksspeicher m	mémoire f de commande	управляющая память
C 740	**control switch**	Steuerschalter m	commutateur m de com-mande	управляющий переклю-чатель
C 741	**control system**	Steuerungssystem n	système m de commande	система управления
C 742	**control task**	Steuerungsaufgabe f	tâche f de commande	задача управления
	control technique	s. C 708		
	control total	s. C 190		
C 743	**control transmitter**	Steuerungssender m, Steuersignalsender m	transmetteur m de com-mande	устройство передачи управляющих сигналов, датчик управляющих сигналов
C 744	**control unit**	Steuereinheit f, Steuerwerk n, Leitwerk n	unité f de commande	устройство управления
C 745	**control word**	Steuerwort n	mot m de commande	управляющее слово
C 746	**convention**	Vereinbarung f ⌐n	convention f	соглашение
C 747	**conventional component**	konventionelles Bauelement	composant m conventionnel	стандартный компонент
C 748	**conventional method**	herkömmliche Methode f	méthode f conventionnelle	стандартный метод
C 749	**conversational com-munication**	Dialogverkehr m	communication f à dialogue	передача [данных] в режиме диалога
C 750	**conversational data entry**	Dialog-Dateneingabe f	entrée f de données par dialogue	ввод данных в режиме диалога
C 751	**conversational language**	Dialogsprache f	langage m de dialogue	язык диалога
	conversational mode	s. I 312		
C 752	**conversational procedure**	Dialogverfahren n	procédé m de dialogue	процедура ведения диалога
C 753	**conversion**, converting	Konvertierung f <einer Informationsdarstellung>, Wandlung f, Umsetzung f	conversion f	преобразование
C 754	**conversion code**	Konvertierungskode m, Umwandlungskode m	code m de conversion	код преобразования
C 755	**conversion constant**	Umrechnungskonstante f	constante f de conversion	константа преобразования
C 756	**conversion precision**	Konvertierungsgenauigkeit f, Umsetzungsgenauig-keit f	précision f de conversion	точность преобразования
C 757	**conversion program**, converting program	Konvertierungsprogramm n	programme m de conversion	программа преобразо-вания
	conversion rate	s. C 759		
C 758	**conversion rule**	Konvertierungsregel f	règle f de conversion	правило преобразования
C 759	**conversion speed**, con-version rate	Konvertierungsgeschwin-digkeit f, Umsetzungs-geschwindigkeit f, Um-setzungsrate f	vitesse f (taux m) de con-version	скорость (частота) пре-образования
C 760	**conversion time**	Konvertierungszeit f, Umsetzungszeit f	temps m de conversion	время преобразования
C 761	**convert / to**	konvertieren, wandeln, umsetzen	convertir	преобразовать, преобразо-вывать
C 762	**converter**	Konverter m, Wandler m, Umsetzer m	convertisseur m	преобразователь, конвер-тер
	converting	s. C 753		
	converting program	s. C 757		
C 763	**cooling air**	Kühlluft f	air m de refroidissement	охлаждающий воздух
C 764	**cooling capacity**	Kühlungsleistung f	puissance f de refroidisse-ment	производительность охлаждающей уста-новки
C 765	**cooling plant**	Kühlsystem n <Belüftungs-system>	système m de refroidisse-ment (ventilation), système d'aération	установка охлаждения
C 766	**coordinate / to**	koordinieren	coordonner	координировать, согласо-вывать
C 767	**coordinate displacement**	Koordinatenverschiebung f	décalage m de coordonnées	координатное смещение (отклонение)
	coordinate plotter	s. C 768		
C 768	**coordinate recorder**, coordinate plotter, X-Y-recorder	Koordinatenschreiber m, XY-Schreiber m	appareil m enregistreur à coordonnées	координатный графо-построитель
C 769	**coordinate store**, matrix store	Koordinatenspeicher m, Matrixspeicher m	mémoire f à coordonnées (matrice)	матричное (координатное) запоминающее устрой-ство
C 770	**coordinate system**	Koordinatensystem n	système m de coordonnées	система координат; координатная система
C 771	**coordinate transfor-mation**	Koordinatentransformation f	transformation f de coordonnées	преобразование коорди-нат
C 772	**copper-clad**	kupferkaschiert	à couche de cuivre	покрытый медью
	coprocessor	s. C 412		
C 773	**copy / to**	kopieren, abschreiben	copier	копировать
C 774	**copy run**	Kopierlauf m	marche f de copiage	прогон [программы] для получения копий
C 775	**core**	Kern m; Magnetkern m	tore m	[магнитный] сердечник, ферритовый сердечник
	core memory	s. M 65		

C 776	core store matrix	Kernspeichermatrix f	matrice f de mémoire à tores	матрица запоминающего устройства на сердечниках
C 777	correct / to	korrigieren	corriger	исправлять, корректировать
C 778	corrected program	korrigiertes Programm n	programme m corrigé	скорректированная (исправленная) программа
C 779	correcting circuit	Korrekturschaltung f	circuit m de correction	схема коррекции
C 780	correcting element	Korrekturelement n	élément m correcteur	элемент коррекции
C 781	correcting term	Korrekturglied n	terme m de correction	поправочный член
C 782	correction	Korrektur f	correction f	коррекция, исправление
C 783	correction bit	Korrekturbit n	bit m de correction	бит коррекции
C 784	correction factor	Korrekturfaktor m	facteur m de correction	поправочный коэффициент
C 785	correction system	Korrektursystem n	système m de correction	система коррекции
C 786	correct operation	fehlerfreies Arbeiten n	travail m correct	правильная (корректная) операция
C 787	cost	Kosten pl	frais mpl, coût m	стоимость
C 788	cost comparison	Kostenvergleich m	comparaison f de coûts	сравнение по стоимости
C 789	cost-performance ratio	Kosten-Leistungs-Verhältnis f	rapport m coût-performance	отношение стоимость-производительность
C 790	count base	Zählbasis f	base f de comptage	основание системы счисления
C 791	count capacity	Zählkapazität f	capacité f de comptage	диапазон счета
C 792	count-down	Rückwärtszählen n, Startzählung f	comptage m en arrière	счет в обратном направлении
C 793	counter	Zähler m	compteur m	счетчик
C 794	counter circuit	Zählerschaltung f	circuit m [de] compteur	счетная схема
C 795	counterclockwise	entgegengesetzt zum Uhrzeigersinn, linksumlaufend	contre le sens des aiguilles d'une montre	против часовой стрелки
C 796	counter-doped	entgegengesetzt dotiert	contre-dopé	легированный противоположно
C 797	counterpart	Gegenstück n	contre-partie f	ответная часть
C 798	counter period	Zählerperiode f	période f de compteur	счетный период
C 799	counter position	Zählerstelle f	position f de compteur	разряд счетчика
C 800	counter reset	Zählerrückstellung f	remise f à zéro du compteur, RAZ f du compteur	установка счетчика в ноль, сброс счетчика
C 801	counter stage	Zählerstufe f	étage m de compteur	ступень пересчета
	counter-timer circuit	s. C 859		
C 802	counter-timer unit	Zähler-Zeitgeber-Einheit f	unité f compteur-rythmeur	устройство задания [интервала] времени, таймер
C 803	counting chain	Zählkette f	chaîne f à compter	счетная цепочка
C 804	counting direction	Zählrichtung f	direction f de comptage	направление счета
C 805	counting frequency, counting rate	Zählfrequenz f, Zählrate f	fréquence f de comptage	частота (скорость) счета
C 806	counting operation	Zählvorgang m	opération f de comptage	операция счета
C 807	counting pulse	Zählimpuls m	impulsion f de comptage	счетный импульс
	counting rate	s. C 805		
	counting sequence	s. C 809		
C 808	count range	Zählbereich m	champ m de comptage	диапазон счета
C 809	count sequence, counting sequence	Zählfolge f	séquence f de comptage	счетная последовательность
C 810	coupled	gekoppelt	couplé	связанный, соединенный
C 811	coupler	Koppler m	coupleur m	соединитель
C 812	coupling	Kopplung f	couplage m, accouplement m	связь, соединение
C 813	coupling circuit	Kopplungsschaltung f, Ankoppelschaltung f	circuit m de couplage	схема связи (соединения)
C 814	CPE, central processing element	CPE-Schaltkreis m, Baustein m (Modul m) der zentralen Verarbeitungseinheit	module m central de processeur	центральный процессорный элемент, ЦПЭ
C 815	CPU, central processing unit	CPU f, ZVE f, zentrale Verarbeitungseinheit f	CPU f, UCT f, unité f centrale de traitement	центральное устройство обработки данных
C 816	CPU board	CPU-Platine f, Prozessorleiterplatte f	plaquette f CPU	плата центрального процессора
C 817	CPU chip	CPU-Schaltkreis m, Verarbeitungseinheit-Schaltkreis m, Prozessorschaltkreis m	circuit m d'unité centrale de traitement, circuit de processeur	БИС центрального процессора
C 818	CPU support chip	CPU-Ergänzungsschaltkreis m, Prozessor-Ergänzungsschaltkreis m	circuit m complémentaire de processeur	вспомогательная микросхема для обеспечения работы центрального процессора
	crest value	s. P 121		
C 819	crimp technique	Quetschtechnik f <Drahtverbindung>	technique f d'écrasement	метод монтажа накруткой
C 820	critical frequency	kritische Frequenz f, Grenzfrequenz f	fréquence f critique	граничная частота, частота среза
C 821	critical matching	kritische Anpassung f	adaptation f critique	согласование по критическим параметрам
C 822	critical value	kritischer Wert m	valeur f critique	критическое значение
C 823	critical voltage	Grenzspannung f	tension f limite	граничное напряжение
	CROM	s. C 733		
C 824	cross assembler	Cross-Assembler m, auf Fremdrechner lauffähiger Programmumsetzer m <für Mikrorechner-Programmentwicklung>	assembleur m cross	кросс-ассемблер <программа преобразования исходного текста, написанного на языке ассемблера, в машинный язык микро-ЭВМ с другой системой команд>
C 825	cross-assembly	Cross-Assemblierung f, auf Fremdrechner durchge-	assemblage m cross	кросс-ассемблирование <трансляция программ

and still: C 825		führte Quellprogramm- übersetzung f <Assembler- niveau>		на языке ассемблера с помощью операционной кросс-системы>
C 826	**cross-bar switch,** cross switch	Koordinatenschalter m	commutateur m à coordon- nées	координатный комму- татор
C 827	**cross compilation**	Cross-Kompilierung f, auf Fremdrechner durch- geführte Quellpro- grammübersetzung f <höheres Programmier- sprachniveau>	compilation f cross	кросс-компиляция <ком- пиляция программ с помощью операционной кросс-системы>
C 828	**cross compiler**	Cross-Kompilierer m, auf Fremdrechner lauffähiges Übersetzungsprogramm n <für Mikrorechner-Pro- grammentwicklung>	compilateur m cross	кросс-компилятор <ком- пилятор, преобразую- щий программу, напи- санную на языке высо- кого уровня, в машин- ные коды [микро-ЭВМ] с системой команд, от- личной от той, на кото- рой проводилась компи- ляция>
C 829	**cross connection**	Querverbindung f	connexion f transversale	перекрестная связь
C 830	**cross-development system**	Cross-Entwicklungssystem n, Entwicklungssystem n auf Fremdrechnerbasis	système m de développe- ment cross	кросс-система проекти- рования [микро-ЭВМ] <комплекс средств про- ектирования микро- ЭВМ с помощью ЭВМ отличающихся архи- тектурой и системой команд>
C 831	**cross direction**	Querrichtung f	direction f transversale	поперечное направление
C 832	**cross editor**	Cross-Editor m, auf Fremd- rechner lauffähiges Auf- bereitungsprogramm n <für Mikrorechner-Pro- grammentwicklung>	éditeur m cross	программа-редактор операционной кросс- системы
C 833	**cross[-over] point**	Kreuzungspunkt m, Koppelpunkt m	point m de croisement (couplage)	точка пересечения, эле- мент коммутации
C 834	**cross reference**	Querverweis m, Querbezug- nahme f <Zuordnung>	référence f de travers	перекрестная ссылка
C 835	**cross reference list (table)**	Querbezugsliste f, Zu- ordnungstabelle f	liste f de référence transver- sale	список перекрестных ссылок
C 836	**cross simulator**	Cross-Simulator m, auf Fremdrechner lauffähiges Simulationsprogramm n <zur Mikrorechner-Pro- grammprüfung>	simulateur m cross	моделирующая программа операционной кросс- системы
C 837	**cross software**	Cross-Software f, auf Fremdrechner lauffähige Systemunterlagen fpl (Programme npl) <Mikrorechnerpro- grammentwicklung>	logiciels mpl cross	кросс-программное обеспечение
C 838	**cross support**	Unterstützung f mit Cross- Systemunterlagen	assistance f par logiciels cross	кросс-система поддержки, предназначенная для разработки программ [микро-ЭВМ] с по- мощью программных средств большой ЭВМ
	cross switch	s. C 826		
C 839	**cross talk**	Übersprechen n	diaphonie f	взаимное влияние между каналами связи; выдача ненужных данных
	CRT	s. C 74		
C 840	**CRT console**	Bildschirmkonsole f auf Katodenstrahlröhrenbasis	console f à tube à rayon cathodique	дисплейный пульт с выда- чей информации на электронно-лучевую трубку, пульт управле- ния с выдачей информа- ции на электронно- лучевую трубку
C 841	**CRT display,** cathode ray tube display	Bildschirm[anzeige]gerät n, Datensichtgerät m mit Katodenstrahlröhre	appareil m à écran (tube cathodique) de visuali- sation	дисплей (устройство отображения) на основе электронно-лучевой трубки
C 842	**CRT terminal**	CRT-Terminal n, Terminal n auf Katodenstrahl- röhrenbasis	terminal m à tube à rayon cathodique	терминал с устройством отображения на ЭЛТ
C 843	**cryogenics**	Kryogenik f	cryogénie f	криогенная техника
C 844	**cryotron**	Kryotron n	cryotron m	криотрон
C 845	**crystal accuracy**	Quarzgenauigkeit f	précision f de quartz	точность обработки кристалла
C 846	**crystal-controlled clock generator**	quarzgesteuerter Takt- generator m	rythmeur m à quartz	кварцевый генератор
C 847	**crystal cutting technique**	Kristalltrenntechnik f	technique f de séparation de cristaux	методы разрезания кри- сталлов
C 848	**crystal defect**	Kristallfehler m	perturbation f de cristal	дефект кристалла (кристаллической решетки)
C 849	**crystal formation**	Kristallzüchtung f	production f de cristaux	изготовление кристалла
C 850	**crystal frequency**	Quarzfrequenz f	fréquence f de quartz	частота [резонирования] кварца
C 851	**crystal growing (growth),** growth of crystals	Kristallwachstum n	croissance f de[s] cristaux	выращивание кристалла (кристаллов)
C 852	**crystal imperfection**	Kristallstörstelle f	imperfection f cristalline	дефект кристалла

C 853	**crystal lattice**	Kristallgitter n	réseau m cristallin	кристаллическая решетка
C 854	**crystalline silicon**	kristallines Silizium n	silicium m cristallin	кристаллический кремний
C 855	**crystal orientation**	Kristallorientierung f	orientation f cristalline	ориентация кристалла
	crystal oscillator	s. Q 20		
C 856	**crystal pulling**	Kristallziehen n	production f de cristaux	вытягивание кристалла
C 857	**crystal size**	Kristallgröße f	grandeur f de cristal	размер кристалла
C 858	**crystal structure**	Kristallstruktur f	structure f cristalline	структура кристалла
	CS signal	s. C 202		
C 859	**CTC, counter-timer circuit**	CTC-Schaltkreis m, Zähler-Zeitgeber-Baustein m	circuit m compteur-rythmeur, circuit CTC	счетчик времени
C 860	**CTD, charge transfer devices**	CTD f, Ladungstransfer-elemente npl	éléments mpl de transfert de charge	схемы с передачей заряда
C 861	**current**	Strom m ‹elektrischer›	courant m	электрический ток
C 862	**current**	laufend, gegenwärtig	courant, actuel	текущий
C 863	**current amplification**	Stromverstärkung f	amplification f de courant	усиление тока
C 864	**current circuit**	Stromkreis m	circuit m électrique	токовая схема
C 865	**current consumption**	Stromverbrauch m	consommation f de courant	потребление тока
C 866	**current-controlled, current-driven**	stromgesteuert	commandé par courant	управляемый током
C 867	**current density**	Stromdichte f	densité f de courant	плотность тока
	current-driven	s. C 866		
C 868	**current-driven device**	stromgesteuertes Bau-element n	module m à commande par courant	возбуждаемое током устройство
C 869	**current-loop signal**	Stromschleifensignal n	signal m de boucle de courant	сигнал, передаваемый по токовой петле
C 870	**current mode**	laufender (gegenwärtiger) Modus m	mode m courant	непрерывный режим; текущий режим
C 871	**current mode logic**	Stromschaltlogik f ‹Schaltungstechnik, z. B. ECL›	logique f de mode à courant	логическая схема с переключением тока ‹например, ЕСЛ-схемы›
C 872	**current page, active page**	derzeitige Speicherseite f, aktuelle Speicherseite	page f de mémoire actuelle	текущая страница [памяти]
C 873	**current-page addressing**	Adressierung f im laufenden Speicherabschnitt ‹bezogen auf Befehlsspeicheradresse›	adressage m dans la page courante de mémoire	адресация внутри текущей страницы [памяти]
C 874	**current segment**	laufendes (derzeitiges) Segment n, derzeitiger Speicherabschnitt m	segment m courant	текущий сегмент
C 875	**current-sinking**	stromaufnehmend	à charge de courant	отводящий ток
C 876	**current-sourcing**	stromspeisend	à source de courant	питаемый током
C 877	**current supply**	Stromquelle f	source f de courant	источник тока
C 878	**current switch**	Stromschalter m	interrupteur m de courant	токовый переключатель (ключ)
C 879	**current systems**	derzeitige Systeme npl	systèmes mpl actuels	существующие системы
C 880	**current value**	gegenwärtiger Wert m	valeur f actuelle	текущее значение
C 881	**cursor**	Cursor m, Läufer m, Positionsanzeiger m ‹Bildschirm›	curseur m	курсор ‹указатель по позиции на экране дисплея›
C 882	**curve plotter**	Kurvenschreiber m	enregistreur m graphique	графопостроитель
C 883	**curve scanner**	Kurvenabtaster m	balayeur m de courbes	устройство считывания графической информации
C 884	**custom-built**	nach Kundenwunsch gefertigt	fabriqué selon option de client	изготовленный по заказу
	custom-built chip	s. C 889		
	custom-built circuit	s. C 889		
C 885	**custom circuit design**	Kunden[wunsch]-Schaltkreisentwurf m ‹Schaltkreisgestaltung nach speziellen Kundenvorgaben›	conception f de circuit de client	проектирование заказных [интегральных] схем
	custom-designed LSI device	s. C 893		
C 886	**customer**	Kunde m	client m	потребитель, заказчик
C 887	**customer-dependent engineering**	kundenabhängige Technik f, kundenspezifische Anpassung f	technique f pour client	разработка и производство [интегральных схем] по заказам потребителей
C 888	**customer engineering**	technischer Kundendienst m	service m technique (après-vente), SAV m	техническое обслуживание потребителей
	custom IC	s. C 889		
C 889	**custom integrated circuit, custom IC, custom-built circuit (chip)**	Kundenschaltkreis m, Kundenwunsch-Schaltkreis m	circuit m intégré de client	заказная интегральная схема, заказная ИС
C 890	**custom interface**	Kunden-Interface n, Schnittstelle f zur kundenspezifischen Schaltung	interface f pour client	интерфейс с нестандартными устройствами пользователя
C 891	**customization**	Kundenproblemanpassung f, Personalisierung f	adaptation f aux problèmes de client	адаптация к требованиям заказчика
C 892	**customize / to**	kundenspezifisch anpassen, einsatzspezifisch zuschneiden ‹einen universellen Basisentwurf›, personalisieren	adapter spécifiquement au client	приводить в соответствие с требованиями заказчика
C 893	**custom LSI device, custom-designed LSI device**	Kunden-LSI-Schaltkreis m, LSI-Schaltkreis m nach Kundenentwurf	circuit m LSI de client	заказная большая интегральная схема, заказная БИС
C 894	**cut-out**	Abschalter m	coupe-circuit m	выключатель
C 895	**cybernetics**	Kybernetik f	cybernétique f	кибернетика
C 896	**cycle, period**	Zyklus m, Periode f	cycle m, période f	цикл, период
C 897	**cycle code**	zyklischer Kode m	code m cyclique	циклический код

	English	German	French	Russian
C 898	cycle control	Zyklussteuerung f	commande f de cycle	циклическое (цикловое) управление
C 899	cycle counter	Zykluszähler m	compteur m de cycles	счетчик циклов
C 900	cycle duration	Zyklendauer f, Periodendauer f	durée f de cycle	длительность цикла
C 901	cycle number	Zyklenzahl f	nombre m de cycles	число циклов
C 902	cycle stealing	„Zyklus-Stehlen" n, Abzweigen n eines Speicherzyklus	branchement m d'un cycle de mémoire	пропуск (занятие) цикла <запоминающего устройства>
C 903	cycle time	Zykluszeit f <Zeitbedarf eines Speicher- oder Prozessorzyklus>	temps m de cycle	время цикла
C 904	cyclic mode, loop mode	zyklische Arbeitsweise (Betriebsart) f	mode m cyclique	циклический режим
C 905	cyclic permutation	zyklische Vertauschung f	permutation f cyclique	циклическая перестановка
C 906	cyclic process	zyklischer (periodischer) Vorgang m	processus m périodique	циклический (периодический) процесс
C 907	cyclic program	zyklisches Programm n	programme m cyclique	циклическая программа
C 908	cyclic redundancy check	zyklische Blockprüfung f, periodische Redundanzkontrolle f	vérification f périodique de redondance	контроль при помощи циклического избыточного кода
	cyclic shift	s. C 242		
C 909	cyclic store, circulating storage	Umlaufspeicher m	mémoire f circulaire	динамическое запоминающее устройство
C 910	cylinder address	Zylinderadresse f <Plattenspeicher>	adresse f de cylindre	адрес цилиндра
C 911	cylinder seek command	Zylindersuchbefehl m <Plattenspeicher>	instruction f de recherche de cylindre	команда установки цилиндра
C 912	cylinder switching	Zylinderumschaltung f <Plattenspeicher>	commutation f de cylindre	переключение цилиндра

D

	English	German	French	Russian
	DAC, D/A converter	s. D 379		
D 1	daisy chain	„Gänseblümchenkette" f <Kette kaskadenartig verbundener Funktionskomplexe mit seriell durchgereichten Steuersignalen>	chaîne f en cascade	последовательно-приоритетная цепочка <в которой устройство, расположенное электрически ближе к процессору, имеет более высокий приоритет>
D 2	daisy-chain bus structure	Daisy-Chain-Busstruktur f <Busstruktur mit kaskadenartig verkettet geführten Gewährungssignalen>	tructure f de bus en chaîne	последовательно-приоритетная структура шины
D 3	daisy-chain connection	Daisy-Chain-Verbindung f <kaskadenartig gestaltete Verbindung von Buseinheiten>	liaison f en chaîne en cascade	соединение в последовательно-приоритетную цепочку
D 4	daisy-chained grant	Busgewährung f auf Daisy-Chain-Basis	assurance f de bus sur base de daisy-chain	предоставление доступа к шине последовательно-приоритетной цепочкой
D 5	daisy-chaining, daisy-chain technique	Signalkettung f, Reihungsverfahren n, Daisy-Chain-Verfahren n, Daisy-Chain-Technik f, „Gänseblümchenketten"-Technik f <Steuerverfahren mit positionsabhängiger Vorrangordnung zur Busmaster-Übertragung auf Basis kaskadenartig verketteten Durchreichen eines Gewährungssignals durch die Bus-Anschlußeinheiten>	procédé m (technique f) de daisy-chain	способ соединения устройств в последовательно-приоритетную цепочку
D 6	daisy-chaining terminals	im Daisy-Chain-Verfahren angeschlossene Terminals npl <kaskadenartig verkettet angeschlossene Terminals>	terminaux mpl raccordés en chaîne	терминалы, объединенные в последовательно-приоритетную цепочку
D 7	daisy-chain interrupt servicing	Daisy-Chain-Interruptbedienung f, Unterbrechungsanforderungsbedienung f nach dem Daisy-Chain-Verfahren <Vorrangstufung gemäß Kettenposition>	service m d'interruption en chaîne	обслуживание источников прерываний, объединенных в последовательно-приоритетную цепочку
D 8	daisy-chain interrupt structure	Daisy-Chain-Interruptstruktur f, Daisy-Chain-Unterbrechungssystemaufbau m <seriell verkettete Interruptgewährungssignalführung>	structure f d'interruption en chaîne	схема формирования сигналов прерываний посредством последовательно-приоритетной цепочки
D 9	daisy-chain priority interrupt logic	Daisy-Chain-Interruptprioritätslogik f, Interruptprioritätskette f <Unterbrechungssystem mit Prioritätsstaffelung entsprechend Kettenposition>	chaîne f de priorités d'interruptions	логика формирования сигналов прерываний посредством последовательно-приоритетной цепочки

D 10	**daisy-chain structure**	Daisy-Chain-Struktur *f*, Struktur *f* mit verketteter Signalführung nach dem Daisy-Chain-Verfahren <Busstruktur>	structure *f* à signaux en chaîne	последовательно-приоритетная структура
	daisy-chain technique	*s.* D 5		
D 11/2	**damping,** attenuation	Dämpfung *f*	atténuation *f*	демпфирование; затухание
D 13	**damping circuit**	Dämpfungskreis *m*	circuit *m* d'atténuation	демпфирующая схема
D 14	**damping of a signal**	Signaldämpfung *f*	atténuation *f* d'un signal	затухание сигнала
D 15	**Darlington power transistor**	Darlington-Leistungstransistor *m*, Darlington-Transistor *m* <monolithische Mehrtransistorschaltung>	transistor *m* de puissance Darlington	мощный транзистор Дарлингтона <монолитный усилительный каскад на 2-х транзисторах>
D 16	**DART,** dual asynchronous receiver/transmitter	zweifacher asynchroner Empfänger/Sender-Schaltkreis *m*, DART-Baustein *m*	émetteur-récepteur *m* asynchrone double, module *m* DART	сдвоенный асинхронный приемопередатчик
D 17	**dash [character]**	Querstrich *m*, Bindestrich *m*, Gedankenstrich *m*	trait *m* d'union	тире
D 18	**dash-dot line**	strichpunktierte Linie *f*	ligne *f* en point-virgule	штрих-пунктирная линия
D 19	**dash marking,** stroke marking	Strichmarkierung *f*	marquage *m* de trait	маркирование с помощью тире
D 20	**data**	Daten *pl* <Angaben, Werte, Informationen>	données *fpl*	данные
D 21	**data acceptance**	Datenannahme *f*, Datenübernahme *f*	acceptation (admission) *f* de données	прием данных
D 22	**data access**	Datenzugriff *m*	accès *m* de données	доступ к данным
D 23	**data acquisition,** data capture (collecting, gathering, logging)	Datenerfassung *f*, Datensammlung *f*	acquisition (saisie) *f* de données	сбор (регистрация) данных
D 24	**data-acquisition system**	Datenerfassungssystem *n* für Analogeingänge, Analogdatenerfassungssystem *n*	système *m* d'acquisition de données	система сбора данных
D 25	**data acquisiton unit**	Datenerfassungseinheit *f*	unité *f* d'acquisition de données	устройство для сбора данных
D 26	**data-addressed memory**	datenadressierter Speicher *m* <Assoziativspeicher>	mémoire *f* adressée sur données	ассоциативная память, память, адресуемая по содержимому
D 27	**data-adjustment instruction**	Datenberichtigungsbefehl *m*, Datenkorrekturbefehl *m* <für BCD- und ASCII-Arithmetik>	instruction *f* de correction de données	команда настройки данных
D 28	**data area**	Datenbereich *m*	domaine *m* de données	область данных
	data array	*s.* D 73		
D 29	**data backup**	Datensicherung *f*	sûreté *f* de données	резервирование данных
D 30	**data bank**	Datenbank *f*, Dateisystem *n*	banque *f* de données	банк данных
D 31	**data bank system**	Datenbanksystem *n*	système *m* de banque de données	система банка данных
D 32	**data base**	Datenbasis *f*, Hauptdatei *f*, Hauptdateisystem *n*, Dateisystem *n*	base *f* de données, fichier *m* de base	база данных
D 33	**data-base file management**	Datenbank-Dateiverwaltung *f*	gestion *f* de fichier de banque de données	управление файлами базы данных
D 34	**data-base inquiry**	Datenbankabfrage *f*	interrogation *f* de banque de données	запрос базы данных
D 35	**data block**	Datenblock *m*	bloc *m* de données	блок данных
D 36	**data block length**	Datenblocklänge *f*	longueur *f* de bloc de données	длина блока данных
D 37	**data buffer**	Datenpuffer *m*, Datenzwischenspeicher *m*	tampon *m* de données	буфер данных
D 38	**data bulk**	große Datenmenge *f*, Datenvolumen *n*	volume *m* de données	большой массив данных; объем данных
D 39	**data bus**	Datenbus *m* <Datenübertragungsweg>	bus *m* de données	шина данных
D 40	**data bus enable**	Datenbusfreigabe *f*	libération *f* de bus de données	разрешение [захвата] шины данных
D 41	**data byte**	Datenbyte *n*	octet *m* de données	байт данных
D 42	**data capacity**	Datenkapazität *f*, Datenaufnahmekapazität *f*	capacité *f* de données	объем данных
	data capture	*s.* D 23		
D 43	**data carrier,** data medium	Datenträger *m*	support *m* de données	носитель данных
D 44	**data carrier compatibility**	Datenträgerkompatibilität *f*	compatibilité *f* de supports de données	совместимость носителей данных
D 45	**data carrier detection**	Datenträgermeldung *f*	message *m* de support de données	сообщение носителя данных
	data carrier initialization	*s.* V 65		
D 46	**data carrier input**	Eingabe *f* vom Datenträger	entrée *f* du (depuis le) support de données	ввод с носителя данных
	data carrier mounting	*s.* V 66		
D 47	**data carrier output**	Ausgabe *f* auf Datenträger	sortie *f* sur support de données	вывод на носитель данных
D 48	**data centre,** data processing centre	Datenverarbeitungszentrum *n*	centre *m* d'informatique	центр обработки данных
D 49	**data chaining**	Datenkettung *f*	enchaînement *m* de données	формирование цепочки данных, сцепление данных
D 50	**data channel**	Datenkanal *m*	canal *m* de données	канал передачи данных, канал ПД
D 51	**data checking**	Datenprüfung *f*	vérification *f* de données	контроль данных
D 52	**data coding**	Datenkodierung *f*	codage *m* de données	кодирование данных
	data collecting	*s.* D 23		
D 53	**data collecting station**	Datenerfassungsstation *f*	station *f* de collection de données	станция сбора данных

D 54	**data communication**	Datenverkehr m, Datenübermittlung f	communication f de données	передача данных
D 55	**data communication control**	Datenverkehrssteuerung f, Datenübermittlungssteuerung f	commande f de communication de données	управление передачей данных
D 56	**data communication control procedure**	Datenübertragungssteuerverfahren n, Datenaustauschsteuerprozedur f	procédure f de commande de communications de données	процедура управления передачей данных
D 57	**data communication equipment**	Datenverkehrseinrichtung n, Datenübermittlungseinrichtung f	équipement (dispositif) m de communication de données	аппаратура передачи данных, АПД
D 58	**data communication protocol**	Datenübertragungsprotokoll n	procès-verbal m de communication de données	протокол передачи данных, протокол обмена данными
D 59	**data communication system**	Datenübermittlungssystem n	système m de communication de données	система передачи данных
D 60	**data communication terminal**	Datenverkehrsterminal n, Datenkommunikationsendgerät n	terminal m de communication de données	терминал для передачи данных
D 61	**data compaction,** data compression (reduction)	Datenverdichtung f, Datenkomprimierung f	compression f de données	сжатие данных
D 62	**data compatibility**	Datenkompatibilität f <Format- und Kodeüber­einstimmung>	compatibilité f de données	совместимость данных
	data compression	s. D 61		
	data-controlled	s. D 67		
D 63	**data convention**	Datenformatvereinbarung f	convention f de données	соглашение о данных
D 64	**data conversion**	Datenumwandlung f, Datenkonvertierung f	conversion f de données	преобразование данных
D 65	**data converter**	Datenwandler m, Datenumsetzer m	convertisseur m de données	устройство преобразования данных
D 66	**data density**	Datendichte f	densité f de données	плотность [записи] данных
D 67	**data-directed,** data-controlled	datengesteuert	commandé par données	управляемый данными
D 68	**data element,** data item	Datenelement n, Datengrundeinheit f	élément m (unité f) de données	элемент данных
D 69	**data entry terminal**	Dateneingabeterminal n	terminal m d'entrée de données	терминал для ввода данных
D 70	**data exchange**	Datenaustausch m	échange m de données	обмен данными
D 71	**data fetch**	Datenholen n, Datenbereitstellung f	mise f à disposition de données	выборка данных
D 72	**data fetch cycle**	Datenholezyklus m, Datenbereitstellungszyklus m	cycle m de saisie (mise à disposition) de données	цикл выборки данных
D 73	**data field,** data array	Datenfeld n	champ m de données	поле данных
D 74	**data file directory,** file directory	Dateiverzeichnis n	relevé m de fichier	оглавление файла
D 75	**data flow**	Datenfluß m	flux m de données	поток данных
D 76	**data flow chart**	Datenflußplan m	schéma m de flux de données	диаграмма потоков данных
D 77	**data format**	Datenformat n	format m de données	формат данных
	data gathering	s. D 23		
D 78	**data generation**	Datengenerierung f	génération f de données	поколение данных
D 79	**data handling**	Datenbearbeitung f <Samm­lung, Übertragung, Ord­nung, Speicherung>	traitement m de données	предварительная обработка данных <сбор, передача, запоминание>
D 80	**data hold time**	Datenhaltezeit f	temps m de maintien de données	время выдержки данных
D 81	**data input**	Dateneingabe f	entrée f de données	ввод данных
D 82	**data input station**	Dateneingabestation f	station f d'entrée de données	станция ввода данных
	data-item	s. D 68		
D 83	**data length**	Datenlänge f	longueur f de données	длина данных
D 84	**data line**	Datenleitung f	ligne f de données	линия данных
D 85	**data link**	Datenverbindung f, Datenverkehrsverbindung f	lien m de données	канал передачи данных, канал связи
D 86	**data link control,** DLC	Datenleitungssteuerung f, Datenverbindungssteuerung f	commande f de liaison de données	управление каналом передачи данных
	data logger	s. D 88		
	data logging	s. D 23		
D 87	**data logging equipment**	Datenaufzeichnungsgeräte npl, Datensammelgeräte npl	appareils mpl d'enregistrement de données, appareils mpl de collection de données	оборудование для регистрации данных
D 88	**data logging system,** data logger	Datenerfassungssystem n, Datensammelsystem n	système m de collection de données	система регистрации данных, регистратор данных
D 89	**data management**	Datenverwaltung f	gestion f de données	управление данными
D 90	**data manipulation**	Datenmanipulation f	manipulation f de données	манипуляция данными
	data medium	s. D 43		
D 91	**data memory,** data store	Datenspeicher m	mémoire f de données	память данных
D 92	**data movement**	Datentransport m, Datenbewegung f <im Rechnersysteminneren>	mouvement (transfert) m de données	перемещение данных
D 93	**data net[work]**	Datennetz n	réseau m de données	сеть передачи данных
D 94	**data output**	Datenausgabe f	sortie f de données	вывод данных
D 95	**data output station**	Datenausgabestation f	station f de sortie de données	станция вывода данных
D 96	**data parity**	Datenparität f	parité f de données	четность данных
D 97	**data path**	Datenweg m	voie f de données	тракт [пересылки] данных
	data plotting	s. D 106		
D 98	**data polling**	Datenabruf m	appel m de données	ввод данных посредством последовательного опроса

D 99	**data positioning in-struction**	Datenpositionierbefehl *m* <Operatiönen wie „Laden", „Speichern", „Move">	instruction *f* de positionne-ment de données	инструкция размещения данных
D 100	**data preparation**	Datenaufbereitung *f*	préparation *f* de données	подготовка данных
D 101	**data presentation**	Datendarstellung *f*	représentation *f* de données	представление данных
D 102	**data processing**	Datenverarbeitung *f*	traitement *m* de données	обработка данных
	data processing centre	*s.* D 48		
D 103	**data processing machine**	Datenverarbeitungsanlage *f*	installation *f* de traitement de données, installation *f* d'informatique	машина для обработки данных
D 104	**data protection**	Datenschutz *m*	protection *f* de données	защита данных
	data rate	*s.* D 131		
D 105	**data ready signal**	Datenbereitschaftssignal *n* <Quittungsbetrieb>	signal *m* de disposition de données	сигнал готовности данных
	data record	*s.* D 113		
D 106	**data recording,** data plotting	Datenaufzeichnung *f*, Datenregistrierung *f*	enregistrement *m* de données	запись (нанесение) данных
	data reduction	*s.* D 61		
D 107	**data register**	Datenregister *n*	registre *m* de données	регистр данных
	data remote com-puting	*s.* D 108		
D 108	**data remote pro-cessing,** remote data processing, data remote computing	Datenfernverarbeitung *f*	traitement *m* de données à distance, informatique *f* à distance	дистанционная обработка данных
D 109	**data remote transfer**	Datenfernübertragung *f*	transmission *f* de données à distance	дистанционная передача данных
D 110	**data scanning**	Datenabtastung *f*	balayage *m* (scrutation *f*) de données	просмотр данных
D 111	**data segment**	Datensegment *n*, Daten-abschnitt *m*	segment *m* de données	сегмент данных
D 112	**data sequence**	Datenfolge *f*	séquence *f* de données	последовательность данных
D 113	**data set,** data record	Datensatz *m*	enregistrement *m* de données	набор данных, запись
D 114	**data set control block,** file control block	Dateisteuerblock *m*	bloc *m* de commande de fichier	блок управления масси-вами (файлами) дан-ных
D 115	**data setup time**	Datenaufstellzeit *f*, Daten-bereitstellzeit *f* <auf Signalleitungen>	temps *m* de mise à dispo-sition de données	время установки данных
D 116	**data sheet**	Datenblatt *n*, Kennblatt *n*	fiche *f* de données	информационная карта
D 117	**data space**	Datenraum *m*, Datenbereich *m* im Speicher	espace *m* de données	пространство данных
	data station	*s.* T 90		
D 118	**data storage**	Datenspeicherung *f*	mémorisation *f* de données	хранение данных
	data store	*s.* D 91		
D 119	**data stream**	Datenstrom *m*	courant *m* de données	поток данных
D 120	**data string**	Datenkette *f* <verkettete Datenfolge>	chaîne *f* de données	строка данных, цепочка данных
D 121	**data strobe**	Datenstrobe *m*, Daten-markierimpuls *m*	impulsion *f* de marquage de données	сигнал стробирования данных, импульс сопро-вождения, строб данных
D 122	**data structure**	Datenstruktur *f*, Daten-aufbau *m*	structure *f* de données	структура данных
D 123	**data switching**	Datenvermittlung *f*	communication *f* de don-nées	коммутация данных
	data time	*s.* D 134		
D 124	**data transceiver**	Daten-Sender/Empfänger *m*	émetteur-récepteur *m* de données	приемопередатчик данных
D 125	**data transfer,** data trans-mission	Datenübertragung *f*	transfert *m* (transmission *f*) de données	передача данных
D 126	**data transfer channel,** data transmission channel	Datenübertragungskanal *m*	canal *m* de transmission de données	канал передачи данных
D 127	**data transfer equip-ment,** data transmission equipment	Datenübertragungseinrich-tung *f*	dispositif *m* de transmission de données	оборудование передачи данных
D 128	**data transfer instruc-tion**	Datenübertragungsbefehl *m*	instruction *f* de transfert de données	инструкция пересылки данных
D 129	**data transfer operation**	Datenübertragungsopera-tion *f*	opération *f* de transfert de données	операция по передаче данных
D 130	**data transfer path**	Datenübertragungsweg *m*	voie *f* de transfert de données	тракт передачи данных
D 131	**data transfer rate,** data rate	Datenübertragungsrate *f*, Datenübertragungs-geschwindigkeit *f*	vitesse *f* de transmission de données	скорость передачи данных
D 132	**data transfer sequence**	Datenübertragungsfolge *f*	séquence *f* de transmission de données	последовательность пере-дачи данных
D 133	**data transfer system,** data transmission system	Datenübertragungssystem *n*	système *m* de transmission de données	система передачи данных
D 134	**data transfer time,** data time	Datenübertragungszeit *f*	temps *m* de transmission de données	время передачи данных
	data transmission	*s.* D 125		
	data transmission channel	*s.* D 126		
	data transmission equipment	*s.* D 127		
D 135	**data transmission link**	Datenübertragungsver-bindung *f*	lien *m* de transmission de données	линия передачи данных
	data transmission system	*s.* D 133		
D 136	**data transmission tech-nique**	Datenübertragungsver-fahren *n*, Datenüber-tragungstechnik *f*	procédé *m* (technique *f*) de transmission de données	метод (техника) передачи данных
D 137	**data type**	Datentyp *m*, Datenart *f*	type *m* de données	тип данных

D 138	data-valid signal	Datengültigkeitssignal n	signal m de validité de données	сигнал истинности (достоверности) данных
D 139	data word	Datenwort n	mot m de données	слово данных
D 140	data word length	Datenwortlänge f	longueur f de mot de données	длина слова данных
	DC	s. D 400		
D 141	DC amplifier, direct-current amplifier	Gleichstromverstärker m	amplificateur m de courant continu	усилитель постоянного тока
D 142	DC bias [voltage]	Gleichstromvorspannung f	polarisation f de courant continu	напряжение смещения, смещение
D 143	DC characteristics	statische Kennwerte mpl	caractéristiques fpl statiques	статические характеристики
D 144	DC converter	Gleichspannungswandler m	convertisseur m de tension continue	преобразователь постоянного напряжения
D 145	DC dump	Gleichstromversorgungsausfall m	manque m de courant continu, panne f de courant continu	внезапное отключение постоянного напряжения
D 146	DCFL, direct-coupled FET logic	DCFL f, direkt gekoppelte FET-Logik f, direkt gekoppelte Feldeffekttransistorlogik f ‹GaAs-Schaltungstechnik›	logique f FET à couplage direct	логика на полевых транзисторах с непосредственными связями
D 147	DC input voltage	Eingangsgleichspannung f	tension f continue d'entrée	постоянная составляющая входного напряжения
D 148	DC level	Gleichspannungspegel m	niveau m de courant continu	уровень постоянной составляющей
D 149	DC output voltage	Ausgangsgleichspannung f	tension f continue de sortie	постоянная составляющая выходного напряжения
D 150	DC plasma-display panel	Gleichstromplasmaanzeige f	affichage m plasma à courant continu	плазменная панель постоянного тока
D 151	DC power amplifier	Gleichstromleistungsverstärker m	amplificateur m de puissance de courant continu	усилитель мощности постоянного тока
D 152	DC power supply, DC supply	Gleichstromversorgung f	alimentation f en courant continu	питание постоянным током, источник постоянного напряжения
D 153	DC reference voltage	Bezugsgleichspannung f	tension f continue de référence	постоянное опорное напряжение
D 154	DC signalling	Gleichstromübertragung f	transmission f à courant continu	связь по постоянному току
	DC supply	s. D 152		
D 155	DCTL, direct-coupled transistor logic	DCTL f, direkt gekoppelte Transistorlogik f ‹Schaltungstechnik›	logique f à transistors couplés directement, DCTL f	транзисторная логика с непосредственными связями, ТЛНС
D 156	DC voltage	Gleichspannung f	tension f continue	постоянное напряжение
	DDC	s. D 403		
D 157	deadlock	gegenseitige Blockierung f, Totalblockierung f, Verklemmung f ‹von Systemkomponenten bei gleichzeitigem Zugriff zu gemeinsamen Ressourcen›	blocage m mutuel (total)	взаимоблокировка, тупиковая ситуация
D 158	deadlock handling	Systemblockierungsbehandlung f	traitement m de blocage [de système]	обработка ситуаций взаимоблокировки
D 159	deadlock problem	Deadlock-Problem n ‹Problem gegenseitiger Blockierung simultan arbeitender Systemkomponenten›	problème m deadlock (de blocage mutuel)	проблема взаимоблокировок
D 160	dead time	Totzeit f	temps m mort	мертвое время
D 161	deblock / to	entblocken	débloquer	деблокировать
D 162	debug / to	fehlerfrei machen, Fehler suchen und beseitigen	dépanner	отлаживать
	debug aids	s. D 165		
D 163	debugged program	fehlerberäumtes (fehlerfreies) Programm n	programme m exempt d'erreurs	отлаженная программа
	debugger	s. D 166		
D 164	debugging	Fehlerausmerzung f, Fehlersuche f und -beseitigung f ‹in Programmen›, Ausprüfung f	dépannage m, débugage m	отладка
D 165	debugging aids, debug aids (tools)	Fehlersuchhilfen fpl, Fehlerkorrekturmittel npl	aides fpl de dépannage, assistance f au débugage	[вспомогательные] средства отладки
D 166	debug[ging] program, debugger	Fehlersuch- und Korrekturprogramm n	programme m de débugage	отладочная программа
	debug tools	s. D 165		
D 167	decade counting	Dekadenzählung f	comptage m de décade	декадный отсчет
D 168	decade divider	Dekadenteiler m	diviseur m décadique	декадный делитель
D 169	decade switch	Dekadenschalter m	commutateur m décadique	декадный переключатель
D 170	decay time	Abklingzeit f	temps m d'affaiblissement	время затухания
D 171	decentralized control	dezentralisierte Steuerung f	commande f décentralisée	децентрализованное управление
D 172	decentralized data acquisition	dezentrale Datenerfassung f	acquisition f de données décentralisée	децентрализованный сбор данных
D 173	decentralized data processing	dezentrale (dezentralisierte) Datenverarbeitung f	traitement m de données décentralisé	децентрализованная обработка данных
D 174	decentralized inquiry unit	dezentrale Abfrageeinheit f	unité f décentralisée d'interrogation	устройство децентрализованного запроса
D 175	decentralized process control	dezentralisierte Prozeßsteuerung f	commande f de processus décentralisée	распределенное (децентрализованное) управление процессом
D 176	decimal	dezimal, Dezimal...	décimal	десятичный
	decimal adjust	s. D 181		
D 177	decimal arithmetic	Dezimalarithmetik f, Dezimalrechnung f	arithmétique f décimale	десятичная арифметика
D 178	decimal-binary conversion, decimal-to-binary conversion	Dezimal-Binär-Umwandlung f	conversion f décimale en binaire	преобразование из десятичной системы в двоичную

D 179	decimal carry	Dezimalübertrag m, Zehner-übertrag m	report m décimal, retenue f décimale	десятичный перенос
D 180	decimal conversion	Dezimalumwandlung f, Dezimalkonvertierung f	conversion f décimale	десятичное преобразование
D 181	decimal correction, decimal adjust	Dezimalkorrektur f <Pseudotetradenkorrektur>	correction f décimale	десятичная коррекция
D 182	decimal digit	Dezimalziffer f, Dezimalstelle f	chiffre m décimal	десятичная цифра
D 183	decimal integer	Dezimalzahl f <ganzzahlig>	nombre m [entier] décimal	десятичное целое [число]
D 184	decimal notation	Dezimalschreibweise f	notation f décimale	представление в десятичной системе
D 185	decimal point	Dezimalkomma n	virgule f décimale	десятичная запятая
D 186	decimal presentation	Dezimaldarstellung f	représentation f décimale	десятичное представление
D 187	decimal processing	Dezimalverarbeitung f	traitement m décimal	обработка десятичных чисел
D 188	decimal string	Dezimalkette f, Dezimalzeichenkette f	chaîne f décimale	строка десятичных чисел
	decimal-to-binary conversion	s. D 178		
D 189	decimal value	Dezimalwert m	valeur f décimale	десятичное значение
D 190	decision criteria	Entscheidungskriterien npl	critères mpl de décision	критерии принятия решения
D 191	decision element	Entscheidungselement n	élément m de décision	решающий элемент
D 192	decision making	Entscheidungsfindung f	découverte f de décision	принятие решения
D 193	decision table	Entscheidungstabelle f	table f de décision	решающая таблица
D 194	decision tree	Entscheidungsbaum m	arbre m de décision	дерево решений
D 195	declaration	Erklärung f	déclaration f	описание
D 196	decode / to	entschlüsseln	décoder	декодировать, дешифрировать
D 197	decoder	Entschlüßler m, Dekodierer m	décodeur m	декодер, дешифратор
D 198	decoder matrix	Entschlüsselungsmatrix f	matrice f de décodage	дешифраторная матрица
D 199	decoding circuit, decryption circuitry	Dekodierschaltung f	circuit m de décodage	декодирующая (дешифрирующая) схема, схема дешифрации
D 200	decoding cycle	Dekodierzyklus m	cycle m de décodage	цикл декодирования
D 201	decomposition	Aufgliederung f, Zerlegung f	décomposition f	декомпозиция
D 202/3	decrement / to	vermindern, stufenweise verringern	décrémenter	декрементировать
	decryption circuitry	s. D 199		
D 204	dedicated	zugeordnet, zweckentsprechend, zweckbestimmt, zweckorientiert	attribué, conforme	специализированный
D 205	dedicated channel	zugeordneter Kanal m, Einzweckkanal m	canal m attribué	выделенный (некоммутируемый) канал
D 206	dedicated control	zugeordnete (zweckorientierte) Steuerung f	commande f attribuée	управление выполнением специальных функций
D 207	dedicated-function application	zweckorientierte Anwendung f, Einsatz m mit zugeschnittenem Funktionsspektrum	application f attribuée à une fonction	применение для выполнения специальных действий
D 208	dedicated memory, dedicated storage	zweckorientierter (speziell zugeordneter) Speicher m	mémoire f attribuée	специальная память
D 209	dedicated microprocessor	zweckorientierter (zugeschnittener) Mikroprozessor m	microprocesseur m attribué	специализированный микропроцессор
D 210	dedicated mode	Einzelverarbeitungsmodus m	mode m de traitement solitaire	специальный режим [работы]
D 211	dedicated stack	gesonderter Stack m, speziell eingerichteter Kellerspeicher m	mémoire-cave f particulière	специальный стек
	dedicated storage	s. D 208		
D 212	dedicated structure	zweckorientierte (speziell zugeschnittene) Struktur f	structure f attribuée	специализированная структура
D 213	dedicated system	zugeschnittenes (zweckbestimmtes) System n	système m attribué	специализированная система
D 214	default <US>	Standard m, Standardwert m	standard m, norme f	стандарт
D 215	default / by <US>	im Normalfall, normalerweise	normalement	по умолчанию
D 216	default declaration <US>	Standardvereinbarung f	déclaration (convention) f standard	стандартное описание
D 217	default vector <US>	Standardvektor m	vecteur m standard	стандартный вектор
D 218	deferred addressing	hinausgeschobene (verwiesene) Adressierung f <indirekte Adressierung>	adressage m reporté	косвенная адресация
D 219	deferred processing	zeitversetzte Verarbeitung f	traitement m décalé	отложенная обработка, выполнение работ с низким приоритетом
D 220	deferred update	zeitversetzte Fortschreibung (Aktualisierung) f	actualisation f décalée	задержанное обновление, задержанная коррективровка
D 221	deflection sensitivity	Ablenkempfindlichkeit f	sensibilité f de déviation	чувствительность отклоняющей системы
	degradation of performance	s. P 372		
D 222	degrade / to	beeinträchtigen, vermindern	dégrader, diminuer	снижать [возможности], деградировать
D 223	degraded performance	verminderte Leistung f	performance f réduite	сниженная производительность
D 224	degree of integration	Integrationsgrad m	degré m d'intégration	степень интеграции
D 225	delay	Verzögerung f	retard m, retardement m	задержка

D 226	**delay circuit,** time-delay circuit	Verzögerungsschaltung f	circuit m de retard	схема задержки
D 227	**delay distortion**	Laufzeitverzerrung f	distorsion f de phase	фазовое искажение
D 228	**delayed feedback**	verzögerte Rückführung f	réaction f retardée (à retardement)	запаздывающая обратная связь
D 229	**delay element**	Verzögerungselement n, Verzögerungsglied n	élément m de retardement	элемент задержки
D 230	**delay equalizer**	Laufzeitentzerrer m	correcteur m de temps de propagation	схема коррекции задержки
D 231	**delay line**	Verzögerungsleitung f, Verzögerungsstrecke f	ligne f de retardement	линия задержки
D 232	**delay line storage**	Verzögerungsleitungs-speicher m, Laufzeit-speicher m	mémoire f à ligne de retardement, mémoire f à temps de propagation	запоминающее устройство на линиях задержки
D 233	**delay time**	Verzögerungszeit f	temps m de retardement	время задержки
D 234	**delay time interval**	Verzögerungsintervall n	intervalle m de retardement	интервал задержки
D 235	**delete / to**	löschen, streichen ‹Speicher-eintragung›	effacer	стирать, вычеркивать
D 236	**deleting, deletion**	Löschen n ‹von Speicher-eintragungen›	effaçage m	стирание
D 237	**delimiter**	Endezeichen n, Begren-zungszeichen n	marque f de fin	ограничитель, раздели-тель
D 238	**delink / to**	entketten, aus einer Kette entfernen	déchaîner	разрывать [цепь], разъе-динять
D 239	**deliver / to**	ausliefern	délivrer	подавать; выдавать
D 240	**delivery date**	Lieferdatum n	date f de livraison (délivrance)	дата поставки
D 241	**demand file**	Bedarfsdatei f, Abrufdatei f	fichier m de demande, fichier d'appel	файл запросов
D 242	**demodulate / to**	demodulieren	démoduler	демодулировать
D 243/4	**demodulator**	Demodulator m	démodulateur m	демодулятор
D 245	**demultiplexer**	Demultiplexer m ‹Ver-teiler›	démultiplexeur m	демультиплексор
D 246	**density**	Dichte f	densité f	плотность
D 247	**deplete / to**	abarbeiten	travailler	обеднять
D 248	**depletion**	Erschöpfung f, Entleerung f, Verarmung f ‹an Ladungsträgern›	épuisement m, appauvrisse-ment m	обеднение
D 249	**depletion layer**	Verarmungsschicht f ‹Ladungsträgerver-armung›	couche f d'appauvrissement	обедненный слой
	depletion layer	s. a. B 47		
	depletion-layer capacitance	s. B 46		
D 250	**depletion load transistor**	Verarmungstyp-Last-transistor m	transistor m de charge à appauvrissement	нагрузочный транзистор, работающий в режиме обеднения
D 251	**depletion mode transistor**	Verarmungstyp-Transistor m	transistor m à appauvrisse-ment	транзистор, работающий в режиме обеднения
D 252	**deposit**	aufgewachsene Schicht f, Niederschlag m	dépôt m, couche f déposée	осажденный слой
D 253	**deposition**	Abscheidung f ‹Beschich-tung›	déposition f	осаждение, напыление
D 254	**derating**	Lastminderung f	réduction f de charge	облегченный режим рабо-ты; выход из диапазона
D 255	**derating factor**	Unterlastfaktor m	facteur m de réduction	коэффициент нагрузки
D 256	**descending order**	s. D 257		
	descending order of priority	absteigende Prioritätsord-nung f	ordre m descendant de priorité	нисходящая приоритетная последовательность
D 257	**descending sequence,** descending order	absteigende Reihenfolge f	séquence f descendante	нисходящая последо-вательность, порядок убывания
D 258	**descriptor register**	Beschreibungsregister n ‹Register für beschrei-bende, kennzeichnende Informationen›	registre m de description, registre descriptif	регистр признака
D 259	**design / to**	entwerfen, anlegen	concevoir	проектировать
D 260	**design**	Entwurf m, Bauplan m	projet m, conception f	проектирование; проект
D 261	**design aids**	Entwurfshilfen fpl	aides fpl de projet, assistance f au projet, aides (assis-tance) à la conception	[вспомогательные] сред-ства проектирования
D 262	**design algorithm**	Entwurfsalgorithmus m	algorithme m de projet (conception)	алгоритм проектирования
D 263	**design analysis**	Entwurfsanalyse f	analyse f de projet (concept)	анализ проекта
D 264	**design automation**	Entwurfsautomatisierung f	automatisation f de projet (conception)	автоматизация проектиро-вания
D 265	**design concept**	Entwurfskonzept n	concept m de projet	концепция проектиро-вания
D 266	**design conditions**	Entwurfsbedingungen fpl	conditions fpl de projet (la conception)	проектные условия
D 267	**design considerations**	Entwurfsüberlegungen fpl	considérations fpl de projet (conception)	обсуждение проекта
D 268	**design criteria**	Entwurfskriterien npl	critères mpl de projet (concept)	критерии разработки
D 269	**design engineer**	Entwurfsingenieur m, Konstrukteur m	ingénieur m de projet (concept)	разработчик; конструк-тор
D 270	**design feature**	Entwurfsmerkmal n, Systemeigenschaft f	propriété f de concept	особенность (характерная черта) разработки
D 271	**design flexibility**	Entwurfsflexibilität f, Systemflexibilität f	flexibilité f de concept	гибкость разработки
D 272	**design goal**	Entwurfsziel n	but m de concept	цель разработки
D 273	**design issues**	Entwurfsabkömmlinge mpl, aus einem Grundentwurf abgeleitete Resultate npl	dérivés mpl de concept	результаты разработки; техническая документа-ция

D 274	design method	Entwurfsmethode f	méthode f de conception	метод проектирования
D 275	design methodology, design technique (procedure)	Entwurfsverfahren n, Entwurfstechnik f	procédé m de conception	методология (процедура) проектирования
D 276	design parameter	Entwurfsbestimmungsgröße f	paramètre m de conception	параметр разработки
D 277	design philosophy	Entwurfsphilosophie f, Entwurfsgedanke m	philosophie f de concept	философия проектирования
D 278	design principle	Entwurfsprinzip n, Entwurfsgrundsatz m	principe m de conception	принцип проектирования
	design procedure	s. D 275		
D 279	design review	Entwurfsüberprüfung f	révision f de concept	рассмотрение проекта
D 280	design rules	Entwurfsregeln fpl	règles fpl de conception	проектные нормы
D 281	design stage	Entwurfsstadium n	stade m de conception	стадия проектирования
D 282	design strategy	Entwurfsstrategie f	stratégie f de conception	стратегия проектирования
	design technique	s. D 275		
D 283	desk calculator	Tischrechenmaschine f	calculateur m de table	настольный калькулятор
D 284	deskew	Schrägversatzberichtigung f	correction f de décalage oblique	коррекция перекоса
D 285	desk mounting	Tischaufbau m	montage m sur table	конструктивное исполнение с расположением оборудования в столе
D 286	desktop computer	Auftischrechner m	calculateur m sur table	настольная ЭВМ
D 287	desktop unit	Auftischeinheit f	unité f sur table	настольное устройство
D 288	destination, target	Ziel n	destination f, but m	пункт назначения, получатель
D 289	destination address, target address	Zieladresse f	adresse f de destination	конечный адрес, адрес получателя
D 290	destination code	Zielkode m	code m de destination	код назначения
D 291	destination operand	Zieloperand m	opérande m de destination	операнд назначения
D 292	destructive	[informations]zerstörend	destructif	разрушающий, стирающий
D 293	destructive reading (read-out), DRO	löschendes (zerstörendes) Lesen n	lecture f destructive	считывание со стиранием [информации]
	detach / to	s. D 422		
D 294	detached	abgesondert, alleinstehend, getrennt	détaché	отдельный, выделенный, независимый
D 295	detected fault	aufgefundener Fehler m	faute f détectée (découverte)	обнаруженный отказ
D 296	detection bit	Kennungsbit n, Erkennungsbit n	bit m de reconnaissance	бит признака
D 297	development cost	Entwicklungskosten pl	coûts mpl de développement	стоимость разработки
D 298	development cycle	Entwicklungszyklus m	cycle m de développement	цикл разработки
D 299	development department	Entwicklungsabteilung f	division f de développement	разрабатывающее подразделение
D 300	development engineer	Entwicklungsingenieur m	ingénieur m de développement	разработчик
D 301	development equipment	Entwicklungsmuster n, Labormuster n	modèle m de développement	лабораторное оборудование, оборудование разработчика
D 302	development level	Entwicklungsniveau n	niveau m de développement	уровень разработки
D 303	development potential	Entwicklungspotential n	potentiel m de développement	потенциал разработки
D 304	development stage	Entwicklungsstufe f	stade m de développement	стадия разработки
D 305	development system	Entwicklungssystem n <Unterstützung der Software- und Hardware-Entwicklung einer Mikroprozessoranwendung>	système m de développement	система проектирования
D 306	development technique	Entwicklungsverfahren n	procédé m de développement	методика разработки
D 307	development time	Entwicklungszeit f	temps m de développement	время разработки; время отладки
D 308	device	Gerät n, gerätetechnische Einrichtung f	appareil m	устройство
D 309	device	Schaltungsbaustein m, Schaltungselement n	module (élément) m de circuit	элемент схемы
D 310	device address	Geräteadresse f	adresse f d'appareil	адрес устройства
D 311	device allocation (assignment)	Gerätezuordnung f	attribution f d'appareil[s]	назначение устройств
D 312	device code	Gerätekode m	code m d'appareil	код [адреса] устройства
D 313	device construction	Geräteaufbau m	construction (structure) f d'appareil	конструкция устройства
D 314	device control	Gerätesteuerung f	commande f d'appareil	управление устройством
D 315	device driver [program]	Gerätesteuerprogramm n	programme m de commande d'appareil	драйвер <программа управления устройством>
D 316	device error	Gerätefehler m	erreur f (défaut m) d'appareil	ошибка [, возникающая] в устройстве
D 317	device-independent	geräteunabhängig	indépendant d'appareil	независимый от устройства
D 318	device priority	Gerätepriorität f	priorité f d'appareil	приоритет устройства
D 319	device selection	Bausteinauswahl f, Geräteauswahl f	sélection f d'appareil	выбор устройства
D 320	device specifications	Geräteangaben fpl, Gerätedaten pl	spécifications fpl d'appareil[s]	спецификации устройств
D 321	device status	Gerätestatus m	état m d'appareil	состояние устройства
D 322	device type	Gerätetyp m, Gerätemodell n	type m (modèle m) d'appareil	тип устройства
D 323	D-flip-flop, D-type-flip-flop	D-Flipflop n <Flipflop mit dynamischem Setzeingang>	bascule f [électronique] à entrée dynamique, bascule de type D	D-триггер, триггер D-типа
	diagnosis	s. D 324		
D 324	diagnostic, diagnosis	Diagnose f	diagnostic m	диагностика
D 325	diagnostic aids	Diagnosehilfen fpl	aides fpl de diagnostic	[вспомогательные] средства диагностики

D 326	**diagnostic bus**	Diagnosebus m	bus m de diagnostic	диагностическая шина
D 327	**diagnostic checking,** diagnostic test	Diagnosetest m	test m de diagnostic	диагностический тест
D 328	**diagnostic data**	Diagnosedaten pl	données fpl de diagnostic	диагностическая информация
D 329	**diagnostic device**	Diagnoseeinrichtung f	dispositif m de diagnostic	устройство диагностики
D 330	**diagnostic message**	Diagnosemitteilung f, Diagnosenachricht f	message m de diagnostic	диагностическое сообщение
D 331	**diagnostic microprogram**	Diagnosemikroprogramm n	microprogramme m de diagnostic	диагностическая микропрограмма
D 332	**diagnostic procedure**	Diagnoseverfahren n	procédé m de diagnostic	диагностическая процедура
	diagnostic program	s. D 333		
D 333	**diagnostic routine,** diagnostic program	Diagnoseprogramm n, Fehlersuchprogramm n	programme m de diagnostic	диагностическая программа
D 334	**diagnostic store**	Diagnosespeicher m, Diagnoseprogrammspeicher m	mémoire f de diagnostic	запоминающее устройство диагностических программ
	diagnostic test	s. D 327		
D 335	**diagnostic test system**	Diagnosetestsystem n	système m de test de diagnostic	контрольно-диагностическая система
D 336	**dial**	Zifferblatt n, Nummernscheibe f, Skalenscheibe f; Telefonwählscheibe f	cadran m [d'appel] <téléphone>	наборный диск; телефонный вызов
D 337	**dial communications lines**	öffentliches Fernsprechnetz n	réseau m téléphonique publique	коммутируемые линии связи
D 338	**dial exchange**	Selbstwählvermittlung f	communication f automatique [téléphonique]	автоматическая телефонная станция; автоматическая связь
D 339	**dialogue capability**	Dialogfähigkeit f	faculté f de dialogue	диалоговая возможность
D 340	**dialogue operation**	Dialogbetrieb m	régime m de dialogue	работа в режиме диалога
D 341	**dialogue request**	Dialoganfrage f	demande f de dialogue	диалоговый запрос
	dialogue terminal	s. I 315		
D 342	**die**	Würfel m <quaderförmiges Scheibchen>	dé m	чип
D 343/4	**die area**	Würfelfläche f, Scheibenfläche f, Schaltungsfläche f auf Chip	surface f de dé (puce), face f à circuit sur la puce	площадь (поверхность) чипа
D 345	**dielectric isolation**	dielektrische Isolation f	isolation f diélectrique	изоляция диэлектриком
D 346	**dielectric layer**	dielektrische Schicht f	couche f diélectrique	диэлектрический слой
D 347	**dielectric scanning**	dielektrische Abtastung f	balayage m diélectrique	диэлектрическое сканирование
D 348	**die size**	Größe f eines quaderförmigen Scheibchens	grandeur f d'une puce	размеры чипа
D 349	**differential amplifier**	Differentialverstärker m	amplificateur m différentiel	дифференциальный усилитель
D 350	**diffusant**	Diffusionsstoff m	matière f à diffusion	диффузант
D 351	**diffuse / to**	diffundieren	diffuser	диффундировать
D 352	**diffused-alloy transistor**	diffusionslegierter Transistor m	transistor m diffusé	диффузионно-сплавной транзистор
D 353	**diffused junction**	diffundierter pn-Übergang m	jonction f diffusée	диффузионный переход
D 354	**diffused layer**	eindiffundierte Schicht f, Diffusionsschicht f	couche f diffusée	диффузионный слой
D 355	**diffused transistor,** diffusion transistor	Diffusionstransistor m	transistor m diffusé	диффузионный транзистор
D 356	**diffusion constant**	Diffusionskonstante f	constante f de diffusion	постоянная (коэффициент) диффузии
D 357	**diffusion depth**	Diffusionstiefe f	profondeur f de diffusion	глубина диффузии
D 358	**diffusion-doped**	diffusionsdotiert	doté par diffusion	легированный методом диффузии
D 359	**diffusion isolation**	Diffusionsisolation f	isolation f de diffusion	изоляция диффузией
D 360	**diffusion limit**	Diffusionsgrenze f	limite f de diffusion	предел диффузии
D 361	**diffusion technique**	Diffusionsverfahren n, Diffusionstechnik f	procédé m (technique f) de diffusion	диффузионная технология, метод диффузии
	diffusion transistor	s. D 355		
D 362	**diffusion velocity**	Diffusionsgeschwindigkeit f	vitesse f de diffusion	скорость диффузии
D 363	**digit**	Ziffer f	nombre m, chiffre m	цифра
D 364	**digital**	digital, ziffernmäßig	numérique, digital	цифровой
D 365	**digital circuit**	Digitalschaltung f, digitale Schaltung f	circuit m numérique	цифровая схема
D 366	**digital clock**	Digitaluhr f	horloge f numérique	цифровой датчик времени
D 367	**digital computer**	Digitalrechner m, digitaler Rechenautomat m	calculateur m numérique	цифровая ЭВМ
D 368	**digital connection**	Digitalverbindung f	connexion f numérique	цифровая связь
D 369	**digital control**	digitale Steuerung f	commande f numérique	цифровое управление
D 370	**digital data processing**	digitale Datenverarbeitung (Meßwertverarbeitung) f	traitement m numérique de données (valeurs de mesure)	цифровая обработка данных
D 371	**digital display,** numerical display	Digitalanzeige f, Ziffernanzeige f, numerische Anzeige f	affichage m numérique	цифровая индикация
D 372	**digital engineering**	Digitaltechnik f	technique f numérique	цифровая техника
D 373	**digital filter**	digitales Filter n	filtre m numérique	цифровой фильтр
D 374	**digital input**	Digitaleingabe f, Digitaleingang m, digitales Eingangssignal n	entrée f digitale	цифровой вход; цифровой ввод
	digitalization	s. D 385		
	digitalize / to	s. D 382		
D 375	**digital output**	Digitalausgabe f, Digitalausgang m, digitales Ausgangssignal n	sortie f numérique	цифровой выход (вывод)
D 376	**digital output transducer**	Meßwertgeber m mit Digitalausgang	transmetteur m à sortie numérique	выходной цифровой преобразователь

D 377	**digital phase-locked loop**	digital phasensynchronisierte Schleife f	boucle f à synchronisation de phase numérique	цифровая петля фазовой автоподстройки [частоты], цифровая ФАП[Ч]
D 378	**digital representation**	Digitaldarstellung f	représentation f numérique	цифровые данные
D 379	**digital-to-analog converter, D/A converter, DAC**	Digital-Analog-Umsetzer m, DAU	convertisseur m numérique-analogique, convertisseur N-A	цифро-аналоговый преобразователь, ЦАП
D 380	**digital transmission**	Digitalübertragung f	transmission f numérique	передача цифровой информации
D 381	**digit delay**	Stellenverzögerung f, Ein-Bit-Verzögerung f	retardement m de position, retardement d'un bit	задержка на один разряд
D 382	**digitize / to, to digitalize**	digitalisieren	représenter numériquement	преобразовывать в цифровую форму
D 383	**digitized drawing**	digitalisierte Zeichnung f	dessin m numérique	преобразованная в цифровую форму графическая информация
D 384	**digitizer**	Digitalisierer m	dispositif m pour représentation numérique	цифровой преобразователь
D 385	**digitizing, digitalization**	Digitalisierung f	digitalisation f	преобразование в цифровую форму
D 386	**digit position**	Ziffernposition f, Ziffernstelle f	position f de chiffre	позиция цифры
D 387	**digit time**	Stellenzeit f, Stellentaktzeit f	temps m de chiffre, temps d'intervalle	цифровой период (интервал)
D 388	**DIL-package, DIP, dual in-line package**	DIL-Gehäuse n, zweireihiges Schaltkreisgehäuse n <Anschlußstiftanordnung in 2 Reihen>	boîtier m DIL	корпус с двухрядным [торцевым] расположением выводом, корпус типа ДИП
D 389	**dimensional informations**	Formangaben fpl	informations fpl sur dimension	данные о формате (размерности), спецификация поля (формата)
D 390	**dimensionless value**	dimensionslose Größe f	valeur f sans dimension	безразмерная величина
D 391	**diode**	Diode f	diode f	диод
	diode transistor logic DTL	s. D 565		
	DIP	s. D 388		
D 392	**direct access**	direkter (unmittelbarer) Zugriff m	accès m direct	прямой (непосредственный) доступ
D 393	**direct-access memory**	Direktzugriffsspeicher m, Speicher m mit direktem Zugriff	mémoire f à accès direct	память с прямым доступом
D 394	**direct-access method**	Direktzugriffmethode f	méthode f d'accès direct	метод прямого доступа
D 395	**direct-addressable device**	direkt adressierbares Gerät n	appareil m directement adressable	прямо адресуемое устройство
D 396	**direct addressing**	Direktadressierung f, direkte Adressierung f	adressage m direct	прямая адресация
D 397	**direct compilation**	Direktkompilierung f, Direktübersetzung f	compilation f directe	прямая компиляция
D 398	**direct connection, direct link**	Direktverbindung f	connexion (liaison) f directe	прямое включение
	direct-coupled FET logic	s. D 146		
	direct-coupled transistor logic	s. D 155		
D 399	**direct coupling**	direkte (galvanische) Kopplung f	raccordement m direct, couplage m galvanique	непосредственная связь
D 400	**direct current, DC**	Gleichstrom m	courant m continu	постоянный ток
	direct-current amplifier	s. D 141		
D 401	**direct data collection**	direkte Datenerfassung f	acquisition f directe de données	прямой сбор данных
D 402	**direct data processing**	direkte (mitlaufende) Datenverarbeitung f	traitement m direct de données	управляемая обработка данных
D 403	**direct digital control, DDC**	direkte digitale Regelung f	réglage m numérique direct	прямое цифровое управление
D 404	**direct digital controller**	direkter digitaler Mehrkanalregler (Regler) m	régulateur m numérique direct	контроллер прямого цифрового управления
D 405	**direct execution**	Direktausführung f <von Anweisungen in einer höheren Programmiersprache>	exécution f directe	непосредственное исполнение
	direct instruction	s. I 42		
D 406	**direct line**	Direktleitung f, Standleitung f	ligne f directe	прямая линия <линия непосредственной связи между двумя абонентами>
	direct link	s. D 398		
D 407	**directly accessible register**	direkt zugreifbares Register n <Register mit direkter Zugangsmöglichkeit>	registre m directement accessible	непосредственно адресуемый регистр
D 408	**directly executed language**	direkt ausgeführte Sprachanweisungen fpl	langage m directement exécuté	язык непосредственно исполняемых инструкций
D 409	**directly interpretable language**	direkt interpretierbare Sprache f <Sprachanweisungen unmittelbar interpretativ abzuarbeiten>	langage m à interpréter directement	непосредственно интерпретируемый язык
	direct memory access	s. D 486		
	direct memory access channel	s. D 489		
	direct memory access system	s. D 495		
	direct numerical control	s. D 500		
	direct operand	s. I 43		
D 410	**direct processing**	Direktverarbeitung f	traitement m direct	прямая обработка
D 411	**direct program**	Geradeausprogramm n	programme m direct	программа на машинном языке

D 412	direct-stepping-on-wafer processing	Technik *f* der direkten Übertragung eines Layout auf eine Halbleiterscheibe *s.* S 151	technique *f* de transmission directe de layout sur une tranche de semi-conducteur	метод непосредственного переноса топологии на полупроводниковую пластину
	direct value			
D 413	direct vectoring system	Direktvektorsystem *n* <System mit Komplettvektorvorgabe durch Interruptquellen>	système *m* de vecteurs directs	система с прямым назначением векторов
D 414	disable / to	unwirksam machen, eine Aktivität blockieren	anéantir, bloquer	запрещать, блокировать
D 415	disabled, disarmed	gesperrt, geblockt	désarmé, bloqué	запрещенный, заблокированный
D 416	disable interrupt / to	Interrupt (Unterbrechung) verhindern, Unterbrechbarkeit sperren	bloquer une interruption	запрещать прерывания
	disable pulse	*s.* I 138		
D 417	disabling of the interrupt system	Sperrung *f* des Interruptsystems	verrouillage *m* du système d'interruption	блокировка системы прерываний
	disabling signal	*s.* I 136		
	disarmed	*s.* D 415		
D 418	disassembler, back-assembler	Rückassembler *m*, Rückübersetzer *m*	désassembleur *m*	дизассемблер, обратный ассемблер, конвертер
D 419	disassembly	Rückassemblierung *f*, Rückübersetzung *f*	désassemblage *m*	обратное ассемблирование, дизассемблирование
D 420	discharge / to	entladen	décharger	разряжать
D 421	discharge time	Entladezeit *f*, Abbauzeit *f*	temps *m* de décharge	время разряда
D 422	disconnect / to, to disjoint, to detach, to isolate	trennen	couper, séparer	разъединять
D 423	disconnection	Abschaltung *f*, Abtrennung *f*	coupure *f*, mise *f* au repos	разъединение, отключение
D 424	discrete circuit	diskrete Schaltung *f* <Schaltung mit diskreten Bauelementen>	circuit *m* discret	дискретная схема
D 425	discrete component	diskretes Bauelement *n*	composant *m* discret	дискретный компонент
D 426	discrete logic	diskrete Logik *f* <Logikschaltung aus diskreten Bauelementen>	logique *f* discrète	дискретная логика
D 427	discrete quantity	diskrete Größe *f*	quantité (grandeur) *f* discrète	дискретная величина
D 428	disjoint / to	*s.* D 422		
D 429	disjunction	Disjunktion *f*	disjonction *f*	дизъюнкция
D 429	disjunction operation	Disjunktionsoperation *f*, Disjunktionsdurchführung *f*	opération *f* de disjonction	операция дизъюнкции
D 430	disjunctive normal form	disjunktive Normalform *f*	forme *f* normale de disjonction	дизъюнктивная нормальная форма
D 431	disk	Platte *f* <Speicher>	disque *m*	диск
D 432	disk access mechanism	Plattenzugriffsmechanismus *m*	mécanisme *m* d'accès de disque	механизм доступа к диску
D 433	disk attachment	Plattenspeicheranschluß *m*	raccordement *m* de disque	подключение диска
D 434	disk cartridge	Plattenkassette *f*	cassette *f* à disque[s]	кассета дискового запоминающего устройства
D 435	disk controller	Plattenspeicher-Steuergerät *n*	appareil *m* de commande de disque	контроллер дискового запоминающего устройства
D 436	disk drive	Plattenspeicherlaufwerk *n*, Plattenspeichergerät *n*	mécanisme *m* de mémoire à disque[s]	привод дискового запоминающего устройства, дисковод
D 437	disk dump	Plattenspeicherausdruck *m*	impression *f* de mémoire à disque	распечатка данных с диска
D 438	diskette	Diskette *f*, flexible Magnetfolienscheibe *f* <Speichermedium eines Floppy-Disk>	disque *m* souple, disquette *f*	дискет, кассета с гибким диском
D 439	disk file	Plattendatei *f*	fichier *m* sur disque	файл на дисках
	disk memory	*s.* D 442		
D 440	disk[-oriented] operating system, DOS	Plattenbetriebssystem *n*, plattenorientiertes Betriebssystem *n* <auf Platte gespeichertes und auf die Plattenspeichernutzung orientierendes Betriebssystem>	système *m* opérationnel sur disque, DOS *m*	дисковая операционная система, ДОС
D 441	disk pack	Plattenstapel *m*	pile *f* de disques	пакет дисков
D 442	disk store, disk memory	Plattenspeicher *m*	mémoire *f* à disques	дисковое запоминающее устройство
D 443	disk store control	Plattenspeichersteuerung *f*	commande *f* de mémoire à disques	управление дисковым запоминающим устройством
D 444	disk surface	Plattenoberfläche *f*	surface *f* de disque	поверхность диска
D 445	disk track	Plattenspur *f*	trace *f* de disque	дорожка на диске, трек
D 446	dispatching	Abfertigungssteuerung *f*, Aufgabendurchlaufsteuerung *f*, Zuteilung *f*	dispatching *m*	диспетчеризация
D 447	dispatching object	Zuteilungsobjekt *n*	objet *m* de dispatching	объект диспетчеризации (присвоения)
D 448	displacement	Verschiebung *f*, Verschiebegröße *f*	déplacement *m*	смещение
D 449	displacement address, offset address	Verschiebeadresse *f*, Versatzadresse *f*	adresse *f* de décalage, adresse d'offset	адрес смещения
D 450	display / to	optisch anzeigen, sichtbar machen	visualiser	отображать
D 451	display, visual display	Sichtanzeige *f*, optische Anzeige *f*	affichage *m* visuel	дисплей, отображение <на экране>
D 452	display console	Bildschirmkonsole *f*	console *f* à écran de visualisation	консоль с дисплеем

D 453	display control	Anzeigesteuerung *f*	commande *f* de l'affichage	управление отображением
D 454	display device, display unit	Anzeigegerät *n*, Anzeige-einheit *f*, Anzeigeein-richtung *f*	appareil *m* (unité *f*) d'affichage	дисплей, устройство отображения
D 455	display modes	Anzeigebetriebsarten *fpl*	modes *mpl* d'affichage	режимы отображения
D 456	display operator	Anzeigeoperator *m*	opérateur *m* d'affichage	оператор дисплея
D 457	display position	Anzeigestelle *f*, Anzeige-position *f*	position *f* d'affichage	позиция на экране дисплея
D 458	display screen	Anzeigeschirm *m*, Bild-schirm *m*	écran *m* de visualisation	экран дисплея
D 459	display technique	Anzeigeverfahren *n*, Anzeigetechnik *f*	procédé *m* d'affichage	техника отображения
	display unit	*s.* D 454		
	dissipation	*s.* P 373		
D 460	distance measurement	Fernmessung *f*	mesure *f* à distance	дистанционное измерение
D 461	distortion	Verzerrung *f*	distorsion *f*	искажение
	distortion elimination	*s.* C 429		
D 462	distribute / to	verteilen	distribuer	распределять
D 463	distributed computer system	verteiltes Rechnersystem *n* <Mehrprozessorsystem mit räumlich und auf-gabenseitig verteilten Komponenten>	système *m* de calculateurs réparti	распределенная вычисли-тельная система
D 464	distributed control	verteilte Steuerung *f*	commande *f* répartie	распределенное управле-ние, децентрализован-ное управлдние
D 465	distributed data entry	verteilte Dateneingabe *f* <dezentrale Anordnung>	entrée *f* de données répartie	децентрализованный ввод данных
D 466	distributed-intelligence microprocessor system	Mikroprozessorsystem *n* mit verteilter Intelligenz, dezentralisiertes Mikro-rechnersystem *n* <Multi-mikroprozessorsystem>	système *m* de microproces-seurs à intelligence répartie	микропроцессорная система с распределен-ной обработкой, децен-трализованная микро-процессорная система
D 467	distributed-intelligence system	System *n* mit verteilter Intelligenz	système *m* à intelligence répartie	система распределенного обслуживания
D 468	distributed logic	verteilte Logik *f*	logique *f* répartie	распределенная логика
D 469	distributed processing	verteilte Verarbeitung *f* <räumlich und aufgaben-mäßig getrennte Verar-beitung in mehreren Prozessoren>	traitement *m* réparti	распределенная обработка
D 470	distributed processing system	verteiltes Datenverarbei-tungssystem *n* <zusam-mengesetzt aus räumlich und aufgabenmäßig getrennten Teilsystemen>	système *m* informatique réparti	распределенная система обработки данных
D 471	distributed system	verteiltes System *n* <mit räumlich verteilten und aufgabenmäßig getrenn-ten Teilsystemen>	système *m* réparti	распределенная (децен-трализованная) система
D 472	distribution bus	Verteilungsschiene *f*	bus *m* de distribution	распределительная шина
D 473	distribution of control	Verteilung *f* der Steuerung	distribution *f* de commande	распределение управле-ния ⌐гистр
D 474	distribution register	Verteilerregister *n*	registre *m* de distribution	распределительный ре-
D 475	distributor	Verteiler *m*	distributeur *m*	распределитель
	disturbance	*s.* T 329		
D 476	disturbance variable, perturbance	Störgröße *f*	grandeur *f* perturbatrice	величина возмущающего воздействия
	disturbed	*s.* O 190		
D 477	disturbed state	gestörter Zustand *m*	état *m* perturbé	возмущенное состояние; разрушенное состояние
D 478	disturb pulse	Störimpuls *m*	impulsion *f* perturbatrice	импульс помехи; разру-шающий импульс
D 479	disturb signal, drop-in signal	Störsignal *n*	signal *m* perturbateur	сигнал помехи
D 480	dividend	Dividend *m*	dividende *m*	делимое
D 481	dividing circuit	Teilerschaltung *f*, Dividier-schaltung *f*	circuit *m* de division	схема деления
D 482	dividing stage	Teilerstufe *f*	étage *m* de division	разряд деления
D 483	division algorithm	Divisionsalgorithmus *m*	algorithme *m* de division	алгоритм деления
D 484	division device (unit)	Divisionseinrichtung *f*	dispositif *m* (unite *f*) de division	устройство деления
D 485	divisor	Divisor *m*, Teiler *m* <Mathematik>	diviseur *m*	делитель
	DLC	*s.* D 86		
D 486	DMA, direct memory access	DMA *m*, direkter Speicher-zugriff *m*	D. M. A., accès *m* direct mémoire	прямой доступ к памяти, ПДП
D 487	DMA acknowledgement	DMA-Bestätigung *f*, DMA-Gewährung *f*	confirmation *f* de D. M. A.	подтверждение ПДП
D 488	DMA capability	DMA-Fähigkeit *f*	faculté *f* D. M. A.	возможность ПДП
D 489	DMA channel, direct memory access channel	DMA-Kanal *m*, direkter Speicherkanal *m*	canal *m* de D. M. A., canal d'accès direct à la mémoire	канал прямого доступа к памяти, канал ПДП
D 490	DMA control	DMA-Steuerung *f*	commande *f* de D. M. A.	управление ПДП
D 491	DMA controller	DMA-Steuerung *f*, Steuer-einheit *f* für direkten Speicherverkehr <DMA>	appareil *m* de commande de D. M. A.	контроллер ПДП
D 492	DMA data transfer	DMA-Datenübertragung *f*, Datenübertragung *f* im DMA-Betrieb	transmission *f* de données D. M. A.	передача данных в режиме ПДП
D 493	DMA operation	DMA-Operation *f*, DMA-Betrieb *m*	opération *f* D. M. A.	режим ПДП, работа в режиме ПДП
D 494	DMA request	DMA-Anforderung *f*	demande *f* de D. M. A.	запрос ПДП

D 495	**DMA system,** direct memory access system	DMA-System n, Direkt-speicherzugriffssystem n, System n des direkten Speicherverkehrs	système m D. M. A., système d'accès direct à la mémoire	система прямого доступа к памяти, система ПДП
D 496	**DMA technique**	DMA-Technik f, Technik f des direkten Speicher-zugriffs	technique f D. M. A.	техника ПДП, способ обмена с использованием ПДП
D 497	**DMA transfer**	DMA-Übertragung f	transfert m D. M. A.	передача в режиме ПДП
D 498	**DMA transfer cycle**	DMA-Übertragungszyklus m	cycle m de transmission D. M. A.	цикл передачи в режиме ПДП
D 499	**D-MOS,** double diffusion MOS technology	D-MOS f, Doppeldiffu-sions-MOS-Technologie f	D-MOS f, technologie f MOS à diffusion double	технология изготовления МОП-структур методом двойной диффузии
D 500	**DNC,** direct numerical control	DNC f, direkte numerische Steuerung f	DNC m, commande f numérique directe	числовое программное управление, ЧПУ
D 501	**document**	Beleg m	document m	документ
D 502	**documentation**	⌐mentation f Belegverwaltung f, Doku-	gestion f de documents	документация
D 503	**document feeding**	Belegzufuhr f	acheminement m de documents	подача документов
D 504	**document handler,** document reader	Belegleser m	lecteur m de documents	устройство считывания документов
D 505	**document handling**	Belegbearbeitung f	travail m de documents	[предварительная] обработка документов
D 506	**document processing** document reader	Belegverarbeitung f s. D 504	traitement m de documents	обработка документов
D 507	**document sorter**	Belegsortierer m	dispositif m de tri documents	устройство сортировки документов
D 508	**document speed**	Belegdurchlaufgeschwin-digkeit f	vitesse f de passage de documents	скорость прохождения документов
D 509	**document stacker**	Belegablage f	dépôt m de documents	устройство приема / выдачи документов
D 510	**domain structure**	Domänenstruktur f	structure f de domaine	доменная структура
D 511	**don[at]or**	Donator m <Elektronen-spender>	donateur m	донор, донорная примесь
D 512	**donor addition**	Donatoreneinbau m <in Kristall>	insertion f de donateur	легирование донорной примесью
D 513	**donor concentration**	Donatorenkonzentration f	concentration f de donateurs	концентрация донорной примеси
D 514	**donor ion**	Donatorion n	ion m donateur	донорный ион
D 515	**dopant,** dope additive	Dotiermittel n, Dotierungs-zusatz m	matière f à doper	легирующий материал, примесь
D 516	**dopant impurity**	dotierte Verunreinigung f	impureté f dopée	легирующая примесь
D 517	**dope / to** dope additive	dopen, dotieren s. D 515	doper	легировать
D 518	**doped junction**	gedopte (dotierte) Schicht f	jonction f dopée	легированный переход
D 519	**doping**	Dotierung f, Dotieren n	dopage m, doping m	легирование
D 520	**doping density**	Dotierungsdichte f	densité f de dopage	концентрация легирую-щей примеси
D 521	**doping junction**	Dotierungsübergang m	jonction f de dopage	переход, образованный легированием
D 522	**doping level**	Dotierungsniveau n	niveau m de dopage	степень легирования
D 523	**doping range**	Dotierungsbereich m	champ m de dopage	зона легирования
D 524	**doping technique**	Dotierungsverfahren n, Dotierungstechnik f	procédé m de dopage	техника легирования
	DOS	s. D 440		
	double computer system	s. D 568		
D 525	**double-diffused tran-sistor**	Doppeldiffusionstransistor m	transistor m à double diffusion	транзистор с двойной диффузией
	double diffusion MOS technology	s. D 499		
D 526	**double-faced printed circuit board**	doppelseitig bedruckte Leiterplatte f, Zweilagen-leiterplatte f	circuit m imprimé à double face	двусторонняя печатная плата
	double-length arithmetic	s. D 530		
	double-length word	s. D 533		
D 527	**double-level polysilicon technique**	Zweiebenen-Polysilizium-technik f <mit 2 Poly-siliziumebenen arbeitende Schaltkreistechnik>	technique f au polysilicium à deux niveaux	двухуровневая технология интегральных схем на поликристаллическом кремнии
	double-operand instruc-tion	s. T 363		
D 528	**double-pole,** two-pole, two-terminal	doppelpolig, zweipolig	bipolaire	двухполюсный
D 529	**double precision**	doppelte Genauigkeit f	précision f double	двойная точность
D 530	**double-precision arithmetic,** double-length arithmetic	Doppelgenauigkeitsarith-metik f, Doppellängen-arithmetik f, Rechnen n mit doppelter Stellenzahl	arithmétique f à précision double	арифметические действия со словами двойной длины
D 531	**double-precision number**	Doppelgenauigkeitszahl f, Zahl f doppelter Stellen-menge	nombre m à précision double	число удвоенной точности
D 532	**double pulse**	Doppelimpuls m	impulsion f double	двойной импульс
D 533	**double word,** double-length word	Doppelwort n, Doppel-längenwort n	mot m [de longueur] double	двойное слово, слово двойной длины
D 534	**double-word access**	Doppelwortzugriff m, Zweiwortzugriff m	accès m de mot double	доступ к словам двой-ной длины
D 535	**double-word instruction**	Doppelwortbefehl m, Zwei-wortbefehl m	instruction f à mot double	инструкция длиной в два слова; инструкция обработки двойных слов
D 536	**down-counter**	Abwärtszähler m	compteur m descendant	счетчик вычитания
D 537	**down-line loading**	Abwärtsladen n, Laden n eines Satellitenrechners durch den Führungs-rechner	chargement m en bas	загрузка периферийной ЭВМ через центральную [ЭВМ]

D 538	downward compatibility	Abwärtskompatibilität f, Verträglichkeit f mit unteren Modellen	compatibilité f vers le bas	совместимость сверху вниз
D 539	drain	Senke f, Abfluß m	drain m	сток
D 540	drain bias, drain voltage	Drain-Spannung f, Senkenspannung f, Saugspannung f	tension f de drain	смещение стока, напряжение на стоке
D 541	drain cutoff current	Drain-Sperrstrom m	courant m de barrage de drain	ток отсечки стока
D 542	drain electrode	Drain-Elektrode f, Senkenelektrode f <stromführende Elektrode eines FET>	électrode f de drain	электрод стока
D 543	drain-gate capacitance	Drain-Gate-Kapazität f <Kapazität zwischen Drain- und Gateelektrode eines FET>	capacité f drain-gate	емкость сток-затвор
	drain voltage	s. D 540		
D 544	drawing digitizing	Zeichnungsdigitalisierung f	chiffrage m de dessin	преобразование графической информации в цифровую форму
D 545	drift	Drift f <Nullpunktverschiebung>	dérive f	дрейф
D 546	drift-corrected amplifier	driftkompensierter Verstärker m	amplificateur m à compensation de dérive	усилитель с коррекцией дрейфа
D 547	drift correction	Driftkorrektur f	compensation f de dérive	коррекция дрейфа
	drift error	s. D 548		
D 548	drift failure, drift error	Driftfehler m	défaut m de dérive	ошибка из-за дрейфа [нуля]
D 549	drift stabilization	Driftstabilisierung f	stabilisation f de dérive	стабилизация дрейфа
D 550	drift transistor	Drifttransistor m	transistor m drift	дрейфовый транзистор
D 551	drive / to	treiben, speisen, lenken	entraîner, alimenter	приводить в действие; вести; запускать
D 552	drive	Antrieb m, Laufwerk n	entraînement m, mécanisme m	привод
D 553	drive capability	Treiberfähigkeit f. Treiberleistungsvermögen n	capacité f d'entraînement, capacité de basculeur	нагрузочная способность
D 554	drive circuit, driving circuit	Treiberschaltung f	circuit m basculeur	формирователь
D 555	drive current	Treiberstrom m, Steuerstrom m	courant m de basculeur (commande)	ток возбуждения
D 556	drive mechanism	Antriebsmechanismus m	mécanisme m d'entraînement	приводной механизм
D 557	drive power	Treiberleistung f	puissance f de basculeur	пусковая мощность
D 558	drive pulse, driving pulse	Treiberimpuls m	impulsion f de basculeur	пусковой импульс
D 559	driver	Treiber m <Verstärkerstufe; E/A-Steuerprogramm>	driver m	формирователь; программа-драйвер
	driving circuit	s. D 554		
D 560	driving motor	Antriebsmotor m	moteur m d'entraînement	приводной двигатель
	driving pulse	s. D 558		
	DRO	s. D 293		
	drop	s. V 60		
	drop-in signal	s. D 479		
D 561	drop out	Signalausfall m, Lesespannungsausfall m	manque m de signal (tension de lecture)	исчезновение сигнала; выпадание <знаков или разрядов>
D 562	drum storage	Trommelspeicher m	mémoire f à tambour	запоминающее устройство на [магнитном] барабане
D 563	dry joint (junction)	kalte Lötstelle f	soudure f incorrecte	«сухой» контакт
D 564	dry run[ning]	Trockenlauf m <Probelauf zur Logik- oder Programmprüfung>	marche f à sec	формальный прогон [программы]
D 565	DTL, diode transistor logic	DTL f, Dioden-Transistor-Logik f <Schaltungstechnik>	logique f diode-transistor, DTL f	диодно-транзисторная логика, ДТЛ
	D-type-flip-flop	s. D 323		
D 566	dual access	Doppelzugriff m	accès m double	двойной доступ
	dual asynchronous receiver/transmitter	s. D 16		
D 567	dual channel	Zweifachkanal m	canal m double	дублированный канал
D 568	dual computer system, double computer system	Doppelrechnersystem n	système m à calculateur double	двухмашинная система
	dual in-line package	s. D 388		
D 569	dual number	Dualzahl f	nombre m dual	двойное число
D 570	dual-port memory	Speicher m mit Doppelzugriffseinrichtung	mémoire f à accès double	двухпортовая память
D 571	dual-register set	zweifacher Registersatz m, Doppel-Registersatz m	jeu m de registres double	двойной набор регистров
D 572	dual-trace oscilloscope	Zweistrahloszillograf m	oscillographe m bicanon	двухлучевой осциллограф
D 573	dumb terminal	Primitivterminal n, nicht-intelligentes Terminal n	terminal m primitif	«немой» (неинтеллектуальный) терминал
D 574	dummy address	Scheinadresse f	adresse f fictive	фиктивный адрес
D 575	dummy argument	Formalargument n	argument m formel	фиктивный аргумент
D 576	dummy character	Blindzeichen n	caractère m blanc	фиктивный символ
D 577	dummy instruction	Scheinbefehl m	instruction f fictive	фиктивная инструкция
D 578	dummy plug	Blindstecker m, Kurzschlußstecker m	fiche f morte (de court-circuit)	изолированный штепсель, короткозамкнутый штепсель
D 579	dummy record	Pseudosatz m	enregistrement m pseudo	пустая запись
D 580	dummy statement	Leeranweisung f, Scheinanweisung f	instruction f vide	пустой оператор
	dump	s. M 266		
D 581	dumping, memory dumping	Kopieren n des Speicherinhaltes	copiage m du contenu de mémoire	копирование данных <из оперативной памяти на средства регистрации>

D 582	**dumping**	programmierter periodischer Speicherauszug *m*	extrait *m* périodique de mémoire programmé	периодический вывод содержимого рабочей области памяти
D 583	**duplex channel**	Duplexkanal *m*, Zweiweg-kanal *m*	canal *m* duplex	дуплексный канал
D 584	**duplex mode,** two-way mode	Duplexbetriebsweise *f*, Zweiwegmodus *m*, doppelgerichtete Betriebs-art *f*	mode *m* duplex	дуплексный режим; режим двухстороннего взаимодействия
D 585	**duplex operation**	Duplexbetrieb *m* <Senden und Empfangen gleich-zeitig>, Zweirichtungs-verkehr *m*	régime *m* duplex	дуплексный режим работы
D 586	**duplicate / to**	duplizieren	doubler	дублировать
D 587	**duplicate routine**	Kopierprogramm *n*	programme *m* de copiage	программа дублирования (копирования)
D 588	**duplicator**	Vervielfältiger *m*	duplicateur *m*	дубликатор, копироваль-ное устройство
D 589	**duty cycle**	Arbeitsphase *f*, Nutzzyklus *m*	cycle *m* de travail, cycle utile	рабочий цикл; активная фаза
D 590	**duty ratio**	Einschalt-Tastverhältnis *n*	rapport *m* de travail	коэффициент заполнения
D 591	**dwell time**	Verweilzeit *f*	temps *m* d'arrêt	программируемая времен-ная задержка; длитель-ность программируемо-го останова
D 592	**dynamic behaviour**	dynamisches Verhalten *n*	comportement *m* dynami-que	динамический режим
D 593	**dynamic characteristics,** AC characteristics	dynamische Kenndaten *pl* (Kennlinie *f*)	caractéristiques *fpl* dynami-ques	динамические характе-ристики
D 594	**dynamic check**	dynamische Prüfung *f*	vérification *f* dynamique	динамический контроль
D 595	**dynamic circuitry**	dynamische Schaltung *f*	circuit *m* dynamique	динамические схемы
D 596	**dynamic dump**	dynamischer Speicherauszug *m* <periodisch während Programmabarbeitung>	extrait *m* dynamique de mémoire	динамическая выдача, динамический дамп
D 597	**dynamic error debug-ging**	Beseitigen *n* dynamischer Fehler	dépannage *m* d'erreurs dynamiques	динамическая отладка, устранение динами-ческих ошибок
D 598	**dynamic memory,** dynamic store (storage)	dynamischer Speicher *m* <Speicherinformation ver-änderlich in Zeit oder Raum>	mémoire *f* dynamique	динамическая память, динамическое запоми-нающее устройство
D 599	**dynamic memory cell**	dynamische Speicherzelle *f* <dyn. RAM-Zelle>	cellule *f* de mémoire dynamique	ячейка динамической памяти
D 600	**dynamic memory device**	dynamischer Speicherbau-stein *m*, Speicherbaustein in dynamischer [MOS-] Technik	module *m* de mémoire dynamique, module de mémoire en technique [MOS] dynamique	модуль динамической памяти
D 601	**dynamic MOS circuit**	dynamische MOS-Schal-tung *f*, MOS-Schaltung in dynamischer Technik	circuit *m* MOS dynamique	динамическая МОП-схема
D 602	**dynamic programming**	dynamische Program-mierung *f*	programmation *f* dynami-que	динамическое програм-мирование
D 603	**dynamic RAM**	dynamischer RAM *m* <Lese-Schreib-Speicher mit dynamischen Spei-cherzellen infolge La-dungsspeicherung>	RAM *f* dynamique <mémoire lecture-écriture dynamique>	динамическое оперативное запоминающее устрой-ство, динамическое ОЗУ
D 604	**dynamic relocation**	dynamische Verschiebung (Zuordnung, Relokali-sierung) *f*	relocation *f* (décalage *m*) dynamique	динамическое переме-щение
D 605	**dynamic scattering mode effect**	DMS-Effekt *m* <Flüssig-kristallanzeige>	effet *m* DMS <affichage à cristaux liquides>	эффект динамического рассеяния
D 606	**dynamic stop**	dynamischer Stopp *m*.	arrêt *m* dynamique	динамический останов
D 607	**dynamic storage**	dynamische Speicherung *f*	mémorisation *f* dynamique	динамическое запо-минание
	dynamic storage (store)	s. D 598		
D 608	**dynamic subroutine**	dynamisches Unterpro-gramm *n*	sous-programme *m* dynami-que	динамическая подпро-грамма

E

E 1	**EAROM,** electrically alterable read-only memory	EAROM *m*, elektrisch änderbarer ROM (Nur-Lese-Speicher) *m*	EAROM *f*, mémoire *f* lecture seule altérable électriquement	постоянное запоминаю-щее устройство с элек-трическим изменением информации
E 2	**earth / to,** to connect to earth	erden, mit Erde verbinden	mettre à terre	заземлять
E 3	**earth-free**	erdfrei	sans terre	незаземленный
E 4	**earthing,** grounding	Erdung *f*	mise *f* à [la] terre	заземление
	easy-flow direction	s. L 319		
	e-beam technology	s. E 72		
E 5	**EBCDIC,** extended binary-coded decimal inter-change code	EBCD-Kode *m*, erweiterter BCD-Austauschkode *m* <8-Bit-Dezimalkode>	code *m* EBCD	расширенный двоично-десятичный код обмена, код EBCDIC
	ECC	s. E 214		
E 6	**Eccles-Jordan circuit**	Eccles-Jordan-Schaltung *f* <bistabile Kippschaltung>	circuit *m* d'Eccles et Jordan	схема с двумя устойчи-выми состояниями
E 7	**ECD,** electrochromeric display	ECD-Element *n*, elektro-chromerische Anzeige *f* <Anzeigeelement mit feld-gesteuerter Durchsichtig-keit>	élément *m* d'affichage ECD	электрохроматический индикатор
E 8	**echo check**	Echotest *m*	test *m* d'écho	эхо-контроль

E 9	**ECL,** emitter-coupled logic	ECL f, ECL-Technik f, emittergekoppelte Logik f	logique f ECL	ЭСЛ-схемы, эмиттерно-связанная логика
	E condition	s. E 187		
E 10	**economic application**	Anwendung f in der Ökonomie	application f dans l'économie	экономическое применение
E 11	**economy circuit**	Sparschaltung f	circuit m économe	экономичная схема
E 12	**edge**	Rand m, Kante f	bord m, arête f	край
E 13	**edge**	Flanke f	flanc m	фронт
E 14	**edge connector,** plug connector	Steckverbinder m	connecteur m à fiches	[торцевой] разъем [платы]
E 15	**edge-level triggered circuit**	flankenzustandsgetriggerte Schaltung f <durch Kombination Schaltflanke-Pegel ausgelöste Schaltung>	circuit m basculé par niveau de flanc	схема со смешанной синхронизацией <управляемая фронтом и уровнем сигнала>
E 16	**edge-triggered circuit**	flankengetriggerte (flankengesteuerte) Schaltung f	circuit m basculé par flancs	схема, переключаемая фронтом импульса
E 17	**edit / to**	aufbereiten, zusammenstellen, neuordnen <Daten>	éditer, composer, classer	редактировать
E 18	**edit character**	Druckaufbereitungszeichen n	caractère m d'édition	редактирующий символ, знак редактирования
E 19	**editing**	Aufbereitung f, Druckaufbereitung f, Textaufbereitung f	édition f, préparation f à l'impression, préparation de textes	редактирование
E 20	**editing program,** editor [routine]	Editor m, Aufbereitungsprogramm n <unterstützt Modifizieren, Speichern und Ausgeben von Quellprogrammen>	programme m éditeur	[программа-]редактор, редактирующая программа
E 21	**editing terminal**	Textaufbereitungsterminal n	terminal m d'édition	редактирующий терминал
E 22	**edit instruction**	Aufbereitungsbefehl m	instruction f d'édition	инструкция редактирования
	editor [routine]	s. E 20		
E 23	**ED-MOS,** enhancement depletion-load MOS technology	ED-MOS f, ED-MOS-Technik f <MOSFET-Schaltungstechnik mit Anreicherungstyp-Schalttransistor und Verarmungstyp-Lasttransistor>	technologie f ED-MOS	МОП-технология с обогащением активных элементов и обеднением нагрузок
E 24	**EDP,** electronic data processing	EDV f, elektronische Datenverarbeitung f	traitement m électronique de données	электронная обработка данных
E 25	**EDP accessories**	EDV-Zubehör n	accessoires mpl d'informatique	[вспомогательные] средства информационной техники
	EDPM	s. E 89		
E 26	**EDP service**	EDV-Dienstleistung f	service m d'informatique	служба [системы] электронной обработки данных
E 27	**educational computer**	Rechner m für Ausbildungszwecke	calculateur m d'enseignement	обучающая вычислительная машина
E 28	**EEROM,** electrically erasable read-only memory	EEROM m, elektrisch lösch- und programmierbarer ROM (Nur-Lese-Speicher) m	EEROM f, mémoire f lecture seule programmable et effaçable électriquement	электрически стираемое постоянное запоминающее устройство
E 29	**effective**	effektiv, wirksam, tatsächlich	effectif, efficace	эффективный, действующий
E 30	**effective address**	effektive Adresse f	adresse f effective	эффективный (исполнительный) адрес
E 31	**effective area**	Nutzfläche f, nutzbare Fläche f	champ m utile, surface f efficace	эффективная площадь; рабочая поверхность
E 32	**effective calculating time**	effektive Rechenzeit f	temps m de calcul effectif	эффективное машинное время
	effective capacity	s. R 64		
E 33	**effective instruction,** actual instruction	effektiver Befehl m	instruction f effective	исполнительная инструкция
E 34	**effective resistance**	Wirkwiderstand m	résistance f [effective]	[действующее] сопротивление
E 35	**effective value**	Effektivwert m	valeur f effective	действующее (эффективное) значение
E 36	**efficiency**	Wirkungsgrad m, Nutzeffekt m, Wirksamkeit f	efficience f	эффективность; коэффициент полезного действия
	EFL	s. E 127		
E 37	**EIA,** electronic industries association	EIA f, Elektronikindustrieverband m <Richtlinienherausgeber>	association f de l'industrie électronique, EIA	Ассоциация электронной промышленности <США>, АЭП
E 38	**EIA interface**	EIA-Standardschnittstelle f, EIA-Schnittstellenstandard m	interface f EIA, standard m d'interface EIA	[стандартный] интерфейс EIA
E 39	**EIA standard code**	EIA-Standardkode m	code m standard EIA	[стандартный] код EIA
	eight-bit arithmetic	s. B 165		
	eight-bit character	s. B 170		
	eight-bit code	s. B 171		
	eight-bit data	s. B 173		
	eight-bit I/O port	s. B 177		
	eight-bit microcomputer	s. B 182		
	eight-bit microprocessor	s. B 185		
	eight-bit operand	s. B 189		
	eight-bit register	s. B 196		
	eight-bit-wide I/O port	s. B 177		
	eight-channel code	s. C 112		
	eight-channel tape	s. C 124		
	eight-level code	s. C 112		
	eight-track code	s. C 112		

	eight-track tape	*s.* C 124		⌐ние
E 40	electric adapting	elektrische Anpassung *f*	adaptation *f* électrique	электрическое сопряже-
E 41	electrical characteristics	elektrische Kenndaten *pl*	caractéristiques *fpl* électriques	электрические характе-ристики
E 42	electrical engineering	Elektrotechnik *f*	électrotechnique *f*	электротехника
E 43	electrical insulation (isolation)	elektrische Isolierung *f*	isolation *f* électrique	электрическая изоляция
	electrical joint	*s.* E 49		
	electrically alterable read-only memory	*s.* E 1		
	electrically erasable read-only memory	*s.* E 28		
	electrically program-mable read-only memory	*s.* E 185		
E 44	electrical measuring and test equipment	elektrische Meß- und Prüf-einrichtung *f*	équipement *m* de mesure et de test électrique	электроизмерительные приборы и испытатель-ное оборудование
E 45	electrical schematic diagram, electric wiring diagram	elektrischer Schaltplan *m*	schéma *m* électrique	электрическая схема
E 46	electrical specifications	Kenndatenblatt *n* elektri-scher Parameter	spécifications *fpl* électriques	требования к электри-ческим параметрам
E 47	electric charge, electric quantity	elektrische Ladung *f*	charge *f* électrique	электрический заряд
E 48	electric conductivity	elektrische Leitfähigkeit *f*	conductibilité *f* électrique	электрическая проводи-мость
E 49	electric connection, electrical joint	elektrische Verbindung *f*	connexion *f* électrique	электрическое соединение
E 50	electric polarization	elektrische Polarisation (Ladungsverschiebung, Verschiebung) *f*	polarisation *f* électrique	электрическая поляри-зация
	electric quantity	*s.* E 47		
E 51	electric signal	elektrisches Signal *n*	signal *m* électrique	электрический сигнал
	electric wiring diagram	*s.* E 45		
	electrochromeric display	*s.* E 7		
E 52	electrode contacting	Elektrodenkontaktierung *f*	formation *f* de contact d'électrode	замыкание электрода
E 53	electrode lead	Elektrodenzuleitung *f*	conducteur *m* d'électrode	вывод электрода
E 54	electrodeposit / to, to electroplate	elektrolytisch aufbringen (niederschlagen), galvani-sieren	appliquer par électrolyse	наносить гальваническим путем, создавать галь-ванопокрытие
E 55	electrodeposition	Galvanisierung *f*	galvanisage *m*	электролитическое осаж-дение, гальваностегия
E 56	electrode shape	Elektrodenform *f*	forme *f* d'électrode	форма электрода
E 57	electrogenerated chemi-luminescence	elektrisch erzeugte Chemi-lumineszenz (Chemo-lumineszenz) *f*	chimiluminescence *f* excitée électriquement	электрически возбуждае-мая хемилюминесцен-ция
E 58	electrographic record-ing	elektrografische Aufzeich-nung *f*	enregistrement *m* électro-graphique	электрографическая запись
E 59	electrohydraulic servo control	elektrohydraulische Servo-steuerung *f*	servocommande *f* électro-hydraulique	электрогидравлическое сервоуправление
E 60	electroluminescent display	Elektrolumineszenzanzeige *f*	affichage *m* électrolumines-cent	электролюминесцентный индикатор
E 61	electrolytic display	elektrolytische Anzeige *f*	affichage *m* électrolytique	электролитический индикатор
E 62	electromagnetic delay line	elektromagnetische Ver-zögerungsleitung *f*	ligne *f* de retardement électromagnétique	электромагнитная линия задержки
E 63	electromagnetic field	elektromagnetisches Feld *n*	champ *m* électromagnétique	электромагнитное поле
E 64	electromagnetic locking	elektromagnetische Ver-riegelung *f*	verrouillage *m* électro-magnétique	электромагнитная блоки-ровка
E 65	electromagnetic screen-ing (shielding)	elektromagnetische Abschirmung *f*	blindage *m* électromagnéti-que	электромагнитное экранирование
E 66	electromagnetic wave	elektromagnetische Welle *f*	onde *f* électromagnétique	электромагнитная волна
E 67	electromechanical drive	elektromechanischer Antrieb *m*	entraînement *m* électro-mécanique	электромеханический привод
E 68	electron attachment	Elektronenanlagerung *f*	dépôt *m* d'électrons	присоединение электрона
E 69	electron avalanche	Elektronenlawine *f*	avalanche *f* d'électrons	электронная лавина
E 70	electron beam	Elektronenstrahl *m*	rayon *m* électronique	электронный пучок
E 71	electron beam direct-stepping-on-wafer lithography	Elektronenstrahllithografie *f* mit direkter Layoutüber-tragung auf eine Halb-leiterscheibe	lithographie *f* au rayon électronique avec trans-fert de layout direct sur tranche de semi-conduc-teur	электроннолучевая лито-графия с непосредствен-ным переносом топо-логии на полупроводни-ковую пластину
E 72	electron beam tech-nology, e-beam tech-nology	Elektronenstrahltechnolo-gie *f*	technologie *f* des rayons électroniques	электроннолучевая технология
E 73	electron camera	elektronische Kamera *f*	caméra *f* électronique	электронная камера
E 74	electron capture	Elektroneneinfang *m*	capture *f* d'électrons	захват электрона
E 75	electron conduction	Elektronenleitung *f*	conduite *f* d'électrons	электронная проводи-мость
E 76	electron deficiency, electron hole	Elektronenlücke *f*, Defekt-elektron *n*, Elektronen-loch *n*	électron-trou *m*	дырка
E 77	electron density	Elektronendichte *f*	densité *f* d'électrons	плотность (концентрация) электронов
E 78/9	electron discharge	Elektronenentladung *f*	décharge *f* d'électrons	электронный разряд
E 80	electron drift, electron flow (stream)	Elektronenwanderung *f*, Elektronenstrom *m*	courant *m* (migration *f*) d'électrons	дрейф (поток) электронов
E 81	electron emission	Elektronenemission *f*	émission *f* d'électrons	электронная эмиссия
	electron flow	*s.* E 80		
	electron hole	*s.* E 76		
E 82	electronic accounting machine	elektronische Abrechnungs-maschine *f*	appareil *m* électronique comptable	электронная счетно-ана-литическая машина

E 83	electronically con-trolled	elektronisch gesteuert	à commande électronique	управляемый электрон-ными средствами
E 84	electronic application	Elektronikanwendung f, Anwendung f der Elek-tronik	application f de l'électro-nique	применение в электро-нике
E 85	electronic circuit tech-nique	elektronische Schaltungs-technik (Schaltkreis-technik) f	technique f des circuits électroniques	электронная схемотехника
E 86	electronic component	elektronisches Bauelement n	composant m électronique	электронный компонент
E 87	electronic computer	elektronische Rechen-anlage f	calculateur m électronique	электронная вычисли-тельная машина, ЭВМ
E 88	electronic control electronic data pro-cessing	elektronische Steuerung f s. E 24	commande f électronique	электронное управление
E 89	electronic data pro-cessing machine, EDPM	elektronische Datenver-arbeitungsanlage f, EDVA f	installation f de traitement électronique des données	ЭВМ для обработки данных
E 90	electronic data pro-cessing system	elektronisches Datenver-arbeitungssystem n	système m de traitement électronique des données	система электронной обработки данных
E 91	electronic device	elektronisches Gerät n	appareil m électronique	электронный прибор, электронное устройство
E 92	electronic display	elektronische Anzeige f	affichage m électronique	электронное устройство отображения
E 93	electronic games	elektronische Spiele npl, Elektronikspiele npl	jeux mpl électroniques	электронные игры
	electronic industries association	s. E 37		
E 94	electronic information processing	elektronische Informations-verarbeitung f	traitement m électronique d'informations, infor-matique f	электронная обработка информации
E 95	electronic pen	elektronischer Stift m	crayon m électronique	световое перо
E 96	electronics	Elektronik f	électronique f	электроника ⌐ность
E 97	electronics industry	Elektronikindustrie f	industrie f électronique	электронная промышлен-
E 98	electronics pack	Elektronikteil n, Elektronik-baustein m	module m électronique	электронный модуль
E 99	electronic switch	elektronischer Schalter m	commutateur m électro-nique	электронный ключ
E 100	electronic typewriter	elektronische Schreib-maschine f	machine f à écrire électronique	электронная пишущая машинка
E 101	electron injection	Elektroneninjektion f	injection f d'électrons	инжекция электронов
E 102	electron mobility	Elektronenbeweglichkeit f	mobilité f d'électrons	подвижность электронов
E 103	electron scanning	Elektronenabtastung f, elektronische Bildzer-legung f	balayage m (scrutation f) à électrons	сканирование электрон-ным лучом
	electron stream	s. E 80		
E 104	electron trap	Elektronenfalle f, Elek-troneneinfangstelle f	piège m à électrons	электронная ловушка
E 105	electrooptical	elektrooptisch	électro-optique	электрооптический
E 106	electrophoretic [image] display, EPD, EPID	elektrophoretische Anzeige f	affichage m par électro-phorèse	индикатор на основе явления электрофореза
	electroplate / to	s. E 54		
E 107	electrostatic field	elektrostatisches Feld n	champ m électrostatique	электростатическое поле
E 108	electrostatic printer electrostatic scanning	elektrostatischer Drucker m s. E 110	imprimante f électrostatique	электростатическое печа-тающее устройство
E 109	electrostatic screen, electrostatic shield	elektrostatischer Schirm m, elektrostatische Abschir-mung f	écran (blindage) m électro-statique	электростатический экран
E 110	electrostatic sensing, electrostatic scanning	elektrostatische Abtastung f	balayage m (scrutation f) électrostatique	электростатическая развертка
E 111	electrostatic shield electrostatic storage electrothermic printer	s. E 109 elektrostatischer Speicher m s. T 149	mémoire f électrostatique	электростатическое запо-минающее устройство
E 112	element	Element n, Baustein m, Glied n	élément m	элемент
E 113	elementary cell	Elementarzelle f	cellule f élémentaire	элементарная ячейка
E 114	elementary circuit	Elementarschaltung f	circuit m élémentaire	элементарная схема
E 115	elementary function	Elementarfunktion f	fonction f élémentaire	элементарная функция
E 116	elementary level	Grundstufe f	niveau m élémentaire	уровень элементов
E 117	elementary operation	Elementaroperation f	opération f élémentaire	элементарная операция
E 118	eliminate / to	eliminieren, beseitigen, aus-sondern	éliminer	устранять, исключать
E 119	emergency power supply	Notstromversorgung f	alimentation f de secours	аварийный источник питания
E 120	emitter	Emitter m <Transistor>	émetteur m	эмиттер
E 121	emitter barrier, emitter depletion layer	Emittersperrschicht f	couche f de barrage d'émetteur	барьер эмиттерного пере-хода, обедненный слой эмиттера
E 122	emitter-base junction	Emitter-Basis-Übergang m	jonction f émetteur-base	переход база-эмиттер
E 123	emitter bias emitter circuit	Emittervorspannung f s. C 372	polarisation f d'émetteur	смещение эмиттера
E 124	emitter contact, emitter terminal	Emitterkontakt m, Emitter-anschluß m	contact m d'émetteur	эмиттерный контакт
	emitter-coupled logic emitter depletion layer	s. E 9 s. E 121		
E 125	emitter doping	Emitterdotierung f	dopage m d'émetteur	легирование эмиттера
E 126	emitter follower	Emitterfolger m	poursuite f d'émetteur	эмиттерный повторитель
E 127	emitter follower logic, EFL	Emitterfolgerlogik f, EFL f	logique f EFL	логические схемы на эмиттерных повтори-телях, ЭПЛ-схемы
E 128	emitter lead	Emitterzuleitung f, Emitter-anschlußleitung f	conduit m d'émetteur	вывод эмиттера
E 129	emitter voltage	Emitterspannung f	tension f d'émetteur	напряжение на эмиттере
	employ / to	s. A 291		
	employment	s. A 277		

E 130	employment case	Einsatzfall *m*	cas *m* d'application	обстоятельства, связанные с применением
E 131	empty	leer, abgearbeitet	vide	незанятый, пустой
E 132	emulation	Emulation *f*, Nachahmung *f* ausgewählter Verhaltenseigenschaften ‹auf Mikrobefehlsebene›	émulation *f*	эмуляция
E 133	emulator	Emulator *m* ‹Programm oder Mikroprogramm, mit dem in einem anderen Maschinenkode geschriebene Programme ausgeführt werden können›	émulateur *m*	эмулятор
E 134	enable / to	wirksam machen	rendre efficace	разрешать
E 135	enable-disable control	Freigabe-Sperr-Steuerung *f*	commande *f* à libération-blocage	управление разрешением-запретом
E 136	enable interrupt / to	Interrupt freigeben, Unterbrechung zulassen, unterbrechbar machen	permettre l'interruption	разрешать прерывание
	enable signal	*s.* E 137		
E 137	enabling signal, enable signal	Freigabesignal *n*	signal *m* de libération	сигнал разрешения
E 138	encapsulating material	Verkapselungsmaterial *n*, Vergußmasse *f*	matériau *m* à encastrer, masse *f* de scellement	герметизирующий материал
E 139	encapsulation	Verkapselung *f*	blindage *m*	герметизация
	encasement	*s.* E 140		
E 140	enclosure, encasement	Gehäuse *n*, Verkleidung *f*	boîtier *m*, revêtement *m*	корпус, упаковка
	encode / to	*s.* C 288		
	encoder	*s.* C 324		
E 141	encryption circuitry	Chiffrierschaltung *f*, Verschlüsselungsschaltung *f*	circuit *m* de chiffrage	схемы криптографической шифрации
E 142	end-around carry	Endübertrag *m*, Rücklaufübertrag *m*, Einerrücklauf *m*	retenue *f* en arrière	циклический перенос
E 143	end connector	Endsteckverbinder *m*, stirnseitiger Steckverbinder *m*	connecteur *m* de fin, connecteur frontal	оконечный разъем
E 144	ending character	Schlußzeichen *n* ‹Block›	caractère *m* final	символ окончания
E 145	ending sequence	Beendigungsfolge *f*	séquence *f* de conclusion	концевая последовательность
	end lead	*s.* T 98		
E 146	end mark	Endmarkierung *f*, Endesteuerzeichen *n*	marque *f* finale	маркер конца файла
E 147	end-of-data-file statement	Dateiendeanweisung *f*	instruction *f* de fin de fichier	оператор конца файла
E 148	end-of-file label	Dateiendeetikett *n*	label *m* de fin de fichier	метка конца файла
E 149	end of message, EOM	Nachrichtenende *n*	terminaison (fin) *f* de message	конец сообщения
E 150	end-of-record character	Satzendezeichen *n*	caractère *m* de fin d'enregistrement	знак конца записи
E 151	end of transmission, EOT	Übertragungsende *n*	fin *f* de transmission	знак конца обмена данными
E 152	end order	Endeanweisung *f*, Endekommando *n*	instruction *f* de fin	команда окончания
	end position switch	*s.* L 121		
E 153	end user	Endnutzer *m*, Endverbraucher *m*	consommateur *m* final, utilisateur *m* final	оконечный пользователь
	end wire	*s.* L 72		
E 154	energy-dependent store	energieabhängiger Speicher *m*	mémoire *f* dépendante d'énergie	энергозависимое запоминающее устройство
E 155	energy-independent store	energieunabhängiger Speicher *m*	mémoire *f* indépendante d'énergie	энергонезависимое запоминающее устройство
E 156	energy level	Energieniveau *n*	niveau *m* d'énergie	энергетический уровень
E 157	engine control	Kraftmaschinensteuerung *f*, Kfz-Motor-Steuerung *f*	commande *f* de moteur, commande d'automobile	управление двигателем
E 158	engineering concept	Konstruktionsprinzip *n*	concept *m* constructif	технический принцип
E 159	engineering constraints	technische Grenzen (Restriktionen) *fpl*	limites (contraintes) *fpl* techniques	технические ограничения
E 160	engineering cost	Technikkosten *pl*, Technikentwicklungskosten *pl*	coûts *mpl* techniques	расходы на техническое развитие
	engineering description	*s.* T 62		
E 161	engineering design	technischer Entwurf *m*	projet *m* (conception *f*) technique	техническое проектирование
E 162	engineering development	technische Entwicklung *f*	développement *m* technique	техническое развитие
E 163	engineering improvement	technische Verbesserung *f*	amélioration *f* technique	техническое усовершенствование
E 164	engineering level	Konstruktionsstand *m*	niveau *m* de construction	технический уровень
E 165	engineering solution	technische Lösung *f*	solution *f* technique	техническое решение
E 166	enhance / to	anreichern	enrichir	обогащать
E 167	enhancement	Erhöhung *f*, Vergrößerung *f*, Anreicherung *f* ‹von Ladungsträgern›	augmentation *f*, agrandissement *m*, enrichissement *m*	увеличение; обогащение
	enhancement depletion-load MOS technology	*s.* E 23		
E 168	enhancement mode transistor	Anreicherungstyp-Transistor *m*	transistor *m* de type à enrichissement	транзистор, работающий в режиме обогащения
	enter position	*s.* E 175		
E 169	entire system	vollständiges System *n*	système *m* entier	законченная (завершенная) система
E 170	entry	Eingang *m*, Eintritt *m*; Eintragung *f* ‹Programm›	entrée *f*	ввод, вход; запись
E 171	entry address	Einsprungadresse *f*, Eintrittsadresse *f*	adresse *f* d'entrée	адрес входа, начальный адрес
E 172	entry condition	Einsprungbedingung *f*	condition *f* d'entrée	начальное условие
E 173	entry instruction	Eingangsbefehl *m* ‹1. Befehl eines Unterprogramms›	instruction *f* d'entrée	инструкция входа в подпрограмму

E 174	entry label	Eintrittsmarke f, Einsprung-marke f	label m d'entrée	метка входа
E 175	entry point, enter position	Eintrittsstelle f	point m d'entrée	точка входа ‹в программу›
	environmental conditions	s. A-230		
E 176	environmental requirements	Umgebungsanforderungen fpl, Klimavorschriften fpl	exigences fpl à l'environnement	требования к внешним условиям
	environmental temperature	s. A 231		
E 177	environment simulation	Umgebungssimulation f, Umweltsimulation f	simulation f de l'environnement	моделирование внешних условий
	EOM	s. E 149		
	EOT	s. E 151		
	EP[I]D	s. E 106		
	epiplanar transistor	s. E 181		
E 178	epitaxial film, epitaxial layer	Epitaxieschicht f	couche f épitaxiale	эпитаксиальная пленка, эпитаксиальный слой
E 179	epitaxial growth	Epitaxialwachstum n, epitaktisches Wachstum n	croissance f épitaxiale	эпитаксиальное выращивание
	epitaxial layer	s. E 178		
E 180	epitaxially grown silicon	epitaktisch aufgewachsenes Silizium n	silicium m à croissance épitaxiale	эпитаксиально выращенный кремний
E 181	epitaxial planar transistor, epiplanar transistor	Epitaxial-Planar-Transistor m	transistor m planaire épitaxial	эпитаксиальный планарный транзистор
E 182	epitaxial technique	Epitaxialtechnik f, Epitaxialverfahren n	technologie f épitaxiale	эпитаксиальная технология ⌐зистор
E 183	epitaxial transistor	Epitaxialtransistor m	transistor m épitaxial	эпитаксиальный тран-
E 184	epitaxy	Epitaxie f, einkristallines Aufwachsen n ‹Halbleiterschicht›	épitaxie f, croissance f monocristalline	эпитаксия
E 185	EPROM, electrically programmable read-only memory	EPROM m, elektrisch programmierbarer ROM (Nur-Lese-Speicher) m	EPROM f, mémoire f lecture seule programmable électriquement	электрически программируемое постоянное запоминающее устройство
E 186	EPROM, erasable programmable read-only memory	EPROM m, lösch- und programmierbarer ROM (Nur-Lese-Speicher) m ‹UV-Löschung: RePROM; elektr. Löschung: EEROM›	EPROM f, mémoire f lecture seule effaçable et programmable	стираемое программируемое постоянное запоминающее устройство ‹с ультрафиолетовым стиранием›
	⌐dition			
E 187	equal condition, E condition	Gleichheitsbedingung f	condition f d'équivalence	эквивалентное состояние; эквивалентное условие
	equality circuit	s. E 199		
E 188	equal sign	Gleichheitszeichen n	signe m d'égalité	знак равенства
E 189	equate / to	gleichsetzen	égaliser	приравнивать
E 190	equipment	Ausrüstung f, Ausstattung f, Anlage f	équipement m	оборудование
E 191	equipment compatibility	Gerätekompatibilität f	compatibilité f d'équipement (d'appareils)	совместимость оборудования
E 192	equipment cost	Ausrüstungskosten pl, Gerätekosten pl	coûts mpl d'équipement	стоимость оборудования
E 193	equipment engineering	Bauweise f	mode m de construction	разработка оборудования
E 194	equipment innovation	Ausrüstungserneuerung f	renouvellement m d'équipement	новшество в оборудовании ⌐ния
E 195	equipment production	Gerätefertigung f	fabrication f d'appareils	производство оборудова-
E 196	equipment reliability	Betriebssicherheit f ‹der Geräte›	sécurité f de fonctionnement, fiabilité f	надежность оборудования
E 197	equipment trouble	Gerätestörung f	perturbation f d'appareil	неисправность оборудования
		⌐keit f		
E 198	equivalence	Äquivalenz f, Gleichwertig-	équivalence f	эквивалентность
E 199	equivalence circuit, equality circuit	Äquivalenzschaltung f	circuit m d'équivalence	эквивалентная схема
	equivalent circuit	s. E 200		
E 200	equivalent network, equivalent circuit	Ersatzschaltung f	circuit m équivalent	эквивалентная схема
E 201	equivalent parameter	Ersatzgröße f	paramètre m équivalent	эквивалентный параметр
	erasable memory	s. E 203		
	erasable programmable read-only memory	s. E 186		
E 202	erasable storage	löschbare Speicherung f	mémorisation f effaçable	запоминающее устройство со стиранием информации
E 203	erasable store, erasable memory	löschbarer Speicher m	mémoire f effaçable	стираемая память
E 204	erase / to	‹Information, Inhalt› löschen	effacer	стирать
E 205	erase bit, erasing bit	Löschbit n ‹Kodeelement›	bit m d'effaçage	бит стирания
E 206	erase current, erasing current	Löschstrom m	courant m d'effaçage	ток стирания
E 207	erase head, erasing head	Löschkopf m	tête f d'effacement	стирающая головка
E 208	erase key	Löschtaste f, Irrungstaste f	touche f d'effacement	кнопка стирания
	erasing	s. E 209		
	erasing bit	s. E 205		
	erasing current	s. E 206		
	erasing head	s. E 207		
E 209	erasure, erasing	Löschung f	effacement m	стирание
E 210	error	Fehler m	erreur f	ошибка
E 211	error analysis	Fehleranalyse f	analyse f d'erreur[s]	обработка (анализ) ошибок
E 212	error burst	Fehlerbündel n, Fehlerhäufung f	tas m (accumulation f) d'erreurs	пакет (пачка) ошибок
E 213	error checking	Fehlerprüfung f	vérification f d'erreurs	контроль ошибок, проверка на наличие ошибок
E 214	error checking and correction, ECC	Fehlerprüfung f und -korrektur f	contrôle m et correction f d'erreurs	обнаружение и исправление ошибок

E 215	error-checking capability	Fehlerprüffähigkeit f, Fehlerprüfungstauglichkeit f	faculté f de vérification d'erreurs	возможность контроля ошибок
E 216	error-checking polynomial	Fehlerprüfpolynom n	polynôme m de vérification d'erreurs	проверочный полином
E 217	error code	Fehlerkode m	code m d'erreur	код с ошибкой
E 218	error compensation	Fehlerkompensation f	compensation f d'erreur	компенсация ошибки
E 219	error condition, fault condition	Fehlerbedingung f, Fehlerzustand m	condition f d'erreur	состояние ошибки
E 220	error control, fault monitoring	Fehlerüberwachung f, Fehlerkontrolle f	surveillance f des erreurs	контроль ошибок
E 221	error-controlled code	fehlerkontrollierender Kode m	code m à surveillance d'erreur[s]	помехоустойчивый код
E 222	error-correcting code	Fehlerkorrekturkode m, fehlerkorrigierender Kode m	code m correcteur (de correction d'erreurs)	код с исправлением ошибок
E 223	error-correcting program	Fehlerkorrekturprogramm n	programme m de correction d'erreurs	программа исправления ошибок
E 224	error correction	Fehlerkorrektur f	correction f d'erreur[s]	коррекция (исправление) ошибок
E 225	error deletion	Fehlerbeseitigung f	élimination f d'erreur[s]	устранение ошибок
E 226	error-detecting code	fehlererkennender Kode m	code m détecteur d'erreurs	код с обнаружением ошибок
E 227	error detection, error discovery, fault detection (discovery)	Fehlererkennung f, Fehlerentdeckung f	détection (reconnaissance) f d'erreur[s]	обнаружение ошибок
E 228	error-detection circuitry, fault-detection circuitry	Fehlererkennungsschaltung f	circuit m de reconnaissance (détection) d'erreurs	схема обнаружения ошибок
E 229	error diagnostic	Fehlerdiagnose f, Fehlerbestimmung f	diagnostic m d'erreur	диагностика ошибок
E 230	error diagnostic signal	Fehlererkennungssignal n	signal m de détection d'une erreur	сигнал распознавания ошибки
	error discovery	s. E 227		
E 231	error distance	Fehlerabstand m	distance f d'erreur	кодовое расстояние
E 232	error distribution	Fehlerverteilung f	distribution f d'erreurs	распределение ошибок
E 233	error evaluation	Fehlerauswertung f	évaluation f d'erreurs	оценка погрешности
E 234	error-free operation	fehlerfreier Betrieb m	régime m sans défaut	режим [работы] без ошибок
E 235	error-free transmission	fehlerfreie Übertragung f	transmission f sans défaut	передача [данных] без ошибок
E 236	error handling	Fehlerbehandlung f	traitement m d'erreurs	обработка ошибок
E 237	error indication, fault indication	Fehleranzeige f	signalement m d'erreur	индикация ошибок
E 238	error indicator, check indicator	Fehleranzeiger m	indicateur m d'erreur	индикатор ошибки
E 239	error interrupt	Fehlerinterrupt m, Fehlerunterbrechung f	interruption f par erreur	прерывание при ошибке
E 240	error localization, fault localization (location)	Fehlerortung f, Fehlerlokalisierung f	localisation f d'erreur	локализация неисправности (ошибок)
E 241	error-location program, fault-location program	Fehlerlokalisierprogramm n, Fehlerortungsprogramm n	programme m de localisation d'erreur	программа локализации ошибок
E 242	error message	Fehlermeldung f	message m d'erreur	сообщение об ошибке
	error of reading	s. R 50		
E 243	error prevention	Fehlerverhütung f	prévention f d'erreur	предотвращение ошибок
E 244	error probability	Fehlerwahrscheinlichkeit f	probabilité f d'erreurs	вероятность ошибки
E 245	error procedure	Fehlerprozedur f, Fehlerbehandlungsroutine f	procédure f d'erreur	процедура обработки ошибок
E 246	error propagation	Fehlerfortpflanzung f	propagation f d'erreur	распространение ошибки
E 247	error protection	Fehlerschutz m, Sicherung f gegen Fehler	protection f contre erreurs	защита от ошибок
E 248	error range	Fehlerbereich m	champ m d'erreur	диапазон ошибок
E 249	error rate, fault rate	Fehlerrate f, Fehlerhäufigkeit f	taux m (fréquence f) d'erreurs	интенсивность (частота появления) ошибок
E 250	error recovery, fault recovery	Fehlerheilung f, Fehlerwiedergutmachung f, Fehlerbeseitigung f ‹Wiederherstellung/Wiederanlauf nach Fehler›	réparation f d'erreur	исправление ошибок
E 251	error report, fault report	Fehlerbericht m, Fehlermitteilung f, Fehlerprotokoll n	rapport m d'erreurs	протокол ошибок
E 252	error routine	Fehlermaßnahmeprogramm n	programme m de mesure contre erreurs	программа контроля ошибок
E 253	error search, fault search	Fehlersuche f	recherche f d'erreurs	поиск ошибок
E 254	error signal	Fehlersignal n	signal m d'erreur	сигнал ошибки
E 255	error source	Fehlerquelle f	source f d'erreur[s]	источник ошибок
E 256	error status code	Fehlerstatuskode m	code m d'état d'erreur	код состояния ошибки
E 257	estimated value	Schätzwert m	valeur f estimée	оценочное значение
	estimation unit	s. E 268		
E 258	etch / to	ätzen	ronger, éroder	травить
E 259	etched circuit	geätzte Schaltung f	circuit m rongé	схема, изготовленная методом травления
E 260	etched wiring	geätzte Verdrahtung (Verbindung) f	câblage m érodé, connexion f érodée	соединение, полученное методом травления
E 261	European standard	Europa-Standard m	standard m européen	европейский стандарт
E 262	evaluate / to	auswerten, erproben	évaluer	оценивать
E 263	evaluation	Auswertung f	évaluation f	оценка
E 264	evaluation kit	Erprobungsbausatz m	ensemble m d'essai	макетный набор ‹для оценки характеристик разрабатываемой микро-ЭВМ при помощи исследования макета-прототипа›
E 265	evaluation module	Erprobungsmodul m ‹Mikrorechner-Leiterplatte zu Entwicklungs- und Trainingszwecken›	module m d'essai	макетный модуль ‹схемная плата›

E 266	evaluation processor module	Mikroprozessor-Erprobungsmodul *m*, Mikroprozessor-Entwicklungsmodul *f*	module *m* d'essai de microprocesseur	макетный процессорный модуль
E 267	evaluation program (routine)	Auswerteprogramm *n*	programme *m* d'évaluation	оценочная программа
E 268	evaluation unit, estimation unit	Auswerteeinheit *f*	unité *f* d'évaluation	устройство для макетирования
E 269	even	gerade, geradzahlig	pair	четный
E 270	even address	gerade Adresse *f*	adresse *f* paire	четный адрес
E 271	even byte	gerades Byte *n* <Byte gerader Adresse innerhalb eines Wortes>	octet *m* pair	четный байт, байт с четным адресом
E 272	even number	gerade Zahl *f*	nombre *m* pair	четное число
E 273	even parity check	geradzahlige Paritätskontrolle *f*	vérification *f* de parité paire	проверка на четность
E 274	event, occurence	Ereignis *n*, Vorgang *m*	événement *m*, occurrence *f*	событие
E 275	event counter	Ereigniszähler *m*	compteur *m* d'événement	счетчик событий
E 276	event-driven	ereignisgesteuert	à commande par événement	управляемый событиями
E 277	event flag	Ereigniskennzeichen *n*	marque *f* d'événement	флаг события
E 278	event identification	Ereigniskennzeichnung *f*	identification *f* d'événement	идентификация события
E 279	evolution	Weiterentwicklung *f*	évolution *f*	эволюция
	EXCEPT	*s.* A 272		
	except gate	*s.* N 1		
E 280/1	exceeding	Überschreitung *f*	dépassement *m*	превышение
E 282	exception	Ausnahme *f*	exception *f*	исключение
E 283	exception condition	Ausnahmebedingung *f*	condition *f* exceptionnelle	исключающее условие
E 284	exception handling	Bearbeitung *f* von Ausnahmebedingungen	traitement *m* d'exceptions	обработка особых случаев
E 285	excess	Überschuß *m*	excès *m*	избыток
E 286	excess-three code	Drei-Exzeß-Kode *m*, Stibitz-Kode *m*	code *m* excès plus trois	код с избытком 3
E 287	exchange / to, to swap	austauschen	échanger	обмениваться
E 288	exchange, switching centre	Vermittlung *f*, Vermittlungsstelle *f* <Nachrichtentechnik>	central *m*	аппаратура обмена; телефонная станция
E 289	exchange, swapping	Austausch *m*	échange *m*	обмен
	exchangeability	*s.* I 316		
	exchangeable	*s.* I 317		
E 290	exchangeable disk storage	Wechselplattenspeicher *m*	mémoire *f* à disques interchangeables	запоминающее устройство со сменными дисками
E 291	exchange buffering	Austauschpufferung *f*	tamponnage *m* d'échange	обменная буферизация
E 292	exchange charge	Austauschladung *f*	charge *f* d'échange	обменный заряд
E 293	exclusive-NOR gate	Exklusiv-NOR-Gatter *n*	porte *f* NON-OU exclusif	схема равнозначности
E 294	exclusive OR, OR-ELSE, XOR	Exklusiv-ODER *n*, ausschließendes ODER *n* <logischer Operator der Antivalenz>	OU exclusif	ИСКЛЮЧАЮЩЕЕ ИЛИ
E 295	exclusive-OR operation	Exklusiv-ODER-Operation *f*	opération *f* OU exclusif	операция ИСКЛЮЧАЮЩЕЕ ИЛИ
E 296	executable	ausführbar	exécutable	выполняемый, исполнительный
E 297	execute / to	ausführen	exécuter	исполнять, выполнять
E 298	execute phase (state)	Ausführungsphase *f*, Ausführungszeitabschnitt *m*	phase *f* d'exécution	фаза исполнения [инструкции]
E 299	execute statement	Ausführungsanweisung *f*	instruction *f* d'exécution	оператор выполнения (шага задания)
E 300	execution cycle, executive cycle	Ausführungszyklus *m*	cycle *m* d'exécution	цикл выполнения [инструкции]
E 301	execution time	Ausführungszeit *f*	temps *m* d'exécution	время выполнения [инструкции]
E 302	execution unit	Ausführungseinheit *f*	unité *f* d'exécution	исполнительное устройство
E 303	executive, executive program (routine)	Exekutivprogramm *n*, Ausführungssteuerprogramm *n*, Ausführungsorganisationsprogramm *n*	programme *m* exécutif, exécutive *f*	исполнительная программа; управляющая программа
E 304	executive control	Exekutivsteuerung *f*, Ausführungssteuerung *f*	commande *f* d'exécution	управление исполнением <программ>
	executive cycle	*s.* E 300		
E 305	executive instruction	Exekutivbefehl *m*, Steuerbefehl *m* für Ausführung	instruction *f* d'exécution	исполнительная инструкция
	executive program	*s.* E 303		
	executive routine	*s.* E 303		
E 306	executive scheduler	Folgesteuerungsprogramm *n*, Ablauforganisationsprogramm *n*	programme *m* de commande de séquence	главный планировщик
E 307	executive system	Ausführungsorganisationssystem *n*	système *m* exécutif	исполнительная система, система управляющих программ
E 308	exercise / to	üben, trainieren	exercer	упражняться, тренировать[ся]
E 309	exit	Austritt *m* <aus einem Programm>	sortie *f* <d'un programme>	выход <из подпрограммы>
E 310	exit connector	Ausgangskonnektor *m* <Programm>	connecteur *m* de sortie	выходной блок объединения <в программе или схеме алгоритма>
E 311	exit decision	Ausgangsentscheidung *f* <Programm>	décision *f* de sortie	решение о выходе <из программы>
	expand / to	*s.* E 328		
E 312	expandability, expansibility, extendibility, extensibility	Erweiterungsfähigkeit *f*, Ausbaufähigkeit *f*	expansibilité *f*, extensibilité *f*	расширяемость
E 313	expandable, extensible	erweiterbar	expansible, extensible	расширяемый
E 314	expander	Erweiterungsbaustein *m*, Erweiterungsmodul *m*	module *m* d'élargissement	расширитель, модуль расширения

E 315	**expander chip**	Erweiterungsschaltkreis *m*	circuit *m* (puce *f*) d'élargissement	схема расширения, микросхема расширителя
	expansibility	*s.* E 312		
E 316	**expansion,** extension	Erweiterung *f*	extension *f*, élargissement *m*	расширение
E 317	**expectation value**	Erwartungswert *m*	valeur *f* attendue	математическое ожидание
E 318	**expected life**	erwartete Lebensdauer *f*	longévité *f* attendue	предполагаемый срок службы
E 319	**expense**	Aufwand *m*, Unkosten *pl*	effort *m*, dépense *f*	расход; цена
E 320	**experimental assembly (set-up)**	Experimentalaufbau *m*, Versuchsaufbau *m*	assemblage *m* expérimental	экспериментальное устройство, макет
E 321	**explicit**	explizit, ausdrücklich	explicite	явный; точный, определенный
E 322	**exponent**	Exponent *m*, Hochzahl *f*	exposant *m*	показатель [степени]; порядок [числа]
E 323	**exponent factor,** exponent key (modifier)	Exponentenfaktor *m*, Exponentenschlüssel *m*	facteur *m* d'exposant	порядковый множитель
E 324	**exponential decrease**	exponentielle Abnahme *f*	diminution *f* exponentielle	экспоненциальное уменьшение
E 325	**exponential distribution**	Exponentialverteilung *f*	distribution *f* exponentielle	экспоненциальное распределение
E 326	**exponential function**	Exponentialfunktion *f*, e-Funktion *f*	fonction *f* exponentielle	экспоненциальная (показательная) функция
	exponent key (modifier)	*s.* E 323		
E 327	**exponent part**	Exponententeil *m* ‹Gleitkommazahl›	partie *f* d'exposant	порядок [числа], разряды порядка
E 328	**extend / to,** to expand	erweitern, ausdehnen	étendre, élargir	расширять
E 329	**extended addressing**	erweiterte Adressierung *f*	adressage *m* élargi	расширенная адресация
E 330	**extended area**	erweiterter Bereich *m*	domaine *m* élargi	расширенная область
E 331	**extended arithmetic**	erweiterte Arithmetik *f*, Zusatzarithmetik *f*	arithmétique *f* élargie (supplémentaire)	расширенная арифметика
	extended binary-coded decimal interchange code	*s.* E 5		
E 332	**extended code**	erweiterter Kode *m*	code *m* élargi	расширенный код
E 333	**extended instruction set**	erweiterter Befehlssatz *m*	jeu *m* élargi d'instructions	расширенный набор инструкций
E 334	**extended-processing unit**	Erweiterungseinheit *f* eines Prozessors	unité *f* d'élargissement d'un processeur	процессор с расширенными функциями
	extendibility	*s.* E 312		
	extensibility	*s.* E 312		
	extensible	*s.* E 313		
	extension	*s.* E 316		
E 335	**extension area**	Erweiterungsbereich *m*	champ *m* d'extension	область расширения
E 336	**extension board**	Verlängerungsplatte *f*	plaque *f* de rallonge	плата расширения
E 337	**extension lead**	Verlängerungsleitung *f*	rallonge *f*	вывод для расширения
E 338	**extension memory**	Erweiterungsspeicher *m*	mémoire *f* d'extension	дополнительная память
E 339	**extension register**	Erweiterungsregister *n*	registre *m* d'extension	регистр расширения
E 340	**extent**	Ausdehnung *f*, Umfang *m*, Belegungsbereich *m*	étendue *f*, volume *m*	экстент, пространство, поле ‹памяти›
E 341	**external bus**	externer Bus *m*, Externbus *m*	bus *m* externe	внешняя шина
E 342	**external clock enable**	externe Taktfreigabe *f*	libération *f* de rythme externe	разрешение внешней синхронизации
E 343	**external clocking**	externe Taktierung *f*	rythme *m* externe	внешняя синхронизация
E 344	**external connection**	Außenanschluß *m*, äußere Verbindung *f*	connexion *f* externe	внешнее соединение
E 345	**external device**	Externgerät *n*	appareil *m* externe	внешнее устройство
E 346	**external disturbance**	äußere Störung *f*	perturbation *f* externe	внешняя помеха
E 347	**external event**	externes (äußeres) Ereignis *n*	événement *m* externe	внешнее событие
E 348	**external interrupt**	externe Unterbrechung *f*	interruption *f* externe	внешнее прерывание
E 349	**external load**	Außenlastwiderstand *m*	charge *f* externe	внешняя нагрузка
E 350	**external magnetic field**	äußeres Magnetfeld *n*	champ *m* magnétique externe	внешнее магнитное поле
E 351	**external representation**	externe Darstellung *f*	représentation *f* externe	внешнее представление
E 352	**external scaling**	externes Untersetzen *n*	démultiplication *f* externe	внешнее преобразование; внешний пересчет
E 353	**external shielding**	äußere Abschirmung *f*	blindage *m* extérieur	внешнее экранирование
E 354	**external signal**	Externsignal *n*	signal *m* externe	внешний сигнал
E 355	**external stack**	externer Kellerspeicher *m*	mémoire-cave *f* externe	внешний стек
E 356	**external storage**	Externspeicher *m*	mémoire *f* externe	внешнее запоминающее устройство
E 357	**external support logic**	externe Hilfslogikschaltung *f* ‹für einen LSI-Schaltkreis›	logique *f* auxiliaire externe	внешняя вспомогательная логика
E 358	**external voltage**	äußere Spannung *f*	tension *f* extérieure	внешнее напряжение
E 359	**extracode**	Zusatzkode *m*	code *m* supplémentaire	экстракод
E 360	**extrapolate / to**	extrapolieren	extrapoler	экстраполировать
E 361	**extremal value**	Extremwert *m*	valeur *f* extrême	экстремум
E 362	**extrinsic conduction**	Störstellenleitung *f*	conduction *f* extrinsèque	несобственная (примесная) проводимость
E 363	**extrinsic semiconductor**	Störstellenhalbleiter *m*	semi-conducteur *m* extrinsèque	несобственный (примесный) полупроводник

F

F 1	**face**	Frontseite *f*, Vorderseite *f*	face *f*	лицевая сторона; плоская поверхность, грань
F 1 a	**FACE,** field-alterable control element	FACE-Schaltkreis *m*, einsatzprogrammierbares Steuerelement *n*, anwenderprogrammierbarer Steuerungsbaustein *m* ‹mikroprogrammiert›	circuit *m* FACE, élément *m* de commande programmable	программируемое пользователем устройство микропрограммного управления
F 1 b	**facsimile,** fax	Bildfunk *m*, Bildtelegrafie *f*	phototélégraphie *f*, téléphotographie *f*	фототелеграфия

F 1c	facsimile transceiver	Faksimileschreiber m ‹Sende-Empfangs-Gerät›	émetteur-récepteur m phototélégraphique	фототелеграфный аппарат (приемопередатчик)
F 1d	factory-programmed memory	herstellerprogrammierter Speicher m ‹Halbleiter-ROM›	mémoire f programmée par le producteur ‹ROM à semiconducteurs›	запоминающая память, программируемая изготовителем
F 1e	factory programming	Herstellerprogrammierung f, Programmierung f durch Hersteller	programmation f du fabricant	программирование изготовителем
F 1f	fail / to	ausfallen	tomber en panne	отказывать
F 1g	fail function	Ausfallfunktion f	fonction f de défaillance	функция отказа
F 1h	fail-safe	ausfallsicher, störsicher	sûr contre perturbations	защищенный от отказов (сбоев)
F 1i	fail-safe system	ausfallsicheres (ausfall-geschütztes) System n	système m sûr contre défaillance	защищенная от оказов система
F 1j	fail-soft system	fehlertolerantes (ausfall-weiches) System n	système m flexible contre perturbations	система с постепенным отказом
F 1k	failure	Ausfall m, Störung f, Fehl-funktion f	défaillance f, panne f, perturbation f	отказ, сбой, неисправность
F 1l	failure condition	Störungszustand m	état m de défaillance	состояние отказов
F 1m	failure logging	Ausfallregistrierung f	enregistrement m de panne	сбор отказов
F 1n	failure prediction	Ausfallvorhersage f	prévision f de panne	предсказание (прогноз) отказов
F 1o	failure rate	Ausfallrate f. Ausfallhäufig-keit f, Fehlerrate f	taux m de panne	частота (интенсивность) отказа
F 1p	failure reason	Ausfallursache f	cause f de panne, origine f de panne	причина отказов
F 1q	failure test	Ausfalltest m	test m de défaillance	тест отказов
F 1r	failure time, fault time	Ausfallzeit f	temps m de panne	время простоя
F 1s	fallback	Ersatzfunktion f ‹im Fehler-fall›	fonction f de réserve	запасная функция
F 1t	falling edge	abfallende Flanke f	flanc m tombant	падающий край
F 2	fall time	Abfallzeit f	temps m de mise au repos	время спада
	FAM	s. F 12		
F 3	family compatibility	Familienkompatibilität f, Familienverträglichkeit f ‹Modellverträglichkeit innerhalb einer Rechner-familie›	compatibilité f de famille	совместимость семейств
F 4	family of characteristics	Kennlinienschar f	ensemble m de caractéristi-ques	семейство характеристик
F 5	family of curves	Kurvenschar f	famille f de courbes	семейство кривых
F 6	FAMOS, floating gate avalanche injection MOS	FAMOS f, MOS-Speicher-elektrodentechnik f mit schwimmendem Gate ‹z. B. für RePROM›	technique f FAMOS, MOS m à électrode à injection	МОП-структура с лавин-ной инжекцией и пла-вающим затвором
F 7	fanfold paper form	Leporello-Papier n, zickzack gefaltetes Formularpapier n	papier m plié en zig-zag	фальцованная бумага
F 8	fan-in	Eingangsfächerung f, Ein-gangslastfaktor m	déploiement m d'entrée	коэффициент объедине-ния по входу
F 9	fanning	Auffächern n	déploiement m	обдув
F 10	fan-out	Ausgangsfächerung f, Aus-gangslastfaktor m	déploiement m à la sortie	коэффициент разветвле-ния по выходу
F 11	fast-access memory	Schnellzugriffsspeicher m, Schnellspeicher m	mémoire f à accès rapide	память с быстрым доступом
F 12	fast auxiliary memory, FAM	schneller Zusatzspeicher m ‹Pufferspeicher›	mémoire f auxiliaire rapide	быстрая вспомогательная память
F 13	fast rise time	kurze Anstiegszeit f	temps m de montée court	малое время нарастания
F 14	fast switching speed	hohe Schaltgeschwindigkeit f	vitesse f de commutation élevée	высокая скорость пере-ключения
F 15	fault	Fehler m ‹technischer›, Defekt m	défaut m	неисправность, ошибка
F 16	fault communication	Fehlerübermittlung f	communication f de défaut	неисправная связь
	fault condition	s. E 219		
	fault detection	s. E 227		
	fault-detection circuitry	s. E 228		
F 17	fault dictionary	Fehlerliste f	liste f de défauts	словарь ошибок
	fault discovery	s. E 227		
F 18	fault-free hardware	fehlerfreie Hardware (Technik) f	technique f sans défaut	исправная аппаратура
	fault indication	s. E 240		
F 19	fault isolation	Fehlerisolierung f	isolement m de défaut	локализация неисправ-ности
	fault loca[liza]tion	s. E 240		
	fault-location program	s. E 241		
	fault monitoring	s. E 220		
F 20	fault population	Fehlerart f	genre m de défaut	совокупность ошибок
	fault rate	s. E 249		
	fault recovery	s. E 250		
F 21	fault register	Fehlerregister n	registre m de défauts	регистр ошибок
	fault report	s. E 251		
	fault search	s. E 253		
	fault time	s. F 1r		
F 22	fault tolerance	Fehlertoleranz f, Fehler-zulässigkeit f	tolérance f de défauts	нечувствительность к от-казам, отказоустой-чивость
F 23	fault-tolerant computer system	fehlertolerantes Rechner-system n	système m de calculateur tolérant des défauts	нечувствительная к от-казам вычислительная система
F 24	faulty element	fehlerhaftes (gestörtes) Element n	élément m défectueux (perturbé)	неисправный (отказав-ший) элемент
F 25	faulty manipulation	fehlerhafte Handhabung f	manipulation f défectueuse	ошибочное действие
F 26	faulty module	fehlerhafter (schadhafter) Modul m	module m défectueux	неисправный (отказав-ший) модуль
	fax	s. F 1b		

F 27	feature / to	aufweisen, kennzeichnen	caractériser, présenter	выделять, характеризовать
F 28	feature	Merkmal n, wesentliche Eigenschaft f, Besonderheit f	propriété f, caractéristique f	особенность, признак; средство
F 29	feed	Zuführung f	acheminement m	подача
F 30	feedback	Rückführung f, Rückfluß m	réaction f	обратная связь
F 31	feedback amplifier	Gegenkopplungsverstärker m	amplificateur m à contre-réaction	усилитель с обратной связью
F 32	feedback channel	Rückführungskanal m	canal m de réaction	канал обратной связи
	feedback control	s. C 277		
F 33	feedback signal	Rückführungssignal n	signal m de réaction	сигнал обратной связи
F 34	feed check	Transportprüfung f	vérification f de transport	контроль подачи
F 35	feed cycle	Zuführungsgang m	cycle m d'acheminement	цикл подачи
F 36	feed forward control	Vorwärtsregelung f	réglage m en avant	прямое управление
F 37	feeding circuit	Speiseschaltung f	circuit m d'alimentation	питающая схема
	feed line	s. S 857		
F 38	ferrite core	Ferritkern m	tore m de ferrite	ферритовый сердечник
F 39	ferroelectric	ferroelektrisch	ferroélectrique	сегнетоэлектрический
F 40	ferromagnetic	ferromagnetisch	ferromagnétique	ферромагнитный
	FET	s. F 51		
F 41	fetch / to	abholen, holen, bringen <Speicherdaten>	apporter	выбирать
F 42	fetch	Abholung f, Bereitstellung f	mise f à disposition	выборка
F 43	fetch cycle	Abholzyklus m, Bereitstellungszyklus m	cycle m de recherche (mise à disposition)	цикл выборки
F 44	fetch phase	Abholphase f, Bringephase f	phase f de recherche	фаза выборки
F 45	fetch state	Abholzustand m, Bringe-zustand m	état m de recherche	состояние выборки
F 46	fibre-optic cable	Faseroptikkabel n, faseroptisches Kabel n, Lichtleiterkabel n	câble m à fibres optiques	волоконно-оптический кабель
F 47	field	Feld n, Gebiet n, Einsatzbereich m	champ m, domaine m	поле
F 48	field-alterable	im Einsatz änderbar, vom Anwender variierbar	variable à l'application, variable par l'usager	изменяемый в эксплуатации, изменяемый пользователем
	field-alterable control element	s. F 1 a		
F 49	field boundary	Feldbegrenzung f	limite f de champ	граница поля
F 50	field definition	Felddefinition f, Feldbestimmung f	définition f de champ	определение поля
F 51	field effect transistor, FET	Feldeffekttransistor m, FET m	transistor m à effet de champ, FET m	полевой транзистор
F 52	field engineer	Wartungsingenieur m, Serviceingenieur m	ingénieur m de service (maintenance)	инженер по эксплуатации
F 53	field installation	Einsatzinstallation f, Vor-Ort-Installation f	installation f sur place (le champ), installation in situ	установка для эксплуатации в полевых условиях
F 54	field length, field width	Feldlänge f	longueur f de champ	длина поля
F 55	field-programmable	im Einsatz programmierbar, vom Anwender programmierbar	programmable à l'application, programmable par l'usager	программируемый в эксплуатации, программируемый пользователем
F 56	field-programmable logic array, FPLA	anwenderprogrammierbare PLA f, FPLA f, einsatzprogrammierbares Logikgatterfeld n	champ m logique programmable par usager	программируемая пользователем логическая матрица
F 57	field-programmable read-only memory	im Einsatz programmierbarer Nur-Lese-Speicher m, anwenderprogrammierbarer ROM m	mémoire f lecture seule programmable à l'application, mémoire lecture seule programmable par l'usager	программируемое пользователем постоянное запоминающее устройство
F 58	field service	Außendienst m, Kundendienst m im Einsatzbereich	service m après-vente, SAV m	эксплуатационное обслуживание
F 59	field test	Einsatztest m, Einsatzerprobung f	test m de mise en œuvre	полевое испытание, испытание в условиях эксплуатации
	field width	s. F 54		
	FIFO ...	= first-in first-out...		
F 60	FIFO memory	FIFO-Speicher m, Silospeicher m <Speicher mit FIFO-Zugriffsprinzip, wobei automatisch das zuerst Gespeicherte beim nächsten Zugriff zuerst ausgelesen wird>	mémoire f FIFO <entré le premier, sorti le premier>	обратный стек, память обратного магазинного типа, память типа FIFO
F 61	FIFO queue	FIFO-Warteschlange f <Datenfolge in einem FIFO-Prinzip-Speicher>	queue f FIFO	очередь, обслуживаемая в соответствии с последовательным алгоритмом, FIFO-очередь
F 62	FIFO register	FIFO-Registerspeicher m <Registerblock nach FIFO-Zugriffsprinzip organisiert>	mémoire f à registre FIFO	регистровая память обратного магазинного типа, FIFO-регистр
F 63	FIFO storage element	FIFO-Speicherbaustein m <mit interner FIFO-Prinzip-Organisation>	élément m de mémoire FIFO	элемент стекового запоминающего устройства типа FIFO
F 64	figure size	Zifferngröße f	grandeur f de chiffres	размер цифр
F 65	file	Datei f, File n	fichier m	файл, массив
F 66	file access	Dateizugriff m	accès m de fichier	доступ к файлу
F 67	file addressing	Dateiadressierung f	adressage m de fichier	адресация файла
F 68	file command	Dateibefehl m	instruction f de fichier	команда обращения к файлу

F 69		file control	Dateisteuerung *f*	commande *f* de fichier	управление файлами
		file control block	*s.* D 114		
F 70		file definition macro	Dateibestimmungsmakro *n*	macro *m* de définition de fichier	макрокоманда определения файла
F 71		file description	Dateierklärung *f*, Dateibeschreibung *f*	description (déclaration) *f* de fichier	описание файла
F 72		file designation	Dateikennzeichnung *f*	désignation *f* de fichier	обозначение файла
		file directory	*s.* D 74		
F 73		file editor	Dateiaufbereiter *m*, Dateiaufbereitungsprogramm *n*	éditeur *m* de fichier	редактор файлов
F 74		file format	Dateiformat *n*	format *m* de fichier	формат файла
F 75		file handling	Dateibearbeitung *f*	travail *m* de fichier	[предварительная] обработка файла
F 76		file header	Dateivorsatz *m*	en-tête *m* de fichier	заголовок файла
F 77		file identification	Dateiidentifizierung *f*, Dateikennung *f*	identification *f* de fichier	идентификация файла
F 78		file label	Dateikennsatz *m*	label *m* de fichier	метка файла
F 79		file maintenance	Dateipflege *f*	maintenance *f* de fichier	обслуживание файла
F 80		file management	Dateiverwaltung *f*	gestion *f* de fichier	управление файлами
F 81		file name	Dateiname *m*	nom *m* (dénomination *f*) de fichier	имя файла
F 82		file opening	Dateieröffnung *f*	ouverture *f* de fichier	открытие файла
F 83		file processing	Dateiverarbeitung *f*	traitement *m* de fichier	обработка файла
F 84		file processor	Fileprozessor *m*, Dateiprozessor *m*	processeur *m* de fichier	процессор управления файлами; программа управления файлами
F 85		file protection	Dateischutz *m*	protection *f* de fichier	защита файла
F 86		file size	Dateigröße *f*	grandeur *f* de fichier	размер файла ⌐файлов
F 87		file store	Dateispeicher *m*	mémoire *f* à (de) fichier	запоминающее устройство
F 88		file structure	Dateiaufbau *m*	structure *f* de fichier	структура файла
F 89		file updating	Dateiaktualisierung *f*	actualisation *f* de fichier	обновление (корректировка) файла
F 90		fill character, pad character	Füllzeichen *n*	caractère *m* de remplissage ⌐final	знак заполнения
F 91		final assembly	Endmontage *f*	montage (assemblage) *m*	окончательная сборка
F 92		final control element	Stellglied *n*	élément *m* final de réglage	исполнительное звено, исполнительный орган
F 93		final inspection	Endprüfung *f*	inspection *f* finale	сдаточное испытание
F 94		final state	Endzustand *m*	état *m* final	конечное состояние
F 95		final value	Endwert *m*	valeur *f* finale	конечное значение
F 96		finite integer	endliche Zahl *f*	nombre *m* fini	ограниченное целое
F 97		finite storage time	begrenzte (endliche) Speicherzeit *f*	temps *m* de mémoire limité	ограниченное время хранения
F 98		firmware	Firmware *f* ‹Bezeichnung für vom Hersteller programmierte und in Festspeichern untergebrachte Strukturlösungen; Mikroprogramme›	firmware *m*	реализованное средствами микропрограммирования специальное программное обеспечение ‹поставляемое изготовителем ЭВМ›
F 99		firmware diagnostic	Firmware-Diagnose *f*, Firmware-Fehlersuche *f*, Diagnose *f* mittels Firmware ‹Mikroprogramm›	diagnostic *m* à l'aide de firmware	реализованное микропрограммно диагностические процедуры
F 100		first-generation microprocessor	Mikroprozessor *m* der ersten [LSI-]Generation	microprocesseur *m* de la première génération [LSI]	микропроцессор первого поколения
		first-in first-out ...	*s.* FIFO ...		
F 101		first-level addressing	Adressierung *f* auf dem ersten Niveau ‹Operandenadresse = Adreßfeldinhalt des Befehls›	adressage *m* au premier niveau	адресация первого уровня
		five-channel code	*s.* C 111		
		five-channel tape	*s.* C 123		
		five-level code	*s.* C 111		
		five-level tape	*s.* C 123		
		five-track code	*s.* C 111		
		five-track tape	*s.* C 123		⌐блока
F 102		fixed block length	konstante Blocklänge *f*	longueur *f* de bloc fixe	фиксированная длина
F 103		fixed costs	Festkosten *pl*, Fixkosten *pl*	coûts *mpl* fixes	фиксированные затраты
		fixed data store	*s.* F 116		
		fixed disk	*s.* F 104		
F 104		fixed-disk device, fixed disk	Festplattenspeicher *m*, Festplattenspeichergerät *n*	appareil *m* à disque fixe, disque *m* fixe	запоминающее устройство с фиксированными дисками
F 105		fixed format	Festformat *n*	format *m* fixe	фиксированный (постоянный) формат
F 106		fixed head	Festkopf *m*, feststehender Magnetkopf *m*	tête *f* fixe	фиксированная головка
F 107		fixed-instruction computer	Rechner *m* mit unveränderlichem Befehlssatz	calculateur *m* à instructions fixes	ЭВМ с фиксированным набором инструкций
F 108		fixed-instruction length	konstante (feste) Befehlslänge *f*	longueur *f* d'instruction fixe	фиксированная длина инструкции
F 109		fixed-length record	Datensatz *m* fester Länge	enregistrement *m* de longueur fixe	запись фиксированной длины
F 110		fixed location, fixed memory location	fester (festgelegter) Speicherplatz *m*	location *f* de mémoire fixe	фиксированная ячейка памяти
		fixed memory	*s.* F 116		
		fixed memory location	*s.* F 110		
F 111		fixed point	Festkomma *n*	virgule *f* fixe	фиксированная запятая
F 112		fixed-point arithmetic	Festkomma-Arithmetik *f*	arithmétique *f* à virgule fixe	арифметика с фиксированной запятой
		fixed-point part	*s.* M 136		
F 113		fixed-point representation	Festkomma-Darstellung *f*	représentation *f* à virgule fixe	представление [чисел] с фиксированной запятой
F 114		fixed program	Festprogramm *n*	programme *m* fixe	фиксированная (постоянная) программа

F 115	fixed-program computer	festprogrammierter Rechner *m*	calculateur *m* à programmation fixe	ЭВМ с фиксированной программой
F 116	fixed storage, fixed memory (data store)	Fest[wert]speicher *m*	mémoire *f* à valeurs fixes	постоянное запоминающее устройство, ЗУ для хранения постоянных величин
F 117	fixed word length	feste Wortlänge *f*	longueur *f* de mot fixe	фиксированная длина слова
F 118	flag, tag, sentinel	Zustandskennzeichen *n*, Zustandsmarke *f*	marque *f* (label *m*) d'état	флаг, признак
F 119	flag bit	Zustandskennzeichenbit *n*	bit *m* de label d'état	флаговый бит
F 120	flag byte	Zustandskennzeichenbyte *n*	octet *m* de label d'état	флаговый байт
F 121	flag manipulation	Flagbehandlung *f*	manipulation *f* de label	действия над флагами
F 122	flat cable	Flachkabel *n*	câble *m* méplat	плоский кабель
F 123	flat-pack	Flachgehäuse *n* <flaches Schaltkreisgehäuse mit Anschlüssen in der Gehäuseebene>	boîtier *m* méplat	размещенное в плоском корпусе [устройство]
F 124	flat-panel display	Flachschirmanzeige *f*	affichage *m* à écran méplat	дисплей с плоским экра- ном
F 125	flexibility	Flexibilität *f*, Vielseitigkeit *f*	flexibilité *f*	гибкость
F 126	flip-flop, bistable multivibrator	Flipflop *n*, bistabile Kippschaltung *f*, bistabiler Multivibrator *m*	bascule *f* électronique	триггер
F 127	flip-flop circuit	Flipflop-Schaltung *f*	circuit *m* de bascule	триггерная схема
F 128	flip-flop register	Flipflop-Register *n*	registre *m* à bascules	регистр на триггерах
F 129	flip-flop storage	Flipflop-Speicher *m*	mémoire *f* à bascules	запоминающее устройство на триггерах
F 130	floating	gleitend, schwimmend <potentialmäßig unbestimmt>	flottant	плавающий
F 131	floating gate	schwimmendes (potentialmäßig freies) Gate *n* <Anwendung als Speicherelektrode>	gate *m* flottant	плавающий затвор
	floating gate avalanche injection MOS	*s.* F 6		
F 132	floating head, flying head	gleitender Magnetkopf (Kopf) *m*	tête *f* [magnétique] volante	плавающая головка
F 133	floating point	Gleitkomma *n*	virgule *f* flottante	плавающая запятая
F 134	floating-point accelerator	Gleitkommarechnungsbeschleuniger *m* <Arithmetikzusatz>	accélérateur *m* de calcul à virgule flottante	дополнительное арифметическое устройство для операций с плавающей запятой, арифметический расширитель для операций с плавающей запятой
F 135	floating-point arithmetic	Gleitkommaarithmetik *f*	arithmétique *f* à virgule flottante	арифметика с плавающей запятой
F 136	floating-point format	Gleitkommaformat *n*	format *m* à virgule flottante	формат [чисел] с плавающей запятой
F 137	floating-point number	Gleitkommazahl *f*	nombre *m* à virgule flottante	число с плавающей запятой
F 138	floating-point operation	Gleitkommaoperation *f*	opération *f* à virgule flottante	операция с плавающей запятой
F 139	floating-point processor, FP processor	Gleitkommaprozessor *m*, GK-Prozessor *m*	processeur *m* à virgule flottante	процессор для [выполнения] операций с плавающей запятой
F 140	floating-point representation	Gleitkommadarstellung *f*	représentation *f* à virgule flottante	представление [чисел] с плавающей запятой
F 141	floating state, high-impedance state, high-Z state	Floating-Zustand *m*, hochohmiger (inaktiver) Zustand *m* <Three-State-Schaltung>	état *m* flottant (à impédance élevée)	высокоимпедансное (третье) состояние
F 142	floor space	Aufstellungsfläche *f*	surface *f* d'installation	площадь под установкой
F 143	floppy disk	Floppy-Disk *m*, Diskettenspeicher *m*, Folienspeicher *m* <flexible, rotierende Magnetfolienscheibe als Speichermedium>	mémoire *f* à disque souple, disque *m* souple	гибкий диск, запоминающее устройство на гибком диске
F 144	floppy disk controller	Folienspeichersteuerung *f*, Diskettenspeichersteuerung *f*	commande *f* de disque souple	контроллер запоминающего устройства на гибких дисках
F 145	floppy disk drive, floppy drive	Floppy-Laufwerk *n*, Diskettenlaufwerk *n*	mécanisme *m* à disque souple	привод памяти на гибких дисках
F 146	floppy disk system floppy drive	Diskettensystem *n* *s.* F 145	système *m* à disque souple	система [памяти] на гибких дисках
F 147	flow chart, flow diagram	Flußdiagramm *n*, Ablaufdarstellung *f*	diagramme *m* de flux, représentation *f* du déroulement	блок-схема
F 148	flow charting	Flußdiagrammtechnik *f*, Programmablaufplanerstellung *f*	technique *f* de diagrammes de flux	составление блок-схем
	flow diagram	*s.* F 147		
	flow direction	*s.* L 319		
F 149	flow line	Flußlinie *f*, Ablauflinie *f*	ligne *f* de flux, ligne d'évolution	линия движения (тока, потока)
F 150	flow-process diagram	Prozeßdiagramm *n*, Prozeßablaufdarstellung *f*	diagramme *m* de processus	блок-схема процесса
F 151	fluorescent display flying head	Fluoreszenzanzeige *f* *s.* F 132	indicateur (affichage) *m* fluorescent	флюоресцентный индикатор
F 152	flying print	fliegender Druck *m*	impression *f* volante	печать летающими литерами
F 153	follower controller	Folgeregler *m*	régulateur *m* de poursuite	контроллер следящего механизма
F 154	force	manuelles Eingreifen *n*	interception *f* manuelle	вмешательство; сила

F 155	forced-air cooling system	Kühlsystem *n* mit Zwangs-belüftung	système *m* de refroidissement à ventilation forcée	система с принудительным воздушным охлаждением
F 156	forced cooling	Zwangskühlung *f*	refroidissement *m* forcé	принудительное охлаждение
F 157	foreground-background mode	Vordergrund-Hintergrund-Betrieb *m* <Mehrfach-programmverarbeitung>	régime *m* de premier plan-arrière plan	основной режим/фоновый режим
F 158	foreground processing	Vordergrundverarbeitung *f*	traitement *m* en premier plan	приоритетная обработка
F 159	foreground program	Vordergrundprogramm *n*	programme *m* de premier plan	приоритетная программа, программа переднего плана
F 160	fork	Mehrfachverzweigung *f*, Gabel *f*	branchement *m* multiple, fourche *f*	разветвление
F 161	form	Formular *n*	formulaire *m*	форма, бланк, формуляр
F 162	format	Format *n*	format *m*	формат
F 163	format code	Formatkode *m*, Format-kennzeichen *n*	code *m* de format	код формата
F 164	format conversion	Formatwandlung *f*	conversion *f* de format	преобразование формата
F 165	format error	Formatfehler *m*	erreur *f* de format	ошибка в формате
F 166	format statement	Formatanweisung *f*	instruction *f* de format	оператор задания формата
F 167	formatted	formatiert, formatgebunden	formaté	форматированный, форматизованный
F 168	formatting form feed	Formatieren *n* *s.* F 169	formatage *m*	задание формата
F 169	form feeding, form feed[out]	Formularvorschub *m*, Papiervorschub *m*	avancement *m* de formu-laire[s] [de papier]	подача бланков (бумаги)
F 170	form feeding device form feedout	Formularvorschubeinrich-tung *f* *s.* F 169	dispositif *m* d'avancement de formulaire[s]	устройство подачи бланков
F 171	formula language	Formelsprache *f*	langage *m* de formules	формульный язык
F 172	formula translation formula translation language	Formelübersetzung *f* *s.* F 174	transposition *f* de formule	преобразование формулы
F 173	form width	Formularbreite *f*	largeur *f* de formulaire[s]	ширина бланка
F 174	FORTRAN, formula translation language	FORTRAN *n*, Formel-übersetzungssprache *f* <höhere Programmier-sprache für technisch-wissenschaftliche Probleme>	FORTRAN *m*	ФОРТРАН <язык высокого уровня для программирования научно-технических задач>
	forward-backward counter	*s.* U 75		
F 175	forward bias	Durchlaßvorspannung *f*	polarisation *f* de passage	прямое смещение
F 176/7	forward current forward direction	Durchlaßstrom *m* *s.* L 319	courant *m* direct	прямой ток
F 178	forward processing	Geradeausverarbeitung *f*	traitement *m* en avant	прямая обработка
F 179	forward spacing four-bit arithmetic four-bit character four-bit data four-bit I/O port four-bit microcomputer four-bit microprocessor four-bit operand four-bit register four-bit-wide I/O port	Vorsetzen *n* *s.* B 164 *s.* B 168 *s.* B 172 *s.* B 176 *s.* B 181 *s.* B 184 *s.* B 188 *s.* B 195 *s.* B 176	espacement *m* en avant	ведущий пробел
F 180	Fourier analysis	Fourier-Analyse *f*	analyse *f* de Fourier	гармонический анализ
F 181	Fourier transformation	Fourier-Transformation *f*	transformation *f* de Fourier	преобразование Фурье
F 182	four-pass compiler	4-Schritt-Kompiler *m*, 4-Schritt-Übersetzer *m* <Programmübersetzung in 4 Durchläufen>	compilateur *m* à quatre pas	четырехпроходный компилятор
	FPLA FP processor fraction	*s.* F 56 *s.* F 139 *s.* M 136		
F 183	frame	Rahmen *m*, Einbaurahmen *m*, Datenblockrahmen *m* <DÜ>	cadre *m*, support *m* de modules	кадр; стойка, рама
F 184	frame connector	ummantelter Mehrkontakt-stecker *m*	connecteur *m* à plusieurs broches enrobé	закрытый разъем
F 185	frame grounding	Gehäuseerdung *f*	mise *f* à terre de boîtier	заземление корпуса
F 186	frame pointer	Bereichszeiger *m*, Sprossen-zeiger *m* <Datenreferenz-register>	pointeur *m* de champ	указатель области
F 187	free-form	formatfrei	sans format	произвольной формы; произвольного формата
F 188	free-programmable control	freiprogrammierbare Steuerung *f*	commande *f* librement programmable	гибко программируемое управление
F 189	frequency modulation	Frequenzmodulation *f*	modulation *f* de fréquence	частотная модуляция
F 190	frequency response	Frequenzgang *m*	réponse *f* harmonique	частотная характеристика
F 191	FROM, fusable ROM, fuse-link programmable ROM	schmelzverbindungspro-grammierbarer ROM *m*, Ausbrenn-ROM *m* <ein-malig programmierbarer ROM>	mémoire *f* lecture seule programmable à fusibles	программируемое током постоянное запоминающее устройство, программируемое постоянное запоминающее устройство с плавкими перемычками
F 192	FROM programmer	Programmiergerät *n* für FROM-Schaltkreise	appareil *m* de programma-tion pour circuits FROM	программатор для постоянных запоминающих устройств, программируемых током
	front edge	*s.* L 64		
F 193	front end	Eingangsseite *f*	côté *m* d'entrée	место входа, передний край

F 194	front-end preprocessing	Eingangsvorverarbeitung f, vorgeschaltete Vorverarbeitung f	prétraitement m d'entrée	предварительная обработка на переднем крае ‹в сетях ЭВМ›
F 195	front-end processor	Eingangsprozessor m, Vorschaltrechner m ⌐feld n	processeur m de prétraitement	фронтальный процессор, процессор переднего края
F 196	front panel	Frontplatte f, Frontbedien-	panneau m frontal	передняя панель
F 197	full adder	Volladdierer m	addeur m complet	полный сумматор
F 198	full-automatic equipment	vollautomatische Einrichtung f	dispositif m entièrement automatique	полностью автоматизированное оборудование
F 199	full-compatible processor	vollkompatibler Prozessor m	processeur m entièrement compatible	полностью совместимый процессор
F 200	full-duplex	vollduplex	duplex entier	дуплексный
F 201	full-duplex communication line	Vollduplexübertragungsleitung f	ligne f de communication duplex	дуплексная линия связи
F 202	full-duplex transmission system	Vollduplexübertragungssystem n	système m de transmission duplex	дуплексная система передачи [данных]
F 203	full-fledged computer	fertiger (kompletter) Rechner m	calculateur m complet	полностью законченная (укомплектованная) ЭВМ
F 204	full-integrated single-chip circuit	vollintegrierte Ein-Chip-Schaltung f	circuit m entièrement intégré sur une puce	полностью интегрированная однокристальная схема
F 205	full load	Vollast f, Vollbelastung f	pleine charge f	полная нагрузка
F 206	fully documented	vollständig dokumentiert	complètement documenté	полностью документированный
F 207	fully equipped	voll bestückt (ausgestattet)	complètement équipé	полностью оборудованный
F 208	functional characteristics	Funktionskennwerte mpl	caractéristiques fpl fonctionnelles	функциональные характеристики
F 209	functional description	Funktionsbeschreibung f	description f de fonctionnement	описание работы (функционирования)
F 210	functional design	[logisch-]funktioneller Entwurf m	conception f fonctionnelle	функциональное проектирование
F 211	functional diagram	Funktionsplan m, Funktionsgruppen-Blockdiagramm n	diagramme m de fonctionnement	функциональная схема
F 212	functional flowchart	funktionelles Flußdiagramm n, funktioneller Ablaufplan m ⌐lung f	diagramme m de déroulement fonctionnel	функциональная схема ⌐вание
F 213	functional interleaving	funktionelle Verschachte-	encastrement m fonctionnel	функциональное чередо-
F 214	functionality	Zweckmäßigkeit f	convenance f, utilité f	функциональность
F 215	functionally divided multi-microprocessor system	funktionell geteiltes Multimikroprozessorsystem n	système m de microprocesseurs multiples à découpage de fonctions	мультимикропроцессорная система с функциональным разделением
F 216	functional module	Funktionsmodul m	module m fonctionnel	функциональный модуль
F 217	functional organization	Funktionsorganisation f	organisation f fonctionnelle	функциональная организация
F 218	functional overview	Funktionsübersicht f	vue f synoptique de fonctionnement	обзор функциональных возможностей
F 219	functional partitioning	funktionelle Teilung f ‹Arbeitsteilung›	partage m fonctionnel	функциональное разделение ⌐вания
F 220	functional requirements	funktionale Forderungen fpl	exigences fpl fonctionnelles	функциональные требования
F 221	functional test	Funktionstest m	test m fonctionnel	функциональная проверка
	functional unit	s. F 228		
F 222	function bit	Funktionsbit n	bit m de fonction	функциональный бит
F 223	function code	Funktionskode m	code m de fonction	код функции
F 224	function element	Funktionselement n	élément m de fonction	функциональный элемент
F 225	function generator	Funktionsgeber m, Funktionsgenerator m	générateur m de fonction	функциональный генератор
F 226	function key	Funktionstaste f	touche f fonctionnelle	функциональная клавиша
F 227	function table	Funktionstafel f ⌐unit	table f de fonctions	таблица функции; функциональная таблица
F 228	function unit, functional fusable ROM	Funktionseinheit f s. F 191	unité f fonctionnelle	функциональное устройство
F 229	fuse	Schmelzsicherung f	fusible m	плавкий предохранитель ‹в программируемом постоянном запоминающем устройстве›
F 230	fuse link	Schmelzverbindung f, aufschmelzbare Verbindung f, Schmelzeinsatz m	liaison f fusible	плавкая перемычка
	fuse-link programmable ROM	s. F 191		

G

G 1	GaAs logic, gallium-arsenide logic	GaAs-Logik f, Gallium-Arsenid-Schaltungstechnik f	logique f Ga-As	логические схемы на основе арсенида галлия
G 2	gain	Gewinn m, Zuwachs m	gain m	усиление
G 3	gain adjustment	Verstärkungsnachstellung f	ajustement m de gain	подстройка усиления
G 4	gain-bandwidth product	Verstärkung-Bandbreite-Produkt n	produit m gain — largeur de bande ⌐tion	добротность ‹произведение коэффициента усиления на ширину полосы пропускания›
G 5	gain characteristic	Verstärkungskennlinie f	caractéristique f d'amplifica-	характеристика усиления
G 6	gain control	Verstärkungsregelung f	réglage m de gain	регулировка усиления
G 7	gain range	Verstärkungsbereich m	champ m d'amplification	диапазон усиления
	gallium-arsenide logic	s. G 1		
G 8	gap digit	Füllziffer f	chiffre m de remplissage	знак пробела
G 9	gap width	Spaltbreite f	largeur f d'interstice	ширина зазора
G 10	garbage, hash	sinnlose Information f, Informationsmüll m, Müll m	information f insensée	устаревшие (ненужные) данные

G 11	garbled information	verstümmelte Information f	information f mutilée	искаженная информация
G 12	gas discharge display	Gasentladungsanzeige f	affichage m à décharge au gaz	газоразрядный индикатор
G 13	gate ‹logic›, gate (gating) circuit	Gatter n, Verknüpfungs-schaltung f, Ausblend-schaltung f, Torschaltung f	gate m, élément m logique de commutation	вентиль; стробируемая схема; стробирующая схема
G 14	gate ‹transistor›	Steuerelektrode f, Gate n	gate m	затвор
G 15	gate array	Gatterfeld n ‹reguläre Anordnung›	champ m de porte	вентильная матрица
G 16	gate array approach	Gatterfeldlösung f ‹Schal-tungsrealisierung mittels regulärer Gatteranord-nung›	solution f de champ de gate	реализация схем на основе вентильных матриц
G 17	gate bias gate circuit	Gate-Vorspannung f s. G 13	polarisation f de gate	смещение затвора
G 18	gate current	Gate-Strom m ‹Steuer-elektrodenstrom›	courant m de gate	ток затвора
G 19	gate delay	Gatterverzögerung f	retardement m de gate	задержка [переключения] вентиля
G 20	gate electrode	Gate-Elektrode f ‹Steuer-elektrode eines Feld-effekttransistors›	électrode f de gate	электрод затвора
G 21	gate insulation (iso-lation)	Gate-Isolierung f	isolement m de gate	изоляция затвора
G 22	gate lead	Gate-Zuleitung f	fil m de gate	вывод затвора
G 23	gate level	Logikgatter-Entwurfs-niveau n, Logikgatter-Niveau n	niveau m de développement de porte	уровень [развития] цифровых схем
G 24	gate-oxide thickness	Gate-Oxiddicke f	épaisseur f gate-oxyde	толщина [слоя] окисла под затвором
G 25	gate positioning	Gatterpositionierung f, Gatteranordnung f	positionnement m de porte	размещение вентилей
G 26	gate pulse	Gatterfreigabeimpuls m, Auftastimpuls m	impulsion f de déblocage (gate, libération)	стробирующий импульс, стробимпульс, строб
G 27	gate signal	Gatterfreigabesignal n, Tor-signal n, Auftastsignal n	signal m de déblocage (gate, porte)	стробирующий (отпираю-щий) сигнал
G 28	gate structure	Gatterstruktur f	structure f de porte	структура вентиля
G 29	gate terminal	Gate-Anschluß m	raccordement m de gate	контакт затвора
G 30	gate time	Gatterlaufzeit f, Gatter-durchschaltzeit f	temps m de commutation de porte	время переключения вентиля
G 31	gate-to-pin ratio	Gatter-Anschlußstift-Ver-hältnis n ‹Packungskenn-wert eines LSI-Schalt-kreises›	rapport m gate/broche	отношение числа вентилей к числу внешних выво-дов [микросхемы]
G 32	gate voltage	Gate-Spannung f ‹Steuer-elektrodenspannung›	tension f de gate	напряжение на затворе
G 33	gathering	Erfassen n, Sammeln n	saisie f, acquisition f	сбор, накопление
G 34	gating	Durchschaltsteuerung f, Ausblenden n	commande f de commu-tation, éclipsage m	стробирование, пропус-кание
	gating circuit	s. G 13		
G 35	gating pulse	Durchschaltimpuls m, Tor-impuls m	impulsion f de porte	импульс совпадения, стробирующий импульс
G 36	general chart	Übersichtsblatt n	fiche f de vue d'ensemble, fiche synoptique	общая схема
G 37	general expense	Gemeinkosten pl	dépenses fpl générales	общий расход
G 38	generalized micropro-cessor architecture	verallgemeinerte Mikro-prozessorstruktur f	structure f de micropro-cesseur généralisée	обобщенная структура микропроцессора
G 39	general-purpose application	Universalanwendung f	application f universelle	универсальное применение
G 40	general-purpose com-puter, all-purpose com-puter	Universalrechner m, All-zweckrechner m	calculateur m universel	универсальная ЭВМ
G 41	general-purpose inter-face	Universalschnittstelle f, Universalanschluß m	interface f universelle	универсальный интерфейс
G 42	general-purpose micro-computer system	universelles Mikrorechner-system n	système m universel de microcalculateur[s]	универсальная микро-ЭВМ
G 43	general-purpose micro-processor	universell ausgelegter Mikroprozessor m, Mehr-zweck-Mikroprozessor m	microprocesseur m universel	универсальный микро-процессор
	general-purpose register	s. G 44		
G 44	general register, general-purpose register	Universalregister n, Mehr-zweckregister n, all-gemeines Register n	registre m universel (général)	регистр общего назначе-ния
G 45	general-register architecture	Universalregisterstruktur f, auf Universalregistern aufbauende Struktur f	structure f à registres généraux	архитектура, базирую-щаяся на регистрах общего назначения
G 46	general reset	allgemeines Rücksetzen n, Rücksetzen der Gesamt-anlage	remise f totale	общий сброс, общая установка в нуль
G 47	general routine	allgemeines (universelles) Programm n	programme m universel	универсальная программа
	general storage	s. M 113		
G 48	generate / to	generieren, erzeugen	générer, engendrer, créer	генерировать, произво-дить, создавать
G 49	generated address	berechnete Adresse f	adresse f générée (calculée)	сформированный (испол-нительный) адрес
G 50	generating program, generator	generierendes Programm n, [programm]erzeugendes Programm, Programm-generator m, Generator m	programme m de généra-tion, générateur m [de programmes]	программа-генератор, генерирующая про-грамма
G 51	generation	Generierung f, Erzeugung f	génération f, création f	генерация, генерирование
G 52	generation	Generation f ‹Entwicklungs-kettenglied›	génération f ‹membre d'une chaîne d'évolution›	поколение
	generator	s. G 50		

G 53	**glass substrate**	Glasunterlage f, Glas-substrat n	substrat[um] m de verre	стеклянная подложка
G 54	**global symbol**	globales Symbol n <Pro-grammiersprache>	symbole m global	глобальный символ
G 55	**global variable**	globale Variable f	variable f globale	глобальная переменная
G 56	**gold-doped**	golddotiert	dopé à l'or	легированный золотом
G 57	**gold-plated plug**	goldplattierter Stecker m	fiche f plaquée d'or	позолоченный разъем
	grant	s. C 464		
G 58	**graph**	Schaubild n, Graph m, Schema n	image f, schéma m, graphe m	график, диаграмма; граф
G 59	**graphic character**	Grafikzeichen n, grafisches Zeichen n	caractère m graphique	графический знак (сим-вол)
G 60	**graphic communication**	grafische Informationsaus-tausch m	communication f graphique	передача графической информации
G 61	**graphic data**	grafische Daten pl, Grafik-daten pl	données fpl graphiques	графические данные
G 62	**graphic data processing**	grafische Datenverarbeitung f, Verarbeitung f grafi-scher Informationen	traitement m d'informations graphiques	обработка графической информации
G 63	**graphic display**	grafisches Display (Sicht-anzeigegerät) n	appareil m de visualisation graphique	графический дисплей
G 64	**graphic information**	grafische Information f	information f graphique	графическая информация
G 65	**graphic input-output**	grafische Eingabe-Ausgabe f	entrée-sortie f graphique	графический ввод-вывод
G 66	**graphic-oriented I/O device**	grafisch orientiertes E/A-Gerät n	appareil m d'E/S graphique	устройство графического ввода-вывода
G 67	**graphic panel**	grafisches Anzeigefeld n, Blindschaltbildtafel f	panneau m graphique	панель индикации графи-ческих данных
G 68	**graphic plotter**	Grafikschreiber m	traceur m graphique	графопостроитель
G 69	**graphic representation**	grafische Darstellung f	représentation f graphique	графическое представ-ление
G 70	**graphic terminal**	Grafikterminal n, grafisches Endgerät n	terminal m graphique	графический терминал
G 71	**grid, raster**	Gitter n, Raster m	grille f, trame f	сетка, растр
G 72	**grid board, raster board**	Rasterplatte f, Rasterleiter-platte f	platine f à grille (trame)	плата с координатной сеткой
G 73	**ground connection**	Masseverbindung f	connexion f de masse	соединение с «землей»
	grounding	s. E 4		
G 74	**ground level**	Grundniveau n, Null-potential n	niveau (potentiel) m de base	нулевой потенциал
G 75	**ground loop**	Erdschleife f, Masseschleife f	boucle f de terre (masse)	цепь возврата [тока] через «землю»
G 76	**ground state**	Grundzustand m	état m de base	основное состояние
G 77	**group code**	Gruppenkode m	code m de groupe	групповой код
G 78	**group item**	Gruppenposten m, Daten-gruppe f	groupe m de données, lot m de groupe	групповое звено данных
G 79	**group mark**	Gruppenmarke f	marque f de groupe	маркер группы
G 80	**grown-diffused tran-sistor**	gezogener Diffusions-flächentransistor m	transistor m à diffusion tiré	тянутый диффузионный транзистор
G 81	**grown junction**	gezogener Zonenübergang m, gezogene Schicht f	jonction f tirée	выращенный (тянутый) переход
G 82	**grown-junction tran-sistor**	gezogener Flächentransistor m	transistor m à jonction tirée	тянутый транзистор, тран-зистор с выращенными переходами
	growth of crystals	s. C 851		
G 83	**guard bit**	Schutzbit n	bit m de protection (garde)	вспомогательный разряд
G 84	**guard digit**	Schutzziffer f	chiffre m de protection (garde)	вспомогательная цифра
	guard ring	s. I 520		
G 85	**guideline**	Richtlinie f	directive f, ligne f de conduite	направляющая линия
G 86	**gulp**	kurze Bytegruppe f, „Schluck" m	groupe m d'octets court, «gorgée » f	группа байтов данных

H

H 1	**half-adder**	Halbadder m	demi-addeur m	полусумматор
H 2	**half-adjust**	aufgerundet <um halben Stellenwert>	arrondi <de la moitié>	округленный до поло-вины младшего знача-щего разряда
H 3	**half-carry**	Halbbyte-Übertrag m <BCD-Arithmetik in 8-Bit-Mikrorechnern>	retenue f de demi-octet	перенос из полубайта
H 4	**half-cycle**	Halbperiode f	demi-période f	полупериод
H 5	**half-duplex channel**	Halbduplexkanal m	canal m demi-duplex	полудуплексный канал
H 6	**half-duplex circuit**	Halbduplexverbindung f	circuit m demi-duplex	полудуплексная схема
H 7	**half-duplex operation**	Halbduplexbetrieb m <nur jeweils in 1 Richtung>	régime m demi-duplex (mi-duplex)	полудуплексный режим
H 8	**half-duplex trans-mission system**	Halbduplex-Übertragungs-system n	système m de transmission mi-duplex	полудуплексная система передачи [данных]
H 9	**half sum**	Halbsumme f	demi-somme f	полусумма
H 10	**half-wave rectifier**	Einweggleichrichter m	redresseur m demi-onde	однополупериодный выпрямитель
H 11	**half word**	Halbwort n	demi-mot m	полуслово
H 12	**halt, stop, hold**	Halt m, Stopp m	arrêt m, halte f, stop m	останов
H 13	**halt instruction, hold instruction**	Haltbefehl m, Stoppbefehl m	instruction f de halte (stop), instruction d'arrêt	команда останова
H 14	**Hamming code**	Hamming-Kode m <Fehler-korrekturkode>	code m Hamming	код Хэмминга
H 15	**Hamming distance**	Hamming-Abstand m	distance f de Hamming	хэммингово расстояние
H 16	**hand assembly**	Handassemblierung f, Pro-grammübersetzung f von Hand	assemblage m manuel	ассемблирование вручную
H 17	**hand-hold device**	Handgerät n <in der Hand zu haltendes Gerät>	appareil m manuel	портативный (переносный) прибор
H 18	**handle / to**	handhaben, bearbeiten, behandeln	manipuler, traiter, travailler	обрабатывать; опериро-вать, манипулировать

H 19	**handling,** manipulating, manipulation	Handhabung *f*, Behandlung *f*, Bearbeitung *f*	manipulation *f*, traitement *m*	оперирование, манипуляция; обработка
H 20	**handling aids**	Handhabungshilfen *fpl*, Bearbeitungshilfen *fpl*	aides *fpl* de traitement (manipulation)	средства обработки (манипулирования)
H 21	**handling condition**	Arbeitsbedingung *f*	condition *f* de travail	режим работы
H 22	**handprinting**	Druckschriftschreiben *n*, Blockschriftschreiben *n* s. M 143	écriture *f* en lettres d'imprimerie	написание типографского шрифта
H 23/4	**hand punch** **handshake**	Quittierung *f*	quittance *f*	⌐вание подтверждение, квитиро-
H 25	**handshake control**	Steuerung *f* auf Quittungsbasis	commande *f* sur base de quittances	асинхронное управление [с подтверждением]
H 26	**handshake I/O control**	Quittungsbetrieb-E/A-Steuerung *f*	commande *f* d'E/S en régime de quittance	асинхронное управление устройствами ввода-вывода [с подтверждением]
H 27	**handshake mode**	Quittungsbetriebsart *f*	mode *m* de régime à quittance	режим асинхронного взаимодействия [двух устройств] с подтверждением
H 28	**handshaking**	Synchronisationsimpuls-austausch *m*, Quittungsbetrieb *m*	échange *m* d'impulsions de synchronisation, régime *m* de quittance	асинхронное взаимодействие [двух устройств] с подтверждением; взаимный обмен сигналами управления
H 29	**handwriting recognition**	Handschrifterkennung *f*	reconnaissance *f* d'écriture	распознавание рукописного текста
H 30	**hang-up**	Ablaufblockierung *f*, unprogrammierter Programmstopp *m*	arrêt *m* de programme non programmé, blocage *m* de déroulement	незапланированный останов, зависание программы
H 31	**hardcopy**	Hartkopie *f*, Druckkopie *f*	copie *f* imprimée	твердая копия, машинный документ
H 32	**hardcopy output**	Hartkopieausgabe *f* <Klarschriftausgabe auf Papier parallel zur Informationsumsetzung in Maschinenkode>	sortie *f* de copie <sortie en écriture lisible sur papier en parallèle à la conversion d'informations en code machine>	получение твердой копии, вывод на печать
H 33	**hardcopy terminal**	Hartkopieterminal *n* <im Gegensatz zum Bildschirmterminal>	terminal *m* à hard copy	терминал с возможностью получения твердой копии
H 34	**hard disk**	Kleinplattenspeicher *m* mit Festplatte <im Gegensatz zu Floppy-Disk>	disque *m* rigide	жесткий диск
H 35	**hardware**	Hardware *f*, Gerätetechnik *f*, materieller Rechnersystemanteil *m*	matériel *m*, hardware *m*	аппаратура, аппаратные (технические) средства
H 36	**hardware assembler**	Hardware-Assembler *m* <1. im Mikrorechner selbst gespeicherter Assembler; 2. PROM-Belegungsmuster erzeugender Assembler>	assembleur *m* hardware <1. assembleur en mémoire du microcalculateur même; 2. assembleur produisant l'occupation de PROM>	аппаратный ассемблер <ассемблер, записанный в программируемое постоянное запоминающее устройство>
H 37	**hardware capability**	Hardware-Fähigkeit *f*, Fähigkeit *f* der technischen Ausstattung	faculté *f* de matériel	возможности технических средств
H 38	**hardware compatibility**	Hardware-Kompatibilität *f*, Verträglichkeit *f* der Gerätetechnik	compatibilité *f* de matériel	аппаратурная совместимость, совместимость аппаратуры
H 39	**hardware configuration**	Hardware-Konfiguration *f*, Konfiguration *f* der Gerätetechnik	configuration *f* de matériel	конфигурация аппаратных средств
H 40	**hardware cost**	Hardware-Kosten *pl*, Gerätetechnikkosten *pl*	coûts *mpl* de matériel	стоимость аппаратуры
H 41	**hardware division**	Divisionsrealisierung *f* mittels Hardware, verdrahtete Division *f*	division *f* par matériel	аппаратная реализация деления
H 42	**hardware failure**	Hardware-Ausfall *m*, Gerätetechnikausfall *m*	défaillance *f* de matériel	отказ аппаратуры
H 43	**hardware fault**	Hardware-Fehler *m*, Gerätetechnikfehler *m*	défaut *m* de matériel	аппаратурная ошибка
H 44	**hardware-implemented**	gerätetechnisch realisiert	réalisé par matériel	аппаратно реализованный
H 45	**hardware interface**	Hardware-Schnittstelle *f*, Gerätetechnikschnittstelle *f*	interface *f* de matériel	аппаратный интерфейс
H 46	**hardware-interrupt**	Hardware-Unterbrechung *f*, gerätetechnisch ausgelöste Unterbrechung *f*	interruption *f* par matériel	прерывание от технических средств
H 47	**hardware multiplication**	Multiplikationsrealisierung *f* mittels Hardware, verdrahtete Multiplikation *f*	multiplication *f* par matériel	аппаратная реализация умножения
H 48	**hardware multiply/ divide**	Hardware-Multiplikation / Division *f*, verdrahtete Multiplikation/Division *f*	multiplication / division *f* par matériel	аппаратное умножение-деление
H 49	**hardware priority interrupts**	Interruptprioritätsstaffelung *f* durch Hardware, verdrahtetes Interruptprioritätssystem (Vorrangunterbrechungssystem) *n*	système *m* d'interruptions à priorité par matériel	система прерываний с аппаратно реализуемыми приоритетами; аппаратная реализация обработки приоритетных прерываний
H 50	**hardware redundancy testing,** hardware-redundant testing	Testung *f* mittels Hardware-Redundanz	test *m* à l'aide de redondance de matériel	метод контроля с помощью введенной аппаратурной избыточности
H 51	**hardware-software tradeoffs**	Hardware-Software-Abstimmung *f*, Abwägung *f* zwischen Hardware- und	accord *m* entre matériel et logiciels	соотношение аппаратных и программных средств, разделение функций

and still: H 51		Software-Realisierung		между аппаратурой и программами
H 52	**hardwired**	festverdrahtet	à montage fixe	монтажный, проводной, запаянный
H 53	**hardwired address**	verdrahtete Adresse *f*, durch Verdrahtung festgelegte Adresse	adresse *f* connectée	проводной адрес, «запаянный» адрес
H 54	**hardwired control**	festverdrahtete Steuerung *f*	commande *f* à montage fixe	«жесткое» управление, непрограммное управление
H 55	**hardwired logic**	festverdrahtete Logik *f* <Gegensatz: programmierbare Logik>	logique *f* connectée	жесткая логика, «запаянная» логика
H 56	**harmonic**	Oberwelle *f*, Harmonische *f*	harmonique *f*	гармоника
H 57	**Harvard-machine architecture**	Harvard-Rechnerstrukturprinzip *n* <Trennung des Programmspeichers vom Datenspeicher>	structure *f* de calculateur Harvard	гарвардская архитектура вычислительной машины <архитектура вычислительной машины с разделением памяти программ и памяти данных>
	hash **HDLC**	*s.* G 10 *s.* H 91		
H 58	**header** header header card	Leitvermerk *m*, Kopfteil *n* *s. a.* H 60 *s.* L 63	en-tête *m*	заголовок
H 59	**header line**	Kopfzeile *f*	ligne *f* d'en-tête	строка заголовка
H 60	**header record**, header	Kopfsatz *m*, Vorsatz *m*	enregistrement *m* d'en-tête	запись заголовка
H 61	**header segment**	Kopfsegment *n*, Vorlaufsegment *n*	segment *m* de tête	сегмент заголовка
H 62	**head gap**	Kopfluftspalt *m*, Kopf-Speichermedium-Luftspalt *m*	entrefer *m* [de tête]	зазор [магнитной] головки; зазор между магнитной головкой и носителем
H 63	**heading**	Überschrift *f*	titre *m*	рубрика
H 64	**head movement**	Kopfbewegung *f*, Lese-Schreib-Kopfbewegung *f*	mouvement *m* de tête [de lecture-écriture]	перемещение головки
H 65	**head positioning**	Kopfpositionierung *f*	positionnement *m* de tête	позиционирование головки
H 66	**head stack**	Magnetkopfgruppe *f*, Mehrspurmagnetkopf *m*	groupe *m* de têtes magnétiques, tête *f* magnétique à plusieurs pistes	пакет [магнитных] головок
H 67	**heat balance**	Wärmebilanz *f*	bilan *m* thermique	тепловой баланс
H 68	**heat dissipation**	Wärmeabgabe *f*, Wärmeabstrahlung *f*	dissipation *f* de chaleur	рассеяние тепла
H 69	**heat-sinked package**	Wärmeabführgehäuse *n*, Schaltkreisgehäuse *n* mit Kühlvorrichtung	boîtier *m* à circuits à dispositif de refroidissement	корпус с теплоотводом
H 70	**hermetically sealed package**	hermetisch verschlossenes Gehäuse *n*	boîtier *m* fermé hermétiquement	герметизированный корпус
H 71	**hermetical seal**	hermetischer Verschluß *m*	fermeture *f* hermétique	герметическое уплотнение
H 72	**heuristic program (routine)**	heuristisches Programm *n*	programme *m* heuristique	эвристическая программа
H 73	**hexadecimal**, sedecimal	hexadezimal, sedezimal	hexadécimal	шестнадцатеричный
H 74	**hexadecimal code**	Hexadezimalkode *m* <Zahlenkode zur Basis 16>	code *m* hexadécimal	шестнадцатеричный код
H 75	**hexadecimal keyboard**	Hexadezimaltastatur *f*	clavier *m* hexadécimal	шестнадцатеричная клавиатура
H 76	**hexadecimal number system**	hexadezimales Zahlensystem *n*, Hexadezimalsystem *n*, Sedezimalsystem *n*	système *m* de nombres hexadécimaux	шестнадцатеричная система счисления
H 77	**hierarchically structured design**	hierarchisch strukturierter Entwurf *m*	conception *f* à structure hiérarchique	иерархически структурированное проектирование
H 78	**hierarchical system**	hierarchisch aufgebautes System *n*, Hierarchiesystem *n*	système *m* hiérarchique	иерархическая система
H 79	**hierarchy**	Rangordnung *f*, Hierarchie *f*	hiérarchie *f*	иерархия
	hierarchy of memories	*s.* M 274		
H 80	**high-active signal,** active-high signal	high-aktives Signal *n*, obenaktives Signal, Signal aktiv im oberen Zustand	signal *m* actif en état supérieur	сигнал, активный при высоком уровне [напряжения]
H 81	**high-capacity storage**	Großraumspeicher *m*	mémoire *f* de grande capacité	запоминающее устройство большой емкости
H 82	**high-density circuit technique**	hochdichte Schaltungstechnik *f*	technique *f* de circuits à haute densité	технология схем с высокой плотностью упаковки
	high-density n-channel silicon-gate MOS technology	*s.* H 126		
H 83	**high-density storage**	hochdichte Speicherung *f*	mémoire *f* à haute densité	запоминающее устройство с высокой плотностью записи
H 84	**high-end microcomputer**	Mikrorechner *m* für das obere Ende des Anforderungsspektrums	microcalculateur *m* supérieur (haut de gamme)	микро-ЭВМ, удовлетворяющая наиболее высоким требованиям
H 85	**highest-priority interrupt**	Interrupt *m* höchster Priorität, Unterbrechung *f* höchster Priorität	interruption *f* de priorité la plus haute	прерывание с высшим приоритетом
H 86	**high-gain amplifier**	Verstärker *m* mit großem Verstärkungsfaktor	amplificateur *m* à gain élevé	усилитель с высоким коэффициентом усиления
H 87	**high-grade component**	hochwertiges Bauteil *n*	composant *m* de degré élevé	высокоуровневый компонент
H 88	**high-impedance output** **high-impedance state**	hochohmiger Ausgang *m* *s.* F 141	sortie *f* à impédance élevée	высокоимпедансный выход

H 89	high input impedance	hoher Eingangswiderstand *m*	impédance *f* d'entrée élevée	высокий входной импеданс
H 90	high level	hoher Pegel *m*, oberes Niveau *n* <Schaltungslogik>	niveau *m* élevé (supérieur)	высокий уровень
H 91	high-level data-link control, HDLC	Hochpegel-Datenleitungssteuerung *f*	commande *f* de liaison de données de niveau élevé	высокоуровневое управление каналами передачи данных, протокол HDLC
H 92	high-level language, HLL	höhere Programmiersprache *f*, HPS *f*	langage *m* de niveau élevé	язык высокого уровня
H 93	high-level logic	Großpegel-Logik *f*, Logikschaltung *f* mit großem Schaltpegel <Störsicherheit>	logique *f* de niveau élevé	логические схемы с высокими уровнями переключения <схемы с повышенной помехоустойчивостью>
H 94	high-level signal	Signal *n* mit hohem Pegel	signal *m* de niveau élevé	сигнал высокого уровня
H 95	high-level software	Programme *npl* (Software *f*) für höhere Programmiersprachen	logiciels *mpl* pour langages de niveau élevé	программное обеспечение на языке высокого уровня
H 96	highlighting display	hervorhebendes Anzeigen *n*	affichage *m* prononcé	дисплей с возможностью выделения заданной информации светотехническими способами
H 97	high-low bias check	Test *m* bei Randwerten der Betriebsspannung	test *m* à des valeurs limites de tension de service	контроль работоспособности при предельных изменениях рабочих параметров
	high-low transition	s. H 122		
H 98	highly doped	hoch dotiert	hautement doté (dopé)	высоколегированный
	high noise immunity logic	s. H 123		
H 99	high-order bit	höchstwertiges Bit *n*, Bit höchsten Stellenwertes <linkes Bit>	bit *m* de valeur supérieure <bit gauche>	бит старшего разряда
H 100	high-order portion	höchstwertiger Teil *m*	partie *f* de valeur supérieure	старшая часть
H 101	high-order position	höchstwertige Stelle *f*	position *f* de valeur supérieure	старший разряд
H 102	high-order zeros	obere Nullen *fpl*	zéros *mpl* supérieurs	нули в старших разрядах, незначащие нули
	high-performance MOS	s. H 125		
	high-performance n-channel MOS technology	s. H 125		
H 103	high-power MOSFET	Hochleistungs-MOSFET *m*, Hochleistungs-MOS-Feldeffekttransistor *m*	MOSFET *m* de performance élevée	мощный МОП-транзистор
H 104	high-precision quartz oscillator	hochpräziser Quarzoszillator *m*, Quarzoszillator hoher Präzision	oscillateur *m* à quartz de haute précision	прецизионный кварцевый генератор
H 105	high-priority event	Ereignis *n* hoher Priorität	événement *m* de haute priorité	событие с высоким приоритетом
H 106	high-purity silicon	hochreines Silizium *n*	silicium *m* de haute pureté	сверхчистый кремний
H 107	high-resistance	hochohmig	à résistance élevée	высокоомный
H 108	high-sensitivity	hochempfindlich	à haute sensibilité	высокочувствительный
H 109	high-speed arithmetic option	Schnellrechenwerk-Zusatzbaustein *m*	module *m* arithmétique supplémentaire à grande vitesse	дополнительный модуль быстрой арифметики, быстродействующий арифметический расширитель
H 110	high-speed bus	Hochgeschwindigkeitsbus *m*	bus *m* à grande vitesse	высокоскоростная шина
H 111	high-speed channel	Hochleistungskanal *m*, Hochgeschwindigkeitskanal *m*	canal *m* à grande vitesse	высокоскоростной (быстрый) канал
H 112	high-speed circuit	Hochgeschwindigkeitsschaltung *f*, Hochgeschwindigkeitsschaltkreis *m*	circuit *m* à grande vitesse	быстродействующая (быстрая) схема
H 113	high-speed logic	Hochgeschwindigkeitslogik *f*	logique *f* à grande vitesse	быстродействующая логика
H 114	high-speed memory	Schnellspeicher *m*	mémoire *f* rapide (à grande vitesse)	быстродействующая (быстрая) память
H 115	high-speed multiplication	Schnellmultiplikation *f*	multiplication *f* rapide	быстрое умножение
H 116	high-speed printer	Schnelldrucker *m*	imprimante *f* rapide	быстродействующее печатающее устройство
H 117	high-speed rewind	Schnellrücklauf *m* <eines Magnetbandes>	rebobinage *m* rapide <d'une bande magnétique>	быстрая перемотка <магнитной ленты>
H 118	high-speed tape reader	schneller Lochstreifenleser *m*	lecteur *m* de bande perforée rapide	быстродействующее устройство считывания с перфоленты
H 119	high-speed version	Hochgeschwindigkeitsversion *f*, schnelle Version *f*	version *f* rapide (à vitesse élevée)	быстрая версия
H 120	high state	High-Zustand *m*, hoher (oberer) Zustand *m* <Eins-Zustand bei positiver Logik>	état *m* supérieur	состояние с высоким уровнем [напряжения]
H 121	high-threshold logic	Logikschaltung *f* mit hohem Schwellwert <Störsicherheit>	logique *f* à seuil élevé	высокопороговая логика
H 122	high-to-low transition, high-low transition	High-Low-Übergang *m*, Übergang *m* vom oberen zum unteren Signalpegel	transition *f* de niveau high à low	переход из состояния с высоким в состояние с низким уровнем напряжения
	high-Z state	s. F 141		
H 123	HiNIL, HNIL, high noise immunity logic	HiNIL *f*, störsichere Logik *f* <störsichere Logikschaltungstechnik>	logique *f* à immunité contre perturbations	логические схемы с высокой помехоустойчивостью

H 124	hit	Treffer *m*, Erfolg *m* <Cache-Zugriff>	impact *m*, succès *m* <accès de cache>	совпадение, результатив-ное обращение <к памяти>
	HLL	*s.* H 92		
H 125	HMOS, high-performance MOS (n-channel MOS technology)	HMOS *f*, Hochleistungs-MOS *f*, Hochleistungs-n-Kanal-MOS-Technologie *f*	HMOS *f*, technologie *f* MOS canal n de haute performance	технология высокопро-изводительных n-ка-нальных МОП-схем
H 126	HMOS technology, high-density n-channel silicon-gate MOS technology	HMOS-Technologie *f*, hochdichte n-Kanal-Siliziumgate-MOS-Technologie *f*	technologie *f* HMOS, tech-nologie MOS canal n à gate au silicium de densité élevée	технология n-МОП схем с кремниевыми затво-рами и высокой плот-ностью упаковки
	HNIL	*s.* H 123		
	hold	*s.* H 12		
H 127	hold circuit, holding (latching) circuit	Haltekreis *m*, Haltestrom-kreis *m*, Halteschaltung *f*	circuit *m* de maintien	схема блокировки, фик-сирующая схема
H 128	hold condition	Haltebedingung *f*, Haltbe-dingung *f*	condition *f* de maintien	состояние блокировки; условие блокировки
	holding circuit	*s.* H 127		
	hold instruction	*s.* H 13		
H 129	hold signal	Haltsignal *n*	signal *m* de halte	сигнал блокировки; сигнал захвата
H 130	hold state	Haltzustand *m*	état *m* de halte	состояние захвата
H 131	hold time	Haltezeit *f*	temps *m* de halte	время удержания
H 132	hole	Loch *n*, Lochstelle *f*; Defektelektron *n*	trou *m*; électron-trou *m*	пробивка <в перфо-ленте>; дырка
H 133	hole conduction	Löcherleitung *f*, Defekt-elektronenleitung *f*	conduction *f* par trous, conduction d'électrons-trous	дырочная проводимость
H 134	hole current	Löcherstrom *m*, Defekt-elektronenstrom *m*	courant *m* d'électrons-trous	дырочный ток
H 135	hole density	Löcherdichte *f*, Defekt-elektronendichte *f*	densité *f* de trous, densité d'électrons-trous	плотность (концентрация) дырок
H 136	hole injection	Löcherinjektion *f*, Defekt-elektroneninjektion *f*	injection *f* d'électrons-trous	инжекция дырок
H 137	hole pattern	Lochmuster *n*, Lochungs-kombination *f*	combinaison *f* de trous	комбинация пробивок
H 138	hole trap	Löchereinfangstelle *f*, Löcherfalle *f*, Defekt-elektronenfalle *f*	piège *m* à trous (électrons-trous)	дырочная ловушка
H 139	home computer	Heimrechner *m*, Wohn-bereichs-Kleinstrechner *m*	calculateur *m* domestique	бытовая ЭВМ
H 140	home down	Anfang *m* letzte Zeile <Bildschirm>	début *m* dernière ligne	начало последней строки <на экране>
H 141	home location	Ausgangsposition *f* <Bildschirm>	position *f* initiale	исходное положение
H 142	home up	Anfang *m* erste Zeile <Bildschirm>	début *m* première ligne	начало первой строки <на экране>
H 143	horizontal micro-programming	horizontale Mikropro-grammierung *f*	microprogrammation *f* horizontale	горизонтальное микро-программирование
H 144	horizontal parity check	horizontale Paritätskon-trolle *f*	vérification *f* de parité horizontale	горизонтальный контроль по четности
H 145	host-based support programs	Unterstützungspro-gramme *npl* auf Wirts-rechnerbasis	programmes *mpl* d'assistance sur base de calculateur-hôte	программы поддержки, выполняемые на глав-ной ЭВМ
H 146	host computer	Wirtsrechner *m* <für Cross-Systemunter-lagen>, Fremdrechner *m*, Gastgeberrechner *m*	calculateur-hôte *m*	главная ЭВМ, хост-машина, ведущая ЭВМ
H 147	host processor, master processor	Leitprozessor *m*, Haupt-prozessor *m*	processeur *m* maître	главный процессор
H 148	hot standby mode	aktiver Reservebetrieb *m*	mode *m* de réserve active	режим горячего резерва
H 149	housekeeping	Systemverwaltung *f*, Systemorganisation *f*, innere Verwaltung *f*	gestion (organisation) *f* de système, gestion interne	организация вычисли-тельного процесса
H 150	housekeeping chores	Systemverwaltungs-Pflichtaufgaben *fpl*, Systemorganisations-Pflichtaufgaben *fpl*	tâches *fpl* obligatoires de gestion de système	вспомогательные дей-ствия для организа-ции вычислительного процесса
H 151	housekeeping function	Systemverwaltungsfunk-tion *f*, Systemorganisa-tionsfunktion *f*	fonction *f* de gestion de système	функция организации [вычислительного процесса]
H 152	housekeeping operation	Systemverwaltungs-operation *f*, System-organisationsarbeit *f*, Vorbereitungsoperation *f*	opération *f* de gestion de système	организационная (служеб-ная) операция
H 153	housekeeping routine	Systemverwaltungsroutine *f*, Systemorganisations-routine *f*, Programm *n* zur inneren Systemvor-bereitung	routine *f* de gestion de système	организационная (обслу-живающая) программа
H 154	housekeeping task	Systemverwaltungs-Auf-gabenelement *n*, System-organisations-Aufgaben-element *n*	tâche *f* de gestion de système	вспомогательная задача для организации вы-числительного процесса
H 155	housing	Unterbringung *f*	logement *m*	корпус
H 156	hunting	Nachlauf *m*	marche *f* de fin	подстройка, слежение
H 157	hunt mode	Fangbetrieb *m* <Synchroni-sationssuche>	mode *m* de saisie	режим активного ожида-ния, режим слежения
H 158	hybrid circuit	Hybridschaltung *f*	circuit *m* hybride	гибридная схема
H 159	hybrid computer	Hybridrechner *m* <ge-mischt analog/digital>	calculateur *m* hybride <analogique/numérique>	гибридная вычислитель-ная машина, аналого-цифровая ЭВМ
H 160	hybrid converter	hybrider Umsetzer *m*	convertisseur *m* hybride	гибридный преобразова-тель

H 161	**hybrid digital-analog circuit**	gemischte Digital-Analog-Schaltung *f*	circuit *m* numérique-analogique hybride	гибридная цифро-аналоговая схема
	hybrid IC	*s.* H 162		
H 162	**hybrid integrated circuit,** hybrid IC	Hybridschaltkreis *m* <mehrere Chips oder mehrere Bauteile in einem Schaltkreisgehäuse>	circuit *m* intégré hybride, CI *m* hybride	гибридная интегральная схема
H 163	**hybrid technique**	Hybridtechnik *f*	technique *f* hybride	гибридная техника
H 164	**hypertape**	Hochgeschwindigkeits-Kassettenmagnetband *n*	bande *f* magnétique en cassette à grande vitesse	кассета с магнитной лентой, работающая с высокой скоростью
	hysteresis loop	*s.* M 66		

I

	IC	*s. a.* integrated circuit...		
	IC...	*s. a.* integrated circuit...		
I 1	**IC device**	IC-Bauelement *n*, integriertes Bauelement *n*, Bauelement mit integrierter Schaltung	module *m* à circuit intégré, module CI	интегральная микросхема, устройство в виде интегральной схемы
I 2	**IC DIL package**	Schaltkreis-DIL-Gehäuse *n*, zweireihiges Schaltkreisgehäuse *n*	boitier *m* DIL de CI	корпус интегральной микросхемы с двухрядным торцевым расположением выводов, корпус интегральной микросхемы типа ДИП
	ICE	*s.* I 71		
	IC layout	*s.* C 227		
	IC maker	*s.* C 200		
I 3	**IC package**	Schaltkreisgehäuse *n*, Gehäuse *n* eines integrierten Schaltkreises	boitier *m* de circuit intégré, boitier CI	корпус интегральной микросхемы
I 4	**IC surface passivation**	Schaltkreis-Oberflächenpassivierung *f*	passivation *f* de surface de CI	пассивация поверхности интегральной схемы
I 5	**IC technology**	SK-Technologie *f*, Schaltkreistechnologie *f*, Technologie *f* integrierter Schaltkreise	technologie *f* de CI (circuits intégrés)	технология интегральных схем
	IC tester	*s.* C 240		
I 6	**IC tri-metal processing**	Trimetall-Schaltkreiserstellung *f*	fabrication *f* de circuits trimétalliques	изготовление интегральных схем с тройной металлизацией
	ICU	*s.* I 405		
I 7	**identifiable**	identifizierbar, erkennbar, nachweisbar	possible à identifier	идентифицируемый
I 8	**identification**	Identifizierung *f*, Bestimmung *f*, Kennzeichnung *f*	identification *f*	идентификация
I 9	**identification check**	Identifizierungsprüfung *f*	vérification *f* d'identification	идентификационный контроль
I 10	**identification code**	Kennzeichnungskode *m*	code *m* d'identification	код идентификации
I 11	**identification division**	Kennungsteil *m*	partie *f* d'identification	раздел идентификации
I 12	**identification field**	Kennfeld *n*	champ *m* d'identification	поле идентификации
	identification label	*s.* I 14		
I 13	**identification number**	Kennzahl *f*, Kennnummer *f*	nombre *m* d'identification	идентификационный (опознавательный) номер
I 14	**identifier,** identification (identifying) label	Identifizierer *m*, Identifizierungskennzeichen *n*	identificateur *m*, label *m* d'identification (d'identité)	идентификатор, метка идентификации
I 15	**identify / to**	identifizieren, bezeichnen	dentifier	идентифицировать
	identifying label	*s.* I 14		
I 16	**identity element**	Identitätsglied *n*	élément *m* d'identité	элемент эквивалентности
I 17	**identity gate**	Identitätsgatter *n*	porte *f* d'identité	схема равнозначности, вентиль, реализующий функцию элемента эквивалентности
I 18	**idle current**	Leerlaufstrom *m*	courant *m* à vide	ток холостого хода; реактивная составляющая тока
I 18a	**idle mode**	Leerlaufbetriebsart *f*	mode *m* à vide	режим простоя
I 19	**idle state**	leerer (operationsloser) Zustand *m*, Leerzustand *m*	état *m* à vide, état sans opération	состояние простоя
I 20	**idle time**	Leerlaufzeit *f*	temps *m* à vide	время простоя, холостое время
I 21	**idling cycle**	Leerlaufgang *m*	cycle *m* à vide	холостой цикл
I 22	**IGFET,** insulated gate field-effect transistor	IGFET *m*, Isolierschicht-Feldeffekttransistor *m* <FET-Grundtyp mit isoliertem Gate>	IGFET *m*, transistor *m* à effet de champ à gate isolé	полевой транзистор с изолированным затвором
I 23	**ignore / to**	ignorieren, nicht beachten	ignorer	игнорировать
I 24	**ignore character**	Auslassungszeichen *n*	caractère *m* de vide	символ удаления (игнорирования)
I 25	**IIL, I²L,** integrated injection logic	I²L *f*, integrierte Injektionslogik *f* <integrationsgünstige bipolare Schaltungstechnik auf Steuerstrominjektionsbasis>	I²L *f*, logique *f* à injection intégrée	интегральная инжекционная логика, И²Л, ИИЛ
I 26	**illegal character**	verbotenes Zeichen *n*	caractère *m* interdit	запрещенный (недопустимый) символ
I 27	**illegal code**	illegaler (unerlaubter) Kode *m*	code *m* interdit	запрещенная кодовая комбинация
I 28	**illegal format**	illegales (unerlaubtes) Format *n*	format *m* illégal	недействительный формат
I 29	**illegal instruction**	verbotener Befehl *m*	instruction *f* interdite	запрещенная инструкция
I 30	**illegal operation**	unzulässige Operation *f*	opération *f* interdite	запрещенная операция
I 31	**illegal value**	unzulässiger Wert *m*	valeur *f* illégale	недопустимое значение

I 32	image	Bild n, Abbildung f, äquivalente Darstellung f	image f, figure f, représentation f équivalente	изображение, отображение
I 33	image machine	Maschinenabbild n, Simulationsmodell n eines Rechners	image f de machine, modèle m de simulation d'un calculateur	гипотетическая машина, модель вычислительной машины
I 34	image processing system	Bildverarbeitungssystem n	système m de traitement d'images	система обработки изображений
I 35	image refresh memory	Bildwiederholspeicher m	mémoire f de rafraîchissement d'image	регенерируемая память для хранения изображения
I 36	image sensor	Bildwandler m	convertisseur m d'image	датчик изображения
I 37	imaginary number	imaginäre Zahl f	nombre m imaginaire	мнимое число
I 38	immediate access	unmittelbarer Zugriff m	accès m immédiat	немедленный доступ <без промежуточных действий>
I 39	immediate address	Direktadresse f	adresse f directe	непосредственный адрес, адрес-операнд
I 40	immediate addressing, zero-level (single-level) addressing	unmittelbare Adressierung f, Nullniveauadressierung f <Operand = Adreßfeldinhalt des Befehls>	adressage m immédiat (à niveau nul)	непосредственная адресация, адресация нулевого уровня
I 41	immediate data	Direktdaten pl	données fpl directes	непосредственные данные
I 42	immediate instruction, direct instruction	Direktbefehl m <Befehl enthält Operand>	instruction f directe	инструкция с непосредственной адресацией
I 43	immediate operand, direct operand	Direktoperand m	opérande m direct	непосредственный операнд
I 44	impact	Auswirkung f	impact m	влияние, воздействие
I 45	impedance	Impedanz f, Scheinwiderstand m	impédance f	импеданс
I 46	impedance converter	Impedanzwandler m	convertisseur m d'impédance	преобразователь импеданса
I 47	impedance matching	Scheinwiderstandsanpassung f, Impedanzanpassung f	adaptation f d'impédance	согласование импедансов
I 48	impedance matrix	Widerstandsmatrix f	matrice f d'impédance	матрица импедансов
I 49	impedance transfer	Impedanzübertragung f	transfert m à impédance	взаимный импеданс
I 50	imperfection	Unvollkommenheit f, Kristallstrukturstörung f	imperfection f	дефект
I 51	implement / to	implementieren, durchführen	exécuter, achever	выполнять, реализовывать
I 52	implementation	Implementierung f, praktische Durchführung f	exécution f	выполнение, реализация, ввод в действие; внедрение
I 53	implication	Implikation f <logische Operation>	implication f	импликация
I 54	implication gate	Implikationsgatter n	porte f d'implication	импликатор
I 55	implicit, implied	implizit, inbegriffen, impliziert, miteinbegriffen	implicite, impliqué	неявный, подразумеваемый, заключающий [в себе]
I 56/7	implicit address	mplizite Adresse f <Adreßangabe im Operationskode enthalten>	adresse f implicite	неявный адрес
	implied	s. I 55		
I 58	implied addressing, inherent addressing	eingeschlossene (implizite) Adressierung f <Adresse ergibt sich aus Op-Kode>	adressage m implicite	неявная адресация
I 59	implied indirect addressing	eingeschlossene Indirektadressierung f <ohne explizite Angabe im Befehl>	adressage m indirect implicite	неявная косвенная адресация
I 60	improved circuit technique	verbesserte Schaltkreistechnik f	technique f améliorée de circuits	усовершенствованная схемотехника
I 61	improvement	Verbesserung f	amélioration f	улучшение, усовершенствование
	impulse	s. P 690		
I 62	impurity	Verunreinigung f, Störstelle f	impureté f	примесь
I 63	impurity atom	Verunreinigungsatom n	atome m d'impureté	атом примеси
I 64	impurity concentration	Störstellenkonzentration f	concentration f des impuretés	концентрация примеси
I 65	impurity diffusion	Störstellendiffusion f	diffusion f d'impureté	диффузия примеси
I 66	impurity level	Störstellenpegel m	niveau m d'impureté	примесный уровень
I 67	in-built	eingebaut	incorporé, encastré	встроенный
I 68	in-circuit	schaltungsintern	interne au circuit	внутрисхемный
I 69	in-circuit check	schaltungsinterne Prüfung f, Prüfung innerhalb einer Schaltung	vérification f interne au circuit	внутрисхемный контроль
I 70	in-circuit emulation	schaltungsinterne Emulation f <in der Anwenderschaltung erfolgende Nachbildung des Mikroprozessors durch Anschluß des Entwicklungssystems>	émulation f interne au circuit	внутрисхемная эмуляция
I 71	in-circuit emulator, ICE	schaltungsinnerer Emulator m, einsteckbarer Mikroprozessor-Emulator m <Echtzeittestsystem für Anwendersysteme>	émulateur m interne au circuit, ICE	внутрисхемный эмулятор, ВСЭ
I 72	in-circuit tester	Schaltkreistester m für Anwendung innerhalb einer Schaltung (Steckeinheit)	examinateur m de circuit interne	внутрисхемный тестер
I 73	include / to	enthalten, unterbringen	contenir, loger, inclure	включать в себя, заключать
I 74	include statement	Einfügungsanweisung f	instruction f d'inclusion	оператор включения
I 75	inclusion	Einfügung f	inclusion f	включение

I 76	inclusive **OR**	inklusives ODER *n* <Disjunktion>	OU *m* inclusif	включающее ИЛИ
	inclusive-OR gate	*s.* O 162		
I 77	incompatibility	Inkompatibilität *f*, Nicht-Kompatibilität *f*, Unverträglichkeit *f*	incompatibilité *f*	несовместимость
I 78	incompatible microprocessor	nicht-kompatibler Mikroprozessor *m*	microprocesseur *m* incompatible	несовместимый микропроцессор
I 79	increment / to	erhöhen, aufzählen	hausser, compter, incrémenter	инкрементировать; увеличивать
I 80	increment	Inkrement *n*, Zuwachs *m*	incrément *m*, croissance *f*	приращение; инкремент
I 81	incremental	inkrementell, schrittweise anwachsend	incrémental	инкрементный, дифференциальный, разностный
I 82	incremental computer	Inkrementrechner *m*	calculateur *m* incrémental	инкрементное вычислительное устройство
I 83	incremental measuring method	Inkremental-Meßverfahren *n*	procédé *m* de mesure incrémental	метод измерений по приращению
I 84	indexed address	indizierte Adresse *f*	adresse *f* indexée	индексированный (модифицированный) адрес
I 85	indexed addressing	indizierte Adressierung *f*	adressage *m* indexé	индексная адресация
I 86	indexing	Indizierung *f*	indexation *f*	индексация
I 87	indexing instruction, index register instruction	Indexbefehl *m*, Indexregisterbefehl *m*	instruction *f* d'indexation, instruction de registre d'index	инструкция обращения к индексному регистру, инструкция индексации
I 88	index register	Indexregister *n* <Adreßmodifikationsregister>	registre *m* d'index	индексный регистр
	index register instruction	*s.* I 87		
I 89	index value	Indexwert *m*	valeur *f* d'index	значение индекса
I 90	indicate / to	anzeigen, hinweisen	indiquer, afficher	указывать, обозначать, индицировать
I 91	indicating instrument	Anzeigeinstrument *n*	instrument *m* d'indication	индикаторный прибор
I 92	indication	Anzeige *f*, Hinweis *m*	indication *f*, affichage *m*	указание, индикация
I 93	indicator	Anzeiger *m*, Meldeeinrichtung *f*	indicateur *m*	указатель, индикатор
I 94	indirect address	indirekte Adresse *f*	adresse *f* indirecte	косвенный адрес
I 95	indirect addressing	indirekte Adressierung *f*	adressage *m* indirect	косвенная адресация
I 96	indirect control	indirekte Steuerung *f*	commande *f* indirecte	непрямое управление
I 97	individual pulse	Einzelimpuls *m* <typbezogen>	impulsion *f* individuelle (solitaire)	одиночный импульс
I 98	individual software	Individual-Software *f*, individuelle Programmausstattung *f*	logiciels *mpl* individuels (particuliers)	индивидуальное программное обеспечение
I 99	individual testing	Einzelprüfung *f*	examen *m* individuel	отдельная проверка, отдельное испытание
I 100	induced charge	induzierte Ladung *f*	charge *f* induite	наведенный (индуцированный) заряд
I 101	induced failure	Sekundärfehler *m*	défaillance *f* induite (secondaire)	наведенный отказ
I 102	inductance coupling	induktive Kopplung *f*	couplage *m* inductif	индуктивная связь
I 103	industrial control	industrielle Steuerung *f*, Industriesteuerung *f*	commande *f* industrielle	управление производственным процессом
I 104	industrial control system	industrielles Steuerungssystem *n*	système *m* de commande industriel	система управления производственным процессом
I 105	industrial electronics	Industrieelektronik *f*	électronique *f* industrielle	промышленная электроника
I 106	industrial microcomputer application	industrielle Mikrorechneranwendung *f*	application *f* industrielle de microcalculateurs	применение микро-ЭВМ в промышленности
I 107	industry specifications	Industrienorm *f*	norme *f* industrielle	промышленные требования (нормы)
I 108	inequality	Ungleichheit *f*	inégalité *f*	неравенство
I 109	information	Information *f*	information *f*	информация
I 110	information build-up	Informationsaufbau *m*, Nachrichtenaufbau *m*	établissement *m* d'information	информационная структура
I 111	information channel	Informationskanal *m*	canal *m* d'information	информационный канал
I 112	information checking	Informationskontrolle *f*	examen *m* (vérification *f*) d'information	контроль информации
I 113	information content	Informationsinhalt *m*	contenu *m* d'information	количество (объем) информации
I 114	information exchange	Informationsaustausch *m*	échange *m* d'informations	информационный обмен, обмен информацией
I 115	information flow	Informationsfluß *m*	flux *m* d'information	поток информации
I 116	information format	Informationsformat *m*	format *m* d'information	формат информации
I 117	information loss	Informationsverlust *m*	perte *f* d'information	потеря информации
I 118	information parameter	Informationsparameter *m*	paramètre *m* d'information	информационный параметр
I 119	information plane	Informationsebene *f* <Leiterplatte>	face *f* d'informations	соединительная печатная плата для передачи информационных сигналов
I 120	information processing	Informationsverarbeitung *f*	informatique *f*, traitement *m* d'information	обработка информации
I 121	information processing system	Informationsverarbeitungssystem *n*	système *m* d'informatique, système de traitement d'information	система обработки информации
I 122	information recording	Informationsaufzeichnung *f*	enregistrement *m* d'information	запись информации
I 123	information-redundant testing	Testung *f* mittels Informationsredundanz	examen *m* par redondance d'information	контроль при помощи [введения] информационной избыточности
I 124	information representation	Informationsdarstellung *f*	représentation *f* d'information	представление информации
I 125	information retrieval	Informationswiedergewinnung *f*, Informationswiederauffindung *f*	récupération *f* d'information	информационный поиск

I 126	information selection	Informationsauswahl f	sélection f d'informations	информационная селек-ция
I 127	information storage	Informationsspeicherung f	mise f en mémoire d'information	запоминание (хранение) информации
I 128	information system	Informationssystem n	système m d'information	информационная система
I 129	information theory	Informationstheorie f	théorie f d'information	теория информации
I 130	information transfer	Informationsübertragung f	transfert m d'information	передача информации
I 131	information unit	Informationseinheit f	unité f d'information	единица [измерения] информации, информационная единица
I 132	information word	Informationswort n	mot m d'information	информационное слово
	inherent addressing	s. I 58		
I 133	inherited error	mitgeschleppter Fehler m	erreur f inhérente	привнесенная (исходная) ошибка
I 134	inhibit / to	sperren, verhindern	inhiber	запрещать, предотвращать, блокировать
I 135	inhibiting input	Sperreingang m	entrée f inhibitrice	вход запрета (блокировки)
I 136	inhibiting signal, disabling signal	Sperrsignal n, Blockiersignal n	signal m inhibiteur (de blocage)	сигнал запрета
I 137	inhibit line	Blockierleitung f, Sperrleitung f	ligne f d'inhibition	линия запрета
I 138	inhibit pulse, disable pulse	Sperrimpuls m, Blockierimpuls m	impulsion f d'inhibition, impulsion de blocage	импульс запрета
I 139	initial address, beginning address	Anfangsadresse f	adresse f initiale	начальный адрес
I 140	initialization, initializing	Initialisierung f, Initialisieren n, Herstellen n von Anfangsbedingungen	initialisation f	инициализация, установка в начальное состояние
I 141	initialize / to	initialisieren, vorbereiten, Anfangsbedingungen einstellen	initialiser	инициализировать
I 142	initialized routine	initialisierte Routine f	routine f initialisée	инициированная программа
	initializing	s. I 140		
I 143	initializing program	Initialisierungsprogramm n	programme m d'initialisation	программа инициализации
I 144	initial program loader	Anfangsprogrammlader m	chargeur m de programme initial	начальный загрузчик
I 145	initial state	Anfangszustand m	état m initial	начальное состояние
I 146	initial value, start value	Anfangswert m, Ausgangswert m, Startwert m	valeur f initiale	начальное значение
I 147	initiate / to	auslösen, einleiten	initier	начинать, инициировать
I 148	in-line	schritthaltend, mitlaufend, in einer Linie	du même pas	линейный; в темпе поступления; в порядке поступления
I 149	in-line array	lineare (einreihige) Anordnung f	placement m linéaire	линейное (однорядное) расположение
I 150	in-line processing	mitlaufende (schritthaltende) Verarbeitung f	traitement m concurrent	оперативная (поточная) обработка, обработка [данных] в темпе [их] поступления; обработка данных в порядке поступления
I 151	in-line subroutine	lineares Unterprogramm n <offen, direkt in Hauptprogramm eingebunden>	sous-programme m linéaire	открытая подпрограмма
I 152	in-phase signal	gleichphasiges Signal n	signal m en phase	синфазный сигнал
I 153	in-plane	in einer Ebene liegend	sur le même niveau	в одной плоскости
I 154	input / to	eingeben	entrer	входить; вводить
I 155	input	Eingabe f, Eingang m	entrée f	вход; ввод
I 156	input-acknowledge signal	Eingabebestätigungssignal n <Quittungsbetrieb>	signal m d'affirmation d'entrée	сигнал подтверждения ввода
I 157	input amplifier	Eingangsverstärker m	amplificateur m d'entrée	входной усилитель
I 158	input amplitude range	Eingangsamplitudenbereich m	champ m d'amplitude d'entrée	амплитудный диапазон входных сигналов
I 159	input area	Eingabebereich m	domaine m d'entrée	область (буферная зона) ввода
I 160	input block	Eingabeblock m	bloc m d'entrée	входной блок
I 161	input buffer	Eingabepuffer m	tampon m d'entrée	входной буфер
I 162	input buffer storage	Eingabepufferspeicher m	mémoire f de tampon d'entrée	входное буферное запоминающее устройство
I 163	input bus type	Eingabe-Bustyp m <Bus mit nur einer Betriebsrichtung, einem Empfänger und mehreren Quellen>	type m de bus d'entrée	входная шина
I 164	input capacitance	Eingangskapazität f	capacité f d'entrée	входная емкость
I 165	input channel	Eingabekanal m	canal m d'entrée	входной канал, канал ввода
I 166	input circuit	Eingabeschaltung f	circuit m d'entrée	входная цепь
I 167	input control	Eingabesteuerung f	commande f d'entrée	управление вводом
I 168	input control program	Eingabesteuerungsprogramm n	programme m de commande d'entrée	программа управления вводом
I 169	input current	Eingangsstrom m	courant m d'entrée	входной ток
I 170	input data	Eingabedaten pl	données fpl d'entrée	входные данные
I 171	input device	Eingabegerät n	appareil m d'entrée	устройство ввода
I 172	input editing	Eingabeaufbereitung f	préparation f d'entrée	редактирование входных данных
I 173	input enable signal	Eingabe-Freigabesignal n, Eingabetor-Aktivierungssignal n	signal m de déblocage (libération) d'entrée	сигнал разрешения ввода
I 174	input facilities	Eingabemöglichkeiten fpl, Eingabeeinrichtungen fpl	possibilités fpl (dispositifs mpl) d'entrée	средства (оборудование) ввода
I 175	input file	Eingabedatei f	fichier m d'entrée	входной файл

I 176	**input format**	Eingabeformat n	format m d'entrée	формат входных данных
I 177	**input high voltage**	Eingangsspannung f oberer Pegel, Eingangs-High-pegelspannung f	tension f d'entrée de niveau supérieur	входное напряжение высокого уровня
I 178	**input impedance**	Eingangsimpedanz f	impédance f d'entrée	входной импеданс
I 179	**input information**	Eingangsinformation f	information f d'entrée	входная информация
I 180	**input instruction**	Eingabebefehl m	instruction f d'entrée	команда ввода
I 181	**input interrupt**	Eingabe-Interrupt m, Eingabeunterbrechung f	interruption f d'entrée	прерывание по вводу
I 182	**input keyboard**	Eingabetastatur f	clavier m d'entrée	клавиатура ввода
I 183	**input leakage current**	Eingangsreststrom m	courant m résiduel d'entrée	входной ток утечки
I 184	**input level**	Eingangspegel m	niveau m d'entrée	входной уровень
I 185	**input line**	Eingabeleitung f	ligne f d'entrée	входная линия
I 186	**input low voltage**	Eingangsspannung f unterer Pegel, Eingangs-Low-pegelspannung f	tension f d'entrée de niveau inférieur	входное напряжение низкого уровня
I 187	**input mode**	Eingabebetriebsart f	mode m d'entrée	режим ввода
I 188	**input operation**	Eingabeoperation f	opération f d'entrée	операция ввода
	input-output	s. I/O...		
I 189	**input-output trunk**	Eingabe-Ausgabe-Sammelschiene f	barre f d'entrée-sortie	[магистральная] шина ввода-вывода
	input-output typewriter	s. I 515		
	input-output unit	s. I 516		
I 190	**input peripherals**	periphere Eingabegeräte npl, Eingabeperipherie f	périphérie f d'entrée	периферийные устройства ввода
I 191	**input port**	Eingabetor n, Eingabe-Anschlußstelle f	porte f d'entrée	входной порт, порт ввода
I 192	**input procedure**	Eingabeverfahren n	procédé m d'entrée	процедура ввода
I 193	**input pulse**	Eingabeimpuls m, Eingangsimpuls f	impulsion f d'entrée	входной импульс
I 194	**input rate**, input speed	Eingaberate f, Eingabegeschwindigkeit f	vitesse f d'entrée	скорость ввода
I 195	**input receiver**	Eingangsempfänger m	récepteur m d'entrée	входной приемник
I 196	**input register**	Eingaberegister n	registre m d'entrée	входной регистр
I 197	**input request**	Eingabeanforderung f	demande f d'entrée	запрос на ввод, требование ввода
I 198	**input routine**	Eingaberoutine f, Einleseprogramm n	routine f d'entrée	программа ввода
I 199	**input section**	Eingabesektion f	secteur m d'entrée	входная область [памяти]
I 200	**input selector**	Eingabeschalter m, Eingabeauswahlschalter m	sélecteur (commutateur) m d'entrée	входной селектор
I 201	**input signal**	Eingabesignal n, Eingangssignal n	signal m d'entrée	входной сигнал
	input speed	s. I 194		
I 202	**input station**, input terminal	Eingabestation f, Eingabeterminal n, Eingabeendgerät n	station f d'entrée, terminal m d'entrée	станция ввода [данных], терминал ввода [данных]
I 203	**input stream**	Eingabedatenstrom m, Eingabefolge f	courant m de données d'entrée	входной поток, поток данных на входе
I 204	**input switching threshold**	Eingangsschal·schwelle f	seuil m de commutation d'entrée	порог переключения [для входного сигнала]
I 205	**input terminal**	Eingabeanschluß m <Kontakt>	raccordement m d'entrée	входной контакт, входная клемма
	input terminal	s. a. I 202		
I 206	**input translator**	Eingabeübersetzer m	traducteur m d'entrée	входной транслятор
I 207	**input unit**	Eingabeeinheit f	unité f d'entrée	устройство ввода
I 208	**input voltage**	Eingangsspannung f	tension f d'entrée	входное напряжение
I 209	**input work queue**	Eingabe-Warteschlange f	queue f d'entrée, queue d'attente à l'entrée	входная очередь заданий
I 210	**inquiry**, interrogation	Abfrage f	interrogation f	опрос; запрос
I 211	**inquiry control**	Abfragesteuerung f	commande f d'interrogation	управление запросами
I 212	**inquiry station**, query station	Abfragestation f	station f d'interrogation	станция ввода запросов
I 213	**inquiry terminal**	Abfrageterminal n	terminal m d'interrogation	справочный терминал
I 214	**inquiry unit**	Abfrageeinheit f	unité f d'interrogation	блок опроса
I 215	**insert / to**	einfügen, bestücken	insérer	вставлять, включать
	insert / to	s. a. J 3		⌐ма
I 216	**inserted subroutine**	eingefügtes Unterprogramm n	sous-programme m inséré	вставленная подпрограм-
I 217	**inserting side**	Bestückungsseite f	face f de garnissage	сторона вставки
I 218	**insertion**	Bestückung f, Einsetzen n	insertion f	вставка, включение
I 219	**insertion subroutine**	Einfügungsunterprogramm n	sous-programme m d'insertion	подпрограмма вставки
I 220	**inspection test**	Prüffeldabnahme f	test m d'inspection	приемочное испытание
	instable	s. A 346		
I 221	**instable state**	instabiler Zustand m	état m instable	неустойчивое состояние
I 222	**installation**	Installation f	installation f	ввод в эксплуатацию
I 223	**installation time**	Aufbauzeit f, Aufstellzeit f <Gerätesystem>	temps m d'installation	время ввода в эксплуатацию
I 224	**instantaneous access**	sofortiger Zugriff m	accès m instantané	немедленный (мгновенный) доступ
I 225	**instantaneous display**	Sofortanzeige f	affichage m immédiat	оперативная индикация
I 226	**instantaneous power**	Momentanleistung f	puissance f instantanée	мгновенная мощность
I 227	**instantaneous value**, actual value	Istwert m	valeur f instantanée (réelle)	мгновенное значение
	in-step	s. S 924		
I 228	**instruction**, order, command	Befehl m	instruction f, ordre m, commande f	команда, инструкция
I 229	**instruction address**	Befehlsadresse f	adresse f d'instruction	адрес команды
I 230	**instruction address register**	Befehlsadressenregister n	registre m d'adresse d'instruction	регистр адреса команды
I 231	**instruction area**, instruction space	Befehlsraum m <Teil eines Speichers zur Aufnahme von Befehlen, Programmspeicherbereich>	champ (domaine) m d'instructions <partie d'une mémoire pour loger des instructions>	память команд <участок памяти для хранения программы>

I 232	instruction array	Befehlsfeld *n*	champ *m* d'instructions	массив команд; поле [в формате] команд
I 233	instruction buffer	Befehlspuffer *m*, Befehls-pufferregister *n*	tampon *m* à instructions	буферный регистр команд
I 234	instruction character	Befehlszeichen *n* <Befehlskode-Element>	caractère *m* d'instruction	управляющий символ
I 235	instruction code	Befehlskode *m*, Befehls-schlüssel *m*	code *m* d'instructions	код команды
I 236	instruction control unit	Befehlssteuereinheit *f*	unité *f* de commande d'instructions	устройство управления, блок обработки инструкций
I 237	instruction counter, program counter	Befehlszähler *m*	compteur *m* d'instructions	счетчик команд
I 238	instruction cycle	Befehlszyklus *m*	cycle *m* d'instruction	цикл команды
I 239	instruction cycle time	Befehlszykluszeit *f* <Befehlszeit>	temps *m* de cycle d'instruction	длительность цикла команды
I 240	instruction decoder	Befehlsentschlüßler *m*	decodeur *m* d'instructions	дешифратор команд
I 241	instruction decoding	Befehlsentschlüsselung *f*	décodage *m* d'instructions	декодирование команд[ы]
I 242	instruction execution	Befehlsausführung *f*, Befehlsabwicklung *f*	exécution *f* d'instructions	выполнение команд[ы]
I 243	instruction execution time	Befehlsausführungszeit *f*, Befehlsabwicklungszeit *f*	temps *m* d'exécution d'instructions	время выполнения команды
I 244	instruction fetch	Befehlsholen *n*, Befehlsbereitstellung *f*	établissement *m* d'instruction	выборка команд[ы]
I 245	instruction fetch cycle	Befehlsholezyklus *m*, Befehlaufstellungszyklus *m*	cycle *m* établissement d'instruction	цикл выборки команды
I 246	instruction format	Befehlsformat *n*	format *m* d'instruction	формат команды
I 247	instruction group	Befehlsgruppe *f*	groupe *m* d'instructions	группа команд
I 248	instruction length	Befehlslänge *f*	longueur *f* d'instruction	длина команды
I 249	instruction list	Befehlsliste *f*	liste *f* d'instructions	список команд
I 250	instruction location	Befehlsspeicherplatz *m*	logement *m* d'instruction	место размещения команды
I 251	instruction loop	Befehlsschleife *f*	boucle *f* d'instructions	программный цикл
I 252	instruction manual, reference manual, operating procedure	Betriebsanleitung *f*	manuel *m* d'instruction	руководство по эксплуатации
I 252 a	instruction modification	Befehlsmodifizierung *f*, Befehlsänderung *f*	modification *f* d'instruction	модификация команды
I 253	instruction name	Befehlsname *m* <Befehlsbezeichnung>	nom *m* d'instruction	имя (наименование) команды
I 254	instruction prefetch	Vorausholen *n* von Befehlen	appel *m* d'instructions d'avance	предварительная выборка команд
I 255	instruction preprocessing unit	Befehlsvorverarbeitungseinheit *f*	unité *f* de prétraitement d'instructions	устройство предварительной обработки команд
	instruction processor	s. C 358		
I 256	instruction queue	Befehlsschlange *f*	queue *f* d'instructions	очередь команд
I 257	instruction register	Befehlsregister *n*, Befehls-koderegister *n*	registre *m* d'instructions	регистр команд
I 258	instruction repertoire (repertory)	Befehlsvorrat *m*	fonds (répertoire) *m* d'instructions	система команд
I 259	instruction repetition	Befehlswiederholung *f*	répétition *f* d'instruction	повторение команды
I 260	instruction representation	Befehlsdarstellung *f*	représentation *f* d'instructions	представление команды
J 261	instruction sequence	Befehlsfolge *f*	séquence *f* d'instructions	последовательность команд
I 262	instruction set	Befehlssatz *m*	jeu *m* d'instructions	набор команд
I 263	instruction set expandability	Befehlssatzerweiterbarkeit *f*	possibilité *f* d'élargissement du fonds d'instructions	возможность расширения набора команд
	instruction space	s. I 231		
I 264	instruction status	Befehlsstatus *m*	état *m* d'instructions	состояние команды
I 265	instruction status indicator	Befehlsstatusanzeiger *m*	indicateur *m* d'état d'instruction	индикатор состояния команд
I 266	instruction stream	Befehlsstrom *m*	courant *m* d'instructions	поток команд
I 267	instruction system	Befehlssystem *n*	système *m* d'instructions	система команд
I 268	instruction time	Befehlszeit *f*	temps *m* d'instruction	время выполнения команды
I 269	instruction type	Befehlstyp *m*	type *m* d'instruction	тип команды
I 270	instruction word	Befehlswort *n*	mot *m* d'instruction	командное слово
	instrumentation	s. M 221		
I 271	instrumentation correcting	Meßgerätekorrektur *f*	correction *f* d'instrument [de mesure]	инструментальная поправка
I 272	instrument programmability	Meßgeräteprogrammierbarkeit *f*	programmabilité *f* d'instrument [de mesure]	программируемость прибора
I 273	instrument transformer	Meßwandler *m*	transformateur *m* de mesure	измерительный трансформатор
I 274	insulate / to, to isolate	isolieren	isoler	изолировать
I 275	insulated gate	isoliertes Gate *n*	gate *m* isolé	изолированный затвор
	insulated gate field-effect transistor	s. I 22		
	insulating film	s. I 276		
I 276	insulating layer, isolation layer, insulating film, insulation sleeving	Isolierschicht *f*	couche *f* d'isolement, couche isolante	изолирующая пленка, изолирующий слой
I 277	insulating substrate	Isoliersubstrat *n*, Isolatorsubstrat *n*	substrat *m* isolant	изолирующая подложка
	insulation sleeving	s. I 276		
I 278	insulation test	Isolationsprüfung *f*	test *m* d'isolation	проверка изоляции
I 279	insulator material	Isoliermaterial *n*	matériel *m*, matériau *m* d'isolation	изоляционный материал
I 280	integer	ganzzahlig	en nombres entiers	целочисленный
	integer	s. I 282		
I 281	integer arithmetic	Ganzzahlarithmetik *f*	arithmétique *f* en nombres entiers	целочисленная арифметика

I 282	**integer value,** integer	ganze Zahl *f*	nombre *m* entier	целочисленное значение, целое [число]
I 283	**integral boundary**	Wortgrenze *f* <bei Datenfeld-Speicherposition>	limite *f* de mot	целочисленная граница
I 284	**integral cassette storage**	integrierter Magnetbandkassettenspeicher *m* <im Rechnergehäuse>	mémoire *f* à cassette à bande magnétique intégrée dans le calculateur	кассетное запоминающее устройство на магнитной ленте, встроенное в основной блок микроЭВМ
I 285	**integral disk**	integrierter Plattenspeicher *m* <im Rechnergehäuse>	mémoire *f* à disque intégrée dans le calculateur	дисковое запоминающее устройство, встроенное в основной блок микроЭВМ
I 286	**integrate / to**	integrieren, zusammenfassen	intégrer	интегрировать; объединять; определять среднее значение
I 287	**integrated**	integriert, eingebaut, zusammenhängend, umfassend	intégré, intégral	проинтегрированный; объединенный, интегральный
I 288	**integrated circuit,** IC	integrierte Schaltung *f*, integrierter Schaltkreis *m*	circuit *m* intégré, CI *m*	интегральная схема, ИС
	integrated circuit ...	*s. a.* IC...		
I 289	**integrated circuit analyzer**	Analysator *m* für integrierte Schaltungen	analyseur *m* pour circuits intégrés	анализатор для интегральных схем
I 290	**integrated circuit design**	Entwurf *m* integrierter Schaltkreise	conception *f* de circuits intégrés	разработка интегральных схем
I 291	**integrated circuit packaging**	Verkapselung *f* integrierter Schaltkreise	encastrement *m* de circuits intégrés	установка интегральных схем в корпусе
I 292	**integrated circuit testing**	Testen *n* integrierter Schaltkreise	test *m* de circuits intégrés	контроль интегральных схем
I 293	**integrated circuit test system**	Testsystem *n* für integrierte Schaltkreise	système *m* de test de circuits intégrés	контрольно-измерительная система для проверки интегральных схем
I 294	**integrated component**	integriertes Bauteil *n*, integrierter Baustein *m*	composant *m* intégré	интегрированный (интегральный) компонент
I 295	**integrated data processing**	integrierte Datenverarbeitung *f* <Verfahren>	traitement *m* de données intégré	интегрированная обработка данных
I 296	**integrated emulator**	integrierter Emulator *m*, programmsystemeingebundener Emulator <im Gegensatz zum Stand-alone-Emulator>	émulateur *m* intégré	интегрированный эмулятор
	integrated injection logic	*s.* I 25		
I 297	**integrated monolithic circuit**	monolithisch-integrierter Schaltkreis *m* <integrierte Schaltung auf einem Chip>	circuit *m* intégré monolithique	монолитная интегральная схема
	integrating circuit	*s.* I 299		
I 298	**integration**	Integration *f*	intégration *f*	интеграция
I 299	**integration circuit,** integrating circuit	Integrierschaltung *f*	circuit *m* d'intégration	интегрирующая схема
I 300	**integration level**	Integrationsniveau *n*	niveau *m* d'intégration	уровень интеграции
I 301	**intelligent cable**	intelligentes Kabel *n* <Kabel mit eingebettetem Pikoprozessor für programmierbare Spezialschnittstellenanpassung>	câble *m* intelligent	«интеллектуальный» кабель, программируемый интерфейсный контроллер на базе микропроцессора
I 302	**intelligent controller**	intelligente Steuereinheit *f* <Steuereinheit mit eingebautem Mikroprozessor>	unité *f* de commande intelligente	интеллектуальный контроллер
I 303	**intelligent device**	intelligentes Gerät *n* <programmierbares Gerät für Rechen- und Steuerfunktion auf Mikro- oder Kleinrechnerbasis>	appareil *m* intelligent	интеллектуальное (программируемое) устройство
I 304	**intelligent disk storage**	intelligenter Magnetplattenspeicher *m* <enthält mikroprozessorgesteuerte Firmware für Datenverwaltung>	mémoire *f* à disque magnétique intelligente	дисковое запоминающее устройство, содержащее [программируемый] контроллер
I 305	**intelligent keyboard**	intelligente Tastatur *f*	clavier *m* intelligent	интеллектуальная клавиатура
I 306	**intelligent terminal**	intelligentes Terminal *n*, intelligente Datenstation *f* <Terminal mit eingebautem Mikrorechner>	terminal *m* intelligent	интеллектуальный терминал
I 307	**interact / to**	zusammenwirken, wechselwirken	collaborer, agir mutuellement	взаимодействовать
I 308	**interacting,** interaction	Wechselwirkung *f*, Zusammenarbeit *f*	coopération *f*	взаимодействие, диалог
I 309	**interacting simulator**	Dialogsimulator *m*	simulateur *m* de dialogue	диалоговая моделирующая программа
	interaction	*s.* I 308		
I 310	**interactive feature**	Dialogeigenschaft *f*	propriété *f* de dialogue	диалоговая возможность
I 311	**interactive I/O device**	Dialogverkehrs-E/A-Gerät *n*, interaktives E/A-Gerät *n*	appareil *m* d'E/S interactif	интерактивное устройство ввода-вывода
I 312	**interactive mode,** conversational mode	Dialogarbeitsweise *f* Bediener-Rechner, interaktive Arbeitsweise *f*	mode *m* à dialogue, mode interactif	режим диалога, интерактивный режим
I 313	**interactive processing**	Dialogverarbeitung *f*	traitement *m* interactif	диалоговая (интерактивная) обработка

I 314	interactive signal processing	Dialogverarbeitung f von Signalen, interaktive Signalverarbeitung f	traitement m interactif de signaux	интерактивная обработка сигналов
I 315	interactive terminal, dialogue terminal	Dialogterminal n, interaktives Terminal n	terminal m de dialogue, terminal interactif	интерактивный (диалоговый) терминал
I 316	interchangeability, exchangeability	Austauschbarkeit f, Auswechselbarkeit f	interchangeabilité f	[взаимо]заменяемость
I 317	interchangeable, exchangeable	austauschbar, auswechselbar	interchangeable, échangeable	[взаимо]заменяемый, сменный
I 318	interconnect / to	zusammenschalten	interconnecter	соединять [внутри], объединять [компоненты]
I 319	interconnecting cable	Zusammenschaltkabel n	câble m d'interconnexions	[внутренний] соединительный кабель
I 320	interconnection	Zwischenverbindung f	interconnexion f	межсхемное соединение
I 321	interconnection line	Zusammenschaltleitung f, Koppelleitung f	ligne f d'interconnexions	[внутренняя] соединительная линия
I 322	interconnection test system	Zusammenschalt-Testsystem n	système m de test d'interconnexions	система контроля [внутренних] соединений
I 323	interface	Interface n, Schnittstelle f, Anschlußstelle f, Anschlußbild n, Anschlußbedingungen fpl	interface f	интерфейс; сопряжение; устройство сопряжения
I 324	interface adapter	Schnittstellen-Anpassungsschaltung f, Schnittstellen-Anpassungsbaustein m	adapteur m d'interface	адаптер интерфейса
I 325	interface channel	Schnittstellenkanal m, Anschlußkanal m	canal m d'interface	канал сопряжения
I 326	interface circuit	Schnittstellenschaltung f, Anschlußschaltung f	circuit m d'interface	интерфейсная схема, схема сопряжения
I 327	interface control	Schnittstellensteuerung f	commande f d'interface	управление интерфейсом
I 328	interface controller	Schnittstellen-Steuerbaustein m, Anschlußsteuereinheit f	module m (unité f) de commande d'interface	модуль управления интерфейсом, контроллер интерфейса
I 329	interface fault	Schnittstellenfehler m	défaut m d'interface	сбой в интерфейсе
I 330	interface logic	Schnittstellen-Logikschaltung f	logique f d'interface	интерфейсная логика
I 331	interface module	Schnittstellenmodul m, Schnittstellenbaustein m	module m d'interface	интерфейсный модуль
I 332	interface procedure	Schnittstellenverfahren n	procédé m à interface	интерфейсная процедура
I 333	interface standard	Schnittstellenstandard m, Interface-Standard m, Anschlußstandard m	norme f (standard m) d'interface	стандарт на интерфейс
I 334	interfacing characteristics	Schnittstellenkenndaten pl	caractéristiques fpl d'interface	характеристики интерфейса
I 335	interfacing kit	Schnittstellenbausatz m	jeu m de construction d'interfaces	набор компонентов для интерфейса
I 336	interfacing technique	Schnittstellentechnik f, Anschlußtechnik f	technique f d'interface	способ сопряжения, метод построения интерфейса
I 337	interlace / to	verflechten, verschränken ‹Speicherzuweisung›	entrelacer	чередовать
I 338	interlaced recording	verschränkte Aufzeichnung f	enregistrement m entrelacé	чередующаяся запись
	interlayer connection	s. T 173		
I 339	interleave / to	verzahnen, ineinander schachteln	engrener	чередоваться, перемежаться
I 340	interleaving	Verzahnung f	engrenage m	чередование
I 341	interleaving memory modules	Speichermodulverschachtelung f, verzahnte Speichermodule mpl	emboîtement m de modules de mémoire	модули расслоенной памяти; чередующиеся модулей памяти
I 342	interleaving operation	verzahnte Operation f	opération f engrenée	чередующаяся операция
I 343	interlock / to	verschränken ‹miteinander›, ineinandergreifen	entrelacer	блокировать, запирать
I 344	interlock, interlocking	gegenseitige Verriegelung f, Verschränkung f	entrelacement m	заблокировка
I 345	interlocked operation	ineinandergreifende (mit anderen starr verschränkte) Operation f ‹in einem Ablauf›	opération f entrelacée	заблокированная операция
I 346	interlocked sequence	ineinandergreifende (starr abzuarbeitende) Folge f ‹eines Vorgangs›	séquence f entrelacée	заблокированная последовательность
	interlocking	s. I 344		
I 347	intermediate data, intermediate quantities	Zwischenwerte mpl	valeurs fpl intermédiaires	промежуточные данные (значения)
I 348	intermediate distribution	Zwischenverteilung f	distribution f intermédiaire	промежуточное распределение
I 349	intermediate language	Zwischensprache f	langage m intermédiaire	промежуточный язык
I 350	intermediate memory, intermediate storage, temporary memory (storage)	Zwischenspeicher m	mémoire f intermédiaire	ЗУ временного хранания данных, ЗУ для хранения промежуточных данных, промежуточное ЗУ
	intermediate quantities	s. I 347		
I 351	intermediate register, temporary register	Zwischenregister n	registre m intermédiaire	промежуточный регистр
I 352	intermediate result	Zwischenergebnis n	résultat m intermédiaire	промежуточный результат
I 353	intermediate storage, temporary storage	Zwischenspeicherung f	mémorisation f intermédiaire	промежуточное запоминающее устройство
	intermediate storage	s. a. I 350		
I 354	intermicroprocessor communication	Kommunikation f zwischen Mikroprozessoren, Aus	communication f entre microprocesseurs	связь между микропроцессорами ‹в мультимикро

		tausch *m* zwischen Prozessoren eines Multimikroprozessorsystems		процессорной системе>
I 355	**intermittent**	intermittierend, aussetzend	intermittent, irrégulier	перемежающийся
	intermittent error	*s.* I 356		
I 356	**intermittent failure (fault, trouble),** transient fault, intermittent error	vorübergehender Fehler *m*, intermittierend auftretende Störung *f*, unregelmäßiger Fehler *m*	erreur *f* intermittente, défaut *m* intermittent (discontinu, irrégulier)	перемежающаяся (нерегулярная) ошибка, нерегулярный сбой; неустойчивое повреждение
I 357	**internal**	intern	interne	внутренний
I 358	**internal architecture**	interner Aufbau *m*, Internarchitektur *f*	architecture *f* interne	внутренняя архитектура
I 359	**internal bus**	interner (innerer) Bus *m*, Internbus *m*	bus *m* interne	внутренняя шина
I 360	**internal circuit**	innere Schaltung *f*	circuit *m* interne	внутренняя схема
I 361	**internal clock**	Interntakt *m*	rythme *m* interne	внутренняя синхронизация; внутренний синхросигнал
I 362	**internal code**	Internkode *m*	code *m* interne	внутренний код
I 363	**internal counter**	interner Zähler *m*	compteur *m* interne	внутренний счетчик
I 364	**internal flag**	Internflag *n*, internes Kennzeichen *n*	label *m* interne	внутренний флаг, внутренняя метка
I 365	**internal interrupt**	interne Programmunterbrechung *f*	interruption *f* interne	внутреннее прерывание
I 366	**internal interrupt mode**	Internunterbrechungsmodus *m*	mode *m* d'interruption interne	режим [обработки] внутреннего прерывания
I 367	**internal interval timer**	interner Intervallzeitgeber *m*	rythmeur *m* interne à intervalles	внутренний интервальный таймер
I 368	**internal layer**	Innenlage *f*, Zwischenebene *f*	couche *f* interne, niveau *m* intermédiaire	внутренний слой
I 369	**internal logic**	interne Logik *f*	logique *f* interne	внутренняя логика
I 370	**internal machine code**	interner Rechnerkode *m*, maschineninterner Kode *m*	code *m* interne de machine	внутренний машинный код
I 371	**internal memory,** internal storage	Internspeicher *m*	mémoire *f* interne	внутренняя память, внутреннее запоминающее устройство
I 372	**internal number representation**	interne Zahlendarstellung *f*	représentation *f* interne de nombres	внутреннее представление чисел
I 373	**internal operation**	Internoperation *f*	opération *f* interne	внутренняя операция
I 374	**internal register display**	Internregisteranzeige *f*	affichage *m* de registres internes	индикация [состояния] внутренних регистров
I 375	**internal scratchpad**	interner Notizspeicher (Zwischenspeicher) *m*	mémoire *f* intermédiaire interne	внутреннее сверхоперативное запоминающее устройство
I 376	**internal signal**	internes Signal *n*	signal *m* interne	внутренний сигнал
	internal storage	*s.* I 371		
I 377	**internal stored program**	intern gespeichertes Programm *n*, Internprogramm *n*	programme *m* interne	программа, хранимая во внутренней памяти
I 378	**internal test**	Interntest *m*	test *m* interne	внутренний тест
I 379	**internal timer**	Internzeitgeber *m*, interner Zeitgeber *m*	rythmeur *m* interne	внутренний таймер
	international standards organization	*s.* I 517		
I 380	**international telegraph (teletype) code**	internationaler Fernschreibkode *m*	code *m* télégraphique (télex) international	международный телеграфный код
I 381	**interpolator**	Interpolator *m*	interpolateur *m*	интерполятор
I 382	**interpole / to**	interpolieren	interpoler	интерполировать
I 383	**interpret / to**	interpretieren	interpréter	интерпретировать
I 384	**interpretable language**	interpretierbare Sprache *f*, interpretativ ausführbare Programmsprache *f*	langage *m* interprétable	интерпретируемый язык
I 385	**interpretation**	Auslegung *f*, Auswertung *f*	interprétation *f*	интерпретация
I 386	**interpretative execution**	interpretierende Ausführung *f*	exécution *f* interprétative	исполнение в режиме интерпретации
I 387	**interpretative simulation**	interpretierende Simulation *f*	simulation *f* interprétative	интерпретационное моделирование
	interpreter	*s.* I 388		
I 388	**interpreting routine, interpret[ive] program,** interpreter	interpretierendes (interpretatives) Programm *n*, Interpreter *m* <Quellsprachenanweisungen werden schrittweise übersetzt und ausgeführt durch Maschinenbefehlsfolgen, Spezialfall: Simulator>	programme *m* d'interprétation, interprétateur *m*	интерпретатор, интерпретирующая программа
I 389	**interprocess communication**	Kommunikation *f* zwischen Einzelprozessen, Informationsaustausch *m* zwischen verschiedenen Programmen <durch Aufbau logischer Verbindungen>	communication *f* entre processus différents	взаимодействие между процессами
I 390	**interprocessor communication**	Interprozessorkommunikation *f*, Austausch *m* zwischen Prozessoren eines Systems	communication *f* entre processeurs	связь между процессорами <в мультипроцессорной системе>
I 391	**interrogate / to**	abfragen	interroger	опрашивать, запрашивать
	interrogation	*s.* I 210		
I 392	**interrogation pulse**	Abfrageimpuls *m*	impulsion *f* d'interrogation	импульс опроса
I 393	**interrogation register**	Abfrageregister *n*	registre *m* d'interrogation	регистр запроса
I 394	**interrogation system**	Abfragesystem *n*	système *m* d'interrogation	система опроса
I 395	**interrupt**	Interrupt *m*, Programmunterbrechung *f*, Unterbrechung *f*, Eingriff *m*	interruption *f*	прерывание

I 396	interrupt acknowledge	Interruptanerkennung f, Unterbrechungsbestätigung f	reconnaissance (confirmation) f d'interruption	подтверждение [запроса] прерывания
I 397	interrupt acknowledge signal	Interruptbestätigungssignal n, Unterbrechungsanerkennungssignal n	signal m de confirmation d'interruption, signal m d'acceptation d'interruption	сигнал подтверждения [запроса] прерывания
I 398	interrupt architecture	Interruptarchitektur f, Unterbrechungssystemaufbau m	architecture f des interruptions	архитектура системы прерываний
I 399	interrupt arm	Interruptquellenfreigabe f, Unterbrechungsquellenfreigabe f	libération f de source d'interruption	разблокировка источника прерываний
I 400	interrupt-based system	System n auf Interruptbasis <E/A-Verkehr>	système m basé sur interruptions	система обмена на основе прерывания
I 401	interrupt button	Interrupttaste f, Unterbrechungstaste f	touche f d'interruption	кнопка прерывания
I 402	interrupt capability	Interruptfähigkeit f, Unterbrechungsfähigkeit f	faculté f d'interruption	возможности прерывания
I 403	interrupt channel	Interruptkanal m, Unterbrechungskanal m	canal m d'interruption	канал с прерыванием, прерываемый канал
I 404	interrupt controller	Interruptsteuerungsgerät n, Unterbrechungssteuerungsgerät n	appareil m de commande d'interruption	контроллер прерываний
I 405	interrupt control unit, ICU	Interruptsteuereinheit f, Unterbrechungssteuereinheit f	unité f de commande d'interruption	блок обработки прерываний
I 406	interrupt disable	Interruptblockierung f, Unterbrechungsblockierung f	blocage m d'interruption	запрет прерывания
I 407	interrupt disarm	Interruptquellenblockierung f, Unterbrechungsquellensperrung f	blocage m de source d'interruption	блокировка источника прерываний
I 408	interrupt-driven environment	interruptbetriebene Systemumgebung f <einer Peripherieeinheit>, auf Unterbrechungssignale reagierende Systemumgebung	environnement m actionné par interruption	оборудование, приводимое в действие сигналом прерывания
I 409	interrupt-driven I/O	interruptgesteuerte E/A f, unterbrechungsgesteuerte Ein-/Ausgabe f	E/S f à commande par interruption	ввод-вывод, управляемый прерываниями
I 410	interrupt-driven operation	interruptgesteuerter (unterbrechungsgesteuerter) Betrieb m	régime m à commande par interruptions	режим работы, управляемый прерываниями
I 411	interrupt-driven system	interruptgesteuertes (unterbrechungsgesteuertes) System n	système m à commande par interruptions	система, управляемая прерываниями
I 412	interrupted program	unterbrochenes Programm n	programme m interrompu	прерванная программа
I 413	interrupt enable	Interruptfreigabe f, Unterbrechungsfreigabe f	libération f d'interruption	разрешение прерывания
I 414	interrupt-enable control	Interruptfreigabe-Steuerung f, Steuerung f der Unterbrechbarkeit	commande f de faculté d'interruption	управление разрешением прерываний
I 415	interrupt facility	Interrupteinrichtung f, Unterbrechungseinrichtung f	dispositif m d'interruption	средство обеспечения прерывания
I 416	interrupt facility	Interruptmöglichkeit f, Unterbrechungsmöglichkeit f	possibilité f d'interruption	возможность обслуживания прерываний
	interrupt handler	s. I 435		
I 417	interrupt handling	Interruptbehandlung f, Unterbrechungsbearbeitung f	traitement m d'interruption	обработка прерывания, управление прерыванием
I 418	interrupt identification	Interruptkennung f, Unterbrechungsidentifizierung f	identification f d'interruption	идентификация прерывания
I 419	interrupt level	Interruptebene f, Unterbrechungsniveau n, Programmunterbrechungsebene f	niveau m d'interruption	уровень прерывания
I 420	interrupt line	Interruptleitung f, Unterbrechungsleitung f	ligne f d'interruption	линия прерывания
I 421	interrupt logic	Interruptlogik f, Unterbrechungslogik f	logique f d'interruption	логика прерывания
I 422	interrupt mask bit	Interruptmaskenbit n, Unterbrechungsmaskierungsbit n	bit m de masque d'interruption	бит маски прерывания
I 423	interrupt mask word	Interruptmaskenwort n, Unterbrechungsmaskierungswort n	mot m de masque d'interruption	слово масок прерываний
I 424	interrupt priority	Interruptvorrang m, Unterbrechungspriorität f	priorité f d'interruption	приоритет прерывания
I 425	interrupt priority level	Interruptprioritätsniveau n, Unterbrechungsvorrangebene f	niveau m de priorité d'interruption	уровень приоритета прерывания
I 426	interrupt priority system	Interruptvorrangsystem n, Unterbrechungsprioritätssystem n	système m de priorité d'interruption	система приоритетов прерываний
I 427	interrupt processing	Interruptverarbeitung f, Unterbrechungsverarbeitung f	traitement m d'interruption	обработка прерывания
I 428	interrupt register	Interruptregister n, Unterbrechungsregister n	registre m d'interruptions	регистр прерываний

I 429	interrupt request	Interruptanforderung f, Unterbrechungsforderung f	demande f d'interruption	запрос прерывания
I 430	interrupt request line	Interruptanforderungsleitung f, Unterbrechungsforderungsleitung f	ligne f de demandes d'interruption	линия запроса прерывания
I 431	interrupt request register	Interruptanforderungs-Sammelregister n	registre m de demandes d'interruption	регистр запросов прерывания
I 432	interrupt request reset signal	Interruptanforderungs-Rücksetzsignal n	signal m de mise à zéro de demandes d'interruption	сигнал установки в нуль запроса прерывания
I 433	interrupt request synchronization register	Interruptanforderungs-Synchronisierungsregister n	registre m de synchronisation de demandes d'interruption	регистр синхронизации запросов прерывания
I 434	interrupt response time	Interruptansprechzeit f, Unterbrechungsreaktionszeit f	temps m de réponse d'interruption	время реакции на прерывание
I 435	interrupt [service] routine, interrupt handler	Interruptprogramm n, Unterbrechungsprogramm n, Unterbrechungsbehandlungsprogramm n	programme m [de traitement] d'interruption	программа [обработки] прерывания
I 436	interrupt signal	Interruptsignal n, Unterbrechungssignal n	signal m d'interruption	сигнал прерывания
I 437	interrupt single multiple line	Interruptsammelleitung f, Unterbrechungssammelleitung f	ligne f collective à interruptions	общая линия прерываний
I 438	interrupt source	Interruptquelle f, Unterbrechungsquelle f, Unterbrechungsverursacher m	source f d'interruption	источник прерывания
I 439	interrupt state	Interruptstatus m, Unterbrechungszustand m	état m d'interruption	состояние прерывания
I 440	interrupt subroutine	Interruptunterprogramm n, Unterbrechungsunterprogramm n	sous-programme m d'interruption	подпрограмма [обработки] прерывания
I 441	interrupt synchronization	Interruptsynchronisierung f, Unterbrechungssynchronisierung f	synchronisation f d'interruptions	синхронизация прерываний
I 442	interrupt system	Interruptsystem n, Unterbrechungssystem n, Eingriffssystem n	système m d'interruptions	система прерываний
I 443	interrupt technique	Interrupttechnik f, Unterbrechungsverfahren n	technique f d'interruptions	техника прерываний
I 444	interrupt terminal	Interruptanschlußstelle f, Unterbrechungssignalanschluß m	terminal m d'interruption	вывод [для подключения к линии] сигнала прерывания
I 445	interrupt vector	Interruptvektor m, Unterbrechungsvektor m, Unterbrechungskennzeiger m	vecteur m d'interruption	вектор прерывания
I 446	interrupt vector address	Interruptvektoradresse f, Unterbrechungsvektoradresse f	adresse f de vecteur d'interruption	адрес вектора прерывания
I 447	interval interval clock	Intervall n s. I 449	intervalle m	интервал
I 448	interval length	Intervallänge f, Intervalldauer f	longueur f (durée f) d'intervalle	длительность (величина) интервала
I 449	interval timer, interval clock	Intervallzeitgeber m, Zeitspannengeber m, Zeitimpulsgeber m	horloge f à intervalles	интервальный таймер, датчик временных интервалов
I 450	intrinsic conduction	Eigenleitung f	conduction f intrinsèque	собственная проводимость
I 451	intrinsic mobility	Elektronenbeweglichkeit f im Eigenhalbleiter	mobilité f intrinsèque	подвижность носителей в собственном полупроводнике
I 452	introduction	Einführung f, Leitfaden m	introduction f	введение, внесение
I 453	invalid	ungültig	non valable	неверный, недействительный
I 454	invalid address	ungültige Adresse f	adresse f non valable	недействительный адрес
I 455	invalid character	ungültiges Zeichen n	caractère m non valable	недействительный символ
I 456	invalid character test	Gültigkeitsprüfung f, Prüfung f ungültiger Zeichen	test m des caractères invalides	проверка знаков на достоверность
I 457	invalid code	ungültiger Kode m	code m non valable	недействительный код
I 458	inverse amplifier, inverted amplifier	Umkehrverstärker m	amplificateur m inverse	инвертирующий усилитель
I 459	inverse feedback, negative feedback	Gegenkopplung f	contre-réaction f	отрицательная обратная связь
I 460	inverse function, inverted function	Umkehrfunktion f	fonction f inverse	обратная функция
	inverse gate	s. I 466		⌐ность
I 461	inverse sequence	umgekehrte Folge f	séquence f inverse	обратная последователь-
I 462	inverse storage	umgekehrte Speicherung f, Speicherung in umgekehrter Folge	mise f en mémoire inverse	запоминание в обратной последовательности
	inversion circuit	s. I 466		
	invert / to	s. R 368		
	inverted amplifier	s. I 458		
	inverted function	s. I 460		
I 463	inverted mode	umgekehrte Betriebsweise f ⟨einer Schaltung⟩	mode m inverti	инверсный режим работы
I 464	inverted operand	invertierter (negierter) Operand m	opérande m inverti	инвертированный операнд
I 465	inverter	Wechselrichter m, Gleichspannungs-Wechselspannungs-Wandler m	convertisseur m continu-alternatif, onduleur m	преобразователь напряжения

I 466	**inverter,** inverting (inverse) gate, inversion circuit	Inverter m, Invertierungsgatter n, Umkehrschaltung f	circuit (montage) m d'inversion	инвертор, элемент НЕ
I 467	**inverting bit**	Negationsbit n	bit m de négation	бит инверсии
I 468	**inverting circuit**	invertierende Schaltung f	circuit m d'inversion	инвертирующая схема
	inverting gate	s. I 466		
I 469	**invoicing**	Fakturierung f	facturation f	ведение экономических операций
I 470	**invoicing computer**	Fakturiercomputer m, Fakturierrechner m	calculateur m de facturation	конторская ЭВМ
I 471	**invoicing machine**	Fakturiermaschine f	machine f de facturation	конторская машина
	invoke / to	s. C 23		
I 472	**I/O,** input-output	E/A, Eingabe-Ausgabe f	E/S, entrée-sortie f	ввод-вывод
I 473	**I/O addressing mode**	E/A-Adressierungsmodus m, E/A-Adressierart f, Eingabe-Ausgabe-Adressierungsmodus m	mode m d'adressage E/S	режим адресации [устройств] ввода-вывода
I 474	**I/O bus,** input-output bus	E/A-Bus m, Eingabe-Ausgabe-Bus m	bus m d'E/S, bus d'entrée-sortie	шина ввода-вывода
I 475	**I/O bus cycle,** input-output bus cycle	E/A-Buszyklus m, Eingabe-Ausgabe-Buszyklus m	cycle m de bus d'entrée-sortie, cycle de bus d'E/S	цикл обращения к шине ввода-вывода, цикл шины ввода-вывода
I 476	**I/O bus structure,** input-output bus structure	E/A-Busstruktur f, Eingabe-Ausgabe-Busstruktur f	structure f de bus d'entrée-sortie, structure de bus d'E/S	структура шины ввода-вывода
I 477	**I/O channel,** input-output channel	E/A-Kanal m, Eingabe-Ausgabe-Kanal m	canal m d'entrée-sortie, canal d'E/S	канал ввода-вывода
I 478	**I/O concept,** input-output concept	E/A-Konzept n, Eingabe-Ausgabe-Konzept n	concept m d'entrée-sortie, concept d'E/S	концепция [организации] ввода-вывода
I 479	**I/O control,** input-output control	E/A-Steuerung f, Eingabe-Ausgabe-Steuerung f	commande f d'entrée-sortie, commande d'E/S	управление вводом-выводом
I 480	**I/O control program,** input-output control program	E/A-Steuerprogramm n, Eingabe-Ausgabe-Steuerprogramm n	programme m de commande d'entrée-sortie, programme de commande d'E/S	программа управления вводом-выводом
I 481	**I/O control system,** input-output control system, IOCS	E/A-Steuersystem n, Eingabe-Ausgabe-Steuersystem n <Programm>	système m de commande d'entrée-sortie, système de commande d'E/S	система управления вводом-выводом
I 482	**I/O control unit,** input-output control unit	E/A-Steuereinheit f, Eingabe-Ausgabe-Steuereinheit f	unité f de commande d'entrée-sortie, unité de commande d'E/S	устройство управления вводом-выводом
	IOCS	s. I 481		
I 483	**I/O cycle,** input-output cycle	E/A-Zyklus m, Eingabe-Ausgabe-Zyklus m	cycle m d'entrée-sortie, cycle d'E/S	цикл ввода-вывода
	I/O data transfer	s. I 514		
I 484	**I/O device,** input-output device (equipment), I/O equipment	E/A-Einrichtung f, Eingabe-Ausgabe-Einrichtung f	dispositif m d'entrée-sortie, dispositif d'E/S	устройство (оборудование) ввода-вывода
I 485	**I/O driver,** input-output driver	E/A-Treiber m, Eingabe-Ausgabe-Treiber m	basculeur m d'entrée-sortie, basculeur d'E/S	[программа-]драйвер [устройств] ввода-вывода
	I/O equipment	s. I 484		
I 486	**I/O executive,** input-output executive	E/A-Organisationsprogramm n, Eingabe-Ausgabe-Organisationsprogramm n	programme m organisationnel d'entrée-sortie, programme organisationnel d'E/S	организационная программа ввода-вывода
I 487	**I/O expansion**	E/A-Erweiterung f, Eingabe-Ausgabe-Systemerweiterung f	élargissement m de système d'E/S	расширение системы ввода-вывода
I 488	**I/O format,** input-output format	E/A-Format n, Eingabe-Ausgabe-Format n	format m d'entrée-sortie, format d'E/S	формат ввода-вывода
I 489	**I/O function,** input-output function	E/A-Funktion f, Eingabe-Ausgabe-Funktion f	fonction f d'entrée-sortie, fonction d'E/S	функция ввода-вывода
I 490	**I/O handler,** input-output handler	E/A-Behandlungsroutine f, Eingabe-Ausgabe-Behandlungsroutine f	routine f de traitement d'entrée-sortie, routine de traitement d'E/S	программа обработки ввода-вывода
I 491	**I/O instruction,** input-output instruction	E/A-Befehl m, Eingabe-Ausgabe-Befehl m	instruction f d'entrée-sortie, instruction d'E/S	команда ввода-вывода
I 492	**I/O instruction modes**	E/A-Befehlsmodi mpl, Eingabe-Ausgabe-Befehlsmodi mpl	modes mpl d'instructions d'E/S	режимы [выполнения] команд ввода-вывода
I 493	**I/O interface,** input-output-interface	E/A-Schnittstelle f, Eingabe-Ausgabe-Schnittstelle f, E/A-Anschlußstelle f	interface f d'entrée-sortie, interface d'E/S	интерфейс ввода-вывода
I 494	**I/O interrupt,** input-output interrupt	E/A-Interrupt m, Eingabe-Ausgabe-Interrupt m	interruption f d'entrée-sortie, interruption d'E/S	прерывание [от устройства] ввода-вывода
I 495	**I/O interrupt program**	E/A-Interruptprogramm n, Eingabe-Ausgabe-Unterbrechungsprogramm n	programme m d'interruption d'E/S	программа [обработки] прерывания ввода-вывода
I 496	**I/O line,** input-output line	E/A-Leitung f, Eingabe-Ausgabe-Leitung f	ligne f d'entrée-sortie, ligne d'E/S	линия ввода-вывода
I 497	**I/O mode,** input-output mode	E/A-Betriebsart f, Eingabe-Ausgabe-Betriebsart f	mode m d'entrée-sortie, mode d'E/S	режим ввода-вывода
I 498	**I/O monitoring,** input-output monitoring	E/A-Überwachung f, Eingabe-Ausgabe-Überwachung f, E/A-Ablaufkontrolle f	surveillance f d'entrée-sortie, surveillance d'E/S	контроль над вводом-выводом
I 499	**I/O multiplexer**	E/A-Multiplexer m, E/A-Mehrfachkoppler m, Eingabe-Ausgabe-Multiplexer m	multiplexeur m d'E/S	мультиплексор ввода-вывода
I 500	**ion implantation**	Ionenimplantation f, Ioneneinbau m <Halbleitertechnik>	implantation f d'ions	ионная имплантация

I 501	**I/O path,** input-output path	E/A-Weg m, E/A-Pfad m, Eingabe-Ausgabe-Pfad m	voie f d'E/S	тракт ввода-вывода
I 502	**I/O pool,** input-output pool	E/A-Gerätesatz m, Eingabe-Ausgabe-Gerätesatz m	jeu m d'appareils d'E/S	набор устройств ввода-вывода
I 503	**I/O port,** input-output port	E/A-Tor n, Eingabe-Ausgabe-Tor n	porte f d'entrée-sortie, porte d'E/S	порт ввода-вывода
I 504	**I/O port address**	E/A-Tor-Adresse f, E/A-An chluß-Adresse f	adresse f de porte d'E/S	адрес порта ввода-вывода
I 505	**I/O processor,** input-output processor	E/A-Prozessor m, Eingabe-Ausgabe-Prozessor m	processeur m d'entrée-sortie, processeur d'E/S	процессор ввода-вывода
I 506	**I/O program,** input-output program	E/A-Programm n, Eingabe-Ausgabe-Programm n	programme m d'entrée-sortie, programme d'E/S	программа ввода-вывода
I 507	**I/O request,** input-output request	E/A-Anforderung f, Eingabe-Ausgabe-Anforderung f	demande f d'entrée-sortie, demande d'E/S	запрос [устройства] ввода-вывода
I 508	**I/O simulation,** input-output simulation	E/A-Simulation f, Eingabe-Ausgabe-Simulation f	simulation f d'E/S	моделирование ввода-вывода
I 509	**I/O space,** input-output space	E/A-Bereich m, Eingabe-Ausgabebereich m	champ m d'entrée-sortie, champ d'E/S	область [памяти для] ввода-вывода
I 510	**I/O strobe /enable signals**	E/A-Markier- und -Freigabesignale npl	signaux mpl de marquage et de libération d'E/S	сигналы стробирования [входных данных] / разрешения [выдачи данных]
I 511	**I/O structure**	E/A-Struktur f, Eingabe-Ausgabe-Struktur f	structure f d'E/S	структура [системы] ввода-вывода
I 512	**I/O switching channel,** input-output switching channel	E/A-Umschaltkanal m, Eingabe-Ausgabe-Umschaltkanal m	canal m de commutation d'entrée/sortie, commutateur f de canal d'E/S	канал коммутации ввода-вывода
I 513	**I/O technique**	E/A-Technik f, E/A-Verfahren n, Eingabe-Ausgabe-Technik f	technique f d'E/S	принцип [организации] ввода-вывода, метод ввода-вывода
I 514	**I/O transfer,** I/O data transfer	E/A-Transfer m, E/A-Datenübertragung f, Eingabe-Ausgabe-Übertragung f	transfert m d'E/S, transmission f de données d'E/S	передача данных при вводе-выводе
I 515	**I/O typewriter,** input-output typewriter	E/A-Schreibmaschine f, Eingabe-Ausgabe-Schreibmaschine f	machine f à écrire d'entrée sortie, machine à écrire d'E/S	пишущая машинка для ввода-вывода
I 516	**I/O unit,** input-output unit	E/A-Einheit f, Eingabe-Ausgabe-Einheit f	unité f d'entrée-sortie, unité d'E/S	устройство ввода-вывода
I 517	**ISO,** international standards organization	ISO, internationale Standard-Organisation f	ISO, organisation f internationale des standards	МОС, международная организация стандартов
I 518	**isolate / to**	s. 1. D 422; 2. I 274		
I 518	**isolated input-output**	getrennte Eingabe-Ausgabe f, getrennte Eingabe-Ausgabe-Adressierung f ‹von Speicheradressierung›	entrée-sortie f isolées	отделенный [от адресного пространства памяти] ввод-вывод
I 519	**isolating circuit**	Entkopplungsschaltung f, Trennstufe f	circuit m de séparation	схема развязки
I 520	**isolation barrier,** guard ring	Isolationswall m, Schutzring m	barrière f d'isolement, anneau m de garde	защитное кольцо
I 520	**isolation layer**	s. I 276		
I 521	**isolation techniques**	Isolationstechniken fpl	techniques fpl d'isolation	методы изоляции
I 522	**isoplanar oxide isolation**	isoplanare Oxidisolation f	isolation f à oxyde isoplanaire	изопланарная оксидная изоляция
I 523	**item**	Einzelheit f, Dateneinheit f, Posten m	détail m, unité f de données	элемент; элементарная группа [данных]
I 524	**iteration**	Iteration f	itération f	итерация
I 525	**iteration loop**	Iterationsschleife f	boucle f d'itération	итерационный цикл, цикл итерации
I 526	**iterative**	iterativ	itératif	итеративный
I 527	**iterative addition**	schrittweise Addition f	addition f itérative	итеративное сложение
I 528	**iterative impedance**	Kettenwiderstand m, Wellenwiderstand m	impédance f itérative	повторный импеданс

J

	jack	s. S 521		
J 1/2	**jack panel**	Buchsenfeld n	panneau m à broches (douilles)	коммутационная панель
J 3	**jam / to,** to insert	einfügen, einmischen	insérer, mélanger	заклинивать[ся], застревать; создавать помехи
J 4	**jamming signal**	Funkstörsignal n	signal m parasite	сигнал помехи
	JFET	s. J 26		
J 5	**JK flip-flop**	JK-Flipflop n	bascule f électronique de type JK	J-K триггер
J 6	**job**	Job m, Arbeitselement n ‹Teilprogramm›, Arbeitsauftrag m	job m, travail m	задание
J 7	**job control**	Jobsteuerung f, Steuerung f des Arbeitselements	commande f de job	управление заданиями
J 8	**job-oriented terminal**	auftragsorientiertes Terminal n, auftragsorientierte Datenstation f	terminal m orienté job	проблемно-ориентированный терминал, специализированный терминал
J 9	**job processing**	Jobbearbeitung f, Bearbeitung f des Arbeitselements	traitement m de job	обработка задания
J 10	**job processing control**	Ablaufsteuerung f eines Auftrages	commande f de travail d'une commission	управление прохождением задания
J 11	**job scheduler**	Jobprioritätssteuerprogramm n, Auftragsablaufplaner m	programme m de commande de job	планировщик заданий

J 12	**Josephson effect**	Josephson-Effekt *m*	effet *m* Josephson	эффект Джозефсона
J 13	**Josephson junction**	Josephson-Übergang *m*	jonction *f* Josephson	переход Джозефсона
J 14	**Josephson-junction device**	Josephson-Bauelement *n*	module *m* Josephson	элемент Джозефсона
J 15	**JOVIAL** <Jules own version of IAL>	JOVIAL *n* <Programmiersprache für numerische Rechnung und Steuerung>	JOVIAL *m* <langage de programmation pour calcul et commande numériques>	ДЖОВИАЛ <язык программирования для числовых расчетов и задач управления>
J 16	**jump**	Sprung *m*	saut *m*	переход; операция перехода
J 17	**jump address**	Sprungadresse *f*, Sprungzieladresse *f*	adresse *f* de saut	адрес перехода
J 18	**jumper [wire]**	Drahtbrücke *f*, Leitungsbrücke *f*	pont *m* de fil	навесной проводник, перемычка
J 19	**jump instruction**	Sprungbefehl *m*	instruction *f* de saut	команда перехода
J 20	**jump routine**	Sprungprogramm *n*	programme *m* de saut	программа перехода
J 21	**junction**	Halbleiterübergang *m* <zwischen unterschiedlich dotierten Zonen>	jonction *f*	[p-n] переход
	junction	*s. a.* B 47		
J 22	**junction area**	Übergangsfläche *f*, Übergangszone *f* <eines pn-Überganges>, Sperrschichtfläche *f*	surface *f* de jonction	площадь [p-n] перехода
J 23	**junction box**	Abzweigdose *f*, Verteilerdose *f*	boîte *f* de branchement	распределительная коробка
	junction capacitance	*s.* B 46		
J 24	**junction depth**	Sperrschichttiefe *f*, Übergangstiefe *f*	profondeur *f* de jonction	глубина перехода
J 25	**junction diode**	Flächendiode *f*, Sperrschichtdiode *f*	diode *f* à jonction	плоскостной диод
J 26	**junction field effect transistor, junction-gate field effect transistor, JFET**	Sperrschicht-Feldeffekttransistor *m* <FET-Grundtyp mit Sperrschichttrennung Gate-Kanal>	transistor *m* à effet de champ à jonction	полевой транзистор с p-n переходом
	junction-gate field effect transistor	*s.* J 26		
J 27	**junction isolation of layer**	Sperrschichtisolierung *f* zwischen Schichten	isolation *f* de jonction entre couches	изоляция p-n переходом
	junction rectifier	*s.* B 48		
J 28	**junction temperature**	Sperrschichttemperatur *f*, Kristalltemperatur *f*	température *f* de jonction	температура [p-n] перехода
J 29	**junction transistor, pn-junction transistor**	Sperrschichttransistor *m*, Transistor *m* mit pn-Übergang	transistor *m* à jonction [p-n]	плоскостной транзистор
J 30	**junction transistor circuit**	Sperrschichttransistorschaltung *f*	circuit *m* à transistor à jonction	схема на плоскостных транзисторах
J 31	**junction transition region**	Sperrschichtübergangsgebiet *n*, pn-Übergangsgebiet *n*	champ *m* (région *f*) de transition de jonction	область [p-n] перехода
J 32	**junction voltage**	Sperrschichtspannung *f*	tension *f* de jonction	напряжение на [p-n] переходе
J 33	**junction width**	Breite *f* der pn-Übergangszone, Sperrschichtdicke *f*, Grenzschichtbreite *f*	largeur *f* de jonction	ширина [p-n] перехода

K

K 1	**K**	K, Kilo *n* <Zahlenfaktor für Vielfache von $2^{10} = 1\,024$>	K, Kilo *m* <facteur pour multiples de $2^{10} = 1\,024$>	K <множитель при единицах емкости памяти, равный 1 024>
K 2	**Karnaugh map**	Karnaugh-Tafel *f*	table *f* de Karnaugh	карта Карно
K 3	**kernel**	Kern *m* <des Betriebssystems>	noyau *m* <de système opérationnel>	ядро <операционной системы>
K 4	**kernel mode**	Kernel-Modus *m*, Kernmodus *m* <Betriebsart>	mode *m* de noyau, mode Kernel	режим ядра <режим работы операционной системы>
K 5	**key / to**	tasten, eintasten	manipuler	манипулировать, работать ключом
K 6	**key**	Taste *f*	touche *f*	клавиша, кнопка
K 7	**key**	Schlüssel *m* <Information>	clé *f*	ключ
K 8	**keyboard, keyset**	Tastatur *f*, Tastenfeld *n*	clavier *m*	клавиатура
K 9	**keyboard control**	Tastatursteuerung *f*	commande *f* par clavier	управление с [помощью] клавиатуры
K 10	**keyboard control keys**	Tastatur-Steuertasten *fpl*	touches *fpl* de commande de clavier	клавиши управления
K 11	**keyboard-controlled**	tastaturgesteuert	à commande par clavier	управляемый клавиатурой
K 12	**keyboard editing display station**	Tastatur-Anzeige-Station *f* mit Aufbereitungsfunktion	station *f* clavier-affichage pour fonctions de préparation	дисплейная станция с клавиатурой редактирования
K 13	**keyboard encoder**	Tastaturkodierer *m*	codeur *m* à clavier	шифратор клавиатуры
K 13a	**keyboard function keys**	Tastatur-Funktionstasten *fpl*	touches *fpl* fonctionnelles de clavier	функциональные клавиши
K 14	**keyboard input, key-in**	Tastatureingabe *f*	entrée *f* par clavier	ввод с клавиатуры
K 15	**keyboard lock**	Tastaturverriegelung *f*	verrouillage *m* de clavier	блокировка клавиатуры
K 16	**keyboard matrix**	Tastaturmatrix *f*	matrice *f* de clavier	клавишная матрица
K 17	**keyboard perforator, key punch**	Tastaturlocher *m*	perforatrice *f* à clavier	клавишный (ручной) перфоратор
K 18	**keyboard scanning**	Tastaturabfrage *f*	interrogation (scrutation) *f* de clavier	опрос (сканирование) клавиатуры

K 19	keyboard send-receive, KSR	Sende-Empfang-Tastatur *f*	clavier *m* émission-réception	клавишный приемопередатчик
K 20	key-driven	tastengesteuert	à commande par touches	с клавишным управлением
K 21	key feature	Schlüsseleigenschaft *f*, Hauptmerkmal *n*, bestimmende Kenngröße *f*	caractéristique-clé *f*	ключевой (отличительный) признак
K 22	key field	Schlüsselfeld *n*	champ-clé *m*	поле ключа
	key-in	s. K 14		
K 23	keylock	Tastensperre *f*	verrou *m* de touche	блокировка клавиш[и]
K 24	keypunch / to	handlochen	perforer à la main	перфорировать вручную
	key punch	s. K 17		
	keyset	s. K 8		⌐тель
K 25	key switch	Tastenschalter *m*	commutateur *m* à touches	клавишный переключа-
K 26	key technique	Schlüsseltechnik *f*, Hauptverfahren *n*	technique *f* clé	главный метод
K 27	key verify / to	prüfen mittels Tastatur, lochprüfen	vérifier par clavier	проверять [перфокарты] с помощью [клавиатуры] контрольника
K 28	keyword	Schlüsselwort *n*	mot-clé *m*	ключевое слово
K 29	kind of operation	Operationsart *f*, Operationstyp *m*	type *m* d'opération	тип операции
K 30	kipp relay	Kipp-Relais *n* ‹monostabiler Multivibrator›	relais-bascule *m*	кипп-реле
K 31	kit	Bausatz *m*	ensemble *m* de construction	набор комплектующих элементов, комплект деталей
K 32	kit component	Bausatzkomponente *f*	composant *m* d'ensemble [de construction]	компонент набора, деталь комплекта
	know-how	s. T 64		
	KSR	s. K 19		

L

L 1	label	Kennzeichen *n*, Etikett *n*, Kennsatz *m*	label *m*	метка, идентификатор
L 2	label-addressed message	kennzeichenadressierte Nachricht *f*	message *m* adressé par label	сообщение, адресуемое меткой
L 3	label area	Kennsatzbereich *m*	domaine *m* à labels	зона метки
L 4	label declaration	Kennsatzvereinbarung *f*	déclaration *f* de label	объявление метки
L 5	label field	Kennsatzfeld *n*	champ *m* de label[s]	поле метки
L 6	label identification	Kennsatzidentifizierung *f*	identification *f* de label	идентификация метки
L 7	labelled statement	markierte Anweisung *f*	instruction *f* marquée (à label)	помеченный оператор
L 8	labelling	Kennsatzzuweisung *f*, Benennung *f*	attribution *f* de label, dénomination *f*	присвоение обозначений; присвоение идентификаторов
L 9	label name	Etikettname *m*	nom *m* de label, nom d'étiquette	имя метки
L 10	label processing	Kennsatzverarbeitung *f*	traitement *m* de label	обработка метки
L 11	label statement	Kennsatzanweisung *f*	instruction *f* de label	оператор-метка
L 12	laboratory logic testing	Labor-Logikprüfung *f*, Laborprüfung *f* der Logik	examen *m* logique au laboratoire	лабораторная проверка [функционирования] логики
L 13	laboratory model	Labormodell *n*	modèle *m* de laboratoire	лабораторная модель
L 14	laboratory use	Laboreinsatz *m*	usage *m* au laboratoire	лабораторное применение
L 15	lack of memory capacity	unzureichende Speicherkapazität *f*	capacité *f* de mémoire insuffisante	недостаточная емкость памяти
L 16	laminated board	Schichtplatte *f*, Mehrschichtplatte *f*	platine *f* laminée	многослойная (слоистая) плата
L 17	laminated structure	Schichtstruktur *f*	structure *f* laminée	многослойная (слоистая) структура
L 18	land, lug	Lötauge *n*, Lötöse *f*, Kontaktlamelle *f*	cosse *f* à souder	контактная пластина
L 19	language interpretation	Sprachinterpretation *f*, Programmsprachinterpretierung *f*	interprétation *f* de langage	интерпретация языка
L 20	language interpreter	Sprachinterpretierer *m*, Programmsprachinterpreterprogramm *n*	interprétateur *m* de langage	интерпретатор языка
L 21	language level	Sprachniveau *n*	niveau *m* de langage	уровень языка
L 22	language list processing	Sprachaufbereitung *f*, Sprachsymbolverarbeitung *f* über Auflistung	préparation *f* de langage	обработка символов языка с помощью списков
L 23	language-oriented architecture	sprachorientierte (programmsprachorientierte) Struktur *f*	structure *f* orientée sur le langage	архитектура, ориентированная на определенный тип языка
L 24	language-oriented computer (machine)	sprachorientierter (programmsprachorientierter) Rechner *m*	calculateur *m* orienté sur le langage	ЭВМ, ориентированная на определенный тип языка
L 25	language rule	Sprachregel *f*	règle *f* de langage	правило языка
L 26	language translator	Sprachübersetzer *m*, Programmsprachübersetzer *m*	traducteur *m* de langage	транслятор языка
L 27	lap / to	läppen	roder	притирать, полировать
	LARAM	s. L 127		
L 28	large-area	großflächig	à grande surface (superficie)	с большой площадью (поверхностью)
L 29	large computer	Großrechner *m*	grand calculateur *m*, ordinateur *m*	большая ЭВМ
	large-scale integration	s. L 327		
L 30	large-scale production	Großserienfertigung *f*	fabrication *f* à grande échelle, fabrication en grande série	крупносерийное производство

L 31	large-signal region	Großsignalbereich *m*	domaine *m* de signaux grands	область большого сигнала
L 32	large-volume applications	Großvolumenanwendungen *fpl*, Massenanwendungen *fpl*	applications *fpl* de grand volume, applications de masse	массовое применение
L 33	laser <light amplification by stimulated emission of radiation>	Laser *m* <Lichtverstärkung durch induzierte Emission von Strahlung>	laser *m*	лазер, оптический квантовый генератор
L 34	laser communication system	Laser-Nachrichtenübertragungssystem *n*	système *m* de [télé]communication par laser	лазерная (оптическая) система связи
L 35	laser-emulsion storage	Laser-Emulsionsspeicherung *f*	mémoire *f* à émulsion à laser	лазерно-эмульсионное запоминающее устройство
	last-in first-out ...	s. LIFO...		
L 36	latch / to	selbsthaltend aufschalten, auffangen	commuter à verrouillage	фиксировать
L 37	latch	Auffang-Flipflop *n*, selbsthaltender Schalter *m*	bascule *f* de maintien, autocommutateur *m*	фиксатор, триггер-защелка, одноступенчатый триггер
L 38/9	latching	Selbsthaltung *f*, Schaltzustandsfixierung *f*, Informationsfang *m*	automaintien *m* [d'état commuté], tamponnage *m* d'informations	фиксация
	latching circuit	s. H 127		
L 40	latching element	Zustandsspeicherelement *n* <eines sequentiellen Schaltnetzwerkes>	élément *m* de mémoire d'état	элемент фиксации [данных]
L 41	latching memory	Haltespeicher *m*	mémoire *f* de maintien	фиксирующая память
L 42	latching output	selbsthaltende Ausgabe *f*	sortie *f* tamponnée	буферизованный выход, выход с фиксацией [состояния]
L 43	latch register	Latchregister *n*, Auffangregister *n*, Informationsfangregister *n*	registre *m* de tampon d'informations	регистр-фиксатор
L 44	latency time	Latenzzeit *f* <Wartezeit>	temps *m* de latence <d'attente>	время ожидания
	lateral parity check	s. V 29		
L 45	lateral transistor	Lateraltransistor *m* <Emitter und Kollektor auf gleicher Seite>	transistor *m* latéral	транзистор с плоским расположением областей
L 46	lattice imperfection	Gitterfehlstelle *f*, Gitterfehler *m*	défaut *m* de réseau	дефект решетки
L 47	lattice parameter	Gitterparameter *m*	paramètre *m* de réseau	параметр решетки
L 48	lattice spacing	Gitterabstand *m*	espace *m* de réseau	период [кристаллической] решетки
L 49	lattice structure	Gitterstruktur *f*	structure *f* de grille	структура решетки
L 50	layer, sheet	Schicht *f*	couche *f*	слой
L 51	layer interface	Zwischeninterface *n*	interface *f* intermédiaire	межуровневый интерфейс
L 52	layer thickness	Schichtdicke *f*	épaisseur *f* de couche	толщина слоя
L 52a	layer-type resistance	Flächenwiderstand *m*	résistance *f* à couche	сопротивление слоя
	layer-type resistor	s. S 312		
L 53	layout / to	belegen, abstecken, auslegen	occuper, déposer, placer	размещать, располагать
L 54	layout	Layout *n*, topografische Anordnung *f*, Belegungsplan *m*	layout *m*, placement *m* topographique, plan *m* d'occupation	план, чертеж; топология
L 55	layout design	Belegungsentwurf *m*, Anordnungsentwurf *m* <topografischer Entwurf einer Schaltung>	conception *f* d'aménagement	компоновка, размещение <процесс>; разработка топологии
L 56	layout error	Layout-Fehler *m*, Fehler *m* in der Schaltungstopografie	défaut *m* de layout	ошибка размещения (в расположении)
L 57	layout rules	Layout-Regeln *fpl*, Entwurfsregeln *fpl* für Schaltungstopografie	règles *fpl* de layout	правила компоновки (размещения)
	LCD	s. L 174		
L 58	lead bonder	Leitungsbonder *m*, Mikrozuleitungsverbinder *m* <Gerät zum Kontaktieren von Chips im Gehäuse über Bondinseln>	élément *m* de bondérisation de microconducteurs	устройство для изготовления контактов кристалла внутри корпуса
L 59	lead capacitance	Zuleitungskapazität *f*	capacité *f* de conducteur	емкость подводящего провода
L 60	leader	Vorspann *m*	amorce *f*, en-tête *m*	заправочный конец ленты
L 61	lead in	hereingeführter Anschluß *m*	raccordement *m* introduit	вводной провод, ввод
L 62	leading bits	führende Bits *npl* (Binärstellen *fpl*)	bits *mpl* de tête	ведущие разряды
L 63	leading card, header card	Leitkarte *f*, Kopfkarte *f*	carte *f* de guidage	управляющая [перфо-]карта
L 64	leading edge, front edge	Vorderflanke *f*, Vorderkante *f*	flanc *m* avant (frontal)	передний фронт [импульса], ведущий край [носителя]
L 65	leading end	Bandanfang *m*	commencement *m* de bande	начало носителя
L 66	leading phase	voreilende Phase *f*	phase *f* d'avance	опережающая фаза
L 67	leading zeros	führende Nullen *fpl*	zéros *mpl* d'en-tête	ведущие нули
L 68	lead length	Zuleitungslänge *f*	longueur *f* d'amenée	длина вывода
L 69	lead out	herausgeführter Anschluß *m*	raccordement *m* sorti	выводной провод, вывод
L 70	lead spacing	Stegabstand *m*, Leiterzugabstand *m*	espace *m* de conducteurs	расстояние от подводящего провода
L 71	lead through	Hindurchführung *f*	traversée *f*	подвод через
	lead time	s. P 416		
L 72	lead wire, end wire	Anschlußdraht *m*	fil *m* de raccordement	подводящий провод
L 73	leak	Ableitung *f*, Streuung *f*, Streuverlust *m*	dérivation *f*, dispersion *f*	утечка; место утечки
L 74	leakage current	Leckstrom *m*, Kriechstrom *m*	courant *m* de fuite	ток утечки

L 75	leakage path	Kriechweg m, Kriech-strecke f	voie f de fuite	путь утечки, токопроводя-щая «дорожка»
L 76	learning machine	Lernmaschine f, lernender Rechenautomat m	machine f élève	[само]обучающаяся машина
L 77	learning program	Lernprogramm n	programme m d'apprentis-sage	обучающая программа
L 78	leased line	Mietleitung f	ligne f louée	выделенная (некомму-тируемая, арендуемая) линия
L 79	leasing	Mietung f, Vermietung f	location f	выделение [линии], сдача в аренду
L 80	least life[time]	Mindestlebensdauer f	longévité f minimum	минимальный срок службы
L 81	least significant bit, LSB	letztes (niederwertigstes) signifikantes Bit n, letzte (niederwertigste) signifi-kante Binärstelle f	dernier bit m significatif [de valeur inférieure], dernier point m binaire significatif [de valeur inférieure]	младший значащий бит
L 82	least significant digit	letzte (niederwertigste) signifikante Ziffer (Ziffernstelle) f	dernier chiffre m significatif [de valeur inférieure]	младшая значащая цифра
	LED	s. L 107		
L 83	LED display	LED-Anzeige f, Leucht-diodenanzeige f	affichage m à diodes lumi-nescentes	светодиодный индикатор
L 84	left-justified	linksbündig	serré à gauche	выравненный влево, вы-равненный по левому знаку (разряду)
L 85	left most position	linke Position f, äußerste linke Stelle f <einer Zahl>	position f [d'extrême] gauche <d'un nombre>	крайний левый разряд [числа]
L 86	left one	linke Eins f, erste mit Eins besetzte Stelle f einer Binärzahl	une f gauche, première position f d'un nombre binaire occupé de un	[крайняя] левая единица <в слове данных>
L 87	left shift	Linksverschiebung f	décalage m à gauche	сдвиг влево
L 88	letters shift	Typenumschaltung f, Buchstabenumschaltung f	commutation f de lettres	переключение на регистр букв <телетайп>
L 89	level	Pegel m, Niveau n	niveau m	уровень
	level of compliance	s. C 465		
L 90	level of interpretation	Interpretierungsniveau n	niveau m d'interprétation	уровень интерпретации
L 91	level of program	Programmstufe f	niveau m de programme	уровень программы
L 92	level of programming	Programmierungsniveau n	niveau m de programmation	уровень программиро-вания
L 93	level regulation	Pegelregelung f	réglage m de niveau	регулирование уровня
L 94	level setting	Pegeleinstellung f	ajustement m de niveau	установка уровня
L 95	level translator	Pegelwandler m	convertisseur m de niveau	преобразователь уровня [сигнала], транслятор уровня
L 96	level-triggered	pegelgetriggert, pegel-geschaltet	basculé par niveau	переключаемый уровнем [сигнала]
L 97	library	Bibliothek f <Programme>	bibliothèque f	библиотека
L 98	library call	Bibliotheksabruf m	appel m de bibliothèque	обращение к библиотеке
L 99	library name	Bibliotheksname m	nom m de bibliothèque	имя библиотеки
L 100	library program (routine)	Bibliotheksprogramm n	programme m de biblio-thèque	библиотечная программа
L 101	library subroutine	Bibliotheksunterprogramm n	sous-programme m de bibliothèque	библиотечная подпро-грамма
L 102	life test	Lebensdauerprüfung f	test m de longévité	испытание на долговеч-ность
	LIFO ...	= last-in first-out...		
L 103	LIFO memory	LIFO-Speicher m <Speicher mit LIFO-Zugriffsprinzip, wobei das zuletzt Gespei-cherte beim nächsten Zu-griff zuerst ausgelesen wird>	mémoire f LIFO <principe d'accès lisant au prochain accès l'information inscrite la dernière>	память типа LIFO, стек, память магазинного типа
L 104	LIFO register	LIFO-Registerspeicher m <Registerblock nach LIFO-Zugriffsprinzip organisiert, siehe LIFO memory>	registre m LIFO <cf. mémoire LIFO>	регистровая память мага-зинного типа, LIFO-регистр
L 105	light barrier	Lichtschranke f	barrière f photo-électrique	фотоэлектрический барьер
L 106	lighted display	Leuchtanzeige f	affichage m lumineux	световая индикация
L 107	light-emitting diode, LED	Lichtemissionsdiode f, Leuchtdiode f, LED-Element n	diode f luminescente, LED f	светодиод, СД
L 108	light indicator	Anzeigelampe f	indicateur m lumineux, lampe f témoin	световой индикатор
L 109	lightly doped	schwach dotiert	faiblement dopé	слабо легированный
L 110	light pen	Lichtstift m	crayon m lumineux	световое перо
L 111	light pen attention	Lichtstiftmarkiersignal n	signal m d'attention de crayon lumineux	сигнал прерывания от светового пера
L 112	light-sensitive	lichtempfindlich	sensible à la lumière	светочувствительный
L 113	light spot, [luminous] spot	Lichtpunkt m, Lichtfleck m, Leuchtfleck m	point m lumineux	световая точка
L 114	limit case, limiting case	Grenzfall m	cas m de limite	предельный случай
L 115	limit check	Grenzwertprüfung f	vérification f de limite[s]	граничное испытание, проверка в граничных условиях
L 116	limit comparator	Grenzwertvergleicher m	comparateur m de limites	блок сравнения предель-ных значений
L 117	limited power	begrenzte Leistung f	puissance f limitée	ограниченная мощность; ограниченная произво-дительность
L 118	limiter	Begrenzer m	limiteur m	ограничитель
L 119	limiter circuit	Begrenzerschaltung f	circuit-limiteur m	ограничительная схема

	limiting case	s. L 114		
	limiting condition	s. B 256		
L 120	limiting frequency	Grenzfrequenz f	fréquence f limite	предельная частота
L 121	limit switch, end position switch	Endlagenschalter m	interrupteur m de fin de course	концевой выключатель
L 122	limit value	Grenzwert m	valeur f limite	предельное значение
L 123	line	Leitung f ‹Verbindung›	ligne f	провод, линия
L 124	line	Zeile f	ligne f	строка
L 125	line adapter	Leitungsadapter m, Leitungsanpassungsteil n	adapteur m de ligne	линейный адаптер
L 126	line adaption	Leitungsanpassung f	adaptation f de ligne	адаптация линии
L 127	line-addressable RAM, LARAM	pfadadressierbarer RAM (Lese-Schreib-Speicher) m	mémoire f lecture-écriture adressable par voie	оперативное запоминающее устройство с линейной адресацией
	line advance	s. L 147		
L 128	linear amplifier	Linearverstärker m, Proportionalverstärker m	amplificateur m linéaire	линейный усилитель
L 129	linear circuit	lineare (linear arbeitende) Schaltung f	circuit m linéaire	линейная схема
L 130	linear distortion	Linearverzerrung f	distorsion f linéaire	линейное искажение
L 131	linear equation	lineare Gleichung f	équation f linéaire	линейное уравнение
L 132	linear function	lineare Funktion f	fonction f linéaire	линейная функция
L 133	linearity error	Linearitätsfehler m	défaut m de linéarité	ошибка линеаризации
L 134	linear-mode region	linearer Arbeitsbereich m	champ m de travail linéaire	линейная область, линейный диапазон [работы]
L 135	linear optimization	lineare Optimierung f	optimisation f linéaire	линейная оптимизация
L 136	linear potentiometer	Linearpotentiometer n	potentiomètre m linéaire	линейный потенциометр
L 137	linear program, linear routine	Linearprogramm n	programme m linéaire	линейная программа
L 138	linear programming	lineare Programmierung f	programmation f linéaire	линейное программирование
L 139	linear rise	linearer Anstieg m	montée f linéaire	линейное возрастание
	linear routine	s. L 137		
L 140	line by line	zeilenweise	ligne par ligne	построчный
L 141	line code	Zeilenkode m, Programmzeilenkode m	code m de ligne	код передачи по линии
L 142	line concentrator	Leitungskonzentrator m	concentrateur m de ligne	линейный концентратор
L 143	line control	Leitungssteuerung f	commande f de ligne	управление линией
L 144	line control character	Leitungssteuerzeichen n	caractère m de commande de ligne	символ управления каналом
L 145	line dialling	Leitungsanwahl f ‹Fernsprechnetz›	sélection f de ligne	линейный вызов
L 146	line driver	Leitungstreiber m	basculeur m de ligne	линейный формирователь
L 147	line feed, line advance	Zeilenvorschub m	avancement m de ligne	перевод строки
L 148	line impedance	Leitungsimpedanz f	impédance f de ligne	импеданс линии
L 149	line interface	Linieninterface n	interface f de ligne	интерфейс линии
L 150	line loss	Leitungsverlust m, Leitungsdämpfung f	atténuation f de ligne	потери на линии
L 151	line occupancy	Leitungsbelegung f	occupation f de ligne	занятость линии
L 152	line printer	Zeilendrucker m	imprimante f de lignes	построчно-печатающее устройство
L 153	line-sharing system	Leitungsteilnehmersystem n, Leitungsteilungssystem n ‹Sammelleitungssystem›	système m de lignes à abonnés	система с разделением линий ‹совместное использование линий устройствами системы›
L 154	line spacing, line-to-line spacing	Zeilenabstand m	écart m de ligne, espace m entre lignes, interligne m	расстояние между строками
	line switching	s. C 237		
L 155/6	line termination	Leitungsabschluß m	terminaison f de ligne	оконечная нагрузка линии
	line-to-line spacing	s. L 154		
L 157	line voltage	Netzspannung f	tension f du secteur	сетевое напряжение; линейное напряжение
L 158	line voltage fluctuations	Netzspannungsschwankungen fpl	variation f de tension du secteur	флуктуации сетевого напряжения
L 159	line voltage regulator	Netzspannungsregler m	régulateur m de tension du secteur	регулятор сетевого напряжения
L 160	line width	Linienbreite f, Strichbreite f	largeur f de ligne	ширина линии
L 161	link / to	verbinden ‹Programmtechnik›, verketten	lier, enchaîner	связывать
	link	s. 1. L 162; 2. L 166; 3. L 168		
L 162	link address, link	Verbindungsadresse f ‹Rückkehradresse›	adresse f de liaison	адрес связи
L 163	link address field	Verbindungsadressenfeld n	champ m d'adresse de lien	поле адреса связи
L 164	linkage	Verbindung f ‹Programmtechnik›, Verkettung f	liaison f	связь
	linkage editor	s. L 169		
L 165	linkage parameter	Verbindungsparameter m ‹Programmtechnik›	paramètre m de liaison	параметр связи
	linkage register	s. L 173		
L 166	link-bit, link	Link-Bit n, Verkettungsbit n, Verbindungsstelle f ‹Akkumulatorerweiterungsstelle›	bit m de liaison	бит расширения [аккумулятора]
	link editor	s. L 169		
L 167	linked subroutine	eingebundenes (geschlossenes) Unterprogramm n	sous-programme m fermé	замкнутая (закрытая) подпрограмма
L 168	link element, link	Verbindungselement n ‹Programmtechnik›, Verbindungsglied n	élément m de liaison, lien m	элемент связи

L 169	linker, link (linkage) editor	Binder *m*, Verkettungs-routine *f*, Programmver-binder *m*	éditeur *m* de lien	редактор связей
L 170	linking	Verbinden *n* einzelner Objektprogrammodule <durch Herstellen von Referenzen zueinander und zu Bibliotheksrou-tinen sowie durch Zuwei-sen von Adressen und Daten>	liaison *f* de différents modules de programme objet	связывание отдельных объектных модулей
L 171	linking loader	Binde-Lader *m*	chargeur *m* de lien	связывающий загрузчик
L 172	linking sequence	Verbindungsfolge *f* <Pro-grammtechnik>, An-schlußbefehlsfolge *f*	séquence *f* de liaison	связывающая последо-вательность
L 173	link register, linkage register	Verbindungsregister *n* <Programmtechnik>	registre *m* de lien	регистр связи
L 174	liquid-crystal display, LCD	Flüssigkristallanzeige *f*, LCD	affichage *m* à cristaux liquides, LCD	индикатор на жидких кристаллах, ЖКИ
L 175	liquid photoresist	flüssiger Fotolack *m*	photolaque *f* liquide	жидкий фоторезист
L 176	LISP, list processing language	LISP *n*, Listenverarbei-tungssprache *f* <Program-miersprache für Symbol-folgen und rekursive Daten>	langage *m* de traitement de listes, LISP *m*	ЛИСП, алгоритмический язык для обработки списков
L 177	list / to	auflisten, listen, in Listen-form ausdrucken	mettre (imprimer) en liste[s]	составлять (вносить в) список
L 178	list	Liste *f*	liste *f*	список
L 179	listing	Auflistung *f*, Ausdruck *m* in Listenform	mise (impression) *f* en liste	составление и печать списков; листинг, рас-печатка
L 180	list processing	Listenverarbeitung *f*	traitement *m* de liste	обработка списков
	list processing language	s. L 176		
L 181	list program, report program	Listenprogramm *n*	programme *m* de liste	программа печати таблиц
L 182	list program generator, LPG	Listenprogrammgenerator *m*	générateur *m* de programme de liste	программный генератор печати таблиц
L 183	list structure	Listenstruktur *f*	structure *f* de liste[s]	списковая структура
L 184	literal	Literal *n*, Selbstgröße *f* <Adreßtyp>	littéral *m*, valeur *f* littérale	литерал, литеральная константа
L 185	load / to	laden, füllen <einlesen>	charger	нагружать; загружать
L 186	load	Last *f*, Belastung *f*	charge *f*	нагрузка
L 187	loadable program format	ladefähiges Programm-format *n*	format *m* de programme chargeable	формат загружаемой про-граммы
L 188	loadable register	ladbares Register *n*	registre *m* chargeable	загружаемый регистр
L 189	load and go	Laden *n* und Ausführen *n*	chargement *m* et exécution *f*	немедленное выполнение, исполнение по загрузке
L 190	load-and-go assembler	Lade-und-Starte-Assembler *m* <Assembler baut Objektprogramm im Spei-cher auf und startet an-schließend dessen Aus-führung>	assembleur *m* « charger et démarrer »	ассемблер с исполнением по загрузке
L 191	load capacity	Belastungsfähigkeit *f*	capacité *f* de charge	емкость нагрузки
L 192	load change	Lastwechsel *m*, Belastungs-änderung *f*	changement *m* de charge	изменение нагрузки; изменение загрузки
L 193	load condition	Belastungszustand *m*, Belastungsbedingung *f*	condition *f* de charge	режим нагрузки, нагру-женное состояние
L 194	load curve, load line	Lastkurve *f*	courbe *f* de charge	нагрузочная кривая, линия нагрузки
L 195	loaded circuit board	bestückte Leiterplatte *f*	circuit *m* imprimé garni	схемная плата с установ-ленными элементами
L 196	loader, loading routine	Lader *m*, Ladeprogramm *n*	chargeur *m*	[программа-]загрузчик
L 197	load factor	Lastfaktor *m*, Belastungs-faktor *m*	facteur *m* de charge	коэффициент нагрузки
L 198	load impedance	Lastwiderstand *m*	impédance (résistance) *f* de charge	нагрузочное сопротивле-ние, импеданс нагрузки
L 199	loading [process]	Beschickung *f*, Laden *n* <Programm>, Ladevor-gang *m*	chargement *m*	загрузка [программы]
	loading routine	s. L 196		
L 200	load instruction	Ladebefehl *m*	instruction *f* de chargement	команда загрузки
L 201	load key	Ladeschalter *m*	commutateur *m* de charge-ment	кнопка загрузки
	load line	s. L 194		
L 202	load mode	Lademodus *m*, Ladebetriebs-art *f*	mode *m* de chargement	режим загрузки
L 203	load module	Lademodul *m*	module *m* de chargement	загрузочный модуль
L 203 a	load resistor	Lastwiderstand *m* <Bauteil>	rhéostat *m* de charge	нагрузочный резистор
L 204	load sharing	Lastteilung *f*, Belastungs-teilung *f*	partage *m* de charge	распределение нагрузки
L 205	load sharing mode	Lastteilverfahren *n*	mode *m* de partage de charge	режим распределения нагрузки
L 206	load test	Belastungstest *m*	test *m* de charge	контроль нагрузки
L 207	load voltage	Lastspannung *f*, Ver-braucherspannung *f*	tension *f* de charge	напряжение на нагрузке
L 208	local data collection	lokale Datenerfassung *f*, Datenerfassung am Ent-stehungsort	acquisition *f* locale de données	локальный сбор данных
L 209	local exchange	Ortsvermittlungsstelle *f* <Nachrichtentechnik>	communication *f* locale	местный коммутатор
L 210	localization	Lokalisierung *f*, Ortung *f*, Eingrenzung *f* <Fehler>	localisation *f*	локализация
L 211	localize / to	lokalisieren	localiser	локализовывать

L 212	**local memory,** local store	lokaler (räumlich zugeordneter, einem Prozessor zugeordneter) Speicher *m* <in Mehrprozessorsystemen>	mémoire *f* locale	локальная память
L 213	**local mode**	lokale (abgegrenzte) Betriebsweise *f*	mode *m* local	локальный режим
L 214	**local network**	lokales Netz *n*	réseau *m* local	локальная сеть
	local oxidation of silicon	*s.* L 226		
L 215	**local processing**	lokale Verarbeitung *f*, Vor-Ort-Verarbeitung *f*	traitement *m* local	локальная обработка
	local store	*s.* L 212		
L 216	**local variable**	lokale Variable *f*	variable *f* locale	локальная переменная
L 217	**locate / to**	aufsuchen, auffinden, orten	chercher, localiser	находить [место]
L 218	**locate function**	Suchfunktion *f*	fonction *f* de recherche	функция поиска
L 219	**locate mode**	Suchmodus *m*, Bereitstellungsmodus *m*	mode *m* de recherche	режим указания
L 220	**location field**	Ortsbestimmungsfeld *n*, Positionierfeld *n* <Plattenspeicher>	champ *m* de positionnement	поле позиционирования
L 221	**location pin**	Positionierstift *m*	crayon *m* de positionnement	штырь позиционирования, направляющий штырь
L 222	**lock / to**	verriegeln	verrouiller	запирать, блокировать
	lock-in	*s.* L 224		
L 223	**locking**	Verriegelung *f*	verrouillage *m*	запирание, блокировка
L 224	**locking-in,** lock-in	Mitnahme *f*, Gleichlaufzwang *m*	entraînement *m*, mise *f* au pas	синхронизм
L 225	**locking type button**	arretierbare Taste *f*	touche *f* d'arrêt	западающая кнопка, кнопка с фиксацией
L 226	**LOCOS,** local oxidation of silicon	LOCOS *f*, lokale Siliziumoxydation *f* <Bipolar-Planar-Technologie>	oxydation *f* locale de silicium	локальное окисление кремния
L 227	**log / to**	registrieren	enregistrer	регистрировать
L 228	**logger**	Registriereinrichtung *f*, Meßwerterfassungsgerät *n*	dispositif *m* d'enregistrement, appareil *m* d'enregistrement de mesure	устройство регистрации [данных]
L 229	**logging mode**	Registriermodus *m*, Erfassungsmodus *m*	mode *m* d'enregistrement	режим регистрации
L 230	**logging typewriter**	Protokollschreibmaschine *f*	machine *f* à écrire de verbalisation	пишущая машинка, использующаяся для печати протокола
L 231/2	**logic**	Logik *f* <digitale Logikschaltung>	logique *f*	логика
	logic[al]	*s.* B 235		
L 233	**logical addition**	logische Addition *f* <ODER-Operation>	addition *f* logique	логическое сложение
L 234	**logical address**	logische Adresse *f*	adresse *f* logique	логический адрес
	logical circuit	*s.* L 254		
L 235	**logical condition**	logische Bedingung *f*	condition *f* logique	логическое условие
L 236	**logical connection**	ogische (Boolesche) Verknüpfung *f*	liaison *f* logique	логическая связка
	logical connector	*s.* L 246		
L 237	**logical decision**	logische Entscheidung *f*	décision *f* logique	логическое (альтернативное) решение
L 238	**logical description**	Logikbeschreibung *f*	description *f* logique	логическое описание
L 239	**logical design,** logic design	logischer Entwurf *m*, logische Struktur *f*, logisches Konzept *n*	projet *m* (conception *f*, structure *f*) logique	логический синтез, логическое проектирование; логический проект
L 240	**logical diagram,** logic diagram, logical flow-chart, logic flowchart	logisches Flußdiagramm *n*, Ablaufplan *m*, Logikdiagramm *n*, Logikschaltbild *n*	diagramme (schéma, organigramme) *m* logique	логическая схема
L 241	**logical element**	logisches Element *n* <Boolescher Elementarausdruck>	élément *m* logique	логический элемент
L 242	**logical error**	logischer Fehler *m*	erreur *f* logique	логическая ошибка
L 243	**logical expression**	logischer (Boolescher) Ausdruck *m*	expression *f* logique	логическое выражение
	logical flowchart	*s.* L 240		
L 244	**logical instruction,** logic instruction	logischer Befehl *m* <Befehl zur Ausführung einer logischen Operation>	instruction *f* logique	логическая инструкция
L 245	**logical operation,** logic (Boolean) operation	logische (Boolesche) Operation *f*	opération *f* logique (booléenne, boolienne)	логическая (булева) операция
L 246	**logical operator,** logic (Boolean) operator, logical connector	logischer (Boolescher) Operator *m*	opérateur *m* logique	логический (булев) оператор
	logical processing power	*s.* P 514		
	logical product	*s.* C 599		
L 247	**logical shift,** logic shift	logische Verschiebung *f*, binäres Verschieben *n*	décalage *m* logique (binaire)	логический сдвиг
L 248	**logical sum**	logische Summe *f*	somme *f* logique	логическая сумма, дизъюнкция
L 249	**logical symbol**	logisches Symbol *n* <Operationszeichen>	symbole *m* logique	логический символ
L 250	**logical term**	logischer (Boolescher) Term *m*	terme *m* logique (booléen, boolien)	логический (булев) терм
L 251	**logical value**	logischer (Boolescher) Wert *m*, Wahrheitswert *m*	valeur *f* logique (booléenne, boolienne, réelle)	логическое значение
L 252	**logical variable,** logic (Boolean) variable	logische (Boolesche) Variable *f* <Schaltvariable>	variable *f* logique (booléenne, boolienne)	логическая (булева) переменная
L 253	**logic analyzer,** logic-state analyzer	Logikanalysator *m* <Testgerät>	analyseur *m* logique	логический анализатор

L 254	**logic circuit,** logical circuit	Logikschaltkreis *m*, logische Schaltung *f*	circuit *m* logique	логическая (цифровая) схема
	logic design	*s.* L 239		
L 255	**logic device**	Logikbauteil *n*	module *m* logique	логическое устройство
	logic diagram	*s.* L 240		
L 256	**logic element**	Logikelement *n* <Grundelement einer Logikschaltung>	élément *m* de logique	логический элемент
L 257	**logic-enhancement memory**	logikerweiterter Speicher *m*, Speicher mit integrierten Logikfunktionen	mémoire *f* à fonctions logiques intégrées	функциональная память, память со встроенной логикой
	logic flowchart	*s.* L 240		
L 258	**logic function**	logische Funktion *f*	fonction *f* logique	логическая функция
L 259	**logic gate**	Logikgatter *n*	porte *f* logique	логический вентиль
L 260	**logic high level**	oberes logisches Niveau *n*, High-Logikpegel *m*	niveau *m* logique supérieur	высокий логический уровень
	logic instruction	*s.* L 244		
L 261	**logic level**	Logikpegel *m*, Logikspannungsniveau *n* <Schaltzustand>	niveau *m* logique	логический уровень
L 262	**logic low level**	unteres logisches Niveau *n*, Low-Logikpegel *m*	niveau *m* logique inférieur	низкий логический уровень
	logic operation	*s.* L 245		
	logic operator	*s.* L 246		
L 263	**logic probe**	Logiktastkopf *m* <Testgerät>	palpeur *m* logique	логический пробник
L 264	**logic replacement**	Logiksubstituierung *f*, Schaltungslogikersatz *m* <durch Mikrorechner>	substitution *f* de logique	логическая подстановка
	logic shift	*s.* L 247		
L 265	**logic simulation**	Logiksimulation *f*	simulation *f* logique	логическое моделирование
	logic state analyzer	*s.* L 253		
L 266	**logic swing**	Logikhub *m*, Logikpegeldifferenz *f*	écart *m* logique, différence *f* de niveau logique	перепад логических уровней
L 267	**logic tester**	Logiktester *m* <Testgerät>	appareil *m* de test logique	логический (цифровой) тестер
	logic variable	*s.* L 252		
L 268	**longevity**	Langlebigkeit *f*	longévité *f*	долговечность
L 269	**long instruction format**	Langbefehlsformat *n*	format *m* d'instruction longue	расширенный формат команд[ы]
L 270	**longitudinal check**	Längsprüfung *f* <einer Information>	vérification *f* longitudinale <d'une information>	продольный контроль <контроль блока информации)
L 271	**longitudinal redundancy check, LRC**	Längsredundanzprüfung *f*, Längsprüfung *f* über Sicherungszeichen	contrôle *m* de redondance longitudinale, LCR	продольный контроль избыточным кодом
L 272	**long-run test,** long-time test	Langzeittest *m*, Dauertest *m*	test *m* d'endurance	длительное испытание
L 273	**long-term stability**	Langzeitstabilität *f*	stabilité *f* à long terme	долговременная стабильность
L 274	**long-term storage**	Langzeitspeicherung *f*	mise *f* en mémoire à long terme, mémorisation *f* à long terme	долговременное запоминание (хранение)
	long-time test	*s.* L 272		
L 275	**longword**	Langwort *n* <Doppelformatwort>	mot *m* long	длинное слово
L 276	**look ahead**	Vorausschau *f*	vue *f* d'avance, prévision *f*	предварительный просмотр
L 277	**look-ahead carry**	vorausermittelter Übertrag *m* <Übertrag aus einer Gruppe von Ziffern, der durch gleichzeitige parallele Analyse aller Ziffernpositionen beschleunigt ermittelt wurde>	retenue *f* évaluée d'avance	ускоренный перенос
L 278	**look-up table**	Nachschlagtabelle *f*, Verweistabelle *f*	table *f* de références, aidemémoire *m*	справочная таблица
L 279	**look-up table technique**	Tabellensuchtechnik *f*	technique *f* de recherche de tables	метод табличного поиска
L 280	**loop checking,** loop testing	Schleifentest *m*	test *m* de boucle	информационная обратная связь, проверка по шлейфу; проверка условия выхода из цикла
L 281	**loop control**	Schleifensteuerung *f*	commande *f* de boucle	управление циклом
L 282	**loop counter**	Schleifenzähler *m*	compteur *m* de boucle	счетчик циклов
L 283	**loop gain**	Schleifenverstärkung *f*	gain *m* de boucle	усиление при замкнутой цепи [обратной связи]
	loop mode	*s.* C 904		
L 284	**loop program**	Schleifenprogramm *n*	programme *m* de boucle	программа цикла
L 285	**loop structure**	Schleifenstruktur *f*, Schleifenaufbau *m*	structure *f* de boucle	структура цикла
	loop testing	*s.* L 280		
L 286	**loose coupling**	lose (schwache) Kopplung *f*	couplage *m* mou	слабая связь
L 287	**loosely coupled processors**	schwach gekoppelte Prozessoren *mpl*, Prozessoren mit loser gegenseitiger Kopplung	processeurs *mpl* couplés mollement (faiblement)	слабо (гибко) связанные процессоры
L 288	**loss factor**	Verlustfaktor *m*, Ausschußfaktor *m*	facteur *m* de perte	коэффициент потерь
L 289	**loss of accuracy**	Genauigkeitsverlust *m*	perte *f* de précision	потеря (снижение) точности
L 290	**low-active signal,** activelow signal	low-aktives Signal *n*, untenaktives Signal, Signal aktiv im unteren Zustand	signal *m* actif en état inférieur	сигнал, активный при низком уровне
L 291	**low address**	untere Adresse *f*	adresse *f* inférieure	нижний (младший) адрес
L 292	**low-capacity**	kapazitätsarm	à faible capacité	с малой емкостью
L 293	**low-cost microcomputer**	billiger Mikrorechner *m*	microcalculateur *m* bon marché	дешевая микро-ЭВМ

L 294	**low-duty cycle**	niedriges Tastverhältnis n, geringe Einschaltdauer f	faible durée f de mise en marche	низкий коэффициент заполнения
L 295	**low-end applications**	Anwendungen fpl im unteren Ende des Spektrums	applications fpl dans le champ inférieur du spectre	области, допускающие применение ЭВМ с малой производительностью
L 296	**low-end microcomputer**	Mikrorechner m für das untere Ende des Anforderungsspektrums	microcalculateur m bas de gamme	микро-ЭВМ с невысокими характеристиками производительности
	low-high transition	s. L 324		
	low-impedance	s. L 318		
L 297	**low-leakage transistor**	Transistor m mit kleinem Reststrom	transistor m à courant résiduel réduit	транзистор с малыми утечками
L 298	**low level**	niedriger Pegel m, unteres Niveau n <Schaltungslogik>	niveau m inférieur	низкий уровень
L 299	**low-level amplifier**	Kleinsignalverstärker m	amplificateur m pour signaux faibles	малосигнальный усилитель
L 300	**low-level circuit**	Niedrigpegelschaltung f	circuit m à niveau inférieur	малосигнальная схема
L 301	**low-level modulation**	Vorstufenmodulation f	modulation f à faible niveau	модуляция на малой мощности, модуляция в каскадах предварительного усиления
L 302	**low-level signal**	Signal n mit niedrigem Pegel	signal m de niveau inférieur	малый сигнал, сигнал с малой амплитудой
L 303	**low-level stage**	Stufe f mit niedrigem Pegel	étage m à faible niveau	маломощный каскад
L 304	**low-loss**	verlustarm	à faible perte	с малыми потерями
L 305	**low-noise amplifier**	rauscharmer Verstärker m	amplificateur m à faible bruit	малошумящий усилитель
L 306	**low-order digit**	niederwertigste Ziffer f <rechte Ziffer>	nombre m de valeur inférieure	младшая цифра
L 307	**low-order portion**	niederwertiger Teil m	partie f de valeur inférieure	младшая часть
L 308	**low-order position**	niedrigste Stelle f, Stelle f geringster Wertigkeit	position f la plus basse	младший разряд [числа]
L 309	**low-pass [filter]**	Tiefpaß m, Tiefpaßfilter n	passe-bas m, filtre m passe-bas	фильтр нижних частот
L 310	**low-power application**	Niederleistungsanwendung f, Einsatzfall m, der niedrige Leistungsaufnahme der Schaltung bedingt <elektronische Uhr, Taschenrechner>	application f à faible puissance	применение, требующее малой потребляемой мощности
L 311	**low-power drain**	geringe Stromaufnahme f	consommation f de courant faible	низкое энергопотребление, низкое потребление [мощности]
L 312	**low-power Schottky TTL circuit, LS-TTL circuit**	Low-Power-Schottky-TTL-Schaltung f, Low-Power-Schottky-TTL-Baustein m, TTL-Schaltung f geringer Leistungsaufnahme mit Schottky-Dioden	circuit m TTL à faible puissance à diodes Schottky	маломощные ТТЛ-схемы с диодами Шоттки
L 313	**low-power source**	geringe Stromabgabe f, Quelle f kleiner Leistung	source f à faible puissance	маломощный источник [питания]
L 314	**low-power system**	Low-Power-System n, System n niedriger Leistungsaufnahme	système m à consommation réduite	система с низким потреблением мощности, маломощная система
L 315	**low-power transistor**	Low-Power-Transistor m, Transistor m niedriger Leistungsaufnahme	transistor m à faible consommation	маломощный транзистор
L 316	**low-power version**	Low-Power-Version f, Ausführung f für niedrigen Leistungsverbrauch, Kleinleistungsversion f	version f à consommation réduite	маломощный вариант, исполнение [схем] с низким потреблением мощности
L 317	**low-priority event**	Ereignis n niederer Priorität	événement m de basse priorité	событие с низким приоритетом
L 318	**low-resistance, low-resistivity, low-impedance**	niederohmig	à faible résistance	низкоомный
L 319	**low-resistance direction, [easy-]flow direction, forward direction**	Durchlaßrichtung f, Flußrichtung f, Vorwärtsrichtung f	direction f de faible résistance, direction de flux, direction avant (de passage)	прямое направление
	low-resistivity	s. L 318		
L 320	**low-resistivity substrate**	niederohmige Unterlage f	substrat m de faible résistance	низкоомная подложка
L 321	**low-speed application**	Anwendung f mit geringer Arbeitsgeschwindigkeit	application f à basse vitesse	применение на низких скоростях [работы]
L 322	**low state**	Low-Zustand m, niedriger (unterer) Zustand m <Null-Zustand bei positiver Logik>	état m inférieur	состояние с низким уровнем [сигнала]
L 323	**low-surface concentration**	niedrige Oberflächenkonzentration f	faible concentration f superficielle	низкая поверхностная концентрация
L 324	**low-to-high transition, low-high transition**	Low-High-Übergang m, Übergang m vom unteren zum oberen Signalpegel	transition f du niveau bas au niveau haut	переход из состояния с низким в состояние с высоким уровнем напряжения
L 325	**low value**	unterer Wert m	valeur f inférieure	нижнее значение
L 326	**low-volume system**	Niedrigstückzahl-System n	système m de volume réduit [de fabrication]	мелкосерийная система
	LPG	s. L 182		
	LRC	s. L 271		
	LSB	s. L 81		
L 327	**LSI, large-scale integration**	LSI f, hohe Integration f, Großbereichsintegration f	LSI f, intégration f élevée	большая интеграция, высокая степень интеграции
L 328	**LSI board tester**	LSI-Leiterplattentester m, LSI-Kartentester m	appareil m de test pour circuits imprimés à LSI	тестер для [проверки] схемных плат с БИС

ID	English	German	French	Russian
L 329	**LSI chip design**	LSI-Chipentwurf m, LSI-Schaltkreisentwurf m	conception f de puce LSI	разработка БИС
L 330	**LSI circuit**	LSI-Schaltkreis m, hochintegrierter Schaltkreis m	circuit m hautement intégré, circuit LSI	большая интегральная схема, БИС
L 331	**LSI technology**	LSI-Technologie f, Technologie f der Herstellung hochintegrierter Schaltkreise	technologie f LSI	технология БИС
	lug	s. L 18		
L 332	**luminous figure display**	Leuchtziffernanzeige f	affichage m à chiffres lumineux	световой индикатор знаков
L 333	**luminous key**	Leuchttaste f	touche f lumineuse	кнопка с подсветкой
	luminous spot	s. L 113		

M

ID	English	German	French	Russian
M 1	**M**	M, Mega n <Zahlenfaktor für Vielfache von 2^{20} = 1 048 576>	M, Méga m <facteur pour multiples de 2^{20} = 1 048 576>	M <множитель, равный 10^6>; <в вычислительной технике M = 2^{20}>
M 2	**machine address**	Maschinenadresse f, Adresse f im Maschinenkode	adresse f machine	машинный адрес
M 3	**machine assembly**	Rechnerassemblierung f, maschinelle Assemblierung f <Programmübersetzung mit Assemblerprogramm>	assemblage m à la machine	машинное ассемблирование
M 4	**machine capacity**	Maschinenkapazität f	capacité f de machine	разрядность машины; производительность машины
M 5	**machine check**	Maschinenprüfung f	vérification f de machine	контроль [работы] аппаратных средств, машинный контроль
M 6	**machine code**	Maschinenkode m	code m [de] machine	машинный код
M 7	**machine-code compatible instruction set**	maschinenkodekompatibler Befehlssatz m, kompatibler Befehlssatz auf Maschinenbefehlsebene	jeu m d'instructions compatible en code machine	система команд, совместимая на уровне машинного кода
M 8	**machine-code instruction**	Maschinenkodebefehl m	instruction f en code machine	команда на машинном языке
M 9	**machine-code level**	Maschinenkodeniveau n	niveau m de code machine	уровень машинного кода
M 10	**machine configuration**	Maschinenkonfiguration f	configuration f de machine	машинная конфигурация
M 11	**machine control, machinery control**	Maschinensteuerung f	commande f de machine	управление с помощью ЭВМ
M 12	**machine cycle**	Maschinenzyklus m, Maschinengang m	cycle m de machine	машинный цикл
M 13	**machine-dependent code**	maschinenabhängiger (maschinentypabhängiger) Kode m	code m dépendant de machine	машинно-зависимый код
M 14	**machine down-time**	Maschinenstillstandszeit f	temps m de repos de machine	время простоя машины
	machine error	s. M 16		
M 15	**machine failure**	Maschinenausfall m, Anlagenausfall m	panne f de machine, panne d'installation	отказ машины
M 16	**machine fault, machine error**	Maschinenfehler m	défaut m (erreur f) de machine	неисправность машины, машинная ошибка
M 17	**machine format**	Maschinenformat n <Datendarstellung im Maschinenkode>	format m de machine	машинный формат
M 18	**machine-independent interface**	maschinenunabhängiges Interface n, maschinentypunabhängige Schnittstelle f	interface f indépendante de machine	машинно-зависимый интерфейс
M 19	**machine-independent language**	maschinenunabhängige Sprache f	langage m indépendant de machine	машинно-независимый язык
M 20	**machine instruction**	Maschinenbefehl m	instruction f de machine	машинная команда
M 21	**machine instruction code**	Maschinenbefehlskode m	code m d'instructions de machine	код операции машинной команды
M 22	**machine language**	Maschinensprache f <maschinenspezifischer Programmkode>	langage m [de] machine	машинный язык
M 23	**machine language programming**	Maschinensprachprogrammierung f, Programmierung f in Maschinensprach-Mnemoniks	programmation f en langage machine	программирование на машинном языке
M 24	**machine load**	Maschinenbelastung f, Maschinenauslastung f	charge f de machine	загрузка машины
M 25	**machine logic**	Maschinenlogik f <Logikstruktur, Schaltungsaufbau>	logique f de machine	машинная логика
M 26	**machine logic design**	Maschinenlogikentwurf m, Logikentwurf m einer Rechenmaschine	conception f logique de machine	разработка логической схемы [вычислительной машины]
M 27	**machine operation**	Maschinenoperation f	opération f de machine	машинная операция
M 28	**machine organization**	Maschinenorganisation f	organisation f de machine	архитектура машины
M 29	**machine-oriented**	maschinenorientiert	orienté machine	машинно-ориентированный
M 30	**machine-oriented language**	maschinenorientierte Programmsprache f	langage m orienté machine	машинно-ориентированный язык
M 31	**machine program**	Maschinenprogramm n <Programm in Maschinensprache, so daß es der Rechner direkt ausführen kann>	programme m machine	машинная программа, программа на машинном языке

M 32	**machine-readable,** machine-sensible	maschinell lesbar (auswertbar)	lisible par machine, lisible mécaniquement	машинно-считываемый, машинно-воспринимаемый
M 33	**machine-readable carrier**	maschinell lesbarer Datenträger *m*	support *m* de données lisible par machine	машинно-считываемый носитель [данных]
M 34	**machine recognition**	maschinelle Erkennung *f*	reconnaissance *f* mécanique	машинное распознавание
M 35	**machine reliability**	Maschinenzuverlässigkeit *f*	fiabilité *f* de machine	надежность машины
M 36	**machine representation**	Maschinendarstellung *f*, maschineninterne (rechnerinterne) Darstellung *f*	représentation *f* de machine	машинное представление
M 37	**machine run,** run	Maschinenlauf *m*, Maschinendurchlauf *m*	marche *f* de machine	машинный прогон, однократное выполнение [программы]
	machinery control	s. M 11		
	machine-sensible	s. M 32		
M 38	**machine set-up time**	Maschinenrüstzeit *f*	temps *m* de préparation de machine	время подготовки машины к работе
	machine state	s. M 39		
M 39	**machine status,** machine state	Maschinenstatus *m*, Maschinenzustand *m*	état *m* de machine	состояние машины
M 40	**machine system**	Maschinensystem *n* ‹Gerätetechniksystem eines Rechners›	système *m* de machine	система машин, аппаратные средства машины
M 41	**machine-tool control**	Werkzeugmaschinensteuerung *f*	commande *f* de machine-outil	программное управление станками
M 42	**machine translation**	maschinelle Übersetzung *f*	traduction *f* par machine	машинная трансляция
M 43	**machine word**	Maschinenwort *n*	mot *m* de machine	машинное слово
	macro	s. M 51		
M 44	**macroassembler**	Makroassembler *m*	assembleur *m* macro, macro-assembleur *m*	макроассемблер
M 45	**macroassembly program**	Makroassemblierprogramm *n*	programme *m* d'assemblage macro, programme de macro-assemblage	программа макроассемблера
M 46	**macrocode**	Makrokode *m*	code *m* macro	макрокод
	macrocommand	s. M 51		
M 47	**macrodefinition**	Makrodefinition *f*, Makrooperationsspezifikation *f*	définition *f* de macro	макроопределение
M 48	**macrofacilities**	Makrosprachmöglichkeiten *fpl*	possibilités *fpl* de langage macro	возможности макроассемблера
M 49	**macrofacility**	Makroeinrichtung *f* ‹Makroübersetzungsfähigkeit›	dispositif *m* à macros	макросредство
M 50	**macrogenerating program, macrogenerator**	Makrogenerierprogramm *n*, Makrogenerator *m*	programme *m* de génération macro, générateur *m* macro	макрогенератор
M 51	**macroinstruction,** macro[command]	Makrobefehl *m*, Makro *n* ‹vereinbarte symbolische Anweisung für häufig benutzte Maschinenbefehlsfolge›	instruction *f* macro, macro *m*, macro-instruction *f*	макрокоманда, макрос
M 52	**macroinstruction library, macrolibrary**	Makrobibliothek *f* ‹Zusammenfassung der vereinbarten Makrodefinitionen›	bibliothèque *f* macro	библиотека макроопределений, макробиблиотека
M 53	**macroprogram**	Makroprogramm *n*, Programm *n* in Makrokode	programme *m* macro	макропрограмма, программа, содержащая макрокоманды
M 54	**macroprogramming**	Makroprogrammierung *f*, Maschinenprogrammierung *f* über Makrobefehle	programmation *f* macro	макропрограммирование, программирование с использованием макрокоманд
M 55	**20 MA current loop**	20-mA-Stromschleife *f* ‹serielles Interface, z. B. für Fernschreiber›	boucle *f* de courant de 20 mA	телеграфный интерфейс с током в линии 20 mA
	magnetic account card	s. M 80		
	magnetic account computer	s. M 81		
M 56	**magnetic bubble,** bubble	Magnetblase *f*	bulle *f* magnétique	магнитный домен
	magnetic bubble memory	s. B 283		
M 57	**magnetic card**	Magnetkarte *f*, magnetische Speicherkarte *f*	carte *f* magnétique	магнитная карта
M 58	**magnetic-card computer**	Magnetkartencomputer *m*, Magnetkartenrechner *m*	calculateur *m* à cartes magnétiques	ЭВМ с вводом информации с магнитных карт
M 59	**magnetic-card store**	Magnetkartenspeicher *m*	mémoire *f* à cartes magnétiques	запоминающее устройство на магнитных картах
M 60	**magnetic character reader**	Magnetschriftleser *m*	lecteur *m* d'écriture magnétique	устройство считывания магнитных символов ‹символов, написанных магнитными чернилами›
M 61	**magnetic character recognition,** magnetic ink character recognition, MICR	Magnetschrifterkennung *f*, Magnetschriftzeichenerkennung *f*	reconnaissance *f* d'écriture magnétique	распознавание магнитных символов, распознавание символов, написанных магнитными чернилами
M 62	**magnetic circuit**	magnetischer Kreis *m*	circuit *m* magnétique	схема на магнитных элементах
M 63	**magnetic coating**	magnetische Beschichtung *f*	recouvrement *m* magnétique	магнитное покрытие
M 64	**magnetic core**	Magnetkern *m*, Ringkern *m*	tore *m* magnétique	магнитный сердечник
M 65	**magnetic-core memory (storage),** core memory	Magnetkernspeicher *m*, Kernspeicher *m*	mémoire *f* à tores [magnétiques]	запоминающее устройство на [магнитных] сердечниках

M 66	**magnetic cycle,** hysteresis loop	Hystereseschleife f, Hysteresisschleife f, Magnetisierungsschleife f	boucle (courbe) f d'hystérésis	цикл намагничивания, петля гистерезиса
M 67	**magnetic delay line**	magnetische Verzögerungsleitung f	ligne f de retardement magnétique	магнитная линия задержки
M 68	**magnetic disk**	Magnetplatte f	disque m magnétique	магнитный диск
M 69	**magnetic drum**	Magnettrommel f	tambour m magnétique	магнитный барабан
M 70	**magnetic field**	Magnetfeld n	champ m magnétique	магнитное поле
M 71	**magnetic field intensity**	magnetische Feldstärke f	intensité f de champ magnétique	напряженность магнитного поля
M 72	**magnetic-film store**	Magnetfilmspeicher m, Magnetschichtspeicher m	mémoire f à film magnétique	запоминающее устройство на магнитных пленках
M 73	**magnetic flux density**	magnetische Flußdichte f	densité f de flux magnétique	плотность магнитного потока
M 74	**magnetic head**	Magnetkopf m	tête f magnétique	магнитная головка
M 75	**magnetic hysteresis**	magnetische Hysterese f	hystérésis f magnétique	магнитный гистерезис
M 76	**magnetic induction**	magnetische Induktion f	induction f magnétique	магнитная индукция
M 77	**magnetic ink**	magnetische Tinte f, Magnetfarbe f	encre f magnétique	магнитные чернила
	magnetic ink character recognition	s. M 61		
M 78	**magnetic latch**	magnetische Verriegelung f	verrouillage m magnétique	магнитный фиксатор, магнитная защелка
M 79	**magnetic leakage**	magnetischer Streufluß m, magnetische Streuung f	dispersion f magnétique	магнитное рассеяние
M 80	**magnetic ledger card,** magnetic account card	Magnetkontokarte f <visuell und maschinell lesbar>	carte f à comptes magnétique	магнитная учетная карта
M 81	**magnetic ledger card computer,** magnetic account computer	Magnetkontencomputer m, Magnetkontenrechner m	calculateur m à comptes magnétiques	вычислительная машина для обработки магнитных учетных карт
M 82	**magnetic ledger memory**	Magnetkontenspeicher m	mémoire f à comptes magnétiques	магнитная память учетных данных
M 83	**magnetic memory,** magnetic storage (store)	magnetischer Speicher m	mémoire f magnétique	магнитная память
M 84	**magnetic recording**	magnetische Aufzeichnung f	enregistrement m magnétique	магнитная запись
M 85	**magnetic recording medium**	magnetisches Aufzeichnungsmedium n	milieu m d'enregistrement magnétique	носитель магнитных записей, магнитный носитель
M 86	**magnetic recording technique**	Magnetaufzeichnungstechnik f	technique f d'enregistrement magnétique	техника магнитной записи
M 87	**magnetic saturation**	magnetische Sättigung f	saturation f magnétique	магнитное насыщение
M 88	**magnetic shield**	magnetische Schirmung f	écran (blindage) m magnétique	магнитный экран
M 89	**magnetic shift register**	magnetisches Schieberegister n	registre m à décalages magnétique	сдвиговый регистр на магнитных элементах
M 90	**magnetic state**	Magnetisierungszustand m	état m d'aimantation	состояние намагниченности
	magnetic storage (store)	s. M 83		
M 91	**magnetic strip**	Magnetstreifen m	ruban m magnétique	магнитная полоска
M 92	**magnetic tape**	Magnetband n	bande f magnétique	магнитная лента
M 93	**magnetic tape cassette,** MTC	Magnetbandkassette f	cassette f à bande magnétique	кассета с магнитной лентой
M 94	**magnetic tape converter**	Magnetbandkonverter m <Umsetzer von Lochkarte oder Lochstreifen auf Magnetband>	convertisseur m à bande magnétique	устройство преобразования и переписи данных с магнитной ленты на другой носитель
M 95	**magnetic tape encoder,** magnetic tape recorder	Magnetbandaufzeichner m	enregistreur m à bande magnétique	устройство записи [данных] на магнитную ленту
M 96	**magnetic tape reader**	Magnetbandleser m	lecteur m à bande magnétique	устройство считывания [данных] с магнитной ленты
	magnetic tape recorder	s. M 95		
M 97	**magnetic tape storage**	Magnetbandspeicher m	mémoire f à bande magnétique	запоминающее устройство на магнитной ленте, память на магнитной ленте
M 98	**magnetic tape unit**	Magnetbandeinheit f	unité f à bande magnétique	блок памяти на магнитной ленте
M 99	**magnetic track**	Magnetspur f	piste f magnétique	магнитная дорожка, дорожка магнитной ленты
M 100	**magnetic wire store**	Magnetdrahtspeicher m	mémoire f à fils magnétiques	запоминающее устройство на магнитной проволоке
M 101	**magnetized spot**	magnetisierte Stelle f, Magnetfleck m	point m magnétisé	намагниченный участок
M 102	**magnetostrictive delay line**	magnetostriktive Verzögerungsleitung f	ligne f de retardement magnétostrictive	магнитострикционная линия задержки
M 103	**magnitude**	Größe f, Größenordnung f	grandeur f	величина, значение
M 104	**mailbox technique**	Briefkastenverfahren n <Datenübergabe>	procédé m à boite à lettre	метод обмена данными при помощи почтовых ящиков
M 105	**main enclosure**	Hauptschrank m	armoire f principale	главный шкаф, главная стойка
M 106	**main file,** master file	Stammdatei f	fichier m maître	основной файл
M 107	**main frame**	Zentraleinheit f, Hauptteil m eines Rechners, Rechnergrundgerät n	unité f centrale	центральный процессор
M 108	**main frame computer**	Rechenanlage f mit großer Zentraleinheit <Bezeichnung für mittlere EDVA>	calculateur m à grande unité centrale	большая ЭВМ
	main line program	s. M 112		

M 109	main line switch	Hauptschalter m	interrupteur m principal	главный коммутатор каналов
M 110	main logic board	Zentral-Steckeinheit f, zentrale Logik-Leiter-platte f	unité f centrale enfichable	главный логический модуль ‹плата с процессором›
	main memory	s. M 113		
M 111	main processor	Hauptprozessor m	processeur m principal	главный процессор
M 112	main program (routine), main line program	Hauptprogramm n	programme m principal	основная (ведущая) программа
M 113	main storage (store), main memory, general storage	Hauptspeicher m	mémoire f principale	главная память
M 114	maintain / to	instand halten, warten	maintenir	обслуживать
M 115	maintainability	Wartbarkeit f, Instand-haltungsmöglichkeit f	faculté f de maintenance	ремонтопригодность
	maintaining	s. M 116		
M 116	maintenance, maintain-ing	Wartung f, Instandhaltung f, Pflege f	maintenance f, entretien m	техническое обслуживание
M 117	maintenance aids	Wartungshilfen fpl	aides fpl à la maintenance	средства технического обслуживания
	maintenance charges	s. M 118		
	maintenance console	s. M 119		
M 118	maintenance costs, maintenance charges	Wartungskosten pl, Instand-haltungskosten pl	frais (coûts) mpl de mainte-nance	эксплуатационные расходы, расходы на техническое обслуживание
M 119	maintenance panel, maintenance console	Wartungspult n	console f de maintenance	инженерный пульт
M 120	maintenance rate	Wartungszeitraum m	délai m d'entretien	продолжительность (длительность) ремонта
M 121	maintenance software	Wartungs-Software f, Wartungsprogramme npl	logiciels mpl de maintenance	программные средства технического обслуживания, комплект программ технического обслуживания
M 122	maintenance task	Wartungsaufgabe f	tâche f de maintenance	задача технического обслуживания
M 123	main timing	Haupttaktierung f, zentrale Taktsteuerung f	rythme m principal	основная синхронизирующая последовательность
M 124	main timing circuitry	zentrale Taktversorgungs-schaltung f	circuit m de rythmeur principal	схемы генерации и распределения основных тактовых сигналов
M 125	major cycle	Hauptzyklus m, Haupt-periode f	cycle m principal	главный (основной) цикл
M 126	majority carrier	Majoritätsladungsträger m	porteur m de charge à majorité	основной носитель [заряда]
M 127	majority element	Majoritätselement n	élément m à majorité	мажоритарный элемент
M 128	majority gate	Majoritätslogikgatter n	porte f logique à majorité	мажоритарный вентиль
M 129	majority logic	Majoritätslogik f, Mehr-heitslogik f	logique f à majorité	мажоритарная логика
M 130	major state	Hauptzustand m	état m principal	основное состояние
	maker	s. M 145		
M 131	malfunction	Fehlfunktion f, fehlerhafte Funktion f	fonction f défectueuse	сбой, неисправность
M 132	man-computer relation-ship	Mensch-Rechner-Bezie-hung f	relation f (rapport m) Homme-calculateur	взаимодействие «человек-ЭВМ»
	manipulating, mani-pulation	s. H 19		
M 133	man-machine commu-nication	Mensch-Maschine-Kom-munikation f	communication f Homme-machine	связь «человек-машина»
M 134	man-machine inter-action	Mensch-Maschine-Wechselwirkung f, Mensch-Maschine-Beziehung f	rapport m Homme-machine	взаимодействие «человек-машина»
M 135	man-machine interface	Mensch-Maschine-Schnitt-stelle f ‹z. B. Dialog-terminal›	interface f Homme-machine	интерфейс «человек-машина»
M 136	mantissa, fraction, fixed-point part	Mantisse f, Festkommateil m einer Gleitkommazahlen-darstellung	mantisse f	мантисса
M 137	manual	Handbuch n	manuel m	руководство
M 138	manual control	Handregelung f; Hand-steuerung f	commande f manuelle	ручное управление
M 139	manual entry (input)	manuelle Eingabe f, Eingabe von Hand, Handeingabe f	entrée f manuelle	ручной ввод
M 140	manual mode	manuelle Betriebsweise f	mode m manuel	ручной режим [работы]
M 141	manual operation	Handbetrieb m	régime m manuel, opération f manuelle	ручная операция; работа вручную
M 142	manual patching	manuelles Durchschalten n	commutation f manuelle	ручное внесение изменений в программу, вставка (удаление) фрагмента программы
M 143	manual perforator, hand punch	Handlocher m	perforatrice f manuelle	ручной перфоратор
M 144	manual switch	Handschalter m	interrupteur m manuel	ручной переключатель
	manufactoring control	s. M 146		
	manufactoring cost	s. M 147		
	manufactoring process	s. M 148		
M 145	manufacturer, producer, maker	Hersteller m, Produzent m	producteur m	[фирма-]производитель, изготовитель
M 146	manufacturing control, manufacturing (produc-tion) control	Fertigungssteuerung f, Produktionssteuerung f	commande f de fabrication	управление производством
M 147	manufacturing cost, manufacturing (produc-tion) cost	Herstellungskosten pl	frais mpl de fabrication	расходы на производство, стоимость производства

M 148	**manufacturing process,** manufactoring process	Herstellungsprozeß *m*, Herstellungsverfahren *n*	processus (procédé) *m* de fabrication	процесс изготовления
M 149	**manufacturing technique**	Herstellungstechnik *f*, Herstellungstechnologie *f*	technique *f* de fabrication	технические средства производства, технология производства
M 150	**map / to**	einteilen, abbilden <einen Größenbereich auf einen anderen, speziell Programmadreßbereich auf Speicheradreßbereich>	découper, représenter	отображать, устанавливать соответствие
M 151	**map**	Einteilungsübersicht *f*, Abbild *n*	synoptique *f*, image *f*, aspect *m*	отображение, соответствие
M 152	**mapping**	Einteilung *f*, Abbildung *f* <Adreßbereiche>	découpage *m*, représentation *f*	отображение <процесс>
M 153	**mapping system**	Einteilungssystem *n*, Abbildungssystem *n*	système *m* de classement (représentation)	система отображения
M 154	**margin**	Spanne *f*, Spielraum *m*	marge *f*	запас <напр. регулирования>, диапазон [действия], поле [печатной страницы]
M 155	**marginal check[ing],** **marginal testing**	Grenzwertkontrolle *f*, Toleranzgrenzentest *m*	test *m* de marge	граничные испытания <испытания при предельных отклонениях рабочих параметров от номинальных значений>
M 156	**marginal voltage check**	Spannungsgrenzwerttest *m*, Test *m* bei reduzierter Betriebsspannung	test *m* à tension limite	испытание при предельном отклонении напряжения питания от номинального значения
M 157	**mark / to**	markieren	marquer	отмечать, размечать
M 158	**mark**	Marke *f*	marque *f*	метка
M 159	**marker**	Markierer *m*	marqueur *m*	маркер
M 160	**marker pulse**	Markierungsimpuls *m*	impulsion *f* de marquage	маркерный импульс
M 161	**market development**	Marktentwicklung *f*	développement *m* du marché	расширение рынка [сбыта]
M 162	**marketing**	Marktarbeit *f*, Absatztätigkeit *f*	marketing *m*	торговля, сбыт
M 163	**market place**	Marktposition *f*	place *f* dans le marché	торговый центр
M 164	**mark-hold**	Ruhestromzustand *m*	état *m* de courant de repos	посылка условного сигнала в линию связи [при отсутствии сообщений], сигнал отсутствия трафика
M 165	**marking**	Markierung *f*	marquage *m*	разметка, обозначение, маркировка
M 166	**mark position**	Markierungsstelle *f*	position *f* de marque	позиция (положение) метки
M 167	**mark reader**	Markierungsleser *m*	lecteur *m* de marquage	устройство считывания меток
M 168	**mask**	Maske *f*, Abdeckschablone *f*, Schaltkreisschablone *f*	masque *m*	маска, трафарет
M 169	**maskable interrupt**	maskierbare Unterbrechung *f*	interruption *f* masquable	замаскированное прерывание
M 170	**mask bit**	Maskierungsbit *n*	bit *m* de masque	разряд [регистра] маски
M 171	**mask contact printing**	Maskenkontaktkopierverfahren *n* <Maskenstrukturübertragung auf Halbleiterscheibe mittels Kontaktkopie>	procédé *m* de copie par contact de masque	нанесение маски способом контактной печати <полупроводниковая техника>
M 172	**masking**	Maskieren *n*	masquage *m*	маскирование
M 173	**masking operation**	Maskieroperation *f*	opération *f* de masquage	операция маскирования
M 174	**mask manufacture**	Maskenherstellung *f*	fabrication *f* de masque	изготовление маски
M 175	**mask process**	Maskenprozeß *m*, Maskierungsprozeß *m*	processus *m* de masque	обработка маски
M 176	**mask-programmable** **read-only memory**	maskenprogrammierbarer Nur-Lese-Speicher *m*	mémoire *f* lecture seule programmable par masque	масочно-программируемое постоянное запоминающее устройство
M 177	**mask-programmed** **memory**	maskenprogrammierter Speicher *m* <Halbleiter-ROM>	mémoire *f* programmée par masque	[постоянное] запоминающее устройство, запрограммированное с помощью масок
M 178	**mask programming**	Maskenprogrammierung *f* <ROM-Speicherinhalt>	programmation *f* de masque	программирование масок
M 179	**mask projection printing**	Maskenprojektionskopierverfahren *n* <Maskenstrukturübertragung auf Halbleiterscheibe mittels Projektion>	procédé *m* de copie par projection de masque	нанесение маски методом проекционной печати
M 180	**mask step**	Maskenschritt *m*, Maskierungsschritt *m*	pas *m* de masquage	шаг маски
M 181	**mask topology**	Maskentopologie *f*, Schaltkreisschablonentopologie *f*	topologie *f* à masque	топология маски
	mass memory (storage)	*s.* B 311		
	master	*s.* M 186		
M 182	**master card**	Hauptkarte *f* <Leitwer>k	carte *f* maître	главная карта
M 183	**master clock**	Haupttaktgeber *m*	rythmeur *m* maître	задающий генератор
M 184	**master control program** **(routine)**	Hauptsteuerprogramm *n*	programme *m* de commande maître	главная управляющая программа
M 185	**master data sheet**	Hauptdatenblatt *n*	fiche *f* de caractéristiques maître	бланк основных данных
M 186	**master device,** master	Hauptgerät *n* [in einem Master-Slave-System], Mastergerät *n*, steuerungsführendes Gerät *n*	appareil *m* maître, maître *m*	ведущее устройство

M 187	master drawing	Leiterbildoriginal *n*, Entwurfsmuster *n*	échantillon *m* de conception	оригинал [топологии печатной платы]; эталонный чертеж
	master file	*s.* M 106		
M 188	master mode	steuerungsführende Betriebsart *f*	mode *m* maître	основной режим, режим ведущего [устройства]
	master processor	*s.* H 147		
M 189	master reset signal	Hauptrücksetzsignal *n*, allgemeines Rücksetzsignal *n*	signal *m* principal (général) de remise	сигнал сброса ведомых устройств со стороны ведущего [устройства]; сигнал общего сброса
M 190	master-slave concept	Master-Slave-Konzept *n*, Hauptgerät-Nebengerät-Konzept *n* <Strukturprinzip mit steuerungsführender und anweisungsausführender Einheit>	concept *m* master-slave	концепция «ведущий-ведомый»
M 191	master-slave configuration	Master-Slave-Konfiguration *f*, Hauptgerät-Nebengerät-Struktur *f*, Konfiguration *f* mit führender und ausführender Einheit	configuration *f* master-slave	структура типа «ведущий-ведомый»
	master-slave flip-flop	*s.* M 517		
M 192	master-slave relationship	Master-Slave-Beziehung *f*, Hauptgerät-Nebengerät-Austauschbeziehung *f* <Signalspiel zwischen führendem und geführtem Gerät eines Systems>	relation *f* master-slave	взаимодействие устройств по принципу «ведущий-ведомый»
M 193	master slice	Stammscheibe *f*, Chip *n* mit maskenprogrammierbarer Universal-Logikstruktur	puce *f* à structure logique universelle programmable par masque	чип-полуфабрикат с базовыми элементами, предназначенный для изготовления заказных БИС
M 194	master tape	Stammband *n*, Systemurband *n*	bande *f* maître	основная лента, лента-оригинал
M 195	master unit	Haupteinheit *f*, steuerungsführende Einheit *f*	unité *f* maître	главное (ведущее) устройство
M 196	matched load	angepaßte Last *f*	charge *f* adaptée	согласованная нагрузка
	matching	*s.* A 90		
	matching circuit	*s.* A 88		
M 197	matching condition	Anpassungsbedingung *f*	condition *f* d'adaptation	условие согласования; условие совпадения
M 198	matching error	Anpassungsfehler *m*	erreur *f* d'adaptation	ошибка несовпадения; ошибка согласования
M 199	matching impedance	Anpassungswiderstand *m*	impédance *f* d'adaptation	согласующее сопротивление
M 200	matching priority	Vergleichspriorität *f*	priorité *f* de comparaison	приоритет сравнения
M 201	matching value	Vergleichswert *m*	valeur *f* de comparaison	контрольное значение
M 202	matrix	Matrix *f*	matrice *f*	матрица
M 203	matrix line	Matrixleitung *f*	ligne *f* de matrice	строка матрицы
M 204	matrix printer	Matrixdrucker *m*	imprimante *f* à matrice	матричное печатающее устройство
	matrix store	*s.* C 769		
M 205	maximum access time	maximale Zugriffszeit *f*	temps *m* d'accès maximal	максимальное время доступа
M 206	maximum load	Höchstbelastung *f*	charge *f* maximale	максимальная нагрузка
M 207	maximum output (performance)	Höchstleistung *f*	puissance *f* maximale	максимальная производительность
M 208	maximum rating	Grenzdaten *pl*	valeurs *fpl* limite	предельные параметры
	MDOS	*s.* M 358		
	MDS	*s.* M 357		
M 209	mean life[time]	mittlere Lebensdauer *f*	longévité *f* moyenne	средний срок службы; среднее время жизни [носителя]
M 210	mean repair time, mean time to repair, MTTR	mittlere Reparaturzeit *f*	temps *m* moyen de réparation	среднее время восстановления
M 211	mean time between failures, MTBF	MTBF *f*, mittlere Zeit *f* zwischen zwei Ausfällen, mittlerer Ausfallabstand *m*	temps *m* moyen entre défaillances	среднее время безотказной работы
M 212	mean time to maintain, MTTM	mittlere Wartungszeit *f*	temps *m* moyen de maintenance	среднее время обслуживания
	mean time to repair	*s.* M 210		
M 213	mean value	Mittelwert *m*	valeur *f* moyenne	среднее значение
	measurand	*s.* M 227		
M 214	measured signal	Meßsignal *n*	signal *m* de mesure	измеряемый сигнал
M 215	measured value	Meßwert *m*	valeur *f* de mesure	измеряемое (измеренное) значение
M 216	measured value reduction	Meßwertverdichtung *f*	compression *f* de valeurs de mesure	предварительная обработка результатов измерений
M 217	measurement error	Meßfehler *m*	erreur *f* de mesure	ошибка измерения
M 218	measurement setup	Meßplatz *m*	place *f* de mesure	установка для измерения
M 219	measuring circuit	Meßschaltung *f*	circuit *m* de mesure	измерительная схема
M 220	measuring device	Meßgerät *n*, Meßeinrichtung *f*	appareil (dispositif) *m* de mesure	измерительное устройство
M 221	measuring equipment, instrumentation	Meßausrüstung *f*, Meßgeräteausstattung *f*	équipement *m* de mesure, instrumentation *f*	измерительное оборудование
M 222	measuring point	Meßstelle *f*	point *m* de mesure	точка замера
	measuring quantity	*s.* M 227		
M 223	measuring range	Meßbereich *m*	champ *m* de mesure	диапазон измерений
M 224	measuring system	Meßsystem *n*	système *m* de mesure	измерительная система
M 225	measuring technique	Meßtechnik *f*, Meßverfahren *n*	technique *f* de mesure	измерительная техника; метод[ы] измерений

M 226	measuring transmitter, transducer	Meßumformer *m*	convertisseur *m* de mesure, transmetteur *m*	измерительный датчик (преобразователь)
M 227	measuring variable, measuring quantity, measurand	Meßgröße *f*	grandeur *f* de mesure	измеряемая величина, измеряемый параметр
M 228	mechanical assembly	mechanische Baugruppe *f*	assemblage (module) *m* mécanique	механический узел
M 229	mechanical design	mechanischer Aufbau *m*	structure *f* mécanique	механическая конструкция
M 230	mechanical specifications	mechanische Spezifikation *f*, Kenndatenblatt *n* mechanischer Parameter	spécification *f* mécanique	требования к механическим параметрам
M 231	medical electronics	Medizinelektronik *f*, elektronische Medizintechnik *f*	électronique *f* médicale	медицинская электроника
M 232	medium duty	mittlere Beanspruchung *f*	charge *f* moyenne	средняя нагрузка
M 233	medium power	mittlere Leistung *f*	puissance *f* moyenne	средняя мощность
	medium scale integration	s. M 518		
M 234	medium-speed version	Mittelgeschwindigkeitsversion *f*, Normalversion *f*	version *f* à vitesse moyenne, version normale	вариант исполнения [устройства] со средним быстродействием, стандартный вариант
M 235	meltback transistor	Schmelzperlentransistor *m*	transistor *m* à perles de fusion	обратнооплавленный транзистор
M 235a	memory, storage, store	Speicher *m*	mémoire *f*	запоминающее устройство, память, ЗУ
M 236	memory access	Speicherzugriff *m*	accès *m* à la mémoire	доступ (обращение) к памяти
M 237	memory access mode	Speicherzugriffsmodus *m*	mode *m* d'accès à la mémoire	режим доступа к памяти
M 238	memory access protection	Speicherzugriffsschutz *m*	protection *f* d'accès à la mémoire	защита от несанкционированного доступа
M 239	memory access time	Speicherzugriffszeit *f*	temps *m* d'accès à la mémoire	время доступа к памяти
M 240	memory address	Speicheradresse *f*	adresse *f* de mémoire	адрес памяти
M 241	memory addressing	Speicheradressierung *f*	adressage *m* de la mémoire	адресация памяти
M 242	memory address register, memory location register	Speicheradreßregister *n*	registre *m* d'adresse de mémoire	регистр адреса памяти
M 243	memory allocation, storage allocation, memory assignment	Speicherplatzzuordnung *f*, Speicherplatzverteilung *f*, Speicherzuweisung *f*	attribution *f* de mémoire	распределение ячеек памяти
M 244	memory area, storage area	Speicherbereich *m*, Speicherfläche *f*	domaine *m* de mémoire	область памяти
M 245	memory array	Speicherfeld *n*, Speicherzellenanordnung *f*	champ *m* de mémoire	поле памяти, массив памяти
	memory assignment	s. M 243		
M 246	memory availability formula	Speicherbelegungsformel *f*	formule *f* d'allocation de mémoire	формула распределения памяти
M 247	memory bank	Speicherbank *f*	banque *f* de mémoire	банк памяти
M 248	memory bank select technique	Speicherbankauswahlverfahren *n*, Speicherbankansteuertechnik *f*	technique *f* de sélection de banque de mémoire	способ выбора банка памяти
M 249	memory bank switching	Speicherbankumschaltung *f*	commutation *f* de banque de mémoire	коммутация банков памяти
M 250	memory battery backup	batteriegestützter Speicher *m*	mémoire *f* soutenue par batterie	резервная батарея питания памяти
M 251	memory bit	Speicherbit *n*	bit *m* de mémoire	разряд запоминающего устройства
M 252	memory block, storage block	Speicherblock *m*	bloc *m* de mémoire	блок памяти
M 253	memory board	Speicherleiterplatte *f*, Speicherkarte *f*	carte *f* de mémoire	плата памяти
M 254	memory bus	Speicherbus *m*	bus *m* de mémoire	шина памяти
M 255	memory capacity, storage capacity	Speicherkapazität *f*	capacité *f* de mémoire	емкость памяти
M 256	memory cell, storage cell	Speicherzelle *f*	cellule *f* de mémoire	ячейка памяти
M 257	memory-cell structure, storage-cell structure	Speicherzellenstruktur *f*, Speicherzellenaufbau *m*	structure *f* de cellule de mémoire	структура ячейки памяти
M 258	memory chip	Speicherchip *n*	puce *f* de mémoire	чип памяти
M 259	memory configuration	Speicherkonfiguration *f*, Speicheraufbau *m*	configuration *f* de mémoire	конфигурация памяти
M 260	memory contents	Speicherinhalt *m*	contenu *m* de mémoire	содержимое памяти
M 261	memory control, storage control	Speichersteuerung *f*	commande *f* de mémoire	управление памятью
M 262	memory cycle, storage cycle	Speicherzyklus *m*	cycle *m* de mémoire	цикл памяти
M 263	memory cycle time	Speicherzykluszeit *f*	temps *m* de cycle de mémoire	длительность цикла памяти
M 264	memory-data register	Speicherdatenregister *n*	registre *m* de données de mémoire	регистр данных памяти
M 265	memory density, storage density	Speicherdichte *f*, Dichte *f* der Speicherelemente	densité *f* de mémoire	плотность записи; плотность размещения элементов памяти
M 266	memory dump, dump	Speicherauszug *m*, Speicherausschrift *f*	extrait *m* de mémoire	дамп, вывод данных (содержимого памяти), разгрузка памяти
	memory dumping	s. D 581		
M 267	memory efficiency, storage efficiency	Speicherausnutzung *f*	efficience *f* de mémoire	эффективность [использования] памяти
M 268	memory element, storage element	Speicherelement *n*	élément *m* de mémoire	элемент памяти, запоминающий элемент

M 269	**memory erasing,** store erasing	Speicherlöschung *f*	effaçage *m* de mémoire	стирание [содержимого] памяти
	memory expander	*s.* M 272		
M 270	**memory expansion**	Speichererweiterung *f*	élargissement *m* de mémoire	расширение памяти
M 271	**memory expansion technique**	Speichererweiterungstechnik *f*, Speichererweiterungsverfahren *n*	technique *f* d'élargissement de mémoire	средства расширения памяти
M 272	**memory extender,** memory expander	Speichererweiterungsbaustein *m*	module *m* d'élargissement de mémoire	схема расширения памяти, расширитель памяти
M 273	**memory fabrication technology**	Speicherherstellungstechnologie *f*	technologie *f* de fabrication de mémoire[s]	технология изготовления памяти
M 274	**memory hierarchy,** storage hierarchy, hierarchy of memories	Speicherhierarchie *f*	hiérarchie *f* de mémoires	иерархия памяти
M 275	**memory IC**	Speicher-SK *m*, Speicherschaltkreis *m*	CI *m* de mémoire	ИС (интегральная схема) памяти
M 276	**memory information**	Speicherinformation *f*	information *f* de mémoire	информация, хранящаяся в памяти
M 277	**memory interleaving**	Speicherverschachtelung *f*	imbrication *f* de mémoire	расслоение памяти
M 278	**memory location,** storage location	Speicherplatz *m*	place *f* de mémoire	адрес ячейки памяти; ячейка памяти
	memory location register	*s.* M 242		
M 279	**memory lockout**	Speichersperre *f*	blocage *m* de mémoire	блокировка памяти
M 280	**memory management**	Speicherverwaltung *f*	gestion *f* de mémoire	управление памятью; управление распределением памяти
M 281	**memory management unit,** MMU	Speicherverwaltungseinheit *f*	unité *f* de gestion de mémoire	устройство управления памяти
M 282	**memory map**	Speicherbelegungsplan *m*	plan *m* d'occupation de mémoire	карта [распределения] памяти
M 283	**memory-mapped**	speicherzugeordnet	attribué à la (une) mémoire	распределенный в памяти
M 284	**memory-mapped I/O addressing**	speicherzugeordnete E/A-Adressierung *f*, E/A-Adressierung im Speicheradreßbereich	adressage *m* d'E/S attribué à la mémoire	выделение части адресного пространства [памяти] под адреса устройств ввода-вывода
M 285	**memory mapping**	Speicherbereichszuordnung *f*, Speicheraufteilung *f*	découpage *m* de mémoire	распределение памяти
M 286	**memory matrix**	Speichermatrix *f*	matrice *f* de mémoire	матрица памяти, запоминающая матрица
M 287	**memory modification**	Speichermodifizierung *f*, Speicherveränderung *f*	modification *f* de mémoire	модификация памяти
M 288	**memory module**	Speichermodul *m*	module *m* de mémoire	модуль памяти
M 289	**memory operand**	Speicheroperand *m* <im Gegensatz zu Registeroperand>	opérande *m* de mémoire	операнд, хранящийся в памяти
M 290	**memory operation**	Speicheroperation *f*	opération *f* de mémoire	операция обращения к памяти
M 291	**memory organization**	Speicherorganisation *f*	organisation *f* de mémoire	организация памяти
M 282	**memory overlay**	Speicherüberlappung *f*	recouvrement *m* de mémoire	наложение [в памяти]
M 293	**memory page**	Speicherseite *f*, Speicherabschnitt (Speicherbereich) *m* konstanter Größe	page *f* de mémoire	страница памяти
M 294	**memory parity**	Speicherparität *f*	parité *f* de mémoire	контроль [содержимого] памяти по четности
M 295	**memory protection,** storage protection	Speicherschutz *m*	protection *f* de mémoire	защита памяти
M 296	**memory protection key,** storage [protection] key	Speicherschutzschlüssel *m*, Speicherschlüssel *m*	clé *f* de protection de mémoire	ключ защиты памяти
M 297	**memory protect violation**	Speicherschutzverletzung *f*	violation *f* de protection de mémoire	нарушение защиты памяти
M 298	**memory read cycle**	Speicherlesezyklus *m*	cycle *m* de lecture de mémoire	цикл чтения [памяти]
M 299	**memory reference**	Speicherbezug *m*	référence *f* à la mémoire	обращение к памяти
M 300/1	**memory reference instruction**	speicherbezogener Befehl *m* <Befehl mit Speicheroperand bzw. Speicheroperation>	instruction *f* relative à la mémoire	команда обращения к памяти
M 302	**memory refresh, memory regeneration**	Speicherinhaltsauffrischung *f*, Speicherregenerierung *f*	régénération *f* de mémoire	регенерация памяти
M 303	**memory register**	Speicherregister *n*	registre *m* de mémoire	регистр памяти
M 304	**memory request**	Speicheranforderung *f*	demande *f* de mémoire	запрос памяти
M 305	**memory requirement**	Speichererfordernis *n*, Speicherbedarf *m*	besoin *m* de mémoire	требование к памяти
M 306	**memory-resident**	speicherresident, im Speicher verbleibend (aufbewahrt)	résident dans la mémoire	хранимый в памяти
M 307	**memory-resident software package**	speicherresidentes (im Speicher verbleibendes) Programmpaket *n*	paquet *m* logiciel résident en mémoire	программное обеспечение, хранящееся в памяти
M 308	**memory sense amplifier**	Speicherleseverstärker *m*	amplificateur *m* de lecture de mémoire	усилитель считывания
M 309	**memory size**	Speichergröße *f*	taille *f* de mémoire	объем памяти
M 310/1	**memory space**	Speicherraum *m*, Speicherumfang *m*	volume *m* de mémoire	пространство памяти
M 312	**memory system,** storage system	Speichersystem *n*	système *m* de mémoire	система памяти, запоминающая система
M 313	**memory technique,** storage technique	Speichertechnik *f*, Speicherverfahren *n*	technique *f* de mémoire	способы построения запоминающих устройств, техника хранения данных

M 314	memory-to-memory architecture	Speicher-Speicher-Architektur f, speicherorientierte Architektur f, Struktur f mit Datenverarbeitung aus dem und in den Speicher <im Gegensatz zur registerorientierten Architektur>	structure f mémoire-mémoire	архитектура типа «память-память»
M 315	memory-to-register architecture	Speicher-Register-Architektur f, Struktur f mit Datenverarbeitung aus dem Speicher in Register <akkumulatororientierte Architektur>	structure f mémoire-registre	архитектура типа «память-регистр»
M 316	memory transfer	Speichertransfer m <Übertragung in den oder aus dem Speicher>	transfert m de mémoire	передача данных в память, передача данных из памяти
M 317	memory type	Speichertyp m, Speicherart f	type m de mémoire	тип памяти
M 318	memory unit, storage unit	Speichereinheit f	unité f de mémoire	блок памяти
M 319	memory word, storage word	Speicherwort n	mot m de mémoire	слово данных памяти; длина ячейки памяти
M 320	memory write cycle	Speicherschreibzyklus m	cycle m d'écriture de mémoire	цикл записи [в память]
M 321	memory write instruction, storage write instruction	Speicherschreibbefehl m	instruction f d'écriture de mémoire	команда записи в память
M 322	merge / to	mischen, zusammenmischen, verschmelzen	fusionner, mélanger	объединять, сливать, смешивать
M 323	merged technology	gemischte Technologie f, Mischtechnik f	technologie f mixte	смешанная технология
M 324	merged transistor logic, MTL	MTL f, gemischte Transistorlogik (Transistorschaltungstechnik) f	logique f à transistors mixte	логические схемы на основе биполярных транзисторов обоих типов проводимости <напр. И²Л-схемы>
M 325	merge instruction	Mischbefehl m	instruction f de fusion	команда слияния (объединения)
M 326	MESFET, metal semiconductor field-effect transistor	MESFET m, Metall-Halbleiter-Feldeffekttransistor m, Schottky-FET m <Sperrschicht-FET mit Metall-Halbleiter-Schottkyübergang>	transistor m métal-semiconducteur à effet champ, MESFET m	полевой транзистор Шоттки, полевой транзистор со структурой «металл-полупроводник»
M 327	message	Nachricht f, Meldung f, Mitteilung f, Botschaft f	message m, information f	сообщение
M 328	message control program	Nachrichtenübertragungs-Steuerprogramm n	programme m de commande de transmission de messages	программа управления сообщениями
M 329	message priority	Nachrichtenpriorität f	priorité f de message	приоритет сообщения
M 330	message queue	Nachrichtenwarteschlange f, Warteschlange f für Botschaften	queue f de messages	очередь сообщений
M 331	message redundancy	Nachrichtenredundanz f	redondance f de message	избыточность сообщения
M 332	message routing	Nachrichtenleitung f, Nachrichtenführung f	acheminement m de messages	маршрутизация сообщений
M 333	message switching, store-and-forward switching	Nachrichtenvermittlung f, Speichervermittlung f	communication f de messages	коммутация сообщений
M 334	meta language	Metasprache f, Zwischensprache f	métalangue f	метаязык
M 335	metal contact	Metallkontakt m	contact m métallique	металлический контакт; металлический вывод
M 336	metal deposit technique	Metallablagerungstechnik f	technique f de dépôt métallique	метод осаждения металла
M 337	metal film resistor	Metallschichtwiderstand m	résistance f à couche métallique	металлопленочный резистор
M 338	metal gate	Metall-Gate n, Metall-Steuerelektrode f <Halbleitertechnik>	gate m métallique	металлический затвор
	metal-insulator semiconductor device	s. M 448		
	metal-insulator semiconductor field effect transistor	s. M 449		
M 339	metallization	Metallisierung f	métallisation f	металлизация
	metal nitride oxide semiconductor technology	s. M 456		
	metal-oxide semiconductor device	s. M 498		
	metal-oxide-semiconductor field effect transistor	s. M 499		
	metal-oxide semiconductor technology	s. M 495		
M 340	metal-rolling application	Anwendung f in Metallwalzwerken	application f aux laminages de métaux	применение в металлопрокатном производстве
	metal semiconductor field-effect transistor	s. M 326		
	MFM	s. M 533		
	MICR	s. M 61		
M 341	microcircuit, microelectronic circuit	Mikroschaltkreis m, mikroelektronischer Schaltkreis m, Mikroschaltung f	microcircuit m	микросхема, микроэлектронная схема
M 342	microcircuit technique	Mikroschaltungstechnik f	technique f des microcircuits	техника микросхем, микросхемотехника

M 343	**microcode**	Mikrobefehlskode m	microcode m	микрокод
M 344	**microcoded operation**	mikrokodierte (mikropro-grammierte) Operation f	opération f microcodée	микропрограммная опера-ция
M 345	**microcode instruction set,** microinstruction set	Mikrokodebefehlssatz m, Mikrobefehlssatz m	jeu m d'instructions en microcode	набор микрокоманд
M 346	**microcoding**	Mikrokodierung f	codage m micro, micro-codage m	микрокодирование
	microcommand	s. M 374		
M 347	**microcomputer**	Mikrorechner m <Rechner auf Mikroprozessorbasis>	microcalculateur m	микро-ЭВМ
M 348	**microcomputer applica-tion**	Mikrorechneranwendung f	application f de micro-calculateur	применение микро-ЭВМ
M 349	**microcomputer-based node**	mikrorechnerbestückter Netzknoten m	nœud m de réseau à micro-calculateur	узел [вычислительной сети] на базе микро-ЭВМ
M 350	**microcomputer-based system**	mikrorechnerbestücktes System n, System auf Mikrorechnerbasis	système m à microcalcula-teurs, système sur base de microcalculateurs	[вычислительная] система на базе микро-ЭВМ
M 351	**microcomputer board**	Mikrorechnerplatine f, Mikrorechner-Leiter-platte f	platine f de microcalculateur	плата микро-ЭВМ
M 352	**microcomputer card module**	Steckeinheitenmodul (Kartenmodul) m eines Mikrorechners	module m de carte d'un microcalculateur	одноплатный модуль микро-ЭВМ
M 353	**microcomputer com-ponent**	Mikrorechnerbauteil n, Mikrorechnerbaugruppe f	composant m de micro-calculateur	компонент (узел) микро-ЭВМ
M 354	**microcomputer-con-trolled device**	mikrorechnergesteuertes Gerät n	appareil m à commande par microcalculateur	устройство, управляемое микро-ЭВМ
M 355	**microcomputer develop-ment**	Mikrorechnerentwicklung f	développement m de micro-calculateur	разработка микро-ЭВМ
M 356	**microcomputer develop-ment kit**	Mikrorechner-Entwick-lungsbausatz m	ensemble m de développe-ment de microcalculateur	макетный набор для про-ектирования микро-ЭВМ
M 357	**microcomputer develop-ment system, MDS**	Mikrorechner-Entwick-lungssystem n	système m de développement de microcalculateur	система проектирования микро-ЭВМ
M 358	**microcomputer disk operating system, MDOS**	Mikrorechner-Disketten-betriebssystem n	système m opérationnel de microcalculateur à disques	дисковая операционная система микро-ЭВМ
M 359	**microcomputer family**	Mikrorechnerfamilie f	famille f de microcalcula-teurs	семейство микро-ЭВМ
M 360	**microcomputer ini-tialization sequence**	Mikrorechner-Initiali-sierungsfolge f, Anfangs-bedingungsherstellungs-folge f eines Mikro-rechners	séquence f d'initialisation de microcalculateur	последовательность дейст-вий для приведения микро-ЭВМ в исходное состояние, последо-вательность инициали-зации микро-ЭВМ
M 361	**microcomputer kit**	Mikrorechnerbausatz m	ensemble m de construction de microcalculateur	набор схемных и конструк-тивных элементов микро-ЭВМ
M 362	**microcomputer proto-typing equipment**	Mikrorechner-Entwick-lungsmusterausstattung f	équipement m prototype de microcalculateur	оборудование резидент-ной отладочной системы
M 363	**microcomputer proto-typing system**	Mikrorechner-Prototyp-system n, Mikrorechner-Entwicklungsmuster-system n	système m prototype de microcalculateur	резидентная отладочная система <система для разработки при клад-ных программ и опреде-ления конфигурации аппаратных средств из стандартного набора под конкретное применение микро-ЭВМ>
M 364	**microcomputer software**	Mikrorechner-Software f, Mikrorechner-Pro-grammausstattung f	logiciels mpl de microcalcu-lateur	программное обеспечение микро-ЭВМ
M 365	**microcomputer start-up**	Mikrorechnerinbetrieb-nahme f	mise f en œuvre (service) de microcalculateur	[за]пуск микро-ЭВМ
M 366	**microcomputer system**	Mikrorechnersystem n, komplettes Rechner-system n auf Mikropro-zessorbasis	système m de microcalcula-teurs	вычислительная система на основе микро-ЭВМ
M 367	**microcontrolled modem**	mikroprozessorgesteuertes Modem n	modulateur-démodulateur m à commande par microprocesseur	модем, управляемый микроконтроллером
M 368	**microcontrolled pro-grammable logic**	mikroprozessorgesteuerte programmierbare Logik f	logique f programmable à commande par micro-processeur	программируемое устрой-ство, управляемое микроконтроллером
	microcontrolled terminal	s. M 396		
M 369	**microcontroller**	Mikrosteuereinheit f, Mikroprozessorsystem n für Steuerungsanwendung	unité f de microcommande	микроконтроллер, кон-троллер, построенный на основе микропроцессора
M 370	**microcycle,** microinstruc-tion cycle	Mikrozyklus m, Mikro-schritt m, Mikrobefehls-zyklus m	microcycle m	цикл микрокоманды, микроцикл
	microelectronic circuit	s. M 341		
M 371	**microelectronic com-ponent**	mikroelektronisches Bauteil n	composant m microélectro-nique	микроэлектронная компо-нента
M 372	**microelectronics**	Mikroelektronik f	microélectronique f	микроэлектроника
M 373	**microfilm**	Mikrofilm m	microfilm m	микрофильм
M 374	**microinstruction,** micro-command	Mikrobefehl m	micro-instruction f	микрокоманда
	microinstruction cycle	s. M 370		
M 375	**microinstruction sequence**	Mikrobefehlsfolge f	séquence f de microinstruc-tions	последовательность микрокоманд
	microinstruction set	s. M 345		
M 376	**microinstruction storage**	Mikrobefehlsspeicher m	mémoire f à microinstruc-tions	память микрокоманд

M 377	**microminiature circuit**	mikrominiaturisierte Schaltung f	circuit m microminiature	микроминиатюрная схема
M 378	**microminiaturization**	Mikrominiaturisierung f	microminiaturisation f	микроминиатюризация
M 379	**micromodule**	Mikromodul m	micromodule m	микромодуль
M 380	**micro-operation**	Mikrooperation f <Arbeitsschritt eines Mikroprogramms; Elementarschritt einer Befehlsabwicklung>	micro-opération f	микрооперация
M 381	**microprocessing unit, MPU, microprocessor unit**	Mikroprozessoreinheit f <eines Mikrorechners>	unité f de microprocesseur	процессорный элемент микропроцессора, модуль центрального процессора
M 382	**microprocessor**	Mikroprozessor m <Prozessor auf LSI-Schaltkreis-Basis>	microprocesseur m	микропроцессор, МП
M 383	**microprocessor analyzer**	Mikroprozessor-Analysator m <Prüfgerät>	analyseur m de microprocesseur	устройство для разработки и контроля аппаратных и программных средств микропроцессорных систем
M 384	**microprocessor application**	Mikroprozessoranwendung f	application f de microprocesseurs	применение микропроцессоров
M 385	**microprocessor architecture**	Mikroprozessorstruktur f, Mikroprozessorarchitektur f	structure f de microprocesseur	архитектура микропроцессора
M 386	**microprocessor-based application**	Anwendung f auf Mikroprozessorbasis	application f sur base de microprocesseurs	применение устройств на основе микропроцессоров
M 387	**microprocessor-based control**	mikroprozessorbestückte Steuerung f, Steuerung auf Mikroprozessorbasis	commande f à microprocesseur[s]	управление на основе микропроцессора
M 388	**microprocessor-based logic board**	mikroprozessorbestückte Leiterplatte f	carte f logique à microprocesseur	плата с микропроцессорной логикой
M 389	**microprocessor-based minicomputer**	Kleinrechner m auf Mikroprozessorbasis	minicalculateur m sur base de microprocesseur	мини-ЭВМ, построенная на основе микропроцессора
M 390	**microprocessor-based product**	mikroprozessorbestücktes Produkt n	produit m à microprocesseur[s]	изделие на базе микропроцессора
M 391	**microprocessor card system**	Mikroprozessorsteckeinheitensystem n, Mikroprozessorsystem n mit Leiterkartenmoduln	système m de cartes à microprocesseurs	система на микропроцессорных платах
M 392	**microprocessor chip**	Mikroprozessorchip n, Mikroprozessor-Schaltkreis m	puce f à microprocesseur	БИС микропроцессора
M 393	**microprocessor chip set**	Mikroprozessor-Schaltkreissatz m, Schaltkreissatz m eines Mikroprozessorsystems	jeu m de circuits de microprocesseurs	микропроцессорный комплект [БИС], МПК [БИС]
M 394	**microprocessor component**	Mikroprozessorbauteil n	composant m de microprocesseur	микропроцессорный компонент
M 395	**microprocessor control**	Mikroprozessorsteuerung f	commande f de microprocesseur	микропроцессорное управление
M 396	**microprocessor-controlled terminal, microcontrolled terminal**	mikroprozessorgesteuertes Terminal n	terminal m à commande par microprocesseur	терминал с микропроцессорным управлением
M 397	**microprocessor development system**	Mikroprozessor-Entwicklungssystem n	système m de développement de microprocesseur	система проектирования микропроцессорных устройств
M 398	**microprocessor-driven control**	mikroprozessorbetriebene Steuerung f	commande f à contrôle par microprocesseur	управление [объектом] с помощью микропроцессора
M 399	**microprocessor education system**	Mikroprozessor-Ausbildungssystem n	système m d'enseignement à microprocesseur	микропроцессорная обучающая система, система для обучения принципам действия микропроцессора
M 400	**microprocessor engineering**	Mikroprozessortechnik f	technique f des microprocesseurs	микропроцессорная техника
M 401	**microprocessor input-output**	Mikroprozessor-Eingabe-Ausgabe-System n, Mikroprozessor-Eingangs-Ausgangs-Gestaltung f	entrée-sortie f de microprocesseur	структура ввода-вывода микропроцессора
M 402	**microprocessor instruction**	Mikroprozessorbefehl m	instruction f de microprocesseur	команда микропроцессора
M 403	**microprocessor instruction set**	Mikroprozessor-Befehlssatz m	jeu m d'instructions de microprocesseur	набор команд микропроцессора
M 404	**microprocessor interrupt system**	Mikroprozessor-Unterbrechungssystem n	système m d'interruption de microprocesseur	система прерываний микропроцессора
M 405	**microprocessor master-slave system**	Mikroprozessor-Master-Slave-System n, Multimikroprozessorsystem n mit Führungs- und Satellitenprozessoren	système m master-slave de microprocesseur	микропроцессорная система, работающая по принципу «ведущий-ведомый»
M 406	**microprocessor net**	Mikroprozessornetz n	réseau m de microprocesseurs	[вычислительная] сеть, построенная на основе микропроцессоров, микропроцессорная сеть
M 407	**microprocessor programming**	Mikroprozessorprogrammierung f	programmation f de microprocesseur	программирование микропроцессора
M 408	**microprocessor simulator**	Mikroprozessorsimulator m, Mikroprozessornachbildner m	simulateur m de microprocesseur	аппаратные (программные) средства моделирования работы микропроцессора

M 409	microprocessor slice	Mikroprozessorscheibe f, Mikroprozessorelement n, LSI-Schaltkreis m zum Aufbau eines kaskadierten Mikroprozessors	tranche f de microprocesseur	центральный процессорный элемент [разрядно-секционированного микропроцессора], ЦПЭ
M 410	microprocessor system	Mikroprozessorsystem n	système m de microprocesseur	микропроцессорная система
M 411	microprocessor system analyzer	Mikroprozessorsystem-Analysator m <Test- und Fehlerdiagnosegerät>	analyseur m de système de microprocesseurs	устройство для разработки и контроля аппаратных и программных средств микропроцессорных систем
	microprocessor unit	s. M 381		
M 412	microprogram	Mikroprogramm n <Folge von Mikrobefehlen zur Abwicklung eines Maschinenbefehls>	microprogramme m	микропрограмма
M 413	microprogram control memory	Mikroprogramm-Steuerspeicher m	mémoire f de commande à microprogrammes	микропрограммная управляющая память
M 414	microprogram control unit	Mikroprogramm-Steuerwerk n <Teil eines mikroprogrammierten Prozessors zur Abwicklung des Maschinenbefehls und zur Erzeugung der Steuersignale>	unité f de commande à microprogramme	устройство микропрограммного управления
M 415	microprogram development	Mikroprogrammentwicklung f	développement m de microprogramme[s]	разработка микропрограмм
	microprogram emulation	s. M 423		
M 416	microprogrammability	Mikroprogrammierbarkeit f	microprogrammabilité f	микропрограммируемость
M 417	microprogrammable instruction	mikroprogrammierbarer Befehl m	instruction f microprogrammable	команда, реализуемая на микропрограммном уровне
M 418	microprogrammable microcomputer	mikroprogrammierbarer Mikrorechner m	microcalculateur m microprogrammable	микро-ЭВМ с микропрограммным управлением
M 419	microprogrammed computer	mikroprogrammierter Rechner m <im Gegensatz zum Mikrorechner>	calculateur m microprogrammé	ЭВМ с микропрограммным управлением
M 420	microprogrammed control	mikroprogrammierte Steuerung f	commande f microprogrammée	микропрограммное управление
M 421	microprogrammed control unit	mikroprogrammiertes Steuerwerk n	unité f de commande microprogrammée	устройство микропрограммного управления
M 422	microprogrammed diagnostics	mikroprogrammierte Fehlersuche f (Fehlersuchprogramme npl)	diagnostic m microprogrammé	средства диагностики, реализованные на микропрограммном уровне
M 423	microprogrammed emulation, microprogram emulation	mikroprogrammierte Emulation f, Mikroprogrammemulation f, Emulation auf Mikroprogrammbasis	émulation f microprogrammée	эмуляция на микропрограммном уровне, микропрограммная эмуляция
M 424	microprogrammed instruction control	mikroprogrammierte Befehlsabwicklung f	commande f par instruction microprogrammée	микропрограммное управление процессом выполнения команд
M 425	microprogrammed queue handling	mikroprogrammierte Warteschlangenbearbeitung f	traitement m de queue microprogrammé	микропрограммная обработка очередей
M 426	microprogrammed sequencer	mikroprogrammierte Ablaufsteuerung f	commande f à microprogramme	микропрограммное устройство управления
M 427	microprogramming	Mikroprogrammierung f <im Gegensatz zu Mikroprozessor-Programmierung>	microprogrammation f	микропрограммирование
M 428	microprogramming techniques	Mikroprogrammiertechniken fpl	techniques fpl de microprogrammation	методы микропрограммирования
M 429	microprogram store	Mikroprogrammspeicher m	mémoire f à microprogrammes	память (запоминающее устройство) микропрограмм
M 430	microstate	Mikrozustand m, Mikroschrittzustand m	état m micro	состояние выполнения шага микрокоманды
M 431	microswitch	Mikroschalter m	micro-interrupteur m	микропереключатель
M 432	midpoint value	Mittelpunktswert m	valeur f de point central	положение средней точки
M 433	midrange	Mittelbereich m	champ m moyen	середина диапазона; полусумма кратных значений [выборки]
M 434	midrange microcomputer	mittlerer Mikrorechner m, Mikrorechner des mittleren Leistungsspektrums	microcalculateur m moyen de gamme	микро-ЭВМ средней производительности
M 435	migration	Wanderung f, Verlagerung f <von Funktionen>	migration f	миграция
	miniaturisation	s. M 436		
M 436	miniaturization, miniaturisation	Miniaturisierung f	miniaturisation f	миниатюризация
M 437	minicartridge	Minikassette f	cassette f mini	мини-кассета
M 438	minicomputer, small computer	Kleinrechner m	minicalculateur m	мини-ЭВМ
M 439	minicomputer-based development system	Entwicklungssystem n auf Kleinrechnerbasis	système m de développement sur base de minicalculateur	система проектирования на основе мини-ЭВМ
M 440	minimum configuration	Minimalausrüstung f	configuration f minimale	минимальная конфигурация
M 441	minimum distance	Mindestabstand m	distance f minimale	минимальное расстояние
M 442	minimum size	Kleinstabmessung f, Kleinstgröße f	dimension (taille) f minimum	минимальный размер, минимальная величина
M 443	minimum time	Mindestzeit f	temps m minimum	минимальное время

M 444	minimum value	Kleinstwert *m*	valeur *f* minimum	минимальное значение
M 445	minimum voltage	Mindestspannung *f*	tension *f* minimum	минимальное напряжение
M 446	minority carrier	Minoritätsladungsträger *m*	porteur *m* de charge minoritaire	неосновной носитель [заряда]
M 447	minterm	Minterm *m* ‹Vollkonjunktion›	conjonction *f* ‹produit logique›	элементарная конъюнктивная форма, минтерм
M 448	**MIS device**, metal-insulator semiconductor device	MIS-Bauelement *n*, Bauelement *n* auf Basis einer Metallgate-Isolator-Halbleiterschicht-Kombination	élément *m* à semi-conducteur métal-isolation	полупроводниковый прибор со структурой «металл-диэлектрик-полупроводник», МДП-прибор
M 449	**MISFET**, metal-insulator semiconductor field effect transistor	MISFET *m*, Metall-Isolator-Halbleiter-Feldeffekttransistor *m*	MISFET *m*, transistor *m* à effet de champ métal-isolateur-semi-conducteur	[полевой] транзистор со структурой «металл-диэлектрик-полупроводник», [полевой] МДП-транзистор
M 450	mismatch	Fehlanpassung *f*	adaptation *f* incorrecte	рассогласование, несовпадение
M 451	miss	Fehlgriff *m* ‹Cache-Zugriff›, Fehlschluß *m*	paralogisme *m*	пропуск, выпадение
M 452	mistake	Irrtum *m*, [menschlicher] Fehler *m*	erreur *f*, faute *f* ‹humaine›	ошибка, неверное действие [оператора]
	MMU	*s.* M 281		
M 453	mnemonic	Mnemonik *n*, mnemonische Abkürzung *f* ‹„Gedächtnishilfe"›	mnémonique *f*	мнемоника
M 454	mnemonic code	mnemonischer Befehlskode (Kode) *m* ‹Kode mit erläuternden Kürzeln›	code *m* mnémonique	мнемонический код, мнемокод
M 455	mnemonic machine code programming	Maschinenkodeprogrammierung *f* mit Mnemoniks	programmation *f* à code machine mnémonique	программирование на мнемоническом машинном языке
M 456	**MNOS**, metal nitride oxide semiconductor technology	MNOS *f*, Metall-Nitrid-Oxid-Halbleitertechnik *f*, MNOS-Technologie *f* ‹MIS-Technik mit Nitrid-Gateisolierung›	technique *f* métal-nitride-oxyde-semi-conducteur, technologie *f* MNOS	технология приборов со структурой «металл-нитрид-окисел-полупроводник», МНОП-технология
M 457	mobile charge	bewegliche Ladung *f*	charge *f* mobile	подвижный заряд
M 458	mobile device	ortsveränderliches Gerät *n*	appareil *m* mobile	переносный прибор
M 459	mode	Modus *m*, Betriebsart *f*	mode *m*	режим; способ, метод
M 460	mode change	Moduswechsel *m*, Betriebsartenänderung *f*	changement *m* de mode	смена режима
M 461	modem	Modem *n*, ‹Modulator/Demodulator, Signalumformer›	modem *m* ‹modulateur/démodulateur›	модем, модулятор-демодулятор
M 462	modem control	Modem-Steuerung *f*	commande *f* de modem	управление модемом
M 463	mode of processing	Verarbeitungsart *f*, Verarbeitungsform *f*	mode *m* de traitement	способ обработки; режим обработки
	mode of transmission	*s.* T 300		
	modification	*s.* A 219		
M 464	modification facilities	Modifizierungsmöglichkeiten *fpl*, Änderungsmöglichkeiten *fpl*	possibilités *fpl* de modification	средства модификации
M 465	modification frequency	Änderungshäufigkeit *f*	fréquence *f* de modification[s]	частота изменений
M 466	modifier	Modifikator *m*, Änderungsgröße *f* ‹Adreßrechnung›	modificateur *m*	модификатор
M 467	modifier register	Modifikatorregister *n*	registre *m* d'index	регистр-модификатор, регистр модификации
M 468	modular	modular, bausteinartig	modulaire	модульный, блочный
M 469	modular construction	modulare Bauweise *f*	construction *f* modulaire	модульная конструкция
M 470	modular design	modularer Entwurf *m*	conception *f* modulaire	модульное построение
M 471	modular expansion	modulare Erweiterung *f*, Ausbau *m* nach dem Baukastenprinzip	élargissement *m* modulaire	модульное расширение ⌐принцип
M 472	modularity	Modularität *f*	modularité *f*	модульность, модульный
M 473	modularization	Modularisierung *f*	modularisation *f*	организация по принципу модульности
M 474	modular language	modulare Programmiersprache *f*	langage *m* modulaire	модульный язык
M 475	modular microcomputer components	Mikrorechner-Modulbauteile *npl*	composants *mpl* modulaires de microcalculateur[s]	компоненты модульной микро-ЭВМ
	modular principle	*s.* B 298		
M 476	modular programming	modulare Programmierung *f*, Programmierung auf Modulbasis	programmation *f* modulaire	модульное программирование
M 477	modular system	Modularsystem *n*, modulares System *n*	système *m* modulaire	модульная система
M 478	modulate / to	modulieren	moduler	модулировать
M 479	modulation code	Modulationskode *m*	code *m* de modulation	модулирующий код
M 480	module	Baustein *m*, Modul *m* ‹austauschbare Funktionsgruppe›	module *m*	модуль
M 481	module board	Modulkarte *f*, Modulplatine *f* ‹Leiterkartenbaustein›	carte *f* de module	плата модуля
M 482	module extender board	Modulverlängerungskarte *f* ‹für Service›	carte *f* à extension de module	переходная плата ‹для проверки и ремонта логических плат›
M 483	modulo N check	Modulo-N-Prüfung *f*	vérification *f* de module N	контроль по модулю N
M 484	monitor / to	[Arbeitsablauf] überwachen, mithören	surveiller	контролировать, управлять
M 485	monitor	Monitor *m*, Überwachungseinrichtung *f*, Kontrolleinrichtung *f*	moniteur *m*	монитор, контрольное устройство

M 486	monitoring	Überwachung f <des Arbeitsablaufes>	surveillance f	контроль, управление
M 487	monitor[ing] program	Überwachungsprogramm n, Ablaufüberwachungsprogramm n	programme m de surveillance	программа-монитор
M 488	monoflop, monostable (one-shot, single-shot) multivibrator, univibrator	Monoflop n, monostabiler Multivibrator m, monostabile Kippstufe f, Univibrator n	monovibrateur m	ждущий мультивибратор, одновибратор
M 489	monolithic	monolithisch <aus einem Block bestehend>	monolithique	монолитный
M 490	monolithic circuit	monolithischer Schaltkreis m, monolithische Schaltung f	circuit m monolithique	монолитная схема
M 491	monolithic clock generator	monolithischer Taktgenerator m <Taktgenerator in monolithischer Halbleitertechnik>	rythmeur m monolithique	микросхема тактового генератора
M 492	monolithic converter	monolithischer Umsetzer m	convertisseur m monolithique	микросхема преобразователя
M 493	monolithic structure	monolithische Struktur f, monolithischer Aufbau m	structure f monolithique	монолитная структура
M 494	monolith-technique monostable multivibrator	Monolithtechnik f s. M 488	technique f monolithique	техника изготовления полупроводниковых интегральных схем
M 495	MOS, MOS (metal-oxide semiconductor) technology	MOS f, MOS-Technologie f, MOS-Technik f, Metalloxidhalbleitertechnologie f	technologie f MOS (métal-oxyde-semi-conducteur)	МОП-технология
M 496	mosaic printer	Mosaikdrucker m	imprimante f matricielle	мозаичное печатающее устройство
M 497	MOS circuit	MOS-Schaltkreis m, unipolarer Schaltkreis m	circuit m MOS (unipolaire)	МОП-схема
M 498	MOS device, metal-oxide semiconductor device	MOS-Bauelement n, Bauelement n auf Basis einer Metallgate-Oxidisolator-Halbleiterschicht-Kombination	module m MOS	прибор со структурой «металл-окисел-полупроводник», прибор на МОП-структурах
M 499	MOSFET, metal-oxide-semiconductor field effect transistor	MOSFET m, MOS-Feldeffekttransistor m, Metalloxidhalbleiter-Feldeffekttransistor m <MISFET mit SiO_2-Gateisolierung>	MOSFET m, transistor m MOS à effet de champ	[полевой] транзистор со структурой «металло-окисел-полупроводник», [полевой] МОП-транзистор
M 500	MOS memory	MOS-Speicher m, unipolarer Speicher m	mémoire f MOS (unipolaire)	память на МОП-структурах, МОП ЗУ
M 501	MOS RAM	MOS-RAM m, unipolarer RAM m, Lese-Schreib-Speicher m in [unipolarer] Metalloxidhalbleitertechnik	RAM f en MOS, RAM unipolaire	оперативное запоминающее устройство на МОП-структурах, МОП ОЗУ
	MOS technology	s. M 495		
M 502	most significant bit, MSB	höchstes signifikantes Bit n	bit m de valeur la plus grande	старший значащий разряд
M 503	most significant character	höchstes signifikantes Zeichen n	caractère m de valeur la plus grande	[самый] старший символ
M 504	most significant digit	höchste signifikante Ziffer f	chiffre m de valeur la plus grande	старшая значащая цифра
M 505	motherboard	Mutterplatine f, Mutterplatte f	plaque f mère	плата второго уровня, соединительная плата
M 506	motor board	Laufwerkplatte f	plaque f de mécanisme	панель привода
M 507	motor control	Motorsteuerung f	commande f de moteur	управление двигателем
M 508	motor punch	Motorlocher m	perforatrice f à moteur	перфоратор с электроприводом
M 509	mounting board, mounting plate	Montageplatte f	plaque f de montage	монтажная панель (плата)
M 510	mounting box	Einbaugehäuse n	boîtier m de montage	монтажный каркас
	mounting plate	s. M 509		
M 511	m-out-of-n-code	m-aus-n-Kode m	code m m de n	код m из n
M 512	movable	beweglich, verstellbar	mobile	перемещаемый, пересылаемый; подвижный
M 513	move instruction	Transportbefehl m	instruction f de transport	команда пересылки
M 514	move operation	Transportoperation f	opération f de transport	операция пересылки
	move time	s. T 267		
M 515	moving head	beweglicher Kopf m	tête f mobile	подвижная головка
M 516	moving head disk	Plattenspeicher m mit positionierbaren (bewegbaren) Köpfen	disque m têtes mobiles	запоминающее устройство на магнитных дисках с подвижными головками
	MPU	s. M 381		
	MSB	s. M 502		
M 517	MS flip-flop, master-slave flip-flop	MS-Flipflop n, Master-Slave-Flipflop n <Flipflop mit Hilfsspeicher>	bascule f master-slave <bascule à mémoire auxiliaire>	двухступенчатый триггер, триггер M-S типа
M 518	MSI, medium scale integration	MSI f, Mittelbereichsintegration f, mittlere Integration f	MSI f, intégration f moyenne	средняя степень интеграции
M 519	MSI circuit	MSI-Schaltkreis m, mittelintegrierter Schaltkreis m	circuit m MSI	схема средней степени интеграции
	MTBF	s. M 211		
	MTC	s. M 93		
	MTL	s. M 324		
	MTTM	s. M 212		
	MTTR	s. M 210		
M 520	multiaccess	Vielfachzugriff m <Teilnehmersystem>	accès m multiple	коллективный доступ

M 521	multiaccess system	Mehrfachzugriffssystem *n*	système *m* à accès multiple	система с коллективным доступом
	multiaddress instruction	*s.* M 542		
	multiaddress machine	*s.* M 543		
M 522	multichannel communication system	Mehrkanalkommunikationssystem *n*	système *m* de communication à canaux multiples	многоканальная система связи
M 523	multichip carrier board	Multichip-Trägerplatte *f*	plaque *f* support pour puces multiples	подложка многокристальной микросхемы
M 524	multichip CPU	Mehrchip-CPU *f*, Multichip-CPU *f* ‹Verarbeitungseinheit aus mehreren LSI-Schaltkreisen›	unité *f* centrale de traitement à circuits multiples	многокристальный модуль центрального процессора
	multichip IC	*s.* M 525		
M 525	multichip integrated circuit, multichip IC	Multichip-Schaltkreis *m* ‹Schaltkreis mit mehreren in einem Gehäuse untergebrachten Chips›	circuit *m* intégré à puces multiples	многокристальная интегральная схема ‹микросхема с несколькими чипами на одной подложке›
M 526	multichip microprocessor	Mehrchip-Mikroprozessor *m*, Multichip-Mikroprozessor *m*, ‹Mikroprozessor aus mehreren LSI-Schaltkreisen›	microprocesseur *m* à puces multiples	многокристальный микропроцессор
M 527	multichip system	Multichipsystem *n*, Multischaltkreissystem *n*	système *m* à puces multiples	многокристальная система
M 528	multi-collector transistor	Multikollektor-Transistor *m*	transistor *m* à collecteurs multiples	многоколлекторный транзистор
M 529	multi-coloured display	mehrfarbige Anzeige *f*	affichage *m* à plusieurs couleurs	многоцветный дисплей
M 530	multi-computer system	Mehrrechnersystem *n*	système *m* à multicalculateurs	многомашинная система
M 531	multicontroller	Mehrfachsteuereinheit *f*	unité *f* de commande multiple	многоконтурный контроллер
M 532	multiemitter transistor	Multiemitter-Transistor *m*	transistor *m* à émetteurs multiples	многоэмиттерный транзистор
M 533	multifunctional memory, MFM	MFM *m*, multifunktionaler Speicher *m* ‹Speicher mit Lese-, Verarbeitungs- und Schreibzyklus›	mémoire *f* multifonctionnelle	многофункциональная память
M 534	multifunction device	Mehrfunktionsgerät *n*	appareil *m* à fonction multiple	многофункциональное устройство
M 535	multifunction instruction	Multifunktionsbefehl *m*, Mehrfachoperationsbefehl *m*	instruction *f* à fonction multiple	многофункциональная команда
M 536	multilayer [printed circuit] board	Mehrlagenleiterplatte *f*	plaque *f* à circuits imprimés en plusieurs couches	многослойная [печатная] плата
	multilevel interrupts	*s.* M 549		
M 537	multilevel subroutines	mehrstufige Unterprogramme *npl*	sous-programmes *mpl* à plusieurs échelons	многоуровневые подпрограммы
M 538	multi-microprocessor system	Multimikroprozessorsystem *n*, Vielfachmikroprozessorsystem *n*	système *m* à microprocesseurs multiples	мультимикропроцессорная система
M 539	multimode	Vielfachbetrieb *m*	mode *m* multiple	режим мультиобработки
M 540	multimode operation	Mehrmodusbetrieb *m*, Betrieb *m* in mehreren Arbeitsweisen	régime *m* à mode multiple	работа в режиме мультиобработки
M 541	multipass assembler	Mehrschritt-Assembler *m*, Assembler *m* mit mehreren Durchläufen arbeitend	assembleur *m* à plusieurs pas	многопроходный ассемблер
M 542	multiple-address instruction, multiaddress instruction	Mehradreßbefehl *m*	instruction *f* à adresses multiples	многоадресная команда
M 543	multiple-address machine, multiaddress machine	Mehradreßmaschine *f*, Mehradreßrechner *m*	machine *f* à adresses multiples	многоадресная машина
M 544	multiple-bit fault detection	Mehrbit-Fehlererkennung *f*	détection *f* de défaut à bits multiples	обнаружение многократной ошибки
M 545	multiple-bus structure	Multibusstruktur *f*, Vielfachbusstruktur *f* ‹Struktur mit mehreren Bussen›	structure *f* à bus multiples	многошинная структура
M 546	multiple-channel data acquisition device	Mehrkanal-Datenerfassungsgerät *n*	appareil *m* d'acquisition de données à canaux multiples	многоканальное устройство сбора данных
M 547	multiple-chip configuration	Multibausteinkonfiguration *f*	configuration *f* à circuits multiples	многокристальная структура
M 548	multiple-length arithmetic	Mehrwortarithmetik *f*, Arithmetik *f* für mehrfache Stellenzahl	arithmétique *f* de longueur multiple	арифметические операции со словами многократной длины
M 549	multiple-level interrupts, multilevel interrupts	Mehrebenen-Interrupts *mpl*, Mehrebenen-Unterbrechungen *fpl*	interruptions *fpl* de niveaux multiples	многоуровневые прерывания
M 550	multiple-position shift	Mehrstellenverschiebung *f*	décalage *m* de plusieurs chiffres	многоразрядный сдвиг
M 551	multiple precision	mehrfache Genauigkeit *f*	précision *f* multiple	многократно увеличенная точность
M 552	multiple-precision arithmetic, multiprecision arithmetic	Mehrfachgenauigkeitsarithmetik *f*, Mehrfachgenauigkeitsrechnung *f*	arithmétique *f* à précision multiple	арифметические операции с многократно увеличенной точностью
M 553	multiple-processor operation, multiprocessor operation	Multiprozessorarbeit *f*, Multiprozessorbetrieb *m*	régime *m* à multiprocesseurs	мультипроцессорная обработка
	multiple-processor system	*s.* M 574		
M 554	multiple register file	mehrfacher Registersatz *m*	fichier *m* de registres multiples	многорегистровый файл

M 555	multiple word	Mehrfachwort n <Datenein-heit mehrfacher Wort-länge>	mot m multiple	слово многократной длины
M 556	multiple-word instruc-tion	Mehrwortbefehl m, Multi-wortbefehl m	instruction f à mots mul-tiples	команда обработки слов многократной длины
M 557	multiplex channel, multi-plexor channel	Multiplex[er]kanal m, multiplexbetriebener Kanal m	canal m multiplex	мультиплексный канал
M 558	multiplexed address-data line set	multiplexbetriebener Adressen-Daten-Leitungs-satz m	jeu m de lignes adresses-données multiplexées	мультиплексированная шина «адрес-данные»
M 559	multiplexed bus, time-shared bus	Multiplexbus m, zeitmulti-plex betriebener (genutz-ter) Bus m	bus m multiplex	мультиплексированная шина
M 560	multiplexed input	Multiplexeingang m, Multi-plexeingangssignal n	entrée f multiplex	мультиплексный вход
	multiplexed operation	s. M 564		
M 561	multiplexer	Multiplexer m, Mehrfach-koppler m	multiplexeur m	мультиплексор
M 562	multiplexing	Bündelung f	multiplexage m	мультиплексирование
M 563	multiplexing	Multiplexarbeit f	travail m multiplex	мультиплексная работа
M 564	multiplex mode, multi-plexed operation	Multiplexbetrieb m	régime m multiplex	мультиплексный режим
	multiplexor channel	s. M 557		
M 565	multiplicand	Multiplikand m	multiplicande m	множимое
M 566	multiplication	Multiplikation f	multiplication f	умножение
M 567	multiplier	Multiplikator m, Multipli-zierer m, Multiplizierein-richtung f, Vervielfacher m	multiplicateur m	множитель, сомножитель; устройство умножения
M 568	multipole connector	Mehrkontaktstecker m	connecteur m multiple	многоконтактный разъем
M 569	multiport memory	Multiport-Speicher m, Mehrfacheingangsspeicher m	mémoire f à portes multiples	многовходовая память
M 570	multiposition switch	Mehrfachpositionsschalter m, Multipositionsschalter m	commutateur m à positions multiples	многопозиционный пере-ключатель
	multiprecision arithmetic	s. M 552		
M 571	multiprocessing	Mehrfachverarbeitung f <durch Multiprozessor-betrieb>	traitement m multiple	мультиобработка
M 572	multiprocessing con-figuration	Konfiguration f für Mehr-fachverarbeitung	configuration f pour traite-ment multiple	мультипроцессорная кон-фигурация
M 573	multiprocessor applica-tion	Multiprozessoranwendung f, Mehrprozessoreinsatz m	application f de multipro-cesseurs	применение мультипро-цессорных систем
	multiprocessor oper-ation	s. M 553		
M 574	multiprocessor system, multiple-processor system	Multiprozessorsystem n, Mehrprozessorsystem n	système m de multiproces-seurs	мультипроцессорная система
M 575	multiprogramming	Multiprogrammierung f, Mehrfachprogrammab-arbeitung f <durch Pro-grammverzahnung und Mehrfachprogramm-steuerung>	multiprogrammation f	мультипрограммная обработка
M 576	multipurpose IC	Mehrzweckschaltkreis m	circuit m intégré d'usage multiple	многоцелевая (универсаль-ная) ИС
M 577	multiregister processor	Multiregister-Prozessor m, Mehrfachregister-Prozes-sor m	processeur m à registres multiples	процессор, содержащий блок универсальных регистров
M 578	multi-step instruction format	Mehrschritt-Befehlsformat n <Format eines in meh-reren Schritten aufzustel-lenden Befehls>	format m d'instruction à plusieurs pas	многошаговый формат команд
M 579	multi-stream processing	Verarbeitung f mehrerer Datenströme	traitement m de plusieurs courants de données	обработка с несколькими потоками данных
M 580	multisystem	Multisystem n <System aus mehreren Computern>	système m multiple	мультисистема
M 581	multitasking	Mehrprozeßbetrieb m, Mehraufgabenbetrieb m <unter einheitlicher Pro-grammregie>	traitement m de tâches multiples	мультизадачный режим
M 582	multitasking software	Multiprozeßbetriebs-systemunterlagen fpl, Systemunterlagen fpl für parallelen Mehraufgaben-betrieb	logiciels mpl pour tâches multiples	программное обеспечение мультизадачной обра-ботки
M 583	multiuser system	Mehrnutzersystem n, Multi-nutzersystem n	système m à usagers multiples	система с множественным (коллективным) досту-пом

N

	NAND	s. A 272		
N 1	NAND circuit (gate), except gate	UND-NICHT-Schaltung f, NAND-Gatter n	circuit m ET-NON	логический элемент И-НЕ, вентиль И-НЕ
N 2	Naperian logarithm, natural logarithm	natürlicher (Neperscher) Logarithmus m	logarithme m naturel (néperien)	натуральный логарифм
N 3	native language	arteigene Sprache (Rechner-sprache) f <im Gegensatz zu Fremdkodes, die z. B.	langage m naturel (propre)	собственный машинный язык

		interpretativ abgearbeitet werden>		
N 4	native mode	natürlicher Modus m, arteigene Betriebsweise f <eines Rechners, der auch in der Art eines anderen Typs arbeiten kann>	mode m naturel	базовый режим <режим работы с собственной системой команд>
N 5	natural base	natürliche Basis f <Zahlensystem>	base f naturelle	натуральное основание
N 6	natural frequency	Eigenfrequenz f	fréquence f naturelle (propre)	собственная частота
N 7	natural language	natürliche Sprache f	langage m naturel	естественный язык
	natural logarithm	s. N 2		
	NC	s. N 128		
N 8	n-channel, n-conducting channel	n-Kanal m, n-leitender Kanal m	canal m n	канал n-типа
N 9	n-channel enhancement mode	n-Kanal-Anreicherungstyp m	type m à enrichissement canal n	n-канал обогащенного типа
N 10	n-channel metal-oxide-semiconductor technology, n-channel MOS, n-channel MOS technology, NMOS technology, NMOS	n-Kanal-Metalloxidhalbleitertechnologie f, n-Kanal-MOS-Technologie f, nMOS-Technologie f, n-Kanal-MOS f, nMOS f	technologie f métal-oxyde-semi-conducteur canal n, technologie MOS canal n	n-канальная МОП-технология, n-МОП технология
N 11	n-channel MOS circuit, nMOS circuit	n-Kanal-MOS-Schaltkreis m, nMOS-Schaltkreis m	circuit m MOS canal n	n-канальная МОП-схема, n-МОП схема
	n-channel MOS technology	s. N 10		
N 12	n-channel silicon gate MOS technology, n-SG-MOS	n-Kanal-Siliziumgate-MOS-Technologie f, n-SGT f, n-SG-MOS f	technologie f MOS à gate au silicium canal n	технология изготовления n-канальных МОП-схем с кремниевыми затворами
	NC machine	s. N 132		
	N condition	s. N 19		
N 13	n-conducting, n-type conducting	n-leitend	conductible n	с проводимостью n-типа
	n-conducting channel	s. N 8		
	NDRO	s. N 71		
N 14	needle printer, stylus printer	Nadeldrucker m	imprimante f à aiguilles	игольчатое печатающее устройство
N 15	negate / to	negieren	nier	инвертировать, отрицать
N 16	negation, NOT operation	Negation f, NICHT-Operation f <Boolesche Komplementierung>	négation f	отрицание, инверсия, операция НЕ
N 17	negative bias	negative Vorspannung f	polarisation f négative	отрицательное смещение
N 18	negative charge	negative Ladung f	charge f négative	отрицательный заряд
N 19	negative condition, N condition	Negativbedingung f	condition f négative	условие отрицательного результата операции
	negative feedback	s. I 459		
N 20	negative impedance	negativer Scheinwiderstand m, negative Impedanz f	impédance f négative	отрицательный импеданс
N 21	negative logic	negative Logik (Schaltungslogik) f <unterer Pegel entspricht logisch Eins>	logique f négative	отрицательная логика
N 22	negative-logic circuit	Negativlogikschaltung f	circuit m logique négatif	схема отрицательной логики
N 23	negative-logic signal	Negativlogiksignal n <niedriger Pegel entspricht logisch Eins>	signal m logique négatif	сигнал отрицательной логики
N 24	negative pulse	negativer Impuls m	impulsion f négative	отрицательный импульс
N 25	negative resistance	negativer Wirkwiderstand (Widerstand) m	résistance f négative	отрицательное сопротивление
N 26	negative sign	Minuszeichen n, negatives Vorzeichen n	signe m négatif	отрицательный знак числа, знак минус
N 27	negative signal	negatives Signal n	signal m négatif	отрицательный сигнал
N 28	negator, NOT circuit, NOT (negation) gate	Negator m, NICHT-Schaltung f, NICHT-Glied n, Negationsgatter n	négateur m, circuit m NON	схема НЕ, инвертор
N 29	nest / to	verschachteln, einschachteln	encastrer	вкладывать
N 30	nested intervals	ineinandergeschachtelte Intervalle npl	intervalles mpl encastrés	вложенные интервалы
N 31	nested subroutine	eingebautes (verschachteltes) Unterprogramm n	sous-programme m encastré	вложенная подпрограмма
N 32	nesting	Einschachtelung f, Verschachtelung f, Einbau m	encastrement m	вложение
N 33	nesting level	Verschachtelungsebene f	niveau m d'encastrement	уровень вложения
N 34	nesting loop	Einbauprogrammschleife f	boucle f d'encastrement	вложенный цикл
N 35	nesting store	Einschachtelungsspeicher m, Speicher m für Programmverschachtelung <Kellerspeicher>	mémoire f d'encastrement	магазинная (стековая) память
	net	s. N 38		
N 36	net amount	Nettobetrag m	montant m net	результирующий остаток
N 37	net loss	Nettoverlust m	perte f nette	полные потери
N 38	network, net	Netz[werk] n, Übertragungsnetz n	réseau m	сеть; сетка
N 39	network analogue	Netzwerknachbildung f	imitation f de réseau	модель сети; моделирующая сетка
N 40	network analysis	Netzwerkanalyse f	analyse f de réseau	анализ цепей
N 41	network analyzer	Netzwerkanalysator m, Netzwerksimulator m	analyseur m de réseau	устройство моделирования [электрических] цепей
N 42	network application	Netzwerkanwendung f, Anwendung f in Netzen	application f dans des réseaux	применение в сетевых структурах
N 43	network calculator	Netzwerkberechner m, Netzwerksimulator m	calculateur m de réseau	устройство моделирования [электрических] сетей

N 44	network communications circuit	Netzwerkübertragungsschaltung f, Netzwerkübertragungsschaltkreis m	circuit m de communication de réseau	схема связи между элементами сети
N 45	network configuration	Netzstruktur f, Netzaufbau m	structure f de réseau	конфигурация (структура) сети
N 46	network topology	Netzwerktopologie f	topologie f de réseau	топология сети
N 47	neutral conductor	Nulleiter m	conducteur m neutre	нулевой провод
N 48	new-line character	Zeilenvorschubzeichen n	caractère m d'avancement de ligne	символ новой строки
N 49	nibble	Nibble n, Halbbyte-Dateneinheit f	mi-octet m	полубайт
N 50	nil	Nichts n	nulle f	пустой символ
N 51	nil report	Fehlanzeige f	rapport m nul	пустое сообщение
N 52	nines complement	Neunerkomplement n	complément m à neuf	дополнение до девяти
	nine-track magnetic tape	s. N 53		
N 53	nine-track tape, nine-track magnetic tape	Neunspurband n, 9-Spur-Magnetband n	bande f magnétique à 9 pistes	9-дорожечная [магнитная] лента
N 54	Nixie tube	Nixie-Röhre f <Ziffernanzeige>	tube m Nixie	газоразрядный цифровой индикатор
	NMOS	s. N 10		
	nMOS circuit	s. N 11		
N 55	nMOS process	nMOS-Prozeß m, nMOS-Herstellungsverfahren n	procédé m n-MOS	n-МОП процесс, процесс изготовления n-МОП схем
	NMOS technology	s. N 10		
N 56	node	Knoten m <Netzwerk>	nœud m	узел; вершина
N 57	node processor	Knotenprozessor m, Einzelrechner m in einem Rechnerverbundnetz	processeur m de nœud	процессор узла
N 58	noise	Rauschen n, Störungen fpl	bruit m	шум[ы], помехи
N 59	noise immunity	Rauschunempfindlichkeit f, Störsicherheit f	insensibilité f contre bruits	помехоустойчивость, помехозащищенность
N 60	noise impulse	Rauschimpuls m <spezieller Störimpuls>	impulsion f de bruit	шумовой импульс
N 61	noise level	Rauschpegel m, Störpegel m	niveau m de bruit	уровень шума
N 62	noise margin	Störabstand m, Störspannungsspanne f	marge f de bruit	запас помехоустойчивости
N 63	noise ratio	Nutz-Stör-Verhältnis n, Rauschzahl f	rapport m de bruit	отношение сигнал-шум
N 64	noise voltage	Störspannung f	tension f de bruit	напряжение шумов
N 65	noisy digit	Störziffer f <Gleitkommaarithmetik>	chiffre m anormal	цифра в освобождающемся при сдвиге разряде
N 66	no-load	unbelastet	non chargé	ненагруженный
N 67	nomenclature	Nomenklatur f, Namensregister n, Fachbezeichnung f	nomenclature f	номенклатура; спецификация; система [условных] обозначений
	nominal current	s. R 32		
	nominal output	s. P 391		
	nominal power	s. P 391		
	nominal value	s. R 38		
	nominal voltage	s. R 34		
N 68	non-addressable memory	nichtadressierbarer Speicher m	mémoire f non adressable	неадресуемое запоминающее устройство
N 69	non-arithmetic shift	nichtarithmetische Verschiebung f	décalage m non arithmétique	неарифметический сдвиг
N 70	non-contiguous constant	unabhängige Konstante f	constante f indépendante	независимая константа
N 71	non-destructive read-out, NDRO	nichtzerstörendes Lesen n, NDRO	lecture f non destructive	неразрушающее считывание, считывание без разрушения
N 72	non-dissipative network	verlustfreies Netzwerk n	réseau m sans pertes	цепь, не рассеивающая мощность
N 73	non-erasable storage	nichtlöschbarer Speicher m <ohne Informationsänderungsmöglichkeit>	mémoire f inaltérable	постоянная память
N 74	non-existent memory module	nichtvorhandener (fehlender) Speichermodul m <im adressierbaren Bereich>	module m de mémoire non existant	несуществующий модуль памяти
	non-impact printer	s. N 81		
N 75	non-linear distortion	nichtlineare Verzerrung f	distorsion f non linéaire	нелинейное искажение
N 76	nonlinearity	Nichtlinearität f	non-linéarité f	нелинейность
N 77	non-linear programming	nichtlineare Programmierung f	programmation f non linéaire	нелинейное программирование
N 78	non-linear resistance (resistor)	nichtlinearer Widerstand m	résistance f non linéaire	нелинейное сопротивление
N 79	non-linear system	nichtlineares System n	système m non linéaire	нелинейная система
N 80	non-maskable interrupt	nichtmaskierbare Unterbrechung f	interruption f non masquable	незамаскированное прерывание
N 81	non-mechanical printer, non-impact printer	nichtmechanischer Drucker m	imprimante f non mécanique	немеханическое печатающее устройство
N 82	non-memory reference instruction	nichtspeicherbezogener (speicherbezugsfreier) Befehl m	instruction f non (pas) relative à la mémoire	команда, выполняемая без обращения к памяти
N 83	non-numerical character	nichtnumerisches Zeichen n	caractère m non numérique	нечисловой символ
N 84	non-numerical data processing	nichtnumerische Datenverarbeitung f	informatique f non numérique	обработка нечисловых данных
N 85	non-powered storage	stromversorgungsunabhängige (energiezuführungsabhängige) Speicherung f	mémorisation f indépendante d'alimentation	хранение информации без потребления энергии
N 86	non-programmable memory	nichtprogrammierbarer Speicher m	mémoire f non programmable	непрограммируемая память
N 87	non-redundant logic	redundanzfreie Logik f	logique f sans redondance	логические схемы, не содержащие избыточность

N 88	non-relocatable program	unverschiebliches Programm n	programme m irrelogeable	неперемещаемая программа
N 89	non-reproducible error	nichtreproduzierbarer Fehler m	erreur f non reproductible	невоспроизводимая ошибка
N 90	non-resident program	nichtresidentes (im Hauptspeicher nicht vorhandenes) Programm n	programme m non résident	нерезидентная программа
N 91	non-segmented addressing	nichtsegmentierte Adressierung f, Adressierung ohne Segmentteilung	adressage m sans segmentation	несегментная адресация
N 92	non-vectored interrupt	ungerichteter Interrupt m, nichtvektorisierte Unterbrechung f	interruption f non vectorisée	невекторное прерывание
N 93	non-volatile storage	nichtflüchtiger Speicher m <bei Stromversorgungsausfall>	mémoire f non volatile	энергонезависимая память <с сохранением информации при отключении питания>
N 94	no-op[eration] instruction	Leerbefehl m	instruction f à vide	холостая команда
N 95	NOR, NOT OR	ODER-NICHT <logische Verknüpfung „negiertes ODER" Pierce-Funktion>	OU-NON	ИЛИ-НЕ
N 96	NOR circuit	NOR-Schaltung f, ODER-NICHT-Schaltung f	circuit m OU-NON	схема ИЛИ-НЕ
	NOR element	s. N 97		
N 97	NOR gate, NOR element, OR-NOT gate	NOR-Gatter n, NOR-Glied n, ODER-NICHT-Gatter n, negierendes ODER-Gatter n	porte f OU-NON	вентиль (элемент) ИЛИ-НЕ
N 98	normal contact, normally closed contact	Ruhekontakt m	contact m de repos	нормально замкнутый контакт
N 99	normal exit	normaler Programmausgang m	sortie f normale [de programme]	нормальный выход [из программы]
N 100	normalization	Normalisierung f, Normierung f	normalisation f	нормализация; нормирование
N 101	normalization routine	Normalisierungsroutine f <Gleitkommaarithmetik>	routine f de normalisation	программа нормализации
N 102	normalize / to	normalisieren, normieren	normaliser	нормализовать, нормировать
N 103	normalized form	normalisierte Form f <Standardform der Gleitkommadarstellung>	forme f normalisée	нормализованная (стандартная) форма
	normally closed contact	s. N 98		
N 104	normally open contact	Arbeitskontakt m	contact m de travail	нормально разомкнутый контакт
N 105	normal state	Normalzustand m	état m normal	нормальное состояние
N 106	NOR operation	NOR-Verknüpfung f, ODER-NICHT-Verknüpfung f	opération f OU-NON	[логическая] операция ИЛИ-НЕ
N 107	NOT	NICHT <Boolescher Negationsoperator>	NON	НЕ
N 108	notation	Schreibweise f	notation f	система счисления
	NOT circuit (gate)	s. N 28		
	NOT operation	s. N 16		
	NOT OR	s. N 95		
N 109	N-pin package	N-poliges Gehäuse n, Gehäuse n mit N Anschlüssen	boîtier m à N fiches	корпус с N выводами
N 110	n-plus-one address instruction	(n+1)-Adreß-Befehl m, N-plus-Eins-Adreß-Befehl m <n-Adreß-Befehl mit Folgeadreßangabe>	instruction f à adresse n+1	(n+1)-адресная команда
N 111	npn junction	npn-Übergang m	jonction f npn	полупроводник с трехслойной структурой «n-p-n»
N 112	npn junction transistor	npn-Flächentransistor m	transistor m à jonction npn	n-p-n транзистор
	n-SG-MOS	s. N 12		
N 113	n-sheet	n-Schicht f, n-leitende Schicht f	couche f n	n-слой, слой n-проводимости
	n-type conducting	s. N 13		
N 114	n-type semiconductor	n-Typ-Halbleiter m	semi-conducteur m de type n	полупроводник n-типа
	n-type well	s. N 135		
N 115	null character	Nullzeichen n <nichtnumerische Null, Steuerzeichen>	caractère m nul	нуль-символ <управляющий символ>
N 116	null cycle	Nullzyklus m <minimale Programmlaufzeit>	cycle m nul	время выполнения программы без учета операций ввода-вывода
N 117	null indicator	Nullanzeiger m, nullanzeigendes Bauteil n	indicateur m de zéro	нуль-индикатор
N 118	null set	Nullmenge f, leere Menge f	quantité f nulle	пустое множество
	null suppression	s. Z 25		
N 119	number cruncher	„Zahlenknacker" m, Arithmetikschaltkreis m	circuit m arithmétique, « casseur m de nombres »	вычислительное устройство для обработки больших массивов чисел
N 120	number crunching	Zahlenverarbeitung f <numerische Rechnung>	traitement m numérique	обработка [больших] массивов чисел
N 121	numbering	Numerierung f	numérotage m	нумерация
N 122	number representation	Zahlendarstellung f	représentation f de nombres	представление чисел
N 123	number system	Zahlensystem n	système m de nombres	система счисления
N 124	numeric[al]	numerisch, zahlenmäßig	numérique	цифровой, числовой
N 125	numerical analysis	numerische Analyse f	analyse f numérique	численный анализ
N 126	numerical code	numerischer Kode m	code m numérique	цифровой код

N 127	**numerical computation**	numerische Berechnung *f*	calcul *m* numérique	решение численными методами
N 128	**numerical control,** numeric control, NC	numerische Steuerung *f*, NC	commande *f* numérique	числовое управление
N 129	**numerical data**	numerische Daten *pl*	données *fpl* numériques	цифровые данные
	numerical display	s. D 371		
N 130	**numerical integration**	numerische Integration *f*	intégration *f* numérique	численное интегрирование
N 131	**numerical keyboard**	numerische Tastatur *f*, Zifferntastatur *f*	clavier *m* numérique	цифровая клавиатура
N 132	**numerically controlled machine,** NC machine	numerisch gesteuerte Maschine *f*, NC-Maschine *f*	machine *f* à commande numérique, machine NC	станок с числовым управлением
N 133	**numerical value**	numerischer Wert *m*, Zahlenwert *m*	valeur *f* numérique	численное значение
	numeric control	s. N 128		
N 134	**numeric input**	Zahleneingabe *f*	entrée *f* numérique	ввод чисел
N 135	**n-well,** n-type well	n-Mulde *f*, n-leitende Mulde *f*	dépression *f* de type n	потенциальная яма n-типа
N 136	**n-zone**	n-leitender Bereich *m*, n-Gebiet *n*, n-Zone *f*	zone *f* n	n-область, зона n-проводимости

O

O 1	**object code**	Objektkode *m* <Kode eines Objektprogramms>	code *m* objet	объектный код
O 2	**object-code compatible**	objektkodekompatibel, verträglich auf Objektkodeebene	compatible en code objet	совместимый на уровне объектного кода
	object machine	s. T 45		
O 3	**object module**	Objektmodul *m*, Objektprogrammodul *m*	module *m* objet	объектный модуль
O 4	**object program**	Objektprogramm *n*, übersetztes Programm *n* <Maschinenprogramm>	programme *m* objet	объектная программа
O 5	**occupation**	Besetzung *f*	occupation *f*	занятие
O 6	**occupy / to**	besetzen, in Anspruch nehmen	occuper	занимать
O 7	**occur / to**	sich ereignen, vorkommen	arriver, survenir	встречать[ся], случаться, происходить
	occurrence	s. E 274		
	OCR	s. O 148		
O 8/9	**OCR-character**	OCR-Zeichen *n* <maschinell lesbares Schriftzeichen>	caractère *m* OCR	символ, воспринимаемый оптической системой считывания
O 10	**octal address**	Oktaladresse *f*	adresse *f* octale	восьмеричный адрес
O 11	**octal digit**	Oktalziffer *f*	chiffre *m* octal	восьмеричная цифра
O 12	**octal notation**	Oktalschreibweise *f*	notation *f* octale	восьмеричное представление
O 13	**octal number**	Oktalzahl *f*	nombre *m* octal	восьмеричное число
O 14	**odd**	ungerade, ungeradzahlig	impair	нечетный
O 15	**odd address**	ungerade Adresse *f*	adresse *f* impaire	нечетный адрес
O 16	**odd byte**	ungerades Byte *n* <Byte ungerader Adresse innerhalb eines Wortes>	octet *m* impair	нечетный байт <байт с нечетным адресом>
O 17	**odd-even check**	Gerade-Ungerade-Prüfung *f* <Kontrollmethode>	vérification *f* pair-impair	контроль [по] четности
O 18	**odd-numbered**	ungeradzahlig	à nombre impair	нечетно-пронумерованный
O 19	**odd party**	ungerade Parität *f*	parité *f* impaire	нечетный паритет
O 20	**OEM,** original equipment manufacturer	Finalprodukthersteller *m*, Endprodukthersteller *m*	fabricant *m* OEM	[фирма-]производитель комплексного оборудования на основе покупных комплектующих изделий, [фирма-]производитель конечной продукции
O 21	**OEM board**	OEM-Leiterplatte *f*, OEM-Steckeinheit *f*, Steckeinheit *f* für Einbau in Finalprodukte	carte *f* OEM	плата, поставляемая изготовителю комплексного оборудования
O 22	**OEM board-level microcomputer**	OEM-Mikrorechner *m* auf Steckeinheitenbasis, Mikrorechner-Steckeinheitensystem *n* für Finalprodukteinsatz	microcalculateur *m* à cartes OEM	модульная микро-ЭВМ, поставляемая изготовителю комплексного оборудования, комплект модулей микро-ЭВМ для использования в конечной продукции
O 23	**OEM microcomputer**	OEM-Mikrorechner *m*, Mikrorechner *m* für Einbau in Finalprodukte	microcalculateur *m* OEM	комплектующая микро-ЭВМ
O 24	**OEM product**	OEM-Produkt *n*, Zulieferprodukt *n* für Finalproduzenten	produit *m* OEM	комплектующая продукция
O 25	**off-chip**	außerhalb des Schaltkreises	en-dehors du circuit	внешний [по отношению к микросхеме]
O 26	**off-chip memory expansion**	Speichererweiterung *f* außerhalb des [Mikrorechner-]Schaltkreises	élargissement *m* de mémoire en-dehors du circuit	расширение памяти внешними [по отношению к БИС микро-ЭВМ] средствами
O 27	**off condition,** off state	Aus-Zustand *m*, Ausschaltzustand *m*	état *m* au repos	выключенное состояние, состояние «выключено»

O 28	off emergency	Notausschalter *m*	interrupteur *m* de secours	устройство аварийного отключения электро-питания
O 29	offer / to	anbieten, bieten	offrir	предлагать, предоставлять
O 30	office automation	Büroautomatisierung *f*	automation *f* de bureau	автоматизация контор-ских работ
O 31	office computer	Bürocomputer *m*, Büro-rechner *m*	calculateur (ordinateur) *m* de bureau	конторская ЭВМ
O 32	off-line	nicht verbunden, getrennt [gegenüber einer Zentrale]	off-line	автономный, «оф-лайн» ‹режим›
O 33	off-line computer	getrennt (ungekoppelt) betriebener Rechner *m*	calculateur *m* off-line	автономная ЭВМ, ЭВМ работающая в режиме, «оф-лайн»
O 34	off-line mode	getrennte (ungekoppelte) Arbeitsweise *f*, Off-line-Modus *m*	mode *m* off-line	автономный режим, режим «оф-лайн»
O 35	off-line operation	getrennter (ungekoppelter) Betrieb *m*, Off-line-Betrieb *m*	régime *m* off-line	автономная работа, работа в режиме «оф-лайн»
O 36	off-line processing	getrennte (ungekoppelte) Verarbeitung *f*, Off-line-Verarbeitung *f*	traitement *m* off-line	автономная обработка
O 37	offset / to	versetzen	décaler	смещать, сдвигать
O 38	offset	Versatz *m*, Abstand *m* konstanter Größe	offset *m*	сдвиг
	offset address	*s.* D 449		
	off state	*s.* O 27		
O 39	off-the-shelf interface	konfektioniertes Interface *n*, gebrauchsfertige Schnitt-stellenlösung *f*	interface *f* confectionnée	покупной интерфейс
O 40	off-the-shelf software	gebrauchsfertig verfügbare Systemunterlagen *fpl*	logiciels *mpl* tout prêts	покупное программное обеспечение
O 41	ohmic drop, resistance drop	ohmscher Spannungsabfall *m*	chute *f* de tension ohmique	омическое падение [на-пряжения], падение [напряжения] на омиче-ском сопротивлении
O 42	ohmic load, resistive load	ohmsche Last (Belastung) *f*, Widerstandslast *f*	charge *f* ohmique	омическая (активная) нагрузка
O 43	ohmic loss	ohmscher Verlust *m*	perte *f* ohmique	омические потери
O 44	on-board	auf der Steckeinheit	sur l'unité enfichable	[размещенный] на плате
O 45	on-board interface	Interface *n* auf der Leiter-platte, Anschlußschnitt-stelle *f* auf der [Mikro-rechner-]Steckeinheit	interface *f* sur l'unité enfichable	интерфейс, размещенный на плате ‹микро-ЭВМ›
O 46	on-board socket	Sockel *m* (Fassung *f*) auf der Leiterplatte	socle *m* sur l'unité enfichable	гнездо на плате ‹микро-ЭВМ›
O 47	on-chip	auf dem Chip, schaltkreis-integriert	sur la puce, intégré sur circuit	размещенный на кри-сталле, интегрирован-ный в кристалле
O 48	on-chip I/O port	auf dem Chip realisierte E/A-Anschlußstelle *f*, schaltkreisintegrierte E/A-Anschlußstelle *f*	raccordement *m* d'E/S sur puce, raccordement d'E/S intégré	порт ввода-вывода, инт-егрированный в кри-сталле
O 49	on-chip memory	schaltkreisintegrierter Spei-cher *m*, Speicher im [Mikrorechner-]Schalt-kreis	mémoire *f* intégrée	память, интегрированная в кристалле ‹микро-ЭВМ›
O 50	on-chip peripheral	schaltkreisintegrierte Peri-pheriesteuerung *f*, Peri-pheriesteuerung im [Mikrorechner-]Schalt-kreis	commande *f* de périphérie intégrée	устройство управления периферийным оборудо-ванием, интегрирован-ное в кристалле ‹микро-ЭВМ›
O 51	on-chip stack	schaltkreisinterner Keller-speicher *m*	mémoire-cave *f* interne de circuit	стековое ЗУ, интегриро-ванное в кристалле ‹микро-ЭВМ›
O 52	on-chip substrate biasing	schaltkreisintegrierte Sub-stratvorspannungs-erzeugung *f*	polarisation *f* de substrat intégrée dans le circuit	интегрированная в кри-сталле схема подачи смещения на подложку
O 53	on condition, on state	Ein-Zustand *m*, Einschalt-zustand *m*	état *m* en marche	включенное состояние, состояние «вклю-чено»
O 54	one-address instruction, single-address instruction	1-Adreß-Befehl *m*, Ein-adreßbefehl *m*	instruction *f* à une adresse, instruction à adresse unique	одноадресная команда
	one-level code	*s.* A 10		
O 55	one-operand instruction	1-Operand-Befehl *m*	instruction *f* à 1 opérande	одноместная команда
O 56	one-pass assembler	Einschritt-Assembler *m*, Assembler *m* mit einem Durchlauf arbeitend	assembleur *m* à un pas	однопроходный ассемблер
O 57	one-pass compiler, single-pass compiler	Einschritt-Kompiler *m*, Übersetzer *m* in einem Durchlauf arbeitend	compilateur *m* à évolution unique	однопроходный компи-лятор
O 58	ones complement, one's complement, 1's com-plement	Einer-Komplement *n*, Kom-plement *n* zu 1	complément *m* à 1	дополнение до единицы, обратный код двоич-ного числа
	one-shot multivibrator	*s.* M 488		
	one-shot operation	*s.* S 492		
O 59	one-shot period	Einzelperiode *f*, einmaliges Intervall *n*	période *f* unique	длительность одиночного импульса
O 60	one state	„Eins"-Zustand *m*	état *m* « un »	состояние «1»
O 61	one-state drain current	erforderlicher Senkenstrom *m* für Eins-Zustand	courant *m* de drain d'état « un »	ток стока [канального] транзистора, находяще-гося в состоянии «1»

	one-step operation	s. S 492		
O 62/3	one-time application	einmalige Anwendung *f*	application *f* unique	однократное применение
O 64	one-to-zero ratio	Null-Eins-Verhältnis *n* <Ausgangssignalverhältnis>	rapport *m* un à zéro	отношение уровня [сигнала] «1» к уровню [сигнала] «0»
O 65	on-line	prozeßgekoppelt, rechnerverbunden, mitlaufend	on-line	неавтономный, управляемый, «он-лайн» <режим>
O 66	on-line acquisition	On-line-Datenerfassung *f*, prozeßgekoppelte Datenerfassung *f*	acquisition *f* de données on-line	неавтономный сбор данных
O 67	on-line data processing	On-line-Datenverarbeitung *f*, prozeßgekoppelte Datenverarbeitung *f*	traitement *m* de données on-line	управляемая обработка данных, обработка данных в режиме «он-лайн»
O 68	on-line debugging	On-line-Fehlerbeseitigung *f*, Programmfehlerkorrektur *f* parallel zur Programmverarbeitung	dépannage *m* on-line	отладка программы в режиме «он-лайн»
O 69	on-line diagnostics	On-line-Diagnose *f*, mitlaufende Diagnose *f*	diagnostic *m* on-line	средства диагностики, работающие в режиме «он-лайн», средства диагностики, работающие под управлением центрального оборудования
O 70	on-line operation	On-line-Betrieb *m*, prozeßgekoppelter Betrieb *m* <eines Rechners>	régime *m* on-line	работа в управляемом режиме, работа в режиме «он-лайн»
O 71	on-line processing	On-line-Verarbeitung *f*, prozeßgekoppelte Verarbeitung *f*	traitement *m* on-line	обработка в управляемом режиме, обработка в режиме «он-лайн»
O 72	on-line test facility	On-line-Testeinrichtung *f*, Testeinrichtung *f* für mitlaufende Prüfung	dispositif *m* de test on-line	средства контроля, работающие под непосредственным управлением центрального оборудования
O 73	on-off control	Ein-Aus-Steuerung *f*	commande *f* marche-arrêt	двухпозиционное управление
O 74	on-off switch	Ein-Aus-Schalter *m*	commutateur *m* marche-arrêt	двухпозиционный переключатель
O 75	on-open site	im Außendienst	en service externe	на внешнем обслуживании
O 76	on-site	an Ort und Stelle, am Einsatzort	sur lieu, in situ	на месте [эксплуатации]
O 77	on-site test	Test *m* am Einsatzort	test *m* sur lieu, test in situ	проверка на месте [эксплуатации]
	on state	s. O 53		
O 78	opcode, operation (operating) code	Operationskode *m*, Op-Kode *m*	code *m* d'opération	код операции
O 79	opcode field	Operationskodefeld *n* <eines Befehls>	champ *m* d'opération d'une instruction	поле кода операции
O 80	open circuit	offene Schaltung *f*, offener Stromkreis *m*	circuit *m* ouvert	разомкнутая цепь
O 81	open-circuited	leerlaufend	à marche à vide	разомкнуто, работающий в холостую
O 82	open-circuit impedance	Leerlaufimpedanz *f*	impédance *f* à vide	сопротивление в разомкнутом состоянии
O 83	open-circuit state	Leerlaufzustand *m*, Schaltungszustand *m* „offen"	état *m* de circuit ouvert	разомкнутое состояние, режим холостого хода
O 84	open-circuit voltage	Leerlaufspannung *f*	tension *f* à vide	напряжение холостого хода
O 85	open-collector gate	Open-Kollektor-Gate *n*, Torschaltung *f* mit offenem Kollektoranschluß	porte *f* à collecteur ouvert	вентиль с открытым коллектором
O 86	open-collector output	Open-Kollektor-Ausgang *m*, Ausgangsschaltung *f* mit offenem Kollektor	sortie *f* à collecteur ouvert	выход с открытым коллектором
O 87	open contact	offener Kontakt *m*	contact *m* ouvert	разомкнутый контакт
O 88	open-drain driver	Open-Drain-Treiber *m*, MOSFET-Treiberstufe *f* mit offener Drainelektrode	basculeur *m* à drain ouvert	формирователь [на МОП-транзисторе] с открытым стоком
O 89	open-drain output	Open-Drain-Ausgang *m*, Ausgangsschaltung *f* mit offenem Drainanschluß	sortie *f* à drain ouvert	выход с открытым стоком
O 90	open loop	offener Wirkungskreis *m*, offene Schleife *f*, offener Regelkreis *m*	boucle *f* ouverte	разомкнутый цикл; разомкнутый контур; разомкнутая петля
O 91	open-loop control	rückführungsfreie Steuerung *f*	commande *f* sans réaction	управление по разомкнутому циклу
O 92	open routine	offenes Programm *n* <einbaufähiges Programm>	programme *m* ouvert	открытая программа
O 93	open shop	offener Betrieb *m*, Rechenzentrumsbetrieb *m* mit direktem Nutzerzugriff	régime *m* ouvert	пультовой режим, режим работы вычислительного центра, при котором пользователь имеет доступ к ЭВМ
O 94	open statement	Eröffnungsanweisung *f*	instruction *f* d'ouverture	оператор открытия
O 95	open subroutine	offenes Unterprogramm *n*	sous-programme *m* ouvert	открытая подпрограмма
O 96	open tube diffusion	offene Diffusion *f*	diffusion *f* ouverte	открытая диффузия
O 97	operand	Operand *m*, Rechengröße *f*	opérande *m*	операнд
O 98	operand address	Operandenadresse *f*	adresse *f* d'opérande	адрес операнда
O 99	operand-address register	Operandenadreßregister *n*	registre *m* d'adresse d'opérande	регистр адреса операнда

O 100	operand register	Operandenregister n, Register n für Rechengröße	registre m d'opérande	регистр операнда
O 101	operand sequence	Operandenfolge f	séquence f d'opérande	последовательность операндов
O 102	operate / to	betreiben, arbeiten, bedienen	opérer, travailler, asservir	оперировать, действовать, работать; управлять
O 103	operating characteristic	Arbeitskennlinie f, Betriebskennlinie f	caractéristique f d'opération	рабочая (эксплуатационная) характеристика
	operating code	s. O 78		
O 104	operating conditions	Betriebsbedingungen fpl	conditions fpl d'opération	условия эксплуатации
	operating console	s. O 143		
O 105	operating costs	Betriebskosten pl	frais mpl d'exploitation	расходы на эксплуатацию
O 106	operating current	Betriebsstrom m	courant m de service	рабочий ток
O 107	operating error	Bedienungsfehler m	erreur f de service	ошибка управления; ошибка оператора
O 108	operating frequency	Betriebsfrequenz f, Arbeitsfrequenz f	fréquence f de service	рабочая частота
O 109	operating instructions, service instruction	Bedienungsanweisung f	instruction f de service	управляющие (служебные) команды
	operating memory	s. O 118		
O 110	operating mode, operation[al] mode	Arbeitsmodus m, Arbeitsweise f, Betriebsweise f	mode m opérationnel (de travail)	рабочий режим; режим обработки
O 111	operating parameter	Betriebsparameter m	paramètre m de service	рабочий параметр
O 112	operating point	Arbeitspunkt m	point m de service	рабочая точка
O 113	operating power requirements	Betriebs-Stromversorgungsanforderungen fpl	besoins mpl d'alimentation de régime	технические требования к рабочей мощности
O 114	operating principle, principle of operation	Operationsprinzip n, Arbeitsprinzip n	principe m d'opération	принцип действия
O 115	operating procedure	Arbeitsverfahren n	procédé m de travail	служебная процедура
	operating procedure	s. a. I 252		
O 116	operating speed, operation speed	Arbeitsgeschwindigkeit f, Operationsgeschwindigkeit f	vitesse f d'opération	рабочая скорость
O 117	operating staff	Bedienungspersonal n	personnel m de service	обслуживающий персонал
O 118	operating store, operating memory, working storage (memory)	Arbeitsspeicher m, Operativspeicher m	mémoire f de travail	оперативная память
O 119	operating system	Betriebssystem n, Operationssystem n ‹umfaßt Steuerprogrammsysteme und Dienstprogramme›	système m opérationnel	операционная система
O 120	operating system nucleus	Betriebssystemkern m	noyau m de système opérationnel	ядро операционной системы
O 121	operating temperature	Betriebstemperatur f	température f de service	рабочая температура
O 122	operating temperature range	Betriebstemperaturbereich m	champ m de température de travail	диапазон рабочих температур
O 123	operating time	Betriebszeit f, Betriebsdauer f	temps m de service	рабочее время
O 124	operating voltage	Arbeitsspannung f, Betriebsspannung f	tension f de service	рабочее напряжение
O 125	operation	Operation f, Arbeitsgang m, Betrieb m	opération f	операция; работа
O 126	operational amplifier	Operationsverstärker m	amplificateur m opérationnel	операционный усилитель
O 127	operational character	Betriebssteuerzeichen n	caractère m opérationnel	управляющий символ
O 128	operational device	Funktionsbauelement n, Funktionseinrichtung f	élément m opérationnel	функциональное (операционное) устройство
O 129	operational input	Funktionseingang m	entrée f opérationnelle	функциональный вход
	operational mode	s. O 110		
O 130	operational output	Funktionsausgang m	sortie f opérationnelle	функциональный выход
O 131	operational software	Betriebs-Software f, Betriebsprogramme npl	logiciels mpl opérationnels	служебное программное обеспечение
	operation code	s. O 78		
O 132	operation control	Operationssteuerung f	commande f d'opération	управление работой
O 133	operation cycle	Operationszyklus m, Arbeitszyklus m	cycle m d'opération	рабочий цикл
	operation mode	s. O 110		
O 134	operation part	Operationsteil n	partie f opérationnelle	операционная часть
O 135	operation register, working register	Operationsregister n, Arbeitsregister n, Rechenregister n	registre m opérationnel	регистр кода операции, рабочий регистр
O 136	operation sequence	Operationsfolge f	séquence f d'opération[s]	последовательность операций
O 137	operations manual	Betriebshandbuch n	manuel m d'opérations	инструкция по эксплуатации
	operation speed	s. O 116		
O 138	operations research	Betriebsforschung f	recherche f d'opérations	исследование операций
O 139	operation time	Operationszeit f	temps m d'opération	время выполнения операции
O 140	operator	Operationssymbol n, Operator m, Bediener m	opérateur m	оператор ‹символ, определяющий операцию›
O 141	operator action, operator intervention	Bedienereingriff m	intervention f d'opérateur	действие (вмешательство) оператора
O 142	operator command	Bedienerkommando n	commande f d'opérateur	директива оператора
O 143	operator console, operating console, operator panel	Bedienkonsole f, Bedienungskonsole f, Bedienpult n	console f (pupitre m) d'opérateur	пульт оператора
	operator intervention	s. O 141		
O 144	operator message	Bedienmeldung f ‹Meldung für Bediener›	message m d'opérateur	сообщение оператору
	operator panel	s. O 143		
O 145	operator station	Bedienstation f	station f d'opérateur	станция оператора
O 146	opposite sign	entgegengesetztes Vorzeichen n	signe m opposé	противоположный знак

O 147	optical character reader	Klarschriftleser *m*, optischer Zeichenleser *m*	lecteur *m* optique de caractères	оптическое устройство ввода символов, оптическое считывающее устройство
O 148	optical character recognition, OCR	optische Zeichenerkennung *f* <maschinelle Eingabe von Schrift- bzw. Druck- zeichen>	reconnaissance *f* optique de caractères	оптическое распознавание символов
O 149	optical coupler, opto- coupler	optischer Koppler *m*, Opto- koppler *m*	coupleur *m* optique	оптрон
O 150	optical fibre	optische Faser *f*	fibre *f* optique	оптическое волокно, световод
O 151	optical image chip	Bildwandlerchip *n*, Halb- leiterbildwandler *m*	puce *f* de conversion d'image	микросхема преобразо- вания изображения
O 152	optical mark reader	optischer Markierungsleser *m*	lecteur *m* de marquage optique	устройство оптического считывания меток
	optical scanner	s. P 201		
O 153	optimal coding	optimale Kodierung *f*, günstigste Verschlüsse- lung *f*	codage *m* optimal	оптимальное кодирование
	optimal value	s. O 157		
	optimization	s. O 155		
O 154	optimize / to	optimieren	optimiser	оптимизировать
O 155	optimizing, optimization	Optimierung *f*	optimisation *f*	оптимизация
O 156	optimum conditions	Optimalbedingungen *fpl*	conditions *fpl* optimales	оптимальные условия
O 157	optimum value, optimal value	Optimalwert *m*, Bestwert *m*	valeur *f* optimale	оптимальное значение
O 158	option	Angebot *n*, wahlfreie Möglichkeit *f*	option *f*	выбор
	option	s. a. O 160		
O 159	optional	wahlfrei, wahlweise	au choix	необязательный, про- извольный; факульта- тивный
O 160	optional facility, option	wahlweise Zusatzeinrich- tung *f*, wahlweiser Zusatz *m*	supplément *m* par option	вспомогательное средство
	optocoupler	s. O 149		
O 161	OR	ODER <logischer Operator der Disjunktion>	OU	ИЛИ <логическая опера- ция дизъюнкции>
O 162	OR-circuit, OR-gate, inclusive-OR gate	ODER-Schaltung *f*, ODER-Gatter *n*	circuit *m* OU	схема (вентиль) ИЛИ
O 163	order	Auftrag *m*	ordre *m*	директива
O 164	order	Rang *m*, Stellenwert *m*	rang *m*, ordre *m*	ранг; разряд числа; степень
	order	s. a. I 228		
O 165	ordered structure	geordnete Struktur *f*	structure *f* ordonnée	упорядоченная структура
O 166	order entry	Auftragseingang *m*	entrée *f* de commission, entrée d'ordre (d'instruc- tion)	ввод директивы
O 167/8	order handling	Auftragsbearbeitung *f*	travail *m* d'ordre	обработка директивы
O 169	orderly close-down	betriebsvorschriftsmäßiges Abschalten *n*	mise *f* au repos ordonnée	останов [системы] с воз- можностью рестарта
O 170	order number	Auftragsnummer *f*	numéro *m* d'ordre, numéro de commission	порядковый номер
O 171	order of priority	Prioritätsordnung *f*	ordre *m* de priorité	приоритетность, порядок приоритета
O 172	ordinary circuit	gebräuchliche (übliche) Schaltung *f*	circuit *m* ordinaire	обычная схема
	OR-ELSE	s. E 294		
	OR-gate	s. O 162		
O 173	oriented	orientiert, ausgerichtet	orienté	ориентированный
O 174	origin	Ursprung *m*, absolute Pro- grammanfangsadresse *f*	origine *f*	начало; абсолютный начальный адрес
O 175	original data	Ausgangsdaten *pl*	données *fpl* originales	исходные данные
	original equipment manufacturer	s. O 20		
O 176	original state	Ausgangszustand *m*, ursprünglicher Zustand *m*	état *m* original	исходное состояние
	OR-NOT gate	s. N 97		
O 177	OR operation	ODER-Verknüpfung *f*, ODER-Operation *f* <Disjunktion>	opération *f* OU	операция ИЛИ <дизъ- юнкция>
O 178	oscillate / to	schwingen	osciller	колебаться
O 179	oscillating crystal	Schwingquarz *m*	cristal *m* oscillant	кварцевый резонатор
O 180	oscillating frequency, oscillation frequency	Schwingungsfrequenz *f*	fréquence *f* d'oscillation	частота колебаний
O 181	oscillation	Schwingung *f*	oscillation *f*	колебание
	oscillation frequency	s. O 180		
O 182	oscillator, resonator	Oszillator *m*, Schwingungs- generator *m*, Schwinger *m*	oscillateur *m*	генератор, осциллятор, резонатор
O 183	oscillator circuit, tank [circuit]	Oszillatorschaltung *f*	circuit *m* oscillateur	схема генератора
O 184	oscilloscope	Oszilloskop *n*	oscilloscope *m*	осциллограф
O 185	outage	Ausfall *m*	manque *m*	отказ; выход из строя
O 186	outer load	äußere Belastung *f*	charge *f* extrême	внешняя нагрузка
O 187	outer macroinstruction	äußerer Makrobefehl *m*	instruction *f* macro extrême	внешняя макрокоманда
O 188	outgoing signal	abgehendes Signal *n*	signal *m* partant	выходной сигнал
O 189	outlet	Austritt *m*, Ausgang *m*	sortie *f*	выход; вывод
O 190	out of order, disturbed	gestört	dérangé, perturbé	нарушенный; поврежден- ный; искаженный
O 191	output	Ausgabe *f*, Ausgang *m*, Ausgangssignal *n*	sortie *f*	вывод; выход
	output	s. a. O 223		
O 192	output amplifier	Ausgangsverstärker *m*	amplificateur *m* de sortie	выходной усилитель

O 193	output area	Ausgabedatenbereich m <eines Speichers>	domaine m de sortie	область (буферная зона) вывода
O 194	output block	Ausgabeblock m, Ausgangsbereich m <Speicher>	bloc m de sortie	выходной блок; блок вывода <область памяти>
O 195	output buffer	Ausgabe-Pufferspeicher m	tampon m de sortie	выходной буфер, буфер вывода
O 196	output bus driver	Ausgangsbustreiber m	basculeur m de bus de sortie	выходной шинный формирователь
O 197	output bus type	Ausgabebustyp m <Bus mit nur einer Betriebsrichtung, einer Quelle und mehreren Empfängern>	type m de bus de sortie	выходная шина
O 198	output capacitance	Ausgangskapazität f	capacité f de sortie	выходная емкость
O 199	output channel	Ausgabekana m	canal m de sortie	выходной канал, канал вывода
O 200	output characteristic	Ausgangskennlinie f	caractéristique f de sortie	выходная характеристика
O 201	output circuit	Ausgangsschaltung f, Ausgabeschaltkreis m	circuit m de sortie	выходная схема
O 202	output connection	Ausgangsverbindung f	connexion f de sortie	выходное соединение
O 203	output control	Ausgabesteuerung f	commande f de sortie	управление выводом
O 204	output current	Ausgangsstrom m	courant m de sortie	выходной ток
O 205	output data	Ausgabedaten pl	données fpl de sortie	выходные данные
O 206	output delay	Ausgangsverzögerung f, Ausgangssignalverzögerung f	retardement m de sortie	задержка вывода; задержка выходного сигнала
O 207	output device	Ausgabegerät n, Ausgabebaustein m	appareil m de sortie	устройство вывода
O 208	output driver [amplifier]	Ausgabetreiber m, Ausgangstreiber m	amplificateur m de sortie	выходной усилитель-формирователь
O 209	output duty cycle	Ausgangstastverhältnis n	rapport m cyclique de sortie	рабочий цикл вывода
O 210	output equipment	Ausgabeausstattung f, Ausgabegeräte npl	équipement m de sortie	оборудование (устройства) вывода
O 211	output file	Ausgabedatei f	fichier m de sortie	выходной файл
O 212	output format	Ausgabeformat n	format m de sortie	выходной формат, формат вывода
O 213	output formatter	Ausgabeformatierer m <Aufbereitungsprogramm>	formateur m de sortie	программа преобразования формата выходных данных
O 214	output high voltage	Ausgangsspannung f oberer Pegel, Ausgangs-High-pegelspannung f	tension f de sortie de niveau élevé	высокий уровень выходного напряжения
O 215	output impedance	Ausgangsimpedanz f	impédance f de sortie	выходное сопротивление, выходной импеданс
O 216	output instruction	Ausgabebefehl m	instruction f de sortie	команда вывода
O 217	output interrupt	Ausgabe-Interrupt m, Ausgabeunterbrechung f	interruption f de sortie	прерывание по выводу
O 218	output latch	Ausgabelatch n, Ausgabeinformations-Halteregister n	registre m de maintien de sortie	схема фиксации выходных данных
O 219	output level	Ausgangspegel m	niveau m de sortie	уровень выходного сигнала
O 220	output line	Ausgabeleitung f, Ausgangsleitung f	ligne f de sortie	выходная линия, линия вывода
O 221	output path	Ausgabeweg m	voie f de sortie	выходной тракт, тракт вывода
O 222	output port	Ausgabetor n, Ausgabeanschlußstelle f	porte f de sortie	выходной порт, порт вывода
O 223	output power, output	Ausgangsleistung f, Ausstoß m	puissance f de sortie	выходная мощность
	output program	s. O 227		
O 224	output pulse	Ausgangsimpuls m, Ausgabeimpuls m	impulsion f de sortie	выходной импульс
O 225	output register	Ausgaberegister n	registre m de sortie	регистр вывода, выходной регистр
O 226	output-request signal	Ausgabe-Anforderungssignal n	signal m de demande de sortie	сигнал запроса на вывод, сигнал требования вывода
O 227	output routine, output program	Ausgaberoutine f, Ausgabeprogramm n	programme m de sortie	программа вывода
O 228	output signal	Ausgangssignal n, Ausgabesignal n	signal m de sortie	выходной сигнал
O 229	output stream	Ausgabedatenstrom m, Ausgabefolge f	courant m de sortie	выходной поток [данных]
O 230	output strobe signal	Ausgabemarkiersignal n, Ausgabetor-Aktivierungssignal n	signal m de marquage de sortie	строб[ирующий сигнал] вывода
O 231	output table	Ausgabetabelle f	table f de sortie	таблица выходных данных
O 232	output terminal	Ausgangsanschluß m, Ausgabeendgerät n	terminal m de sortie	выходная клемма
O 233	output time constant	Ausgangszeitkonstante f	constante f de temps de sortie	постоянная времени выходной цепи
O 234	output typewriter	Ausgabeschreibmaschine f	machine f à écrire de sortie	выходная пишущая машинка
O 235	output unit	Ausgabeeinheit f	unité f de sortie	выходное устройство; устройство вывода
O 236	output value	Ausgangswert m, Ausgabewert m	valeur f de sortie	выходное значение
O 237	output voltage	Ausgangsspannung f	tension f de sortie	выходное напряжение
O 238	outside loop	äußere Schleife f	boucle f extérieure	внешний цикл
O 239	overall costs	Gesamtkosten pl	frais mpl totaux	общие расходы, общая стоимость
O 240	overall loading	Gesamtbelastung f	charge f totale	общая (суммарная) нагрузка
O 241	overall loss	Gesamtverlust m	perte f totale	общие (суммарные) потери

O 242	overall system	Gesamtsystem n	système m total	полная система
O 243	overall system performance	Gesamtsystemleistung f	performance f du système entier	общая производительность системы
O 244	overflow	Überlauf m	dépassement m, débordement m	переполнение
O 245	overflow bit, V-bit	Überlaufbit n, V-Bit n <Statusbit>	bit m de dépassement	двоичный разряд переполнения, V-бит регистра состояния [процессора]
O 246	overflow condition, V condition	Überlaufbedingung f	condition f de dépassement	состояние переполнения <V-бит регистра состояния равен 1>
O 247	overflow flag, V-flag	Überlaufkennzeichen n	marque f de dépassement	флаг переполнения, V-флаг регистра состояния [процессора]
O 248	overflow indicator	Überlaufanzeiger m	indicateur m de dépassement	индикатор переполнения
O 249	overflow position	Überlaufstelle f	position f de dépassement	разряд переполнения
O 250	overhead	Organisationsaufwand m, Verwaltungsaufwand m	effort m d'organisation	время, затрачиваемое операционной системой на вспомогательные операции; затраты на вспомогательные операции
O 251	overhead area	zusätzlicher Flächenverbrauch m <Reduzierung der für eine Logikschaltung nutzbaren Chipfläche durch Bondstellen, Anpaßelektronik usw.>	surface f supplémentaire	дополнительно затрачиваемая площадь [кристалла] <уменьшение полезной площади кристалла за счет контактных площадок, согласующих элементов и т.д.>
O 252	overhead operation	Operation f im Rahmen des Organisationsaufwandes <keine Nutzoperation>	opération f dans le cadre de l'organisation	организационная [вспомогательная] операция
O 253	overlap / to	überlappen, überdecken, überschneiden	chevaucher	перекрывать; совмещать
O 254	overlap, overlapping	Überlappung f	chevauchement m	перекрытие; совмещение
O 255	overlapped access	überlappter (überlappender) Zugriff m	accès m chevauché	совмещенный доступ, перекрывающийся [во времени] доступ
O 256	overlapped machine	überlappende Maschine f, Rechner m mit Überlappungsstruktur	machine f à chevauchement	машина с совмещенным [во времени] выполнением операций
O 257	overlapped processing overlapping	überlappte Verarbeitung f s. O 254	traitement m à chevauchement	совмещенная обработка
O 258	overlapping execution	überlappende Ausführung f	exécution f à chevauchement	выполнение [операций] с совмещением во времени
O 259	overlay / to	überlagern	superposer	налагать; совмещать
O 260	overlay	Überlagerung f <Programmtechnik>	overlay m <programmes>, superposition f	наложение, оверлей; оверлейный
O 261	overlay area	Überlagerungsbereich m <Speicher>	champ m à overlay	область наложения, оверлейная область [памяти]
O 262	overlay structure	Überlagerungsstruktur f <Programmaufbau>	structure f d'overlay	оверлейная структура
O 263	overload	Überlastung f	surcharge f	перегрузка
O 264	overload protection	Überlastschutz m	protection f contre surcharges	защита от перегрузки
O 265	overpunch	Überlochung f <zum Löschen gestanzter Informationen>	perforation f totale <pour effacer des informations perforées>	зонная перфорация; перфорация в специальной зоне перфокарты
O 266	override / to	übergehen, außer Kraft setzen <eine Regel oder Begrenzung>	passer <en ignorant>, mettre hors effet	перейти, перешагнуть
O 267	overrun	Aufnahmekapazitätsüberschreitung f <Datenübertragung>	dépassement m	выход за границы; перегрузка канала передачи данных
O 268	overshoot	Überschwingen n	suroscillation f	перерегулирование; отклонение от заданного значения; выброс сигнала
O 269	overview	Überblick m	vue f synoptique	обзор
O 270	overvoltage protection	Überspannungsschutz m	protection f contre surtensions	защита от перенапряжения
O 271	overwrite / to	überschreiben <einen Speicherinhalt>	transcrire <contenu du mémoire>	перезаписывать
O 272	oxide growth	Oxidwachstum n	croissance f d'oxyde	выращивание окисла
O 273	oxide insulator	Oxidisolator m	isolateur m à oxyde	оксидный изолятор
O 274	oxide isolation	Oxidisolation f	isolation f à oxyde	оксидная изоляция, изоляция окислом
O 275	oxide layer	Oxidschicht f	couche f d'oxyde	оксидный слой, слой окисла
O 276	oxide thickness	Oxiddicke f, Oxidschichtdicke f	épaisseur f [de couche] d'oxyde	толщина оксидного слоя

P

	pack	s. P 10		
P 1	package, packaging	Packung f, Bausteingehäuse n, Schaltkreisgehäuse n	boîtier m	корпус интегральной схемы

	English	German	French	Russian
P 2	package power dissipation constraints	gehäusebedingte Leistungsverbrauchsgrenzen *fpl* (Verlustleistungsbeschränkung *f*)	contraintes *fpl* de dissipation de puissance dans le boîtier	ограничения на рассеиваемую мощность корпусом [интегральной схемы]
P 3	package reliability	Gehäusezuverlässigkeit *f*	fiabilité *f* de boîtier	надежность корпуса
P 4	package size	Gehäusegröße *f*, Gehäuseform *f*	grandeur *f* de boîtier	размер корпуса
	packaging	*s.* P 1		
P 5	packaging style	Gehäusetyp *m*, Verpackungsart *f*	type *m* de boîtier	тип корпуса; тип упаковки
P 6	packaging technology	Schaltkreisverkapselungstechnologie *f*, Gehäusetechnologie *f*	technologie *f* de boîtier	технология корпусирования [интегральных схем]
P 7	packed BCD data, packed binary-coded decimal data	gepackte BCD-Daten *pl*, gepackte binär kodierte Dezimaldaten *pl* <2 Dezimalziffern in 1 Byte>	données *fpl* BCD groupées	упакованное двоично-десятичное число <две десятичных цифры в одном байте>
P 8	packed format	gepacktes Format *n*	format *m* groupé	упакованный формат
P 9	packed mode	gepackte Darstellungsform *f*	mode *m* groupé	режим работы с упакованными данными
P 10	packet, pack	Paket *n*, Datenpaket *n*, Programmpaket *n*	paquet *m*	пакет
P 11	packet-switched network, packet switching network	Paketvermittlungsnetz *n*, Datenpaketvermittlungsnetz *n* mit Knotenrechnern <Speichervermittlung>	réseau *m* de communication de données	сеть с коммутацией пакетов
P 12	packet-switched service on public networks	Paketvermittlung *f* in öffentlichen Netzen	service *m* de transmission de données sur réseaux de communications publics	служба коммутации пакетов сетей общественного пользования
P 13	packet switching	Paketvermittlung *f*, Datenpaketvermittlung *f* <Rechnerkommunikation>	communication *f* de paquet	коммутация пакетов
	packet switching network	*s.* P 11		
P 14	packet switching network line	Vermittlungsleitung *f* für Datenpaketübertragung	ligne *f* de communication de paquets	линия сети с коммутацией пакетов
P 15	packet switching protocol	Paketvermittlungsprotokoll *n*, Datenpaketvermittlungsprozedurvorschrift *f*	procès-verbal *m* de communication de données	протокол коммутации пакетов
P 16	packet switching system	Speichervermittlungssystem *n*, Datenpaketvermittlungssystem *n*	système *m* de communication de paquets	система с коммутацией пакетов
P 17	packet system	Datenpaketsystem *n*	système *m* de paquet	пакетная система
P 18	packet transmission	Datenpaketübertragung *f*	transmission *f* de paquet	передача пакета
P 19	packing density	Packungsdichte *f* <Schaltelemente, Informationen>	densité *f* d'emballage	плотность упаковки
P 20	packing factor	Packungsfaktor *m*	facteur *m* d'emballage	коэффициент [плотности] упаковки; коэффициент [плотности] записи
P 21	pad	Dämpfungsglied *n* <Anpassung>	élément *m* d'atténuation	выравнивающий элемент, элемент согласования
P 22	pad	Anschlußinsel *f* <Chip>	ilôt *m* de branchement <puce>	контактная площадка <чип>
	pad character	*s.* F 90		
P 23	padding	Auffüllen *n*	remplissage *m*	заполнение, дополнение, набивка <заполнение блоков данных незначащей информацией>
P 24	page	Seite *f*, Abschnitt *m* konstanter Größe, Kachel *f* <Speicher>	page *f*	страница
P 25	page addressing	Page-Adressierung *f*, Seitenadressierung *f*	adressage *m* de page	страничная адресация; адресация страницы
P 26	page address register	Page-Adreßregister *n*, Seitenadreßregister *n*	registre *m* d'adresse de page	регистр адреса страницы
	page-at-a-time printer	*s.* P 28		
P 27	page number	Page-Nummer *f*, Seitennummer *f*	numéro *m* de page	номер страницы
P 28	page printer, page-at-a-time printer	Blattschreiber *m*, Blattdrucker *m*, Seitendrucker *m*	imprimante *f* à pages	построчно-печатающее устройство
P 29	page protection	Seitenschutz *m*	protection *f* de page	защита страниц
P 30	page register	Page-Register *n*, Seitenregister *n*	registre *m* de pages	регистр страниц
P 31	page zero	Page Null *m*, Seite Null *f* <erster Speicherabschnitt>	page *f* zéro	страница с нулевым номером, нулевая страница
P 32	page-zero addressing	Page-Null-Adressierung *f*, Seite-Null-Adressierung *f* <Adressierung nur von Speicherplätzen auf Seite Null>	adressage *m* en page zéro	адресация нулевой страницы
P 33	paging	Seitenbildung *f* <Speicherorganisation>	pagination *f*	разбивка [памяти] на страницы; страничный обмен
	p-AIG-MOS	*s.* P 103		
	PAM	*s.* P 693		
P 34	panel	Tafel *f*, Frontplatte *f*	panneau *m*	панель; пульт управления
P 35	paper feed	Papiervorschub *m*, Papierzuführung *f*	avancement *m* de papier	подача бумаги
P 36	paper tape, punch tape	Lochstreifen *m*	bande *f* perforée	перфолента
P 37	paper tape punch, tape punch (perforator)	Lochstreifenlocher *m*, Lochstreifenstanzer *m*	perforatrice *f* de bande perforée	ленточный перфоратор
P 38	paper tape reader, [punch] tape reader	Lochstreifenleser *m*	lecteur *m* de bande perforée	устройство считывания [данных] с перфоленты
P 39	paper tape unit, punch tape unit	Lochstreifeneinheit *f*, Lochstreifengeräteeinheit *f*	unité *f* de bande perforée	устройство ввода [данных] с перфоленты, фотоввод

P 40	parallel / to	parallel betreiben, parallel-schalten	exploiter (mettre) en parallèle	распараллеливать; соединять параллельно; сравнивать; соответствовать
P 41	parallel access	Parallelzugriff *m*	accès *m* parallèle	параллельный доступ
P 42	parallel adder	Paralleladdierwerk *n*	addeur *m* parallèle	параллельный сумматор
P 43	parallel arbitration technique	Parallelentscheidungsverfahren *n* <Busprioritätstechnik>	procédé *m* d'arbitrage parallèle	параллельный арбитраж
P 44	parallel arithmetic unit	Parallelrechenwerk *n*	unité *f* de calcul parallèle	параллельное арифметическое устройство
P 45	parallel by character	zeichenparallel	parallèle en caractères	параллельный по символам
P 46	parallel computer	Parallelrechner *m* <im Gegensatz zum Seriellrechner>	calculateur *m* (calculatrice *f*) parallèle	ЭВМ параллельного действия; ЭВМ с совмещением операций
	parallel computer	s. a. S 433		
P 47	parallel connection	Parallelschaltung *f*	montage *m* parallèle	параллельное соединение
P 48	parallel input	Paralleleingabe *f*, Paralleleingang *m*	entrée *f* parallèle	параллельный вход; параллельный ввод
P 49	parallel input/output, parallel I/O	Parallel-Ein-/Ausgabe *f*, Parallel-E/A *f*	entrée/sortie *f* parallèle, E/S parallèle	параллельный ввод-вывод
P 50	parallel interface	Parallelinterface *n*, Parallelschnittstelle *f*, Parallelanschluß *m*	interface *f* parallèle	параллельный интерфейс
	parallel I/O	s. P 49		
P 51	parallel I/O controller, PIO	Parallel-Ein-/Ausgabe-Steuerbaustein *m*, Schaltkreis *m* für parallele Ein-/Ausgabe	circuit *m* de commande d'E/S parallèle	контроллер параллельного ввода-вывода
	parallel mode	s. S 436		
P 52	parallel operation	Paralleloperation *f*, Parallelarbeit *f* <Arbeit mit allen Elementen einer Informationseinheit gleichzeitig>	opération *f* (travail *m*) parallèle	параллельная работа
	parallel operation	s. a. S 437		
P 53	parallel output	Parallelausgabe *f*, Parallelausgang *m*	sortie *f* parallèle	параллельный выход; параллельный вывод
P 54	parallel printer	Paralleldrucker *m*	imprimante *f* parallèle	параллельное печатающее устройство
	parallel processing	s. S 438		
	parallel-processing system	s. S 439		
P 55	parallel search	Parallelsuche *f*, Parallelabfrage *f* <inhaltsadressierter Speicher>	recherche *f* parallèle	параллельный поиск
P 56	parallel search memory	Parallelsuchspeicher *m* <Assoziativspeicher>	mémoire *f* de recherche parallèle	память параллельного поиска
	parallel technique	s. S 440		
P 57	parallel-to-serial conversion	Parallel-Seriell-Umsetzung *f*	conversion *f* parallèle en série	параллельно-последовательное преобразование
P 58	parallel transfer	Parallelübertragung *f*	transfert *m* parallèle	параллельная передача
P 59	parameter acceptance	Parameterannahme *f*	acceptation *f* de paramètre	прием параметра
P 60	parameter-dependent instruction	parameterabhängiger Befehl *m*	instruction *f* dépendant de paramètre[s]	параметрически настраиваемая команда, команда, зависящая от параметров
P 61	parameter list	Parameterliste *f*, Werteliste *f*	liste *f* de paramètres	список параметров
	parameter passing	s. P 88		
P 62	parameter region	Parameterbereich *m*, Wertebereich *m*	domaine *m* de paramètres	область (зона) параметров; диапазон параметров
P 63	paraphase amplifier	Phasenumkehrverstärker *m*	amplificateur *m* inverseur de phase	фазоинверсный (парафазный) усилитель
	paraphase amplifier	s. a. P 751		
P 64	parasitic capacitance	parasitäre Kapazität *f*	capacité *f* parasitaire	паразитная емкость
P 65	parasitic frequency	Störfrequenz *f*	fréquence *f* parasitaire	частота [сигнала] помехи; частота возмущающего воздействия
P 66	parasitic oscillation	parasitäre Schwingung *f*, Störschwingung *f*	oscillation *f* parasitaire	паразитное колебание
P 67	parasitics	Störeffekte *mpl*	parasites *mpl*	паразитные помехи
P 68	parenthesis	runde Klammer *f*	parenthèse *f* [ronde]	круглая скобка
P 69	parity	Parität *f*	parité *f*	равенство; четность
P 70	parity bit	Paritätsbit *n*	bit *m* de parité	бит [контроля по] четности
P 71	parity check	Paritätsprüfung *f*	vérification *f* de parité	контроль по четности
P 72	parity digit	Paritätsziffer *f*	chiffre *m* de parité	контрольная цифра, контрольный разряд
P 73	parity error	Paritätsfehler *m*	erreur *f* de parité	ошибка [контроля по] четности
P 74	parity flag, P-flag	Paritätskennzeichen *n*	marque *f* de parité	флаг [контроля по] четности, P-бит регистра состояния [процессора]
P 75	parity generator	Paritätsgenerator *m*	générateur *m* de parité	генератор разряда четности
P 76	part-failure rate	Teilausfallrate *f*	cote *f* de manque partiel	интенсивность [возникновения] частичных отказов
P 77	partial carry	Teilübertrag *m*	retenue *f* partielle	частичный перенос
P 78	partial overlap	partielle (teilweise) Überlappung *f*	recouvrement *m* partiel	частичное перекрытие (совмещение), неполное совмещение
P 79	partial product	Teilprodukt *n* <Multiplikation>	produit *m* partiel	частичное произведение
	participant	s. S 308		
P 80	partition / to	aufteilen, unterteilen	partager	разделять, расчленять; секционировать

P 81	partitioned	aufgeteilt, untergliedert	partagé	разделенный, расчленен-ный; секционированный
P 82	partitioning	Aufteilung f	partage m	разделение, расчленение, разбиение; секционирование
P 83	parts list	Stückliste f, Teileliste f	liste f des pièces détachées	спецификация
P 84	parts number	Stückzahl f	nombre m de pièces	число элементов
P 85	party line	Partyline f, Gemeinschafts-leitung f <Kommuni-kationssystem>	ligne f commune	линия коллективного пользования, групповая линия
P 86	pass	Durchlauf m, Lauf m, Arbeitsgang m	course f, passage m	просмотр, проход; прогон
P 87	passing of control	Übergabe f der Steuerung	remise f de la commande	передача управления
P 88	passing parameter, parameter passing	Parameterbereitstellung f, Parameterübergabe f <Unterprogramm>	mise f à disposition des paramètres	передача параметра
P 89	passivate / to	passivieren	passiver	пассивировать
P 90	passive component (element)	passives Bauelement n	élément m passif	пассивный компонент (элемент)
P 91	patch / to	flicken, stöpseln <proviso-risch verbinden>	boucher	ставить «заплату» <делать временное соединение или исправление>
P 92	patch	Ausbesserung f	réparation f	склейка, «заплата»
	patchboard	s. P 266		
P 93	path	Weg m, Pfad m, Bahn f	voie f, chemin m	тракт; траектория; путь, маршрут
P 94	path control	Bahnsteuerung f <Numerik>	commande f de voie	управление маршрутом (выбором пути)
P 95	path length	Weglänge f	longueur f de voie	длина пути; длина пробега
P 96	pattern	Muster n, Schablone f, Figur f	échantillon m, modèle m, figure f	образец; шаблон; модель; образ; комбинация, [конкретный] набор
P 97	pattern classification	Musterklassifizierung f	classification f d'échantillons	классификация образцов
P 98	pattern feature	Schablonengestaltung f, Schablonenraster n	aspect m de modèle	вид шаблона, растр шаб-лона
P 99	pattern mask	Mustermaske f, Wafer-schablone f	masque m de modèle	рисунок маски; фото-шаблон
P 100	pattern plane	Leiterzugebene f, Leiter-ebene f	face f à conducteurs	слой сигнальных провод-ников; слой межсоеди-нений
P 101	pattern recognition	Mustererkennung f, Struk-turerkennung f	reconnaissance f de modèle	распознавание образов
P 102	payroll	Lohnabrechnung f, Lohn-liste f	liste f de paie	расчетная ведомость, пла-тежная ведомость
	PC board	s. P 448		
	PC edge connector	s. P 450		
P 103	p-channel aluminium gate MOS technology, p-AlG-MOS	p-Kanal-Aluminiumgate-MOS-Technologie f, p-AlG-MOS f	technologie f MOS à gate à l'aluminium canal p	р-канальные МОП-схемы с алюминиевыми зат-ворами
P 104	p-channel metal oxide semiconductor tech-nology, p-channel MOS, p-channel MOS technology, PMOS-tech-nology, PMOS, pMOS	p-Kanal-Metalloxidhalb-leitertechnologie f, p-Kanal-MOS-Technologie f, pMOS-Technologie f, p-Kanal-MOS f, pMOS f	technologie f métal-oxyde-semi-conducteur canal p	р-канальная МОП-техно-логия, р-МОП техно-логия, р-МОП
P 105	p-channel MOS circuit, pMOS circuit	p-Kanal-MOS-Schaltkreis m, pMOS-Schaltkreis m	circuit m MOS canal p	р-канальная МОП-схема, схема на р-МОП струк-турах
	p-channel MOS tech-nology	s. P 104		
P 106	p-channel silicon gate MOS technology, p-SG-MOS, p-SGT	p-Kanal-Siliziumgate-MOS-Technologie f, p-SG-MOS f, p-SGT f	technologie f MOS à gate au silicium canal p	р-канальные МОП-схемы с кремниевыми затво-рами
P 107	PCI, programmable com-munication interface	PCI-Baustein m, program-mierbarer Übertragungs-netzwerks-Anschlußbau-stein m, programmierbare Kommunikationsschnitt-stellenschaltung f	interface f de communica-tion programmable	программируемый связной интерфейс
	PC layout	s. P 451		
	PCM	s. P 698		
	PC master	s. P 452		
	P condition	s. P 352		
P 108	p-conducting	p-leitend	conductible p	р-проводящий, характери-зующийся р-проводи-мостью
	PDM	s. P 707		
	pd product	s. P 371		
P 109	peak amplitude	Spitzenamplitude f	amplitude f de pointe	максимальная амплитуда
P 110	peak collector current	Kollektorspitzenstrom m	courant m de collecteur de pointe	[максимальный] импульс-ный ток коллектора
P 111	peak data transfer rate	Spitzen-Datenüber-tragungsgeschwindigkeit f, Spitzenrate f der Datenübertragung	vitesse f de transmission de données maximale	максимальная скорость передачи данных
P 112	peak frequency	Spitzenfrequenz f	fréquence f de pointe	максимальная частота
P 113	peak limiter	Spitzenbegrenzer m	délimiteur m de pointe	пиковый ограничитель
P 114	peak load	Spitzenbelastung f	charge f de pointe	пиковая нагрузка
P 115	peak output power	Ausgangsspitzenleistung f	puissance f de pointe de sortie	[максимальная] импульс-ная выходная мощность
P 116	peak point	Scheitelpunkt m	point m de crête	пиковая (высшая) точка, точка максимума
P 117	peak power	Spitzenleistung f	puissance f de pointe	максимальная мощность
P 118	peak pulse power	Impulsspitzenleistung f	puissance f de pointe d'impulsion	максимальная мощность импульса

P 119	peak signal	Spitzensignal *n*	signal *m* de pointe	пиковый сигнал
P 120	peak-to-peak value	Wert *m* von Spitze zu Spitze, Maximal-Minimal-Wert *m*	valeur *f* de pointe à pointe	полный размах колебаний, двойная амплитуда
P 121	peak value, crest value	Spitzenwert *m*	valeur *f* de pointe	пиковое значение
P 122	peak voltage	Spitzenspannung *f*	tension *f* de pointe	пиковое напряжение
P 123	pending interrupt	anstehender Interrupt *m*, anstehende Unterbrechungsanforderung *f* <noch nicht angenommener Interrupt einer Peripherieeinheit>	interruption *f* pendante	отложенное (отсроченное) прерывание
P 124	penetration depth	Eindringtiefe *f*	profondeur *f* de pénétration	глубина проникновения
P 125	perception	Wahrnehmung *f*	perception *f*	перцепция, ощущение
P 126	perforate / to, to punch	perforieren, lochen, stanzen	perforer, poinçonner	перфорировать, пробивать
P 127	perforator, punch[er]	Locher *m*, Stanzer *m*	perforatrice *f*, perforateur *m*, poinçonneuse *f*	перфоратор
P 128	perform / to	leisten, verrichten	exécuter	выполнять <операцию>
P 129	performance	Leistungsvermögen *n*	performance *f*	производительность
	performance	*s. a.* P 368		
P 130	performance characteristics	Leistungscharakteristik *f*, Leistungskennwerte *mpl*	caractéristiques *mpl* de performance	рабочие характеристики, характеристики производительности
P 131	performance comparison	Leistungsvergleich *m*	comparaison *f* de performance	сравнение производительности
P 132	performance reference	Leistungsreferenz *f*	référence *f* de performance	эталонная производительность
P 133	performance requirement	Leistungsanforderung *f*	exigence *f* de performance	требование по производительности; требование к техническим характеристикам
	period	*s.* C 896		
P 134	periodic duty	Aussetzbetrieb *m*, periodisch wiederkehrende Belastung *f*	régime *m* intermittent, charge *f* périodique	периодический режим; периодическая нагрузка
P 135	periodic rating	Nennleistung *f* für Aussetzbetrieb	puissance *f* nominale pour régime intermittent	номинальное значение периодической нагрузки
P 136	periodic signal	periodisches Signal *n*	signal *m* périodique	периодический сигнал
P 137	peripheral	peripher	périphérique	периферийный
P 138	peripheral board	Peripheriesteckeinheit *f*, Leiterplatte *f* mit Peripherieschaltung	carte *f* périphérique	плата сопряжения с периферийным устройством
P 139	peripheral bus	peripherer Bus *m*, Peripheriebus *m*	bus *m* périphérique	периферийная шина
P 140	peripheral chip	Peripherieschaltkreis *m*	circuit *m* périphérique	периферийная микросхема
P 141	peripheral control	periphere Steuerung *f*, Peripheriesteuerung *f*	commande *f* périphérique	управление периферийным оборудованием
P 142	peripheral controller	Peripheriesteuerungsbaustein *m*	module *m* commande périphérique	контроллер периферийного оборудования
P 143	peripheral device	Peripheriegerät *n*	appareil *m* périphérique	периферийное устройство
P 144	peripheral device allocation	Peripheriegerätezuordnung *f*	attribution *f* d'appareils périphériques	распределение внешних устройств
P 145	peripheral device controller	Peripheriegerätesteuereinheit *f*	unité *f* de commande de périphériques	контроллер периферийного устройства
P 146	peripheral equipment	periphere Ausstattung *f*, externe Ausrüstung *f*	équipement *m* périphérique (externe)	периферийное (внешнее) оборудование
P 147	peripheral interface adapter, PIA	PIA-Schaltkreis *m*, Peripherieschnittstellen-Anpassungsbaustein *m*	adapteur *m* d'interface périphérique	адаптер периферийного интерфейса
P 148	peripheral processor	Peripherieprozessor *m*	processeur *m* périphérique	периферийный процессор
P 149	peripherals	Peripheriegeräte *npl*	périphériques *mpl*	периферийные устройства
P 150	peripheral subsystem	Peripherie-Untersystem *n*	sous-système *m* de périphérie	периферийная подсистема
P 151	peripheral transfer	periphere Übertragung *f*	transmission *f* périphérique	внешний перенос
P 152	peripheral units	periphere Einheiten *fpl*	unités *fpl* périphériques	периферийные (внешние) устройства
P 153	permanent data	Fixdaten *pl*	données *fpl* permanentes	постоянные (фиксированные) данные
P 154	permanent error (fault), stuck-at fault	permanenter Fehler *m*, bleibende Störung *f*	erreur *f* permanente	устойчивая ошибка; неисправность типа залипания
P 155	permanent magnet	Dauermagnet *m*, Permanentmagnet *m*	aimant *m* permanent	постоянный магнит
P 156	permanent memory (storage, store)	Permanentspeicher *m*, Dauerspeicher *m*	mémoire *f* permanente	постоянная память
P 157	permissible value	zulässiger Wert *m*	valeur *f* admissible	допустимое значение
P 158	permittivity	Dielektrizitätskonstante *f*	permittivité *f*	диэлектрическая проницаемость
P 159	persist / to	nachwirken	persister	сохраняться; продолжаться; действовать
P 160	persistence	Nachleuchtdauer *f*	persistance *f*	послесвечение
P 161	persistency checking	Stetigkeitsprüfung *f*	vérification *f* de persistance	проверка устойчивости
P 162	personal computer	persönlicher Rechner *m* <persönlich verfügbar>, arbeitsplatzgebundener Rechner, Personalcomputer *m*	calculateur *m* privé	персональная ЭВМ, ЭВМ индивидуального пользования
P 163	PERT, program evolution and review technique	PERT *n*	PERT *m*	ПЕРТ, система планирования и руководства разработками
	perturbance	*s.* D 476		
	PFE	*s.* P 204		
	P-flag	*s.* P 74		
	PFM	*s.* P 711		
P 164	phantom circuit	Phantomschaltkreis *m*	circuit *m* fantôme	фантомная (искусственная) цепь
P 165	phase advancing, phase shift	Phasenschiebung *f*	décalage *m* de phase	фазовый сдвиг

P 166	**phase angle**	Phasenwinkel *m*	angle *m* de phase	фазовый угол, угол сдвига фаз
P 167	**phase change**	Phasenwechsel *m*	échange (changement) *m* de phase	смена фаз
P 168	**phase coincidence**	Phasenübereinstimmung *f*	coincidence *f* des phases	синфазность, совпадение по фазе
P 169	**phase control**	Phasenregelung *f*	réglage *m* de phase	регулирование фазы; фазовое регулирование
P 170	**phase delay**	Phasenlaufzeit *f*, Phasenverzögerung *f*	décalage *m* de phase	задержка по фазе
P 171	**phase deviation**	Phasenabweichung *f*	déviation *f* de phase	фазовый сдвиг
P 172	**phase difference**	Phasendifferenz *f*	différence *f* de phase	разность фаз
P 173	**phase error**, phasing error	Phasenfehler *m*	erreur *f* de phase	фазовая погрешность
P 174	**phase frequency distortion**	Phasenverzerrung *f*	distorsion *f* de phase	частотно-фазовое искажение
P 175	**phase inversion**, phase reversal	Phasenumkehr *f*	inversion *f* de phase	инверсия фазы
P 176	**phase inverter circuit**	Phasenumkehrschaltung *f*	circuit *m* d'inversion de phase	фазоинверсная схема
P 177	**phase lag**	Phasennachlauf *m*	retard *m* de phase	отставание (запаздывание) по фазе
P 178	**phase lead**	Phasenvorlauf *m*	avancement *m* de phase	опережение по фазе
P 179	**phase lock**	Phasenrastung *f*, Phasenmitnahme *f*	entraînement *m* de phase	захват фазы, фазовая автоподстройка
P 180	**phase-locked loop**, PLL	Phasenregelkreis *m*, phasenstarre Schleife *f*	boucle *f* à verrouillage de phase	контур фазовой автоподстройки
P 181	**phase-locked loop motor control**, PLL motor control	phasenstarre Gleichstrommotorsteuerung *f*, PLL-Schaltkreis-Motorsteuerung *f*	commande *f* de moteur à phase rigide	управление двигателем постоянного тока с фазовой автоподстройкой
P 182	**phase logic**	Phasenlogik *f*	logique *f* de phase	фазовая логика ‹схемы переключения ЭВМ из одного состояния на другое›
P 183	**phase modulation**	Phasenmodulation *f*	modulation *f* de phase	фазовая модуляция
P 184	**phase position**	Phasenlage *f*	position *f* de phase	значение фазового угла, фаза колебаний; фазировка сигнала
P 185	**phase reversal**	*s.* P 175		
	phase sequence	Phasenfolge *f*	séquence *f* de phase	фазовая последовательность
	phase shift	*s.* P 165		
P 186	**phase splitter**	Phasenteiler *m*	diviseur *m* de phase	схема расщепления фазы
P 187	**phasing**	Phasenlageeinstellung *f*, Phasenabgleich *m* ⌐*m*	ajustement *m* de phase	фазирование, фазировка
P 188	**phasing capacitor**	Phasenabgleichkondensator *m*	condensateur *m* d'ajustement de phase	фазовыравнивающий конденсатор
	phasing error	*s.* P 173		
P 189	**phosphorescence**	Phosphoreszenz *f*, Nachleuchten *n*	phosphorescence *f*	фосфоресценция; послесвечение
P 190	**photoactive layer**	fotoaktive (lichtelektrisch aktive) Schicht *f*	couche *f* photoactive	фотоэлектрический слой
P 191	**photocell**, photoelement	Fotozelle *f*, Fotoelement *n*, lichtelektrisches Element *n*	cellule *f* photo-électrique	фотоэлемент
P 192	**photoconductive**	lichtelektrisch leitend	photoconductible	фотопроводящий, характеризующийся фотопроводимостью
P 193	**photoconductive cell**, photoresistance	Fotowiderstand *m*, Fotowiderstandszelle *f*	cellule *f* photorésistante	фотосопротивление
P 194	**photoconductive effect**	innerer fotoelektrischer Effekt *m*, Fotoleitungseffekt *m*	effet *m* photo-électrique interne	эффект фотопроводимости
P 195	**photoconductive layer**	Fotowiderstandsschicht *f*, lichtelektrisch leitende Schicht *f*	couche *f* photo-électrique	фотопроводящий слой
P 196	**photoconductivity**	Fotoleitfähigkeit *f*	conductibilité *f* photo-électrique	фотопроводимость
P 197	**photodiode**	Fotodiode *f*	diode *f* photo-électrique	фотодиод
P 198	**photoelectric effect**	[äußerer] fotoelektrischer Effekt *m*	effet *m* photo-électrique	фотоэлектрический эффект
P 199	**photoelectric emission**, photoemission	Fotoemission *f*, lichtelektrische Emission *f*	émission *f* photo-électrique	фотоэлектрическая эмиссия, фотоэмиссия
P 200	**photoelectricity**	Fotoelektrizität *f*	photo-électricité *f*	фотоэлектричество
P 201	**photoelectric reader**, optical scanner	fotoelektrischer Leser *m*, optischer Abtaser *m*	balayeur *m* optique, lecteur *m* photo-électrique	фотосчитывающее устройство, фотосчитыватель
P 202	**photoelectric receiver**	fotoelektrischer (lichtelektrischer) Empfänger *m*	récepteur *m* photo-électrique	фотоэлектрический приемник
P 203	**photoelectric yield**	fotoelektrische Ausbeute *f*	gain *m* photo-électrique	фотоэлектрический выход
	photoelement	*s.* P 191		
	photoemission	*s.* P 199		
P 204	**photoferroelectric effect**, PFE	fotoferroelektrischer Effekt *m* ‹Bildspeicherung›	effet *m* ferro-photo-électrique	сегнетоэлектрический эффект
P 205	**photographic storage**	fotografischer Speicher *m*	mémoire *f* photographique	фотографическое запоминающее устройство
P 206	**photolithographic diffusion window**	fotolithografisches Diffusionsfenster *n*	fenêtre *f* à diffusion photolithographique	диффузионное окно, полученное методом фотолитографии
	photolithographic mask	*s.* P 210		
P 207	**photolithographic pattern**	fotolithografisches Muster *n*	dessin *m* photolithographique	фотолитографический шаблон; рисунок, нанесенный методом фотолитографии
P 208	**photolithographic process**	fotolithografischer Prozeß *m*	processus *m* photolithographique	фотолитографический процесс
P 209	**photolithography**	Fotolithografie *f*	photolithographie *f*	фотолитография
P 210	**photomask**, photolithographic mask	Fotomaske *f*, fotolithografische Maske (Schablone) *f*	masque *m* photo[lithographique]	фотомаска, фотолитографическая маска

P 211	photomasking	Fotomaskierung f	masquage m photo	фотомаскирование, фотолитография ‹процесс›
P 212	photomask technology	Fotomaskentechnologie f	technologie f à masque photo	технология фотолитографии
P 213	photoprinting	Fotodruck m	impression f photo	фотопечать
P 214	photoresist photoresistance	Fotolack m s. P 193	laque f photo	фоторезист
P 215	physical address	physische (reale) Adresse f	adresse f physique	физический адрес
P 216	physical constraints	physikalische Grenzbedingungen (Beschränkungen) fpl	contraintes fpl physiques	физические ограничения
P 217	physical device	physisches Gerät n	appareil m physique	физическое устройство
P 218	physical layout	physische (räumliche) Anordnung f	aménagement m physique	физическое размещение
P 219	physical size	physische Abmessungen fpl, Baugröße f	dimensions fpl physiques	физический размер
	PIA	s. P 147		
P 220	pickup / to	aufnehmen	enregistrer	снимать, считывать; срабатывать
P 221	pickup	Aufnehmer m, Meßwertaufnehmer m	capteur m de mesure	считывающий (чувствительный) элемент
P 222	pickup value	Ansprechwert m	valeur f de réponse	порог срабатывания
P 223	picoprocessor	Picoprozessor m ‹Subprozessor eines Mikrorechners, z. B. im „intelligenten Kabel"›	picoprocesseur m	пикопроцессор ‹процессор нижнего уровня микро-ЭВМ›
P 224	picosecond	Picosekunde f	picoseconde f	пикосекунда
P 225	piezoelectric crystal	piezoelektrischer Kristall m ‹z. B. Quarz›	cristal m piézo-électrique	пьезоэлектрический кристалл, пьезокристалл
P 226	piezoelectric device	piezoelektrisches Bauteil n	module m piézo-électrique	пьезоэлектрический элемент
P 227	piggy-back EPROM	EPROM-Schaltkreis m in Huckepack-Montage	circuit m EPROM en montage à califurchon	плата электрически программируемого ПЗУ с микросхемами, установленными в контактных панелях
P 228	piggy-back socket	Huckepack-Sockel m, Fassung f auf Schaltkreisgehäuse ‹zur Aufnahme eines weiteren Schaltkreises›	socle m à califurchon	контактная панель для установки микросхем
P 229	pilot reference	Pilotton m, Bezugswelle f	référence f pilote	контрольный сигнал тональной частоты
P 230	pilot run	Piloteinsatz m, Ersteinsatz m	application f pilote	опытное применение
P 231	pilot system	Pilotsystem n, Erkundungssystem n	système m pilote	система проведения опытных испытаний, система сбора экспериментальных данных
P 232	pin	Pin m, Stift m ‹Schaltkreis-Anschlußstift›	fiche f	контактный вывод (штырек)
P 233	pin assignment, pin configuration pinboard	Pinbelegung f, Anschlußbelegung f ‹Schaltkreis› s. P 266	configuration f de fiches	расположение выводов; распределение выводов
P 234	pinch	Einzug m, Karteneinzug m	introduction f [de cartes]	закладка [перфокарт]
P 235	pinch off	Abschnürung f ‹FET-Kanal›	étranglement m	сужение канала [полевого транзистора]; максимальное уменьшение тока [полевого транзистора]
P 236	pin-compatible	pinkompatibel, anschlußbelegungskompatibel	enfichable	совместимый на уровне электрического соединения, совместимый по выводам
	pin configuration	s. P 233		
P 237	pin connect	Pinanschluß m	connexion f à fiche[s]	штырь, подключаемый через внешние контакты
P 238	pin contact	Stiftkontakt m	contact m de fiche	штыревой контакт разъема
P 239	pin count	Pinanzahl f, Anschlußstiftzahl f	nombre m de fiches	число выводов; число контактов
P 240	pinout	Pinausgang m, Anschlußstiftabgang m, Schaltkreisausgang m	sortie f de circuit (fiches)	наружный вывод [микросхемы]
	PIO	s. P 51		
P 241	pipelined architecture	zeitverschachtelt arbeitende Struktur f, Pipeline-Architektur f ‹überlappende Ausführung der Phasen aufeinanderfolgender Operationen›	structure f à travail à la chaîne, structure pipeline	конвейерная архитектура
P 242	pipeline execution	zeitverschachtelte Ausführung f der Befehlsabwicklung, Fließbandausführung f, Pipeline-Ausführung f ‹überlappende Ausführung der Phasen aufeinanderfolgender Befehle›	exécution f pipeline	конвейерная работа
P 243	pipelining	Zeitverschachtelung f der Befehlsabwicklung, Fließband-Arbeitsprinzip n, Pipeline-Arbeitsweise f ‹überlappende Bearbeitung der Phasen aufein-	principe m à travail à la chaîne, principe pipeline	конвейерный принцип

		anderfolgender Befehle durch zueinander parallel und in sich kontinuierlich arbeitende Teilwerke>		
P 244	**PL/1,** programming language 1	PL/1 n, Programmiersprache 1 f <universelle höhere Programmiersprache>	PL/1 m, langage m de programmation 1	PL/1, ПЛ/1 <язык программирования высокого уровня>
P 245	**PLA,** programmable logic array	PLA f, programmierbares Logikgatterfeld n	champ m logique programmable	ПЛМ, программируемая логическая матрица
P 246	**place / to**	plazieren, unterbringen	placer	помещать, размещать
P 247	**placement**	Plazierung f, Unterbringung f	placement m	размещение
P 248	**placement algorithm**	Plazierungsalgorithmus m	algorithme m de placement	алгоритм размещения
P 249	**planar epitaxial process**	Planarepitaxieverfahren n	procédé m épitaxial planaire	эпитаксиально-планарная технология
P 250	**planar MOSFET**	Planar-MOSFET m, Planar-MOS-Feldeffekttransistor m, MOSFET m mit Oberflächenstruktur	FET m MOS planaire	планарный МОП-транзистор, МОП-транзистор, изготовленный по планарной технологии
P 251	**planar process**	Planarprozeß m	processus m planaire	планарный процесс
P 252	**planar structure**	Planarstruktur f, flächenhafte (ebene) Struktur f	structure f planaire	планарная структура
P 253	**planar technique (technology)**	Planartechnik f	technique f planaire	планарная технология
P 254	**planar transistor**	Planartransistor m, Flächentransistor m	transistor m planaire	планарный транзистор
P 255	**plasma display**	Plasmaanzeige f	affichage m au plasma	плазменный (газоразрядный) дисплей
P 256	**plastic package**	Plastgehäuse n	boîtier m en matière plastique	пластмассовый корпус
P 257	**plate / to**	plattieren, überziehen, galvanisieren	plaquer, recouvrir, galvaniser	покрывать, гальванизировать
	plate	s. B 225		
P 258	**plated-through hole**	durchkontaktiertes Loch n	trou m contacté	металлизированное отверстие
P 259	**playback**	Wiedergabe f	reproduction f	воспроизведение, считывание
	PLL	s. P 180		
	PLL motor control	s. P 181		
P 260	**PL/M,** programming language for microcomputer	PL/M n <universelle höhere Programmiersprache für Mikrorechner>	PL/M m <langage de programmation pour microcalculateurs>	PL/M, ПЛ/М <язык программирования высокого уровня для микроЭВМ>
P 261	**plot / to**	plottern, maschinell zeichnen, grafisch darstellen	dessiner mécaniquement, représenter graphiquement	наносить, представлять графически
P 262	**plotter**	Plotter m <Kurvenschreiber mit Zeichentrommel und Schrittmotorantrieb>	traceur m	графопостроитель
P 263	**plotting**	maschinelles Zeichnen n, grafisches Darstellen n	dessin m mécanique	построение, графическое представление
P 264	**plug / to**	stecken, stöpseln	enficher	вставлять
P 265	**plug**	Stecker m	fiche f	[штепсельный] разъем; штекер
P 266	**plugboard,** pinboard, patchboard	Stecktafel f	tableau m à enficher	наборное поле, коммутационная панель
P 267	**plug-compatible**	steckkompatibel	compatible par fiches	совместимый на уровне разъемов
P 268	**plug connection**	Steckverbindung f	connexion f à fiches	разъемное соединение
	plug connector	s. E 14		
P 269	**plug contact**	Steckkontakt m	contact m à fiche	штепсельный контакт
P 270	**pluggable**	steckbar	enfichable	сменный, съемный
P 271	**plugging chart**	Steckschema n	schéma m de fiches	схема коммутации
P 272	**plug-in arrangement**	Einschubanordnung f	disposition f en tiroir	расположение сменных блоков; монтаж сменных блоков
P 273	**plug-in board**	Steckeinheit f, steckbare Leiterplatte f	unité f enfichable	сменная плата с разъемом
P 274	**plug-in cabling**	Steckkabeltechnik f, Steckverkabelung f	câblage m à fiches	разъемное соединение кабеля
P 275	**plug-in card**	Steckkarte f	carte f enfichable	сменная [печатная] плата
P 276	**plug-in chassis**	Geräteeinschub m, steckbarer Montagerahmen m	tiroir m d'appareil, châssis m enfichable	съемное шасси, вставляемое шасси
P 277	**plug-in console**	Steckkonsole f <Mikrorechnerservicegerät>	console f enfichable	вспомогательный пульт, подключаемый через разъем
P 278	**plug-in construction**	Einschubkonstruktion f, Einschubaufbau m	construction f en tiroirs	конструкция на основе сменных блоков [с разъемами]
P 279	**plug-in IC**	Einsteck-SK m, steckbarer Schaltkreis m	CI m enfichable	сменная (вставляемая) ИС
P 280	**plug-in module**	Steckmodul m, steckbarer Modul m, steckbare Baugruppe f	module m enfichable	сменный модуль [с разъемом], съемный модуль
P 281	**plug-in printed circuit board**	einsteckbare gedruckte Leiterplatte f	circuit m imprimé enfichable	вставляемая печатная плата [с разъемом]
P 282	**plug-in technique**	Einschubtechnik f	technique f enfichable	компоновка системы на основе сменных модулей
P 283	**plug-in unit**	Einschub m, Einsteckeinheit f	tiroir m, unité f enfichable	сменный (вставляемый) блок
P 284	**plug-PROM**	Steck-PROM m	mémoire f lecture seule programmable enfichable, PROM f enfichable	модуль программируемого ПЗУ, подключаемый с помощью разъема
P 285	**plug strip**	Steckerleiste f	réglette f à fiches	колодка [штепсельного] разъема

P 286	**plug-to-plug com-patibility**	Steckkompatibilität *f*, Steckverträglichkeit *f*	compatibilité *f* de fiches	полная совместимость, совместимость на уровне разъемов
P 287	**plug wire**	Steckdraht *m*	fil *m* à fiche	[сменная] проводная перемычка
P 288	**PLUS** ‹programming language for microcomputer systems›	PLUS *n* ‹Programmiersprache für Mikrorechnersystem, entwickelt für Typ 2650›	PLUS *m* ‹langage de programmation pour système de microcalculateurs›	PLUS ‹язык программирования микропроцессорных систем› ‹система 2650 фирмы Signetics›
P 289	**plus sign**	Pluszeichen *n*	signe *m* plus	знак «плюс»
	pMOS, PMOS	s. P 104		
	pMOS circuit	s. P 105		
	PMOS-technology	s. P 104		
P 290	**p-n barrier, p-n junction**	pn-Sperrschicht *f*, pn-Barriere *f*, pn-Übergang *m*	barrière *f* p-n, jonction *f* p-n	барьер p-n перехода, p-n переход
P 291	**p-n boundary**	pn-Grenzschicht *f*	couche *f* limite p-n	граничный слой p-n перехода
	p-n junction	s. P 290		
	pn-junction transistor	s. J 29		
P 292	**p-n-p transistor**	pnp-Transistor *m*	transistor *m* de type p-n-p	p-n-p транзистор
P 293	**pocket calculator (computer)**	Taschenrechner *m*	calculateur *m* de poche	карманный калькулятор
P 294	**pocket-sized**	ın Taschenformat	en format de poche	карманный
P 295	**point**	Punkt *m*	point *m*	точка; пункт; место
P 296	**point contact**	Spitzenkontakt *m*	contact *m* de pointe	точечный контакт
P 297	**point contact diode**	Spitzenkontaktdiode *f*	diode *f* à pointe	точечный диод
P 298	**pointer**	Zeiger *m*, Hinweisadresse *f*	pointeur *m*	указатель
P 299	**pointer register**	Zeigerregister *n*, Hinweisregister *n* ‹Referenzadressenregister›	registre *m* de pointeur	регистр-указатель
P 300	**point of sale**	Verkaufsplatz *m*	place *f* de ventes	пункт для выполнения финансовых операций ‹торговля, кредит, и т.д.›
P 301	**point of sale terminal**	s. C 71		
P 301	**point position**	Kommastellung *f*	position *f* de virgule	положение запятой
P 302	**point shifting**	Kommaverschiebung *f*	décalage *m* de virgule	сдвиг запятой
P 303	**point-to-point [positioning] control, positioning control**	Punktsteuerung *f*	commande *f* par points	позиционное управление
P 304	**point transistor**	Spitzentransistor *m*	transistor *m* à pointe	точечный транзистор
P 305	**polar coordinates**	Polarkoordinaten *fpl*	coordonnées *fpl* polaires	полярные координаты
P 306	**polar display**	Polarkoordinatendarstellung *f*	représentation *f* en coordonnées polaires	индикация в полярных координатах
P 307	**polarity**	Polarität *f*	polarité *f*	полярность
P 308	**polarization**	Polarisation *f*	polarisation *f*	поляризация; поляризованность
P 309	**polarization state**	Polarisationszustand *m*	état *m* de polarisation	состояние поляризации, поляризованное состояние
P 310	**polarize / to**	polarisieren, polen	polariser	поляризовать
P 311	**polarized plug**	gepolter Stecker *m*	fiche *f* polarisée	разъем с [защитным] ключом ‹конструкция разъема с защитой от неправильного соединения›
P 312	**polish notation**	polnische Notation *f*	notation *f* polonaise	польская [инверсная] запись
P 313	**poll / to**	abrufen, ausgewählt abfragen	interroger	опрашивать
P 314	**polled environment**	auswählend abzufragende Systemumgebung *f*	environnement *m* interrogeant	опрашиваемое оборудование
P 315	**polling**	Abrufen *n* ‹zyklisches Abfragen von Eingabestationen über Testbefehle›, Abfrageverfahren *n*	interrogation *f*	опрос, запрос передачи ‹периодический опрос оконечных устройств для определения запроса на обслуживание›
P 316	**polling architecture**	Abruf-Strukturprinzip *n* ‹auf Testabfrage orientierte Architektur›	structure *f* d'interrogation	структура, построенная на принципе периодического опроса
P 317	**polling character**	Abrufzeichen *n*	caractère *m* d'interrogation	опросный символ
P 318	**polling interrupt system**	Abruf-Interruptsystem *n* ‹Unterbrechungssystem mit programmierter zyklischer Anforderungsabfrage›	système *m* d'interruption d'interrogation	система определения источника прерывания методом опроса
P 319	**polling interval**	Abrufintervall *n*	intervalle *m* d'interrogation	интервал опроса
P 320	**polling loop**	Abrufschleife *f* ‹zyklische Abfragefolge›	boucle *f* d'interrogation	петля опроса
P 321	**polling mode**	Abruf-Betriebsart *f*	régime *m* d'interrogation	режим опроса
P 322	**polling operation**	Abrufoperation *f*	opération *f* d'interrogation	операция опроса
P 323	**polling procedure**	Abrufverfahren *n*	procédé *m* d'interrogation	процедура опроса
P 324	**polling technique**	Abruftechnik *f*	technique *f* d'interrogation	способ выполнения процедуры опроса
P 325	**polycristalline structure**	polykristalline Struktur *f*, mehrkristalliner Aufbau *m*	structure *f* polycristalline	поликристаллическая структура
P 326	**polyphase**	mehrphasig	polyphasé	многофазный
P 327	**polysilicon**	Polysilizium *n*	polysilicium *m*	поликремний, поликристаллический кремний
P 328	**polysilicon gate**	Polysiliziumgate *n*, Polysiliziumgateelektrode *f*	gate *m* au polysilicium	поликремниевый затвор

P 329	**polysilicon layer**	Polysiliziumschicht f	couche f au polysilicium	слой поликремния
P 330	**polysilicon resistor**	Polysiliziumwiderstand m, Widerstand m aus Polysilizium	résistance f au polysilicium	поликремниевый резистор
P 331	**polyvalence**	Mehrwertigkeit f	polyvalence f	многозначность; многовалентность; многопараметрическая представимость
P 332	**pop instruction,** pull instruction	Kellerdatenholebefehl m, Auskellerungsbefehl m	instruction f de sortie de mémoire-cave	команда извлечения (вывода) из стека
P 333	**pop off stack / to**	vom Kellerspeicher holen, auskellern	chercher de la mémoire-cave	извлечь из стека, вывести из стека
P 334	**pop up / to**	hervorholen, auftauchen	relever, surgir	доставать, извлекать
P 335	**port**	Tor n, Anschlußstelle f	porte f	порт; место подключения
P 336	**portability**	Übertragbarkeit f <von Programmen, Entwürfen, Lösungen usw.>, Portabilität f	portabilité f	портативность
P 337	**portable**	übertragbar, tragbar	portable	портативный, переносной
P 338	**portable data collection terminal**	tragbares Datenerfassungsterminal n	terminal m de collection de données portable	переносное устройство сбора данных
P 339	**portable data entry terminal**	tragbares Dateneingabeterminal n	terminal m d'entrée de données portable	переносной терминал ввода данных
P 340	**portable terminal**	tragbares Terminal (Datenendgerät) n, Handterminal n	terminal m portable	переносной терминал, портативное оконечное устройство
P 341	**portable use**	Trageinsatz m, Verwendung f in Trageform	usage m sous forme portable	применение в качестве переносного устройства
P 342	**port controller**	Torsteuerung f	commande f de porte	контроллер порта
P 343	**port selection**	Torauswahl f, Anschlußstellenauswahl f	sélection f de porte	выбор порта
P 344	**position**	Stelle f, Lage f, Ort m, Stellung f	position f	позиция, местоположение
P 345	**positional operand**	Stellenoperand m	opérande m de position	позиционный операнд
P 346	**position code**	Positionskode m, Stellenkode m	code m de position	позиционный код
P 347	**position-dependent code**	positionsabhängiger (stellungsabhängiger) Kode m	code m dépendant de position	позиционно-зависимый код
P 348	**position-independent code**	positionsunabhängiger (stellungsunabhängiger) Kode m	code m indépendant de position	позиционно-независимый код
P 349	**positioning**	Positionierung f	positionnement m	позиционирование
P 350	**positioning control**	s. P 303		
P 350	**positive bias**	positive Vorspannung f	polarisation f positive	положительное смещение
P 351	**positive charge**	positive Ladung f	charge f positive	положительный заряд
P 352	**positive condition,** P condition	Positiv-Bedingung f	condition f positive	условие положительного результата [операции]
P 353	**positive feedback,** regenerative feedback	Mitkopplung f, positive Rückkopplung f	réaction f positive	положительная обратная связь
P 354	**positive logic**	positive Logik (Schaltungslogik) f <oberer Pegel entspricht logisch Eins>	logique f positive	положительная логика <логической 1 соответствует высокий уровень сигнала>
P 355	**positive-logic circuit**	Positivlogikschaltung f	circuit m à logique positive	схема положительной логики
P 356	**positive-logic signal**	Positivlogiksignal n <hoher Pegel entspricht logisch Eins>	signal m à logique positive	сигнал положительной логики
P 357	**post-editing**	Nachedieren n	édition f postérieure	постредактирование
P 358	**postfix**	Postfix m <Operator am Ausdrucksende>	postfix m	постфикс
P 359	**post-indexing**	Nachindizierung f	postindexage m	постиндексация
P 360	**post-mortem routine**	Post-mortem-Programm n, Fehlersuchprogramm n auf Basis Speicherinhaltsausgabe	programme m post mortem	постпрограмма, программа вывода после останова <обслуживающая программа вывода содержимого памяти для выявления ошибок>
P 361	**postprocessor**	Postprozessor m, Nachverarbeitungsprogramm n, Anpassungsprogramm n <NC-Steuerung>	postprocesseur m	постпроцессор
	pot	s. P 367		
P 362	**potential application**	potentielle Anwendung f, Anwendungsmöglichkeit f	application f potentielle	потенциальное (перспективное) применение
P 363	**potential barrier**	Potentialschwelle f, Potentialwall m	seuil m (barrière f) de potentiel	потенциальный барьер
P 364	**potential distribution**	Potentialverteilung f, Potentialverlauf m	distribution f de potentiel	распределение потенциала
P 365	**potential drop**	Potentialabfall m	chute f de potentiel	падение потенциала
P 366	**potential jump**	Potentialsprung m	saut m de potentiel	скачок потенциала, потенциальный скачок
P 367	**potentiometer,** pot	Potentiometer n	potentiomètre m	потенциометр
P 368	**power,** performance	Leistung f	puissance f	мощность
P 369	**power amplifier**	Leistungsverstärker m	amplificateur m de puissance	усилитель мощности
P 370	**power consumption,** power drain	Leistungsverbrauch m, Leistungsaufnahme f	consommation f de puissance	потребляемая мощность; потребление мощности
P 371	**power-delay product,** pd product	pd-Produkt n, Leistung-Verzögerungszeit-Pro-	produit m pd	произведение потребляемой мощности на время

and still: P 371		dukt n ‹Produkt der Ver- lustleistung und der Ver- zögerungszeit eines Logik- gatters›		задержки сигнала, про- изведение «задержка × мощность» ‹характерис- тика качества инте- гральных схем›
P 372	power derating, degra- dation of performance	Leistungsverminderung f	réduction (diminution) f de puissance	снижение мощности
P 373	power dissipation, dis- sipation	Verlustleistung f	puissance f dissipée, dissi- pation f	рассеяние мощности
P 374	power-down	Ausschalten n der Strom- versorgung	mise f au repos de l'alimen- tation	отключение электро- питания
	power drain	s. P 370		
P 375	power driver	Leistungstreiber m	basculeur m de puissance	формирователь с мощным выходом, силовой фор- мирователь
	power dump	s. P 376		
P 376	power fail[ure], power outage (dump)	Netzausfall m, Stromausfall m, Stromversorgungsaus- fall m	manque m d'alimentation, manque de secteur	неисправность [источ- ника] питания, отказ [источника] питания
P 377	power fail[ure] interrupt	Stromausfallinterrupt m	interruption f de manque de courant	прерывание при отказе питания
P 378	power fail[ure]/restart	Stromausfall/Neuanlauf m	manque m de courant/ redémarrage m	отключение/восстановле- ние электропитания
P 379	power frequency	Netzfrequenz f	fréquence f du secteur	частота сети электро- питания
P 380	powerful	leistungsfähig	puissant	мощный; производитель- ный; эффективный
P 381	power gain	Leistungsverstärkung f, Leistungsgewinn m	gain m de puissance	усиление по мощности; коэффициент усиления по мощности
P 382	power ground	Stromversorgungsmasse f	masse f de l'alimentation	заземление источника пи- тания, «земля» источ- ника питания
P 383	power input	aufgenommene Leistung f	puissance f consommée	входная мощность
P 384	power level	Leistungspegel m	niveau m de puissance	уровень мощности
P 385	power line	Netzleitung f	ligne f de secteur	линия сети
P 386	power loss	Leistungsverlust m	perte f de puissance	потери мощности
P 387	power MOSFET	MOS-Feldeffekt-Leistungs- transistor m	transistor m MOS de puis- sance à effet de champ	мощный МОП-транзистор
P 388	power-on reset	Grundzustandseinstellung f bei Netzeinschaltung	établissement m de l'état initial à l'enclenchement du secteur	установка микро-ЭВМ в начальное состояние при включении питания
	power outage	s. P 376		
P 389	power output	abgegebene Leistung f	puissance f de sortie	отдаваемая мощность
P 390	power pack	Netzgerät n, Netzteil n	bloc m secteur	блок питания
P 391	power rating, rated (nominal) power, rated (nominal) output, rated performance	Nennleistung f	puissance f nominale	номинальная мощность
P 392	power requirements	Leistungsbedarf m, Strom- versorgungsanforderun- gen fpl	exigences fpl à l'alimentation	требования по мощности
P 393	power strobing	Stromversorgungstastung f	manipulation f d'alimen- tation	импульсное питание
P 394	power supply	Stromversorgung f	alimentation f en courant	электропитание
P 395	power supply sensitivity	Empfindlichkeit f gegen- über Versorgungsspan- nungsschwankungen	sensibilité f d'alimentation	чувствительность к изме- нению напряжения питания
	power supply voltage	s. S 859		
P 396	power switch	Leistungsschalter m	disjoncteur m	силовой выключатель
P 397	power transistor	Leistungstransistor m	transistor m de puissance	силовой (мощный) тран- зистор
P 398	power-up	Einschalten n der Stromver- ⌐sorgung	mise f en marche de l'ali- mentation	включение (подача) электропитания
	PPI	s. P 589		
	PPM	s. P 726		
P 399	preamplifier	Vorverstärker m	préamplificateur m	предварительный усили- тель, предусилитель
P 400	preceding	vorhergehend, vorangehend	précédant	предшествующий
P 401	precharge / to	vorladen ‹elektrisch›	précharger ‹électrique›	предварительно заряжать, подзаряжать
P 402	precharge set-up time	Vorladezeit f, Vorladezeit- bedarf m	temps m de préchargement	время подзаряда
P 403	predecessor	Vorgänger m	prédécesseur m	предшествующий образец
P 404	prediction	Vorhersage f, Prognose f	prévision f, pronostic m	предсказание
P 405	predictive control	vorausschauende Steuerung f	commande f préventive	управление с предсказа- нием
P 406	preferred value	Vorzugswert m	valeur f de préférence	стандартный номинал, номинал стандартной шкалы ‹резисторы, конденсаторы›
P 407	prefetch / to	vorausholen, vorlaufend holen	chercher d'avance	предварительно вызывать (выбирать)
P 408	prefetch buffer	Puffer m für vorausgeholte Informationen	tampon m pour informations cherchées d'avance	буфер предварительной выборки
P 409	prefetching	vorausschauende Speicher- abruftechnik f	technique f d'appel de mémoire préventif	предварительный вызов, предварительная вы- борка
P 410	prefix	Präfix n ‹Operator am Aus- drucksanfang›	préfixe m	префикс
P 411	p-region	p-Bereich m, p-leitende Zone f	région f p	p-область, область про- водимости p-типа
P 412	pre-indexing	Vorindizierung f	préindexage m	предварительная индек- сация
P 413	preliminary data pro- cessing	vorbereitende Datenver- arbeitung f	traitement m préliminaire de données	предварительная (под- готовительная) обра- ботка данных

P 414	preliminary logic	vorläufige Logik (Logik-schaltung) f	logique f préliminaire	логические схемы пред-варительной обработки
P 415	preliminary program	vorläufiges Programm n	programme m préliminaire	предварительная про-грамма
P 416	preparation time, lead time	Vorbereitungszeit f	temps m de préparation	время подготовки
P 417	preprocessing	Vorverarbeitung f	prétraitement m	предварительная обра-ботка
P 418	preprocessor	Vorprozessor m, Vorver-arbeitungsprozessor m	processeur m de prétraite-ment	предпроцессор, препро-цессор
P 419	preprogrammed	vorprogrammiert	préprogrammé	предварительно запро-граммированный
P 420	prepulse	Vorimpuls m	impulsion f préalable	предварительный (под-готавливающий) импульс
P 421	prerunning	Vorlaufen n	marche f d'avance	предварительный прогон
P 422	prescaler	Voruntersetzer m	prédémultiplicateur m	[предварительный] делитель частоты
P 423	preselection	Vorauswahl f	présélection f	предварительная селек-ция, предварительный выбор
P 424	presence	Vorhandensein n, Anwesen-heit f	présence f	присутствие
P 425	present-day state of the art	gegenwärtiger Stand m der Technik	l'état m actuel de la tech-nique	современное состояние [развития] техники
P 426	preset counter, batch counter	Vorwahlzähler m	compteur m à présélection	счетчик с предваритель-ной установкой
P 427	presettable	voreinstellbar	ajustable d'avance	предварительно устана-вливаемый
P 428	presettable I/O con-ditions	voreinstellbare E/A-Bedin-gungen fpl	conditions fpl d'E/S ajustables d'avance	предварительно устана-вливаемое состояние устройств ввода-вы-вода
P 429	presetting	Voreinstellen n, Festlegen n von Anfangsbedingungen	fixation f d'une condition initiale	предварительная уста-новка
P 430	prestage	Vorstufe f	étage m préliminaire	предварительный каскад
P 431	prestore / to	vorspeichern	mettre en mémoire d'avance	предварительно запоми-нать
P 432	pretested	vorgeprüft	contrôlé d'avance	предварительно про-веренный
P 433	pretranslator	Vorübersetzer m	traducteur m d'avance	предтранслятор
P 434	preventive maintenance	vorbeugende Wartung f	maintenance f prophylacti-que	профилактическое обслуживание
P 435	previous contents	vorhergehender (vorheriger) Inhalt m	contenu m précédent	предыдущее (предшест-вующее) содержимое
P 436	previous mode	vorhergehender Modus m, vorherige Betriebsart f	mode m précédent	предшествующий режим
P 437	previous status	vorhergehender (vorheriger) Status m	état m précédent	предшествующее (преды-дущее) состояние
P 438	prewired PRF	vorverdrahtet s. P 730	câblé d'avance	предварительно закомму-тированный
P 439	price-performance improvement	Verbesserung f des Preis-Leistungs-Verhältnisses	amélioration f du rapport prix-performance	улучшение соотношения стоимость / произво-дительность
P 440	price-performance ratio	Preis-Leistungs-Verhältnis n	rapport m prix-performances	отношение стоимость/ производительность
P 441	primary current	Primärstrom m	courant m primaire	ток в первичной цепи
P 442	primary data	Primärdaten pl	données fpl primaires	первичные данные
P 443	primary memory (store)	Primärspeicher m	mémoire f primaire	основная память, первич-ное запоминающее устройство
P 444	principle of construction principle of operation	Aufbauprinzip n s. O 114	principe m de construction	принцип построения
P 445	print buffer	Druckpuffer m	tampon m d'impression	буферная память печатаю-щего устройства, буфер печати
P 446	print control	Drucksteuerung f	commande f d'impression	управление выводом на печать, управление печатью
P 447	printed circuit	gedruckte Schaltung f	circuit m imprimé	печатная схема
P 448	printed circuit board, PC board	gedruckte Leiterplatte f	circuit m imprimé	печатная плата
P 449	printed circuit bread-board	gedruckte Universalraster-leiterplatte f	carte f universelle à circuit imprimé	универсальная печатная плата
P 450	printed circuit edge con-nector, PC edge con-nector, board connector	Leiterplatten-Steckver-binder m, Steckverbinder m einer gedruckten Leiterplatte	connecteur m de circuit imprimé	торцевой разъем печатной платы
P 451	printed circuit layout, PC layout	LP-Layout n, Leiterplatten-l belegungsplan m <Leiter-zugführung und Baustein-anordnung>	ayout m de circuit imprimé	топология печатных ком-понент; топология печати
P 452	printed circuit master, PC master	Leiterplattenoriginal n	circuit m imprimé maître	чертеж печатной платы; фотооригинал печатной платы
P 453	printed contact	gedruckter Kontakt m	contact m imprimé	печатный контакт
P 454	printed element	gedrucktes Bauelement n	élément m imprimé	печатный элемент (компонент)
P 455	printed wiring	gedruckte Verdrahtung f	câblage m imprimé	печатный монтаж
P 456	printer	Drucker m	imprimante f	печатающее устройство
P 457	printer (printing) con-trol	Druckersteuerung f	commande f d'imprimante	управление печатающим устройством
P 458	printing format	Druckformat n	format m d'impression	формат печати
P 459	printing rate (speed)	Druckgeschwindigkeit f	vitesse f d'impression	скорость печати

P 460	print-out	Ausdruck m <Drucker>, Druckbild n	impression f, aspect m d'impression	распечатка
P 461	print suppression	Schreibunterdrückung f	suppression f d'écriture	блокировка печати
P 462	print unit	Schreibwerk n, Druckwerk n	unité f d'impression	блок печати (печатающего устройства)
P 463	print wheel	Typenrad n	roue f à types	печатающее (литерное) колесо
P 464	prioritize / to	priorisieren, bevorrechten	accorder des priorités	устанавливать (назначать) приоритет
P 465	prioritized interrupt	priorisierter Interrupt m, vorrangige Unterbrechung f	interruption f prioritaire	приоритетное прерывание
P 466	priority	Priorität f, Vorrang m	priorité f	приоритет; приоритетность
P 467	priority arbitration	Prioritätsentscheidung f, Vorrangentscheidung f	arbitrage m de priorité	разрешение конфликтов на основе приоритетов
P 468	priority chain	Prioritätskette f <serielles Vorrangentscheidungsprinzip>	chaîne f de priorités	приоритетная последовательность (цепочка)
P 469	priority circuit	Vorrangschaltung f, Prioritätsschaltung f	circuit m prioritaire	приоритетная схема
P 470	priority comparator	Prioritätsvergleicher m	comparateur m de priorité	приоритетный компаратор, схема сравнения приоритетов
P 471	priority control	Vorrangsteuerung f, Prioritätssteuerung f	commande f de priorité	управление по приоритету, приоритетное управление
P 472	priority dispatching	Prioritätszuteilung f	attribution f de priorité	приоритетная диспетчеризация, упорядочивание по приоритету
P 473	priority encoder	Prioritätsverschlüßler m <erzeugt Schlüsselnummer für den vorrangigsten der anliegenden prioritätsgestuften Interrupts>	codeur m de priorité	приоритетный шифратор
P 474	priority fashion	Prioritätstyp m, Vorrangtyp m	type m de priorité	структура приоритетов
P 475	priority hierarchy	Prioritätenhierarchie f, Vorrangstufung f	hiérarchie f de priorité	иерархия приоритетов, приоритетная иерархия
P 476	priority indicator	Prioritätsanzeiger m, Vorranganzeiger m	indicateur m de priorité	указатель приоритета
P 477	priority interrupt	Prioritätsinterrupt m, Vorrangunterbrechung f	interruption f de priorité	приоритетное прерывание
P 478	priority interrupt control	Prioritätsinterruptsteuerung f, Vorrangunterbrechungssteuerung f	commande f d'interruption de priorité	управление приоритетными прерываниями
P 479	priority interrupt system	vorranggestuftes (hierarchisches) Unterbrechungssystem n, Prioritätsinterruptsystem n	système m d'interruption de priorité	система приоритетных прерываний
P 480	priority level	Vorrangebene f, Prioritätsebene f	niveau m de priorité	уровень приоритета
P 481	priority processing	Prioritätsverarbeitung f, vorranggerechte Verarbeitung f	traitement m prioritaire	обработка по приоритетам
P 482	priority program	Prioritätsprogramm n, Vorrangprogramm n	programme m prioritaire	приоритетная программа
P 483	priority resolver	Prioritätsauflöser m, Vorrangauflöser m	découpeur m de priorités	блок разрешения конфликтов на приоритетной основе
P 484	priority scheduling	Prioritätsplanung f, Prioritätseinteilung f	planning m de priorités	планирование [заданий] по приоритетам
P 485	priority status	Prioritätsstatus m, Vorrangstatus m	état m de priorités	приоритетное состояние
P 486	priority structure	Prioritätsstruktur f, Vorrangstruktur f	structure f de priorités	структура приоритетов; приоритетная структура
P 487	priority system	Prioritätssystem n, Vorrangsystem n	système m prioritaire	система приоритетов; приоритетная система
P 488	privileged instruction	privilegierter Befehl m	instruction f privilégiée	привилегированная команда
P 489	privileged operation	privilegierte Operation f	opération f privilégiée	привилегированная операция
P 490	probe	Taster m, Sonde f	sonde f, palpeur m	пробник, зонд
P 491	problem definition	Problemdefinition f, Problembestimmung f	définition f de problème	постановка задачи
P 492	problem description	Problembeschreibung f	description f de problème	описание задачи
P 493	problem-oriented language	problemorientierte Programmiersprache f	langage m orienté problèmes	проблемно-ориентированный язык
P 494	problem-oriented software package	problemorientiertes Softwarepaket (Systemunterlagenpaket) n	paquet m [de] logiciel[s] orienté problème	проблемно-ориентированный пакет системного программного обеспечения
P 495	procedure	Prozedur f, Verfahren n	procédure f, procédé m	процедура
P 496	procedure declaration	Prozedurvereinbarung f	déclaration f de procédure	описание процедуры
P 497	procedure-oriented language	prozedurorientierte (verfahrensorientierte) Programmiersprache f	langage m orienté procédé	процедурно-ориентированный язык
P 498	procedure statement	Prozeduranweisung f	instruction f de procédure	оператор процедуры
P 499	process / to	verarbeiten	traiter	обрабатывать
P 500	process algorithm	Prozeßalgorithmus m	algorithme m de processus	алгоритм управления объектом
P 501	process automation	Prozeßautomatisierung f	automation f de processus	автоматизация производственных процессов

P 502	process control	Prozeßsteuerung f	commande f de processus	управление производственными процессами
P 503	process control computer	Prozeßrechner m	calculateur m de processus	управляющая ЭВМ, ЭВМ для управления производственными процессами
P 504	process control language	Prozeßsteuerungssprache f	langage m de commande de processus	язык управления производственными процессами, язык описания задач управления объектом
P 505	process data	Prozeßdaten pl, Prozeßinformationen fpl	données fpl de processus	информация об объекте управления, информация о процессе
P 506	processing	Verarbeitung f	traitement m	обработка
P 507	processing capability	Verarbeitungsfähigkeit f	faculté f de traitement	возможности обработки
P 508	processing capacity	Verarbeitungskapazität f	capacité f de traitement	производительность обработки
	processing centre	s. C 550		
P 509	processing cycle	Verarbeitungszyklus m	cycle m de traitement	цикл обработки
P 510	processing equipment	Fertigungsausrüstung f	équipement m de traitement	оборудование для обработки
P 511	processing monitoring	Prozeßüberwachung f	surveillance f de traitement	контроль обработки
P 512	processing operation	Verarbeitungsoperation f	opération f de traitement	операция обработки
P 513	processing part	Verarbeitungsteil m	partie f de traitement	частная функция обработки [данных]
P 514	processing power, logical processing power	Verarbeitungsleistung f, logische Verarbeitungsleistung	performance f de traitement	производительность вычислительного оборудования
P 515	processing section	Verarbeitungsabschnitt m	section f de traitement	устройство обработки [процессора]
P 516	processing speed	Verarbeitungsgeschwindigkeit f	vitesse f de traitement	скорость обработки
P 517	processing step	Prozeßschritt m, Bearbeitungsschritt m, Verarbeitungsschritt m	pas m de traitement	стадия обработки; шаг обработки
P 518	processing throughput	Verarbeitungsdurchsatz m	volume m de traitement	пропускная способность обработки
	processing unit	s. P 519		
P 519	processor, processing (processor) unit	Prozessor m, Verarbeitungseinheit f	processeur m, unité f de traitement (processeur)	процессор, процессорный блок
P 520	processor chip	Prozessorschaltkreis m	circuit m de processeur, puce f à processeur	БИС [центрального] процессора
P 521	processor clock	Prozessortakt m	rythme m de processeur	синхронизация процессора
P 522	processor-controlled exchange	prozessorgesteuerte Vermittlungsstelle f	point m de communication à commande par processeur	коммутатор с процессорным управлением
P 523	processor cycle	Prozessorzyklus m	cycle m de processeur	[рабочий] цикл процессора
P 524	processor element	Prozessorelement n, Baustein m einer Verarbeitungseinheit	élément m de processeur	процессорный элемент
P 525	processor interface	Prozessorschnittstelle f	interface f de processeur	интерфейс процессора
P 526	processor interrupt	Prozessorunterbrechung f	interruption f de processeur	прерывание процессора
P 527	processor intervention	Prozessoreingriff m	intervention f de processeur	вмешательство (воздействие) процессора
P 528	processor module	Prozessormodul m	module m de processeur	процессорный модуль
P 529	processor portion	Prozessorteil n	partie f de processeur	процессорная часть
P 530	processor power	Prozessorleistung f	performance f de processeur	производительность процессора
P 531	processor register	Prozessorregister n	registre m de processeur	регистр процессора
P 532	processor status word, PSW	Prozessorstatuswort n	mot m d'état de processeur	слово состояния процессора, ССП
	processor unit	s. P 519		
	producer	s. M 145		
P 533	production automation	Produktionsautomatisierung f	automation f de production	автоматизация производства
	production control	s. M 146		
	production cost	s. M 147		
P 534	production equipment	Produktionsausrüstung f, Fertigungsanlage f	équipement m de fabrication	производственное оборудование
P 535	production rate	Produktionsrate f, Fertigungsquote f	cote f de fabrication	скорость изготовления
	production series	s. S 274		
P 536	production test	Fertigungsprüfung f	test m de fabrication	производственный контроль, производственные испытания
P 537	productive sampling test	Produktionsstichprobe f	test m d'échantillon de production	выборочный производственный контроль, выборочные производственные испытания
P 538	product line	Produktlinie f	ligne f de produit	производственная линия
P 539	product scheduling	Produktionsplanung f	planning m de production	планирование производства
P 540	program	Programm n	programme m	программа
P 541	program analyzer	Programmanalysator m	analyseur m de programme	программный анализатор
P 542	program bank	Programmbank f	banque f de programmes	банк программ
P 543	program branch	Programmzweig m	branche f (branchement m) de programme	ветвь программы; ветвление программы
P 544	program carrier	Programmträger m	support m de programme	программный носитель
P 545	program change	Programmwechsel m	échange m de programme	смена программ
P 546	program code	Programmkode m	code m de programme	код программы
P 547	program compatibility	Programmkompatibilität f, Programmverträglichkeit f	compatibilité f de programmes	программная совместимость
	program compilation	s. P 649		
P 548	program control	Programmsteuerung f	commande f de programme	программное управление

P 549	program control instruction	Programmsteuerbefehl m	instruction f de commande de programme	команда программного управления
P 550	program-controlled device	programmgesteuertes Gerät n	appareil m à commande programmée	программно-управляемое устройство
P 551	program-controlled priority interrupt system	programmgesteuertes Vorrangunterbrechungssystem n	système m d'interruption de priorités à commande programmée	программно-управляемая система приоритетных прерываний
P 552	program control unit	Programmsteuereinheit f	unité f de commande de programme	устройство управления прохождением программы
	program counter	s. I 237		
P 553	program debugging	Programmaustesten n, Programmfehlersuche f	essai (test) m de programme	отладка программы
P 554	program-dependent	programmabhängig	dépendant de programme	программно-зависимый; программно-обнаруживаемый
P 555	program description	Programmbeschreibung f	description f de programme	описание программы
P 556	program design	Programmentwurf m	conception f de programme	разработка программы
P 557	program development system	Programmentwicklungssystem n	système m de développement de programmes	система разработки программ
P 558	program documentation	Programmdokumentation f	documentation f de programme	документация на программу
P 559	program entry	Programmeingang m, Programmeintrittsstelle f	entrée f de programme	вход в программу, точка входа в программу
P 560	program error	Programmfehler m	erreur f de programme	программная ошибка
	program evolution and review technique	s. P 163		
P 561	program fetch	Programmabruf m, Programmholen n	appel m de programme	вызов (выборка) программы
P 562	program flow	Programmablauf m, Programmfluß m	flux (déroulement) m de programme	процесс выполнения программы; блок-схема программы
P 563	program flow chart	Programmablaufplan m	diagramme m de cheminement d'un programme	графическая блок-схема программы
P 564	program flow control	Programmablaufsteuerung f	commande f de déroulement de programme	управление выполнением программы
P 565	program generator	Programmgenerator m	générateur m de programme	генератор программ
P 566	program identifier	Programmkennzeichner m, Programmidentifizierer m	identificateur m de programme	идентификатор программы
P 567	program input	Programmeingabe f	entrée f de programme	ввод программы
P 568	program interrupt[ion]	Programmunterbrechung f	interruption f de programme	программное прерывание
P 569	program jump	Programmsprung m	saut m de programme	переход в программе
P 570	program language, programming language	Programmsprache f, Programmiersprache f	langage m de programmation	язык программирования
P 571	program library	Programmbibliothek f	bibliothèque f de programmes	библиотека программ
P 572	program link[age]	Programmverbindung f	liaison f de programme[s]	компоновка программы; межпрограммные связи
P 573	program loading	Programmladen n	chargement m de programme[s]	загрузка программы
P 574	program loop	Programmschleife f	boucle f de programme	программный цикл
P 575	programmability	Programmierbarkeit f	programmabilité f	программируемость
P 576	programmable assembly system	programmierbares Montagesystem n	système m de montage programmable	программно-настраиваемая система компоновки
P 577	programmable calculator	programmierbarer Taschenrechner m	calculateur m programmable	программируемый калькулятор
	programmable communication interface	s. P 107		
P 578	programmable control	programmierbare Steuerung f	commande f programmable	программируемое управление
P 579	programmable counter/timer	programmierbarer Zähler-Zeitgeber m	compteur/rythmeur m programmable	программируемый счетчик/таймер
P 580	programmable desk calculator	programmierbarer Tischrechner m	calculateur m programmable de table	программируемый настольный калькулятор
P 581	programmable features	programmierbare Eigenschaften fpl	propriétés fpl programmables	программируемые функции
P 582	programmable function	programmierbare Funktion f	fonction f programmable	программируемая функция
P 583	programmable interface	programmierbares Interface n, programmierbare Schnittstelle (Anschlußstelle) f	interface f programmable	программируемый интерфейс
P 584	programmable interface adapter	programmierbarer Interface-Adapter m, programmierbare Schnittstellenanpassung f	adapteur m d'interface programmable	программируемый интерфейсный адаптер
P 585	programmable interrupt controller	programmierbare Interruptsteuereinheit (Unterbrechungssteuereinheit) f	unité f de commande d'interruptions programmable	программируемый контроллер прерываний
P 586	programmable I/O line	programmierbare E/A-Leitung (E/A-Verbindung) f	ligne f d'E/S programmable	программируемая линия ввода-вывода
P 587	programmable I/O port	programmierbares E/A-Tor n, programmierbarer E/A-Anschluß m	porte f d'E/S programmable	программируемый порт ввода-вывода
P 588	programmable logic	programmierbare Logik (Schaltung) f	logique f programmable	программируемая логика; схема с программируемой логикой
	programmable logic array	s. P 245		
P 589	programmable peripheral interface, PPI	PPI-Schaltkreis m, programmierbarer Peripherieschnittstellenbaustein m	interface f périphérique programmable	программируемый интерфейс периферийных устройств
P 590	programmable peripherals	programmierbare Peripheriebaugruppe f	périphériques mpl programmables	программируемые периферийные устройства

P 591	programmable procedure	programmierbare Prozedur f, programmierbares Verfahren n	procédure f (procédé m) programmable	программируемая процедура (операция)
	programmable read-only memory	s. P 654		
P 592	programmable segmentation	programmierbare Segmentierung (Programmunterteilung) f	segmentation f programmable	программируемая сегментация
P 593	programmable system component	programmierbare Systemkomponente f, programmierbares Systembauteil n	composant m programmable	программируемый компонент системы
P 594	programmable timer	programmierbarer Zeitgeber m	rythmeur m programmable	программируемый таймер
P 595	program maintenance	Programmpflege f	maintenance f de programme[s]	обслуживание программ[ы]
P 596	programmed check, programmed testing	programmierte Prüfung f	test m programmé, vérification f programmée	программный контроль
P 597	programmed input/output	programmierte Ein-/Ausgabe f	entrée/sortie f programmée	программированный ввод-вывод
P 598	programmed learning	programmiertes Lernen n	enseignement m programmé	программированное обучение
P 599	programmed logic	programmierte Logik f	logique f programmée	программированная логика
P 600	programmed stop	programmierter Halt m	arrêt m programmé	программный останов; запрограммированный останов
	programmed testing	s. P 596		
P 601	program memory, program storage	Programmspeicher m	mémoire f de programme	программная память, память программ
P 602	programmer	Programmierer m	programmeur m	программист
P 603	programmer, programming machine	Programmiergerät n	machine f de programmation	программатор
P 604	programmer tools	Programmiererhilfen fpl	moyens mpl auxiliaires de programmeur	вспомогательные средства программиста
P 605	programming	Programmierung f	programmation f	программирование
P 606	programming costs	Programmierkosten pl	frais mpl de programmation	расходы программирования, стоимость разработки программного обеспечения
P 607	programming ease	Programmiererleichterung f	facilité f de programmation	легкость (свобода) программирования
P 608	programming expense	Programmieraufwand m	effort m de programmation	затраты на программирование
P 609	programming flexibility	Programmierflexibilität f	flexibilité f de programmation	гибкость программирования
	programming form	s. P 637		
P 610	programming handbook, programming manual	Programmierhandbuch n	manuel m de programmation	руководство по программированию
P 611	programming instruction	Programmieranleitung f	instruction f de programmation	инструкция по программированию
	programming language	s. P 570		
	programming language 1	s. P 244		
	programming language for microcomputer	s. P 260		
	programming machine	s. P 603		
	programming manual	s. P 610		
P 612	programming procedure	Programmierverfahren n	procédé m de programmation	метод (способ) программирования
P 613	programming style	Programmierstil m	style m de programmation	стиль программирования
P 614	programming support	Programmierunterstützung f	assistance f de programmation	программное обеспечение
P 615	programming system	Programmiersystem n	système m de programmation	система программирования
P 616	programming technique	Programmiertechnik f	technique f de programmation	техника (технология) программирования
P 617	programming time	Programmierzeit f, PROM-Informationseinschreibzeit f	temps m de programmation	время программирования; время записи информации в программируемое ПЗУ
P 618	programming tools	Programmiermittel npl, Programmierhilfen fpl	moyens mpl de programmation	[вспомогательные] средства программирования
P 619	program module	Programmodul n	module m de programme	программный модуль
P 620	program name	Programmname m	nom m de programme	имя программы
P 621	program notation	Programmschreibweise f	notation f de programme	запись (представление) программы
P 622	program optimization	Programmoptimierung f	optimisation f de programme	оптимизация программы
P 623	program output	Programmausgabe f	sortie f de programme	вывод программы; выход из программы
P 624	program parameter	Programmparameter m	paramètre m de programme	параметр программы
P 625	program part	Programmteil n	partie f de programme	часть программы
P 626	program preparation	Programmvorbereitung f	préparation f de programme	подготовка программы
P 627	program protection	Programmschutz m	protection f de programme	защита программы
P 628	program request	Programmanforderung f	exigence f de programme	запрос программы
P 629	program restart	Programm-Wiederanlauf m	redémarrage m de programme	повторный пуск программы, рестарт программы
P 630	program run, run of the program	Programmlauf m, Programmdurchlauf m	marche f de programme	пуск (прогон) программы
P 631	program scheduler	Programmablaufplaner m ‹Ablauffolgesteuerung›	scheduler m de programme	планировщик программ
P 632	program segment	Programmabschnitt m, Programmsegment n	segment m de programme	программный сегмент
P 633	program segmentation	Programmsegmentierung f, Programmunterteilung f	segmentation f de programme	сегментация программы

P 634	program segment relocation	Programmsegmentver-schiebung f, Programm-segmentumspeicherung f	décalage m de segment de programme	перемещение сегмента программы
P 635	program-sensitive fault	programmabhängiger Fehler m ‹von Programm-schrittfolge abhängiger Fehler›	défaut m dépendant du pro-gramme	программно-зависимый отказ ‹встречается только при определен-ном сочетании про-грамм›
P 636	program sequence	Programmfolge f	séquence f de programme	последовательность про-грамм
P 637	program sheet, pro-gramming form	Programmformular n, Pro-grammierbogen m	formulaire m de programme	программный бланк
P 638	program simulation	Programmsimulation f, Programmablaufnach-bildung f	simulation f de programme	моделирование [испол-нения] программы
P 639	program size	Programmgröße f, Pro-grammumfang m	volume m de programme	величина программы
P 640	program space	Programmraum m, Pro-grammbereich m im Speicher	espace m de programme	область [памяти] про-грамм
P 641	program statement	Programmanweisung f	instruction f de programme	инструкция программы
P 642	program status word	Programmstatuswort n	mot m d'état de programme	слово состояния про-граммы, ССП
P 643	program step	Programmschritt m	pas m de programme	шаг программы
P 644	program storage program storage	Programmspeicherung f s. a. P 601	mémorisation f de pro-gramme	хранение программ в памяти
P 645	program structure	Programmaufbau m, Pro-grammstruktur f	structure f de programme	структура программы
P 646	program system	Programmsystem n	système m de programmes	система программ
P 647	program tape	Programmband n	bande f de programme	лента программы
P 648	program test	Programmtest m	test m de programme	программный тест, тест программы
P 649	program translation, program compilation	Programmübersetzung f	traduction f de programme	трансляция программы
P 650	program verification	Programmüberprüfung f, Programmrichtigkeits-prüfung f	vérification f de programme	проверка (верификация) программы
P 651	projection display	Projektionsanzeige f	affichage m de projection	проекционный дисплей
P 652	projection mask	Projektionsmaske f	masque m de projection	проекционная маска
P 653	projection screen	Projektionsschirm m	écran m de projection	проекционный экран
P 654	PROM, programmable read-only memory	PROM m, programmier-barer ROM (Nur-Lese-Speicher) m ‹Oberbegriff›	PROM f, ROM f pro-grammable	программируемое ПЗУ (постоянно запоминаю-щее устройство), ППЗУ
P 655	PROM programmer	Programmiergerät n für PROM-Schaltkreise	appareil m de programma-tion pour PROM	программатор ППЗУ
P 656	propagating error	sich fortpflanzender Fehler m, mitlaufender Fehler	erreur f propagée	распространяющаяся ошибка
P 657	propagation delay	Ausbreitungsverzögerung f, Schaltverzögerung f	retardation f de propagation	задержка распростра-нения
P 658	propagation time	Laufzeit f ‹einer physikali-schen Größe›, Ausbrei-tungszeit f	temps m de propagation	время распространения
P 659	proportional control	Proportionalregelung f	réglage m proportionnel	линейное регулирование, регулирование по от-клонению, пропорцио-нальное регулирование
P 660	proportional gain	proportionale Verstärkung f	gain m proportionnel	линейное усиление
P 661	proportional integral control	Proportional-Integral-Regelung f	réglage m proportionnel et par intégration	пропорционально-инте-гральное регулирование
P 662	proportioning	Bemessung f, Dimensionie-rung f	dimensionnement m	определение размеров (размерности)
P 663	protected instruction	geschützter Befehl m	instruction f protégée	защищенная команда
P 664	protected location	geschützter Speicherplatz m	logement m de mémoire protégé	защищенная ячейка памяти
P 665	protected storage	geschützter Speicher m	mémoire f protégée	запоминающее устройство со средствами защиты, защищенная память
P 666	protected terminal key	geschützte Terminaltaste f	touche f protégée de termi-nal	[терминальная] клавиша защиты символа
P 667	protection	Schutz m	protection f	защита
P 668	protection facility	Schutzeinrichtung f	dispositif m de protection	устройство защиты
P 669	protection field	Schutzfeld n, Schutzkode-feld n	champ m de protection	поле защиты
P 670	protection key	Schutzschlüssel m	clé f de protection	ключ защиты
P 671	protection surface	Schutzoberfläche f	surface f de protection	защитная поверхность
P 672	protective coating	Schutzüberzug m	recouvrement m de pro-tection	защитное покрытие, защитная оболочка
P 673	protocol	Protokoll n, Regel f, Übermittlungsvorschrift f ‹Übertragungsprozedur-vereinbarung›	procès-verbal m	протокол
P 674	prototype	Prototyp m, Baumuster n	prototype m	прототип; макет
P 675	prototyping card	Prototypenplatine f	carte-prototype f	макетная плата; плата ППЗУ ‹системы проек-тирования микро-ЭВМ›
P 676	prototyping system	Prototypsystem n, Muster-system n	système m prototype	резидентная отладочная система
P 677	pseudoaddress	Pseudoadresse f	pseudo-adresse f	псевдоадрес
P 678	pseudocode, abstract code	Pseudokode m	pseudo-code m	псевдокод
P 679	pseudoinstruction	Pseudobefehl m	pseudo-instruction f	псевдокоманда
P 680	pseudo-operation	Pseudooperation f	pseudo-opération f	псевдооперация
P 681	pseudostatic memory, quasi-static memory	pseudostatischer (quasi-statischer) Speicher m ‹dynamischer Speicher	mémoire f quasi-statique	псевдостатическая (квазистатическая) память

		mit interner Selbstregenerierung>		
P 682	pseudostatic RAM	pseudostatischer RAM *m*, quasistatischer Lese-Schreib-Speicher *m* <dyn. RAM mit interner Selbstregenerierung>	mémoire *f* écriture lecture pseudo-statique, RAM *f* pseudo-statique	псевдостатическое ОЗУ <память на динамических БИС с внутренней регенерацией>
P 683	pseudotetrade	Pseudotetrade *f*	pseudo-tétrade *f*	псевдотетрада
	p-SG-MOS	*s.* P 106		
	p-SGT	*s.* P 106		
P 684	p-sheet	p-Schicht *f*	couche *f* p	p-слой, слой с p-проводимостью
P 685	p-substrate	p-Substrat *n*, p-Halbleitersubstrat *n*, p-leitendes Substrat *n*	substrat *m* P	подложка с p-проводимостью
	PSW	*s.* P 532		
P 686	p-type semiconductor	p-Halbleiter *m*	semi-conducteur *m* de type p	полупроводник p-типа
	p-type well	*s.* P 753		
	pull instruction	*s.* P 332		
P 687	pull up / to	hochziehen	tirer en haut	повышать <уровень>, подключать к источнику питания
P 688	pull-up device	Ziehelement *n* <Arbeitswiderstandsrealisierung einer Transistorschaltung>	élément *m* de tirage	нагрузочный элемент транзисторного ключа <например: в схемах с открытым коллектором>
P 689	pull-up resistor	Ziehwiderstand *m*, Arbeitswiderstand *m* einer Transistorschaltung	résistance *f* de tirage	нагрузочный резистор транзисторного ключа <например: в схемах с открытым коллектором>
P 690	pulse, impulse	Impuls *m*	impulsion *f*	импульс
P 691	pulse amplifier	Impulsverstärker *m*	amplificateur *m* d'impulsions	импульсный усилитель
P 692	pulse amplitude	Impulsamplitude *f*	amplitude *f* d'impulsion	амплитуда импульса
P 693	pulse-amplitude modulation, PAM	Pulsamplitudenmodulation *f*	modulation *f* d'impulsions en amplitude	амплитудно-импульсная модуляция, АИМ
P 694	pulse bandwidth	Impulsbandbreite *f*	largeur *f* de bande d'impulsion	частотная полоса импульса
P 695	pulse burst	Impulsbündel *n*	faisceau *m* d'impulsions	пучок импульсов
P 696	pulse carrier	Impulsträger *m*	support *m* d'impulsion	несущая [частота] импульса
P 697	pulse code	Impulskode *m*	code *m* d'impulsion	импульсный код
P 698	pulse-code modulation, PCM	Pulskodemodulation *f*, PCM	modulation *f* de code d'impulsion	импульсно-кодовая модуляция, ИКМ
P 699	pulse-controlled	impulsgesteuert	à commande par impulsions	с импульсным управлением
P 700	pulse counter	Impulszähler *m*	compteur *m* d'impulsions	счетчик импульсов
P 701	pulsed current	getasteter Strom *m*	courant *m* palpé	импульсный ток
P 702	pulse decay time	Impulsabfallzeit *f*	temps *m* de chute d'impulsion	время спада импульса
P 703	pulse delay	Impulsverzögerung *f*	retardement *m* d'impulsion	задержка импульса
P 704	pulse distortion	Impulsverzerrung *f*	distorsion *f* d'impulsion	искажение импульса
P 705	pulse driver	Impulstreiber *m*	basculeur (driver) *m* d'impulsions	формирователь импульсов
	pulse droop	*s.* P 736		
P 706	pulse duration	Impulsdauer *f*	durée *f* d'impulsion	длительность импульса
P 707	pulse duration modulation, PDM	Pulsdauermodulation *f*	modulation *f* de durée d'impulsion	широтно-импульсная модуляция, ШИМ
P 708	pulse duty factor	Impulstastverhältnis *n*	rapport *m* cyclique d'impulsion	коэффициент заполнения импульса
P 709	pulse equalizer	Impulsentzerrer *m*	égaliseur *m* d'impulsion	схема коррекции [формы] импульсов
P 710	pulse frequency, pulse rate	Impulsfrequenz *f*, Impulsrate *f*	fréquence *f* d'impulsion	частота импульсов
P 711	pulse-frequency modulation, PFM	Pulsfrequenzmodulation *f*	modulation *f* d'impulsions en fréquence	частотно-импульсная модуляция
P 712	pulse-frequency multiplier	Impulsfrequenzvervielfacher *m*	multiplicateur *m* de fréquence d'impulsions	умножитель частоты [импульсов]
P 713	pulse generator	Impulsgenerator *m*	générateur *m* d'impulsion	генератор импульсов
P 714	pulse height	Impulshöhe *f*	hauteur *f* d'impulsion	высота импульса
P 715	pulse interleaving	Impulsverschachtelung *f*	imbriquage *m* d'impulsions	чередование импульсов
P 716	pulse interval	Impulsabstand *m*	intervalle *m* d'impulsions	интервал между импульсами
P 717	pulse length	Impulslänge *f*	longueur *f* d'impulsion	длительность импульса
P 718	pulse-length modulation	Impulslängenmodulation *f*	modulation *f* de longueur d'impulsion	широтно-импульсная модуляция, ШИМ
P 719	pulse level	Impulspegel *m*	niveau *m* d'impulsion	уровень импульса
P 720	pulse modulation	Impulsmodulation *f*	modulation *f* d'impulsions	импульсная модуляция
P 721	pulse noise	Impulsrauschen *n*	bruit *m* d'impulsion	импульсная (кратковременная) помеха
P 722	pulse-operated	impulsbetrieben	opéré par impulsions	в импульсном режиме
P 723	pulse operation	Impulsbetrieb *m*	régime *m* à impulsions	импульсный режим
P 724	pulse output	Impulsausgang *m*, impulsgetragener Ausgang *m* <dynamische Ausgabe>	sortie *f* à impulsions	импульсный выход <динамический выход>
P 725	pulse peak	Impulsspitze *f*	crête *f* d'impulsion	пик (вершина) импульса
P 726	pulse-position modulation, PPM	Pulslagenmodulation *f*, Pulsphasenmodulation *f*	modulation *f* de position d'impulsion	фазо-импульсная модуляция
P 727	pulse power	Impulsleistung *f*	puissance *f* d'impulsion	импульсная мощность
	pulse rate	*s.* P 710		
P 728	pulse ratio	Impulsverhältnis *n*	rapport *m* d'impulsion	скважность импульсов
P 729	pulse repeater, transponder	Impulswiederholer *m*	répétiteur *m* d'impulsions	импульсный повторитель
	pulse repetition frequency	*s.* P 730		

Code	English	German	French	Russian
P 730	pulse repetition rate, pulse repetition frequency, PRF	Impulsfolgefrequenz f, Impulswiederholfrequenz f	fréquence f de répétition d'impulsions	частота повторения (следования) импульсов
P 731	pulse resolution	Impulsauflösung f	résolution f d'impulsions	разрешение импульсов
P 732	pulse rise time	Impulsanstiegszeit f	temps m de montée d'impulsion	время нарастания импульса, длительность фронта
P 733	pulse sequence, pulse train	Impulsfolge f, Impulszug m	séquence f d'impulsion	импульсная последовательность
P 734	pulse shaper	Impulsformer m	circuit m de mise en forme	формирователь импульсов
P 734 a	pulse spacing	Impulszwischenraum m	espace m d'impulsion	промежуток между импульсами
P 735	pulse stretcher	Impulsdehner m	dilatateur m d'impulsion	расширитель импульсов
P 736	pulse tilt, pulse droop	Impulsdachschräge f, Impulsdachneigung f	inclinaison f de toit d'impulsion	наклон вершины импульса
P 737	pulse-time modulation pulse train	Impulszeitmodulation f s. P 733	modulation f de temps d'impulsion	время-импульсная модуляция
P 738	pulse width	Impulsbreite f	largeur f d'impulsion	ширина импульса
P 739	pulse-width modulation punch / to punch	Impulsbreitenmodulation f s. P 126 s. P 127	modulation f de largeur d'impulsion	широтно-импульсная модуляция, ШИМ
P 740	punch block, punching block	Locherblock m, Stanzblock m	bloc m de perforation	перфорирующий блок
P 741	punch capacity	Stanzleistung f	capacité f de perforation	производительность перфорирования
P 742	punch card, [punched] card	Lochkarte f	carte f perforée	перфокарта
P 743	punch code, punched code	Stanzkode m, Lochkode m	code m perforé	код перфорации
P 744	punch column	Lochspalte f	colonne f perforée	колонка перфорации
P 745	punch device	Lochgerät n, Stanzeinrichtung f	appareil (dispositif) m de perforation	перфоратор
	punched card	s. P 742		
	punched code	s. P 743		
	puncher	s. P 127		
	punching block	s. P 740		
P 746	punch row	Lochzeile f	ligne f perforée	строка перфокарты
P 747	punch station	Lochstation f, Stanzgerätestation f	station f de perforation	перфораторная станция
	punch tape	s. P 36		
	punch tape reader	s. P 38		
	punch tape unit	s. P 39		
P 748	pushbutton	Druckknopf m, Drucktaste f	touche f, bouton-poussoir m	клавиша, кнопка
	push down / to	s. P 750		
	push-down storage	s. S 646		
P 749	push instruction	Kellerspeicherungsbefehl m, Einkellerungsbefehl m	instruction f en mémoire-cave	команда обращения к стеку, команда записи в стековое ЗУ
P 750	push onto stack / to, to push down	in den Kellerspeicher bringen, einkellern	mettre en mémoire-cave	поместить (записать) в стек
	push-pop memory	s. S 646		
P 751	push-pull amplifier, paraphase amplifier	Gegentaktverstärker m	amplificateur m push-pull	двухтактный усилитель
P 752	push-pull output	Gegentaktausgang m <Gegentaktausgangsschaltung>	montage m de sortie push-pull	двухтактный выход
	push-push mode	s. C 378		
P 753	p-well, p-type well	p-Mulde f, p-leitende (p-dotierte) Mulde f	trou m de type P	потенциальная яма p-типа

Q

Code	English	German	French	Russian
	Q factor	s. Q 11		
	QIL package	s. Q 4		
Q 1	Q-output state	Q-Ausgangs-Zustand m <Zustand des wahren Ausgangs eines Flipflop>	état m de sortie Q	состояние прямого выхода триггера
Q 2	QTAM, queued telecommunications access method	QTAM n, Warteschlangen-Fernübertragungsverfahren n	méthode f d'accès de télécommunication à queue, méthode QTAM	телекоммуникационный метод доступа с очередями
Q 3	quad-in-line	vierreihig <Anschlußstift-Anordnung>	quad-in-line	четырехрядный
Q 4	quad-in-line package, QIL package	QIL-Gehäuse n, Quad-In-Line-Gehäuse n, <Schaltkreisgehäuse mit vier Anschlußstiftreihen>	boîtier m quad-in-line, boîtier QIL	корпус с четырехрядным расположением выводов
Q 5	quadruple word	Vierfachwort n	mot m quadruple	четырехкратное слово
Q 6	qualification testing	Qualifikationsprüfung f	examen m de qualification	квалификационное испытание
Q 7	qualifier tester	Bauteiletester m	examinateur m de composants	устройство проверки интегральных схем
Q 8	quality assurance	Gütesicherung f	assurance f de qualité	гарантия качества
Q 9	quality control	Gütekontrolle f	contrôle m de qualité	контроль качества
Q 10	quality engineering	Qualitätstechnik f	technique f de qualité	техника проверки качества
Q 11	quality factor, Q factor	Gütefaktor m	facteur m de qualité	показатель качества; коэффициент добротности
Q 12	quality grade	Güteklasse f	degré m de qualité	сорт; класс точности
Q 13	quality test	Qualitätstest m	test m de qualité	проверка качества
Q 14	quantization	Quantelung f, Quantisierung f	quantification f	квантование
Q 15	quantize / to	quantisieren, quanteln	quantifier	квантовать

Q 16	quartz	Quarz *m*	quartz *m*	кварц
	quartz-controlled	*s.* Q 19		
Q 17	quartz crystal	Quarzkristall *m*	cristal *m* de quartz	кристалл кварца
Q 18	quartz crystal clock	Quarzuhr *f,* quarz- gesteuerte Uhr *f*	horloge *f* à quartz	кварцевые часы
Q 19	quartz crystal con- trolled, quartz-con- trolled	quarzgesteuert	commandé par quartz	управляемый кварцем
Q 20	quartz oscillator (reso- nator), crystal oscillator	Quarzschwinger *m,* Quarz- oszillator *m*	oscillateur *m* à quartz	кварцевый осциллятор (резонатор)
Q 21	quartz-stabilized	quarzstabilisiert	stabilisé par quartz	с кварцевой стабили- зацией [частоты]
Q 22	quartz window	Quarzfenster *n*	fenêtre *f* à quartz	кварцевое окно
Q 23	quasi-stable state	quasistabiler Zustand *m*	état *m* quasi-stable	квазиустойчивое состояние
	quasi-static memory	*s.* P 684		
	query station	*s.* I 212		
Q 24	queue	Warteschlange *f*	queue *f*	очередь
Q 25	queued access method	Warteschlangen-Zugriffs- verfahren *n*	méthode *f* d'accès de queue	метод доступа с очередями
Q 26	queue discipline	Warteschlangenverfahren *n*	procédé *m* de queue	дисциплина обслужива- ния очередей
	queued telecommuni- cations access method	*s.* Q 2		
Q 27	queue entry	Warteschlangeneintragung *f*	inscription *f* de queue	вхождение в очередь
Q 28	queue priority	Warteschlangenpriorität *f*	priorité *f* de queue	приоритет очереди
Q 29	queuing	Einreihen *n* in Warte- schlange	mise *f* en queue	образование (органи- зация) очередей
Q 30	queuing list	Warteschlangenliste *f*	liste *f* de queue	список очередей
Q 31	queuing theory	Warteschlangentheorie *f*	théorie *f* des queues	теория массового обслу- живания, теория очередей
Q 32	quiescent current	Ruhestrom *m*	courant *m* de repos	ток покоя
Q 33	quiescent current drain	Ruhestromaufnahme *f*	prise *f* de courant de repos	потребление тока в ре- жиме покоя
	quiescent power	*s.* S 693		
Q 34	quiescent state	Ruhezustand *m*	état *m* de repos	состояние покоя
Q 35	quiet operation	geräuschloser Betrieb *m*	service *m* silencieux	бесшумная работа
Q 36	quill	Sockel *m* (Fassung *f*) für QIL-Gehäuse	socle *m* pour boîtier QIL	гнездо для корпуса с четырехрядным распо- ложением выводов
Q 37	quotient	Quotient *m*	quotient *m*	частное; коэффициент

R

R 1	rack	Gestellrahmen *m,* Einschub- schrank *m*	cadre *m* du bâti, armoire *f* à tiroirs, châssis *m*	стойка, шасси
R 2	rack-mounted version, rack-mounting version	Ausführung *f* für Gestell- einbau, Gestelleinbauaus- führung *f*	version *f* pour montage en bâti	стоечный вариант
R 3	rack mounting	Gestelleinbau *m*	montage *m* en bâti	монтаж в стойке
	rack-mounting version	*s.* R 2		
R 4	radio interference, RI	Funkstörung *f*	perturbation *f* radio	радиопомехи
R 5	radix	Zahlenbasis *f*	base *f,* nombre *m* de base	основание системы счисления
R 6	radix notation	Radix-Schreibweise *f,* Stellenwertschreibweise *f*	notation *f* de racine (base)	позиционная система счисления
R 7	radix point	Komma *n,* Zahlenkomma *n*	virgule *f* [numérique]	запятая ‹разделение целой и дробной части числа›
R 8	RALU, register and arithmetic logic unit	Register- und arithmetisch- logische Einheit *f* ‹Pro- zessorkomponente›	unité *f* arithmétique- logique et à registres	регистровое арифмети- ческо-логическое устройство, РАЛУ
R 9	RALU chip	RALU-Schaltkreis *m,* Register/Arithmetik- Logik-Einheit-Schalt- kreis *m*	circuit *m* d'unité arith- métique-logique et à registres	БИС РАЛУ, микросхема регистрового арифмети- ческо-логического устройства
R 10	RAM, random access memory	RAM *m,* Lese-Schreib- Speicher *m* ‹im Gegen- satz zu ROM› mit wahl- freiem Zugriff	mémoire *f* écriture-lecture, RAM *f*	оперативное запоминаю- щее устройство, ОЗУ
R 11	RAM-located stack	RAM-realisierter Keller- speicher *m,* im Arbeits- speicher angeordneter Kellerspeicher	mémoire *f* cave logée dans la mémoire opérative	стек, размещенный в оперативном запоми- нающем устройстве
R 12	RAM memory save option	Speicherinhaltssicherungs- Zusatzeinrichtung *f* für RAMs	dispositif *m* de sauvegarde de mémoire écriture- lecture	дополнительные средства защиты содержимого ОЗУ [в случае наруше- ния питания] ‹постав- ляются по заказу пользователя›
R 13	RAM refresh cycle	RAM-Regenerierungs- zyklus *m,* RAM- Refresh-Zyklus *m* ‹dyn. RAM›	cycle *m* de rafraîchissement de mémoire lecture- écriture	цикл регенерации ОЗУ ‹динамические ОЗУ›
R 14	RAM refresh operation	RAM-Regenerierungs- operation *f,* RAM- Refresh-Operation *f* ‹dyn. RAM›	opération *f* de rafraîchisse- ment de mémoire lecture- écriture	процесс регенерации ОЗУ ‹динамические ОЗУ›
R 15	random access	wahlfreier Zugriff *m*	accès *m* libre	произвольный доступ
R 16	random access memory, random memory	Randomspeicher *m,* Spei- cher *m* mit wahlfreiem Zugriff	mémoire *f* à accès libre	память с произвольным доступом
	random access memory	*s. a.* R 10		

R 17	**random access storage**	Speicherung f mit wahl-freiem Zugriff	mise f en mémoire à accès libre	запоминающее устройство с произвольным досту-пом
R 18	**random error,** accidental error	Zufallsfehler m	erreur f accidentelle	случайная ошибка
R 19	**random failure**	zufälliger Ausfall m, Zufallsausfall m	défaut m aléatoire	случайный сбой
R 20	**random logic**	frei gestaltete Logik f, will-kürlich angeordnete Logik <Gegensatz: reguläre Logik>	logique f de structure libre	логические схемы с не-регулярной структурой
	random memory	s. R 16		
R 21	**random number**	Zufallszahl f	nombre m aléatoire	случайное число
R 22	**random number generator**	Zufallszahlengenerator m	générateur m de nombres aléatoires	генератор случайных чисел
R 23	**random point**	willkürlicher Punkt m	point m arbitraire	произвольная (нерегуляр-ная) точка
R 24	**random sequence**	Zufallsfolge f	séquence f aléatoire	случайная последователь-ность
R 25	**range changing,** range switching	Bereichsumschaltung f	commutation f de domaine	переключение диапазонов
R 26	**range limit,** bound	Bereichsgrenze f, Schranke f	limite f de domaine	граница диапазона
R 27	**range of applications,** application field	Anwendungsbereich m, Anwendungsgebiet n, Einsatzspektrum n, Ein-satzgebiet n, Einsatzfeld n	champ m d'application	область (диапазон) при-менения
R 28	**range of components**	Bauelementesortiment n	assortiment m de compo-sants	набор (ассортимент) элементов
R 29	**range of values**	Wertebereich m	domaine (champ) m de valeurs	диапазон значений
	range switching	s. R 25		
	raster	s. G 71		
	raster board	s. G 72		
R 30	**raster count**	Rasterzählung f	comptage m de grilles	отсчет адресуемых коорди-нат экрана дисплея
R 31	**rate / to**	bemessen, veranschlagen	évaluer	оценивать, измерять
R 32	**rated current,** nominal current	Nennstrom m	courant m nominal	номинальный ток
R 33	**rated load**	Nennlast f	charge f nominale	номинальная нагрузка
	rated output (perform-ance, power)	s. P 391		
R 34	**rated voltage,** nominal voltage	Nennspannung f	tension f nominale	номинальное напряжение
R 35	**rate-grown transistor**	stufengezogener (gezogener) Transistor m	transistor m tiré	тянутый транзистор, тран-зистор с выращенными переходами
R 36	**rate of change**	Änderungsgeschwindigkeit f, Änderungsrate f	vitesse f de changement	скорость изменения
R 37	**rate test**	Bewertungstest m	test m d'évaluation	оценочное испытание
R 38	**rating,** nominal value	Nennwert m, Sollwert m	valeur f nominale	номинальное значение, номинальный параметр
R 39	**ratio control**	Verhältnisregelung f	réglage m du rapport	регулирование соотно-шения
	RC circuit	s. R 329		
	RCTL	s. R 330		
	R & D	s. R 304		
	R dump	s. R 303		
R 40	**react / to**	reagieren, [zu]rückwirken	réagir	реагировать; [воз]дейст-вовать
R 41	**reactance**	Blindwiderstand m, Reaktanz f	réactance f	реактивное сопротивле-ние, реактанс
R 42	**reaction time**	Reaktionszeit f	temps m de réaction	время реакции
R 43	**read-back test**	Rücklesekontrolle f <Wiederholtest>	test m de lecture répétée	эхо-контроль
R 44	**read cycle**	Lesezyklus m	cycle m de lecture	цикл считывания (чтения)
R 45	**read data**	Lesedaten pl	données fpl de lecture	считываемые данные
R 46	**read enable**	Lesefreigabe f, Leseaktivie-rung f	libération f de lecture	готовность считывания
R 47	**reader**	Leser m	lecteur m	считыватель, считываю-щее устройство
R 48	**read head,** reading head	Lesekopf m	tête f de lecture	головка считывания
R 49	**read in / to**	einlesen <eines externen Datenträgers in eine interne Speichereinrich-tung>	lire dans, entrer	считать [в память] <про-цесс считывания дан-ных с внешнего носи-теля и помещение их во внутреннюю память>
R 50	**reading error,** error of reading	Lesefehler m, Ablesefehler m	erreur f de lecture	ошибка считывания
	reading head	s. R 48		
	reading operation	s. R 52		
R 51	**reading rate (speed)**	Lesegeschwindigkeit f, Leserate f	vitesse f de lecture	скорость считывания
	read-mostly memory	s. R 386		
	read-only memory	s. R 393		
R 52	**read operation,** reading operation	Leseoperation f, Lese-betrieb m	opération f de lecture	операция считывания
R 53	**read out / to**	auslesen <einer internen Speichereinrichtung für ein externes Gerät>	lire, extraire	считать [из памяти] <про-цесс считывания данных из памяти и запись их на внешний носитель>
R 54	**read pulse**	Leseimpuls m	impulsion f de lecture	импульс считывания
R 55	**read signal**	Lesesignal n	signal m de lecture	сигнал считывания (чтения)
R 56	**read-write cycle**	Lese-Schreib-Zyklus m	cycle m de lecture-écriture	цикл чтения/записи

R 57	read-write head	Lese-Schreib-Kopf *m*	tête *f* de lecture-écriture	[универсальная] головка чтения/записи
R 58	read-write memory, RWM	Lese-Schreib-Speicher *m*	mémoire *f* lecture-écriture	память с возможностью чтения/записи
R 59	read-write memory testing	Lese-Schreib-Speichertest *m*	test *m* de mémoire lecture-écriture	проверка чтения/записи
R 60	ready line	Bereit-Leitung *f*, Fertig-meldeleitung *f*	ligne *f* de libération	линия [сигнала] готов-ности
R 61	ready pulse	Freigabeimpuls *m* ‹Fertig-meldesignal›	impulsion *f* de libération	сигнал готовности
R 62	real number	reelle Zahl *f*	nombre *m* réel	действительное число
R 63	real part	Realteil *m*	partie *f* réelle	действительная часть
R 64	real power, active power, effective capacity	Wirkleistung *f*, Nutz-leistung *f*	puissance *f* réelle (active, efficace, utile)	активная мощность
R 65	real time	Echtzeit *f*	temps *m* réel	реальное время
R 66	real-time application	Echtzeitanwendung *f*, Echtzeiteinsatz *m*	application *f* en temps réel	применение в системах реального времени
R 67	real-time clock	Echtzeituhr *f*, Echtzeittakt *m*	horloge *f* en temps réel	датчик сигналов времени ‹таймер, использую-щий, например, сигналы сети переменного тока›
R 68	real-time computer	Echtzeitrechner *m*, Rechner *m* im Echtzeitbetrieb	calculateur *m* en temps réel	ЭВМ, работающая в реальном времени
R 69	real-time control	Echtzeitsteuerung *f*, Real-zeitsteuerung *f*	commande *f* en temps réel	управление в реальном времени
R 70	real-time executive	Echtzeitsteuerprogramm *n*	programme *m* exécutif en temps réel	монитор реального времени
R 71	real-time input	Echtzeiteingabe *f*; Echtzeit-dateneingang *m*	entrée *f* en temps réel	ввод [данных] в реальном времени; вход системы реального времени
R 72	real-time mode	Echtzeitarbeitsmodus *m*	mode *m* en temps réel	режим работы в реальном времени
R 73	real-time operating system	Echtzeitbetriebssystem *n*	système *m* opérationnel en temps réel	операционная система реального времени, ОСРВ
R 74	real-time operation	Echtzeitbetrieb *m*	opération *f* en temps réel	работа в реальном времени
R 75	real-time output	Echtzeitausgabe *f*, Echtzeit-datenausgang *m*	sortie *f* en temps réel	вывод [данных] в реаль-ном времени; выход системы реального времени
R 76	real-time processing	Echtzeitverarbeitung *f*, Sofortverarbeitung *f*	traitement *m* en temps réel	обработка в реальном времени
R 77	real-time simulation	Echtzeitsimulation *f*, Simu-lation *f* von Echtzeit-bedingungen	simulation *f* en temps réel	моделирование в реальном времени
R 78	real-time system	Echtzeitverarbeitungs-system *n*	système *m* en temps réel	система реального вре-мени
R 79	real-time task	Echtzeitaufgabe *f*	tâche *f* en temps réel	задача, выполняемая в реальном времени
R 80	real value	Realwert *m*, reeller Wert *m*	valeur *f* réelle	действительное значение
R 81	rearrangement	Umordnung *f*, Neuordnung *f*	réarrangement *m*	перестройка
R 82	reassignment	Neuzuweisung *f*	réattribution *f*	перераспределение, пере-назначение
R 83	receive / to	empfangen, aufnehmen	recevoir, acquérir	получать, принимать
R 84	receive channel	Empfangskanal *m*	canal *m* de réception	приемный канал
R 85	receive clock	Empfängertakt *m*	rythme *m* de récepteur	синхронизация приема
R 86	receive data	Empfangsdaten *pl*	données *fpl* de réception	принимаемые данные
R 87	receive end, receiving end	Empfangsseite *f*	côté *m* récepteur	приемная сторона
R 88	receive mode	Empfangsbetrieb *m*	mode (régime) *m* de récep-tion	режим приема
R 89	receiver	Empfänger *m*, Empfangsein-richtung *f*	récepteur *m*	приемник
R 90	receiver gating	Empfängertastung *f*	suppression *f* de récepteur	стробирование приемника
R 91	receiver unit, receiving device	Empfangsgerät *n*	appareil *m* récepteur	приемное устройство
R 92	receive terminal, receiv-ing terminal (station)	Empfangsterminal *n*, Empfangsendstelle *f*, Empfangsstation *f*	terminal *m* récepteur	принимающий терминал, принимающая (прием-ная) станция
	receiving device	*s.* R 91		
	receiving end	*s.* R 87		
R 93	receiving speed	Empfangsgeschwindigkeit *f*	vitesse *f* de réception	скорость приема
	receiving station (terminal)	*s.* R 92		
R 94	reception	Empfang *m*, Aufnahme *f*	réception *f*	прием, получение
R 95	recharge	Umladung *f*	recharge *f*	перезарядка
R 96	rechargeable	umladbar	rechargeable	перезаряжаемый
R 97	reciprocal	reziprok, umgekehrt	réciproque	обратный; взаимный
R 98	recirculating, circulating, rotary	umlaufend	circulaire	циркулирующий
R 99	recognition	Erkennung *f*	reconnaissance *f*	распознавание; различе-ние
R 100	recognition algorithm	Erkennungsalgorithmus *m*	algorithme *m* de reconnais-sance	алгоритм распознавания
R 101	recognition logic	Erkennungslogik *f*	logique *f* de reconnaissance	логика распознавания
R 102	recognition matrix	Erkennungsmatrix *f*	matrice *f* de reconnaissance	матрица распознавания
	recognition method	*s.* R 103		
R 103	recognition procedure, recognition method	Erkennungsverfahren *n*	procédé *m* (méthode *f*) de reconnaissance	метод распознавания
R 104	recombination	Rekombination *f* ‹Ladungs-träger›	recombinaison *f*	рекомбинация
R 105	record / to	niederschreiben, aufzeichnen	enregistrer	записывать

R 106	record	Niederschrift *f*, Aufzeich-nung *f*, Satz *m*	enregistrement *m*	запись
R 107	record address	Satzadresse *f*	adresse *f* d'enregistrement	адрес записи
R 108	record block	Satzblock *m*, Aufzeich-nungsblock *m*	bloc *m* d'enregistrement	блок записей
R 109	record deletion	Satzlöschung *f*	effaçage *m* d'enregistrement	стирание записи
R 110	recorder	Aufzeichnungsgerät *n*, Registriergerät *n*, Schreiber *m*	enregistreur *m*	записывающее (регистри-рующее) устройство, регистратор
R 111	record format	Aufzeichnungsformat *n*	format *m* d'enregistrement	формат записи
R 112	recording carrier, recording medium	Aufzeichnungsträger *m*	support *m* d'enregistrement	носитель записи
R 113	recording density	Aufzeichnungsdichte *f*, Speicherdichte *f*	densité *f* d'enregistrement	плотность записи
R 114	recording head	Aufzeichnungskopf *m*, Auf-nahmekopf *m*	tête *f* d'enregistrement	головка записи
	recording medium	*s.* R 112		
R 115	recording speed, record speed	Aufzeichnungsgeschwin-digkeit *f*	vitesse *f* d'enregistrement	скорость записи
R 116	recording surface	Aufzeichnungsplattenseite *f*	face *f* d'enregistrement	рабочая поверхность носителя
R 117	recording technique	Aufzeichnungsverfahren *n*	procédé *m* d'enregistrement	техника записи; метод записи
R 118	record length	Satzlänge *f*	longueur *f* d'enregistrement	длина записи
R 119	record size	Satzgröße *f*	grandeur *f* d'enregistrement	размер записи
	record speed	*s.* R 115		
R 120	recover / to	wiedererlangen, wiedergut-machen, sich erholen	rétablir	возвращаться [к задан-ному значению], вос-станавливаться
R 121	recoverable error	heilbarer (wiedergutzu-machender) Fehler *m*	erreur *f* rémédiable	исправимая ошибка
R 122	recovery	Erholung *f*, Rückgewin-nung *f* <Werte>, Wieder-herstellung *f* <Arbeits-fähigkeit>	restauration *f*, restitution *f*	возврат к заданному зна-чению, восстановление
R 123	recovery management	Organisation *f* der Wieder-herstellung	organisation *f* de restau-ration	управление восстановле-нием
R 124	recovery period	Erhol[ungs]dauer *f*	période *f* de restauration	период восстановления
R 125	recovery procedure	Rückstellvorgang *m* <nach Fehlern>	procédure *f* de restauration	процедура восстановления
R 126	recovery program, automatic recovery program	Programm *n* zur Betriebs-fähigkeitswiedererlan-gung, Erholungspro-gramm *n* <nach Geräte-ausfall>	programme *m* de restau-ration (restitution)	программа восстановления
R 127	recovery time	Erhol[ungs]zeit *f*, innere Totzeit *f*	temps *m* de restauration	время восстановления
R 128	rectangular loop	Rechteckschleife *f* <Hysterese>	boucle *f* rectangulaire	прямоугольная петля гистерезиса, ППГ
R 129	rectangular pulse, square pulse	Rechteckimpuls *m*	impulsion *f* rectangulaire (carrée)	прямоугольный импульс
R 130	rectangular shape	Rechteckform *f*	forme *f* rectangulaire	прямоугольная форма
R 131	rectangular waveform	Rechteckwellenform *f*	forme *f* d'onde rectangulaire	прямоугольная форма колебания
R 132	rectification	Gleichrichtung *f*	redressage *m*	выпрямление; детектиро-вание
R 133	rectified alternating current	gleichgerichteter Wechsel-strom *m*	courant *m* alternatif redressé	выпрямленный перемен-ный ток
R 134	rectifier circuit	Gleichrichterschaltung *f*	montage *m* redresseur	схема выпрямителя
R 135	rectifier converter	Gleichrichterwandler *m*	convertisseur *m* à redresseur	выпрямительный пре-образователь
R 136	rectifying characteristics	Gleichrichterkennwerte *mpl*	caractéristiques *fpl* de redresseur	вольтамперные характе-ристики [выпрямитель-ного] диода
R 137	rectifying junction	gleichrichtender pn-Über-gang *m*	jonction *f* de redresseur	выпрямляющий переход
R 138	recurrent, recursive	rekursiv, wiederkehrend, zurückkehrend	récursif	рекурсивный
R 139	recursion	Rekursion *f*, Wiederkehr *f*	récursion *f*	рекурсия
	recursive	*s.* R 138		
R 140	recursive procedure	rekursives Verfahren *n*, Rekursionsverfahren *n*	procédure *f* récursive	рекурсивная процедура
R 141	recursive program	rekursives Programm *n* <Programm, das sich selbst als Unterprogramm benutzen kann>	programme *m* récursif	рекурсивная программа
R 142	recursive structure	rekursive Struktur *f*	structure *f* récursive	рекурсивная структура
R 143	recursive subroutine	rekursives Unterprogramm *n*	sous-programme *m* récursif	рекурсивная подпро-грамма
R 144	recycling	zyklisch zurückführend, zyklisch erneuernd <Speicherregenerierung>	à recyclage	возвратный
R 145	recycling program	Rückführungsprogramm *n*	programme *m* de réaction	программа возврата
R 146	redesign	Neuentwurf *m*, Reentwurf *m*, Umentwicklung *f*	projet *m* nouveau	реконструкция; переделка
R 147	redistribution	Umverteilung *f*, Neuver-teilung *f*	redistribution *f*	перераспределение
R 148	reduce / to	reduzieren, verringern	réduire	уменьшать, сокращать
R 149	reduced size	reduzierte Größe *f*, ver-kleinerte Abmaße *npl*	grandeur *f* réduite	приведенный размер; уменьшенная величина
R 150	reducing, reduction	Reduzierung *f*, Verringe-rung *f*	réduction *f*	редукция, уменьшение, сокращение; приведение
R 151	redundancy	Redundanz *f*, Weitschwei-figkeit *f*	redondance *f*	избыточность

R 152	redundancy check	Redundanzprüfung f	contrôle m de redondance	контроль с введением избыточности
R 153	redundancy technique	Redundanztechnik f, Redundanzverfahren n	technique f à redondance	способ введения избыточности
R 154	redundant character	redundantes Zeichen n	caractère m à redondance	избыточный символ
R 155	redundant circuit	redundante Schaltung f	circuit m à redondance	избыточная схема
R 156	redundant code	redundanter Kode m	code m à redondance	избыточный код
R 157	redundant module	redundanter Modul m, Redundanzbaustein m	module m à redondance	избыточный модуль
R 158	redundant representation	redundante Darstellung f	représentation f à redondance	избыточное представление
R 159	redundant system	redundantes System n	système m à redondance	избыточная система
R 160	reel	Spule f, Rolle f	bobine f, rouleau m	катушка, бобина; рулон
R 161	reenterable, reentrant	wiedereintrittsfähig, wiederverwendungsfähig, eintrittsinvariant	réutilisable	реентерабельный, абсолютный <свойства программы, позволяющие использовать ее несколькими задачами в мультипрограммном режиме>
R 162	reentrant code	wiederverwendungsfähiger (eintrittsinvarianter) Kode m <wird durch Ausführung nicht verändert>	code m réutilisable	реентерабельный (многократно используемый) код
R 163	reentrant program	wiedereintrittsfähiges Programm n <bei bereits begonnener Abarbeitung>, eintrittsinvariantes Programm	programme m réutilisable	реентерабельная (многократно используемая) программа
R 164	reentrant subroutine	wiederaufrufbares Unterprogramm n <nach bereits begonnener Nutzung>, eintrittsinvariantes Unterprogramm	sous-programme m réutilisable	реентерабельная (многократно используемая) подпрограмма
R 165	reentry	Wiedereintritt m	entrée f de retour	повторный вход
R 166	reentry point	Wiedereintrittsstelle f <Rücksprungstelle>	point m d'entrée de retour	точка повторного входа
R 167	refer / to	verweisen, sich beziehen	référer, se rapporter	ссылаться, относиться
R 168	reference	Bezug m, Bezugnahme f, Verweis m, Hinweis m, Referenz f	référence f	ссылка
R 169	reference address	Bezugsadresse f	adresse f de référence	исходный адрес, адрес ссылки
R 170	reference data	Bezugsdaten pl	données fpl de référence	справочные данные; эталонные данные
R 171	reference input	Führungsgröße f	valeur f de référence	заданная (контрольная) величина
R 172	reference level	Bezugspegel m	niveau m de référence	опорный уровень; уровень отсчета
R 173	reference line	Bezugslinie f	ligne f de référence	линия отсчета; ось координат
R 174	reference manual	s. I 252		
	reference pattern	Bezugsmuster n	échantillon m de référence	эталонный образец; эталонный образ
R 175	reference point	Bezugspunkt m	point m de référence (repère)	контрольная точка; опорная точка
R 176	reference possibility	Bezugsmöglichkeit f	possibilité f de référence	возможность ссылки
R 177	reference potential	Bezugspotential n	potentiel m de référence	опорный потенциал; эталонный потенциал
R 178	reference program table	Referenzprogrammtabelle f <Speicherabschnitt>	table f de programmes de référence	таблица программных ссылок <секция памяти>
R 179	reference signal	Bezugssignal n	signal m de référence	опорный (эталонный) сигнал
R 180	reference voltage	Bezugsspannung f, Referenzspannung f	tension f de référence	опорное (эталонное) напряжение
R 181	reformatting	Formatänderung f	modification f de format	изменение формата
R 182	refresh	Auffrischung f, Datenregenerierung f <in dynamischen Speicher- und Anzeigeelementen>	rafraîchissement m	регенерация
R 183	refresh circuit	Refresh-Schaltung f, Auffrischungschaltung f, Datenregenerierungsschaltung f	circuit m de rafraîchissement	схема регенерации
R 184	refresh control	Refresh-Steuerung f, Auffrischungssteuerung f, Datenregenerierungssteuerung f	commande f de rafraîchissement	управление регенерацией
R 185	refresh cycle	Refresh-Zyklus m, Auffrischungszyklus m, Datenregenerierungszyklus m	cycle m de rafraîchissement	цикл регенерации
R 186	refresh period	Refresh-Periode f, Auffrischungsperiode f, Datenregenerierungsperiode f	période f de rafraîchissement	период регенерации
R 187	regenerate / to	regenerieren, erneuern, wiederherstellen	régénérer	регенерировать, восстанавливать
R 188	regeneration	Regenerierung f, Wiederherstellung f	régénération f	регенерация, восстановление
R 189	regeneration period	Regenerierungsperiode f	période f de régénération	период регенерации

R 190	regenerative	rückkoppelnd	régénératif	регенеративный; с положительной обратной связью
	regenerative feedback	s. P 353		
R 191	regenerative reading	zurückschreibendes Lesen *n*	lecture *f* régénérative	считывание с регенерацией
R 192	register	Register *n*	egistre *m*	регистр
R 193	register address	Registeradresse *f*	adresse *f* de registre	адрес (номер) регистра
R 194	register address field	Registeradreßfeld *n*	champ *m* d'adresse de registre	поле адреса регистра
	register and arithmetic logic unit	s. R 8		
R 195	register architecture, register structure	Registerarchitektur *f*, Registerstruktur *f* <eines Systems>	structure *f* de registres	регистровая архитектура
R 196	register arrangement	Registeranordnung *f*	arrangement *m* de registres	[функциональное] назначение регистров
R 197	register array	Registerfeld *n*, Registerblock *m* <räumlich>	champ *m* de registre	регистровый файл, блок регистров
	register bank	s. R 210		
R 198	register contents	Registerinhalt *m*	contenu *m* de registre	содержимое регистра
R 199	register content storage	Registerinhaltsspeicherung *f* <Zustandsrettung>	mise *f* en mémoire du contenu de registres	запоминание содержимого регистра
R 200	register direct addressing	Registerdirektadressierung *f* <adressiertes Register enthält Operand>	adressage *m* direct de registre	прямая адресация регистра, прямая регистровая адресация
	register file	s. R 210		
R 201	register indirect addressing	Registerindirektadressierung *f* <Speicheradressierung über Registerinhalt>	adressage *m* indirect à registre[s]	косвенная адресация через регистр, косвенно-регистровая адресация
R 202	register instruction	Registerbefehl *m*, Registeroperationsbefehl *m*	instruction *f* de registre	регистровая команда, команда работы с регистром
R 203	register length	Registerlänge *f*	longueur *f* de registre	длина (разрядность) регистра
R 204	register memory	Registerspeicher *m*	mémoire *f* à registres	регистровая память
R 205	register operand	Registeroperand *m* <Operand aus Register>	opérande *m* de registre	операнд, хранящийся в регистре
R 206	register-oriented architecture	registerorientierte Struktur *f*	structure *f* à registres	регистровая архитектура
R 207	register pair	Registerpaar *n*	paire *f* de registres	пара регистров
R 208	register save instruction	Registerrettungsbefehl *m*	instruction *f* de sauvegarde de registres	команда сохранения содержимого регистра
R 209	register selection	Registerauswahl *f*	sélection *f* de registre	выбор регистра
R 210	register set, register file (bank)	Registersatz *m*, Registerblock *m* <logisch>	jeu *m* de registres	блок регистров, регистровый файл, банк регистров
	register structure	s. R 195		
R 211	register-to-register architecture	Register-Register-Architektur *f*, Register-Register-Struktur *f* <Struktur mit Informationsverarbeitung aus und in Register>	structure *f* registre-registre	архитектура типа «регистр-регистр»
R 212	regular cell structure	reguläre (regelmäßige) Zellenstruktur *f*	structure *f* de cellule régulière	регулярная структура
R 213	regular interconnection	regelmäßige Zwischenverbindung *f* <in einer regulären Schaltungsstruktur>	interconnexion *f* régulière	регулярные внутренние соединения, регулярные межсоединения
R 214	regular logic	reguläre Logik *f*, regelmäßige Logikschaltungsstruktur *f* <z. B. zellulare Struktur>	logique *f* régulière	регулярная логика
R 215	regulate / to	regulieren, regeln	régler	регулировать
R 216	regulated supply	geregelte Stromversorgung *f*	alimentation *f* réglée	стабилизированный источник питания
R 217	regulated value	geregelter (stabilisierter) Wert *m*	valeur *f* réglée	регулируемое значение; стабилизированное значение
R 218	regulating and control system	Regelungs- und Steuerungssystem *n*	système *m* de réglage et de commande	система регулирования и управления
R 219	regulating circuit	Regelschaltung *f*	circuit *m* de réglage	схема регулирования
R 220	regulation	Regelung *f*, Regulierung *f*	réglage *m*, régulation *f*	регулирование
R 221	regulator	Regler *m*	régulateur *m*	регулятор
R 222	reinsertion	Wiedereinfügen *n*	réinsertion *f*	восстановление
R 223	reject / to	zurückweisen, aussteuern	rejeter	отвергать, отклонять
R 224	reject	Ausschuß *m*, Zurückweisung *f*	rebut *m*, rejet *m*	брак
R 225	relative address	relative Adresse *f*, Relativadresse *f*	adresse *f* relative	относительный адрес
R 226	relative addressing	Relativadressierung *f*	adressage *m* relatif	относительная адресация
R 227	relative addressing instruction	Relativadreßbefehl *m*	instruction *f* à adresse relative	команда с относительной адресацией
R 228	relative code	relativer Kode *m*	code *m* relatif	код с относительным адресом, относительный код
	relative coding	s. R 232		
R 229	relative displacement	relativer Versatz *m*, relative Verschiebung *f*	décalage *m* relatif	относительное смещение, относительный сдвиг
R 230	relative error	relativer Fehler *m*	erreur *f* relative	относительная погрешность (ошибка)
R 231	relative magnitude	relative Größe *f*	grandeur *f* relative	относительная величина
R 232	relative programming, relative coding	relative Programmierung *f*, Programmieren *n* mit relativen Adressen	programmation *f* relative (à adresses relatives)	программирование в относительных адресах
R 233	relative timing relationship of signals	relative zeitliche Beziehung *f* zwischen Signalen	rapport *m* relatif dans le temps entre signaux	относительная временная взаимосвязь сигналов

R 234	release / to	freigeben, auslösen	libérer, déclencher	освобождать, отпускать; разъединять, разблокировать
R 235	release-guard signal	Auslösequittungssignal n	signal m de garde de déclenchement	ответный сигнал готовности
R 236	release key	Auslösetaste f	touche f de déclenchement	кнопка разблокировки
R 237	release pulse	Auslöseimpuls m	impulsion f de déclenchement	пусковой импульс
R 238	release statement	Freigabeanweisung f	instruction f de libération	оператор разблокировки
R 239	reliability	Zuverlässigkeit f, Betriebssicherheit f	fiabilité f	надежность
R 240	reliability data	Zuverlässigkeitswerte mpl	valeurs fpl de fiabilité	показатели надежности
R 241	reliability index, RI	Zuverlässigkeitsindex m	index m de fiabilité	коэффициент надежности
R 242	reliability testing	Zuverlässigkeitsprüfung f	test m de fiabilité	испытание на надежность
R 243	reliable	zuverlässig, betriebssicher	fiable	надежный; достоверный
R 244	relocatability	Verschieblichkeit f	relogeabilité f	перемещаемость
R 245	relocatable address	verschiebliche Adresse f	adresse f relogeable	перемещаемый адрес
R 246	relocatable assembler	verschieblicher Assembler m	assembleur m relogeable	перемещаемый ассемблер
R 247	relocatable format	verschiebliches Format n	format m relogeable	перемещаемый формат
R 248	relocatable library	verschiebliche Programmbibliothek f, Bibliothek f für verschiebliche Programme <Objektmodulnbibliothek>	bibliothèque f de programmes relogeables	перемещаемая библиотека <библиотека объектных модулей>
R 249	relocatable loader, relocating loader	Verschiebelader m, verschiebendes Ladeprogramm n, Lader m für verschiebliche Programme	chargeur m à décalage	перемещающий загрузчик
R 250	relocatable object code	verschieblicher Objektkode m	code m objet relogeable	перемещаемый объектный код
R 251	relocatable program	verschiebliches Programm n	programme m relogeable	перемещаемая программа
R 252	relocate / to	verschieben im Speicher, umspeichern	reloger	перемещать; перераспределять <память>
	relocating loader	s. R 249		
R 253	relocation	Verschiebung f <im Adreßraum>, Umsiedlung f	décalage m, relogement m	перемещение
R 254	rely on / to	bauen auf, sich stützen auf	s'appuyer sur	полагаться <на>; основываться <на>
R 255	remainder	Rest m <Math.>	reste m	остаток; остаточный член [ряда]
R 256	remanence	Remanenz f	rémanence f	остаточная намагниченность (магнитная индукция)
R 257	remote access	Fernzugriff m	accès m à distance	дистанционный доступ
R 258	remote access storage and retrieval	Datenspeicherung und -wiedergewinnung f mit Fernzugriff	mémorisation f et recherche f de données à l'accès à distance	хранение и поиск с дистанционным доступом
R 259	remote batch processing	Stapelfernverarbeitung f	traitement m à distance à empilage	дистанционная пакетная обработка [данных]
R 260	remote communications	Fernkommunikation f, Nachrichtenfernverkehr m, Nachrichtenfernverbindung f	communication f à distance, télécommunications fpl	дистанционная связь
R 261	remote console, remote station (terminal)	Fernbedienplatz m, Fernterminal n, entfernt aufgestellte Datenendstation f	console f (station f, terminal m) à distance	удаленный терминал, удаленная станция
R 262	remote control	Fernsteuerung f	commande f à distance	дистанционное управление
R 263	remote control system	Fernwirksystem n	système m de télécommande	система дистанционного управления
	remote data processing	s. D 108		
R 264	remote diagnostic	Ferndiagnose f, Fernfehlersuche f	diagnostic m à distance	дистанционная диагностика
R 265	remote display	Fernanzeige f	affichage m à distance	удаленный дисплей
R 266	remote inquiry	Fernabfrage f	interrogation f à distance	дистанционный запрос (опрос)
R 267	remote job entry	Job-Ferneingabe f	entrée f de job à distance	дистанционный ввод заданий
R 268	remote monitoring, remote supervision	Fernüberwachung f	surveillance f à distance	дистанционный контроль
R 269	remote operation	Fernbedienung f, Fernsteuerung f	télécommande f	дистанционное управление
	remote processing	s. T 75		
	remote station	s. R 261		
	remote supervision	s. R 268		
	remote terminal	s. R 261		
R 270	remote transfer (transmission)	Fernübertragung f	télétransmission f	дистанционная передача
R 271	removable cartridge	Wechselkassette f	cassette (cartouche) f interchangeable	сменная кассета
R 272	removable disk	auswechselbare Platte f	disque m interchangeable	съемный (сменный) диск
R 273	removing	Beseitigung f, Rücknahme f, Wegnahme f	enlèvement m, retrait m	удаление; устранение
R 274	repeatability, reproducibility	Reproduzierbarkeit f	reproductibilité f	повторяемость; воспроизводимость
R 275	repeat counter	Wiederholungszähler m	compteur m de répétition	счетчик циклов
R 276	repeater	Zwischenverstärker m <Übertragungsleitung>	amplificateur m intermédiaire	промежуточный усилитель
R 277	repeater station	Relaisstelle f, Verstärkerstelle f, Zwischenstation f <Nachrichtentechnik>	station f de relais	ретранслятор
R 278	repeat scanning	nochmalige Abtastung f	balayage m répété	повторное сканирование
R 279	repetition factor	Wiederholungsfaktor m	facteur m de répétition	коэффициент повторения
R 280	repetition rate, repetitive rate	Wiederholungsfrequenz f, Folgefrequenz f	fréquence f de répétition	частота повторения (следования)

R 281	repetitive	sich wiederholend	répétitif	повторяющийся; повторный
	repetitive rate	s. R 280		
R 282	replacement	Ersatz m	remplacement m	замена
R 283	replacement character	Ersetzungszeichen n —	caractère m de remplacement	символ замены
	replacement part	s. S 592		
R 284	replacing discrete logic	Ersatz m diskreter Logikbausteine	remplacement m de modules logiques discrets	замена дискретной логики
R 285	reply pulse	Antwortimpuls m	impulsion f de réponse	ответный импульс
R 286	report file	Listendatei f	fichier m de liste[s]	файл отчетов
R 287	report generation	Listenerstellung f	génération f de liste[s]	генерирование отчетов
	report program	s. L 181		
	report program generator language	s. R 415		
	reproducibility	s. R 274		
R 288	reproducible error	reproduzierbarer Fehler m	erreur f reproductible	воспроизводимая ошибка
	reprogrammable read-only memory	s. R 290		
R 289	reprogramming	Umprogrammierung f, Neuprogrammierung f	reprogrammation f	репрограммирование, перепрограммирование
R 290	RePROM, reprogrammable read-only memory	RePROM m, neuprogrammierbarer ROM (Nur-Lese-Speicher) m <nach Löschung des Inhalts mittels UV-Lichts>	RePROM f, PROM f reprogrammable	репрограммируемое постоянное запоминающее устройство, репрограммируемое ПЗУ, РПЗУ <электрическая запись информации, стирание ультрафиолетовыми лучами>
R 291	RePROM programmer	Programmiergerät n für RePROM-Schaltkreise	appareil m de programmation pour RePROM	программатор для репрограммируемых ПЗУ
R 292	request / to	anfordern, anfragen	demander, exiger	запрашивать, требовать
R 293	request	Anfrage f, Anforderung f	demande f, exigence f	запрос
R 294	request repeat	Wiederholungsanforderung f	demande f de répétition	запрос повторения <передачи>
R 295	request-repeat system	System n mit automatischer Wiederholungsanforderung	système m à demande de répétition	система с автоматическим перезапросом
R 296	request signal	Anforderungssignal n	signal m de demande	сигнал запроса
R 297	request to send	Sendeanforderung f	demande f d'émission	запрос передачи
R 298	requirement	Anforderung f, Forderung f, Erfordernis n	nécessité f	требование
R 299	requirements tracer	Anforderungsverfolger m, Anforderungsfolge-Prüfprogramm n	programme m de poursuite de demandes	программа прослеживания требований
R 300	rerun / to	wiederablaufen, Programm wiederholen	répéter la marche, répéter le programme	запускать (прогонять) повторно
R 301	rerun	Wiederholungslauf m	marche f de répétition	повторный пуск (прогон)
R 302	rerun point	Wiederholungspunkt m	point m de répétition	точка повторного пуска
R 303	rescue dump, R dump	Rettungsumspeicherung f <z. B. RAM-Magnetband bei Stromausfall>	changement m de mémoire de sauvegarde	аварийная разгрузка, аварийный дамп
R 304	research and development, R&D	Forschung f und Entwicklung f, FuE	recherche f et développement m	научно-исследовательские и опытно-конструкторские работы
R 305	research-oriented processing	forschungsorientierte Verarbeitung f, wissenschaftlich-technische Datenverarbeitung f	traitement m orienté recherche	обработка экспериментальных данных, обработка результатов научных исследований
R 306	reset / to	zurücksetzen, in Grundstellung bringen	remettre	возвращать в исходное состояние, сбрасывать
R 307	reset button	Rücksetztaste f	touche f de RAZ	кнопка сброса
	reset command	s. R 310		
R 308	reset condition	Rücksetzbedingung f	condition f de RAZ	условие возврата в исходное состояние
R 309	reset input	Rücksetzeingang m	entrée f de RAZ	вход сброса
R 310	reset instruction, reset command	Rücksetzbefehl m	instruction f de RAZ	команда сброса
R 311	reset line	Rücksetzleitung f	ligne f de RAZ	линия сброса
R 312	reset pulse	Rücksetzimpuls m	impulsion f de RAZ	импульс сброса
R 313	reset signal	Rücksetzsignal n <Anfangszustands-Einstellung>	signal m de mise à zéro	сигнал сброса
R 314	reset switch	Rücksetzschalter m	commutateur m de RAZ	переключатель возврата в исходное состояние
R 315	residence	Aufenthalt m	résidence f	область размещения [в памяти]
R 316	resident	resident <1. ständig im Hauptspeicher befindlich; 2. auf dem eigenen Rechner laufend>	résident	резидентный <размещенный в главной памяти>
R 317	resident compiler	residenter Kompilierer m, auf dem eigenen [Mikro-]Rechner laufender Kompilierer	compilateur m résident	резидентный компилятор
R 318	resident macro-assembler	residenter Makroassembler m, Makroassembler auf dem eigenen Rechner laufend	assembleur m macro résident	резидентный макроассемблер
R 319	resident program	residentes (im Hauptspeicher ständig vorhandenes) Programm n	programme m résident	резидентная программа
R 320	resident software	residente Systemunterlagen fpl, auf dem Objektrechner lauffähige Systemprogramme npl	logiciels mpl résidents	резидентное программное обеспечение

R 321	residual charge	Restladung f	charge f résiduelle	остаточный заряд
R 322	residual class code	Restklassenkode m	code m de classe résiduel	код в остаточных классах, код в остатках
R 323	residual current	Reststrom m	courant m résiduel	остаточный ток; ток утечки
	resistance coupling	s. R 326		
	resistance drop	s. O 41		
R 324	resistant	widerstandsfähig	résistant	резистивный
R 325	resistive component	ohmsche Komponente f	composante f ohmique	резистивный компонент
R 326	resistive coupling, resistance coupling	Widerstandskopplung f	couplage m par résistance	резистивная связь
	resistive load	s. O 42		
R 327	resistivity	spezifischer Widerstand m	résistance f spécifique	удельное сопротивление
R 328	resistor	Widerstand m <Bauteil>	résistance f	резистор
R 329	resistor-capacitor circuit, RC circuit	RC-Schaltung f <Netzwerk aus Widerständen und Kapazitäten>	circuit m RC	RC-цепь
R 330	resistor-capacitor-transistor-logic, RCTL	RCTL f, Widerstand-Kondensator-Transistor-Logik f <Schaltungstechnik>	logique f résistance-capacité-transistor	резисторно-емкостная транзисторная логика, транзисторная логика с резистивно-емкостными связями
	resistor-transistor-logic	s. R 418		
R 331	resolution capability (power), resolving power	Auflösungsvermögen n	pouvoir m de résolution	разрешающая способность
R 332	resolve / to	auflösen	résoudre	разрешать
R 333	resolver	Koordinatenwandler m, Auflöser m, Resolver m	convertisseur m de coordonnées	координатный преобразователь
	resolving power	s. R 331		
	resonator	s. O 182		
R 334	resonator circuit	Schwingkreis m	circuit m d'oscillation	колебательный контур
R 335	resource	Ressource f, Systemmittel n, Betriebsmittel n, verfügbare Einrichtung f	ressource f	ресурс
R 336	resource allocation	Ressourcenzuordnung f, Systemmittelzuordnung f	attribution f de ressource	распределение ресурсов
R 337	resource allocation processor	Ressourcen-Zuordnungsprozessor m, Systemmittel-Zuordnungsprozessor m <in Master-Slave-Multiprozessorsystemen>	processeur m d'attribution de ressources	процессор распределения ресурсов
R 338	resource control	Ressourcensteuerung f, Systemmittelsteuerung f, Steuerung f der verfügbaren Einrichtungen	commande f des ressources	управление ресурсами
R 339	resource management	Ressourcenverwaltung f, Systemmittelverwaltung f	gestion f de ressources	управление запасами; управление ресурсами
R 340	resource sharing	Ressourcenteilung f, anteilige Nutzung f gemeinsamer Systemmittel	partage m des ressources	разделение ресурсов
R 341	resource-sharing capability	Ressourcenteilungsfähigkeit f, Fähigkeit f zur anteiligen Nutzung gemeinsamer Systemmittel	faculté f de partage des ressources	возможность разделения ресурсов
R 342	response	Antwort f, Ansprechen n, Reaktion f	réponse f	ответ; чувствительность; зависимость; реакция
R 343	response curve	Empfindlichkeitskurve f, Frequenzgang m	courbe f de réponse	частотная характеристика
R 344	response rate	Ansprechrate f, Antwortrate f <Reaktionskoeffizient>	cote f de réponse	коэффициент ответа <отношение времени ответа ко времени обслуживания задания>
R 345	response threshold	Ansprechschwelle f	seuil m de réponse	порог чувствительности
R 346	response time	Antwortzeit f, Ansprechzeit f	temps m de réponse	время ответа; время запаздывания; время доставки сообщения <сети ЭВМ>
R 347	restart	Re-Start m, Wiederanlauf m eines Programms	redémarrage	рестарт, повторный пуск ⌈ного пуска)
R 348	restart address	Wiederanlaufadresse f	adresse f de redémarrage	адрес рестарта (повтор-
R 349	restart point	Wiederanlaufpunkt m <Stützpunkt im Programm für Wiederanlauf>	point m de redémarrage	точка рестарта (повторного пуска)
R 350	restart procedure	Wiederanlaufverfahren n	procédé m de redémarrage	процедура рестарта (повторного пуска)
R 351	restore / to	rückspeichern, wiedereinsetzen	remettre en mémoire, replacer	восстанавливать
R 352	restore status / to, to unsave status	Status rückspeichern (wiedereintragen)	remettre l'état en mémoire	восстанавливать состояние
R 353	restoring	Rückspeichern n	remise f en mémoire	восстановление, возврат в исходное состояние
R 354	restrict / to	einschränken	restreindre	ограничивать
R 355	restriction	Beschränkung f, Einschränkung f	restriction f	ограничение; препятствие
R 356	result	Ergebnis n, Resultat n	résultat m	результат, исход
R 357	retail terminal	Einzelhandelsterminal n, Datenstation f für den Einzelhandel	terminal m de commerce en détail	кассовый аппарат сети сбора данных
R 358	retrieval	Wiederauffindung f, Wiederauffinden n	recouvrement m, recherche f	поиск; вызов данных
R 359	return / to	zurückkehren, zurückführen	retourner	возвращать[ся]
R 360	return	Rückkehr f, Rücksprung m	retour m, saut m de retour	возврат
R 361	return address	Rückkehradresse f, Rücksprungadresse f	adresse f de retour	адрес возврата

R 362	return code	Rückkehrkode m	code m de retour	код возврата
	return command	s. R 363		
R 363	**return instruction,** return command	Rückkehrbefehl m, Rücksprungbefehl m	instruction f de retour	команда возврата
R 364	**return location**	Rückkehrplatz m, Rückkehrspeicherzelle f	place f de retour	ячейка [адреса] возврата
R 365	**return-to-zero recording,** RZ recording	Rückkehr-zur-Null-Aufzeichnung f	enregistrement m retour à zéro	запись с возвращением к нулю
R 366	reuse	Wiederverwendung f	réusage m	повторное использование
R 367	**reversal of sign,** sign reversal (inversion)	Vorzeichenumkehr[ung] f	inversion f de signe	смена (инверсия) знака
R 368	**reverse / to,** to invert	umkehren, umdrehen	inverser	реверсировать, обращать
	reverse bias	s. B 1		
	reverse current	s. B 4		
R 369	**reverse direction,** back direction	Sperrichtung f	direction f inverse	обратное направление
R 370	**reversely doped transistors**	umgekehrt (entgegengesetzt) dotierte Transistoren mpl \<bei CMOS-Technik\>	transistors mpl dopés inversement	противоположно легированные транзисторы \<КМОП-технология\>
R 371	**reverse phase**	Gegenphase f	phase f inverse	противоположная (обратная) фаза
R 372	**reverse resistance,** backward resistance	Sperrwiderstand m	résistance f inverse	обратное сопротивление
R 373	**reverse scan**	umgekehrte Abtastung f \<Editieroperation\>	balayage m inverse	редактирование [текста] с подавлением незначащих нулей
R 374	**reverse translator**	umgekehrter Übersetzer m, Gegenrichtungsübersetzer m \<generiert eine Programmiersprachversion aus Maschinenkodeprogramm\>	traducteur m inverse	обратный транслятор \<генератор текста программы из машинного кода\>
	reverse voltage	s. B 24		┌тимый
R 375	reversible	umkehrbar	reversible	реверсируемый, обра-
R 376	**reversible process**	umkehrbarer Vorgang m	processus m reversible	обратимый процесс
R 377	**rewrite / to**	rückschreiben, wiedereinschreiben	écrire (inscrire) de nouveau	перезаписывать
	RI	s. 1. R 4; 2. R 241		
R 378	**right-aligned, right-justified**	rechtsbündig	aligné à droite	выравненный вправо; выравненный по правому краю
R 379	**right shift**	Rechtsverschiebung f	décalage m à droite	сдвиг вправо
R 380	**ring counter**	Ringzähler m	compteur m circulaire	кольцевой счетчик
R 381	**ripple carry**	durchrieselnder Übertrag m \<Übertragsbildung durch aufeinanderfolgenden Durchlauf aller Positionen\>	retenue f ruisselante	[последовательно] распространяющийся перенос
R 382	**ripple counter**	durchlaufender Zähler m \<Zählimpuls bewirkt aufeinanderfolgende Inhaltsänderung in den einzelnen Stufen\>	compteur m courant	счетчик с последовательным переносом
R 383	**ripple factor**	Welligkeitsfaktor m, Brummfaktor m	facteur m d'ondulation	коэффициент пульсаций
R 384	**rise time**	Anstiegszeit f	temps m de montée	время нарастания
R 385	**rising edge**	ansteigende Flanke f	flanc m montant	фронт нарастания
R 386	**RMM,** read-mostly memory	RMM m, Meist-Lese-Speicher m, Halbfestspeicher m, \<Prinzipbezeichnung für einen ROM mit Inhaltsänderungsmöglichkeit, z. B. EAROM\>	mémoire f RMM	память преимущественно для чтения \<репрограммируемые ПЗУ\>
	RMS value	s. R 397		
R 387	robot	Roboter m, Handhabungssystem n	robot m	робот
R 388	**robotics**	Robotertechnik f	technique f des robots, robotique f	робототехника
R 389	**roll down / to**	Bildschirmzeilen abwärts verschieben	décaler des lignes de l'écran vers le bas	сдвигать строки [текста на экране дисплея] в обратном направлении
R 390	**roll in / to**	einspeichern \<Rückkehr nach Auslagerung\>	mettre en mémoire	развертывать, подкачивать \<возвращать данные в главную память из внешней памяти\>
R 391	**roll out / to**	ausspeichern \<Registerinhalte; Diagnose\>	rejeter	свертывать, сбрасывать \<переписывать содержимое главной памяти во внешнюю память\>
R 392	**roll up / to**	Bildschirmzeilen aufwärts verschieben	décaler des lignes de l'écran vers le haut	сдвигать строки [текста на экране дисплея] в прямом направлении
R 393	**ROM,** read-only memory	ROM m, Nur-Lese-Speicher m \<Festspeicher\>	ROM f, mémoire f fixe	постоянное запоминающее устройство, ПЗУ
R 394	**ROM bootstrap**	ROM-Urlader m \<ROM-gespeichertes Anlaufprogramm\>	chargeur m primitif en mémoire lecture seule	хранящийся в ПЗУ первичный загрузчик
R 395	**ROM-less microcomputer**	ROM-loser Mikrorechner m, Mikrorechner-Schaltkreis m ohne internen ROM	microcalculateur m sans mémoire lecture seule	микро-ЭВМ без внутреннего ПЗУ
R 396	**ROM simulator**	ROM-Simulator m, Simulationsgerät n für ROM	simulateur m pour mémoire lecture seule	имитатор ПЗУ \<модуль ОЗУ, имеющий харак-

		‹Festspeicherersatz durch äquivalente RAM›		теристики аналогичные моделируемому ПЗУ и используемый в системе проектирования›
R 397	root-mean-square value, RMS value	quadratischer Mittelwert m	valeur f moyenne quadratique	среднеквадратичное значение
	rotary	$s.$ R 98		
R 398	rotate / to, to circulate	umlaufen	circuler	вращать[ся]
R 399	rotation, circulation	Umlauf m	rotation f, circulation f	вращение
	rotational delay	$s.$ R 400		
	rotational speed	$s.$ R 401		
R 400	rotation delay, rotational delay	Umlaufverzögerung f ‹Platte›, Umdrehungsverzögerung f	retardement m circulaire	замедление вращения
R 401	rotation speed, rotational (circulation) speed	Umlaufgeschwindigkeit f	vitesse f de rotation (circulation)	скорость вращения
R 402	round / to	runden	arrondir	округлять
R 403	rounding	Runden n, Rundung f	arrondissement m	округление
R 404	rounding error	Rundungsfehler m	erreur f d'arrondissement	ошибка округления
R 405	round off / to	abrunden	arrondir en dessous	округлять с недостатком
R 406	round up / to	aufrunden	arrondir au-dessus	округлять с избытком
R 407	route / to	zuführen, zuleiten	acheminer	проводить путь; трассировать; определять маршрут
R 408	routine	Routine f ‹Programm oder Programmteil, das häufig wiederholt wird›	routine f	стандартная программа
R 409	routing	Leitweglenkung f, Übertragungswegfestlegung f, Wegesuche f	guidage m sur voie [de transmission]	маршрутизация; трассировка
R 410	routing system	Leitwegsystem n	système m de voie guide	система маршрутизации
R 411	routing technique	Leitwegverfahren n, Wegesuchverfahren n	technique f de voie guide	метод маршрутизации
R 412	row	Reihe f; Zeile f ‹Matrix, Lochkarte›	ligne f	ряд; строка ‹матрица, перфокарта›
R 413	row decoder	Zeilenentschlüßler m ‹Matrix›, Reihendekoder m	décodeur m de ligne	дешифратор строки
R 414	row selection	Zeilenauswahl f ‹Matrix›, Reihenauswahl f	sélection f (choix m) de ligne	выбор строки
R 415	RPG, report program generator language	RPG n, Listenprogrammgeneratorsprache f ‹einfache Sprache für kommerzielle Programmierung›	RPG m, langage m de génération de programme à liste	РПГ, генератор программ отчетов, язык программирования для обработки экономических и статистических данных ‹фирма IBM›
R 416	RS flip-flop	RS-Flipflop n ‹Flipflop mit statischen Setz- und Rücksetzeingängen›	bascule f électronique de type RS	RS-триггер
R 417	RS format	Register-Speicher-Befehlsformat n	format m d'instruction registre-mémoire	формат [команды] типа регистр-память
R 418	RTL, resistor-transistor logic	RTL f, Widerstand-Transistor-Logik f ‹Schaltungstechnik›	logique f résistance-transistor	резисторно-транзисторная логика, РТЛ
R 419	rule	Regel f, Vorschrift f	règle f, prescription f	правило; масштаб
	run	$s.$ M 37		
R 420	running costs	laufende Kosten pl	frais mpl courants	текущие расходы
R 421	running time, run time	Laufzeit f ‹Programm, Aufgabenbearbeitung›	temps m de marche	время прогона (выполнения программы)
	run of the program	$s.$ P 630		
	run time	$s.$ R 421		
R 422	run-time system	Laufzeitsystem n ‹Softwareunterstützung für Programmiersprache›	système m de temps de marche	исполнительная система ‹система, управляющая процессом исполнения программы›
	RWM	$s.$ R 58		
	RZ recording	$s.$ R 365		

S

S 1	safety device	Sicherheitsvorrichtung f	dispositif m de sûreté	устройство защиты
S 2	safety requirements	Sicherheitsanforderungen fpl	exigences fpl de sûreté	требования техники безопасности
	SAG	$s.$ S 141		
S 3	SAGMOS, self-aligning gate MOS	SAGMOS f, MOS-Technik f mit selbstjustierendem Transistorgate	SAGMOS f, technique f MOS à gate autoajusté	МОП-структуры с самосовмещенными затворами
	SAM	$s.$ S 243		
S 4	SAMOS, stacked-gate avalanche injection MOS	SAMOS f, MOS-Speicherelektrodentechnik f mit Stapelgate ‹für FROM, EAROM, RePROM›	technique f de semi-conducteurs M. O. S. à injection d'électrons par gate, SAMOS f	лавиноинжекционные МОП-приборы с составными затворами
S 5	sample / to	austasten, [ausgewählt] abtasten	scruter	производить выборку
S 6	sample	Stichprobe f	échantillon m d'essai	выборка, выборочная совокупность; замер; эталон ⌐выборки
S 7	sample amplifier	Abtastverstärker m	amplificateur m de balayage	усилитель [сигнала]
S 8	sample-and-hold amplifier	Abtast-Speicher-Verstärker m	amplificateur m de palpage et de mémorisation	усилитель [устройства] выборки и хранения
S 9	sample-and-hold circuit	Abtast-Halte-Schaltung f, Abtast-Speicher-Schaltung f ‹Analogsignalerfassung›	circuit m de palpage et de mémorisation	схема выборки и хранения

S 10	sampled-data control	Abtastregelung f	commande f de balayage	дискретное управление; импульсное управление
S 11	sampled-data system	Abtastsystem n, Datenabtastsystem n	système m de palpage de données	дискретная система [управления]; импульсная следящая система; система сканирования данных
S 12	sample facility, sampler, scanner	Abtasteinrichtung f, Abtaster m	dispositif m de balayage	сканирующее устройство
S 13	sampling, scanning	Abfragen n, Abtastung f	balayage m	выборка: дискретизация
S 14	sampling circuit	Abtastschaltung f	circuit m de balayage	схема выборки
S 15	sampling frequency, scan frequency	Abtastfrequenz f	fréquence f de balayage	частота выборки
S 16	sampling gate	Abtastgatter n	porte f de balayage	коммутатор выборки
	sampling impulse	s. S 19		входного сигнала
S 17	sampling oscilloscope	Sampling-Oszillograf m	oscilloscope m de sampling	стробоскопический осциллограф
S 18	sampling period	Sampling-Periode f, Abtastperiode f	période f de balayage	период дискретизации
S 19	sampling pulse, sampling (scanning) pulse	Abtastimpuls m, Tastimpuls m	impulsion f de balayage	импульс выборки
S 20	sampling rate, scanning (sensing) rate	Abtastrate f	cote f de scrutation (balayage)	скорость выборки
S 21	sampling speed, scanning (sensing) speed	Abtastgeschwindigkeit f	vitesse f de balayage	скорость развертки
S 22	sandwich	Schichtelement n, Schichtkörper m	élément m sandwich	конструкция слоистого типа, конструкция типа «сэндвич»
S 23	sapphire	Saphir m	saphir m	сапфир
S 24	sapphire substrate	Saphir-Substrat n, Saphir-Trägermaterial n	substrat m au saphir	сапфировая подложка
S 25	satellite computer	Satellitenrechner m	calculateur m satellite	сателлитная (периферийная) ЭВМ
S 26	saturated logic	Übersteuerungslogik f, Sättigungslogik f	logique f de saturation	насыщенная логика, логика на насыщающихся транзисторах
S 27	saturation	Sättigung f, Übersteuerung f	saturation f	насыщение
S 28	saturation current	Sättigungsstrom m	courant m de saturation	ток насыщения
S 29	saturation state	Sättigungszustand m	état m de saturation	состояние насыщения
S 30	save / to	retten, aufbewahren, sichern, sparen	sauvegarder	сохранять, экономить
S 31	save area	Sicherungsbereich m, Rettungsbereich m	champ m de sauvegarde	область сохранения
S 32	save status / to	Status retten	sauvegarder l'état	сохранять состояние
S 33	saving in logic	Logikelementeeinsparung f	économie f d'éléments logiques	экономия логических элементов
S 34	saving in size	Größeneinsparung f, Flächeneinsparung f <Chip>	économie f de surface	сокращение габаритов; экономия площади [кристалла]
	SBC	s. S 449		
S 35	scalar	skalar	scalaire	скалярный
	scalar	s. a. S 37		
S 36	scalar product	Skalarprodukt n	produit m scalaire	скалярное произведение
S 37	scalar quantity, scalar	skalare Größe f, Skalar m	quantité f scalaire	скаляр, скалярная величина
S 38	scale / to	skalieren, maßstabsgerecht ändern	modifier à l'échelle	масштабировать, изменять масштаб; приводить к масштабу
S 39	scaled[-down] MOS circuit, SMOS chip	skalierter (maßstäblich verkleinerter) MOS-Schaltkreis m, MOS-Schaltung f mit linear reduzierten Dimensionen	circuit m MOS réduit	МОП-схема с уменьшенной площадью кристалла
S 40	scale down / to	maßstabsgerecht verkleinern	réduire à l'échelle	уменьшать масштаб; уменьшать в масштабе
S 41	scaled value	untersetzter Wert m	valeur f réduite	приведенное к масштабу значение
S 42	scale factor, scaling factor	Skalenfaktor m, Maßstabsfaktor m, Skalierungsfaktor m, Untersetzungsfaktor m	facteur m d'échelle	масштабный множитель (коэффициент)
S 43	scaler	Untersetzer m	démultiplicateur m	счетчик
S 44	scale range (span)	Skalenbereich m	champ m d'échelle	диапазон шкалы
S 45	scaling	Skalierung f, Maßstabsänderung f, Untersetzung f	modification f d'échelle	масштабирование; пересчет
S 46	scaling circuit	Untersetzerschaltung f	circuit m démultiplicateur	пересчетная схема
S 47	scaling control	Skalierungssteuerung f, Maßstabssteuerung f	commande f d'échelle	управление масштабированием
	scaling factor	s. S 42		
S 48	scaling ratio	Untersetzungsverhältnis n	rapport m de démultiplication	коэффициент пересчета
S 49	scan / to	durchmustern, [punktweise] abtasten	balayer	сканировать, развертывать
S 50	scan counter	Abtastzähler m	compteur m de scrutation (balayage)	счетчик сканирования
	scan frequency	s. S 15		
S 51	scan matrix	Abtastmatrix f	matrice f de balayage	сканирующая матрица
	scanner	s. S 12		
S 52	scanning	Absuchen n	scrutation f	сканирование
	scanning	s. a. S 13		
S 53	scanning action	Abtastvorgang m	action f de balayage	процесс сканирования
S 54	scanning cycle	Abtastzyklus m	cycle m de balayage	цикл сканирования; цикл развертки

S 55	scanning line	Abtastzeile f	ligne f de balayage	строка развертки
S 56	scanning pulse	Rasterimpuls m	impulsion f de scrutation	импульс развертки
	scanning pulse	s. a. S 19		
	scanning rate	s. S 20		
	scanning speed	s. S 21		
S 57	scanning spot	Abtastfleck m	tache f de balayage	развертывающее (бегущее, сканирующее) пятно
S 58	scan size	Abtastfläche f, Abtastformat n	surface f (format m) de balayage	сканируемая площадь; формат развертки
S 59	scatter / to	streuen, zerstreuen	distribuer, disséminer	разбрасывать; рассеивать[ся]
S 60	scattered	gestreut	distribué	разбросанный, несплошной; рассеянный
S 61	scattering	Streuung f	dispersion f	разброс; рассеяние
S 62	scatter loading	Streuladung f <Programmspeicherung>	chargement m diffusé	загрузка вразброс
S 63	scatter read	Streulesung f, gestreutes Lesen n <Lesen aus verschiedenen Speicherbereichen>	lecture f diffusée	чтение вразброс
	SCC	s. 1. S 249; 2. S 457		
	SCCD	s. S 873		
S 64	schedule / to	zeitlichen Ablauf planen	planifier le déroulement	составлять расписание (план)
S 65	schedule	Ablaufplan m, Zeitplan m	plan m de déroulement	расписание, план
S 66	scheduler	Scheduler m, Ablaufauflister m <Steuerprogramm>	programme m d'établissement de déroulement	планировщик
S 67	scheduling	Ablauffolgeplanung f	planning m de séquence	составление расписания (плана)
S 68	schematic circuit diagram	Blockschema n, Prinzipschaltbild n	schéma m de principe	принципиальная [электрическая] схема
S 69	Schmitt limiter	Schmitt-Begrenzer m	limitateur m Schmitt	усилитель-ограничитель
S 70	Schmitt trigger circuitry	Schmitt-Triggerschaltung f	bascule f de Schmitt	триггер Шмитта
S 71	Schottky barrier	Schottky-Barriere f, Schottky-Sperrschicht f <Metall-Halbleiter-Übergangspotentialwall>	barrière f Schottky	барьер Шоттки
S 72	Schottky barrier diode, Schottky diode	Schottky-Sperrschichtdiode f <im Gegensatz zur pn-Sperrschichtdiode>, Schottky-Diode f	diode f Schottky	диод Шоттки
S 73	Schottky bipolar electrically programmable ROM	elektrisch programmierbarer ROM m in bipolarer Schottky-Technik	mémoire f lecture seule programmable électriquement en technique bipolaire Schottky	электрически программируемое постоянное запоминающее устройство на биполярных элементах с диодами Шоттки
S 74	Schottky bipolar memory	bipolarer Speicher m in Schottky-Technik	mémoire f bipolaire en technique Schottky	память на биполярных элементах с диодами Шоттки
S 75	Schottky bipolar microcomputer set	Mikrorechner-Schaltkreissatz m in bipolarer Schottky-Technik	jeu m de circuits bipolaires Schottky pour microcalculateurs	микропроцессорный набор на основе биполярных схем с диодами Шоттки
	Schottky circuit	s. S 77		
S 76	Schottky-clamped transistor	Schottky-Transistor m, Transistor m mit Schottky-Diode geklammert	transistor m à diode Schottky	транзистор с [фиксирующим] диодом Шоттки, транзистор Шоттки
	Schottky diode	s. S 72		
	Schottky-diode FET logic	s. S 92		
S 77	Schottky TTL circuit, Schottky circuit	Schottky-TTL-Schaltung f, Schottky-Schaltung f <TTL-Schaltung mit Schottky-Klammerdioden>	circuit m Schottky TTL	ТТЛ-схема с диодами Шоттки
S 78	scientific computer	wissenschaftlicher Rechner m, Rechner für wissenschaftliche Aufgaben	calculateur m scientifique	ЭВМ для научных расчетов
S 79	scientific instrumentation	wissenschaftliche Gerätetechnik (Instrumentierung) f	instrumentation f scientifique	[измерительные] приборы для научных исследований
S 80	scientific instrument manufacture	wissenschaftlicher Gerätebau m	fabrication f d'appareils scientifiques	производство [измерительных] приборов для научных исследований
	SCLT	s. S 583		
S 81	scope	Spielraum m, Gültigkeitsbereich m	champ m de validité	диапазон; сфера действия
S 82	scratch area	Notizbereich m, Arbeitsbereich m <Speicher>	domaine m de travail	рабочая область (зона) <памяти>
	scratch file	s. W 50		
S 83/4	scratch-pad memory	Notizblockspeicher m, Notizspeicher m	mémoire f de bloc-notes	сверхоперативное запоминающее устройство, СОЗУ
S 85	scratch-pad register	Notizregister n	registre m de bloc-notes	регистр сверхоперативной памяти
S 86	screen	Bildschirm m	écran m	экран
S 87	screen area	Schirmfläche f	surface f d'écran	площадь экрана; поверхность экрана
S 88	screen device	Bildschirmgerät n	appareil m à écran	устройство визуального отображения
S 89	screen formatting	Bildschirmformatierung f	formation f d'écran	задание формата [данных] для вывода на экран
	screening	s. S 314		
S 90	screen terminal	Bildschirmterminal n	terminal m à écran	экранный терминал

S 91	**scrolling**	Bildlauf *m*, vertikale Bildschirmzeilenverschiebung *f* s. S 874	décalage *m* vertical d'image	отображение на дисплее в рулонном режиме
	SCT			
S 92	**SDFL**, Schottky-diode FET logic	SDFL *f*, Schottky-Dioden-Feldeffekttransistortechnik *f*, <GaAs-Schaltungstechnik>	SDFL *f*, logique *f* à diode Schottky-transistor à effet de champ	логические схемы на МОП-транзисторах с диодами Шоттки
S 93	**SDLC**, synchronous data link control	SDLC *f*, synchrone Datenleitungssteuerung *f* <Übertragungsverfahren>	commande *f* de liaison de données synchrone	синхронное управление каналом передачи данных, протокол SDLC
S 94	**SDLC mode**, synchronous data link control mode	SDLC-Modus *m*, Betriebsart *f* mit synchroner Datenleitungssteuerung	mode *m* SDLC, mode à commande synchrone de liaison de données	режим синхронного управления каналом передачи данных
S 95	**search algorithm**	Suchalgorithmus *m*	algorithme *m* de recherche	алгоритм поиска
S 96	**searching method**, searching procedure	Suchverfahren *n*	méthode *f* de recherche	метод (процедура) поиска
S 97	**searching operating**, seek operation	Suchvorgang *m*, Suchoperation *f*	opération *f* de recherche	операция поиска
	searching procedure	s. S 96		
S 98	**search instruction**	Suchbefehl *m*	instruction *f* de recherche	команда поиска
S 99	**search key**	Suchschlüssel *m*	clé *f* de recherche	ключ поиска
S 100	**search process**	Suchprozeß *m*	processus *m* de recherche	процесс поиска
S 101	**secondary memory (storage)**	Sekundärspeicher *m*	mémoire *f* secondaire	вторичная (вспомогательная) память
S 102	**secondary storage system**	Sekundärspeichersystem *n*	système *m* secondaire de mémoire	вспомогательная система памяти, система вторичной памяти
S 103	**second-generation microprocessor**	Mikroprozessor *m* der zweiten [LSI-]Generation	microprocesseur *m* de la deuxième génération [LSI]	микропроцессор второго поколения
S 104	**second-level addressing**	Adressierung *f* auf dem zweiten Niveau <Adreßfeldinhalt des Befehls = Adresse der Operandenadresse>	adressage *m* au second niveau	адресация второго уровня
S 105	**second-level polysilicon**	zweite Polysiliziumebene *f*	second niveau *m* de polysilicium	второй уровень поликремния
S 106	**second source**	Zweitquelle *f*, Zweitbezugsquelle *f*, Zweithersteller *m*	seconde source *f*, second fabricant *m*	второй поставщик
S 107	**second-source product**	Produkt *n* mit Zweithersteller	produit *m* de second fabricant	изделие второго поставщика
S 108	**sector address**	Sektoradresse *f*	adresse *f* de secteur	адрес сектора
	sedecimal	s. H 73		
S 109	**seek check bit**	Suchprüfbit *n*	bit *m* de contrôle de recherche	контрольный бит поиска
	seek operation	s. S 97		
S 110	**seek time**	Suchzeit *f*, Einstellzeit *f* <Plattenspeicher>	temps *m* de recherche	время установки <запоминающее устройство на магнитных дисках>
S 111	**segment / to**	segmentieren, unterteilen	segmenter	сегментировать; делить на части
S 112	**segment address**	Segmentadresse *f*	adresse *f* de segment	адрес сегмента
S 113	**segmentation**	Segmentierung *f*, Unterteilung *f* <Programm, Speicher>	segmentation *f*	сегментация
S 114	**segment base**	Segmentbasis *f*	base *f* de segment	база сегмента
S 115	**segment base address**	Segmentbasisadresse *f*	adresse *f* de base de segment	адрес базы сегмента
S 116	**segment boundary**	Segmentgrenze *f*	limite *f* de segment	граница сегмента
S 117	**segment decoder**	Segmententschlüßler *m*	décodeur *m* de segment	дешифратор сегмента
S 118	**segmented addressing**	segmentierte (gegliederte) Adressierung *f*	adressage *m* segmenté	сегментная адресация
S 119	**segmented address space**	segmentierter (unterteilter, abschnittsweise gegliederter) Adreßraum	espace *m* d'adresse segmenté	сегментированное адресное пространство
S 120	**segmented mode**	segmentierte Betriebsweise *f*, Betrieb *m* mit Segmenten	mode *m* segmenté	режим [работы] с сегментацией
S 121	**segment header**	Segmentvorsatz *m*	en-tête *m* de segment	заголовок сегмента
S 122	**segment limit protection**	Segmentgrenzenschutz *m*	protection *f* de limite de segment	защита границы сегмента
S 123	**segment management**	Segmentverwaltung *f*	gestion *f* de segment	управление сегментами
S 124	**segment number**	Segmentnummer *f*, Abschnittsnummer *f*	numéro *m* de segment	номер сегмента
S 125	**segment register**	Segmentregister *n*	registre *m* de segment	регистр сегмента
S 126	**select / to**	auswählen	sélectionner	выбирать; отбирать
S 127	**selected I/O port**	ausgewähltes E/A-Tor *n*, angesteuerter E/A-Anschluß *m*	porte *f* d'E/S sélectionnée	выбранный порт ввода-вывода
S 128	**select input**	Auswahleingang *m*	entrée *f* de sélection	вход выбора
S 129	**selection**	Auswahl *f*, Ansteuerung *f*	sélection *f*	выбор[ка]; селекция
	selection circuit	s. S 130		
S 130	**selection logic**, selection circuit, select logic	Auswahlschaltung *f*, Ansteuerschaltung *f*	circuit *m* de sélection	схема селекции
S 131	**selection signal**, select signal	Auswahlsignal *n*	signal *m* de sélection	сигнал выбора
S 132	**selection technique**	Auswahlverfahren *n*	procédé *m* de sélection	способ селекции
S 133	**selective dump**	selektiver Speicherauszug *m*	extrait *m* [de mémoire] sélectif	выборочный дамп, выборочная разгрузка
	select logic	s. S 130		
S 134	**selector**	Auswahlschalter *m*, Selektor *m*	commutateur *m* de sélection, sélecteur *m*	селекторный переключатель, селектор
S 135	**selector channel**	Selektorkanal *m*	canal *m* sélecteur	селекторный канал
	select signal	s. S 131		
S 136	**self-adapting**	selbstanpassend	auto-adaptif	самоадаптирующийся
S 137	**self-adapting control**, adaptive control	selbstanpassende (adaptive) Steuerung *f*	commande *f* autoadaptive	адаптивное управление

	English	German	French	Russian
S 138	self-adjusting	selbsteinstellend	à auto-ajustement	самонастраивающийся; саморегулирующийся
S 139	self-aligned polysilicon gate	selbstausrichtendes Polysiliziumgate n	gate m au polysilicium à autoalignement	самосовмещенный поликремниевый затвор
S 140	self-aligning	selbstausrichtend	auto-alignant	автоматически выравнивающийся, самовыравнивающийся
S 141	self-aligning gate MOS	s. S 3		
	self-alignment gate, SAG	Selbstjustierungsgate n, selbsteinstellendes Gate n	gate m à auto-alignement	самосовмещенный затвор
S 142	self-assembly	Selbstassemblierung f <Quellprogrammübersetzung auf dem Rechnertyp bzw. dessen Entwicklungssystem, auf dem das Objektprogramm laufen soll>	auto-assemblage m	ассемблирование на целевой машине
S 143	self-balancing	selbstabgleichend	auto-equilibré	самобалансирующийся, самоуравновешивающийся
S 144	self-check, self-test	Selbstprüfung f, Selbstkontrolle f	autocontrôle m	самопроверка, самоконтроль
S 145	self-checking circuit	selbstprüfende Schaltung f	circuit m à autocontrôle	самопроверяемая схема
S 146	self-checking code	selbstprüfender Kode m	code m de vérification [autonome]	самоконтролируемый код
S 147	self-checking number	selbstprüfende Zahl f, Zahl mit Selbstprüfungsteil	nombre m à autocontrôle	число с разрядами контроля
S 148	self-clocking	Selbsttaktierung f	rythme m propre	самосинхронизация, автосинхронизация
S 149	self-correcting code	selbstkorrigierender Kode m	code m à autocorrection	самокорректируемый код
S 150	self-defining term	selbstdefinierender Ausdruck m	terme m à propre définition	самоопределяемый терм
S 151	self-defining value, direct value	Direktwert m	valeur f directe	самоопределяемая величина
S 152	self-development system	Selbstentwicklungssystem n <Mikrorechnerentwicklungssystem, das mit dem Objektrechnertyp aufgebaut ist>	système m d'autodéveloppement	микро-ЭВМ, содержащая в себе систему проектирования и выполняющая функции целевой машины
S 153	self-diagnostic ability	Selbstdiagnosefähigkeit f	possibilité f d'autodiagnostic	возможность самодиагностики
S 154	self-diagnostic method	Selbstdiagnosemethode f	méthode f de propre diagnostic	метод самодиагностики
S 155	self-discharge	Selbstentladung f, Eigenentladung f	décharge f propre	саморазряд
S 156	self-gating	Selbststeuerung f	autocommande f	самоуправление
S 157	self-gating	selbststeuernd	à autocommande	саморегулирующийся
S 158	self-loading	selbstladend	à propre chargement	самозагружаемый
S 159	self-loading program	Programm n mit Selbstladeeigenschaft, sich selbst ladendes Programm <Objektprogramm mit vorgesetztem Bootstraplader>	programme m à propre chargement	самозагружаемая программа
S 160	self-organizing machine, self-scheduling machine	[sich] selbst organisierende Rechenmaschine f	machine f à organisation autonome	самоорганизующаяся машина
S 161	self-oscillation	Eigenschwingung f	oscillation f propre	самовозбуждение
S 162	self-powered device	selbstversorgtes Gerät n, Gerät mit netzunabhängiger Stromversorgung	appareil m à alimentation autonome	устройство с автономным питанием
S 163	self-refreshing	Selbstregenerierung f <SK-interne Speicherauffrischung bei pseudostatischen RAM-SK>	rafraîchissement m propre	внутренняя регенерация
S 164	self-relocating program	selbstverschiebendes Programm n <sich an jedem Speicherbereich selbst organisierendes Programm>	programme m à relogement autonome	самоперемещаемая программа
	self-scheduling machine	s. S 160		
	self-test	s. S 144		
S 165	self-test electronics	Selbsttestelektronik f, Selbstprüfungselektronik f	électronique f à test propre	самотестируемая электроника
S 166	self-testing computer	selbsttestender Rechner m, automatisch sich selbstprüfender Rechner	calculateur m à propre test	самоконтролируемая (самотестируемая) ЭВМ
S 167	self-test method	Selbstprüfmethode f	méthode f de test autonome	метод самопроверки (самоконтроля)
S 168	self-timed	selbstsynchronisierend, selbst ablaufsteuernd <im Gegensatz zu „getaktet">	à propre synchronisation	с внутренней синхронизацией
S 169	self-triggering	Selbsttriggerung f, Selbstauslösung f	autobasculage m	самовозбуждение, самозапуск <схемы>
S 170	semantic error	semantischer Fehler m	erreur f sémantique	семантическая ошибка
S 171	semantics	Semantik f	sémantique f	семантика
S 172	semianalytic code	halbanalytischer Befehlskode m	code m semi-analytique	полуаналитический код
S 173	semi-automatic	halbautomatisch	semi-automatique	полуавтоматический
S 174	semiconductor	Halbleiter m	semi-conducteur m	полупроводник
S 175	semiconductor circuit	Halbleiterschaltung f, Halbleiterschaltkreis m	circuit m à semi-conducteurs	полупроводниковая схема
S 176	semiconductor density	Halbleiterschaltungsdichte f	densité f de semi-conducteurs	плотность упаковки полупроводниковых схем
S 177	semiconductor development	Halbleiterentwicklung f	développement m de semi-conducteurs	развитие полупроводниковой техники; проектирование полупроводниковых схем

11*

S 178	**semiconductor device**	Halbleiterbaustein *m*	module *m* à semi-conducteurs	полупроводниковое устройство
S 179	**semiconductor doping**	Halbleiterdotierung *f*	dopage *m* de semi-conducteurs	легирование полупроводника
S 180	**semiconductor junction**	Halbleitersperrschicht *f*	jonction *f* de semi-conducteur	переход в полупроводнике
S 181	**semiconductor manufacture,** semiconductor production	Halbleiterfertigung *f*, Halbleiterproduktion *f*	fabrication *f* de semi-conducteurs	полупроводниковое производство
S 182	**semiconductor material**	Halbleitermaterial *n*	matériau *m* de semi-conducteur	полупроводниковый материал
S 183	**semiconductor memory**	Halbleiterspeicher *m*	mémoire *f* à semi-conducteurs	полупроводниковая память
S 184	**semiconductor-metal contact**	Halbleiter-Metall-Kontakt *m*	contact *m* semi-conducteur-métal	контакт металл-полупроводник
S 185	**semiconductor product**	Halbleiterprodukt *n*, Halbleitertechnik-Produkt *n*	produit *m* de semi-conducteur	полупроводниковое изделие
	semiconductor production	*s.* S 181		
S 186	**semiconductor slice,** semiconductor wafer	Halbleiterscheibe *f*	disque *m* (tranche *f*) de semi-conducteur	полупроводниковая пластина
S 187	**semiconductor technology**	Halbleitertechnologie *f*	technologie *f* des semi-conducteurs	полупроводниковая технология
	semiconductor wafer	*s.* S 186		
S 188	**semipermanent memory**	Halbfestspeicher *m*	mémoire *f* semi-permanente	полупостоянная память
S 189	**send / to,** to transmit	senden, aussenden, abgeben	émettre	посылать
S 190	**send line,** transmit line	Sendeleitung *f*	ligne *f* d'émission	линия передачи
S 191	**send out / to**	aussenden	diffuser	выпускать; излучать
S 192	**sense / to**	abfühlen, ‹erkennend› abtasten	palper	воспринимать; опознавать; считывать
S 193	**sense amplifier**	Leseverstärker *m*, Lesesignalverstärker *m*	amplificateur *m* de lecture	усилитель считывания
S 194	**sense bit**	Lesebit *n*	bit *m* de lecture	бит считывания
S 195	**sensed signal**	ausgelesenes Signal *n*	signal *m* lu	считанный сигнал
S 196	**sense line**	Leseleitung *f*	ligne *f* de lecture	линия считывания
S 197	**sensibility,** sensitivity	Empfindlichkeit *f*	sensibilité *f*	чувствительность
S 198	**sensing**	Abfühlen *n*	palpage *m*	восприятие; опознавание
	sensing element	*s.* S 205		
S 199	**sensing method**	Abfühlverfahren *n*, Abtastverfahren *n*	procédé *m* de palpage	метод восприятия; метод считывания
S 200	**sensing program**	Abfühlprogramm *n*, Abtastprogramm *n*	programme *m* de palpage	программа считывания ‹информации с датчиков›
	sensing rate	*s.* S 20		
	sensing speed	*s.* S 21		
S 201	**sensing station**	Abfühlstation *f*, Abtaststation *f*, Lesestation *f*	station *f* de palpage	устройство считывания
S 202	**sensitive**	empfindlich	sensible	чувствительный
	sensitivity	*s.* S 197		
S 203	**sensitize / to**	sensibilisieren, empfindlich machen	sensibiliser	увеличивать чувствительность
S 204	**sensitized path**	kritischer Weg (Signalpfad) *m*	chemin *m* critique	критический путь
S 205	**sensor,** sensing element	Meßfühler *m*, Meßwertaufnehmer *m*, Sensor *m*	capteur *m*	датчик, сенсор, чувствительный элемент
S 206	**sensor-based computer**	auf Sensoren basierender Rechner *m*, Rechner mit Sensoren ‹Prozeßrechner›	calculateur *m* à éléments sensitifs, calculateur de processus	управляющая ЭВМ с датчиками [состояния физического процесса]
S 207	**sensor chip**	Sensorschaltkreis *m*	circuit *m* de capteur	интегральная схема датчика
S 208	**sentence**	Anweisungssatz *m*	sentence *f*	предложение
	sentinel	*s.* F 118		
S 209	**separate component**	Einzelbauelement *n*	composant *m* solitaire	отдельный компонент
S 210	**separated data**	separierte (getrennte) Daten *pl*	données *fpl* séparées	отдельные данные
S 211	**separate I/O address space**	separater (getrennter) E/A-Adreßraum *m*	espace *m* d'adresse d'E/S séparé	отдельное пространство адресов [устройств] ввода-вывода
S 212	**separate keyboard**	separate Tastatur *f*	clavier *m* séparé	отдельная клавиатура
S 213	**separate unit**	getrennte Einheit *f*	unité *f* séparée	отдельное устройство
S 214	**separation**	Trennung *f*, Separierung *f*	séparation *f*	разделение
S 215	**separation of instruction storage and data storage** ‹Havard architecture›	Trennung *f* von Befehls- und Datenspeicher ‹Havard-Architektur›	séparation *f* de la mémoire à instructions de la mémoire à données ‹architecture Havard›	разделение памяти программ и памяти данных ‹гавардская архитектура›
S 216	**separation of tasks**	Aufgabentrennung *f*	séparation *f* de tâches	разделение задач
S 217	**separator**	Trennzeichen *n*	séparateur *m*	разделитель, разделительный символ
S 218	**sequence**	Folge *f*, Reihenfolge *f*, Sequenz *f*	séquence *f*	последовательность; порядок следования
S 219	**sequence checking**	Ablauffolgeprüfung *f* ‹Diagnoseprogramm›	vérification *f* de séquence	контроль последовательности (выполнения команд); контроль порядка следования
S 220	**sequence control**	Ablauffolgesteuerung *f*	commande *f* de séquence	управление последовательностью
S 221	**sequence counter**	Folgezähler *m*	compteur *m* de séquence	счетчик последовательности
S 222	**sequenced**	geordnet	classé	упорядоченный; включенный в последовательность
S 223	**sequencer**	Ablauffolgesteuereinrichtung *f*, Befehlsabwicklungsfolgesteuerung *f*	commande *f* de séquence	устройство, задающее последовательность; устройство [микропрограммного] управления

S 224	**sequence register**	Folgeregister n, Folge-adreßregister n	registre m de séquence	регистр хранения содержимого счетчика команд; регистр, определяющий последовательности
S 225	**sequence timer**	Folgezeitgeber m	rythmeur m de séquence	последовательный таймер
S 226	**sequencing**	Reihenfolgebestimmung f	détermination f de séquence	установление последовательности
S 227	**sequential**	zeitlich nacheinander, auf-einanderfolgend, sequentiell	séquentiel	последовательный, последующий; последовательностный
S 228	**sequential access**	sequentieller Zugriff m ‹Zu-griff zu aufeinanderfol-genden Informationen›	accès m séquentiel	последовательный доступ
	sequential-access memory	s. S 240		
S 229	**sequential circuit**	sequentielle Schaltung f, Folgeschaltung f ‹Schal-tung mit Zustandsspei-chern und zustandsabhän-giger Reaktion auf Ein-gangsgrößen›	circuit m séquentiel	последовательностная схема, схема последовательного действия
S 230	**sequential computer**	sequentiell arbeitender Rechner m ‹normales Arbeitsprinzip im Gegen-satz zur simultanen Arbeitsweise›	calculateur m séquentiel	ЭВМ последовательного действия
S 231	**sequential control**	Folgesteuerung f	commande f séquentielle	последовательное управление
S 232	**sequential execution**	sequentielle Ausführung f	exécution f séquentielle	последовательное исполнение
S 233	**sequential file access**	sequentieller Filezugriff (Dateizugriff) m	accès m de fichier séquentiel	последовательный доступ к файлу
S 234	**sequential logic**	sequentielle Logik f	logique f séquentielle	последовательностная логика
S 235	**sequential network**	sequentielles Schaltnetz (Schaltwerk) n, Folge-schaltsystem n	réseau m séquentiel	последовательная цепь
S 236	**sequential operation**	sequentieller Betrieb m	régime m séquentiel	последовательная работа, последовательный режим работы
S 237	**sequential processing**	sequentielle Verarbeitung f ‹im Gegensatz zur simul-tanen Verarbeitung Aus-führung der Einzelschritte einer Aufgabe zeitlich nacheinander›	traitement m séquentiel	последовательная обработка
S 238	**sequential scheduling**	Folgeverarbeitungssteue-rung f	commande f séquentielle de traitement	последовательное планирование
S 239	**sequential searching**	sequentielles Suchen n	recherche f séquentielle	последовательный поиск
S 240	**sequential store,** sequential-access memory	Sequenzspeicher m, sequen-tieller Speicher m ‹Spei-cher mit datenanord-nungsabhängigem Zu-griffsverhalten›	mémoire f séquentielle	память с последователь-ным доступом
S 241	**serial**	seriell, nacheinander, in Reihe	sériel	последовательный
S 242	**serial access**	serieller Zugriff m	accès m sériel	последовательный доступ
S 243	**serial access memory,** SAM	Speicher m mit seriellem Zugriff, Seriellspeicher m	mémoire f à accès seriel	память с последователь-ным доступом
S 244	**serial adder**	Serielladdierwerk n, serieller Addierer m ‹verarbeitet die Binärstellen einer Dateneinheit nachein-ander›	addeur m sériel	последовательный сумма-тор
S 245	**serial arithmetic unit**	serielles Rechenwerk n	unité f arithmétique sérielle	арифметическое устрой-ство последовательного действия
S 246	**serial BCD arithmetic**	serielle BCD-Arithmetik f, serielle Dezimalzahlen-rechnung f	arithmétique f BCD sérielle	последовательная дво-ично-десятичная ариф-метика
S 247	**serial by bit**	bitseriell	sériel par bit	последовательно по битам, бит-последовательно
S 248	**serial by character**	zeichenseriell	sériel par caractère	последовательно по симво-лам
S 249	**serial communication controller,** SCC	Seriellübertragungs-Steuerschaltkreis m, SCC-Baustein m	circuit m de commande de communication sérielle, circuit SCC	связной контроллер для последовательной пере-дачи данных
S 250	**serial communications interface**	serielles Übertragungsinter-face f, serielle Über-tragungsschnittstelle f	interface f sérielle de com-munication	последовательный связной интерфейс
S 251	**serial computer**	Seriellrechner m, seriell arbeitender Rechner m	calculateur m sériel	ЭВМ последовательного действия
S 252	**serial data channel**	serieller Datenkanal m	canal m de données sériel	последовательный канал обмена данными
S 253	**serial data input**	serieller Dateneingang m	entrée f de données sérielle	последовательный вход данных; последователь-ный ввод данных
S 254	**serial data line**	serielle Datenleitung f	ligne f de données sérielle	линия последовательного обмена данными
S 255	**serial data transfer**	serielle Datenübertragung f	transmission f de données sérielle	последовательная пере-сылка данных
S 256	**serial format**	serielles Format n	format m sériel	последовательный формат
S 257	**serial input-output**	serielle Eingabe-Ausgabe f	entrée-sortie f sérielle	последовательный ввод-вывод

S 258	serial interface	serielles Interface n, serielle Schnittstelle f	interface f sérielle	последовательный интерфейс
S 259	serial I/O controller, SIO	SIO m, Seriell-E/A-Steuerschaltkreis m, Baustein m für serielle Ein-/Ausgabe	circuit m de commande d'E/S sérielle	контроллер последовательного вводa-вывода
S 260	serial I/O port	serielle E/A-Anschlußstelle f, serieller E/A-Kanal m	porte f d'E/S sérielle	порт последовательного ввода-вывода
S 261	serializer	Seriellumsetzer m	convertisseur m en sériel	[параллельно-]последовательный преобразователь
S 262	serial mode	serielle Arbeitsweise f, Seriellmodus m	mode m sériel	последовательный метод
S 263	serial operation	serieller Betrieb m	régime m sériel	последовательная работа, последовательный режим работы
S 264	serial-parallel	seriell-parallel, serienparallel	parallèle-sériel	последовательно-параллельный
S 265	serial-parallel processing	seriell-parallele Verarbeitung f	traitement m sériel-parallèle	последовательно-параллельная обработка
S 266	serial priority technique	serielles Prioritätsentscheidungsverfahren n, serielles Vorrangsprinzip n	technique f sérielle des priorités	метод последовательного назначения приоритетов
S 267	serial processing	serielle Verarbeitung f <Verarbeitung der Informationselemente einer Dateneinheit nacheinander mit der gleichen Einrichtung — auch im Sinne von „sequentielle Verarbeitung" benutzt>	traitement m sériel	последовательная обработка
S 268	serial programming	serielle Programmierung f <Programmierung für rein sequentielle Arbeitsweise>	programmation f sérielle	программирование с учетом последовательного выполнения операций
S 269	serial technique	serielle Technik f, Seriellverfahren n	technique f sérielle	последовательный способ
S 270	serial-to-parallel conversion	Seriell-Parallel-Umsetzung f	conversion f sérielle en parallèle	последовательно-параллельное преобразование
S 271	serial-to-parallel converter	Seriell-Parallel-Umsetzer m	convertisseur m sériel en parallèle	последовательно-параллельный преобразователь
S 272	serial transfer	serielle Übertragung f	transfert m sériel	последовательная передача, поочередная пересылка
S 273	serial workflow	serieller Arbeitsfluß m	déroulement m sériel du travail	последовательный поток работ
S 274	series, production series	Baureihe f, Herstellungsreihe f	série f, série de fabrication	серия, ряд унифицированных конструктивных модулей
S 275	series connection	Serienschaltung f, Reihenschaltung f	montage m en série	последовательное включение (соединение)
S 276	service / to	pflegen, bedienen	vérifier	обслуживать
S 277	service	Kundendienst m, Dienst m	service m	служба, обслуживание
S 278	service contract	Wartungsvertrag m	contrat m de service	контракт на обслуживание
S 279	service file	Änderungsdatei f s. O 109	fichier m de service	служебный файл, файл изменений
	service instruction			
S 280	service program, service routine, utility program (routine)	Dienstprogramm n	programme m de service	сервисная программа
S 281	service request	Bedienanforderung f	demande f de service	запрос на обслуживание
	service routine	s. S 280		
S 282	service utilities	Unterstützungsprogramme npl	programmes mpl d'assistance	вспомогательные (сервисные) программы
S 283	servocontrol	Folgeregelung f	servocommande f	сервоуправление
S 284	servo drive	Servoantrieb m, Stellantrieb m, Folgeregelantrieb m	servo-entraînement m	сервопривод, следящий привод
S 285	servo motor	Servomotor m	servomoteur m	сервомотор, серводвигатель
S 286	servo system	Folgeregelungssystem n	servosystème m	сервосистема, следящая система
S 287	session mode	Dialogmodus m, Dialogbetriebsweise f	mode m de dialogue	режим диалога (сеанса)
S 288	set breakpoint / to	Haltepunkt setzen	mettre un point d'arrêt	установить контрольную точку, установить точку [контрольного] останова
S 289	setpoint	Sollwert m, Einstellwert m	valeur f mise	уставка
S 290	set pulse	Einstellimpuls m	impulsion f de mise, impulsion d'ajustage	импульс установки; импульс установки в состояние логической «1»
S 291	setter	Einsteller m	ajusteur m	механизм установки; механизм включения
S 292	setting	Einstellung f	ajustage m, ajustement m	регулировка, настройка; установка
S 293	setting accuracy	Einstellgenauigkeit f	précision f d'ajustage, précision de calibrage	точность установки; точность настройки
S 294	setting range	Einstellbereich m	champ m d'ajustement	диапазон регулирования (установки)
S 295	setting time	Einstellzeit f	temps m d'ajustement, temps de mise au point	время установки
S 296	set up / to	einrichten, aufbauen, aufstellen	aménager, établir	устанавливать; настраивать

S 297	set-up	Aufstellung f	établissement m	установка, сборка
S 298	set-up diagram	Aufbaudiagramm n, Konfigurator m	diagramme m d'aménagement, configurateur m	схема (таблица) настройки диаграмма соединений
S 299	set-up time	Aufstellzeit f <Informationssignal>	temps m d'établissement	время установки [опережения] <сигнала>
S 300	seven-segment code	Siebensegmentkode m, 7-Segmentkode m <Kode zur Zeichenabbildung auf 7-Segment-Anzeigen>	code m à sept segments	семисегментный код
S 301	seven-segment LED display	Siebensegment-LED-Anzeige f	affichage m LED à sept segments	семисегментный светодиодный индикатор
	S-flag	s. S 384		
	SG	s. S 404		
	SGT	s. S 407		
S 302	shaper	Former m, Formierungseinrichtung f	dispositif m de formation	формирователь
S 303	share / to	anteilig nutzen, teilhaben	partager, utiliser en commun	разделять, совместно использовать
S 304	shared bus system	anteilig genutztes Bussystem n	système m de bus partagé	система с общей шиной, система с шиной коллективного пользования
S 305	shared regions	geteilte (anteilig genutzte) Bereiche mpl	domaines mpl partagés	разделяемые области, совместно используемые области
S 306	shared resources	anteilig genutzte gemeinsame Einrichtungen fpl	ressources fpl partagées	общие (разделяемые) ресурсы
S 307	shared storage	anteilig genutzter Speicher m	mémoire f partagée	разделяемая (совместно используемая) память
S 308	sharer, participant	Teilnehmer m	abonné m, participant m	абонент, участник
S 309	share resources / to	Ressourcen teilen, Systemmittel anteilig nutzen <gemeinsame Einrichtungen anteilig nutzen>	partager les ressources	разделять [общие] ресурсы, совместно использовать [общие] ресурсы
S 310	sharing	anteilige Nutzung f, Teilhaben n	utilisation f partagée, participation f	разделение, совместное использование
S 311	sharp edge	steile Flanke f	flanc m raide	крутой фронт
	sheet	s. L 50		
S 312	sheet resistor	Schichtwiderstand m	rhéostat m à couche	пленочный резистор
S 313	Sheffer-stroke operation	Sheffer-Strich-Operation f, Sheffer-Operation f	opération f Sheffer	операция «штрих Шеффера», операция И-НЕ
S 314	shield, shielding, screening	Abschirmung f, Schirmung f	blindage m	экранирование, экранировка
S 315	shielded-conductor cable	Abschirmkabel n	câble m blindé	экранированный кабель
S 316	shielded line	abgeschirmte Leitung f	ligne f blindée	экранированный провод, экранированная линия
	shielding	s. S 314		
S 317	shift / to	schieben, verschieben <der Stellenposition>	décaler	сдвигать; смещать
S 318	shift, shifting	Schieben n, Verschiebung f <der Stellenposition>	décalage m	сдвиг; смещение
S 319	shift circuit	Schiebeschaltung f, Stellenverschiebeschaltung f	circuit m de décalage	схема сдвига; цепь сдвига
S 320	shift counter	Schiebezähler m, Verschiebestellenzähler m	compteur m de décalage	счетчик сдвигов
	shifter	s. S 327		
	shifting	s. S 318		
S 321	shift instruction	Schiebebefehl m	instruction f de décalage	команда сдвига
S 322	shift key	Umschalttaste f	touche f de commutation	клавиша переключения
S 323	shift operation	Schiebeoperation f, Stellenverschiebeoperation f	opération f de décalage	операция сдвига
S 324	shift pulse	Schiebeimpuls m	impulsion f de décalage	импульс сдвига
S 325	shift register	Schieberegister n	registre m de décalage	регистр сдвига, сдвиговый регистр
S 326	shift register memory (storage)	Schieberegisterspeicher m	mémoire f à registres à décalage	память на регистрах сдвига
S 327	shift unit, shifter	Schiebeeinrichtung f, Verschiebeeinrichtung f	dispositif m de décalage	схема сдвига, сдвигатель
S 328	short circuit	Kurzschluß m	court-circuit m	короткое замыкание, к.з.; короткозамкнутая цепь
S 329	short-circuit current	Kurzschlußstrom m	courant m de court-circuit	ток короткого замыкания
S 330	short-circuited input	kurzgeschlossener Eingang m	entrée f en court-circuit	короткозамкнутый вход
S 331	short-circuit proof	kurzschlußfest	résistant aux courts-circuits	с защитой от короткого замыкания, защищенный от короткого замыкания
S 332	short-circuit protection	Kurzschlußschutz m	protection f contre courts-circuits	защита от короткого замыкания
S 333	shortcoming	Unzulänglichkeit f	insuffisance f	недостаток; дефект
S 334	short-cut operation	abgekürzte Operation f	opération f abrégée	укороченная операция
S 335	shorted out	überbrückt	court-circuité	закороченный, шунтированный
S 336	short-instruction format	Kurzbefehlsformat n	format m d'instruction court	формат короткой команды
S 337	short recovery time	kurze Erholzeit f	temps m de repos court	короткое время восстановления
S 338	short-time duty	Kurzzeitbetrieb m, Kurzzeitbelastung f	régime m à temps court	кратковременный режим; кратковременная нагрузка
S 339	short-time storage	Kurzzeitspeicherung f	mise f en mémoire à temps court	кратковременное хранение
S 340	short word computer	Kurzwortmaschine f	machine f à mots courts	ЭВМ с малой длиной [машинного] слова

S 341	shunt / to	überbrücken; nebenschlie-ßen ‹parallelschalten›	shunter	шунтировать
S 342	shunt	Nebenschluß m, Shunt m	shunt m	шунт; шунтирование, параллельное подключение
S 343	shut-down, shut-off	Abschalten f, Abstellen n	mise f hors circuit	выключение, отключение; остановка
S 344	sign / to	mit Vorzeichen versehen (behaften)	munir de signe	присваивать знак
S 345	sign	Vorzeichen n	signe m	знак
S 346	signal code	Signalkode m	code m de signal	сигнальный код
S 347	signal conditioning	Signalformung f, Signalaufbereitung f	formation f de signaux	приведение сигнала к заданным нормам
S 348	signal conversion equipment	Signalwandlungseinrichtung f	équipement (dispositif) m à conversion de signaux	устройство преобразования сигнала ‹данных›, УПС
S 349	signal converter	Signalumsetzer m, Zeichenwandler m	convertisseur m de signaux	преобразователь сигнала
S 350	signal decoding	Signalentschlüsselung f	décodage m de signal	декодирование сигнала
S 351	signal delay	Signalverzögerung f	retardement m de signal	задержка сигнала
S 352	signal duration	Signaldauer f	durée f de signal	длительность сигнала
S 353	signal element	Signalelement n ‹Übertragungsschrittlänge›	élément m de signal	элемент [цифрового] сигнала ‹данных›
S 354	signal generator, signalizer	Signalgeber m, Prüfsender m	générateur m de signaux	сигнал-генератор; генератор сигналов
S 355	signal handling signalizer	Signalbehandlung f s. S 354	manipulation f de signaux	обработка сигналов
S 356	signal level	Signalpegel m	niveau m de signal	уровень сигнала
S 357	signal line	Signalleitung f	ligne f de signaux	сигнальная линия; линия передачи сигналов
S 358	signalling	Signalisierung f, Zeichengebung f	signalisation f	сигнализация; передача сигналов
S 359	signalling type	Signalisierungsart f	type m de signalisation	вид сигнализации
S 360	signal output level	Ausgangssignalpegel m	niveau m de signal sortie	уровень выходного сигнала
S 361	signal power	Signalleistung f	puissance f de signal	мощность сигнала
S 362	signal processing	Signalverarbeitung f	traitement m de signaux	обработка сигналов ‹например цифровая фильтрация, дискретное преобразование Фурье и т.п.›
S 363	signal processor	Signalprozessor m, Signalverarbeitungseinheit f	processeur m de signaux	процессор [для] обработки сигналов, сигнальный процессор
S 364	signal recognition	Signalerkennung f	reconnaissance f de signaux	распознавание сигналов
S 365	signal representation	Signaldarstellung f	représentation f de signaux	представление сигналов
S 366	signal scanning	Signalabtastung f	balayage m de signaux	сканирование сигналов; развертывание сигнала
S 367	signal selection	Signalauswahl f	sélection f de signal	селекция сигналов
S 368	signal skew	Signalschrägverzerrung f, Signalversatz m	distorsion f oblique de signal	перекос сигнала
S 369	signal timing	Signaldiagramm n, Signalablauf m	diagramme m de signal	временные соотношения сигнала; синхронизация сигнала
S 370	signal-to-noise ratio	Rauschabstand m, Signal-Rausch-Verhältnis n	rapport m signal-bruit	отношение сигнал-шум
S 371	signal tracing	Signalverfolgung f	poursuite f de signal	прослеживание (трассировка) сигнала
S 372	signal transducer	Signalwandler m, Wandler m für standardisierte Übertragungssignale	transformateur m de signaux	преобразователь сигнала
S 373	signature	Signatur f, Informationsprüfkennung f	signature f	сигнатура
S 374	signature analysis	Signaturanalyse f ‹Fehlersuchmethode›	analyse f de signature	сигнатурный анализ
S 375	signature analyzer	Signaturanalysator m	analyseur m de signature	сигнатурный анализатор
S 376	sign bit	Vorzeichenbit n	bit m de signe	знаковый разряд (бит)
S 377	sign change	Vorzeichenwechsel m	échange m de signe	смена знака
S 378	sign control	Vorzeichensteuerung f	commande f de signe	контроль по знаку
S 379	sign digit	Vorzeichenziffer f	chiffre m de signe	знаковая цифра
S 380	signed	vorzeichenbehaftet	muni de signe	со знаком
S 381	signed data	vorzeichenbehaftete Daten pl	données fpl munies de signe	данные со знаком
S 382	signed number	vorzeichenbehaftete Zahl f, Zahl mit Vorzeichen	nombre m muni de signe	число со знаком
S 383	sign extension	Vorzeichenerweiterung f ‹auf vordere Binärpositionen›	extension f de signe	расширение поля знака
S 384	sign flag, S-flag	Vorzeichenkennzeichen n, Vorzeichenzustandskennung f	marque f de signe	флаг знака, знаковый признак ‹S-бит регистра флагов процессора›
S 385	significant digits	signifikante Ziffern fpl, relevante (bedeutsame) Stellen fpl	chiffres mpl significatifs (révélateurs)	значащие цифры
S 386/7	significant fraction sign inversion	bestimmender Anteil m s. R 367	fraction f révélatrice	значащая часть
S 388	sign manipulation	Vorzeichenbehandlung f	manipulation f de signe	манипулирование знаком
S 389	sign representation sign reversal	Vorzeichendarstellung f s. R 367	représentation f de signe	представление знака
S 390	sign test	Vorzeichenprüfung f	test m de signe	проверка знака
S 391	silicon	Silizium n	silicium m	кремний
S 392	silicon alloy transistor	Siliziumlegierungstransistor m	transistor m en alliage de silicium	кремниевый сплавной транзистор

S 393	**silicon anodization**	Siliziumanodisierung *f* <Technologie>, anodische Oxydation *f* von Silizium	anodisation *f* au silicium	анодирование (электролитическое окисление) кремния
S 394	**silicon chip**	Siliziumchip *n*	puce *f* au silicium	кремниевый чип
S 395	**silicon crystal**	Siliziumkristall *m*	cristal *m* de silicium	кремниевый кристалл
S 396	**silicon-diffused transistor**	Siliziumdiffusionstransistor *m*	transistor *m* de diffusion de silicium	кремниевый диффузионный транзистор
S 397	**silicon diode**	Siliziumdiode *f*	diode *f* au silicium	кремниевый диод
S 398	**silicon dioxide**	Siliziumdioxid *n*	dioxyde (bioxyde) *m* de silicium	двуокись кремния
S 399	**silicon dioxide insulating layer**	Siliziumdioxid-Isolationsschicht *f*	couche *f* d'isolation au bioxyde de silicium	изолирующий слой двуокиси кремния
S 400	**silicon dioxide layer**	Siliziumdioxidschicht *f*	couche *f* de bioxyde de silicium	слой двуокиси кремния ⌐соединение
S 401	**silicone**	Silikon *n*	silicone *m*	кремнийорганическое
S 402	**silicon epitaxial planar transistor**	Silizium-Epitaxialplanar-Transistor *m*	transistor *m* épitaxial planaire au silicium	кремниевый эпитаксиально-планарный транзистор
S 403	**silicon field-effect transistor**	Silizium-Feldeffekttransistor *m*	transistor *m* à effet de champ au silicium	кремниевый полевой транзистор
S 404	**silicon gate,** SG	Siliziumgate *n*, Siliziumsteuerelektrode *f*, Si-Gate *n*	gate *m* au silicium	поликремниевый затвор
S 405	**silicon-gate CMOS technology**	Siliziumgate-CMOS-Technologie *f* <Komplementär-MOS-Schaltungen mit Steuerelektroden aus Polysilizium anstelle von Metall>	technologie *f* CMOS à gate au silicium	технология КМОП-схем с поликремниевыми затворами
S 406	**silicon-gate process**	Siliziumgateprozeß *m*, Siliziumgate-Schaltkreisherstellungstechnik *f*	processus *m* à gate au silicium	процесс изготовления схем с поликремниевыми затворами
S 407	**silicon gate technology,** SGT	SGT *f*, Siliziumgatetechnologie *f* <MOSFET mit Polysilizium-Steuerelektrode>	technologie *f* de gate au silicium	технология схем с поликремниевыми затворами
S 408	**silicon nitride passivation**	Siliziumnitridpassivierung *f*	passivation *f* de nitride de silicium	пассивация нитридом кремния
S 409	**silicon-on-sapphire microprocessor**	Mikroprozessor *m* in Silizium-auf-Saphir-Technik	microprocesseur *m* en technique silicium sur saphir	микропроцессор, изготовленный по технологии «кремний на сапфире», КНС-микропроцессор
	silicon-on-sapphire technology	s. S 562		
S 410	**silicon planar technique**	Siliziumplanartechnik *f*	technique *f* planaire au silicium	кремниевая планарная технология
S 411	**silicon rectifier**	Siliziumgleichrichter *m*	redresseur *m* au silicium	кремниевый выпрямитель
S 412	**silicon semiconductor device**	Silizium-Halbleiterbauelement *n*	module *m* semi-conducteur au silicium	кремниевый полупроводниковый прибор
S 413	**silicon substrate**	Siliziumsubstrat *n*, Siliziumunterlage *f*	substrat *m* au silicium	кремниевая подложка
S 414	**silicon technology**	Siliziumtechnologie *f*, Siliziumschaltkreistechnologie *f*	technologie *f* au silicium	технология кремниевых схем
S 415	**silicon transistor**	Siliziumtransistor *m*	transistor *m* au silicium	кремниевый транзистор
S 416	**silicon wafer**	Siliziumscheibe *f*, Siliziumsubstratplättchen *n*	puce *f* de silicium	кремниевая пластина
S 417	**SIMOS,** stacked-gate injection MOS	SIMOS *f*, MOS-Speicherelektrodentechnik *f* mit Stapelgate <für RePROM, EAROM>	technologie *f* MOS à injection de gate empilé, SIMOS	инжекционные МОП-приборы с составными затворами
S 418	**simple statement**	einfache Anweisung *f*	instruction *f* simple	простой оператор
S 419	**simplex channel**	Simplexkanal *m*, Ein-Richtungs-Kanal *m*	canal *m* simplex	симплексный (односторонний) канал
S 420	**simplex operation**	Simplexbetrieb *m*, Einfachbetrieb *m*	régime *m* simplex	симплексный режим, односторонняя передача
S 421	**simplification**	Vereinfachung *f*	simplification *f*	упрощение
S 422	**simplified**	vereinfacht	simplifié	упрощенный
S 423	**simulate / to**	nachbilden, simulieren	simuler	моделировать; имитировать ⌐моделирования
S 424	**simulated design**	simulierter Entwurf *m*	conception *f* simulée	разработка с применением
S 425	**simulation**	Simulation *f*, Nachbildung *f* wesentlicher Eigenschaften <Modellbildung auf Maschinenbefehlsebene>	simulation *f*	моделирование, имитация
S 426	**simulation language**	Simulationssprache *f*	langage *m* de simulation	язык моделирования
S 427	**simulation technique**	Simulationstechnik *f*, Simulationsverfahren *n*	technique *f* de simulation	метод моделирования
S 428	**simulator,** simulator program	Simulator *m*, Simulationsprogramm *n* <Programm zur Ausführung und Testung von für einen anderen Rechner geschriebenen Maschinencode-Programmen>	simulateur *m*	моделирующая программа, программа моделирования ⌐щей системой
S 429	**simulator control**	Simulatorsteuerung *f*	commande *f* de simulateur	управление моделирую-
S 430	**simulator processor**	Simulationsprozessor *m*	processeur *m* de simulation	процессор моделирующей системы
	simulator program	s. S 428		
S 431	**simultaneity**	Gleichzeitigkeit *f*	simultanéité *f*	одновременность
S 432	**simultaneous**	gleichzeitig, simultan	simultané	одновременный
S 433	**simultaneous computer,** parallel computer	Simultanrechner *m*	calculateur *m* simultané	вычислительная машина параллельного действия, вычислительная машина с совмещением операций

S 434	**simultaneous executing,** concurrent execution	simultane (gleichzeitige) Ausführung f	exécution f simultanée (concurrente)	одновременное исполнение
S 435	**simultaneous I/O (input/output),** concurrent input/output, concurrent I/O	simultane E/A f, simultane Ein-/Ausgabe f, gleichzeitige E/A <parallel zur Prozessorarbeit>	E/S f concurrente, entrée/ sortie f concurrente	одновременный (параллельный) ввод-вывод
S 436	**simultaneous mode,** parallel (concurrent) mode	Simultanarbeitsweise f, Parallelarbeitsweise f <gleichzeitige Ausführung verschiedener Arbeitsprozesse in mehreren Einheiten>	mode m simultané	параллельный метод
S 437	**simultaneous operation,** parallel (concurrent) operation	Simultanbetrieb m, Parallelbetrieb m	régime m simultané	режим [работы] с совмещением операций
S 438	**simultaneous processing,** parallel (concurrent) processing	Simultanverarbeitung f, Parallelverarbeitung f <Verarbeitung verschiedener Elemente einer Aufgabe gleichzeitig in mehreren Einheiten — im Gegensatz zu sequentieller Verarbeitung>	traitement m simultané	параллельная обработка; обработка з совмещением операций
S 439	**simultaneous-processing system,** parallel-processing system, concurrent-processing system	Simultanverarbeitungssystem n, Parallelverarbeitungssystem n	système m de traitement parallèle	система с параллельной (совмещенной) обработкой
S 440	**simultaneous technique,** parallel technique	Simultantechnik f	technique f simultanée	метод параллельной (совмещенной) обработки
S 441	**single-accumulator architecture**	Einzelakkumulatorarchitektur f <Struktur mit nur einem Akkumulator>	structure f à un seul accumulateur	архитектура с одним аккумулятором
	single accuracy	s. S 480		
S 442	**single-action printer**	Einzelzeichendrucker m	imprimeuse f de lettre à lettre	печатающее устройство, печатающее одиночными символами
	single-address instruction	s. O 54		
S 443	**single-address machine**	Einadreßmaschine f	machine f à une adresse	одноадресная машина
S 444	**single-bit fault correction**	Einbitfehlerkorrektur f	correction f de défaut d'un bit	исправление одиночных ошибок
S 445	**single-bit fault detection**	Einbitfehlererkennung f	détection f de défaut à un bit	обнаружение одиночных ошибок
S 446	**single-bit I/O**	Einzelbit-E/A f, Einzelbit-Eingabe-Ausgabe f	E/S f à un bit	одноразрядный ввод-вывод
S 447	**single-bit operation**	Einzelbitoperation f	opération f à bit unique	битовая операция
S 448	**single-bit register**	Einzelbitregister n, Einbitregister n	registre m à bit unique	одноразрядный регистр
S 449	**single-board computer,** SBC	Einkartenrechner m, Einzelsteckeinheit-Rechner m, ESR <[Mikro-]Rechner auf nur 1 Leiterplatte>	calculateur m sur carte unique, SBC m	одноплатная ЭВМ
S 450	**single-board microprocessor,** single-printed circuit board microprocessor	Einzelsteckeinheit-Mikroprozessor m, <Mikroprozessorsystem auf 1 Leiterkarte konzentriert>	microcalculateur m sur circuit imprimé unique	одноплатная микропроцессорная система
S 451	**single bus structure**	Einzelbusstruktur f <Struktur mit einem einzigen, für Speicher- und E/A-Verkehr gemeinsamen Bus>	structure f à bus unique	одношинная структура
S 452	**single-bus-transfer mode**	Einzelübertragungs-Busbetriebsweise f, Betriebsweise f mit Einzel-Busübertragungen <Rückgabe der Steuerung nach jedem Transfer>	mode m de bus à transfert unique	обмен данными по одной общей шине
S 453	**single-byte instruction**	Einzelbytebefehl m, Befehl m im 1-Byte-Format	instruction f à un octet	однобайтная команда
S 454	**single-byte transfer**	Einzelbyteübertragung f	transfert m d'octet unique	передача одного байта
S 455	**single character**	Einzelzeichen n	caractère m unique	одиночный символ
S 456	**single-chip application**	Einzelchipanwendung f, Einzelschaltkreisanwendung f	application f de puce unique	применение однокристальных изделий <область применения однокристальных изделий>
S 457	**single-chip computer,** SCC	Einchiprechner m, 1-Chip-Mikrorechner m, EMR m <Mikrorechner auf 1 Schaltkreis konzentriert>	calculateur m sur une puce, SCC m	однокристальная микро-ЭВМ
S 458	**single-chip processor**	Einchipprozessor m, 1-Chip-Mikroprozessor m <Mikroprozessor auf 1 Schaltkreis konzentriert>	processeur m sur une puce	однокристальный [микро]процессор
S 459	**single crystal**	Einkristall m	monocristal m, cristal m unique	монокристалл
S 460	**single-cycle operation**	Einzyklusoperation f, Einzelzyklusbetrieb m	opération f à cycle unique	операция, исполняемая за один цикл
S 461	**single-diffused epitaxial base transistor**	Epibasis-Transistor m, einfachdiffundierter Transistor m mit epitaxialer Basis	transistor m à base épitaxiale à diffusion simple	транзистор с одинарной диффузией и эпитаксиальной базой
S 462	**single-diffused transistor**	einfachdiffundierter Transistor m	transistor m à diffusion simple	транзистор с одинарной диффузией
S 463	**single-disk cartridge**	Einzelplattenkassette f	cassette f à disque unique	кассета с одним диском
S 464	**single-error correction**	Einzelfehlerkorrektur f	correction f d'erreur unique	исправление одиночных ошибок
	single-layer board	s. S 466		

	single-layer metalliza- tion package	s. S 507		
S 465	single-layer polysilicon technique, single-level polysilicon technique	Einschichtpolysilizium- technik f, Einebenenpoly- siliziumtechnik f	technique f au polysilicium à couche unique	технология одноуровне- вых поликремниевых структур
S 466	single-layer printed circuit board, single- layer board	Einebenen-Leiterplatte f, Einlagen-Leiterplatte f	circuit m imprimé à une seule couche	однослойная печатная плата
S 467	single-length arithmetic	Einfachlängenarithmetik f	arithmétique f à simple longueur	арифметические действия над операндами одинар- ной длины
S 468	single-length operand	Einfachlängen-Operand m, Operand m einfacher Länge	opérande m de simple longueur	операнд одинарной длины
	single-level addressing	s. I 40		
S 469	single-level interrupt system	Einebenen-Interruptsystem n <Unterbrechungssystem ohne Prioritätsstaffelung>	système m d'interruption à niveau unique	одноуровневая система прерываний
	single-level polysilicon technique	s. S 465		
S 470	single-level storage system	Einebenen-Speichersystem n <Speichersystem ohne hierarchische Staffelung>	système m de mémoire à niveau unique	одноуровневая система памяти
S 471	single-line controller	Einzelleitungssteuereinheit f	unité f de commande de ligne unique	одноконтурный контрол- лер
S 472	single-line transfer	Einzelleitungsübertragung f, Ein-Leitungs-Über- tragung f	transfert m à ligne unique	передача по одной линии
S 473	single-mask technology	Ein-Masken-Technologie f <Blasenspeicherherstel- lung>	technologie f à masque unique	одномасочная технология
S 474	single-memory archi- tecture <von Neumann architecture>	Einzelspeicherarchitektur f <Struktur mit gemein- samem Speicher für Daten und Programm>	structure f à mémoire unique	архитектура вычисли- тельной машины с еди- ной памятью [программ и данных] <архитектура фон-Неймана>
	single-operand oper- ation	s. U 12		
	single-pass compiler	s. O 57		
S 475	single-pass program	Einzeldurchgangsprogramm n <Programm mit Ergeb- nisermittlung in einem einzigen Durchlauf>	programme m à passage unique	однопроходная программа
S 476	single-phase	einphasig	monophasé	однофазный, однотактный
S 477	single-phase clock	Einphasentakt m	rythme m à phase unique	однотактная (однофазная) синхронизация
S 478	single-pole switch	einpoliger Schalter m	commutateur m unipolaire	однополюсный переклю- чатель
S 479	single-power supply, single-voltage supply	Einzelspannungs-Strom- versorgung f	alimentation f à tension unique	источник питания на одно выходное напряжение
S 480	single precision, single accuracy	einfache Genauigkeit f	précision f simple	одинарная точность
	single-printed circuit board micropro- cessor	s. S 450		
S 481	single-program mode	Einzelprogrammbetriebsart f, Einprogrammbetrieb m	mode m à programme unique	однопрограммный режим
S 482	single pulse	Einzelimpuls m <mengen- bezogen>	impulsion f unique	одиночный импульс
S 483	single-purpose computer	Einzweckrechner m, Rech- ner m für eine spezielle Aufgabe	calculateur m pour une tâche unique	одноцелевая ЭВМ
S 484	single-shot circuit	monostabile Schaltung f	circuit m monostable	моностабильная (спуско- вая) схема <схема фор- мирования стандартного сигнала>
	single-shot multi- vibrator	s. M 488		
S 485	single-shot trigger circuit	Univibratorkippschaltung f	circuit m basculeur mono- stable	одновибратор
S 486	single signal	Einzelsignal n	signal m unique	одиночный сигнал
S 487	single-stage amplifier	einstufiger Verstärker m	amplificateur m à un étage	однокаскадный усилитель
S 488	single step	Einzelschritt m	pas m unique	[один] шаг; [одна] ступень
S 489	single-step control	Einzelschrittsteuerung f	commande f à pas unique[s]	одноступенчатое управле- ние
S 490	single-step debugging	Einzelschrittfehlersuche f	dépannage m pas à pas	пошаговая отладка
S 491	single-step mode	Einzelschrittarbeitsweise f	mode m de travail pas à pas	пошаговый режим
S 492	single-step operation, single stepping, one- step (step-by-step, one- shot) operation	Einzelschrittbetrieb m, Schrittbetrieb m	régime m pas à pas, régime à pas	пошаговая работа, по- шаговый режим
S 493	single-tasking	Einzelaufgabenverarbei- tung f, Einzelverarbeitung f	traitement m de tâches particulières	однозадачная обработка
S 494	single-trace	einspurig	à voie unique	однодорожечный, одно- канальный
S 495	single-transistor cell	1-Transistor-Zelle f, Ein- transistorzelle f	cellule f à transistor unique	однотранзисторная ячейка
	single-voltage supply	s. S 479		
S 496	single-word instruction format	Einwortbefehlsformat n	format m d'instruction à mot unique	формат команды длиной в одно слово
S 497	sink current	Aufnahmelaststrom m <Bauelement>, Senken- strom m	courant m de charge con- sommé	ток, поступающий в нагрузку
	SIO	s. S 259		

S 498	**SI unit**	SI-Einheit *f*	unité *f* de SI	единица системы СИ
	six-bit character	*s.* B 169		<международная система
	sixteen-bit arithmetic	*s.* B 166		ма единиц измерений
	sixteen-bit data	*s.* B 174		физических величин>
	sixteen-bit microcom- puter	*s.* B 183		
	sixteen-bit micropro- cessor	*s.* B 186		
	sixteen-bit operand	*s.* B 190		
	sixteen-bit register	*s.* B 197		
S 499	**size / to**	dimensionieren	dimensionner	определять величину
S 500	**size reduction**	Größenreduzierung *f*, Flächenreduzierung *f* <Chip>	réduction *f* de taille	сокращение размеров
S 501	**skew**	Schrägverzerrung *f*, Schrägversatz *m*	distorsion *f* oblique	перекос
S 502	**skin effect**	Skineffekt *m*, Hauteffekt *m*	effet *m* pelliculaire	скин-эффект, поверхностный эффект
S 503	**skip / to**	überspringen, auslassen	sauter, surpasser	пропускать
S 504	**skip**	Übersprung *m* <der Folgeposition>, Auslassung *f* <der Folgeposition>	surpassement *m*	пропуск
S 505	**skip instruction**	Übersprungbefehl *m*, Skipbefehl *m*	instruction *f* de surpassement	команда пропуска
S 506	**slab**	Tafel *f*, Platte *f* <Halbleiterkristallrohling>	table *f*, plaque *f*	кристалл полупроводника, из которого нарезают пластины
S 507	**SLAM package,** singlelayer metallization package	SLAM-Gehäuse *n*, Einschichtmetallisierungsgehäuse *n*	boîtier *m* métallisé à une couche	корпус с однослойной металлизацией
	slave	*s.* S 508		
S 508	**slave device,** slave	Nebengerät *n* [in einem Master-Slave-System], Slave-Gerät *n*, abhängiges (anweisungsausführendes) Gerät *n*	appareil *m* slave, slave *m*	ведомое устройство
S 509	**slave processor**	Nebenprozessor *m*, Slave-Prozessor *m*, abhängiger Prozessor *m*	processeur *m* slave	ведомый процессор
S 510	**slave station**	Nebenstation *f*, Slave-Station *f*, Passivstation *f*	station *f* slave (auxiliaire)	ведомая станция
S 511	**slice / to**	in Scheiben schneiden (zerteilen)	découper en disques	нарезать, вырезать
S 512	**slice**	Scheibenteil *n* <eines scheibenstrukturierten Mikroprozessors>	tranche *f*	процессорная секция
S 513	**slice architecture**	Scheibenarchitektur *f*, Bitscheibenarchitektur *f* eines Prozessors	architecture *f* en tranches	архитектура разрядносекционируемых микропроцессоров
S 514	**slice handling ·**	Teilwortverarbeitung *f*	traitement *m* en tranches	обработка по частям
S 515	**slot**	Einsteckschlitz *m*; Steckplatz *m*	place *f* de logement, place à enficher	[щелевое] отверстие; позиция для подключения платы
	SLT	*s.* S 548		
	small computer	*s.* M 438		
	small-scale integration	*s.* S 640		
S 516	**small signal current gain**	Kleinsignalstromverstärkung *f*	amplification *f* de courant de petits signaux	усиление по току в режиме малого сигнала
S 517	**smooth scrolling**	stetiger Schriftbildlauf *m* <Bildschirm>	évolution *f* continue d'écriture	непрерывное отображение на экране дисплея в рулонном режиме
	SMOS chip	*s.* S 39		
S 518	**snapshot debugging**	„Schnappschuß"-Fehlersuche *f* <Fehlersuchtechnik>	dépannage *m* en instantané	режим отладки <сегментов> программы с индикацией содержимого регистров и выбранных ячеек памяти
S 519	**snapshot dump**	Momentanausdruck *m*, Momentanspeicherauszug *m*	expression *f* instantanée	избирательный вывод, моментальный дамп
S 520	**socket**	Sockel *m*, Fassung *f*	socle *m*, culot *m*	гнездо
S 521	**socket connector,** jack	Buchse *f*	douille *f*	[штепсельная] розетка, [контактное] гнездо, фишка
S 522	**socket strip**	Experimentiersteckplatte *f*	plaque *f* à douilles expérimentale	панель с контактными гнездами под выводы микросхем
S 523	**software**	Software *f*, Systemunterlagen *fpl*, Programm- und Dokumentationsausrüstung *f*	logiciels *mpl*, software *m*	средства программирования; программное обеспечение
S 524	**software aids**	Software-Hilfen *fpl*	aides *fpl* logicielles	программные средства
S 525	**software architecture**	Software-Struktur *f*, Programmsystemstruktur *f*	structure *f* logicielle	структура программного обеспечения
S 526	**software-compatible**	software-kompatibel, programmkompatibel	software-compatible	программно совместимый
S 527	**software-controlled**	software-gesteuert, programmgesteuert	à commande logicielle	программно управляемый
S 528	**software design aids**	Software-Entwicklungshilfen *fpl*	assistance *f* au développement logiciel	средства разработки программного обеспечения
S 529	**software development**	Software-Entwicklung *f*, Systemunterlagenentwicklung *f*	développement *m* de logiciel[s]	разработка программного обеспечения
S 530	**software development** system	Software-Entwicklungssystem *n*	système *m* de développement logiciel	система разработки программного обеспечения

S 531	software diagnostic	Software-Diagnose f, Software-Fehlersuche f, Diagnose f mittels Programms	diagnostic m logiciel	программная диагностика, программный диагностический контроль
S 532	software documents	Software-Unterlagen fpl	documents mpl logiciels	документация по программному обеспечению
S 533	software engineering	Software-Technik f, Software-Entwicklungstechnik f, Programmtechnik f	technique f logicielle	техника разработки программного обеспечения
S 534	software house	Software-Dienstleistungsfirma f	entreprise f de services logiciels, société f de services et de conseils en informatique	фирма, специализирующаяся в области разработки программного обеспечения
S 535	software interrupt	Software-Interrupt m, programmierte Unterbrechung f	interruption f de logiciel	программное прерывание
S 536	software library	Software-Bibliothek f	bibliothèque f de logiciels	библиотека программ
S 537	software maintenance	Software-Wartung f, Software-Pflege f	maintenance f de logiciels	сопровождение программного обеспечения
S 538	software package	Software-Paket n	paquet m logiciel	пакет программного обеспечения
S 539	software stack	Software-Stapelspeicher m, programmtechnisch organisierter Kellerspeicher m <Arbeitsspeicherbereich>	empilage m logiciel	программный стек
S 540	software support	Software-Unterstützung f	assistance f logicielle	программная поддержка, вспомогательные программные средства
S 541	software tools	Software-Werkzeuge npl, Hilfsmittel npl in Form von Systemunterlagen	moyens mpl logiciels	программные средства
S 542	solder	Lötmetall n	métal m à souder	припой
S 543	solder connection	Lötverbindung f	connexion f soudée	паяное соединение
S 544	soldering	Löten n	soudage m	пайка
S 545	solderless	lötfrei	sans soudage	беспаечный
S 546	solder-mask protection	Lötmaskenschutz m <Schutz nicht zu lötender Flächen durch Abdeckung mit einer Maske — Lötmaske>	protection f à masque de soudage	защита от припоя
S 547	solder side	Lötseite f	face f soudée	сторона паек
S 548	solid logic technology, SLT	Festkörperschaltkreistechnik f	technologie f logique solide	твердотельные (полупроводниковые) логические схемы
S 549	solid state	Festkörperzustand m, fester Zustand m	corps (état) m solide	твердое (кристаллическое) состояние
S 550	solid-state integrated circuit	integrierte Festkörperschaltung f	circuit m intégré à corps solide	твердотельная (монолитная) интегральная схема
S 551	solid-state memory	Festkörperspeicher m <im Gegensatz zum Kernspeicher>	mémoire f à corps solide	полупроводниковая память
S 552	solid-state technique	Festkörpertechnik f	technique f des corps solides	твердотельная техника
S 553	solution	Lösung f, Auflösung f	solution f, résolution f	решение, разрешение
S 554	solve / to	lösen	résoudre	решать
	SOM	s. S 703		вать
S 555	sort / to	sortieren	assortir, trier	сортировать; упорядочивать
S 556	sorting	Sortierung f	tri m, triage m	сортировка; упорядочение
S 557	sorting process	Sortiervorgang m	processus m de tri	процесс сортировки
S 558	sorting program, sort program	Sortierprogramm n	programme m de tri	программа сортировки
S 559	sort instruction	Sortierbefehl m	instruction f de tri	команда сортировки
S 560	sort key	Sortierschlüssel m, Sortierbegriff m	clé f de triage	ключ сортировки
S 561	sort/merge program	Sortier/Misch-Programm n	programme m de tri/fusion	программа сортировки-слияния (сортировки-объединения)
	sort program	s. S 558		
S 562	SOS technology, silicon-on-sapphire technology	SOS-Technologie f, Silizium-auf-Saphir-Technologie f <Halbleitertechnologie mit Isolatorsubstrat>	technologie f SOS (silicium-sur-saphir)	технология «кремний на сапфире», КНС-технология
S 563	source	Quelle f, Einspeisung f	source f	источник, исток
S 564	source address	Quelloperandenadresse f	adresse f d'opérande source	адрес источника
S 565	source code	Quellkode m, Ursprungskode m	code m source	исходный код
S 566	source current	Source-Strom m, Einspeisungsstrom m	courant m de source	ток истока
S 567	source data	Quelldaten pl, Ursprungsdaten pl	données fpl de source	исходные данные; данные источника
S 568	source-drain spacing	Source-Drain-Abstand m, Quellenelektrode-Senkenelektrode-Abstand m eines Feldeffekttransistors	espace m source-drain	промежуток сток-исток
S 569	source editor	Quellenkode-Editorprogramm n	éditeur m source	редактор исходного текста
S 570	source electrode	Source-Elektrode f, Quellenelektrode f eines Feldeffekttransistors	électrode f de source	электрод истока
S 571	source-gate capacitance	Source-Gate-Kapazität f <Kapazität zwischen Quellen- und Gate-Elektrode eines Feldeffekttransistors>	capacité f source-gate	емкость затвор-исток

S 572	source impedance	Quellimpedanz f	impédance f de source	импеданс истока
S 573	source language	Quellsprache f, Quellkode-sprache f	langage m source	исходный язык
S 574	source library	Quellenprogrammbiblio-thek f	bibliothèque f de pro-grammes source	библиотека программ на исходном языке
S 575	source module	Quellprogrammodul m	module m de programme source	исходный модуль
S 576	source operand	Quelloperand m	opérande m source	исходный операнд, опе-ранд источника
S 577	source program	Quellprogramm n	programme m source	исходная программа
S 578	source statement	Quellenkodeanweisung f	instruction f source	исходный оператор
S 579	source voltage	Source-Spannung f, Span-nung f der Source-Elektrode	tension f de source	напряжение истока
S 580	space	Raum m	espace m	пространство
S 581	space	Zwischenraum m, Leerstelle f	intervalle m, espace m	промежуток; пробел
	space bar	s. S 584		
S 582	space charge	Raumladung f	charge f spatiale	пространственный заряд
S 583	space-charge-limited transistor, SCLT	raumladungsbegrenzter Transistor m	transistor m à charge d'espace limitée, SCLT m	транзистор с ограничен-ным пространственным зарядом
S 584	space key, space bar	Leertaste f	touche f de vide, touche d'espacement	клавиша пробела
S 585	space lattice	Raumgitter n <Kristall-struktur>	réseau m spatial	пространственная решетка
S 586	space-multiplexed	raummultiplex, raumgeteilt <Speicher>	multiplex dans l'espace	пространственно распре-деленный
S 587	space requirement	Raumbedarf m, Platzbedarf m	besoin m de place, encom-brement m	требование к простран-ству, требуемый объем
S 588	space-saving	platzsparend	peu encombrant	занимающий мало места, малогабаритный
S 589	space-sharing	Platzteilung f, Raum-teilung f <anteilige Raum-nutzung im Speicher>	partage m de place	разделение пространства
S 590	space switching	Zeilenschaltung f	interlignage m	пространственная комму-тация
S 591	spacing	Abstand m	distance f	расстояние, интервал, промежуток
S 592	spare, replacement part	Ersatzteil n, Reserveteil n	pièce f de rechange (réserve)	заменяемая часть, запас, резерв
S 593	special application	Spezialanwendung f	application f spéciale	специальное применение
S 594	special character	Sonderzeichen n	caractère m spécial	специальный символ
S 595	special circuitry	Spezialschaltung f	circuit m spécial	специальные схемы
S 596	special-function key	Spezialfunktionstaste f	touche f de fonction spéciale	специальная (функцио-нальная) клавиша
S 597	special hardware	Spezialgerätetechnik f	matériel m spécial	специальная аппаратура, специальные аппарат-ные средства
S 598	special instruction	Spezialbefehl m, Sonder-befehl m	instruction f spéciale	специальная инструкция
S 599	specialized device	Spezialbaustein m, speziali-sierter Baustein m	module m spécialisé	специализированное устройство
S 600	specialized register	spezialisiertes Register n, Spezialregister n	registre m spécialisé	регистр специального назначения
S 601	special-purpose com-puter	Spezialzweckrechner m, Spezialrechner m	calculateur m spécial	специализированная ЭВМ
S 602	special-purpose logic chip	Spezialzweck-Logikschalt-kreis m	circuit m logique spécial	специализированная логическая микросхема
S 603	special-purpose micro-processor	Spezialzweck-Mikro-prozessor m	microprocesseur m spécial	специализированный микропроцессор
	specific address	s. A 7		
S 604	specification	Spezifikation f, Vorschrift f, detaillierte Angabe f	spécification f	спецификация
S 605	specifications	Kenndatenblatt n, tech-nische Daten pl (Bedin-gungen fpl)	spécifications fpl	технические условия (требования)
	specific code	s. A 10		
S 606	specific conductivity	spezifischer Leitwert m	conductance f spécifique	удельная проводимость
S 607	specific program	spezifisches (spezielles) Pro-gramm n	programme m spécifique	специальная программа, программа для решения частной задачи
S 608	specific use	spezifische Verwendung f	usage m spécifique	конкретное применение
S 609	specify / to	spezifizieren, bestimmen, festlegen	spécifier	точно определять, устана-вливать, специфициро-вать
S 610	speech	Sprechen n, Sprechweise f	parole f	речь
S 611	speech-based I/O (input-output)	sprachbasierende E/A f, Eingabe-Ausgabe f auf Sprachlauten basierend	entrée-sortie f sur base de la parole	речевой ввод-вывод
S 612	speech channel, voice channel	Sprachkanal m	canal m de parole	речевой (телефонный) канал, канал тональной частоты
S 613	speech generator	Sprachgenerator m, Sprach-lauterzeuger m	générateur m de parole	генератор искусственной речи
S 614	speech input, voice input	Spracheingabe f	entrée f parlée	речевой ввод
S 615	speech module	Sprachmodul m, Sprachbau-gruppe f	module m de parole	речевой модуль
S 616	speech output, voice output	Sprachausgabe f	sortie f parlée	речевой вывод
S 617	speech output capabil-ity, voice output capabil-ity	Sprachausgabefähigkeit f	faculté f de sortie parlée	возможность речевого вывода

S 618	speech recognition, voice recognition	Spracherkennung f, Sprachlauterkennung f	reconnaissance f de la parole	распознавание речи
S 619	speech recognition system, voice recognition system	Spracherkennungssystem n	système m de reconnaissance de la parole	система распознавания речи
S 620	speech signal	Sprachsignal n	signal m de parole	речевой сигнал
S 621	speech synthesis	Sprachsynthese f, Lautsynthese f	synthèse f de la parole	синтез речи
S 622	speech-synthesis chip, voice-synthesis chip	Sprachsyntheseschaltkreis m, Sprachsynthetisatorchip m	circuit m de synthèse de la parole	микросхема синтезатора речи
S 623	speech synthesizer, voice synthesizer	Sprachsynthetisator m, Lautsynthetisator m	synthétisateur m de la parole	синтезатор речи
S 624	speed control	Geschwindigkeitsregelung f, Geschwindigkeitssteuerung f	régulation f (réglage m) de vitesse	регулирование скорости
S 625	speed-power product	Geschwindigkeits-Leistungs-Produkt n <Produkt der Verzögerungszeit und der Verlustleistung eines Logikgatters>	produit m vitesse-puissance	произведение показателя быстродействия на величину рассеиваемой мощности <показатель качества цифровой схемы>
S 626	speed range	Geschwindigkeitsbereich m	champ m de vitesse	диапазон скоростей
S 627	speed-up	Voreilen n	avancement m	опережение, ускорение
S 628	split / to	aufspalten, aufteilen, splitten	fractionner, découper	разбивать, разделять <текст>
S 629	split load	aufgeteilte Belastung f	charge f partagée	разделенная нагрузка
S 630	split screen	geteilter Bildschirm m	écran m partagé	разделенный экран
S 631	spoken language	gesprochene Sprache f	langage m parlé	разговорный язык
S 632	spooling	Ausspulen n <Datenzwischenspeicherung auf Platte oder Band>	exécution f de SPOOL <opération périphérique simultanée on-line>	спулинг, режим подкачки <совмещение обработки с вводом-выводом>
	spot	s. L 113		
S 633	sprocket channel	Transportspur f <Lochstreifen>	piste f de transport <bande perforée>	дорожка ведущей перфорации, синхродорожка
S 634	sprocket hole	Führungsloch n, Transportloch n <Lochstreifen>	trou m de transport <bande perforée>	ведущее перфорационное отверстие
S 635	spurious pulse	Fehlimpuls m	impulsion f fautive	паразитный импульс
S 636	square chip-carrier	quadratischer Chipträger m (Chiprahmen) m	cadre m à puces quadratique	прямоугольный кристаллоноситель
	square pulse	s. R 129		
S 637	square root	Quadratwurzel f	racine f carrée	квадратный корень
S 638	square wave	Rechteckwelle f	onde f carrée (rectangulaire)	колебание прямоугольной формы
S 639	SS-format	Speicher-Speicher-Befehlsformat n	format m d'instruction mémoire-mémoire	формат команды «память-память»
S 640	SSI, small-scale integration	SSI f, Kleinintegration f, einfache Integration f	SSI f, intégration f simple	малая интеграция, малая степень интеграции
S 641	SSI circuit	SSI-Schaltkreis m, einfach (niedrig) integrierter Schaltkreis m	circuit m SSI	микросхема малой [степени] интеграции
S 642	stabilized power supply	stabilisierte Stromversorgung f	alimentation f stabilisée	стабилизированный источник питания
S 643	stable data	stabile Daten pl, eingeschwungene Datensignale npl	données fpl stables	установившиеся данные (сигналы данных)
	stable power source	s. C 636		
S 644	stable state	stabiler Zustand m	état m stable	устойчивое состояние
S 645	stack / to	stapeln	empiler	помещать (записывать) в стек
S 646	stack, push-down storage, push-pop memory	Kellerspeicher m, Keller m, Stapelspeicher m	mémoire f d'empilage, cave f	стек, память магазинного типа
S 647	stack addressing	Stackadressierung f, Kellerspeicheradressierung f <Adresse im Kellerzeiger>	adressage m de mémoire-cave	адресация стека, адресация по указателю стека
S 648	stack architecture	Kellerspeicherstruktur f, Kellerspeicheraufbau m	structure f de mémoire-cave	стековая архитектура
S 649	stack depth	Kellerspeichertiefe f, Kellerungstiefe f	profondeur f de mémoire-cave	глубина стека
S 650	stacked gate	geschichtetes Gate n, Stapel-Gate n	gate m empilé	составной затвор
	stacked-gate avalanche injection MOS	s. S 4		
	stacked-gate injection MOS	s. S 417		
S 651	stack frame	Stackrahmen m, Kellerspeichersprosse f <Datenstrukturaufbau im Stack>	échelon m de mémoire-cave	граница стека
S 652	stack frame pointer	Stackrahmenzeiger m, Kellerdatenreferenzregister n	pointeur m d'échelon de mémoire-cave	указатель границы стека
S 653	stack handling	Kellerspeichersteuerung f	commande f de mémoire-cave	управление стеком
S 654	stacking	Kellerung f, Stapelung f	mise f en cave, empilage m	запись (помещение) в стек
S 655	stack instruction	Kellerbefehl m, Kellerspeicherbefehl m	instruction f de mémoire-cave	команда работы со стеком
S 656	stack-oriented computer	stackorientierter Rechner m, Rechner mit Kellerspeicherarchitektur	calculateur m de structure à cave	ЭВМ со стековой организацией
S 657	stack pointer	Kellerzeiger m, Stapelzeiger m, Stackadreßregister n	pointeur m de cave	указатель стека
S 658	stack segment	Kellerspeichersegment n, Arbeitsspeichersegment n für Kellerspeicheraufbau	segment m de mémoire-cave	стековый сегмент [памяти], область памяти, отведенная для стека

S 659	stage	Stufe *f*, Stadium *n*	étage *m*, degré *m*	каскад; разряд, ступень; стадия
S 660	stage delay time	Stufenverzögerungszeit *f*, Stufenverzögerung *f*	retardement *m* graduel	время задержки каскада
S 661	stand-alone	unabhängig, selbständig	indépendant, autonome	автономный, независимый
S 662	stand-alone configuration	selbständig arbeitsfähige Konfiguration *f*	configuration *f* autonome	автономная конфигурация
S 663	stand-alone emulator	selbständiger (hilfsprogrammunabhängiger) Emulator *m*	émulateur *m* autonome	автономный (внесистемный) эмулятор
S 664	stand-alone microcomputer system	selbständiges Mikrorechnersystem *n* ‹Ausführungsvariante eines Mikrorechners als unabhängiger Rechner›	système *m* de microcalculateur autonome	автономная вычислительная система на базе микро-ЭВМ
S 665	stand-alone mode	unabhängige Betriebsweise *f*, Betriebsweise ohne Umgebungseinbindung	mode *m* autonome	автономный режим
S 666	stand-alone program	selbständiges (autonomes) Programm *n* ‹unabhängig von Systemprogrammen arbeitend›	programme *m* autonome	автономная программа, [системно-]независимая программа
S 667	stand-alone system, autonomous system	unabhängiges System *n*, selbständiges Rechnersystem *n*	système *m* autonome	автономная система
S 668	standard	Standard *m*, Norm *f*	standard *m*, norme *f*	стандарт
S 669	standard assembly	Standardbaugruppe *f*	assemblage *m* standard	стандартный узел
S 670	standard circuit	Standardschaltkreis *m*	circuit *m* standard	стандартная схема
S 671	standard component	Standardbauteil *n*, Standardbauelement *n*	composant *m* standard	стандартный компонент
S 672	standard data format	Standarddatenformat *n*	format *m* standard de données	стандартный формат данных
	standard design	s. S 687		
S 673	standard deviation	Standardabweichung *f*	déviation *f* standard	среднеквадратичное отклонение
S 674	standard equipment	Standardausrüstung *f*, Normalausrüstung *f*	équipement *m* standard	стандартное оборудование
S 675	standard input unit	Standardeingabeeinheit *f*	unité *f* standard d'entrée	стандартное устройство ввода
S 676	standard instruction set	Standardbefehlssatz *m*	jeu *m* d'instructions standard	стандартный набор команд
S 677	standard interface	Standardinterface *n*, Standardschnittstelle *f*, genormte Anschlußstelle *f*	interface *f* standard	стандартный интерфейс
S 678	standard I/O peripheral	Standard-E/A-Peripherie *f*	périphérie *f* d'E/S standard	стандартная периферия [ввода-вывода]
S 679	standardized device	standardisierter Baustein *m*	module *m* standardisé	стандартизированный модуль
S 680	standardized structure	standardisierte Struktur *f*, standardisierter Aufbau *m*	structure *f* standardisée	стандартизированная структура
S 681	standard memory component	Standardspeicherbaustein *m*	composant *m* standard de mémoire	стандартный компонент памяти
S 682	standard sheet	Normblatt *n*	feuille *f* de normes	стандартный формат
S 683	standard size	Standardformat *n*, Normalgröße *f*	format *m* standard	стандартный размер; стандартная величина
S 684	standard software	Standardprogrammausstattung *f*	software *m* standard	стандартное программное обеспечение
S 685	standard subroutine	Standardunterprogramm *n*, einheitliches Unterprogramm *n*	sous-programme *m* standard (unifié)	стандартная подпрограмма
S 686	standard TTL circuit	TTL-Standardschaltkreis *m* ‹TTL-Schaltkreis einer unifizierten Baureihe›	circuit *m* standard TTL	стандартная ТТЛ-схема
S 687	standard version, standard design	Standardversion *f*, Normalausführung *f*	version *f* standard	стандартный вариант, стандартная версия
S 688	standby application	Bereitschaftseinsatz *m*, Einsatz *m* als Hilfseinrichtung	application *f* de disponibilité	использование в качестве резерва; использование в качестве вспомогательного оборудования
S 689	standby computer	Reserverechner *m*, Bereitschaftsrechner *m*	calculateur *m* de réserve	резервная ЭВМ
	standby condition	s. S 696		
S 690	standby consumption	Leistungsverbrauch *m* im Bereitschaftszustand	puissance *f* consommée en état d'attente	энергопотребление в режиме резерва
S 691	standby current	Notstrom *m*, Bereitschaftsbetriebsstrom *m* ‹erforderlicher Strom zum Informationserhalt in RAM-Schaltkreisen›	courant *m* de régime d'attente	ток в режиме резерва
S 692	standby mode	Bereitschaftsbetrieb *m*, Reservebetrieb *m*	mode *m* de réserve	режим резерва
S 693	standby power, quiescent power	Ruheleistungsaufnahme *f*, Leistungsbedarf *m* im Bereitschaftszustand	consommation *f* au repos	резервная мощность
S 694	standby power dissipation	Verlustleistung *f* im Bereitschaftszustand (Ruhezustand)	puissance *f* de perte au repos	рассеиваемая мощность в состоянии резерва
S 695	standby register	Reserveregister *n*	registre *m* de réserve	резервный регистр
S 696	standby status, standby condition	Bereitschaftszustand *m*	état *m* de disponibilité	состояние резерва, резервное состояние
	standby system	s. B 23		
S 697	standby unit	Reserveeinheit *f*	unité *f* de réserve	резервное устройство
S 698	start / to	beginnen, starten	démarrer, commencer	начинать, стартовать

S 699	start	Start m	démarrage m	начало; старт, [за]пуск
S 700	start address	Startadresse f	adresse f de commencement	начальный адрес
S 701	start bit	Startbit n <DÜ>	bit m de démarrage	стартовый бит, стартовый элемент [сигнала]
	start button	s. A 75		
S 702	start key	Starttaste f	touche f de démarrage	клавиша пуска, пусковая кнопка
S 703	start of message, SOM	Nachrichtenbeginn m	début m de message	начало сообщения
S 704	start point	Startpunkt m	point m start (de départ)	начальная точка, точка старта
S 705	start routine	Startprogramm n	programme m de démarrage	программа начального пуска, стартовая программа
S 706	start-stop transmission	Start-Stopp-Übertragung f	transmission f marche-arrêt	стартстопная передача
S 707/8	start-up	Anlauf m, Betriebsstart m	démarrage m	пуск
	start value	s. I 146		
S 709	start vector	Startvektor m, Startadressenzeiger m	vecteur m de commencement	начальный вектор
S 710	state, status	Zustand m, Status m	état m	состояние
S 711	state change, status change	Statuswechsel m, Zustandswechsel m	changement m d'état	смена (изменение) состояния
S 712	statement	Anweisung f	instruction f	инструкция, оператор
S 713	state of technology	Technologiestand m, Technologieniveau n	niveau m technologique	уровень [развития] технологии
S 714	state of the art	Stand m der Technik	niveau m de la technique	современный технический уровень
S 715	state signal, status signal	Statussignal n, Zustandssignal n	signal m d'état	сигнал состояния
S 716	state transition	Zustandsübergang m	transition f d'état	переход между состояниями
S 717	state transition diagram	Zustandsübergangsdiagramm n <Graph>	diagramme m de transition d'état	диаграмма переходов между состояниями
S 718	static characteristic	statische Kennlinie f	caractéristique f statique	статическая характеристика
	static charge	s. S 721		
S 719	static circuitry	statische Schaltung f	circuit m statique	статические схемы
S 720	static dump	statischer Speicherauszug m	extrait m statique de mémoire	статический дамп, статическая разгрузка
S 721	static electrification, static charge	[elektro]statische Aufladung f	charge f [électro]statique	[электро]статический заряд
S 722	static gain	statische Verstärkung f	gain m statique	статическое усиление
S 723	static memory	statischer Speicher m	mémoire f statique	статическая память
S 724	static RAM	statischer RAM m <Lese-Schreib-Speicher mit statischen Speicherzellen>	RAM f statique	статическое оперативное запоминающее устройство, статическое ОЗУ
S 725	static shift register	statisches Schieberegister n <mit statischen Speicherzellen, informationserhaltend bei Taktabschaltung>	registre m de décalage statique	статический сдвигающий регистр, статический регистр сдвига
S 726	static subroutine	statisches Unterprogramm n	sous-programme m statique	статическая подпрограмма
S 727	statistical error	statistischer Fehler m	erreur f statistique	статистическая ошибка
	status	s. S 710		
S 728	status bit	Statusbit n, Zustandsbit n	bit m d'état	бит состояния
S 729	status byte	Statusbyte n, Zustandsbyte n	octet m d'état	байт состояния
	status change	s. S 711		
S 730	status code	Statuskode m, Zustandskode m	code m d'état	код состояния
S 731	status condition	Statusbedingung f, Zustandsbedingung f	condition f d'état	условие, отвечающее данному состоянию
S 732	status flags	Statusflags npl, Statuskennzeichen npl	signes mpl d'état	флаги (признаки) состояния
S 733	status line	Statusleitung f	ligne f d'état	линия состояния
S 734	status panel	Statusanzeigefeld n	panneau m d'affichage d'état	панель индикации состояния
S 735	status poll	Statusabfrage f	interrogation f de l'état	опрос состояния
S 736	status register	Statusregister n	registre m d'état	регистр состояния
S 737	status saving	Statusrettung f	sauvegarde f d'état	сохранение состояния
S 738	status-saving hardware	Statusrettungsschaltung f, technische Lösung f zur Statusrettung	montage m de sauvegarde d'état	аппаратные средства для сохранения состояния
S 739	status-saving procedure	Statusrettungsverfahren n	procédé m de sauvegarde d'état	процедура сохранения состояния
	status signal	s. S 715		
S 740	status test	Statusprüfung f, Zustandsprüfung f	vérification f (test m) d'état	проверка состояния
S 741	status word	Statuswort n	mot m d'état	слово состояния
S 742	steady state	eingeschwungener Zustand m	état m stationnaire (établi)	установившееся состояние
S 743	steady-state characteristic	stationärer Kennwert m	caractéristique f stationnaire	характеристика установившегося режима
S 744	steady-state deviation	stationäre (bleibende) Abweichung f	déviation f stationnaire	установившаяся (статическая) ошибка
S 745	steady-state oscillation	stationäre Schwingung f	oscillation f stationnaire	установившиеся колебания
S 746	stencil	Matrize f	stencil m	шаблон; трафарет
	step-by-step	s. S 756		
	step-by-step operation	s. S 492		
S 747	step-by-step switch, stepping switch	Schrittschaltwerk n	commutateur m pas à pas	шаговый искатель
S 748	step counter	Schrittzähler m	compteur m de pas	счетчик шагов [операции процессора]
S 749	step-down	Abwärtsübersetzung f	démultiplication f	понижение, преобразование с понижением
S 750	step function	Sprungfunktion f	fonction f de saut	ступенчатая функция
S 751	stepless	stufenlos	continu, sans paliers	плавный, непрерывный
S 752	stepped	gestuft	étagé	ступенчатый, ярусный

S 753	**stepper (stepping) motor**	Schrittmotor m	moteur m pas à pas	шаговый двигатель
	stepping switch	s. S 747		
S 754	**step response**	Sprungantwort f, Sprungübergangsfunktion f	réponse f indicielle (de saut)	переходная характеристика
S 755	**step-up**	Aufwärtsübersetzung f	rapport m [multiplicateur]	повышение, преобразование с повышением
S 756	**stepwise, step-by-step**	schrittweise	pas à pas	[по] шаговый, скачкообразный
S 757	**stochastic simulation**	stochastische Simulation f	simulation f stochastique	статистическое (стохастическое) моделирование
S 758	**stock control**	Lagersteuerung f, Bestandskontrolle f	commande f (contrôle m) de stock[s]	управление запасами
	stop	s. H 12		
S 759	**stop bit**	Stoppbit n	bit m d'arrêt	стоповый бит, стоповый элемент [сигнала]
S 760	**stop condition**	Haltbedingung f	condition f d'arrêt	условие останова
S 761	**storable**	speicherbar	apte à mise en mémoire	запоминаемый
S 762	**storage**	Speicherung f, Lagerung f	mise f en mémoire, mémorisation f	запоминание, хранение
	storage	s. a. M 235a		
	storage allocation	s. M 243		
	storage area	s. M 244		
	storage block	s. M 252		
	storage capacitor	s. S 763		
	storage capacity	s. M 255		
	storage cell	s. M 256		
S 763	**storage cell capacitor, storage capacitor**	Speicherzellenkondensator m, Speicherkondensator m <dyn. RAM>	condensateur m de cellule de mémoire	запоминающий конденсатор
	storage-cell structure	s. M 257		
S 764	**storage circuit**	Speicherschaltung f	circuit m de mémoire	схема запоминающего устройства
	storage control	s. M 261		
	storage cycle	s. M 262		
	storage density	s. M 265		
S 765	**storage device**	Speichereinrichtung f, Speichergerät n	dispositif m de mémoire	устройство памяти
S 766	**storage duration, store duration**	Speicherdauer f	durée f de mise en mémoire	длительность хранения [в памяти]
	storage efficiency	s. M 267		
	storage element	s. M 268		
	storage hierarchy	s. M 274		
	storage key	s. M 296		
	storage location	s. M 278		
S 767	**storage medium**	Speichermedium n	milieu m de mémoire	запоминающая среда
S 768	**storage oscilloscope**	Speicheroszillograf m	oscilloscope m à mémoire	запоминающий осциллограф, осциллограф с запоминающей ЭЛТ
	storage protection	s. M 295		
	storage protection key	s. M 296		
	storage system	s. M 312		
	storage technique	s. M 313		
S 769	**storage temperature**	Lagerungstemperatur f	température f de stockage	температура хранения
S 770	**storage time**	Speicherzeit f	temps m d'accumulation	время хранения; время накопления [зарядов]; время хранения накопленных зарядов
	storage unit	s. M 318		
	storage word	s. M 319		
	storage write instruction	s. M 321		
S 771	**store / to**	speichern	emmagasiner, mémoriser	запоминать, хранить
	store	s. M 235a		
	store-and-forward switching	s. M 333		
S 772	**stored charge**	gespeicherte Ladung f	charge f accumulée	накопленный заряд
S 773	**stored data**	gespeicherte Daten pl	données f pl accumulées	запомненные (хранимые) данные
S 774	**stored instruction**	gespeicherter Befehl m	instruction f mise en mémoire	хранимая в памяти команда
S 775	**stored-program computer**	speicherprogrammierter Rechner m	calculateur m programmé en mémoire	ЭВМ с хранимой [в памяти] программой
S 776	**stored-program control**	speicherprogrammierte Steuerung f	commande f programmée en mémoire	управление по хранимой [в памяти] программе
	store duration	s. S 766		
	store erasing	s. M 269		
S 777	**store instruction**	Speicherbefehl m, Abspeicherbefehl m	instruction f de mémoire	команда обращения к памяти
S 778	**store through / to, to write through**	durchspeichern, durchschreiben <in den Arbeits­speicher mit Datenein­tragung in den zwischen­liegenden Cache-Puffer­speicher>	mettre en mémoire avec écriture dans le tampon intermédiaire	записывать через промежуточный буфер
S 779	**straight-cut control**	Streckensteuerung f <Numerik>	commande f de parcours (trajet)	маршрутное управление
S 780	**straightforward design**	geradliniger (einfacher, direkter) Entwurf m	conception f linéaire (simple)	прямой (линейный) метод проектирования
S 781	**straight-line**	geradlinig	droit, en ligne droite, rectiligne	прямолинейный
S 782	**straight-line coding**	lineare Kodierung f <Pro­grammierung ohne Ver­zweigungen und Schlei­fen>	codage m linéaire	бесцикловое кодирование
S 783	**straight-through**	direkt durchgehend, durchlaufend	à passage direct	проходящий <через что-либо>
S 784	**strapping plug**	Brückenstecker m	fiche-pont f	перемычка
	string	s. C 93		
S 785	**string handling**	Kettenbehandlung f, Zeichenkettenbehandlung f	traitement m de chaîne	обработка строк [данных]

S 786	string manipulation	Kettenmanipulierung f, Zeichenkettenbearbeitung f	manipulation f de chaîne	манипулирование строками [данных]
S 787	string operation	Kettenoperation f, Zeichenkettenoperation f	opération f de chaîne	работа со строками [данных]
S 788	string translation	Zeichenkettenübersetzung f	traduction f de chaîne	преобразование строки
S 789	strip / to	abstreifen; abisolieren	retirer; dénuder	зачищать, снимать изоляцию
S 790	strip	Streifen m; Leiste f	bande f; réglette f	полоса; шина
S 791	stripper	Schichtentferner m; Abisolierer m	dispositif m à éliminer des couches; dispositif à dénuder	инструмент для зачистки проводов
S 792	strip printer	Streifendrucker m	imprimante f à ruban	ленточное печатающее устройство
S 793	strobe / to strobe	markieren; einblenden s. S 796	marquer	стробировать
S 794	strobe input	Strobesignal-Eingang m	entrée f de signal stroboscopique	стробирующий вход, вход стробирования
S 795	strobe line	Strobe-Leitung f, Markierimpulsleitung f	ligne f d'impulsion de marquage	линия стробирования
S 796	strobe pulse, strobe	Markierimpuls m, Kennungsimpuls m, Strobe m \<Aktivierungsimpuls\>	impulsion f de marquage	строб, стробирующий импульс
S 797	strobe signal	Strobe-Signal n, Markiersignal n, Kennungssignal n, Aktivierungssignal n	signal m de marquage	сигнал стробирования, стробирующий сигнал
S 798	stroke	Strich m	trait m	штрих, черта
	stroke marking	s. D 19		
S 799	structural	strukturell	structurel	структурный
S 799 a	structure	Struktur f	structure f	структура
S 800	structured circuit	strukturierte Schaltung f \<kombinatorische und speichernde Anteile getrennt\>	circuit m structuré	структурированная схема
S 801	structured programming	strukturierte Programmierung f	programmation f structurée	структурное программирование
S 802	stuck at	ständig (festgelegt) auf	tenu sur	фиксированный
	stuck-at fault	s. P 154		
S 803	stuck at low level	auf Lowpegel festgehalten	tenu sur niveau bas (low)	фиксированный на низком уровне
S 804	stuck fault	haftender (ständiger) Fehler m	défaut m permanent	постоянная неисправность \<типа залипания\>
S 805	stylus	Nadel f, Schreibstift m	aiguille f, style m	перо самописца
	stylus printer	s. N 14	renregistreur	
S 806	subaddress	Unteradresse f	sous-adresse f	субадрес, подадрес
S 807	subchannel	Subkanal m, Unterkanal m	sous-canal m	подканал
S 808	sublibrary	Teilbibliothek f, Unterbibliothek f	sous-bibliothèque f	подбиблиотека
S 809	subload	Teillast f	charge f partielle	частичная нагрузка
S 810	subprocessor	Subprozessor m, Unterprozessor m	sub-processeur m	субпроцессор
S 811	subprogram, subroutine	Unterprogramm n	sous-programme m, sous-routine f	подпрограмма
S 812	subroutine call	Unterprogrammaufruf m	appel m de sous-programme	вызов подпрограммы
S 813	subroutine calling	Unterprogrammaufruftechnik f	technique f de l'appel de sous-programmes	способ вызова подпрограммы
S 814	subroutine library	Unterprogrammbibliothek f	bibliothèque f de sous-programmes	библиотека подпрограмм
S 815	subroutine linkage	Unterprogrammeinbindung f	liaison f de sous-programme	связь подпрограмм
S 816	subroutine nesting	Unterprogrammverschachtelung f	encastrement m de sous-programmes	вложение подпрограмм
S 817	subroutine package	Unterprogrammpaket n	paquet m de sous-programmes	пакет подпрограмм
S 818	subroutine sequence	Unterprogrammfolge f	séquence f de sous-programmes	последовательность подпрограмм
S 819	subroutine starting address	Unterprogrammstartadresse f	adresse f de démarrage de sous-programme	стартовый адрес подпрограммы
S 820	subscript	Index m, Indexzahl f	index m	[нижний] индекс
S 821	subsequent	nachfolgend, folgend	subséquent	последующий
S 822	subset	Teilsatz m, Untermenge f	sous-ensemble m, sous-multitude f	подмножество
S 823	subsidiary	behilflich, beigeordnet, untergeordnet	subsidiaire	вспомогательный
S 824	substitute / to	substituieren, ersetzen	substituer	заменять, подставлять
S 825	substitution	Substitution f	substitution f	подстановка
S 826	substitution facility	Substitutionsmöglichkeit f	possibilité f de substitution	возможность замены
S 827	substrate	Substrat n, Trägerschicht f, Unterlage f	substrat m	подложка
S 828	substructure	Substruktur f, Teilstruktur f	structure f partielle	подструктура, субструктура
S 829	subsystem	Untersystem n, Teilsystem n	système m partiel	подсистема, субсистема
S 830	subtask	Unteraufgabe f	tâche f partielle	подзадача
S 831	subtract / to	subtrahieren	soustraire	вычитать
S 832	subtracter	Subtrahierer m	terme m soustractif, dispositif m de soustraction	вычитающее устройство, вычитатель
S 833	subtraction	Subtraktion f	soustraction f	вычитание
S 834	subunit	Untereinheit f	subunité f	субблок
S 835	successive	aufeinanderfolgend	successif	последующий, следующий один за другим, последовательный
S 836	successive-approximation converter	Stufenumsetzer m, Umsetzer m mit schrittweiser Annäherung	convertisseur m à approximation successive	преобразователь, работающий по методу последовательных приближений
	successive cycles	s. B 17		

S 837	successive stages	aufeinanderfolgende Stufen *fpl*	étages *mpl* successifs	последовательные стадии; смежные каскады
S 838	successor	Nachfolger *m*	successeur *m*	преемник; последующий элемент
S 839	suffix	Suffix *n*, nachgesetzter Operator *m*	suffixe *m*	суффикс
S 840	suitability	Eignung *f*	qualification *f*	пригодность
S 841	suitable microprocessor system	geeignetes Mikroprozessorsystem *n*	système *m* de microcalculateur approprié	микропроцессорная система, удовлетворяющая заданным требованиям
S 842	sum	Summe *f*	somme *f*	сумма, итог
S 843	summarize / to	zusammenfassen	sommer	суммировать; подводить итог
S 844	superconductivity	Supraleitfähigkeit *f*	supraconductivité *f*	сверхпроводимость
S 845	supervising system, supervisor system	Ablaufüberwachungssystem *n*, Aufsichtssystem *n*	système *m* de supervisor (surveillance)	супервизорная система
S 846	supervisor, supervisor program	Supervisor *m*, Supervisorprogramm *n*, Aufsichtsprogramm *n*, Kontrollprogramm *n* ‹für systeminterne Abläufe›	supervisor *m*, programme *m* de supervisor	[программа-]супервизор
S 847	supervisor call	Supervisoraufruf *m*	appel *m* de supervisor, appel-supervisor *m*	вызов супервизора
S 848/9	supervisor mode	Supervisormodus *m*, Supervisorregime *n*	mode *m* de supervisor	режим супервизора
	supervisor program	s. S 846		
	supervisor system	s. S 845		
S 850	supervisory instruction	Supervisorbefehl *m*	instruction *f* de supervisor	команда супервизора, супервизорная команда
S 851	supplement / to	ergänzen, hinzufügen, nachtragen	ajouter, compléter	добавлять; прилагать
S 852	supplement	Ergänzung *f*, Zusatz *m*	supplément *m*	добавление; приложение
S 853	supplier	Lieferant *m*	fournisseur *m*	поставщик
S 854	supply	Versorgung *f*, Speisung *f*	alimentation *f*	питание
S 855	supply current	Netzstrom *m*, Speisestrom *m*	courant *m* d'alimentation	ток питания
S 856	supply frequency	Speisefrequenz *f*	fréquence *f* d'alimentation	частота источника питания
S 857	supply line, feed line	Speiseleitung *f*, Versorgungsleitung *f*	ligne *f* d'alimentation	линия (шина) питания
S 858	supply source	Speisequelle *f*	source *f* d'alimentation	источник питания
S 859	supply voltage, power supply voltage	Speisespannung *f*, Versorgungsspannung *f*	tension *f* d'alimentation	напряжение питания
S 860	support / to	unterstützen	supporter	поддерживать
S 861	supporting hardware	Unterstützungs-Hardware *f*, unterstützende Gerätetechnik *f*	matériel *m* d'assistance	вспомогательные аппаратные средства, аппаратные средства поддержки
S 862	support program	Unterstützungsprogramm *n*	programme *m* d'assistance	программа поддержки, вспомогательная программа
S 863	support software	Unterstützungs-Software *f*, Unterstützungsprogrammpaket *n*	logiciels *mpl* d'assistance	вспомогательное программное обеспечение, программные средства поддержки
S 864	support system	Unterstützungsprogrammsystem *n*	système *m* d'assistance	система поддержки
S 865	support tools	Unterstützungshilfsmittel *npl* ‹Entwicklungshilfen›	moyens *mpl* d'assistance	средства поддержки
S 866	suppress / to	unterdrücken	supprimer	подавлять, гасить
S 867	suppression	Unterdrückung *f*	suppression *f*	подавление, гашение
S 868	surface barrier	Oberflächenschwelle *f*, Oberflächensperrschicht *f*	barrière *f* superficielle	поверхностный барьер
S 869	surface barrier transistor	Oberflächensperrschicht-Transistor *m*, Oberflächensperrschicht-FET *m*	transistor *m* à barrière superficielle	поверхностно-барьерный транзистор
S 870	surface channel	Oberflächenkanal *m*	canal *m* de surface	поверхностный канал
S 871	surface-channel structure	Struktur *f* mit Oberflächenkanälen ‹Schaltkreistechnik›	structure *f* à canaux de surface	структура с поверхностными каналами
S 872	surface charge	Oberflächenladung *f*	charge *f* superficielle (de surface)	поверхностный заряд
S 873	surface charge-coupled devices, SCCD	oberflächenladungsgekoppelte Elemente *npl*, Oberflächenladungsverschiebeschaltung *f*, Oberflächen-CCD *f*	éléments *mpl* couplés par charge de surface	приборы с поверхностно-зарядовой связью
S 874	surface-controlled transistor, SCT	SCT *m*, Oberflächenladungstransistor *m* ‹Ladungstransferstruktur›	transistor *m* à commande de surface	поверхностно-управляемый транзистор
S 875	surface impurity	Oberflächenverunreinigung *f*	impureté *f* de surface	поверхностная примесь
S 876	surface layer	Oberflächenschicht *f*, Deckschicht *f*	couche *f* superficielle (de surface)	поверхностный слой
S 877	surface leakage current	Kriechstrom *m*, Oberflächenkriechstrom *m*, Oberflächenisolationsstrom *m*	courant *m* rampant de surface, courant de fuite [superficielle]	поверхностная утечка
S 878	surface passivation	Oberflächenpassivierung *f*	passivation *f* de surface	пассивация поверхности
S 879	surface recombination velocity	Oberflächenrekombinationsgeschwindigkeit *f*	vitesse *f* de recombinaison superficielle (de surface)	скорость поверхностной рекомбинации
S 880	suspend / to	suspendieren, aufschieben	suspendre	приостанавливать

S 881	**suspending**	Zurückstellung *f*, Aussetzen *n*, Suspendierung *f* *s.* E 287	suspension *f*	приостановка
S 882	**swap / to** **swap-byte function**	Byteaustausch-Funktion *f*	fonction *f* d'échange d'octet	функция перестановки байтов
S 883	**swap in / to**	einlagern <Datenstruktur oder Aufgabe vom Externspeicher in den Arbeitsspeicher bringen>	emmagasiner	загружать память <считывать задание или шаг задания из внешней памяти в оперативную>
S 884	**swap out / to**	auslagern	mettre hors le dépôt	разгружать память <перезаписывать задание или шаг задания из оперативной памяти во внешнюю>
S 885	**swapper** **swapping**	Austauscher *m* *s.* E 289	échangeur *m*	обменник
S 886	**switch / to**	schalten	commuter	переключать; коммутировать
S 887	**switch**	Schalter *m*	commutateur *m*	переключатель
S 888	**switchable**	umschaltbar	commutable	переключаемый; коммутируемый
S 889	**switch board**	Schalttafel *f*	panneau *m* à commutateurs, tableau *m* de commande	распределительный щит
S 890	**switching**	Schalten *n*	commutation *f*	переключение
S 891	**switching algebra** **switching centre**	Schaltalgebra *f* *s.* E 288	algèbre *f* de Boole (commutation)	алгебра логики (переключательных схем)
S 892	**switching characteristic**	Schaltcharakteristik *f*	caractéristique *f* de commutation	характеристика переключения, ключевая характеристика
S 893	**switching circuit**	Schaltkreis *m*	circuit *m* de commutation	переключательная схема
S 894	**switching device**	Schalteinrichtung *f*, Schaltelement *n*	dispositif *m* de commutation	переключающее устройство
S 895	**switching frequency**	Schaltfrequenz *f*	fréquence *f* de commutation	частота переключения
S 896	**switching function**	Schaltfunktion *f*	fonction *f* de commutation	переключательная функция
S 897	**switching network**	Vermittlungsnetz *n*, Koppelnetz *n* <Nachrichtentechnik>	réseau *m* de communication	коммутационная схема; коммутационная сеть
S 898	**switching pulse**	Schaltimpuls *m*	impulsion *f* de commutation	переключающий импульс
S 899	**switching speed**	Schaltgeschwindigkeit *f*	vitesse *f* de commutation	скорость переключения
S 900	**switching system**	Vermittlungssystem *n* <Nachrichtentechnik>	système *m* de communication	система коммутации
S 901	**switching technique**	Vermittlungstechnik *f*	technique *f* de communication	коммутационная техника, техника коммутации
S 902	**switching time**	Schaltzeit *f*	temps *m* de commutation	время переключения
S 903	**switching transistor**	Schalttransistor *m*	transistor *m* de commutation	переключательный (ключевой) транзистор
S 904	**switching unit**	Schalteinheit *f*, Schaltbaustein *m*	unité *f* de commutation	блок коммутации
S 905	**switching variable**	Schaltvariable *f*	variable *f* de commutation	переменная типа «переключатель»
S 906	**switch off / to**	abschalten	couper	выключать
S 907	**switch on / to**	einschalten	enclencher	включать
S 908	**symbol**	Symbol *n*	symbole *m*	символ, знак
S 909	**symbolic address**	symbolische Adresse *f*	adresse *f* symbolique	символический адрес
S 910	**symbolic addressing**	symbolische Adressierung *f*	adressage *m* symbolique	символическая адресация
S 911	**symbolic assembler**	symbolischer Assembler *m*	assembleur *m* symbolique	символический ассемблер
S 912	**symbolic coding**	symbolische Kodierung *f*	codage *m* symbolique	символическое кодирование
S 913	**symbolic language**	symbolische Sprache *f*, Symbolsprache *f*	langage *m* symbolique	символический язык
S 914	**symbolic programming system**	symbolisches Programmiersystem *n*	système *m* de programmation symbolique	система символического программирования
S 915	**symbol table**	Symboltabelle *f* <Namentabelle>	table *f* de symboles	таблица символов
S 916	**symmetrical clock**	symmetrischer Takt *m*	intervalle *m* symétrique	симметричный такт
S 917	**symmetrically located**	symmetrisch angeordnet	placé symétriquement	симметрично расположенный
S 918	**sync character**	Synchronisationszeichen *n*	caractère *m* de synchronisation	синхросимвол, символ синхронизации
S 919	**synchronism**	Gleichlauf *m*	synchronisme *m*	синхронизм
S 920	**synchronism check**	Gleichlaufprüfung *f*	essai *m* synchrone, vérification *f* de synchronisme	контроль синхронизма
S 921	**synchronization, synchronizing**	Synchronisation *f*, Synchronisierung *f*, Gleichlaufsteuerung *f*	synchronisation *f*	синхронизация
S 922	**synchronization buffer**	Synchronisationspuffer *m*	tampon *m* de synchronisation	буфер синхронизации
S 923	**synchronize / to** **synchronizing**	synchronisieren *s.* S 921	synchroniser	синхронизировать
S 924	**synchronous, in-step**	synchron, gleichlaufend	synchrone, au pas	синхронный
S 925	**synchronous adapter**	Synchronadapter *m*	adapteur *m* synchrone	синхронный адаптер
S 926	**synchronous clock**	Synchrontakt *m*	rythme *m* synchrone	синхронный такт
S 927	**synchronous communications interface**	synchrone Übertragungsschnittstelle *f*	interface *f* de communication synchrone	синхронный связной интерфейс
S 928	**synchronous computer**	Synchronrechner *m*, taktgesteuerter Rechner *m*	calculateur *m* synchrone	вычислительная машина синхронного действия, синхронная ЭВМ
S 929	**synchronous controller** **synchronous data link control** **synchronous data link control mode**	Synchronsteuergerät *n* *s.* S 93 *s.* S 94	appareil *m* de commande synchrone	синхронный контроллер

	synchronous data transfer	s. S 930		
S 930	synchronous data transmission, synchronous data transfer	synchrone Datenübertragung f	transmission f synchrone de données	синхронная передача данных
S 931	synchronous input	Synchroneingabe f	entrée f synchrone	синхронный ввод
S 932	synchronous logic	synchrone (getaktete) Logik f	logique f synchrone	синхронная логика
S 933	synchronous mode	Synchronmodus m, synchrone Betriebsart f	mode m synchrone	синхронный режим
S 934	synchronous operation	Synchronbetrieb m, synchroner Betrieb m	opération f à durée définie, opération synchrone	синхронная работа
S 935	synchronous output	Synchronausgabe f	sortie f synchrone	синхронный вывод
S 936	synchronous transmission	Synchronübertragung f	transmission f synchrone	синхронная передача
S 937	sync line	Synchronisierleitung f	ligne f de synchronisation	линия синхронизации
S 938	sync pulse	Synchronisationsimpuls m	impulsion f de synchronisation	импульс синхронизации
S 939	sync signal	Synchronisiersignal n	signal m de synchronisation	синхросигнал, сигнал синхронизации
S 940	syntax check	Syntaxprüfung f	vérification f syntactique	синтаксический контроль
S 941	syntax error	Syntaxfehler m, Formfehler m	erreur f syntactique	синтаксическая ошибка
S 942	synthesize / to	künstlich erzeugen	produire synthétiquement	синтезировать
S 943	synthetic language	synthetische Sprache f	langage m synthétique	синтезированный (синтетический) язык
S 944	system approach	Systemlösung f	solution f [approximative] de système	системный подход
S 945	system architecture	Systemarchitektur f, Systemaufbau m	architecture f de système	архитектура системы
S 946	systematic error	systematischer Fehler m	erreur f systématique	систематическая (постоянная) ошибка
S 947	system behaviour	Systemverhalten n	comportement m de système	поведение системы; режим работы системы
S 948	system bus	Systembus m ‹gemeinsamer Übertragungsweg aller angeschlossenen Systemkomponenten eines Rechners›	bus m de système	системная шина ‹общая шина, объединяющая системные компоненты микро-ЭВМ›
	system check	s. S 979		
S 949	system clock	Systemtakt m	rythme m de système	такт системы
S 950	system command	Systemkommando n	commande f de système	системная команда
S 951	system compatibility	Systemkompatibilität f	compatibilité f de système	совместимость с системой; совместимость систем
S 952	system component	Systemkomponente f	composant m de système	системный компонент, компонент системы
S 953	system configuration	Systemkonfiguration f, Systemgestaltung f	configuration f de système	конфигурация системы
S 954	system control	Systemsteuerung f	commande f de système	управление системой, системное управление
S 955	system control language	Systemsteuersprache f	langage m de commande de système	язык управления системой
S 956	system controller	Systemsteuerbaustein m	appareil m de commande de système	системный контроллер
S 957	system control logic	Systemsteuerungslogik f	logique f de commande de système	логические средства управления системой
S 958	system crash	Systemabsturz m, Systemzusammenbruch m	effondrement m de système	авария в системе, катастрофический отказ системы
S 959	system deadlock	Systemblockierung f, Systemverklemmung f	blocage m de système	блокировка системы
S 960	system design	Systementwurf m	conception f (projet m) de système	разработка (проектирование) системы
S 961	system designer	Systementwerfer m	concepteur m de système	разработчик системы
S 962	system development	Systementwicklung f	développement m de système	развитие (совершенствование) системы
S 963	system diagnostic	Systemdiagnose f	diagnostic m de système	системная диагностика, диагностика системы
S 964	system disk	Systemplatte f ‹plattengespeichertes Betriebssystem›	disque m de système	системный диск ‹магнитный диск операционной системы›
S 965	system engineering	Systemplanung f, System[entwurfs]technik f	ingénierie f de système, technique f du système	системотехника
S 966	system environment	Systemumgebung f	environnement m de système	окружение системы ‹внешние условия по отношению к системе›
S 967	system generation	Systemgenerierung f	génération f de système	генерация системы
S 968	system level	Systemebene f	niveau m de système	системный уровень
S 969	system-level compatibility	Kompatibilität f auf Systemebene	compatibilité f au niveau de système	совместимость на системном уровне
S 970	system library	Systembibliothek f	bibliothèque f de système	системная библиотека
S 971	system memory chip	systemspezifischer Speicherschaltkreis m	circuit m de mémoire spécifique de système	микросхема системной памяти
S 972	system reliability	Systemzuverlässigkeit f	fiabilité f de système	надежность системы
S 973	system residence	Systemresidenz f ‹Programmresidenz im System›	résidence f de système	резиденция (размещение) системы
S 974	system resource	Systemressource f, Systemmittel n, Systembetriebsmittel n	ressource f de système	ресурс системы, системный ресурс
S 975	system restart	Systemwiederanlauf m	redémarrage m de système	повторный пуск системы, рестарт системы
S 976	system security	System[betriebs]sicherheit f	sûreté f de système	защита системы

S 977	**system software**	System-Software f, System-programmpaket n	logiciels mpl de système	системное программное обеспечение
S 978	**system support**	Systemunterstützung f	assistance f de système	системная поддержка
S 979	**system test**, system check, checkout of system	Systemtest m, System-prüfung f	test m (vérification f) de système	испытание системы; проверка системы; системный тест (контроль)
S 980	**system throughput**	Systemdurchsatz m	capacité f de système	производительность системы

T

	tab	s. T 12		
	TAB	s. T 18		
T 1	**table / to**, to tabulate	tabellieren, in Tabelle eintragen	tabuler	табулировать, составлять таблицы
T 2	**table entry**	Tabelleneingang m, Tabelleneintritt m	entrée f de table	вход в таблицу
T 3	**table handling**	Tabellenbearbeitung f, Tabellenbehandlung f	traitement m de tables	обработка таблиц
T 4	**table item**	Tabelleneinheit f	unité f de table	элемент таблицы
T 5	**table lookup**, table searching	Tabellensuchen n	recherche f de table	просмотр таблицы, поиск в таблице
T 6	**table-mounted device**	Tischgerät n, Gerät n in Arbeitsplatzausführung	appareil m sur table	устройство, смонтированное в столе, устройство в составе рабочего места
	table searching	s. T 5		
T 7	**tablet**	Tafel f, Täfelchen n	tablette f	планшет; блокнот
T 8	**table top mounting**	Auftischmontage f, Montage f in Auftischgehäuse	montage m sur table	настольное исполнение
T 9	**tabular**	tabellarisch	tabulaire	табличный
	tabulate / to	s. T 1		
T 10	**tabulated data**	tabellierte Daten pl, Tabellenwerte mpl	données fpl en tables	табличные данные
	tabulating	s. T 11		
T 11	**tabulation**, tabulating	Tabellierung f	mise f en table	табулирование, составление таблицы
T 12	**tabulator**, tab	Tabulator m	tabulateur m	табулятор
	tag	s. F 118		
T 13	**tagged storage** <self-identifying storage>	gekennzeichnete Speicherung f <selbstidentifizierende Speicherung>	mémorisation f marquée	запоминание [данных] с признаком <само-идентифицирующее запоминание (накопление)>
T 14	**tailoring** <to an application>	Zuschneiden n, Zuschnitt m <auf eine Anwendung>	taille f <sur une application>	адаптация <к применению>
T 15	**take-up reel**	Aufwickelspule f	bobine f d'enroulement	приемная бобина
T 16	**tandem circuit**	Tandemschaltung f <Kaskadenschaltung>	circuit m tandem	каскадная схема
	tank [circuit]	s. O 183		
T 17	**tape**	Band n	ruban m, bande f	лента
T 18	**tape automated bonding**, TAB	TAB n, automatisches Bonden n mit Leiterbahn-Film	bondérisation f automatique à film	автоматическая сборка на ленте
T 19	**tape cable**	Bandkabel n	câble m en ruban	ленточный кабель
	tape cartridge	s. T 20		
T 20	**tape cassette**, tape cartridge	Bandkassette f	cassette f à bande	кассета с лентой
T 21	**tape collation**	Bandmischen n	fusion f de bande	объединение записей на магнитной ленте
T 22	**tape-controlled**	lochstreifengesteuert	à commande par bande perforée	управляемый перфолентой
T 23	**tape controller**	Bandsteuerung f <Magnetband, Lochstreifen>	commande f à bande	контроллер запоминающего устройства на магнитной ленте; контроллер устройства считывания с перфоленты
T 24	**tape control unit**	Bandsteuereinheit f	unité f de commande à bande	устройство управления накопителем на магнитной ленте
T 25	**tape conversion program**	Lochstreifenformatwandlungsprogramm n	programme m de conversion de bande perforée	программа преобразования форматов представления данных на перфоленте
T 26	**tape deck**	Bandgerätesatz m, Bandgeräteeinheit f	jeu m de bandes	комплект (набор) лент
T 27	**tape device**	Bandgerät n	appareil m à bande	блок магнитной ленты
T 28	**tape drive**	Bandlaufwerk n, Bandantrieb m	mécanisme m à ruban (bande)	лентопротяжный механизм
T 29	**tape drive controller**	Bandlaufwerk-Steuereinheit f	unité f de commande de mécanisme à bande	контроллер лентопротяжного механизма
T 30	**tape dump**	Bandauszug m	extrait m de bande	дамп ленты, вывод данных с ленты [на печать]
T 31	**tape feed**	Bandvorschub m, Lochstreifentransport m	avancement m de bande	протяжка ленты
T 32	**tape file**	Banddatei f	fichier m de bande	ленточный файл
T 33	**tape gap**	Bandlücke f	interstice m de bande	пробел на ленте
	tape label	s. T 35		
T 34	**tape loadpoint**	Bandladepunkt m	point m de chargement de bande	начало рабочей зоны магнитной ленты
T 35	**tape mark**, tape label	Bandmarke f	marque f de bande	метка (маркер) на ленте
T 36	**tape operating system**	Band-Betriebssystem n	système m opérationnel de bande	ленточная операционная система
	tape perforator (punch)	s. P 37		

	tape reader	*s.* P 38		
T 37	**tape record**	Bandsatz *m*	enregistrement *m* de	запись на ленте
			стековое ЗУ	
T 38	**tape-resident**	bandresident, auf dem Band ständig vorhanden	résident sur bande	[постоянно] размещенный на ленте
T 39	**tape speed**	Bandgeschwindigkeit *f*	vitesse *f* de bande	скорость ленты
T 40	**tape start**	Bandanlauf *m*	démarrage *m* de bande	пуск ленты
T 41	**tape store**	Bandspeicher *m*	mémoire *f* à bande	память на лентах
T 42	**tape transport**	Bandtransport *m*	transport *m* de bande	подача ленты
T 43	**tape unit**	Bandeinheit *f*	unité *f* de bande [perforée, magnétique]	ленточный блок, блок ленты
	target	*s.* D 288		
	target address	*s.* D 289		
	target computer	*s.* T 45		
T 44	**target language**	Zielsprache *f*	langage *m* de destination	целевой язык
T 45	**target machine**, object machine, target computer	Objektmaschine *f*, Zielmaschine *f*, Zielrechner *m*	machine *f* de destination	целевая ЭВМ <ЭВМ, на которой должна исполняться составляемая программа>
T 46	**target program**	Zielprogramm *n*	programme *m* de destination	целевая (объектная) программа
T 47	**target system**	Zielsystem *n*	système *m* de destination	целевая система
T 48	**task**	Aufgabe *f*, Teilaufgabe *f* <Programm>, Problemstellung *f*, Task *f*	tâche *f*, devoir *m*	задача; проблема
T 49	**task builder**	Taskbildner *m*	concepteur *m* de tâche	построитель задач
T 50	**task control**	Tasksteuerung *f*, Aufgabensteuerung *f*	commande *f* de tâche	управление задачами
T 51	**task-control block**	Tasksteuerblock *m*, Aufgabensteuerblock *m*	bloc *m* de commande de tâche	блок управления задачей
T 52	**task dispatcher**	Taskzuteiler *m*, Aufgabenzuteiler *m*	dispatcher *m* de tâches	диспетчер задач
T 53	**task distribution**	Aufgabenverteilung *f*	distribution *f* de tâches	распределение задач
T 54	**task-divided multi-microprocessor system**	aufgabengeteiltes Multimikroprozessorsystem *n*	système *m* à microcalculateurs multiples à tâches découpées	мультимикропроцессорная система с распределением задач
T 55	**task image**	Taskabbild *n* <auf Speicher>	image *f* de tâche	образ задачи
T 56	**tasking**	Aufgabenzuweisung *f*	attribution *f* de tâches	размещение задач
T 57	**task management**	Taskführung *f*, Aufgabendurchlaufsteuerung *f*	commande *f* de tâches	управление задачами
T 58	**task monitor**	Taskmonitor *m*, Aufgabenüberwacher *m*	moniteur *m* de tâches	монитор задач
T 59	**task queue**	Aufgabenwarteschlange *f*	queue *f* de tâches	очередь задач
T 60	**task scheduling**	Taskreihenfolgeplanung *f*, Aufgabenablaufplanung *f*	planning *m* de séquence de tâches	составление расписания для задач, планирование [решения] задач
T 61	**task switch[ing]**	Aufgabenumschaltung *f*, Aufgabenbearbeitungs-Umschaltung *f*	commutation *f* de tâches	переключение задач
	TCAM	*s.* T 69		
	teaching machine	*s.* A 404		
T 62	**technical description,** engineering description	technische Beschreibung *f*	description *f* technique	техническое описание
T 63	**technological innovation**	technologische Neuerung *f*	nouveauté *f* technologique	технологическое новшество
T 64	**technological know-how**, know-how	technologische Erfahrung *f*, technisches Wissen *n*	savoir-faire *m* technologique	технологические секреты, «ноу-хау» <оригинальная технология, являющаяся предметом торговли>
T 65	**technological premises**	technologische Prämissen (Voraussetzungen) *fpl*	conditions *fpl* technologiques	технологическая база, достигнутый уровень технологии
T 66	**technology development**	Technologieentwicklung *f*	développement *m* de la technologie	разработка технологии
T 67	**technology limitations**	Technologiebegrenzungen *fpl*, Einschränkungen *fpl* durch die Technologie	limites *fpl* de la technologie	технологические ограничения
T 68	**telecommunication[s]**	Fernübertragung *f* von Informationen, Fernmeldetechnik *f*	télécommunication *f*	электросвязь, телекоммуникация; дистанционная передача данных
T 69	**telecommunication access method**, TCAM	Fernübertragungs-Zugriffsmethode *f*, TCAM *f*	méthode *f* d'accès de télécommunication, TCAM *f*	телекоммуникационный метод доступа
T 70	**telemet[e]ring**	Telemetrie *f*, Entfernungsmessung *f*	télémétrie *f*	телеметрия
T 71	**telephone dialer circuit**	Telefonwählerschaltung *f*	circuit *m* chercheur de téléphone	схема телефонного номеронабирателя
T 72	**telephone network**	Fernsprechnetz *n*	réseau *m* téléphonique	телефонная сеть
T 73	**teleprinter**, teletype[writer]	Fernschreiber *m*	téléscripteur *m*, téléimprimeur *m*	телетайп
T 74	**teleprinter exchange,** telex	Fernschreibverkehr *m*	trafic *m* télex	телекс, автоматическая коммутируемая телеграфная связь
T 75	**teleprocessing**, remote processing	Fernverarbeitung *f*	traitement *m* à distance	телеобработка, дистанционная обработка
T 76	**teleticketing**	Fernbuchung *f*	notation *f* à distance	резервирование билетов при подаче заявок с удаленных абонентских пунктов
	teletype	*s.* T 73		
T 77	**teletypesetting**	Fernsetzen *n*	position *f* à distance	абонентский телетайпный пункт
T 78	**teletype terminal**	Fernschreibterminal *n*	terminal *m* à téléscripteur	терминал, оснащенный телетайпом
	teletypewriter	*s.* T 73		

T 79	**teletypewriter trans-mission procedure**	Fernschreiber-Über-tragungsverfahren *n*	procédé *m* de transmission par téléscripteur	процедура передачи [сооб-щения] с телетайпа
	telex	*s.* T 74		
T 80	**temperature dependence**	Temperaturabhängigkeit *f*	dépendance *f* de la tempéra-ture	температурная зависи-мость
T 81	**temperature range (span)**	Temperaturbereich *m*	champ *m* de température	температурный диапазон
T 82	**temperature test**	Temperaturtest *m*	test *m* de température	температурное испытание
T 83	**temporary memory,** temporary storage	temporärer (zeitweiliger) Speicher *m*	mémoire *f* temporaire	временная (промежуточ-ная) память
	temporary memory	*s. a.* I 350		
T 84	**temporary register**	temporäres (zeitweilig speicherndes) Register *n*	registre *m* temporaire	регистр временного хра-нения, регистр-фикса-тор
	temporary register	*s. a.* I 351		
T 85	**temporary run file**	vorläufige Laufdatei *f*	fichier *m* de marche provisoire	временный файл прогона
T 86	**temporary storage**	temporäre (zeitweilige) Speicherung *f*	mémorisation *f* temporaire	временное хранение, про-межуточное запомина-ние
	temporary storage	*s. a.* 1. I 350; 2. I 353; 3. T 83		
T 87	**temporary storage register**	Zwischenspeicherregister *n*	registre *m* de mémoire intermédiaire	регистр промежуточной памяти
T 88	**tens complement**	Zehnerkomplement *n*	complément *m* à dix	дополнение до десяти
T 89	**terminal**	Endstelle *f*, Anschluß-klemme *f*, Anschluß *m*	terminal *m*	зажим, клемма, подвод
T 90	**terminal,** data station	Datenendeinrichtung *f*, Datenendgerät *n*, Daten-station *f*, Bediengerät *n*, Terminal *n*	terminal *m*, station *f* de données	терминал, оконечное устройство; абонент-ский пункт
T 91	**terminal area**	Anschlußfläche *f*, Lötauge *n*	surface *f* de raccordement	контактная поверхность
T 92	**terminal communica-tion**	Terminalverkehr *m*	communication *f* à termi-naux	связь с терминалами
T 93	**terminal computer**	Endstellenrechner *m*, Terminalrechner *m*	calculateur *m* terminal	оконечная ЭВМ, терми-нальная машина
T 94	**terminal control**	Terminalsteuerung *f*, Daten-endgerätesteuerung *f*	commande *f* de terminal	управление терминалом
T 95	**terminal controller**	Terminalsteuergerät *n*	appareil *m* de commande de terminal	терминальный контроллер
T 96	**terminal equipment**	Terminaleinrichtung *f*	équipement *m* terminal	терминальное оборудо-вание
T 97	**terminal impedance**	Klemmenimpedanz *f*	impédance *f* aux bornes	полное сопротивление между зажимами
T 98	**terminal lead,** end lead	Anschlußleitung *f*	ligne *f* de raccordement	подводящий провод
T 99	**terminal multiplexer**	Anschlußmultiplexer *m*; Mehrfachterminal-anschluß *m*	multiplexeur *m* terminal	мультиплексор терми-налов
T 100	**terminal-oriented system**	terminalorientiertes (auf Terminalarbeit ausgerich-tetes) System *n*	système *m* orienté terminal	терминально-ориентиро-ванная система
T 101	**terminal pin**	Anschlußstift *m*	fiche *f* de raccordement	выводной штырек, око-нечный вывод
T 102	**terminated line**	abgeschlossene Leitung *f*	ligne *f* fermée	замкнутая [на конце] линия, нагруженная линия
	terminate flag	*s.* C 455		
T 103	**termination require-ments**	Abschlußanforderungen *fpl*	exigences *fpl* de raccorde-ment	требования к оконечной нагрузке
T 104	**termination resistance**	Abschlußwiderstand *m*	résistance *f* terminale	сопротивление оконечной нагрузки
T 105	**ternary**	ternär, dreiwertig	ternaire	троичный
T 106	**ternary arithmetic**	Ternärarithmetik *f*, Arith-metik *f* für dreiwertige Variable	arithmétique *f* ternaire	троичная арифметика
T 107	**ternary output**	Ternärausgang *m*, drei-wertiger Ausgang *m*	sortie *f* ternaire	троичный выход
T 108	**test / to**	prüfen, untersuchen, testen	vérifier, examiner	испытывать, проверять
	test	*s.* C 169		
T 109	**testability**	Prüfbarkeit *f*, Testmöglich-keit *f*	faculté *f* de test	тестопригодность, тести-руемость
T 110	**testable system**	prüfbares System *n*	système *m* vérifiable	тестируемая система
T 111	**test aids**	Testhilfen *fpl*	aides *fpl* de test	средства контроля
T 112	**test arrangement**	Prüfanordnung *f*	aménagement *m* de test	тестовая конфигурация
T 113	**test assembly,** test place (set)	Prüfplatz *m*, Prüfgerätesatz *m*	dispositif *m* de test	испытательная установка
	test bit	*s.* C 171		
T 114	**test certificate**	Abnahmeprotokoll *n*	certificat *m* de test	сертификат качества; свидетельство о приемке
	test circuit	*s.* C 174		
T 115	**test cycle**	Prüfzyklus *m*, Testschritt *m*	cycle *m* de test	цикл испытаний
T 116	**test data**	Prüfdaten *pl*	données *fpl* de test	тестовые данные
T 117	**test data generator**	Prüfdatengenerator *m*	générateur *m* de données de test	генератор тестовых данных ⌐вание
T 118	**test equipment**	Prüfeinrichtung *f*	équipement *m* de test	испытательное оборудо-
T 119	**tester,** testing in-strument	Prüfgerät *n*, Tester *m*	instrument *m* de test	тестер, контрольно-измерительный прибор
T 120	**testing of digital logic circuits**	Testen *n* digitaler Logik-schaltungen	test *m* de circuits logiques numériques	проверка цифровых логических схем
	testing technique	*s.* C 181		
T 121	**testing terminal,** test terminal	Prüfklemme *f*, Prüfan-schluß *m*	borne *f* de test	контрольный вывод
T 122	**testing time**	Prüfzeit *f*, Testzeit *f*	temps *m* de test	время тестирования
	testing tools	*s.* T 134		
T 123	**test instruction**	Testbefehl *m*	instruction *f* de test	тестовая команда
T 124	**test lead**	Prüfkabel *n*, Prüfzuleitung *f*	câble *m* de test	контрольный вывод
T 125	**test line**	Prüfleitung *f*	ligne *f* de test	тестовая линия, тестовый провод
	test method	*s.* C 181		

T 126	**test monitor**	Testmonitor *m*, Prüfablauf-überwacher *m*	moniteur *m* de test	тест-монитор
T 127	**test operation**	Prüfvorgang *m*, Testoperation *f*	opération *f* de test	тестовый режим работы, процесс тестирования
T 128	**test pattern**	Testmuster *n*	échantillon *m* de test	тестовая комбинация
T 129	**test-pattern generation**	Testmustererzeugung *f*, Prüffolgenerzeugung *f*	génération *f* d'échantillons de test	генерация тестовых комбинаций
	test place	s. T 113		
	test point	s. C 187		
	test procedure	s. C 181		
	test program	s. C 188		
T 130	**test requirements**	Prüfbedingungen *fpl*	conditions *fpl* de test	требования контроля
T 131	**test result**	Prüfergebnis *n*	résultat *m* de test	результат проверки
	test routine	s. C 188		
T 132	**test run,** check run	Testlauf *m*, Prüflauf *m*	marche *f* de test	тестовый прогон
	test sequence	s. C 182		
	test set	s. T 113		
T 133	**test socket**	Prüffassung *f*	socle *m* de test	контрольное гнездо
	test system	s. T 183		
	test terminal	s. T 121		
T 134	**test tools,** testing tools	Testhilfsmittel *npl*, Testwerkzeuge *npl*, Prüfwerkzeuge *npl*	moyens *mpl* de test	контрольные приспособления, испытательные средства
T 135	**tetrad**	Tetrade *f*	tétrade *f*	тетрада
T 136	**text analysis**	Textanalyse *f*	analyse *f* de texte	анализ текста
T 137	**text editing**	Textaufbereitung *f*, Textedierung *f*	édition *f* de texte	редактирование текста
T 138	**text editing facilities**	Textaufbereitungsmöglichkeiten *fpl*, Textaufbereitungsmittel *npl*	possibilités *fpl* d'édition de texte	средства редактирования текста
T 139	**text editor**	Texteditor *m*, Textaufbereiter *m*, Programmtextaufbereitungsprogramm *n*	éditeur *m* de texte	редактор текста
T 140	**text modification**	Textmodifizierung *f*, Textänderung *f*	modification *f* de texte	внесение изменений в текст, исправление текста
T 141	**text processing,** word processing ‹US›	Textverarbeitung *f* ‹Aufbereiten und Manipulieren von Worttexten mittels Computers›	traitement *m* de texte	обработка текстов
T 142	**thermal compensation**	thermische Kompensation *f*, Wärmekompensation *f*	compensation *f* thermique	компенсация теплового воздействия
T 143	**thermal conductivity**	thermische Leitfähigkeit *f*, Wärmeleitfähigkeit *f*	conductibilité *f* thermique	удельная теплопроводность
T 144	**thermal exchange**	Wärmeaustausch *m*	échange *m* thermique	теплообмен
T 145	**thermal power**	thermische Leistung *f*, Wärmeleistung *f*	puissance *f* thermique	тепловая энергия
	thermal printer	s. T 149		
T 146	**thermal printing technique**	thermisches Druckverfahren *n*	procédé *m* d'impression thermique	метод термопечати
T 147	**thermal protection**	thermischer Schutz *m*, Wärmeschutz *m*	protection *f* thermique	теплозащита, тепловая защита
T 148	**thermal shock**	thermischer Schock *m*, Wärmestoß *m*	choc *m* thermique	тепловой (термический) удар
T 149	**thermoprinter,** thermal (electrothermic) printer	Thermodrucker *m*, elektrothermischer Drucker *m*	imprimante *f* thermique	устройство термопечати
T 150	**thick-film circuit technology**	Dickschichtschaltungstechnologie *f*	technologie *f* des circuits à couches épaisses	толстопленочная технология
T 151	**thin-film device**	Dünnschichtbauelement *n*	élément *m* à couche mince	тонкопленочный элемент, тонкопленочная схема
T 152	**thin-film evaporation technique**	Dünnschichtaufdampfverfahren *n*	procédé *m* d'évaporation de couches minces	метод [вакуумного] напыления тонких пленок
T 153	**thin-film integrated circuitry**	integrierte Dünnschichtschaltung *f*	circuit *m* intégré à couches minces	тонкопленочная интегральная схема
T 154	**third-generation microprocessor**	Mikroprozessor *m* der dritten [LSI-]Generation	microprocesseur *m* de la trosième génération	микропроцессор третьего поколения
T 155	**three-digit**	dreistellig	à trois positions	трехзначный
T 156	**three-dimensional**	dreidimensional	à trois dimensions	трехмерный
T 157	**three-layer structure**	Dreischichtstruktur *f*, Dreischichtanordnung *f*	structure *f* à trois couches	трехслойная структура
T 158	**three-phase net**	Dreiphasennetz *n*, Drehstromnetz *n*	réseau *m* triphasé	трехфазная сеть
T 159	**three-pole,** three-terminal	dreipolig	tripolaire	трехполюсный
T 160	**three-state buffer,** tri-state buffer	Tri-State-Puffer *m*, Drei-Zustands-Puffer *m*, Pufferschaltung *f* mit Tri-State-Charakteristik	tampon *m* à caractéristique à trois états	буфер с тремя [устойчивыми] состояниями, трехстабильный буфер
T 161	**three-state characteristic,** tri-state characteristic	Tri-State-Charakteristik *f*, Drei-Zustands-Charakteristik *f* ‹Ausgangsverhalten mit 3 möglichen Zuständen: high, low, hochohmig/offen/floating›	caractéristique *f* à trois états	характеристика третьего состояния ‹высокоомное [отключенное от нагрузки] состояние выхода цифровой схемы›
T 162	**three-state device,** tri-state device	Tri-State-Bauelement *n*, Bauelement *n* mit Tri-State-Ausgang	élément *m* à sortie à trois états	устройство с тремя [устойчивыми] состояниями, трехстабильное устройство
T 163	**three-state driver,** tri-state driver	Tri-State-Treiber *m*, Treiberstufe *f* mit Tri-State-Charakteristik	basculeur *m* à caractéristique à trois états	[шинный] формирователь с тремя [устойчивыми] состояниями, трехстабильный формирователь

T 164	**three-state enable signal,** tri-state enable signal, trit-state enable (select)	Tri-State-Freigabesignal m, Tri-State-Ansteuersignal n <Steuersignal, das den Ausgang eines Tri-State-Elements in den dritten, gesperrt hochohmigen, Zustand setzt>	signal m de libération à trois états	сигнал выбора третьего состояния; сигнал выбора (разблокировки выхода) трехстабильной схемы
T 165	**three-state output,** tri-state output	Tri-State-Ausgang m, Ausgangsschaltung f mit Tri-State-Charakteristik <Ausgangszustände: high, low, offen/hochohmig/floating>	sortie f à caractéristique à trois états	выход с тремя [устойчивыми] состояниями, трехстабильный выход
T 166	**three-terminal**	s. T 159		
T 167	**threshold circuit**	Schwellwertschaltung f	circuit m de seuil	пороговая схема
T 167	**threshold control**	Schwellwertsteuerung f	commande f de seuil	регулирование порога
T 168	**threshold element**	Schwellwertelement n	élément m de seuil	пороговый элемент
T 169	**threshold logic**	Schwellwertlogik f	logique f de seuil	пороговая логика
T 170	**threshold region**	Grenzbereich m, Schwellenbereich m ⌐wert m	région f limite	пороговая область
T 171	**threshold value**	Ansprechwert m, Schwell-	valeur f de seuil	пороговое значение
T 172	**threshold voltage**	Schwellspannung f, Ansprechspannung f	tension f de seuil	пороговое напряжение
T 173	**through connection,** interlayer connection	Durchkontaktierung f	connexion f entière	сквозное (межслойное) соединение
T 174	**through hole**	Durchgangsloch n	trou m de passage	сквозное отверстие
T 175	**through-plated circuit board**	durchplattierte (durchkontaktierte) Leiterplatte f	circuit m imprimé entièrement contacté	соединительная печатная плата
T 176	**throughput rate**	Durchsatzrate f	cote f de passage	скорость прохождения
T 177	**throughput time**	Durchsatzzeit f	temps m de passage	время прохождения
T 178	**tight coupling**	enge (starke) Kopplung f	couplage m rigide	сильная комплексация
T 179	**tightly-coupled processors**	eng gekoppelte Prozessoren mpl, Prozessoren mit starker gegenseitiger Kopplung	processeurs mpl à couplage rigide	сильно связанные процессоры, процессоры с непосредственной связью
T 180	**time-addressed signal**	zeitlagenadressiertes Signal n	signal m à adressage temporaire	сигнал с адресацией по времени передачи
T 181	**time base**	Zeitbasis f, Zeitmaßstab m, Zeitablenkung f	base f de temps	временная ось, масштаб времени
T 182	**time check**	Zeitkontrolle f	contrôle m de temps	контроль по времени
T 183	**time constant**	Zeitkonstante f	constante f de temps	постоянная времени
T 184	**time constraints**	Zeitbeschränkung f, Zeiteinschränkungen fpl	contrainte f de temps	временные ограничения
T 185	**time-consuming**	zeitaufwendig	coûtant du temps	требующий больших затрат времени
T 186	**time-consuming operation**	zeitaufwendige Operation f	opération f nécessitant beaucoup de temps	операция с большими затратами времени
T 187	**time control**	Zeitsteuerung f	commande f de temps	управление по временной диаграмме
T 188	**time converter**	Zeitlagenumsetzer m <Nachrichtentechnik>	convertisseur m de temps	преобразователь время-код
	time-delay circuit	s. D 226		
T 189	**time-dependent**	zeitabhängig	dépendant du temps	зависящий от времени, времязависимый
T 190	**time displacement**	Zeitverschiebung f	décalage m de temps	временной сдвиг
	time division multiplexed	s. T 195		
	time-division multiplexing	s. T 197		
T 191	**time duration**	Zeitdauer f	durée f	длительность, продолжительность ⌐тельность
T 192	**time interval**	Zeitabschnitt m, Zeitintervall n, Zeitraum m, Zeitspanne f	intervalle m de temps	временной интервал, интервал времени
T 193	**time lag**	zeitliche Nacheilung f, Zeitverzögerung f	temporisation f	запаздывание по времени
T 194	**time limit**	Zeitgrenze f	limite f de temps	предел по времени, временная граница
T 195	**time-multiplexed,** time division multiplexed	zeitgeschachtelt, zeitmultiplex	multiplex [de division de temps]	с временным мультиплексированием
T 196	**time-multiplexed address**	zeitmultiplex übertragene Adresse f <Adreßübertragung in Teilen zeitlich nacheinander>	adresse f multiplex	мультиплексированный адрес, адрес, передаваемый с временным мультиплексированием [шины]
T 197	**time-multiplex technique,** time-division multiplexing	Zeitmultiplexverfahren n	procédé m multiplex	метод временного мультиплексирования, мультиплексирование с временным уплотнением
T 198	**timeout**	Zeitsperre f, Auszeit f, Grenzzeitüberschreitung f	temps m de suspension	тайм-аут <интервал времени, выделяемый для наступления определенного события, например, ответа на обращение>, блокировка по [интервалу] времени
T 199	**timeout function**	Zeitbegrenzerfunktion f <zwangsweises Beenden eines eingeleiteten Vorganges nach Erreichen einer Zeitgrenze>	fonction f de limitation de temps	функция ограничения по времени
T 200	**timeout interval**	Auszeitintervall n <Zeitbereich bis zum Ansprechen der Zeitbegrenzerfunktion>	intervalle m de suspension	длительность тайм-аута (контрольного интервала времени)

T 201	timeout violation	Zeitvorgabeverletzung f, Zeitüberschreitung f	dépassement m de temps	превышение тайм-аута (контрольного интервала времени)
T 202	time-pulse distributor timer timer circuit	Zeitimpulsverteiler m s. T 217 s. T 214	distributeur m d'impulsions de temps	распределитель тактовых импульсов, распределитель синхроимпульсов
T 203	timer/counter	Zeitgeber/Zähler m	rythmeur/compteur m	счетчик-таймер
T 204	time response	Zeitverhalten n, Zeitverlauf m	réponse f de temps	временная характеристика
T 205	time-saving	zeitsparend	à économie de temps	не требующий больших затрат времени
T 206/7	time schedule controller	Zeitablaufplan-Steuereinrichtung f	dispositif m de commande de déroulement	контроллер распределения времени
	time-shared bus	s. M 559		
T 208	time sharing	Zeitteilung f, zeitliche Verschachtelung f, Teilnehmerverfahren n <für ein Rechnersystem>	partage (découpage) m de temps	разделение времени
T 209	time-sharing operation	Teilnehmerbetrieb m, Zeitteilungsbetrieb m <eines Rechnersystems>	régime m à abonnés (découpage de temps)	работа в режиме разделения времени
T 210	time-sharing system	Teilnehmersystem n, System n mit Zeitteilverfahren <für gleichzeitige Arbeit mit mehreren Nutzern>	système m à découpage de temps, système à abonnés	система с разделением времени
T 211	time slice	Zeitscheibe f <Zeitabschnitt im Teilnehmersystem>	tranche f de temps	квант времени
T 211 a	timing	Taktierung f, Zeitsteuerung f <zeitliche Ablaufsteuerung>	commande f de temps (déroulement)	синхронизация
T 212	timing and control	Taktierung f und Steuerung f	rythme m et commande f	синхронизация и управление
T 213	timing characteristics	Taktierungskennwerte mpl	caractéristique f de rythme	характеристики синхронизации
T 214	timing circuit, timer circuit	Zeitgeberschaltung f	circuit m de rythmeur	схема времязадающего устройства, схема таймера
T 215	timing diagram	Taktierungsdiagramm n, Darstellung f der zeitlichen Ablaufsteuerung	diagramme m de rythme	временная диаграмма
T 216	timing error, clocking error	Taktierungsfehler m, Zeitsteuerungsfehler m, Gleichlauffehler m	défaut m de rythme	ошибка синхронизации
T 217	timing generator, timer	Zeitsignalgenerator m, Zeitgeber m	rythmeur m	генератор синхросигналов, таймер
T 218	timing pulse	Taktierungsimpuls m, Zeitsteuerimpuls m	impulsion f de rythme	синхроимпульс, тактовый импульс
T 219	timing sequence	Taktierungsfolge f, zeitliche Ablauffolge f	séquence f de rythme	синхронизирующая (тактирующая) последовательность
T 220	timing signal	Taktierungssignal n, Zeitsteuerungssignal n	signal m de rythme	сигнал синхронизации, тактовый сигнал
T 221	timing specification	Taktierungsvorschrift f, detaillierte Angabe f zur Zeitsteuerung	spécification f de rythme	требование к синхронизации
T 222	timing unit	Zeitsteuereinheit f, Zeitgebereinheit f	unité f de rythmeur	устройство синхронизации, синхронизатор
T 223	tiny BASIC	Einfach-BASIC n <BASIC-Untermenge für Mikrorechner>	BASIC m simple	упрощенный БЕЙСИК
T 224	tiny size	Minimalgröße f	grandeur f minime	уменьшенный размер
T 225	toggle / to	kippen	basculer	генерировать релаксационные колебания
T 226	toggle rate	Kippgeschwindigkeit f	vitesse f de bascule	скорость переключения, частота релаксаций
T 227	toggle switch	doppelpoliger Umschalter m, Kippschalter m	interrupteur m à bascule	двухпозиционный переключатель, тумблер
T 228	top-down design	Entwurf m von oben nach unten <Entwurfsverfahren vom Gesamtsystemkonzept zur Detailaspektlösung vorangehend>	conception f de haut en bas	метод проектирования сверху вниз
T 229	total system cost	Gesamtsystemkosten pl	coûts mpl de système totaux	общая стоимость системы
T 230	trace / to	schrittweise verfolgen, protokollierend verfolgen	poursuivre	трассировать, отыскивать [неисправность]
T 231	trace	Ablaufverfolgung f <schrittweise Programmausführung mit Protokollierung>	poursuite f de déroulement	след, слежение, трассировка
				⌐ность
T 232	traced fault	aufgespürter Fehler m	défaut m détecté	обнаруженная неисправ-
T 233	trace memory	Ablaufverfolgungsspeicher m, Echtzeittestspeicher m	mémoire f de poursuite	трассировочная память, память трассировки
T 234	trace mode	Ablaufverfolgungs-Betriebsart f <Diagnosemodus>	mode m de poursuite	режим трассировки
T 235	trace program, tracing routine	Ablaufverfolgungsprogramm n, Programmablauf-Überprüfungsprogramm n	programme m de poursuite	программа трассировки
T 236	track	Spur f	trace f, piste f	дорожка; след, траектория
T 237	track selection	Spurauswahl f, Spuransteuerung f	sélection f de piste	выбор дорожки
T 238	track switching	Spurumschaltung f	commutation f de piste	переключение дорожек

T 239	**track width**	Spurbreite *f*	largeur *f* de piste	ширина дорожки
T 240	**tradeoff**	Abstimmung *f*, Abwägen *n*, Kompromiß *m*, Koordinierung *f*	accord *m*, coordination *f*	компромисс
T 241	**tradeoff decision**	Kompromißentscheidung *f*, abgewogene Entscheidung *f*	décision *f* de compromis	компромиссное решение
T 242	**traffic control**	Verkehrssteuerung *f*	commande *f* de trafic	управление трафиком (движением)
T 243	**traffic-light controller**	Verkehrsampel-Steuergerät *n*	appareil *m* de commande de feux de circulation	контроллер светофора
T 244	**traffic load**	Verkehrsbelastung *f* <Vermittlungsnetz>	charge *f* de trafic	интенсивность трафика
	trailing edge	*s.* B 5		
T 245	**training aid**	Übungshilfe *f*	aide *f* d'entraînement	средство обучения
T 246	**training centre**	Schulungszentrum *n*	centre *m* d'enseignement	центр обучения
T 247	**transaction**	Vorgang *m*	transaction *f*	транзакция
T 248	**transaction editing**	Vorgangsaufbereitung *f*	préparation *f* de transaction	подготовка транзакции
T 249	**transaction file**	Vorgangsdatei *f*, Bewegungsdatei *f*	fichier *m* de mouvement	файл транзакций, вспомогательный файл, временный файл, файл сообщений
T 250	**transaction processing**	Vorgangsverarbeitung *f* <Teilhaberbetrieb>	traitement *m* de transaction	обработка записей о событиях
T 251	**transceiver** <transmitter-receiver>	Sendeempfänger *m* <Sender-Empfänger-Kombination>	émetteur-récepteur *m*	приемопередатчик
	transducer	*s.* M 226		
T 252	**transfer / to**, to transmit	übertragen	transmettre	передавать, пересылать
T 253	**transfer, transmission**	Übertragung *f*, Übermittlung *f*, Transfer *m*	transfert *m*, transmission *f*	передача, пересылка
T 254	**transfer channel**	Übertragungskanal *m*	canal *m* de transfert	канал передачи
T 255	**transfer characteristic**	Übertragungskennlinie *f*, Übertragungscharakteristik *f*	caractéristique *f* de transfert	передаточная характеристика
T 256	**transfer check**	Übertragungskontrolle *f*	vérification *f* de transfert	контроль передачи
T 257	**transfer command**, transfer instruction	Übertragungsbefehl *m*	instruction *f* de transfert	команда передачи
T 258	**transfer control / to**	die Steuerung übertragen (weitergeben)	transmettre la commande	передавать управление
T 259	**transfer element**	Übertragungsglied *n*, Übertragungselement *n*	élément *m* de transfert	передаточный элемент
T 260	**transfer error**, transmission error	Übertragungsfehler *m*	erreur *f* de transmission	ошибка передачи
T 261	**transfer function**	Übertragungsfunktion *f*	fonction *f* de transfert	передаточная функция
	transfer instruction	*s.* T 257		
T 262	**transfer line**, transmission line	Übertragungsleitung *f*	ligne *f* de transfert	линия передачи
T 263	**transfer of control**	Übertragen *n* der Programmsteuerung (Steuerung), Weitergabe *f* der Steuerung	transmission *f* de la commande	передача управления
T 264	**transfer operation**	Übertragungsoperation *f*	opération *f* de transfert	операция передачи
T 265	**transfer path**	Übertragungsweg *m*	voie *f* de transfert	тракт передачи
T 266	**transfer rate (speed)**	Übertragungsrate *f*, Übertragungsgeschwindigkeit *f*	vitesse *f* de transfert	скорость передачи
T 267	**transfer time**, move time	Übertragungszeit *f*, Transferzeit *f*	temps *m* de transfert	время передачи
T 268	**transform / to**	transformieren, umwandeln	transformer	трансформировать, преобразовывать
T 269	**transformation program**	Umwandlungsprogramm *n*	programme *m* de transformation	программа преобразования
T 270	**transformer**	Transformator *m*, Umformer *m*, Übertrager *m*	transformateur *m*	трансформатор, преобразователь
T 271	**transient**	Ausgleichsvorgang *m*, Einschwingvorgang *m*, Übergangsvorgang *m*	transitoire *m*	переходный процесс
T 272	**transient**	vorübergehend	transitoire	переходный
T 273	**transient characteristic**	Übergangscharakteristik *f*, Übertragungseigenschaft *f*, Einschwingeigenschaft *f*	caractéristique *f* transitoire	переходная характеристика, характеристика переходного процесса
T 274	**transient condition**	Übergangsbedingung *f*	condition *f* transitoire	условие перехода
T 275	**transient current**	Ausgleichsstrom *m*, Übergangsstrom *m* <instationärer Strom>	courant *m* transitoire	переходный ток, ток переходного процесса
	transient fault	*s.* I 356		
T 276	**transient library**	vorläufige Bibliothek *f*	bibliothèque *f* provisoire	временная библиотека
T 277	**transient period**, transient time	Einschwingzeit *f*	période *f* transitoire	длительность переходного процесса; время установления
T 278	**transient process**	Umschaltvorgang *m*	processus *m* transitoire	переходный процесс
T 279	**transient pulse**	Einschwingimpuls *m*	impulsion *f* transitoire	импульс переходного процесса
T 280	**transient response**	Einschwingverhalten *n*	réponse *f* transitoire	переходная характеристика <реакция на ступенчатый входной сигнал>
T 281	**transient state**	Einschwingzustand *m*, Übergangszustand *m*	état *m* transitoire	переходное состояние
	transient time	*s.* T 277		
T 282	**transient waveform**	Einschaltkurve *f*	courbe *f* transitoire	кривая (форма сигнала) переходного процесса
T 283	**transistor amplifier**	Transistorverstärker *m*	amplificateur *m* à transistors	транзисторный усилитель
T 284	**transistor characteristic**	Transistorkennlinie *f*	caractéristique *f* de transistor	характеристика транзистора

T 285	**transistor circuit**	Transistorschaltung f	circuit m de transistor	транзисторная схема
T 286	**transistor-controlled**	transistorgesteuert	à commande par transistor	с транзисторным управлением
T 287	**transistor current gain**	Transistorstromverstärkung f	gain m de courant de transistor	усиление тока в транзисторе
T 288	**transistorized**	transistorisiert	transistorisé	выполненный на транзисторах, транзисторный
T 289	**transistor supply voltage**	Transistorspeisespannung f	tension f d'alimentation de transistor	напряжение питания транзистора
T 290	**transistor switching speed**	Transistorschaltgeschwindigkeit f	vitesse f de commutation de transistor	скорость переключения транзистора
T 291	**transistor technique**	Transistortechnik f	technique f des transistors	транзисторная техника
	transistor-transistor logic	s. T 341		
T 292	**transition region**	Übergangsbereich m	région f de transition	область перехода
T 293	**transit time**	Durchgangszeit f <eines Ladungsträgers>	temps m de transit	время пролета <заряженной частицы>
T 294	**translate / to**	übersetzen	traduire	транслировать
	translating	s. T 295		
T 295	**translation,** translating	Übersetzung f	traduction f	трансляция
T 296	**translator**	Übersetzungsprogramm n	programme m de traduction	транслирующая программа, транслятор
	transmission	s. T 253		
T 297	**transmission code**	Übertragungskode m	code m de transmission	код передачи
T 298	**transmission direction**	Übertragungsrichtung f	direction f de transmission	направление передачи
	transmission error	s. T 260		
T 299	**transmission interface**	Übertragungsschnittstelle f	interface f de transmission	интерфейс с системой передачи
	transmission line	s. T 262		
T 300	**transmission mode,** mode of transmission	Übertragungsart f, Übertragungsmodus m $\ulcorner f$	mode m de transmission	способ передачи
T 301	**transmission repetition**	Übertragungswiederholung	répétition f de transmission	повторение передачи
	transmit / to	s. 1. S 189; 2. T 252		
T 302	**transmit buffer**	Übertragungspuffer m	tampon m de transmission	буфер передатчика
T 303	**transmit clock**	Sendetakt m	rythme m de transmission	синхронизация передачи
T 304	**transmit data**	Sendedaten pl	données fpl de transmission	передаваемые данные
	transmit line	s. S 190		
T 305	**transmitter**	Sender m	émetteur m	передатчик
T 306	**transmitter**	Geber m	transmetteur m	трансмиттер
T 307	**transparency**	Transparenz f, Durchlässigkeit f, Durchsichtigkeit f	transparence f	прозрачность
T 308	**transparent refresh**	transparente Speicherregenerierung f <ohne Beeinträchtigung der Prozessorarbeit>	régénération f transparente [de mémoire]	прозрачная регенерация [памяти]
	transponder	s. P 729		
T 309	**trap**	Falle f, Trap m <unprogrammierter bedingter Programmsprung auf vereinbarten Speicherplatz>	piège m	центр захвата, ловушка <в полупроводнике>; захват <незапрограммированное прерывание с условным переходом в заданную ячейку, автоматически выполняемое аппаратурой>; программная ловушка <прерывание, выполняемое в определенной точке программы при соблюдении некоторого условия, используется при отладке>
T 310	**trap handling**	Trap-Behandlung f	traitement m de piège	обработка состояния захвата
T 311	**trap instruction**	Trap-Befehl m <Software-Interrupt>	instruction f piège	команда захвата
T 312	**trapping mode**	Fangbetriebsart f, Haltepunktmodus m	mode m de capture	режим захвата
T 313	**trap vector**	Trap-Vektor m	vecteur m de piège	вектор прерывания при захвате
T 314	**tree structure**	Baumstruktur f	structure f d'arbre	древовидная структура
T 315	**trial equipment**	Versuchsanlage f	équipement m d'essai	экспериментальное оборудование
T 316	**trial production**	Versuchsproduktion f, Probeproduktion f	production f d'essai	опытная (экспериментальная) продукция
T 317	**trial run**	Probelauf m, Versuchslauf m	marche f d'essai	тестовый прогон
T 318	**trigger / to**	triggern <Zustand wechseln, Umschaltung auslösen>	basculer, déclencher	запускать
T 319	**trigger**	Trigger m, Auslöser m	basculeur m, trigger m	триггер
	trigger	s. a. T 323		
T 320	**trigger circuit**	Triggerschaltung f	circuit m de basculeur	триггерная схема
T 321	**triggering**	Triggerung f	basculage m	запуск
T 322	**trigger input**	Triggereingang m	entrée f de basculeur	вход запуска
T 323	**trigger pulse,** trigger	Triggerimpuls m	impulsion f de basculeur	запускающий сигнал, сигнал перехода в другое состояние
T 324	**trim down / to**	zurechtstutzen, abrüsten	réduire, dégarnir	разбирать, демонтировать
	trimmer	s. A 165		
T 325	**trip computer**	Fahrtrechner m, Bordrechner m in Kraftfahrzeugen	calculateur m de bord	возимая [бортовая] ЭВМ
T 326	**triple-diffused transistor**	dreifachdiffundierter Transistor m	transistor m à triple diffusion	транзистор с тройной диффузией
T 327	**triplication**	Verdreifachung f	action f de tripler	троирование, утрование
T 328	**tri-state**	Dreifachzustand m <three-state>	état m triple	трехстабильное состояние, трехустойчивое состояние
	tri-state buffer	s. T 160		
	tri-state characteristic	s. T 161		

	tri-state device	s. T 162		
	tri-state driver	s. T 163		
	tri-state enable [signal]	s. T 164		
	tri-state output	s. T 165		
	tri-state selection	s. T 164		⌐дение
T 329	trouble, disturbance	Störung f	perturbation f	неисправность, повреж-
T 330	trouble location	Störungslokalisierung f	localisation f de panne	локализация неисправ- ностей
T 331	trouble shooting	Störungssuche f	recherche f de panne	устранение неисправно- стей, отладка
T 332	true complement	wahres Komplement n <B- Komplement>	complément m vrai	дополнение до основания системы счисления
T 333	true output	wahrer Ausgang m	sortie f vraie	выход истинного значе- ния [логической функ- ции]
T 334	true value	wahrer Wert m	valeur f vraie	истинное значение
T 335	truncate / to	abschneiden, abbrechen <einen Rechenprozeß bei Erreichen der Genauig- keitsschranke>	interrompre, couper	обрывать <вычислитель- ный процесс>; усекать, отбрасывать
T 336	truncation	Abschneiden n, Runden n <durch Weglassen von Stellen>	arrondissement m <en sup- primant des positions>	прерывание [процесса]; усечение
T 337	truncation condition	Abbruchbedingung f	condition f d'interruption	условие выхода из цикла; условие прерывания
T 338	truncation error	Abbruchfehler m	erreur f d'interruption	ошибка отбрасывания (усечения)
T 339	trunk	Verbindungsstrang m, Leitungssatz m <Nach- richtentechnik>	jeu m de lignes	канал связи, шина
T 340	truth table	Wahrheitswertetabelle f	table f de valeurs vraies	таблица истинности
T 341	TTL, transistor-transistor logic	TTL f, Transistor-Tran- sistor-Logik f <Schal- tungstechnik>	logique f transistor-tran- sistor, TTL f	транзисторно-транзистор- ная логика, ТТЛ
T 342	TTL compatibility	TTL-Kompatibilität f, TTL-Standardschaltkreis- Anschlußkompatibilität f	compatibilité f TTL	совместимость с ТТЛ- схемами
T 343	TTL compatible	TTL-kompatibel, anschluß- verträglich mit TTL- Bausteinen	compatible TTL	совместимый с ТТЛ- схемами
T 344	TTL component	TTL-Baustein m	composant (module) m TTL	микросхема ТТЛ, ТТЛ- компонент
T 345	TTL level	TTL-Pegel m	niveau m TTL	ТТЛ-уровень <входного или выходного сиг- нала>
T 346	TTL load	TTL-Last f, TTL-Lastein- heit f	charge f TTL	нагрузка, соответствую- щая одному (стандарт- ному) входу ТТЛ- схемы
T 347	TTL voltage level	TTL-Spannungspegel m	niveau m de tension TTL	уровень напряжения ТТЛ-схем
T 348	tube	Röhre f, Bildröhre f	tube m	[электронно-лучевая] трубка, [электронная] лампа
T 349	tube display	Bildröhrenanzeige f, An- zeige f mit Bildröhre	affichage m à écran	дисплей на электронно- лучевой трубке
T 350	tubeless display	röhrenlose Anzeige f, An- zeige ohne Bildröhre	affichage m sans tube	дисплей без использова- ния электронно-лучевой трубки
	tuned circuit	s. T 351		
T 351	tuned tank circuit, tuned circuit	abgestimmter Schwingkreis m	circuit m oscillant syntonisé	настроенный резонансный контур
T 352	tunnel effect	Tunneleffekt m	effet m de tunnel	туннельный эффект
T 353	tunnelling	Durchtunnelung f, Tunnel- bau m	établissement m de tunnel	туннельное прохождение через потенциальный барьер
T 354	turnaround time	Durchlaufzeit f	temps m de marche continue	время реверсирования на- правления [передачи данных]
T 355	turnkey system	schlüsselfertiges System n	système m clés en main	система, готовая к непо- средственному исполь- зованию
T 356	turn-off delay	Ausschaltverzögerung f	retardement m de mise au ⌐repos	задержка выключения
T 357	turn-off time	Ausschaltzeit f	temps m de mise au repos	время выключения
T 358	turn-on delay	Einschaltverzögerung f	retardement de mise en marche	задержка включения
T 359	turn-on time	Einschaltzeit f	temps m de mise en marche	время включения
	TV games	s. V 33		
T 360	twisted-pair cable	verdrilltes Doppelleitungs- kabel n	câble m à ligne double torsadé	кабель из витых (скру- ченных) пар
T 361	two-address instruction	Zweiadreßbefehl m	instruction f à deux adresses	двухадресная команда
T 362	two-dimensional	zweidimensional	bidimensionnel	двумерный
T 363	two-operand instruction, double-operand instruc- tion	Zweioperandenbefehl m	instruction f à deux opérandes	двуместная команда
T 364	two-operand operation, binary operation	Zweioperandenoperation f, Zweioperandenverknüp- fung f	opération f à deux opérandes	операция над двумя операндами, двуместная операция
T 365	two-pass assembler	2-Schritt-Assembler m <übersetzt Quellkode in zwei Durchläufen>	assembleur m à deux cycles	двухпроходный ассемблер
T 366	two-pass macro- assembler	2-Schritt-Makroassembler m <Makroassembler mit zwei Durchläufen arbeitend>	assembleur m macro à deux cycles	двухпроходный макро- ассемблер

T 367	two-phase clock	Zweiphasentakt m	rythmeur m biphasé	двухфазная (двухтактная) синхронизация, двухфазный синхросигнал
	two-pole	s. D 528		
T 368/9	two's complement, 2's complement	Zweierkomplement n	complément m de deux	дополнительный код двоичного числа
T 370	two-stage	zweistufig	à deux étages	двухступенчатый, двухэтажный; двухкаскадный
	two-terminal	s. D 528		
	two-way mode	s. D 584		
T 371	type declaration	Typvereinbarung f, Variablentypvereinbarung f	déclaration f de type	описание типа
T 372	type spacing	Typenabstand m	espace m de types	интервал (пробел) между литерами
T 373	typical current requirement	typischer Strombedarf m	consommation f typique de courant	типовые требования по току

U

U 1	UART, universal asynchronous receiver/transmitter	UART m, universeller asynchroner Empfänger/Sender m <Parallel-Serie-Wandler- und Übertragungssteuerungsbaustein>	récepteur-émetteur m universel asynchrone	универсальный асинхронный приемопередатчик, УАПП
	UJT	s. U 41		
U 2	ULA, uncommitted logic array	ULA-Baustein m, unverdrahtete Logikanordnung f <kundenwunschentsprechend maskenprogrammierbare Universalschaltung, Master-Slice-Schaltkreis>	module m ULA, assemblage m logique non commuté	логическая матрица с несвязанными элементами <БИС>
U 3	ultimate load	höchstmögliche Belastung f, Grenzlast f	charge f limite	предельная нагрузка
U 4	ultraviolet erasable PROM, UV erasable PROM	UV-löschbarer PROM m <RePROM>	mémoire f lecture seule programmable effaçable aux rayons ultraviolets	программируемое постоянное запоминающее устройство с ультрафиолетовым стиранием
U 5	ultraviolet lamp, UV lamp	Ultraviolettlampe f, UV-Lampe f	lampe f ultraviolette	ультрафиолетовая лампа
U 6	ultraviolet light, UV light	ultraviolettes Licht n, UV-Licht n	lumière f ultraviolette	ультрафиолетовое излучение
U 7	ultraviolet light erasing, UV erasing	Löschen n mittels UV-Lichts	effaçage m par lumière ultraviolette	стирание [информации] ультрафиолетовым излучением
U 8	ultraviolet ray, UV ray	Ultraviolettstrahl m, UV-Strahl m	rayon m ultraviolet	ультрафиолетовый луч
U 9	UMOS transistor	U-Gruben-MOS-Transistor m <Modifikation des VMOS-FET>	transistor m UMOS	U-МОП транзистор
U 10	unactivated	unaktiviert	non activé	неактивированный
U 11	unallowable digit	unerlaubtes Zeichen n	nombre m non permis	запрещенный символ
U 12	unary operation, single-operand operation	Einoperanden-Operation f	opération f à opérande unique	унарная (одноместная) операция
U 13	unary operator	Einzeloperator m	opérateur m unique	унарный оператор
U 14	unassigned	nicht zugeordnet	non assigné	незакрепленный, неназначенный
U 15	unattended	unbewacht, ohne Bedienung	non surveillé, sans service	несопровождаемый, неконтролируемый
U 16	unbalanced	unabgeglichen, nicht im Gleichgewicht	déséquilibré	несбалансированный, рассогласованный
U 17	unbalanced line	unsymmetrische Leitung f	ligne f déséquilibrée	несимметричная (несбалансированная) линия
U 18	unbiased	nichtvorgespannt	sans polarisation	несмещенный
U 19	unblocked	ungeblockt	non bloqué	незаблокированный, несблокированный
U 20	unbuffered	ungepuffert	non tamponné	небуферизованный, безбуферный
U 21	unbundling	ungebunden <Verfahren der separaten Software- und Gerätetechnik-Kostenberechnung>	non lié	несвязанный
U 22	unburden / to, to unload	entlasten	décharger	разгружать
U 23	uncased	gehäuselos	sans boitier, nu	бескорпусной, без корпуса
U 24	unclocked	ungetaktet	non rythmé	несинхронизированный
	uncommitted logic array	s. U 2		
U 25	unconditional branch	unbedingte Verzweigung f	branchement m inconditionnel	безусловное ветвление
U 26/7	unconditional jump	unbedingter Sprung m	saut m inconditionnel	безусловный переход
	uncorrectable error	s. U 67		
U 28	undefined symbol	undefiniertes Symbol n	symbole m indéfini	неопределенный символ
U 29	undercut / to	unterätzen	sous-ronger	подтравливать
U 30	underflow	Unterlauf m, Unterschreitung f <des Zahlendarstellungs- oder -gültigkeitsbereichs>	dépassement m vers le bas	потеря, исчезновение
U 31	underload	Unterlast f, Unterbelastung f	sous-charge f	недогрузка, неполная нагрузка
U 32	underscore	Unterstreichung f	soulignement m	подчеркивание
U 33	undervoltage	Unterspannung f	sous-tension f	пониженное напряжение
U 34	undisturbed	ungestört	non perturbé	невозмущенный, невозбужденный

	English	German	French	Russian
U 35	unformatted	unformatiert, formatfrei	non formaté	без [задания] формата, свободного формата
U 36	unformatted record	formatfreier Datensatz *m*	enregistrement *m* non formaté	неформатная запись, запись в свободном формате
U 37	unidirectional bus	Einzelrichtungsbus *m*, Bus *m* mit nur einer Übertragungsrichtung	bus *m* unidirectionnel	однонаправленная шина
U 38	unidirectional pulses	Impulse *mpl* gleicher Richtung	impulsions *fpl* unidirectionnelles	однополярные импульсы
U 39	unidirectional transfer	Ein-Richtungs-Übertragung *f*	transfert *m* unidirectionnel	однонаправленная передача
U 40	uniform	gleichmäßig, gleichförmig	uniforme	однородный, равномерный, единообразный
U 41	unijunction transistor, UJT	Ein-pn-Übergang-Transistor *m*, Zweibasistransistor *m*, Doppelbasisdiode *f*	transistor *m* à une jonction pn	однопереходный транзистор
U 42	unimplemented instruction	nichtrealisierter Befehl *m*	instruction *f* non réalisée	нереализованная инструкция
U 43	uninterruptable mode	nichtunterbrechbare Betriebsweise *f*	mode *m* non interruptible	режим [работы] с запрещенными прерываниями
U 44	union	Vereinigung *f* <logischer Operator>	union *f*	объединение <логический оператор>
U 45	unipolar transistor	Unipolartransistor *m*	transistor *m* unipolaire	униполярный транзистор
U 46	unique	eindeutig, einmalig	unique	единственный, уникальный
U 47	unit	Einheit *f*, Baugruppe *f*, Geräteeinheit *f*	unité *f*	единица, устройство, узел, блок
U 48	unit costs	Stückpreis *m*	prix *m* à la pièce	стоимость в расчете на единицу
U 49	unit element	Einheitselement *n*, Elementarelement *n*	élément *m* unitaire	единичный элемент <цифрового сигнала данных>
U 50	unit interval	Einheitsintervall *n*, Elementarintervall *n*	intervalle *m* unitaire	единичный интервал <цифрового сигнала данных>
U 51	unit status	Status *m* der Geräteeinheit	état *m* de l'unité	состояние устройства
U 52	universal development system	universelles Entwicklungssystem *n*	système *m* universel de développement	универсальная система проектирования
U 53	universal instruction set	universeller Befehlssatz *m*	jeu *m* d'instructions universel	универсальный набор команд
U 54	universal microcomputer	universeller Mikrorechner *m*	microcalculateur *m* universel	универсальная микро-ЭВМ
	universal peripheral controller	*s.* U 71		
U 55	universal peripheral interface	universelle Peripherieschnittstelle *f*, Universalinterface *n* für Peripherieanschluß	interface *f* périphérique universelle	универсальный периферийный интерфейс
	universal synchronous/ asynchronous receiver/ transmitter	*s.* U 82		
U 56	universal terminator board	universelle Anschlußplatte *f*	plaque *f* de fin universelle	универсальная плата для оконечных устройств
	univibrator	*s.* M 488		
U 57	unknown	Unbekannte *f*	inconnue *f*	неизвестное
U 58	unknown quantity	unbekannte Größe *f*	quantité *f* inconnue	неизвестная величина
U 59	unlabelled	nicht etikettiert	non étiqueté, sans label	непомеченный
U 60	unlimited	unbegrenzt	illimité	неограниченный
	unload / to	*s.* U 22		
U 61	unloaded circuit board	unbestückte Leiterplatte (Steckeinheit) *f*	circuit *m* imprimé non équipé	плата без схемных элементов
U 62	unmatched	ungleich, unpaarig	inégal, impair	несогласованный
U 63	unpack / to	entpacken, auspacken	déballer	распаковывать
U 64	unpacked BCD data	ungepackte BCD-Daten *pl*, ungepackte binär kodierte Dezimalwerte *mpl*	données *fpl* BCD dégroupées	распакованные двоично-десятичные данные
U 65	unpacked format	ungepackte Form *f*	format *m* dégroupé	распакованный формат
U 66	unpredictable	unvorhersehbar, unbestimmt	imprévisible	непредсказуемый
U 67	unrecoverable error, uncorrectable error	nichtbehebbarer (unkorrigierbarer) Fehler *m*	erreur *f* incorrigible	неисправимая ошибка
	unsave status / to	*s.* R 352		
U 68	unsigned number	vorzeichenlose Zahl *f*	nombre *m* sans signe	число без знака
	unstable	*s.* A 346		
U 69	unused	unbenutzt	inusé	неиспользуемый
U 70/1	UPC, universal peripheral controller	universeller Peripheriesteuerungs-Schaltkreis *m*, UPC-Baustein *m*	circuit *m* de commande périphérique universel	универсальный периферийный контроллер
U 72	update / to	aktualisieren, fortschreiben	actualiser	обновлять, корректировать
U 73	update	Aktualisierung *f*, Fortschreibung *f*	actualisation *f*	дополнительная запись
U 74	updating maintenance	Änderungsdienst *m*	service *m* d'actualisation	служба [внесения] изменений
U 75	up-down counter, forward-backward counter, bidirectional counter	Vorwärts-Rückwärts-Zähler *m*, Zweirichtungszähler *m*	compteur *m* avant-arrière, compteur réversible	реверсивный счетчик
U 76	upgrade / to	ausbauen, aufstocken, steigern	augmenter	поднимать, повышать, надстраивать
U 77	upgrade	Steigung *f*, Steigerung *f*	montée *f*	подъем, повышение, увеличение

U 78	upper bound[ary]	obere Grenze f	limite f supérieure	верхняя граница, верхний предел
U 79	upper limit	oberer Grenzwert m	valeur f limite supérieure	верхнее предельное значение
U 80	uptime	Betriebszeit f <Gegensatz von „down time">	temps m de service (marche)	полезное [машинное] время, рабочее [машинное] время
U 81	upward compatibility	Aufwärtskompatibilität f	compatibilité f vers le haut	совместимость снизу вверх
U 82	USART, universal synchronous/asynchronous receiver/transmitter	USART-Schaltkreis m, universeller Synchron/Asynchron-Empfänger/Sender m	récepteur-émetteur m synchrone-asynchrone universel	универсальный синхронно-асинхронный приемопередатчик, УСАПП
	use	s. A 277		
	use / to	s. A 291		
U 83	user	Benutzer m, Anwender m	usager m, utilisateur m	пользователь, потребитель
U 84	user code	Benutzerkode m, Nutzerkode m	code m d'usager	код пользователя
U 85	user command	Nutzerbefehl m, Anwenderbefehl m, Nutzerkommando n	commande f d'usager (d'application)	команда пользователя
U 86	user interface	nutzerspezifischer Anschluß m, Anwenderschnittstelle f	interface f d'usager	интерфейс пользователя
U 87	user level	Nutzerebene f, Anwenderebene f	niveau m d'usager	уровень пользователя
U 88	user library	Anwenderbibliothek f, Nutzerbibliothek f <Programmbibliothek für Anwender eines Rechnersystems>	bibliothèque f d'usager	библиотека пользователя
U 89	user memory	Nutzerspeicher m	mémoire f d'usager	память [программы и рабочей области] пользователя
U 90	user-microprogrammable processor	anwendermikroprogrammierbarer Prozessor m	processeur m microprogrammable d'usager	процессор, программируемый пользователем на уровне микрокоманд
U 91	user-oriented design	nutzerorientierter (anwendungsorientierter) Entwurf m	conception f orientée usager	разработка, ориентированная на пользователя
U 92	user program	Nutzerprogramm n, Anwenderprogramm n	programme m d'usager	прикладная программа, программа пользователя
U 93	user programmability	Anwenderprogrammierbarkeit f, Programmierbarkeit f durch den Anwender	programmabilité f par l'usager	возможность программирования пользователем
U 94	user-programmable product	anwenderprogrammierbares Produkt n	produit m programmable par l'usager	программируемое пользователем изделие
U 95	user-programmable single-chip microcomputer	anwenderprogrammierbarer Einchip-Mikrorechner m	microcalculateur m sur une puce, programmable par l'usager	программируемая пользователем однокристальная микро-ЭВМ
U 96	user terminal	Benutzerstation f, Nutzerterminal n	terminal m d'usager	терминал пользователя
U 97	USRT, universal synchronous receiver/transmitter	USRT-Schaltkreis m, universeller synchroner Empfänger/Sender m	récepteur-émetteur m synchrone universel	универсальный синхронный приемопередатчик, УСПП
	utility program (routine)	s. S 280		
	UV erasable PROM	s. U 4		
	UV erasing	s. U 7		
	UV lamp	s. U 5		
	UV light	s. U 6		
	UV ray	s. U 8		

V

V 1	vacant	unbesetzt, frei	vacant	незанятый, свободный
V 2	vacuum deposition	Vakuumbedampfung f	dépôt m sous vide	вакуумное напыление
V 3	vacuum fluorescent display	Vakuumfluoreszenzanzeige f	affichage m fluorescent au vide	вакуумный флюоресцентный индикатор
V 4	valence, valency	Wertigkeit f	valence f	валентность
V 5	valid address	gültige Adresse f	adresse f valable	действительный адрес
V 6	validation	Gültigkeitsbestätigung f	confirmation f de validité	подтверждение достоверности
V 7	valid data	gültige Daten pl	données fpl valables	истинные (достоверные) данные
V 8	validity	Gültigkeit f, Richtigkeit f	validité f	истинность, достоверность, точность
V 9	validity check	Gültigkeitskontrolle f	vérification f de validité	проверка достоверности
V 10	value assignment	Wertzuweisung f	attribution f de valeur	присвоение значений
V 11	variable connector	veränderbarer Programmverbinder m	connecteur m variable	переключаемый [логический] блок объединения
V 12	variable field length	veränderliche Datenfeldlänge f	longueur f de champ variable	переменная длина поля
V 13	variable identification	Variablenbezeichnung f	identification f de variable	идентификация переменной
V 14	variable-length computer	Stellenmaschine f, Rechner m für variable Wortlänge	calculateur m pour longueur de mots variable	ЭВМ, работающая со словами переменной длины
V 15	variable-length instructions	Befehle mpl variabler Länge, verschieden lange Befehle	instructions fpl de longueur variable	инструкции переменной длины
V 16	variable master clock	veränderlicher Haupttakt m	rythme m principal variable	переменная [основная] тактовая частота
V 17	variable symbol	variables Symbol n	symbole m variable	переменный символ

V 18	**variable word length**	variable Wortlänge *f*	longueur *f* de mots variable	переменная длина слова
V 19	**VATE,** vertical anisotrope etching	VATE *f*, vertikal-anisotrope Ätztechnik *f* <Schaltkreis- technologie>	technique *f* VATE	вертикально-анизотроп- ный метод травления
	V-bit	*s.* O 245		
	V condition	*s.* O 246		
V 20	**vectored interrupt,** vector interrupt	Vektorinterrupt *m*, gerich- tete Unterbrechung *f* <Interrupt mit Ziel- angabe>	interruption *f* à vecteur	векторное прерывание
V 21	**vectoring**	Vektorisierung *f* <Selbst- kennung durch Vektor- angabe>	indication *f* de vecteur	векторизация
	vector interrupt	*s.* V 20		
V 22	**verification**	Richtigkeitsprüfung *f*, Verifizierung *f*	vérification *f*	контроль, проверка, вери- фикация
V 23	**verifier**	Prüfer *m*, Lochprüfgerät *n*	vérificateur *m*	контрольник
	verify / to	*s.* C 168		
V 24	**versatile structure**	vielseitige Struktur *f*	structure *f* diverse	универсальная структура
V 25	**versatility**	Vielseitigkeit *f*, vielseitige Verwendbarkeit *f*	variété *f*	универсальность
	vertical anisotrope etching	*s.* V 19		
V 26	**vertical check**	Querprüfung *f*, vertikale Prüfung *f*	vérification *f* verticale	вертикальный контроль
V 27	**vertical microprogram- ming**	vertikale Mikroprogram- mierung *f*	microprogrammation *f* verticale	вертикальное микропро- граммирование
	vertical MOS	*s.* V 45		
V 28	**vertical parity**	Querparität *f*, vertikale Pari- tät *f* <Zeichenparität>	parité *f* verticale	четность по вертикали
V 29	**vertical parity check,** lateral parity check	vertikale Paritätskontrolle *f*	test *m* de parité vertical	вертикальный контроль по четности
V 30	**vertical redundancy check,** VRC	Querredundanzprüfung *f*, Querprüfung *f* über Sicherungszeichen	contrôle *m* vertical de redondance	вертикальный контроль избыточным кодом
	very large scale integration	*s.* V 44		
	V-flag	*s.* O 247		
V 31	**V-groove**	V-Graben *m*, Graben *m* mit V-förmigem Querschnitt	fosse *f* en V	V-[образная] канавка
	V-groove MOS tech- nology	*s.* V 45		
V 32	**video data terminal**	Datensichtstation *f*	station *f* de visualisation	видеотерминал
V 33	**video games,** TV games	Bildschirmspiele *npl*, TV- Spiele *npl*	jeux *mpl* vidéo	телевизионные игры
V 34	**violation**	Verletzung *f*, Übertretung *f* <z. B. einer Speicher- schutzvorschrift>	violation *f*	повреждение, нарушение
V 35	**virtual address**	virtuelle Adresse *f*	adresse *f* virtuelle	виртуальный адрес
V 36	**virtual file**	virtuelle Datei *f*	fichier *m* virtuel	виртуальный файл
V 37	**virtual instruction set**	virtueller Befehlssatz *m* <Be- fehlssatz eines mikropro- grammierten Mikro- rechners>	jeu *m* d'instructions virtuelles	виртуальный набор команд
V 38	**virtual machine**	virtuelle Maschine *f*	machine *f* virtuelle	виртуальная машина
V 39	**virtual memory,** virtual storage	virtueller Speicher *m*	mémoire *f* virtuelle	виртуальная память
V 40	**virtual memory concept**	virtuelles Speicherkonzept *n*, Virtuellspeicherkonzept *n*	concept *m* de mémoire virtuelle	концепция виртуальной памяти
	virtual storage	*s.* V 39		
V 41	**virtual storage tech- nique**	virtuelle Speichertechnik *f*	technique *f* de mémoire virtuelle	методы виртуальной памяти
	visual display	*s.* D 451		
V 42	**visual pattern recogni- tion system**	optisches (visuelles) Zeichen- erkennungssystem *n*	système *m* visuel de recon- naissance de caractères	визуальная (оптическая) система распознавания образов
V 43	**visual perception system**	optisches Wahrnehmungs- system *n*, visuelles Erken- nungssystem *n*	système *m* de perception visuelle	система визуального вос- приятия, система опти- ческого считывания
V 44	**VLSI,** very large scale integration	VLSI *f*, Größtbereichs- integration *f*, sehr hohe Integration *f*	intégration *f* extrêmement haute	сверхбольшая интеграция
V 45	**VMOS,** vertical MOS, V- groove MOS technology	VMOS *f*, Vertikal-MOS *f*, V-Graben-MOS-Tech- nologie *f*	technologie *f* VMOS, tech- nologie MOS à fosse en V	МОП-технология с изо- ляцией V-[образными] канавками, V-МОП технология
V 46	**voice**	Stimme *f*	voix *f*	голос
V 47	**voice analyzer**	Sprachanalysator *m*	analyseur *m* de la parole	анализатор речи
	voice channel	*s.* S 612		
V 48	**voice communication**	Sprachverbindung *f*	communication *f* vocale	голосовая связь
	voice input	*s.* S 614		
V 49	**voice-operated device**	sprachgesteuertes Gerät *n*, sprachgesteuerte Anlage *f*	appareil *m* à commande vocale	устройство, управляемое голосом
	voice output	*s.* S 616		
	voice output capability	*s.* S 617		
	voice recognition	*s.* S 618		
	voice recognition system	*s.* S 619		
V 50	**voice response**	Sprachreaktion *f*, Sprach- antwort *f*	réponse *f* vocale	ответ в речевой форме
	voice-synthesis chip	*s.* S 622		
V 51	**voice synthesis system**	Sprachsynthesesystem *n*	système *m* de synthèse de la parole	система синтеза речи
	voice synthesizer	*s.* S 623		
V 52	**volatile**	flüchtig	volatile	непостоянный, измен- чивый

V 53	**volatile information**	flüchtige (unbeständige) Information *f*	information *f* volatile	изменяемая информация
	volatile memory	*s.* V 54		
V 54	**volatile storage,** volatile memory	flüchtiger Speicher *m* ‹energieabhängiger Speicher, regenerativer Speicher›	mémoire *f* volatile	энергозависимая (разрушаемая) память
V 55	**voltage**	[elektrische] Spannung *f*	tension *f*	напряжение
V 56	**voltage adjustment**	Spannungseinstellung *f*	ajustement *m* de tension	регулировка напряжения
V 57	**voltage comparator**	Spannungskomparator *m*, Spannungsvergleicher *m*	comparateur *m* de tension	компаратор напряжений
V 58	**voltage divider**	Spannungsteiler *m*	diviseur *m* de tension	делитель напряжения
V 59	**voltage-driven device**	spannungsgesteuertes Bauelement *n*	composant *m* commandé par tension	[электронный] прибор, управляемый напряжением
V 60	**voltage drop,** drop	Spannungsabfall *m*	chute *f* de tension	падение напряжения
V 61	**voltage gain**	Spannungsverstärkung *f*	gain *m* de tension	усиление напряжения; коэффициент усиления по напряжению
V 62	**voltage jump**	Spannungssprung *m*	saut *m* de tension	скачок напряжения
V 63	**voltage level**	Spannungspegel *m*	niveau *m* de tension	уровень напряжения
V 64	**voltage regulation**	Spannungsregelung *f*	réglage *m* de tension	регулирование напряжения
V 65	**volume initialization,** data carrier initialization	Datenträgerinitialisierung *f*	mise *f* en état initial de supports de données	инициализация тома
V 66	**volume mounting,** data carrier mounting	Datenträgereinrichtung *f*, Datenträgereinbau *m*	dispositif *m* à supports de données	установка тома
V 67	**volume production,** batch production	Großproduktion *f*, Serienproduktion *f*	production *f* de série	массовое (серийное) производство
V 68	**volume swap**	Datenträgerwechsel *m*	changement *m* de support de données	замена тома
V 69	**volume table of contents, VTOC**	Datenträgerinhaltsverzeichnis *n*	table *f* des matières des supports de données	оглавление тома
V 70	**voluntary interrupt**	beabsichtigte (programmierte) Unterbrechung *f*	interruption *f* volontaire	запрограммированное прерывание
V 71	**voucher**	Quittungsbeleg *m*	quittance *f*	квитанция
	VRC	*s.* V 30		
	VTOC	*s.* V 69		

W

W 1	**wafer**	Scheibe *f*, Halbleitersubstratplättchen *n*	disque *m*, puce *f*	пластина ‹полупроводник›
W 2	**wait condition**	Wartebedingung *f*	condition *f* d'attente	состояние ожидания
W 3	**wait[ing] cycle**	Wartezyklus *m*	cycle *m* d'attente	цикл ожидания
W 4	**waiting list**	Warteliste *f*	liste *f* d'attente	список очередности ‹входная очередь заданий›
W 5	**waiting state,** wait state	Wartezustand *m*	état *m* d'attente	состояние ожидания
	waiting time	*s.* W 7		
W 6	**wait loop**	Warteschleife *f*	boucle *f* d'attente	цикл ожидания
	wait state	*s.* W 5		
W 7	**wait time,** waiting time	Wartezeit *f*	temps *m* d'attente	время ожидания
W 8	**warm-up time**	Aufwärmzeit *f*, Anheizzeit *f*	temps *m* de réchauffement	время прогрева
W 9	**watchdog timer**	Zeitüberwachungseinrichtung *f*, Programmausführungszeit-Überwachungseinheit *f*	dispositif *m* de surveillance de temps	контрольный таймер
W 10	**wave carrier**	Trägerwelle *f*	onde *f* porteuse	несущая частота
W 11	**waveform**	Wellenform *f*, Impulssignalform *f*	forme *f* d'onde	форма колебания
W 12	**wave impedance**	Wellenwiderstand *m*	impédance *f* caractéristique	волновое (характеристическое) сопротивление
W 13	**wave length**	Wellenlänge *f*	longueur *f* d'onde	длина волны
W 14	**weakness**	Schwachstelle *f*	point *m* faible	слабое место
W 15	**wear-out failure**	Ermüdungsausfall *m*, Erschöpfungsausfall *m*	défaillance *f* de fatigue	отказ за счет износа
W 16	**well**	Mulde *f*, Potentialtopf *m*	cuvette *f*	потенциальная яма
W 17	**wheel printer**	Typenraddrucker *m*	imprimante *f* à roue à types	печатающее устройство барабанного типа
W 18	**wire / to**	verdrahten	enfiler	соединять проводами
W 19	**wire**	Draht *m*, Schaltkabel *n*	fil *m*	провод, проводник
W 20	**wired-AND**	verdrahtetes UND *n*	ET *m* câblé	проводное И, монтажное И
W 21	**wired-OR**	verdrahtetes ODER *n*	OU *m* incorporé	проводное (монтажное) ИЛИ
W 22	**wired-program computer**	Rechner *m* mit verdrahtetem Programm	calculateur *m* à programme câblé	ЭВМ с коммутируемой программой
W 23	**wireless network**	drahtfreies Netzwerk *n*, Schaltung *f* ohne Verbindungsdrähte	réseau *m* sans fil	беспроводная сеть
W 24	**wire-ORed signals**	verdrahtet geoderte Signale *npl*	signaux *mpl* OU câblés	сигналы, объединенные по схеме проводного ИЛИ
W 25	**wire printer**	Drahtdrucker *m* ‹Matrixdruckertyp›	imprimante *f* à fils	матричное печатающее устройство
W 26	**wire-wrap**	Drahtwickelverbindung *f*, ‹lötfreie Drahtverbindung›, Drahtwickeln *n*	connexion *f* wrappée	накрутка [проводов]
W 27	**wire-wrap technique**	Wire-Wrap-Technik *f*, Wickelverbindungstechnik *f*	wrapping *m*	метод накрутки
W 28	**wiring**	Verdrahtung *f*	câblage *m*	монтаж; межсоединения
W 29	**wiring diagram**	Verdrahtungsschema *n*	schéma *m* de câblage	монтажный чертеж
W 30	**wiring error**	Verdrahtungsfehler *m*	erreur *f* de câblage	ошибка в соединениях (монтаже)

W 31	word	Wort *n*, Maschinenwort *n*	mot *m*	[машинное] слово
W 32	word access	Wortzugriff *m*	accès *m* de mot	пословный доступ; выборка слова
W 33	word addressing	Wortadressierung *f*	adressage *m* de mots	пословная адресация, адресация слов
W 34	word boundary	Wortgrenze *f*	limite *f* de mot	граница слова
W 35	word format	Wortformat *n*	format *m* de mot	формат слова
W 36	word generator	Wortgenerator *m*	générateur *m* de mot	генератор [машинных] слов
W 37	word length, word size	Wortlänge *f*	longueur *f* de mot	длина слова
W 38	word mark	Wortmarke *f*	marque *f* de mot	маркер слова
W 39	word-organized storage	wortorganisierter Speicher *m*	mémoire *f* organisée par mots	память с пословной организацией
W 40	word-oriented application	wortorientierte (wortstruktur-orientierte) Anwendung *f*	application *f* orientée sur mot	применение, ориентированное на пословную структуру данных
W 41	word pattern	Wortmuster *n*	échantillon *m* de mot	эталонное слово
W 42	word period, word time	Wortzeit *f*, Worttaktzeit *f*	période *f* (temps *m*) de mot	период слова
W 43	word-processed document <US>	textverarbeitete Unterlage *f*, mittels Textverarbeitung erstellte Unterlage	document *m* créé par traitement de texte	документ, полученный при помощи обработки текстов
W 44	word processing	Wortverarbeitung *f*	traitement *m* de mots	обработка слов
	word processing	*s. a.* T 141		
W 45	word-processing application <US>	Textverarbeitungsanwendung *f*	application *f* de traitement de texte	применение в обработке текстов
W 46	word-processing station <US>	Textverarbeitungsplatz *m*	place *f* de traitement de texte	станция обработки текстов
	word size	*s.* W 37		
	word time	*s.* W 42		
W 47	word-wide organization	wortbreite Organisation *f*	organisation *f* de largeur de mot	пословная структура
W 48	work area, working area	Arbeitsbereich *m*	domaine (champ) *m* de travail	рабочая область (зона)
W 49	work disk, working disk	Arbeitsplatte *f* <Plattenspeicher>	disque *m* de travail	рабочий диск
W 50	work file, scratch file	Arbeitsfile *n*, Arbeitsdatei *f*, Notizdatei *f*	fichier *m* de travail	рабочий файл
	working area	*s.* W 48		
	working disk	*s.* W 49		
	working memory	*s.* O 118		
	working register	*s.* O 135		
W 51	working set	Arbeitssatz *m*	jeu *m* de travail	рабочий комплект
	working storage	*s.* O 118		
W 52	work place computer, work station computer	Arbeitsplatzrechner *m* <ständig verfügbarer Mikrorechner am Arbeitsplatz>	calculateur *m* de place de travail	ЭВМ в составе рабочего места [пользователя]
W 53	work space	Arbeitsraum *m* <Arbeitsbereich *m*>	espace *m* de travail	рабочая область
W 54	work-space pointer	Arbeitsbereichszeiger *m*	pointeur *m* de champ de travail	указатель рабочей области
W 55	work station	Arbeitsplatz *m* <Benutzerstation>	place *f* de travail	рабочее место <пользователя>
	work station computer	*s.* W 52		
W 56	work-station-oriented data processing equipment	arbeitsplatzorientierte Datenverarbeitungsausrüstung *f*	équipement *m* de traitement de données orienté sur place de travail	оборудование [для] обработки данных, ориентированное на размещение в составе рабочего места
W 57	worst case	ungünstigster Fall *m*	cas *m* le plus défavorable	наихудший случай
W 58	worst-case circuit analysis	Schaltungsanalyse *f* unter Grenzbedingungen	analyse *f* de circuit sous conditions limites	анализ схемы на наихудшее сочетание параметров, анализ схемы в граничных условиях
W 59	worst-case design	Entwurf *m* auf Grenzbedingungen	conception *f* sous conditions limites	расчет [схем] на наихудшее сочетание параметров
W 60	writable control store	beschreibbarer (umschreibbarer) Steuerspeicher *m*	mémoire *f* de commande à écrire	управляющая память с возможностью перезаписи
W 61	write / to	schreiben, einschreiben <in einen Speicher>	écrire	писать, записывать
W 62	write amplifier	Schreibverstärker *m*	amplificateur *m* d'écriture	усилитель записи
W 63	write control	Schreibsteuerung *f*	commande *f* d'écriture	управление записью
W 64	write current	Schreibstrom *m*	courant *m* d'écriture	ток записи
W 65	write cycle	Schreibzyklus *m*	cycle *m* d'écriture	цикл записи
W 66	write data	Schreibdaten *pl*	données *fpl* d'écriture	записываемые данные
W 67	write enable signal	Schreib-Freigabesignal *n* <Steuersignal>	signal *m* d'autorisation d'écriture	сигнал разрешения записи
W 68	write head, writing head	Schreibkopf *m*	tête *f* d'écriture	головка записи
W 69	write lockout	Schreibsperre *f*	verrouillage *m* d'écriture	блокировка записи
W 70	write operation	Schreiboperation *f*	opération *f* d'écriture	операция записи
W 71	write protection	Schreibschutz *m*	protection *f* d'écriture	защита при записи
W 72	write pulse	Schreibimpuls *m*, Schreibtaktimpuls *m*	impulsion *f* d'écriture	импульс записи
W 73	write-read process	Schreib-Lese-Vorgang *m*	processus *m* de lecture-écriture	процесс «запись-считывание» <совмещение процессов считывания, обработки и записи результатов>
	write through / to	*s.* S 778		
	writing head	*s.* W 68		
W 74	writing rate, writing speed	Schreibgeschwindigkeit *f*	vitesse *f* d'écriture	скорость записи

X

X 1	**xerographic printer**	xerografischer Drucker *m*	imprimante *f* xérographique	ксерографическое (электрографическое) печатающее устройство
	XOR	*s.* E 294		
X 2	**X-ray**	Röntgenstrahl *m*	rayon *m* X	рентгеновские лучи
X 3	**X-ray lithography**	Röntgenstrahllithografie *f*	lithographie *f* aux rayons X	рентгенолучевая литография
X 4	**X-Y presentation,** X-Y representation	XY-Darstellung *f*	représentation *f* XY	двухкоординатное представление, представление в двумерной прямоугольной системе координат
	X-Y-recorder	*s.* C 768		
	X-Y representation	*s.* X 4		

Y

Y 1	**yoke**	Joch *n* ‹Magnetkopfgruppe›	joug *m*	блок магнитных головок

Z

	Z-bit	*s.* Z 8		
	Z-condition	*s.* Z 10		
Z 1	**Zener breakdown**	Zener-Durchbruch *m*	décharge *f* de Zener	зеноровский пробой
Z 2	**Zener diode**	Zener-Diode *f*, Z-Diode *f*	diode *f* Zener	опорный диод, стабилитрон, зеноровский диод
Z 3	**Zener voltage**	Zener-Spannung *f*	tension *f* Zener	напряжение зеноровского пробоя, напряжение стабилизации
Z 4	**zero**	Null *f*	zéro *m*	нуль
Z 5	**zero-address instruction**	adreßloser Befehl *m*	instruction *f* sans adresse	безадресная команда
Z 6	**zero adjust**	Nullabgleich *m*	ajustement *m* de zéro	установка в нуль; установка нуля
	zero balancing	*s.* Z 9		
Z 7	**zero bias Schottky diode**	Schottky-Diode *f* mit sehr niedriger Schwellspannung	diode *f* Schottky à très basse tension de seuil	диод Шоттки с малым прямым смещением
Z 8	**zero bit,** Z-bit	Nullbit *n*	bit *m* zéro	разряд нуля, Z-бит
T 9	**zero check,** zero balancing	Nullkontrolle *f*	vérification *f* de zéro	настройка (контроль) нуля
	zero compression	*s.* Z 25		
Z 10	**zero condition,** Z-condition	Nullbedingung *f*	condition *f* de zéro	нулевое состояние, состояние «0»
Z 11	**zero deletion**	Nullenlöschung *f*, Nullenstreichung *f*	effaçage *m* de zéros	исключение нулей
Z 12	**zero error**	Nullpunktfehler *m*	faute *f* de point zéro	ошибка в нулевой точке; уход нуля
Z 13	**zero filling**	Auffüllen *n* mit Nullen	remplissage *m* de zéros	заполнение нулями
Z 14	**zero flag,** Z-flag	Nullzustandskennzeichen *n*	marque *f* de zéro	признак нуля, флаг нуля ‹Z-бит регистра состояния процессора›
Z 15	**zero insertion**	Nulleinfügung *f*	insertion *f* de zéro	введение нулей
Z 16	**zero level**	Nullpegel *m*	niveau *m* zéro	нулевой уровень
	zero-level addressing	*s.* I 40		
Z 17	**zero-page addressing**	Page-Null-Adressierung *f*, indirekte Adressierung *f* über Speicherseite Null	adressage *m* sur page zéro	адресация в режиме нулевой страницы
Z 18	**zero point**	Nullpunkt *m*	point *m* zéro	нулевая точка
Z 19	**zero position**	Nullstellung *f*, Nullposition *f*	position *f* zéro	нулевое положение
Z 20/1	**zero potential**	Nullpotential *n*	potentiel *m* zéro	нулевой потенциал
	zero reset	*s.* C 249		
Z 22	**zero shift**	Nullpunktverschiebung *f*	décalage *m* du point zéro	уход (смещение) нуля
Z 23	**zero stability**	Nullpunktstabilität *f*	stabilité *f* du point zéro	стабильность нуля
Z 24	**zero state**	Nullzustand *m*	état *m* zéro	состояние логического «0»
Z 25	**zero suppression,** null suppression, zero compression	Nullunterdrückung *f* ‹Datenkompression durch Unterdrückung führender Nullen›	suppression *f* de zéros	подавление [незначащих] нулей
Z 26	**zero voltage**	Nullspannung *f*	tension *f* zéro	нулевое напряжение
	Z-flag	*s.* Z 14		
Z 27	**zoned**	gezont, in Zonen geteilt	en zones	разделенный на зоны
Z 28	**zoned format**	gezontes Format *n* ‹vorzeichenloses ungepacktes Format›	format *m* en zones	зонный формат
Z 29	**zone digit**	Bereichsziffer *f*	chiffre *m* de zone	знак зоны
Z 30	**zone melting**	Zonenschmelzen *n*	raffinage *m* zonal	зонная плавка ‹полупроводниковая технология›

DEUTSCH

FRANÇAIS

diagramme de déroulement fonctionnel F 212
diagramme de flux F 147
diagramme de fonctionnement F 211
diagramme de processus F 150
diagramme de rythme C 272, T 215
diagramme de signal S 369
diagramme de transition d'état S 717
diagramme logique L 240
diaphonie C 839
différence de niveau logique L 266
différence de phase P 172
diffuser D 351, S 191
diffusion dépendant de la concentration C 566
diffusion d'impureté I 65
diffusion ouverte O 96
digital D 364
digitalisation D 385
digit binaire B 161
dilatateur d'impulsion P 735
dimension minimum M 442
dimensionnement P 662
dimensionner S 499
dimensions physiques P 219
diminuer D 222
diminution de puissance P 372
diminution exponentielle E 324
diode D 391
diode agrafe C 246
diode à jonction J 25
diode à pointe P 297
diode au silicium S 397
diode d'avalanche A 425
diode luminescente L 107
diode photo-électrique P 197
diode Schottky S 72
diode Schottky à très basse tension de seuil Z 7
diode Zener Z 2
dioxyde de silicium S 398
direction avant L 319
direction de comptage C 804
direction de faible résistance L 319
direction de flux L 319
direction de passage L 319
direction de transmission T 298
direction inverse R 369
direction transversale C 831
directive G 85
disjoncteur D 396
disjonction D 428
dispatcher de tâches T 52
dispatching D 446
dispersion L 73, S 61
dispersion magnétique M 79
disponibilité A 420
disponible à l'émission C 250
dispositif à conversion de signaux S 348
dispositif à dénuder S 791
dispositif à éliminer des couches S 791
dispositif à macros M 49
dispositif à supports de données V 66
dispositif automatique de test A 405
dispositif d'avancement de formulaire[s] F 170
dispositif de balayage S 12
dispositif de codage C 324
dispositif de commande de déroulement T 206/7
dispositif de communication de données D 57
dispositif de commutation S 894
dispositif de décalage S 327
dispositif de diagnostic D 329
dispositif de division D 484
dispositif de formation S 302
dispositif de mémoire S 765
dispositif de mesure M 220
dispositif d'enregistrement L 228
dispositif d'entrée-sortie I 484

dispositif de perforation P 745
dispositif de protection P 668
dispositif de protection incorporé P 306
dispositif d'E/S I 484
dispositif de sauvegarde de mémoire écriture-lecture R 12
dispositif de soustraction S 832
dispositif de sûreté S 1
dispositif de surveillance de temps W 9
dispositif de test T 113
dispositif de test de composants C 474
dispositif de test on-line O 72
dispositif de transmission de données D 127
dispositif de tri de documents D 507
dispositif de visualisation de calculateur C 513
dispositif d'interruption I 415
dispositif entièrement automatique F 198
dispositif pour représentation numérique D 384
dispositifs d'entrée I 174
dispositif supplémentaire A 95
disposition correcte A 182
disposition en tiroir P 272
disque D 431, W 1
disque de semi-conducteur S 186
disque de système S 964
disque de travail W 49
disque fixe F 104
disque interchangeable R 272
disque magnétique M 68
disque rigide H 34
disque souple D 438, F 143
disque têtes mobiles M 516
disquette D 438
disséminer S 59
dissipation P 373
dissipation de chaleur H 68
distance S 591
distance de branchement B 267
distance de Hamming H 15
distance d'erreur E 231
distance minimale M 441
distorsion D 461
distorsion de phase D 227, P 174
distorsion d'impulsion P 704
distorsion linéaire L 130
distorsion non linéaire N 75
distorsion oblique S 501
distorsion oblique de signal S 368
distribué S 60
distribuer D 462, S 59
distributeur D 475
distributeur d'impulsions de temps T 202
distribution de charge C 158
distribution de commande D 473
distribution de concentration C 567
distribution de potentiel P 364
distribution d'erreurs E 232
distribution de tâches T 53
distribution exponentielle E 325
distribution intermédiaire I 348
dividende D 480
diviseur D 485
diviseur décadique D 168
diviseur de phase P 186
diviseur de tension V 58
division de développement D 299
division par matériel H 41
D.M.A. D 486
D-MOS D 499
DNC D 500
document D 501
documentation de programme P 558

document créé par traitement de texte W 43
documents logiciels S 532
domaine F 47
domaine actif A 82
domaine à labels L 3
domaine commun C 366
domaine consécutif C 628
domaine de données D 28
domaine de mémoire M 244
domaine d'entrée I 159
domaine de paramètres P 62
domaine de signaux grands L 31
domaine de sortie O 193
domaine de travail S 82, W 48
domaine de valeurs R 29
domaine d'instructions I 231
domaine élargi E 330
domaines partagés C 305
donateur D 511
données D 20
données à 4 bits B 172
données à 8 bits B 173
données à 16 bits B 174
données accumulées S 773
données analogiques A 252
données BCD dégroupées U 64
données BCD groupées P 7
données caractéristiques C 134
données de cache C 5
données de chaînes de bits B 205
données de commande C 702
données de compatibilité B 233
données d'écriture W 66
données de diagnostic D 328
données de lecture R 45
données d'entrée I 170
données de processus P 505
données de réception R 86
données de référence R 170
données de sortie O 205
données de source S 567
données de test T 116
données de transmission T 304
données directes I 41
données d'octet[s] B 375
données en chaîne C 563
données en tables T 10
données graphiques G 61
données munies de signe S 381
données numériques N 129
données originales O 175
données permanentes P 153
données primaires P 442
données séparées S 210
données stables S 643
données valables V 7
dopage D 519
dopage d'émetteur E 125
dopage de semi-conducteurs S 179
dopé à l'or G 56
doper D 517
doping D 519
dos B 13
DOS D 440
dotation d'accepteur A 29
doté par diffusion D 358
doublé D 244
doubler D 586
douille S 521
drain D 539
dresser B 301
driver D 559
driver d'impulsions P 705
droit S 781
DTL D 565
dual B 137
duplex entier F 200
duplicateur D 588
durée T 191
durée de cycle C 900
durée de mise en mémoire S 766
durée de signal S 352
durée d'impulsion P 706
durée d'intervalle I 448

E

EAROM E 1
écart de colonne C 349
écart de contact C 648
écart de ligne L 154
écart de réglage C 704
écart logique L 266
écart moyen A 429
échange E 289
échangeable I 317
échange de bus B 333
échange de charge C 159
échange de données D 70
échange de phase P 167
échange de programme P 545
échange de signe S 377
échange d'impulsions de synchronisation H 28
échange d'informations I 114
échange d'octets B 383
échanger E 287
échange thermique T 144
échangeur S 885
échantillon P 96
échantillon de conception M 187
échantillon de mot W 41
échantillon de référence R 174
échantillon d'essai S 6
échantillon de test T 128
échelon de mémoire-cave S 651
éclipsage G 34
éclipser B 209
économie d'éléments logiques S 33
économie de surface S 34
économie de temps / à T 205
écran S 86
écran de projection P 653
écran de visualisation D 458
écran électrostatique E 109
écran magnétique M 88
écran partagé S 630
écrire W 61
écrire de nouveau R 377
écriture en lettres d'imprimerie H 22
éditer E 17
éditeur cross C 832
éditeur de fichier F 73
éditeur de lien L 169
éditeur de texte T 139
éditeur source S 569
édition E 19
édition de texte T 137
édition postérieure P 357
éducation sur base de calculateur C 498
EEROM E 28
effaçage D 236
effaçage de mémoire M 269
effaçage d'enregistrement R 109
effaçage de zéros Z 11
effaçage par lumière ultraviolette U 7
effacement E 209
effacer D 235, E 204
effectif E 29
effet de réaction B 3
effet de tunnel T 352
effet DMS D 605
effet ferro-photoélectrique P 204
effet Josephson J 12
effet pelliculaire S 502
effet photo-électrique P 198
effet photo-électrique interne P 194
efficace E 29
efficience E 36
efficience de mémoire M 267
efficience de réglage C 705
effondrement de système S 958
effort E 319
effort de programmation P 608
effort d'organisation O 250
égaliser E 189
égaliseur d'impulsion P 709

quantifier Q 15
quantité complexe C 462
quantité discrète D 427
quantité inconnue U 58
quantité nulle N 118
quantité scalaire S 37
quartz Q 16
queue Q 24
queue d'attente à l'entrée I 209
queue de messages M 330
queue d'entrée I 209
queue de tâches T 59
queue d'instructions I 256
queue FIFO F 61
quittance A 70, H 23/4, V 71
quotient Q 37

R

raccordement C 612
raccordement de disque D 433
raccordement de gate G 29
raccordement d'entrée I 205
raccordement d'E/S intégré
(sur puce) O 48
raccordement direct D 399
raccordement introduit L 61
raccordement sorti L 69
raccorder C 602
racine carrée S 637
raffinage zonal Z 30
rafraîchissement R 182
rafraîchissement propre S 163
rallonge E 337
RAM R 10
RAM bipolaire B 155
RAM couplée par charge
C 76
RAM dynamique D 603
RAM en MOS M 501
RAM orientée bloc B 221
RAM pseudo-statique P 682
RAM statique S 724
RAM unipolaire M 501
rang O 164
rapport S 755
rapport coût-performance
C 789
rapport cyclique de sortie
O 209
rapport cyclique d'impulsion
P 708
rapport de bruit N 63
rapport de démultiplication
S 48
rapport d'erreurs E 251
rapport de travail D 590
rapport d'impulsion P 728
rapporter / se R 167
rapport gate / broche G 31
rapport Homme-calculateur
M 132
rapport Homme-machine
M 134
rapport multiplicateur S 755
rapport nul N 51
rapport prix-performances
P 440
rapport relatif dans le temps
entre signaux R 233
rapport signal-bruit S 370
rapport un à zéro O 64
rayon électronique E 70
rayon ultraviolet U 8
rayon X X 2
RAZ C 249
RAZ automatique A 400
RAZ du compteur C 800
réactance R 41
réactance capacitive C 36
réaction F 30
réaction à retardement D 228
réaction positive P 353
réaction retardée D 228
réagir R 40
réalisé par matériel H 44
réarrangement R 81
réattribution R 82
rebobinage rapide H 117
rebondissement de contact
C 645
rebut R 224
récepteur R 89

récepteur de bus B 354
récepteur d'entrée I 195
récepteur-émetteur de bus
B 362
récepteur-émetteur syn-
chrone-asynchrone univer-
sel U 82
récepteur-émetteur synchrone
universel U 97
récepteur-émetteur universel
asynchrone U 1
récepteur photo-électrique
P 202
réception R 94
recevoir R 83
recharge R 95
rechargeable R 96
recherche R 358
recherche binaire B 144
recherche de caractères C 142
recherche de panne T 331
recherche d'erreurs E 253
recherche de table T 5
recherche d'opérations O 138
recherche et développement
R 304
recherche parallèle P 55
recherche séquentielle S 239
réciproque R 97
recombinaison R 104
reconnaissance A 70, R 99
reconnaissance automatique de
caractères A 384
reconnaissance automatique de
la parole A 402
reconnaissance de caractères
C 140
reconnaissance d'écriture H 29
reconnaissance d'écriture
magnétique M 61
reconnaissance de la parole
S 618
reconnaissance de la parole
automatisée A 380
reconnaissance de modèle
P 101
reconnaissance d'erreur[s]
E 227
reconnaissance de signaux
S 364
reconnaissance d'interruption
I 396
reconnaissance mécanique
M 34
reconnaissance optique de
caractères O 148
recouvrement R 358
recouvrement de mémoire
M 292
recouvrement de protection
P 672
recouvrement magnétique
M 63
recouvrement partiel P 78
recouvrir R 257
rectiligne S 781
récupération d'information
I 125
récursif R 138
récursion R 139
recyclage / à R 144
redémarrage R 347
redémarrage automatique
A 401
redémarrage de programme
P 629
redémarrage de système S 975
redistribution R 147
redondance R 151
redondance de code C 314
redondance de message M 331
redressage R 132
redresseur à couche de barrage
B 48
redresseur au silicium S 411
redresseur demi-onde H 10
réduction R 150
réduction de charge D 254
réduction de puissance P 372
réduction de taille S 500
réduire R 148, T 324
réduire à l'échelle S 40
référence R 168
référence à la mémoire M 299

référence de performance
P 132
référence de travers C 834
référence pilote P 229
référer R 167
refroidissement forcé F 156
régénératif R 190
régénération R 188
régénération de mémoire
M 302
régénération transparente [de
mémoire] T 308
régénérer R 187
régime à abonnés T 209
régime à commande par interruptions I 410
régime à coups B 318
régime à découpage de temps
T 209
régime à impulsions P 723
régime à mode multiple
M 540
régime à multiprocesseurs
M 553
régime à octets B 377
régime à pas S 492
régime asynchrone A 357
régime à temps court S 338
régime automatique A 410
régime de bits B 187
régime de dialogue D 340
régime demi-duplex H 7
régime d'empilage B 101
régime de premier plan-arrière
plan F 157
régime de quittance H 28
régime de réception R 88
régime d'interrogation P 321
régime duplex D 585
régime fermé C 278
régime intermittent P 134
régime manuel M 141
régime mi-duplex H 7
régime multiplex M 564
régime off-line O 35
régime on-line O 70
régime ouvert O 93
régime pas à pas S 492
régime push-push C 378
régime sans défaut E 234
régime séquentiel S 236
régime sériel S 263
régime simplex S 420
régime simultané S 437
région de transition T 292
région de transition de jonction
J 31
région limite T 170
région p P 411
registre R 192
registre à bascules F 128
registre à 4 bits B 195
registre à 8 bits B 196
registre à 16 bits B 197
registre à bit unique B 448
registre à décalages couplé par
charge C 156
registre à décalages magnétique
M 89
registre arithmétique A 312
registre chargeable L 188
registre circulaire C 243
registre cyclique C 243
registre d'adresse A 148
registre d'adresse de mémoire
M 242
registre d'adresse de page P 26
registre d'adresse d'instruction
I 230
registre d'adresse d'opérande
O 99
registre d'adresses de banque
B 42
registre de base B 66
registre de bloc-notes S 85
registre de code de condition
C 585
registre de commande C 734
registre de commande de cache
C 4
registre de décalage S 325
registre de décalage statique
S 725
registre de défauts F 21

registre de demandes d'interruption I 431
registre de description D 258
registre de distribution D 474
registre de données D 107
registre de données de
mémoire M 264
registre de lien L 173
registre de maintien d'adresse
A 137
registre de maintien de sortie
O 218
registre de mémoire M 303
registre de mémoire intermédiaire T 87
registre d'entrée I 196
registre de pages P 30
registre de pointeur P 299
registre de processeur P 531
registre de réserve S 695
registre descriptif D 258
registre de segment S 125
registre de séquence S 224
registre de sortie O 225
registre de synchronisation de
demandes d'interruption
I 433
registre de tampon d'informations L 43
registre d'état S 736
registre de test C 189
registre d'extension E 339
registre d'index I 88, M 467
registre d'instructions I 257
registre d'interrogation I 393
registre d'interruptions I 428
registre directement accessible
D 407
registre d'opérande O 100
registre général G 44
registre hit de cache C 6
registre intermédiaire I 351
registre LIFO L 104
registre opérationnel O 135
registre spécialisé S 600
registre tampon B 295
registre temporaire T 84
registre universel G 44
réglage R 220
réglage à réaction C 277
réglage de gain G 6
réglage de niveau L 93
réglage de phase P 169
réglage de tension V 64
réglage de vitesse S 624
réglage du rapport R 39
réglage en avant F 36
réglage numérique direct
D 403
réglage proportionnel P 659
réglage proportionnel et par
intégration P 661
règle R 419
règle de calcul C 560
règle de conversion C 758
règle de langage L 25
régler R 215
règles de conception D 280
règles de layout L 57
réglette S 790
réglette à fiches P 285
régulateur R 221
régulateur automatique A 388
régulateur continu C 673
régulateur de poursuite F 153
régulateur de tension du
secteur L 159
régulateur numérique direct
D 404
régulation R 220
régulation de vitesse S 624
réinsertion R 222
rejet R 224
rejeter R 223, R 391
relais-bascule K 30
relation Homme-calculateur
M 132
relation master-slave M 192
relevé de fichier D 74
relever P 334
relocation dynamique D 604
relogeabilité R 244
relogement R 253
reloger R 252

РУССКИЙ

A

абонент S 308
абонентский пункт T 90
абонентский телетайпный
   пункт T 77
абсолютная адресация A 8
абсолютная загрузка A 14
абсолютная погрешность
   A 12
абсолютное значение A 17
абсолютный R 161
абсолютный адрес A 7
абсолютный ассемблер A 9
абсолютный загрузчик
   A 13
абсолютный код A 10
абсолютный начальный
   адрес O 174
аварийная разгрузка R 303
аварийное сообщение A 188
аварийный дамп R 303
аварийный источник
   питания E 119
авария в системе S 958
ABM A 251
автодекрементный способ
   адресации A 372
автоиндексация A 375
автоинкрементный способ
   адресации A 374
автокод A 370
автоматизация A 409
автоматизация конторских
   работ O 30
автоматизация проектиро-
   вания D 264
автоматизация проектиро-
   вания микросхем с умень-
   шенными размерами
   чипов C 10
автоматизация произ-
   водства P 533
автоматизация производ-
   ственных процессов P501
автоматизированная об-
   работка данных A 389
автоматизированная об-
   работка текстов C 493
автоматизированная сборка
   A 377
автоматизированная система
   обработки данных A 390
автоматизированное кон-
   струирование A 378
автоматизированное логи-
   ческое проектирование
   A 379
автоматизированное про-
   граммирование C 492
автоматизированное проек-
   тирование C 9
автоматизированное произ-
   водство с применением
   ЭВМ C 491
автоматизированное распо-
   знавание речи A 380
автоматическая загрузка
   [программ] B 246
автоматическая коммутация
   сообщений A 398
автоматическая коммути-
   руемая телеграфная связь
   T 74
автоматическая коррекция
   ошибок A 393
автоматическая обработка
   текстов A 407
автоматическая подача
   бланков A 394
автоматическая регистрация
   A 397
автоматическая сборка на
   ленте T 18
автоматическая связь
   (телефонная станция)
   D 338
автоматическая трансляция
   A 408
автоматическая установка
   в ноль A 400
автоматически выравни-
   вающийся S 140
автоматический A 381

автоматический загрузчик
   A 396
автоматический коммутатор
   A 403
автоматический контроллер
   A 388
автоматический контроль
   A 385
автоматический обмен A 386
автоматический опрос
   A 412
автоматический повторный
   запуск A 401
автоматический режим
   A 410
автоматический рестарт
   A 401
автоматическое декремен-
   тирование A 371
автоматическое инкремен-
   тирование A 373
автоматическое испытатель-
   ное оборудование A 405
автоматическое испытатель-
   ное оборудование, рабо-
   тающее под управлением
   ЭВМ C 529
автоматическое преобразо-
   вание графической ин-
   формации в цифровую
   форму A 392
автоматическое приемо-
   передающее устройство
   A 322
автоматическое програм-
   мирование A 399
автоматическое распозна-
   вание речи A 402
автоматическое распозна-
   вание символов A 384
автоматическое усреднение
   A 382
автономная вычислительная
   система на базе микро-
   ЭВМ S 664
автономная конфигурация
   S 662
автономная обработка O 36
автономная программа S 666
автономная работа O 35
автономная система S 667
автономная ЭВМ O 33
автономный S 661
автономный режим S 665
автономный эмулятор S 663
авторизованный A 369
автосинхронизация S 148
адаптация A 90, T 14
адаптация к требованиям
   заказчика C 891
адаптация линии L 126
адаптер A 87
адаптер интерфейса I 324
адаптер канала C 107
адаптер периферийного
   интерфейса P 147
адаптер [схемы] управления
   C 687   ГА 91
адаптивная архитектура
   A 86, A 92
адаптивная система
   A 86, A 92
адаптивное управление
   S 137
адаптивность A 85
адрес A 105
адресация A 127
адресация, базирующая на
   принципе допустимости
   C 32
адресация внутри текущей
   [страницы] памяти C 873
адресация в режиме нуле-
   вой страницы Z 17
адресация второго уровня
   S 104
адресация нулевого уровня
   I 40
адресация нулевой страни-
   цы P 32
адресация памяти M 241
адресация первого уровня
   F 101
адресация по указателю
   стека S 647

адресация слов W 33
адресация стека S 647
адресация страницы P 25
адресация файла F 67
адрес базы сегмента S 115
адрес байта B 372
адрес блока B 211
адрес буфера B 287
адрес вектора прерывания
   I 446
адрес возврата R 361
адрес входа E 171
адрес доступа A 32
адрес записи R 107
адрес источника S 564
адрес канала C 108
адрес команды I 229
(n + 1)-адресная команда
   N 110
адресная константа A 118
адресная линия A 138
адресная часть A 143
адресное пространство
   A 151
адресное слово A 160
адресные сигналы A 135
адресный байт A 113
адресный стек A 153
адресный тракт A 144
адрес обращения A 32
адресованная память A 123
адресовать A 104
адрес-операнд I 39
адрес операнда O 98
адрес памяти M 240
адрес, передаваемый с вре-
   менным мультиплексиро-
   ванием [шины] T 196
адрес перехода J 17
адрес повторного пуска
   R 348
адрес получателя D 289
адрес порта ввода-вывода
   I 504
адрес продолжения C 669
адрес регистра R 193
адрес рестарта R 348
адрес связи L 162
адрес сегмента S 112
адрес сектора S 108
адрес смещения D 449
адрес ссылки R 169
адресуемая память A 108
адресуемое устройство
   A 122
адресуемость A 106
адресуемый регистр-фик-
   сатор A 107
адрес устройства D 310
адрес цилиндра C 910
адрес ячейки памяти M 278
АИМ P 693
аккумулятор A 56
активизация A 76
активировать A 74
активная зона A 82
активная мощность R 64
активная нагрузка O 42
активная область A 77
активная фаза D 589
активность канала C 106
активный компонент A 78
активный преобразователь
   A 83
активный элемент A 80
акцептор A 28
алгебраическая функция
   A 190
алгебраическое выражение
   A 189
алгебра логики (переключа-
   тельных схем) S 891
АЛГОЛ A 191
алгоритм A 192
алгоритм деления D 483
алгоритмический A 194
алгоритмический язык для
   обработки списков L 176
алгоритм контроля C 170
алгоритм поиска S 95
алгоритм проверки C 170
алгоритм проектирования
   D 262
алгоритм размещения P 248

алгоритм распознавания
   R 100
алгоритм распознавания
   образов A 193
алгоритм управления C 688
алгоритм управления
   объектом P 500
АЛУ A 308
алфавитно-цифровая
   клавиатура A 216
алфавитно-цифровое пред-
   ставление A 218
алфавитно-цифровой
   A 212/3
алфавитно-цифровой вы-
   ход A 217
алфавитно-цифровой
   дисплей A 215
алфавитно-цифровой код
   A 214
алфавитный A 209
алфавитный код A 211
алфавитный символ A 210
альтернативное ветвление
   A 226
альтернативное решение
   L 237
альтернативный A 225
альтернативный код A 221
алюминиевый затвор A 229
американский стандартный
   код информационного
   обмена A 321
амплитуда импульса P 692
амплитудная характери-
   стика A 243
амплитудно-импульсная
   модуляция P 693
амплитудный диапазон
   входных сигналов I 158
амплитудный уровень A 244
анализатор A 267
анализатор для интеграль-
   ных схем I 289
анализатор речи V 47
анализ изделий E 211
анализ проекта D 263
анализ схемы в граничных
   условиях W 58
анализ схемы на наихудшее
   сочетание параметров
   W 58
анализ текста T 136
анализ условия ветвления
   B 264
анализ цепей N 40
аналитический код A 266
аналоговая вычислительная
   машина A 251
аналоговая схема A 248
аналоговая схемотехника
   A 249
аналоговое представление
   A 261
аналоговый A 245
аналоговый вход A 254
аналоговый выход A 259
аналоговый интерфейс
   A 256
аналоговый компаратор
   A 250
аналоговый модуль A 258
аналоговый переключатель
   A 262
аналого-цифровая ЭВМ
   H 159
аналого-цифровой интер-
   фейс A 265
аналого-цифровой преоб-
   разователь A 263
анизотропное травление
   A 274
анизотропный полупровод-
   ник A 275
анодирование кремния
   S 393
АПД D 57
аппаратная реализация
   деления H 41
аппаратная реализация об-
   работки приоритетных
   прерываний H 49
аппаратная реализация
   умножения H 47

знак зоны Z 29
знак конца записи E 150
знак конца обмена данными E 151
знак минус N 26
знаковая цифра S 379
знаковый бит S 376
знаковый признак S 384
знаковый разряд S 376
знакогенератор C 129
знаком / со S 380
знакопечатающее устройство последовательного типа C 137
знак «плюс» P 289
знак присвоения A 341
знак пробела G 8
знак равенства E 188
знак редактирования E 18
значащая часть S 386/7
значащие цифры S 385
значение S 191
значение адреса A 159
значение индекса I 89
значение фазового угла P 184
зона легирования D 523
зона метки L 3
зона параметров P 62
зона n-проводимости N 136
зонд P 490
зонная перфорация O 265
зонная плавка Z 30
зонный формат Z 28
ЗУ M 235a
ЗУ временного хранения данных I 350
ЗУ для хранения постоянных величин F 116
ЗУ для хранения промежуточных данных I 350

И

И A 269
игнорировать I 23
игольчатое печатающее устройство N 14
идентификатор I 14, L 1
идентификатор программы P 566
идентификационные данные C 134
идентификационный контроль I 9
идентификационный номер I 13
идентификация I 8
идентификация метки L 6
идентификация переменной V 13
идентификация прерывания I 418
идентификация события E 278
идентификация файла F 77
идентифицировать I 15
идентифицируемый I 7
иерархическая система H 78
иерархически структурированное проектирование H 77
иерархия H 79
иерархия памяти M 274
иерархия приоритетов P 475
иерархия управления C 713
избирательный A 225
избирательный вывод S 519
избыток E 285
избыточная система R 159
избыточная схема R 155
избыточное представление R 158
избыточность R 151
избыточность кода C 314
избыточность сообщения M 331
избыточный код R 156
избыточный модуль R 157
избыточный символ R 154
извлекать P 334

извлечь из стека P 333
изготовитель M 145
изготовитель микросхем C 200
изготовление интегральных схем с тройной металлизацией I 6
изготовление кристалла C 849
изготовление маски M 174
изготовление с поддержкой ЭВМ C 491
изготовленный по заказу C 884
изделие второго поставщика S 107
изделие на базе микропроцессора M 390
излучать S 191
изменение A 219
изменение адреса A 142
изменение загрузки (нагрузки) L 192
изменение состояния S 711
изменение формата R 181
изменчивый V 52
изменяемая информация V 53
изменяемый в эксплуатации F 48
изменяемый пользователем F 48
изменять масштаб S 38
измерение относительно нуля в центре шкалы C 90
измеренное значение M 215
измерительная система M 224
измерительная схема M 219
измерительная техника M 225
измерительная установка, управляемая с помощью ЭВМ C 530
измерительное оборудование M 221
измерительное устройство M 220
измерительные приборы для научных исследований S 79
измерительный датчик M 226
измерительный преобразователь M 226
измерительный трансформатор I 273
измеряемая величина M 227
измеряемое значение M 215
измеряемый параметр M 227
измеряемый сигнал M 214
измерять R 31
изображение I 32
изолированный затвор I 275
изолированный штепсель D 578
изолировать I 274
изолирующая пленка I 276
изолирующая подложка I 277
изолирующий слой I 276
изолирующий слой двуокиси кремния S 399
изоляционный материал I 279
изоляция диффузией D 359
изоляция диэлектриком D 345
изоляция затвора G 21
изоляция окислом O 274
изоляция p-n переходом J 27
изопланарная оксидная изоляция I 522
ИИЛ I 25
ИКМ P 698
И²Л I 25
ИЛИ O 161
ИЛИ-НЕ N 95
имитатор ПЗУ R 396
имитация S 425

имитировать S 423
импеданс I 45
импеданс истока S 572
импеданс линии I 148
импеданс нагрузки L 198
импликатор I 54
импликация I 53
импульс P 690
импульс выборки S 19
импульс записи W 72
импульс запрета I 138
импульсная выходная мощность P 115
импульсная модуляция P 720
импульсная мощность P 727
импульсная помеха P 721
импульсная последовательность P 733
импульсная следящая система S 11
импульсное питание P 393
импульсное управление S 10
импульсно-кодовая модуляция P 698
импульсном режиме / в P 722
импульсный выход P 724
импульсный код P 697
импульсный повторитель P 729
импульсный режим P 723
импульсный ток P 701
импульсный ток коллектора P 110
импульсный усилитель P 691
импульсным управлением / с P 692
импульс опроса I 392
импульс переходного процесса T 279
импульс помехи D 478
импульс предварительной установки B 105
импульс развертки S 56
импульс сброса R 312
импульс сдвига S 324
импульс синхронизации S 938
импульс совпадения G 35
импульс сопровождения D 121
импульс считывания R 54
импульс установки [в состояние логической «1»] S 290
импульс чтения R 54
имя библиотеки L 99
имя команды I 253
имя метки L 9
имя программы P 620
имя файла F 81
инверсия N 16
инверсия знака R 367
инверсия фазы P 175
инверсный режим работы I 463
инвертированный операнд I 464
инвертировать N 15
инвертирующая схема I 468
инвертирующий усилитель I 458
инвертор I 466, N 28
индекс S 820
индексация I 86
индексированный адрес I 84
индексная адресация I 85
индексный регистр I 88
индивидуальное программное обеспечение I 98
индикатор I 93
индикатор на жидких кристаллах L 174
индикатор на основе явления электрофореза E 106
индикаторный прибор P 91
индикатор ошибки E 238
индикатор переполнения O 248
индикатор состояния команды I 265

индикация I 92
индикация в полярных координатах P 306
индикация ошибок E 237
индикация состояния внутренних регистров I 374
индицировать I 90
индуктивная связь I 102
индуцированный заряд I 100
И-НЕ A 272
инжекционные МОП-приборы с составными затворами S 417
инжекция дырок H 136
инжекция носителей C 53
инжекция электронов E 101
инженерный пульт M 119
инженер по эксплуатации F 52
инициализация I 140
инициализация тома V 65
инициализировать I 141
инициированная программа I 142
инициировать I 147
инкремент I 80
инкрементирование адреса A 126
инкрементировать I 79
инкрементное вычислительное устройство I 82
инкрементный I 81
инструкции переменной длины V 15
инструкция I 228, S 712
инструкция ассемблера A 336
инструкция входа в подпрограмму E 173
инструкция длиной в два слова D 535
инструкция индексации I 87
инструкция настройки аккумулятора A 57
инструкция обработки двойных слов D 535
инструкция обращения к индексному регистру I 87
инструкция пересылки данных D 128
инструкция по программированию P 611
инструкция поразрядной обработки B 180
инструкция по управлению C 700
инструкция по эксплуатации O 137
инструкция присваивания A 339
инструкция программы P 641
инструкция размещения данных D 99
инструкция редактирования E 22
инструкция с непосредственной адресацией I 42
инструкция условного перехода C 578
инструментальная поправка I 271
инструмент для зачистки проводов S 791
интегральная инжекционная логика I 25
интегральная микросхема I 1
интегральная схема I 288
интегральная схема датчика S 207
интегральная схема памяти M 275
интегральный I 287
интегральный компонент I 294
интеграция I 298
интегрированная в кристалле схема подачи смещения на подложку O 52
интегрированная обработка данных I 195

непостоянный V 52
непредсказуемый U 66
непрерывная переменная C 683
непрерывная подача документов C 675
непрерывная работа C 679
непрерывная функция C 677
непрерывно действующий C 678
непрерывное отображение на экране дисплея в рулонном режиме S 517
непрерывность C 672
непрерывный S 751
непрерывный режим C 870
непрерывный режим работы C 680
непрерывный сигнал C 681
непрограммируемая память N 86
непрограммное управление H 54
непрямое управление I 96
неравенство I 97
неразрушающее считывание N 71
нереализованная инструкция U 42
нерегулярная ошибка I 356
нерегулярная точка R 23
нерегулярный сбой I 356
нерезидентная программа N 90
несбалансированная линия U 17
несбалансированный U 16
несблокированный U 19
несвязанный U 21
несегментная адресация N 91
несимметричная импульсная последовательность A 348
несимметричная линия U 17
несинхронизированный U 24
несмещенный U 18
несобственная проводимость E 362
несобственный полупроводник E 363
несовместимость I 77
несовместимый микропроцессор I 78
несовпадение M 450
несогласованный U 62
несопровождаемый U 15
несплошной S 60
несущая импульса P 696
несущая частота W 10
несущая частота импульса P 696
несуществующий модуль памяти N 74
не требующий больших затрат времени T 205
неустойчивое повреждение I 356
неустойчивое состояние I 221
неустойчивый A 346
неформатная запись U 36
нечетно-пронумерованный O 18
нечетный O 14
нечетный адрес O 15
нечетный байт O 16
нечетный паритет O 19
нечисловой символ N 83
нечувствительная к отказам вычислительная система F 23
нечувствительность к отказам F 22
неявная адресация I 58
неявная косвенная адресация I 59
неявный I 55
неявный адрес I 56/7
нижнее значение L 325
нижний адрес L 291
нижний индекс S 820

нижний слой B 251
нижний уровень напряжения B 254
нижняя граница B 252
низкая поверхностная концентрация L 323
низкий коэффициент заполнения L 294
низкий логический уровень L 262
низкий уровень L 298
низкое потребление [мощности] L 311
низкое энергопотребление L 311
низкоомная подложка L 320
низкоомный L 318
нисходящая последовательность D 257
нисходящая приоритетная последовательность D 256
новшество в оборудовании E 194
номенклатура N 67
номер регистра R 193
номер сегмента S 124
номер страницы P 27
номинал стандартной шкалы P 406
номинальная мощность P 391
номинальная нагрузка R 33
номинальное значение R 38
номинальное значение периодической нагрузки P 135
номинальное напряжение R 34　　⌐R 38
номинальный параметр
номинальный ток R 32
нормализация N 100
нормализованная форма N 103
нормализовать N 102
нормальное состояние N 105
нормально замкнутый контакт N 98
нормально разомкнутый контакт N 104
нормальный выход [из программы] N 99
нормирование N 100
нормировать N 102
носитель данных D 43
носитель записи R 112
носитель заряда C 151
носитель кристалла C 193
носитель кристалла с керамической подложкой C 91
носитель магнитных записей N 85
«ноу-хау» T 64
нулевая страница P 31
нулевая точка C 89, Z 18
нулевое напряжение Z 26
нулевое положение Z 19
нулевое состояние Z 10
нулевой потенциал G 74, Z 20/1
нулевой провод N 47
нули в старших разрядах H 102
нуль Z 4
нуль-индикатор N 117
нуль-символ N 115
нумерация N 121

О

обдув F 9
обеднение D 248
обеднение носителями C 52
обедненный слой D 249
обедненный слой коллектора C 332
обедненный слой эмиттера E 121
обеднять D 247
обзор O 269
обзор функциональных возможностей F 218

области, допускающие применение ЭВМ с малой производительностью L 295
n-область N 136
p-область P 411
область базы B 65
область большого сигнала L 31
область ввода I 159
область ввода-вывода I 509
область вывода O 193
область данных D 28
область коллектора C 341
область коллекторного перехода C 342
область наложения O 261
область памяти M 244
область памяти для ввода-вывода I 509
область памяти, зарезервированная под начальный загрузчик B 244
область памяти, отведенная для стека S 658
область памяти программ P 640
область параметров P 62
область перехода J 31, T 292
область p-n перехода J 31
область применения R27
область проводимости p-типа R 411
область программ P 640
область размещения [в памяти] R 315
область расширения E 335
область сохранения S 31
область управления C 710
облегченный режим работы D 254
обмен E 289
обмен данными D 70
обмен данными по одной общей шине S 452
обмениваться E 287
обмен информацией I 114
обменная буферизация E 194
обменник S 885
обменный заряд E 292
обнаружение и исправление ошибок E 214
обнаружение многократной ошибки M 544
обнаружение одиночных ошибок S 445
обнаружение ошибок E 227
обнаруженная неисправность T 232
обнаруженный отказ D 295
обновление файла F 89
обновлять U 72
обобщенная структура микропроцессора G 38
обогащать E 166
обогащение E 167
обозначать I 90
обозначение M 165
обозначение файла F 72
оборудование E 190
оборудование ввода I 174
оборудование ввода-вывода I 484
оборудование вывода O 210
оборудование для обработки P 510
оборудование для обработки данных, ориентированное на размещение в составе рабочего места W 56
оборудование для регистрации данных D 87
оборудование для обработки данных, ориентированное на размещение в составе рабочего места W 56
оборудование передачи данных D 127
оборудование, приводимое в действие сигналом прерывания I 408
оборудование разработчика D 301

оборудование резидентной отладочной системы M 362
оборудованный средствами вычислительной техники C 528
обрабатывать H 18, P 499
обрабатывать в пакетном режиме B 96
обработка H 19, P 506
обработка больших массивов чисел N 120
обработка булевых переменных B 237
обработка в пакетном режиме B 101
обработка в реальном времени R 76
обработка в режиме «он-лайн» O 71
обработка в темпе поступления I 150
обработка в управляемом режиме O 71
обработка графической информации G 62
обработка данных D 102
обработка данных в порядке поступления I 150
обработка данных в режиме «он-лайн» O 67
обработка данных в темпе [их] поступления I 150
обработка десятичных чисел D 187
обработка директивы O 167/8
обработка документов D 505, D 506
обработка задания J 9
обработка записей о событиях T 250
обработка информации I 120
обработка информационных массивов B 308
обработка маски M 175
обработка массива A 317
обработка массивов чисел N 120
обработка метки L 10
обработка нечисловых данных N 84
обработка особых случаев E 284　　⌐E 236
обработка ошибок E 211, обработка по приоритетам P 481
обработка по частям S 514
обработка прерывания I 417, I 427
обработка результатов научных исследований R 305
обработка сигналов S 355, S 362
обработка символов C 130, C 138
обработка символов языка с помощью списков L 22
обработка ситуаций взаимоблокировки D 158
обработка слов W 44
обработка с несколькими потоками данных M 579
обработка сообщений C 405
обработка состояния захвата T 310
обработка списков L 180
обработка с совмещением операций S 438
обработка строк [данных] S 785
обработка таблиц T 3
обработка текстов T 141
обработка файла F 75, F 83
обработка экономической информации C 363
обработка экспериментальных данных R 305
образ[ец] P 96
образ задачи T 55
V-образная канавка V 31
образование дополнения C 445

поколонный двоичный код C 347
покрывать P 257
покрытие C 283
покрытый C 244
покрытый медью C 772
покупное программное обеспечение O 40
покупной интерфейс O 39
полагаться R 254
поле E 340, F 47, M 154
поле адреса A 110
поле адреса регистра R 194
поле адреса связи L 163
полевое испытание F 59
полевой МДП-транзистор M 449
полевой МОП-транзистор M 499
полевой транзистор F 51
полевой транзистор с изолированным затвором I 22
полевой транзистор со структурой «металл-диэлектрик-полупроводник» M 449
полевой транзистор со структурой «металл-окисел-полупроводник» M 499
полевой транзистор со структурой «металл-полупроводник» M 326
полевой транзистор с p-n переходом J 26
полевой транзистор Шоттки M 326
поле в формате команд I 232
поле данных D 73
поле для обозначения типа адресации A 141
поле защиты P 669
полезное [машинное] время U 80
поле идентификации I 12
поле инструкции для обозначения типа адресации A 141
поле ключа K 22
поле кода операции O 79
поле кодирования C 325
поле команд I 232
поле метки L 5
поле памяти M 245
поле печатной страницы M 154
поле позиционирования L 220
поле строки символов C 148
поликремниевый затвор P 328, S 404
поликремниевый резистор P 330
поликремний P 327
поликристаллическая структура P 325
поликристаллический кремний P 327
полировать L 27
полная нагрузка F 205
полная совместимость P 286
полное сопротивление между зажимами T 97
полностью автоматизированное оборудование F 198
полностью документированный F 206
полностью законченная ЭВМ F 203
полностью интегрированная однокристальная схема F 204
полностью оборудованный F 207
полностью совместимый процессор F 199
полностью транзисторный C 457
полностью укомплектованная ЭВМ F 203
полные потери N 37

полный отказ C 453
полный перенос C 454
полный размах колебаний P 120
полный сумматор F 197
половина периода A 224
положение запятой P 301
положение метки M 166
положение средней точки M 432
положительная логика P 354
положительная обратная связь P 353
положительное смещение P 350
положительной обратной связью / с R 190
положительный заряд P 351
полоса S 790
полуавтоматический S 173
полуаналитический код S 172
полубайт N 49
полудуплексная система передачи [данных] H 8
полудуплексная схема H 6
полудуплексный канал H 5
полудуплексный режим H 7
полупериод H 4
полупостоянная память S 188
полупроводник S 174
полупроводниковая память S 183, S 551
полупроводниковая пластина S 186
полупроводниковая схема S 175
полупроводниковая технология S 187
полупроводниковое изделие S 185
полупроводниковое производство S 181
полупроводниковое устройство S 178
полупроводниковые логические схемы S 548
полупроводниковый кристалл с размещенной схемой C 191
полупроводниковый материал S 182
полупроводниковый прибор со структурой «металл-диэлектрик-полупроводник» M 448
полупроводник с трехслойной структурой «n-p-n» N 111
полупроводник n-типа N 114
полупроводник p-типа P 686
полуслово H 11
полусумма H 9
полусумма кратных значений [выборки] M 433
полусумматор H 1
получатель D 288
получать R 83
получение R 94
получение твердой копии H 32
пользователь U 83
польская [инверсная] запись P 312
поляризация P 308
поляризованное состояние P 309
поляризованность P 308
поляризовать P 310
полярность P 307
полярные координаты P 305
поместить в стек P 750
помехи N 58
помехозащищенность N 59
помехоустойчивость N 59
помехоустойчивый код E 221
помеченный оператор L 7

помещать P 246
помещать в стек S 645
помещение в стек S 654
понижение S 749
пониженное напряжение U 33
поочередная пересылка S 272
поперечное направление C 831
поправочный коэффициент C 784
поправочный член C 781
поразрядная установка A 182
пороговая логика T 169
пороговая область T 170
пороговая схема T 166
пороговое значение T 171
пороговое напряжение T 172
пороговый элемент T 168
порог переключения [для входного сигнала] T 204
порог срабатывания P 222
порог чувствительности R 345
порождать G 48
порт P 335
портативное оконечное устройство P 340
портативность P 336
портативный P 337
портативный прибор H 17
порт ввода I 191
порт ввода-вывода I 503
порт ввода-вывода, интегрированный в кристалле O 48
порт вывода O 222
порт последовательного ввода-вывода S 260
порядке поступления / в I 148
порядковый множитель E 323
порядковый номер O 170
порядок E 327
порядок приоритета O 171
порядок следования S 218
порядок убывания D 257
порядок числа E 327
посимвольно кодированный C 127
последовательная адресация C 94
последовательная двоично-десятичная арифметика S 246
последовательная нумерация C 630
последовательная обработка S 237, S 267
последовательная обработка битов B 199
последовательная передача S 272
последовательная пересылка данных S 255
последовательная работа S 236, S 263
последовательная схема S 229
последовательная цепь S 235
последовательное включение S 275
последовательное исполнение S 232
последовательное планирование S 238
последовательное соединение S 275
последовательное управление S 231
последовательно-параллельная обработка S 265
последовательно-параллельное преобразование S 270
последовательно-параллельный S 264
последовательно-параллельный преобразователь S 271

последовательно по битам S 247
последовательно по символам S 248
последовательно-приоритетная структура D 10
последовательно-приоритетная структура шины D 2
последовательно-приоритетная цепочка D 1
последовательно распространяющийся перенос R 381
последовательно соединенные каскады C 68
последовательностная логика S 234
последовательностный S 227
последовательность C 93, S 218
последовательность данных D 112
последовательность двоичных разрядов B 203
последовательность действий для приведения микро-ЭВМ в исходное состояние M 360
последовательность инициализации микро-ЭВМ M 360
последовательность команд I 261
последовательность коммутации шин B 338
последовательность микрокоманд M 375
последовательность операндов O 101
последовательность операций O 136
последовательность передачи данных D 132
последовательность подпрограмм S 818
последовательность программ P 636
последовательность символов C 144
последовательные стадии S 837
последовательные такты B 17
последовательный C 626, S 227, S 241, S 835
последовательный ввод-вывод S 257
последовательный ввод (вход) данных S 253
последовательный доступ C 627, S 228, S 242
последовательный доступ к файлу S 233
последовательный интерфейс S 258
последовательный канал обмена данными S 252
последовательный метод S 262
последовательный поиск S 239
последовательный поток работ S 273
последовательный преобразователь S 261
последовательный режим S 236
последовательный режим работы S 263
последовательный связной интерфейс S 250
последовательный способ S 269
последовательный сумматор S 244
последовательный таймер S 225
последовательный формат S 256
последующий S 227, S 821, S 835
последующий элемент S 838
послесвечение P 160